Let's Go Publications

Let's Go: Alaska & the Pacific Northwest 2002
Let's Go: Amsterdam 2002 **New Title!**
Let's Go: Australia 2002
Let's Go: Austria & Switzerland 2002
Let's Go: Barcelona 2002 **New Title!**
Let's Go: Boston 2002
Let's Go: Britain & Ireland 2002
Let's Go: California 2002
Let's Go: Central America 2002
Let's Go: China 2002
Let's Go: Eastern Europe 2002
Let's Go: Egypt 2002 **New Title!**
Let's Go: Europe 2002
Let's Go: France 2002
Let's Go: Germany 2002
Let's Go: Greece 2002
Let's Go: India & Nepal 2002
Let's Go: Ireland 2002
Let's Go: Israel 2002
Let's Go: Italy 2002
Let's Go: London 2002
Let's Go: Mexico 2002
Let's Go: Middle East 2002
Let's Go: New York City 2002
Let's Go: New Zealand 2002
Let's Go: Paris 2002
Let's Go: Peru, Ecuador & Bolivia 2002
Let's Go: Rome 2002
Let's Go: San Francisco 2002
Let's Go: South Africa with Southern Africa 2002
Let's Go: Southeast Asia 2002
Let's Go: Southwest USA 2002 **New Title!**
Let's Go: Spain & Portugal 2002
Let's Go: Turkey 2002
Let's Go: USA 2002
Let's Go: Washington, D.C. 2002
Let's Go: Western Europe 2002

Let's Go *Map Guides*

Amsterdam	New Orleans
Berlin	New York City
Boston	Paris
Chicago	Prague
Dublin	Rome
Florence	San Francisco
Hong Kong	Seattle
London	Sydney
Los Angeles	Venice
Madrid	Washington, D.C.

Let's Go

NEW ZEALAND
INCLUDING FIJI
2002

Holly E. Fling editor
Chris Clayton associate editor

researcher-writers
Jesse Green
Maja Groff
Jongsoo Lee
Steven Most
Ann Robinson
Mica Root

Dan Barnes map editor
Marly Ohlsson managing editor

Macmillan

HELPING LET'S GO If you want to share your discoveries, suggestions, or corrections, please drop us a line. We read every piece of correspondence, whether a postcard, a 10-page email, or a coconut. Please note that mail received after May 2002 may be too late for the 2003 book, but will be kept for future editions. **Address mail to:**

> Let's Go: New Zealand including Fiji
> 67 Mount Auburn Street
> Cambridge, MA 02138
> USA

Visit Let's Go at **http://www.letsgo.com,** or send email to:

> feedback@letsgo.com
> Subject: "Let's Go: New Zealand including Fiji"

In addition to the invaluable travel advice our readers share with us, many are kind enough to offer their services as researchers or editors. Unfortunately, our charter enables us to employ only currently enrolled Harvard students.

Published in Great Britain 2002 by Macmillan, an imprint of Pan Macmillan Ltd.
20 New Wharf Road, London N1 9RR
Basingstoke and Oxford
Associated companies throughout the world
www.panmacmillan.com

Maps by David Lindroth copyright © 2002, 2001, 2000, 1999, 1998, 1997, 1996, 1995, 1994, 1993, 1992, 1991, 1990, 1989, 1988 by St. Martin's Press.

Published in the United States of America by St. Martin's Press.

ISBN: 0-333-90595-4
First edition
10 9 8 7 6 5 4 3 2 1

Let's Go: New Zealand including Fiji is written by Let's Go Publications, 67 Mount Auburn Street, Cambridge, MA 02138, USA.

Let's Go® and the thumb logo are trademarks of Let's Go, Inc.
Printed in the USA on recycled paper with biodegradable soy ink.

ACKNOWLEDGMENTS

The Let's Go 2002 series is dedicated to the memory of Haley Surti

NEW ZEALAND TEAM THANKS: To Marly for leading the way (and cooking dinner). To all the MEs for holding our hands. To Production for making it all work. To Dan for such wonderful new maps. To Ann for making *our* job easy. To Harris for helping us start and finish 2002, with some karaoke along the way. To the Down Under Pod for laughs...many many laughs. To Backspace, our favorite key. To 7-Eleven, Bertucci's, and Lee's Beehive. To our fish, may their flippery souls rest in peace.

HOLLY FLING THANKS: Chris for computer skills, late hours, and an unbelievable ability to tolerate me. You gave it 100% and it shows. To Marly for weights, treats, and bitchin'. To Gretchen for the poop game. A big shout out to Loran and Krishnany for distinctive entertainment. To Stephles for Tim McGraw and Mayme for inspiration and for the last four years. To Ve for always being there. To Anna for Paul Simon and Tom Petty. To Justin for Shrek and macaroni and cheese. To Mary for keeping me nourished and sane. To Christopher for Florida and the flash. To Radcliffe Crew, it's never been so fun. Keep the music playin'. To all of my family. Thanks for all coming to see me finish it all. To Mom and Dad for letting me travel the world and for your unconditional support and love.

CHRIS CLAYTON THANKS: To Hol, who edits like she rows—bad-assed. I never knew that cutting could feel so good. To Marly for snacks, endless patience, and lots of help. To Kiri (my dinner) and Jason (my dishes). To Collin, for putting up with it all and making this summer perfect. To Sharmi, Krishnany, Loran, and Gretchen, a unique pod. SEAS wasn't bad, either. To Sharon Wilson, Craig Weston, and the rest of the '98 SJA expedition. To Max, my favorite pooch despite his penchant for wildlife. And finally, a very special thanks to Steve and Terry Irwin, Masaharu Morimoto, Kenichi Chen, Masahiko Kobe, and Hiroyuki Sakai for endless inspiration.

Editor
Holly E. Fling
Associate Editor
Chris Clayton
Managing Editor
Marly Ohlsson
Map Editor
Dan Barnes

Publishing Director
Sarah P. Rotman
Editor-in-Chief
Ankur N. Ghosh
Production Manager
Jen Taylor
Cartography Manager
Dan Barnes
Design & Photo Manager
Vanessa Bertozzi
Editorial Managers
Amélie Cherlin, Naz F. Firoz, Matthew Gibson, Sharmi Surianarain, Brian R. Walsh
Financial Manager
Rebecca L. Schoff
Marketing & Publicity Managers
Brady R. Dewar, Katharine Douglas, Marly Ohlsson
New Media Manager
Kevin J. Yip
Online Manager
Alex Lloyd
Personnel Manager
Nathaniel Popper
Production Associates
Steven Aponte, Chris Clayton, Caleb S. Epps, Eduardo Montoya, Melissa Rudolph
Some Design
Melissa Rudolph
Office Coordinators
Efrat Kussell, Peter Richards

Director of Advertising Sales
Adam M. Grant
Senior Advertising Associates
Ariel Shwayder, Kennedy Thorwarth
Advertising Associate
Jennie Timoney
Advertising Artwork Editor
Peter Henderson

President
Cindy L. Rodriguez
General Manager
Robert B. Rombauer
Assistant General Manager
Anne E. Chisholm

RESEARCHER-WRITERS

Jesse Green *The Mamanuca Group, Viti Levu, Auckland, and Northland*

DayTwo.WakeUp.GetHitByTruck. Write stylishly formatted, witty commentary and refreshing copy without skipping a beat. His mettle proven as a researcher for *Let's Go: San Francisco 2001*, Jesse braved hit-and-run drivers, email poltergeists, and Kings Road brothels without even flinching, adding a touch of class and discerning artistic sensibility to our New Zealand and Fiji coverage.

Maja Groff *Great Walks, the Southland, Stewart Island, Southern Lakes*

Dependable and adventurous, Maja ventured off the beaten path to fan out our coverage of the South Island. With high-seasoned writing, this former *Let's Go: Alaska & the Pacific Northwest 2000* researcher and *Let's Go: Ireland 2001* editor proved that she could not only walk the Great Walk, but talk the low-season talk as well. Her calm foray into Wanaka and Queenstown left us wondering whether maybe she had already been there and done that.

Jongsoo "James" Lee *Outlying Fijian Islands, northeastern North Island*

Bravely choosing sun and surf over the Trans-Siberian Railway, Secret Agent James Lee quietly slipped out of Moscow to accept his latest assignment in the Pacific. With superior researching techniques honed while writing for *Let's Go: South Africa 2001*, James never shied from brutal interrogation techniques or shameless seduction in compiling his descriptive reports. Chalk another one up for the SupeRW.

Steven Most *Coromandel, western North Island, and South Island*

Covering the most ground in *Let's Go: New Zealand* history, Steve drove the lengths of both islands on a whirlwind itinerary. He perpetually and punctually delighted us with his flawless and impressive copy, even busting out his dancing shoes in Christchurch. Steve wishes to express his gratitude to all the people who made his trip great, and to the kea who ravaged his car.

Ann Robinson *Wellington, Marlborough, and Nelson*

Ann wrote the book on travel in New Zealand. No, really. A researcher for *Let's Go: New Zealand 2000* and editor of *Let's Go: New Zealand 2001*, Ann pitched in one last time to lend her resident's perspective to the book. Fearlessly stripping down to her skivvies to swim with random fur seals, not all of her exploits can be attributed to the Tui's. With superlative prose, one hell of a graybox, and hilarious marginalia, ◼Ann is simply perfect in every way.

Mica Root *Great Walks, West Coast, Taranaki, Wanganui, Marlborough, and Fiordland*

Mica Root traveled north to south to cover most of the Great Walks. A researcher for *Let's Go: Southeast Asia 1999* and *Peru & Ecuador 2000*, and the editor of *Let's Go: Peru, Bolivia & Ecuador 2001*, this three-time vet was given a fourth chance to show her stuff. With meticulous research and timely prose, she left us ever anticipating her next report from the road.

CONTENTS

✚ Hospital	✈ Airport	🏛 Museum	┈ Pedestrian Zone
🚓 Police	🚌 Bus Station	🏨 Hotel/Hostel	Park
✉ Post Office	🚉 Train Station	⛺ Camping	
ⓘ Tourist Office	⛪ Church	🍔 Food & Drink	Beach
💵 Bank	✡ Synagogue	🛍 Shopping	
Embassy/Consulate	⚓ Ferry Landing	♪ Nightlife & Clubs	Water
▪ Site or Point of Interest	Theater	Bars	
☎ Telephone Office	🏔 Mountain	Internet Access	The Let's Go thumb always points NORTH.

-10   0   10   20   30   40   °Celsius

°Fahrenheit 30   40   50   60   70   80   90   100   110   120

100 meters (m) = 328 feet (ft.)   500m = 1640 ft. = 0.31 miles (mi.)
1 kilometer (km) = 0.625 mi.   50km = 31.25 mi.   1 hectare (ha) = 2.47 acres

MAPS

HOW TO USE THIS BOOK

Kia Ora! Bula! Welcome to *Let's Go: New Zealand including Fiji 2002*, this year including new coverage of Fiji. We dispatched a crack team of six researchers to storm down under and report back to you their first-hand experiences: they sky-dived; they tramped; they partied; they skied; they zorbed; they got loopy on kava. Their insightful coverage of culture, cities, outdoors, and adventure will make this an indispensable guide for seeing it all and doing it all—with style.

ORGANIZATION OF THIS BOOK

DISCOVER. **Discover New Zealand** and **Discover Fiji** provide you with an overview of travel in New Zealand and Fiji, including **Suggested Itineraries** that give you an idea of what you shouldn't miss and how long it will take to see it.

NEW ZEALAND AND FIJI. The **New Zealand** and **Fiji** chapters provides you with a general introduction to the culture, history, and flavor of these countries.

ESSENTIALS. This section may seem long and boring. You're right, it is. But it does outline the practical information you will need to prepare for and execute your trip. It may save you money, keep you out of jail, or get you laid. It may not. Read it anyways.

COVERAGE. New Zealand coverage is divided into 14 chapters, beginning with Auckland and then moving roughly from north to south; Fiji is detailed in an additional two chapters at the end of the book. The **black tabs** in the margins will help you to navigate between chapters quickly and easily.

TRAMPING. Check out the **Tramping** chapter at the end of the New Zealand coverage for comprehensive info on all the Great Walks and tramping in general.

APPENDIX. The appendix contains a **phrasebook** of handy Kiwi phrases, Maori-English and Fijian-English dictionaries highlighting some important words and concepts, and climate charts for several cities in New Zealand and Fiji.

A FEW NOTES ABOUT LET'S GO FORMAT

RANKING ESTABLISHMENTS. In each section (accommodations, food, etc.), we list establishments in order from best to worst. Our absolute favorites are so denoted by the highest honor given out by Let's Go, the Let's Go thumbs-up (🏆).

PHONE CODES AND TELEPHONE NUMBERS. The **phone code** for each New Zealand region, city, or town appears opposite the name of that region, city, or town, and is denoted by the ☎ icon. **Phone numbers** in text are also preceded by the ☎ icon. Mobile and snowphones are noted where appropriate. There are no phone codes in Fiji.

GRAYBOXES AND WHITEBOXES. **Grayboxes** at times provide wonderful cultural insight, at times simply crude humor. In any case, they're usually amusing, so enjoy. **Whiteboxes,** on the other hand, provide important practical information, such as warnings (⚠) and helpful hints and further resources (📌).

A NOTE TO OUR READERS The information for this book was gathered by *Let's Go* researchers from May through August of 2001. Each listing is based on one researcher's opinion, formed during his or her visit at a particular time. Those traveling at other times may have different experiences since prices, dates, hours, and conditions are always subject to change. You are urged to check the facts presented in this book beforehand to avoid inconvenience and surprises.

DISCOVER

NEW ZEALAND AND FIJI

If you spin a globe and stop it with the tip of your finger, your chances of landing on New Zealand or Fiji will always be next to none. The countries' isolation from the rest of the world evokes images of exotic lands—and so it should. New Zealand's startling landscapes can only be described as otherworldly; psychedelic lakes perfectly mirror volcanic peaks, constellations of aqua-blue glow-worms glitter in black-water caves, and twin glaciers creep toward the nearby beach and ocean. Several thousand kilometers to the north, Fiji's pristine beauty and untouched natural and cultural splendor can only be experienced in such a tropical paradise: cool misty waterfalls cascade through lush virgin rainforests, remote mountain villages offer visitors complete immersion into tradition, and some of the most spectacular reefs and underwater scenery in the world present a once-in-a-lifetime diving opportunity. The sheer diversity of earthly wonders in these two very different nations is matched only by the number of ways to enjoy them. To get to New Zealand and Fiji you will cross oceans, perhaps even circumnavigate the globe. In return, local Kiwis and Fijians will make the edge of the world accessible and hospitable. With an ever-growing travel industry for exploration and adventure, New Zealand and Fiji perpetually surprise, amaze, and inspire travelers.

NEW ZEALAND FACTS

CAPITAL: Wellington

AGE OF THE INDEPENDENT NEW ZEALAND: 54 years

AGE OF THE OLDEST WORKING BREWERY: 125 years

AGE OF THE NEW ZEALAND RUGBY FOOTBALL UNION: 109 years

SHEEP POPULATION AT LAMBING TIME: 130 million

RATIO OF SHEEP TO PEOPLE AT LAMBING TIME: 35:1

AVERAGE AMOUNT OF SHEEPMEAT CONSUMED: 17kg per person annually

DRINKING AGE: 18

AMOUNT OF BEER CONSUMED PER YEAR: 11 million liters

NUMBER OF ALL-BLACKS, THE NATIONAL RUGBY TEAM: 27

CHANCE OF BECOMING A MEMBER OF THE ALL-BLACKS: Slim to none

FIJI FACTS

CAPITAL: Suva

AGE OF THE INDEPENDENT FIJI: 32 years

NUMBER OF ISLANDS Over 300

PERCENT OF POPULATION LIVING ON VITI LEVU: 70%

ANNUAL NUMBER OF VISITORS TO FIJI: Over 400,000

YEAR OF FIRST TV BROADCAST IN FIJI: 1991

% OF YOUNG GIRLS WHO BEGAN PURGING THANKS TO TV: 15%

DRINKING AGE: 18

LAST TIME HUMAN MEAT WAS CONSUMED: late 1800s

LENGTH OF COASTLINE: 1129km

CHANCE OF LEAVING FIJI HAVING NEVER EXPERIENCED KAVA: None

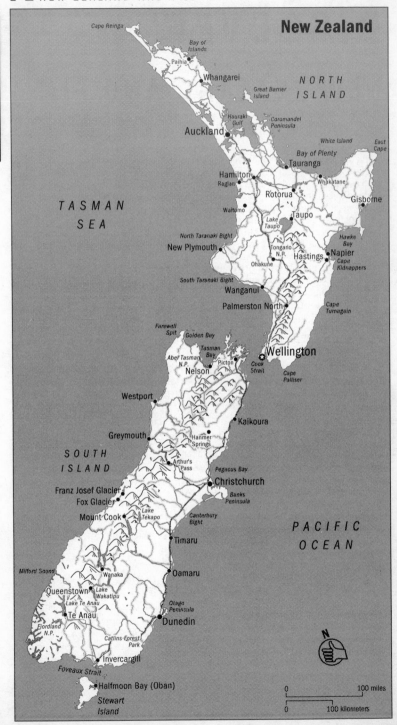

New Zealand

Cape Reinga

Bay of Islands

Paihia

Whangarei

NORTH ISLAND

Great Barrier Island

Hauraki Gulf

Coromandel Peninsula

Auckland

White Island

East Cape

Bay of Plenty

Tauranga

Hamilton

Raglan

Whakatane

Rotorua

Gisborne

TASMAN SEA

Waitomo

Taupo

Lake Taupo

North Taranaki Bight

New Plymouth

Tongariro N.P.

Hawke Bay

Hastings

Napier

Ohakune

Cape Kidnappers

South Taranaki Bight

Wanganui

Palmerston North

Cape Turnagain

Farewell Spit

Golden Bay

Tasman Bay

Abel Tasman N.P.

Picton

Nelson

Cook Strait

Wellington

Cape Palliser

Westport

Kaikoura

Greymouth

Hanmer Springs

SOUTH ISLAND

Arthur's Pass

Pegasus Bay

Christchurch

Franz Josef Glacier

Banks Peninsula

Fox Glacier

Mount Cook

Lake Tekapo

Canterbury Bight

PACIFIC OCEAN

Timaru

Milford Sound

Wanaka

Oamaru

Queenstown

Lake Wakatipu

Otago Peninsula

Lake Te Anau

Te Anau

Dunedin

Fiordland N.P.

Catlins Forest Park

Invercargill

Foveaux Strait

Halfmoon Bay (Oban)

Stewart Island

N

| 0 | 100 miles |
| 0 | 100 kilometers |

WHEN TO GO

The best time to visit **New Zealand** depends on the type of activities (warm or cold weather) you are most interested in, and your sensitivity to crowds. If you are traveling from the Northern Hemisphere, be aware that the seasons are reversed. Summer arrives in December and lasts roughly until February; winter is from June to August. New Zealand enjoys its high season in the warmest months (Nov.-Feb.), but major national holidays add considerable traffic congestion. Advance reservations for transportation and accommodations can become necessary. To avoid crowds, you might consider traveling toward the beginning (Oct.-Nov.) or end (Mar.-Apr.) of the summer. While the crowds largely disappear during low season, some areas and activities shut down. In contrast to New Zealand's climatic fluctuations, **Fiji** is warm and tropical year-round. While travel to Fiji is most popular during the summer months (Nov.-Feb.) for Kiwis and Aussies, milder temperatures and less rain may make a stay more enjoyable from May through October; visibility for diving is also greatly increased from April through November. For charts detailing climate and major national holidays and festivals in both New Zealand and Fiji, see the **Appendix** p. 439 and **Holidays and Festivals** p. 9.

THINGS TO DO

Simply put, New Zealand has it all. From adventure activities to breathtaking natural attractions, from kickin' nightlife to occasional smatterings of culture, from the refined sport of the yachties to the bone-crunching madness of the scrum, the Kiwis have managed to build an all-encompassing paradise. In order to make the most of your time Down Under, we have suggested a few routes you may wish to consider (see p. 5). The **Adventure New Zealand** itinerary is tall-tale friendly, if your wallet can handle it. On the other hand, the **Tramping New Zealand** trip offers more serene enjoyment. If you only have a brief stay, we suggest the **Whirlwind New Zealand and Fiji** approach; for a more leisurely trip, the **Best of New Zealand** hits all the right spots.

Fiji is an earthly tropical paradise, and it has the resorts and prices to prove it. Along with the potential to thoroughly clean your wallet, however, Fiji also has natural (free) attractions and a rapidly growing infrastructure for budget travelers. Whether lounging on tranquil white-sand beaches or diving amidst the shimmering rainbow of soft coral reefs, those who spend time in Fiji discover the perfect mix of relaxation and excitement to suite their tastes. The **Whirlwind New Zealand and Fiji** itinerary provides a quick stopover in heaven on the shore of the Blue Lagoon, while the **Best of Fiji** allows for in-depth exploration of Fiji's unique offerings. Check out the **Diving Spots** box for some must-stops for the diving fanatic.

For more specific regional attractions, see the **Highlights of the Region** section at the beginning of each chapter. On the other hand, spontaneity and independence are the two biggest perks of a budget trip—take our suggestions for what they are worth and build a trip to your own liking.

WINE, BEER, AND KAVA

It would be difficult to determine whether Kiwis take more pride in their wine or their beer. O.K., it's their beer. Still, New Zealand is known for its quality production of both. Beer drinkers (in New Zealand that's pretty much everyone) are loyal to the beer made in their region. For example, in Dunedin, locals are ever-faithful to Speight's, whereas CD is the pride of Canterbury. To contemplate the wonder and majesty of beer, there are brewery tours in **Dunedin** (p. 328), **Timaru** (p. 281), **Gisborne** (p. 167), and **Greymouth** (p. 290), among others. New Zealand's vineyards make for a more extensive—if not more tipsy—daytrip. From Auckland, you can take a ferry to **Waiheke Island** (p. 98), where you can sample both sea-salty air and wine and the wines in **Martinborough** (p. 241) and **Blenheim** (p. 240).

Though Fiji may be lacking in vineyards, it surely makes up for it with **kava** (see I Can't Feel My Lips p. 363). While the Fijian national drink is traded, shared, and enjoyed just about everywhere in the islands, for a cultural experience "grog" must be enjoyed at traditional ceremony in a Fijian village. The **Interior Highlands** (p. 406) of Viti Levu are filled with welcoming and hospitable villages in which to partake in this integral piece of Fijian life. Be sure to read **Fijian Village Etiquette** (p. 385) before you visit.

OFF THE BEATEN PATH

The best way to stay outside the main veins of tourism is to rent a car and explore more remote regions. There is no shortage of one-horse towns in New Zealand, many of which have nearby beaches, lagoons, and tramps for casual exploration. The **Marlborough Sounds** (p. 239) is a web of waterways called home by dolphins, seals, penguins, and seduced travelers alike. Take a water taxi to any one of the many impressive hostels interspersed among the Sounds that you can call home. The **Coromandel Peninsula** (p. 123) has unsealed roads in its northern reaches that extend to hippie outposts and relaxing coastal views. A bit farther south, the splendid coastline, friendly penguin colonies, and unpeopled expanse of the **Catlins** (p. 340) lead travelers further and further into the wilds.

A less frequently touristed destination, **Taveuni** (p. 430) has some of the greatest hiking and diving in Fiji. Although transportation is a little complicated, the extreme natural beauty and lack of tourists make the trip well worth it. For a true Fijian experience, venture into the Nausori Highlands of Viti Levu to **Navala** () and get a dose of traditional hospitality and comfort.

OFF THE *UNBEATEN* PATH

We can't even call these places towns with a straight face; they are magical nowheres barely offering the essentials. Each can be visited for a peaceful escape for a day or more. Up the coast from Wellington, **Paekakariki** (p. 227) is the perfect break from urbanity—and the views of the Tasman Sea and across to the South Island are unparalleled. **Opoutere** (p. 133) in the Coromandel Peninsula is a road with a canopy of trees that leads to a lagoon. People? Nope. Except at the lone backpackers. Giant bull kelp litters the beach at **Papatowai** (p. 343) in the Catlins; you can't escape the stunning and practically uninterrupted beach views. Just a short dash from the glaciers, **Okarito** (p. 296) seems miles away. While Fiji is full of tiny villages rarely visited, tiny **Naiserelagi Village** (p. 401) on the Kings Road is home to the intriguing Black Christ mural of St. Francis Xavier Parish. All of these places prove that even going nowhere is often worth the trip.

ISLAND GETAWAYS

There aren't even paths to be beaten to these escapes, but that's all the more reason to venture onwards by sea. **Kapiti Island** (p. 227), hosts some of New Zealand's endangered species, while nearby **Mana Island** (p. 227), is seclusion. The **Poor Knight's Islands** (p. 107) were a favorite of the late Jacques Cousteau. Don't question Jacques Cousteau.

With so many islands to choose from Fiji is full of island getaways. However **Nananu-i-ra** (p. 402) boasts some of the best wind surfing in the world. And although **Beachcomber Island** (p. 418) in the Mamanucas is a sleekly packaged tourist destination, it doesn't get much more wild (or relaxed) than this party hotspot.

SUGGESTED ITINERARIES

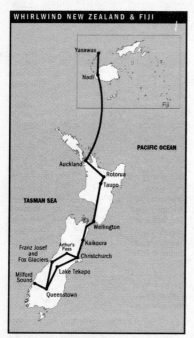

WHIRLWIND NEW ZEALAND & FIJI

and crampons to protect you. Take a deep breath before dashing to the madness of **Queenstown** (p. 302) where jumping off bridges and up onto bars to dance is all in a day's work. As much as your wallet may hurt at this point, a day trip to the awe-inspiring **Milford Sound** (p. 322) is worth the expense for a grand finale before a last breathtaking stop at **Lake Tekapo** (p. 282). Back in **Christchurch**, drop by the International Antarctic Center (p. 272) on the way to the airport to become reacquainted with the cold, cruel world before you hop on your plane to rejoin it.

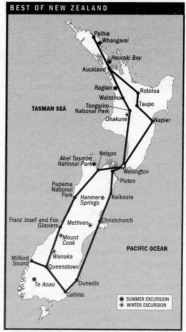

BEST OF NEW ZEALAND

WHIRLWIND NEW ZEALAND & FIJI (2 WEEKS)

After flying into bustling **Nadi** (p. 393), the gateway to Fiji, take a deep breath and catch the first seaplane to Tavewa Island in the **Yasawas** (p. 418). After a couple days of indulgence in the brilliant waters of the Blue Lagoon, regretfully head back to Nadi and hop a flight to **Auckland** (p. 74). After a day in this metropolitan mecca's flavorful neighborhoods, and a throbbing night on the town, gather your pack and your throbbing head and immediately aim south for **Wellington** (p. 214), stopping at the hot spas and bubbling mud pools of **Rotorua** (p. 152) to rejuvenate, and at the adrenaline factory of **Taupo** (p. 182) on the way. After taking in Te Papa, Wellington's capital national museum in the capital city, make the ferry crossing to the **South Island** and head further south, stopping for the day in **Kaikoura** (p. 241) to swim with the dolphins. After refueling at the cafes of **Christchurch** (p. 263), take the spectacular train ride through **Arthur's Pass** (p. 279) to the rugged **West Coast**. Continue south to the enormous **Franz** and **Fox Glaciers** (p. 296) where you attack a behemoth of blue ice, with only your ice axe

BEST OF NEW ZEALAND (5 WEEKS)

Beginning in **Auckland** (p. 74), the trendy neighborhood of Ponsonby is pleasant for an afternoon's exploration and the nightclubs along K. Rd. (p. 86) will keep you grooving until dawn. After Auckland, loop through Northland, up to the **Bay of Islands** (p. 108), a hot spot for watersports, and back down past the enormous trees of the **Kauri Coast** (p. 120). Next, **Rotorua's** (p. 152) geothermal wonders and Maori *hangi* will make a camera-happy tourist out of you. Farther south, **Taupo** (p. 182), set on

New Zealand's largest lake, is the high-adrenaline capital of the North Island, and the site of the most frequent backpacker skydives. To calm your frayed nerves, the Art Deco town of **Napier** (p. 175), offers relaxation in liquid form—a day (or two) with a bottle (or two) of wine from one of the surrounding vineyards will leave you well prepared to catch the train to the nation's compact cosmopolitan capital. Absorb

SUMMER SPOTS

Grab your togs and your shades and hit the surfer's safari to **Raglan** (p. 141), the "city kids on a rampage" nightlife of **Whangarei** (p. 105), the **Hauraki Gulf's** (p. 98) collection of seaside respites and sun worshipers, **Abel Tasman National Park** (p. 254), the playground of the tramped and tented, and **Te Anau** (p. 324), the walking capital of the world.

some culture at **Wellington's** Te Papa (p. 223) before crossing the Cook Strait to the beautiful and remote reaches of the South Island; save anything you can't quite get to for your return trip. Once you are back on dry land, the small gateway town of **Picton** (p. 236) and the nearby **Marlborough Sounds** (p. 239), encourage returning to the water, with stunning sanctuaries for seals, penguins, dolphins and laid-back travelers. If not before, **Kaikoura** (p. 241) is the place to get all wet, swimming with playful dolphins in the stunning surf before moving on to **Christchurch** (p. 263), where New Zealand shows its British colors.

WINTER SPOTS

In frosty weather, you shouldn't miss the North Island slopes around **Ohakune** (p. 193), or the South Island snowbunnies in **Methven** (p. 277) and **Wanaka** (p. 313), the majesty of **Mt. Cook National Park** (p. 284), or the revitalizing hot springs of **Hanmer Springs** (p. 245).

Christchurch is a great base for fantastic day trips to **Akaroa** and the **Banks Peninsula** (p. 274). From Christchurch, you can continue south to the university pub town of **Dunedin** (p. 328), where rugby, beer, and music represent the Father, Son, and Holy Ghost. The youthful exuberance of the students supports both vibrant nightlife and active sport. From Dunedin, explore the rugged pastures, forests, and beaches of the **Catlins** (p. 340) before blitzkrieging **Queenstown** (p. 302), where all of New

Zealand's heart-stopping adventure activities converge. In the middle of the Queenstown insanity (plan on 3-4 days and NZ$300-400), take a daytrip into the heart of the spectacular **Fiordland National Park** to the mystical **Milford Sound** (p. 322). Nearby **Wanaka** and **Glenorchy** are also worthwhile stops. As you head north, you'll pass the ice palaces of **Franz and Fox Glaciers** (p. 296), several billion cubic meters of moving solid blue ice that you can, and should, explore in shorts. One of the most explosive West Coast highlights is the pancake rocks of **Paparoa National Park** (p. 289), which stupefy both tourists and scientists with their unique formations. To pay a fond farewell to the South Island, stay a day in **Nelson** (p. 246), one of its sunniest cities. The weekend flea market is an especially bright spot, and a great farewell to the South Island before you zip back through Picton to Wellington and northward on the TranzScenic to the volcanic moonscapes of Tongariro National Park for the **Tongariro Crossing** (p. 360), one of New Zealand's finest one-day tramps. Then, it's on to **Waitomo** (p. 145) for spelunking, glowworms, and rafting, before tracing a weary but reluctant path back toward Auckland.

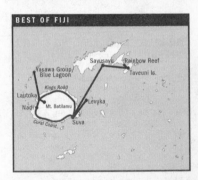

BEST OF FIJI

BEST OF FIJI (3 WEEKS) Sleep off your jetlag in **Nadi** (p. 393), and head north to friendly **Lautoka** (p. 397) to check out the Garden of the Sleeping Giant. Oil yourself up and grab your togs on your way to the **Yasawa Group** (p. 418). Keep your eyes peeled for Hollywood's favorites as you island hop from beach to beach. Be sure to hit the **Blue Lagoon** before heading back to Lautoka. At this point head east along the **Kings Road** (p. 399) for a rough taste of rural Fiji or head south along the Queens Road and the **Coral Coast** (p. 403) if glitzy resorts are up your alley. From both roads, interior treks are a definite must to meet, greet, and eat the Fijian way. Take a day

DIVING

Do soft corals and pelagic fish get you wild? Head to the Somosomo Strait between **Vanua Levu** (p. p. 427) and **Taveuni** (p. 430) for some of the world's best diving. More easily accessible from Viti Levu, **Beqa Lagoon** (p. 406) also offers world-class underwater scenery.

to hike over **Mt. Batilamu** (p. 409), the highest peak in Fiji. Regardless of your path, head to **Suva** (p. 410) for a small taste of the modern Fiji. Hop on a boat (with life jackets) to **Levuka** (p. 424) on the island of **Ovalau** (p. 423). Lap up some historical Fiji and stop by Lovoni Village with Epi before cruising back to Suva to catch a ride to **Savusavu** (p. 428) on **Vanua Levu** (p. 427). Enjoy the remote waters of this under-touristed island by kayak and catch a ferry to **Taveuni** (p. 430), Fiji's Garden Island. Have your pick of some of Fiji's greatest accommodations and enjoy the world's best diving in the **Rainbow Reef** (p. 433).

knowledge that you have done New Zealand in the most heart-racing, memory-erasing, and death-defying way possible. **Scuba** to the wreck of the *Rainbow Warrior* in Paihia (p. 112) or among Jacques Cousteau's preferred marine friends on the Poor Knight's Islands (p. 107). **Offer yourself** to the one **active volcano** in New Zealand, White Island from Whakatane (p. 163). Learn why you just can't beat the life of a hamster while **zorbing** in Rotorua (p. 152). **Raft** through extensive subterranean cave systems in Waitomo (p. 145). **Skydive** over the geothermal beauty and mountainous majesty of Taupo (p. 182). **Kayak** the Marlborough Sounds to see sealife galore (p. 239). **Swim with dolphins** or sea lions in the sparkling blue waters of Kaikoura (p. 241). **Raft** the tempestuous Buller River on Grade 4-5 rapids (p. 290). **Climb** one of New Zealand's twin glaciers (p. 296) and **descend** through subtropical rainforest. Depending on the season, **canyon, ski,** or **snowboard** in versatile Wanaka (p. 313). **Bungy** in the original capital of the sport, Queenstown (p. 302). Scream, scrum, and spectate at a **rugby match** in Dunedin (p. 328). And finally, **fly** out of Christchurch (p. 263) with the clothes on your back, the memory of financial solvency, and enough adrenaline to last a lifetime.

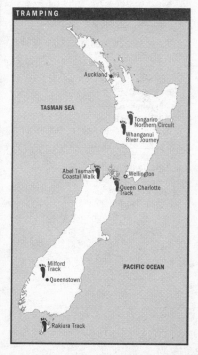

ADVENTURE NEW ZEALAND Though this tour might leave you a little light in the wallet, you can return home secure in the

DISCOVER

TRAMPING NEW ZEALAND (4 WEEKS) A tramping tour of New Zealand for the serious tramper might start with the **Tongariro Northern Circuit** (4 days) which includes the breath-taking **Tongariro Crossing** (p. 360). From this central point, day trips to Wellington, Rotorua and Auckland are possible after completing the track. Then, after you have gotten your fill of civilization, head to **Taumarunui** (p. 212) to start the **Whanganui River Journey** (5 days). The only Great Walk over water, this paddle is peppered with phenomenal accommodations, from a loft above a microbrewery to a Maori *marae*. Ultimately, all trampers in New Zealand will want to hop over to the South Island where the scenery is even more spectacular. Luckily, the **Queen Charlotte Track** (3-5 days), accessible from Picton (p. 376), is just a quick hop across the Strait. Although not the most strenuous or technical trip, the tramp offers a unique way to see the beauty of the Marlborough Sounds. Also a part of the north of the South, the **Abel Tasman Coastal Track** (3 days; p. 363) through the National Park (p. 254) of the same name is a relatively mellow tramp past the coves and golden beaches of the northern coast. After two laid-back journeys, make your way down the west coast where the Southern Alps, Mount Aspiring Park (p. 318) and Fiordland National Park (p. 319) provide stereotypically gorgeous New Zealand scenery. Glenorchy (p. 312), just north of Queenstown, is the starting point of the world famous **Milford Track** (4 days; p. 370), often heralded as the "finest walk in the world." Finally, it doesn't get more remote than the Great Walk along Stewart Island's **Rakiura Track** (2-3 days; p. 375) which winds through lush forest in the southernmost part of New Zealand.

▨ LET'S GO PICKS

BEST PLACE TO BOOZE: You won't be alone atop the tables in **The Holy Cow** in Taupo (p. 182). On the other hand, if you prefer to get smashed, try the **Smash Palace** in Gisborne (p. 167). And who wouldn't order a Fiji Baby on **Beachcomber Island** (p. 418) as the sun sets over the Mamanucas.

BEST PLACE TO TEMPT FATE: The skydive over **Taupo** (p. 182), or **Franz Josef** and **Fox Glaciers** (p. 296,, p. 300). Or, the world's most famous bungy jump in adrenaline-happy **Queenstown** (p. 302).

BEST AND WORST USE OF "PROTECTION": A.J. Hackett made his first commercial **bungy** (p. 320) with a latex rubber cord, making Queenstown the bungy capital of the world. **Te Urewera National Park** (p. 173), meaning "burnt penis," illustrates the perils of forgetting to make sure the fire is *out* before falling asleep.

BEST PLACE TO SEE THE KING: Elvis himself still lives on in **Hawera** (p. 205), thanks to one Kiwi's obsession with the rock 'n' roll legend.

BEST PLACE TO SNOG: When you roll into **Whangarei** (p. 105) late at night, you'll find urban cowboys from Auckland whooping it up to DJ rhythms. In **Queenstown,** The World (p. 302) will keep you turning all night long. In **Ohakune** (p. 193), everyone knows each other by name by day, but forgets them by night.

BEST PLACE TO DIG YOUR OWN GRAVE AND LIE IN IT: You have to dig the thermal pools at **Hot Water Beach** (p. 133) yourself.

BEST PLACE TO MEET THE LOCALS: Stay with Fijian families in **Navala** (p. 407) and **Bukuya** (p. 408). Visit a marae and enjoy a hangi with Maori in Rotorua (p. 152).

BEST PLACE TO BE WASHED UP: Swimming with dolphins in **Kaikoura** (p. 241), surfing in **Raglan** (p. 141), soaking in the hot pools of **Hanmer Springs** (p. 245), and learning how to snowboard at **Cardrona** (p. 276).

BEST PLACES TO DIVE: Get deep and wet in the **Somosomo Strait,** accessed from Taveuni (p. 430). See what Jacques was talkin' about at Poor Knight's Island (p. 107).

ESSENTIALS

FACTS FOR TRAVELERS

ENTRANCE REQUIREMENTS
Passport (p. 12). Required for all visitors to New Zealand and Fiji.
Visa (p. 13). Not usually required unless you are planning to work or study. Contact an embassy or consulate for specific information.
Work Permit (p. 13). Required for all foreigners, except those from Australia who plan to work in New Zealand.
Driving Permit (p. 42). Required for all those planning to drive.

CLIMATE

For a detailed climate chart of several major destinations in New Zealand and Fiji see the **Appendix** p. 437.

NEW ZEALAND. Year-round, temperature fluctuation in New Zealand is far from extreme; however weather systems in mountainous areas can change instantaneously, so be prepared. Rainfall in most of the North Island and the northern South Island is heaviest in the winter (June-Aug.), though the infamous rainfall on the West Coast of the South Island knows no season, often totalling 7-8m annually.

FIJI. The Fijian islands experience a relatively constant tropical climate, free from extreme heat or cold. The wet season (Dec.-Feb.) sees heavy rainfall and the occasional violent storm, as well as the warmest weather of the year.

TIME ZONES

New Zealand and Fiji lie in the same time zone, 12 hours ahead of Greenwich Mean Time (GMT). If the world ran only on standard time, they would be two hours ahead of Sydney, 12 hours ahead of London, 16 hours ahead of New York and Toronto, and 19 hours ahead of California and Vancouver. But due to different **Daylight Savings Times (DST)**, calculations can easily be confused. In **New Zealand,** DST runs from the first Sunday in October, when clocks are sprung ahead one hour, until the last Sunday in March, when time falls back one hour. In **Fiji,** DST runs from the first Sunday in November until the last Sunday in February. Both of these schedules contrast sharply with DST in most of the Northern Hemisphere, which typically runs from the last Sunday in March until the first Sunday in October. See the **Inside Back Cover** for charts listing relative times in large cities world-wide.

HOLIDAYS AND FESTIVALS

Public holidays in New Zealand and Fiji can put a crimp in your plans. During the days listed below, banks, restaurants, stores, and museums may close, and public transport may be considerably more difficult to find. During the New Zealand **school holidays** in the summer (roughly Christmas to Waitangi Day) finding a place to stay in the major vacation destinations can be harder than spotting a kiwi in the bush; book ahead whenever possible. Certain areas such as the Tongariro region in the North Island and the ski fields of the South Island draw their biggest crowds in the winter (June-Aug.), especially during the first two weeks of July when the schools get out for vacation. Travelers to Fiji should be aware that with the changes of government in the last 15 years there has been a strong movement to desecularize **Sundays;** currently accessibility of stores and services remains

2002 DATE	HOLIDAY NAME
January 1	New Year
February 6	Waitangi Day **(NZ)**
March 13	National Youth Day **(F)**
March 29	Good Friday
March 31	Easter
April 1	Easter Monday
April 25	Anzac Day **(NZ)**
May 31	Ratu Sir Lala Sukuna Day **(F)**
June 12	Queen's Birthday
July 7	Mohammed's Birthday **(F)**
July 26	Constitution Day **(F)**
October 11	Fiji Day **(F)**
October 22	Labour Day **(NZ)**
December 25	Christmas
December 26	Boxing Day

extremely limited, so plan accordingly. Cities and towns across **New Zealand** hold countless **festivals and fairs** throughout the year. Most take place between December and February; ask the local tourist office for information. If you're near a festival, it pays to alter your plans to attend; most are ebullient explosions that draw Kiwis from the surrounding area. **Fijian festivals** can be extremely disruptive to travel plans. The celebration of certain religious holidays can last for up to a week, with entire villages often turning out to enjoy the occasions. Activities range from firewalking to squirting each other with colored water (Festival of Colours).

2002 DATE	FESTIVAL	LOCATION
January-February	Summer City Festival	Wellington **(NZ)**
February 15-24	Festival of Flowers	Christchurch **(NZ)**
February 10-25	HERO Gay and Lesbian Festival	Auckland **(NZ)**
February or March	Holi (Hindu Festival of Colours)	Fiji
March or April	Ram Naumi (Hindu Birth of Lord Rama)	Fiji
April	Auckland-Suva Yacht Race	Auckland/Suva **(NZ/F)**
June 13-16	National Fieldays	Hamilton/Cambridge **(NZ)**
July	International Film Festival	Auckland **(NZ)**
August	Winter Festival	Christchurch **(NZ)**
August	Hibiscus Festival	Suva **(F)**
September	Wearable Art Awards	Nelson **(NZ)**
August	Ritual Fire Walking (Hindu)	Suva **(F)**
September	Sugar Festival	Lautoka **(F)**
November 8-11	Rhododendron Festival	Dunedin **(NZ)**
November 8	Diwali (Hindu Festival of Light)	Fiji

EMBASSIES & CONSULATES

NZ CONSULAR SERVICES ABROAD

Australia: High Commission, Commonwealth Ave., **Canberra** ACT 2600 (☎02 6270 4211; fax 6273 3194).

Canada: High Commission 99 Bank St. (Suite 727), **Ottawa** ON K1P 6G3 (☎613-238-5991; fax 238-5707; www.nzhcottawa.org). All visa queries ☎613-238-6097.

Fiji: Embassy & High Commission, Reserve Bank Building, P.O. Box 1378, **Suva** (☎311 422; fax 300 842; nzhc@is.com.fj; www.embassy.kcom.ne.jp/newzealand/).

Ireland: Consulate General, 37 Leeson Park, **Dublin** 6 (☎01 660 4233; fax 660 4228).

Japan: Embassy, 20-44 Kamiyama-cho, Shibuya-ku, **Tokyo** 150 0047 (☎03 3467 2271; fax 3467 6843; nzemb@gol.com).

South Africa: High Commission, Block C, 2nd fl., Hatfield Gardens, 1110 Arcadia St., **Pretoria** 0028 (☎012 342 8656; fax 342 8640).

UK: High Commission, New Zealand House, The Haymarket, **London** SW1Y 4TQ. Passport queries ☎020 7930 8422; fax 839 4580.

US: Embassy, 37 Observatory Circle NW, **Washington, D.C.** 20008 (☎202-328-4848; fax 667-5227). Consulate-General, 12400 Wilshire Blvd. (Suite 1150), **Los Angeles,** CA 90025 (☎310-207-1605; fax 207-3605).

FIJIAN CONSULAR SERVICES ABROAD

Australia: High Commission, P.O. Box 159, 19 Beale St., Deakin, **Canberra** ACT 2600 (☎06 260 5115; fax 260 5105). Embassy, 9 Beagle St., Red Hill, **Canberra** ACT 2600; P.O. Box E159, Queen Victoria Terrace (☎06 239 6872; fax 295 3283).

Canada: Honorary Consul, 130 Slatter St. (Suite 750), **Ottawa,** ON KIP 6E2 (☎613-233-9252; fax 594-8705).

Japan: Embassy, NOA Building, 3-5, 2 Chome Azabudai, Minato-ku, **Tokyo** 106 0047 (☎03 3587 2038; fax 3587 2563).

New Zealand: High Commission, 31 Pipitea St., Thorndon, **Wellington** (☎04 473 5401; fax 499 1011).

UK: Embassy & High Commission, 34 Hyde Park Gate, **London** SW7 5BN (☎020 7584 3661; fax 7584 2838; fijirepuk@compuserve.com).

US: Embassy & High Commission, 2233 Wisconsin Ave. NW (Suite 240), **Washington, D.C.** 20007 (☎202-337-8320; fax 337-1966; fijiemb@earthlink.com).

CONSULAR SERVICES IN NEW ZEALAND

Australia: High Commission, 72-78 Hobson St., P.O. Box 4036, **Wellington** (☎04 473 6411; fax 498 7118). Consulate General, Union House, 7th-8th fl., 132-138 Quay St., (Private Bag 92023) **Auckland** (☎09 303 2429; fax 377 0798).

Canada: High Commission, 3rd fl., 61 Molesworth St., P.O. Box 12049, **Wellington** (☎04 473 9577; fax 471 2082).

Fiji: High Commission, 31 Pipitea St., **Wellington** (☎04 473 5401; fax 499 1011).

Ireland: Consulate General, Dingwall Building, 2nd fl., 87 Queen St., P.O. Box 279, **Auckland** (☎09 302 2867; fax 302 2420).

UK: High Commission, 44 Hill St., P.O. Box 1812, **Wellington** (☎04 472 6049; fax 473 4982). Consulate General, 151 Queens St. (Private Bag 92014), **Auckland** (☎09 303 2973; fax 303 1836).

US: Consular Services, General Building, 29 Shortland St. (Private Bag 92022), **Auckland** (☎09 303 2724; fax 366 0870). American Embassy, 29 Fitzherbert Terrace, Thorndon, **Wellington** (☎04 472 2068; fax 471 2380).

CONSULAR SERVICES IN FIJI

Australia: High Commission, 37 Princes Rd., P.O. Box 214, **Suva** (☎382 211; fax 382 065; austembassy@is.com.fj).

Japan: Embassy, 2nd fl. Dominion House, P.O. Box 13045, **Suva** (☎302 122; fax 301 452).

New Zealand: High Commission Reserve Bank Building P.O. Box 1378, **Suva** (☎311 422; fax 300 842; nzhc@is.com.fj).

UK: High Commission, Victoria House, Government Buildings, P.O. Box 1355, **Suva** (☎311 033; fax 301 406; richard_emmerson@bhc.org.fj).

US: Embassy 31 Loftus St., P.O. Box 218, **Suva** (☎314 466; fax 300 081; usemb-suva@is.com.fj)

NEW ZEALAND TOURIST BOARD

The ever-helpful **New Zealand Tourism Board (NZTB)** offices can provide information galore about any aspect of the country. Their web page (www.purenz.com/indexnz.cfm) is easy to use and enormously helpful, offering concise travel info and links to other travel pages. NZTB has offices in the following countries:

Australia: 35 Pitt St., Level 8, **Sydney** NSW 2000 (☎02 9247 5222; fax 9241 1136).

Japan: Meiji Seimei Sakaisuji Honmachi Building, 2nd fl., 1-7-15 Minami Honmachi, Chuo-ku, **Sosaka** 541 (☎06 268 8335; fax 268 8412).

South Africa: Holiday House, 158-160 Hendrik Verwoerd Dr., **Randberg** 2125 (☎011 289 8186; fax 289 8023)

UK: New Zealand House, Haymarket, **London** SW1Y 4TQ (☎0171 930 1662; fax 839 8929; enquiries@nztb.govt.nz).

US: 501 Santa Monica Blvd. (Suite 300), **Santa Monica, California** 90401 (☎800-388-5494 (headquarters) or 310-395-7480; fax 310-395-5453).

VISITORS INFORMATION NETWORK (VIN). In most towns, all cities, and many airports you should watch for the green "i" symbol denoting one of the 81 independently owned and operated **Visitor's Information Network (VIN)** tourist offices throughout New Zealand. Coordinated by the New Zealand Tourism Board, these offices will help plan your travel, from booking accommodations to transport to activities. You can also tune into 88.2 FM, the 24-hour tourist radio station.

FIJI VISITORS BUREAU

While perhaps not providing the same depth of information as its New Zealand counterpart, the **Fiji Visitors Bureau (FVB)** staffs a number of extremely friendly and helpful tourist offices in the islands and the rest of the world. Their impressive website (www.bulafiji.com) is a great starting point for planning your trip; be aware that, like most government tourism organizations, the FVB has no interest in showcasing the less savory aspects of their country. Travelers should take note that the FVB is the *only* official tourist organization in Fiji. Many travel agencies masquerade as tourist centers in an attempt to sign unwary visitors up for cruises and package deals. Be prepared to be bombarded in the Nadi Airport.

Australia: St. Martins Tower, 31 Market St., Level 12, **Sydney** 2000 (☎02 9264 3399; fax 9264 3060; infosyd@bulafiji.au.com).

Canada: ☎800-932-3454; fax 310-670-2318; fiji@primenet.com.

Japan: 14th fl., NOA Building, 3-5, 2 Chome Azabudai, Minato-ku, **Tokyo** 106 (☎03 3587 2038; fax 3587 2563; fijijp@magical.egg.or.jp).

New Zealand: P.O. Box 1179, **Auckland** (☎09 373 2133; fax 309 4720; infor@bulafiji.co.nz; www.BulaFiji.co.nz).

US: 5777 West Century Blvd. (Suite 220), **Los Angeles,** CA 90045 (☎310-568-1616; fax 670-2318; info@bulafiji_americas.com).

UK: 203 Sheen Lane, East Sheen, **London** SW14 8LE (☎020 8876 1938; fax 8878 9876; uk@interface-tourism.com

DOCUMENTS AND FORMALITIES

PASSPORTS

REQUIREMENTS. All visitors need valid passports to enter New Zealand or Fiji. Passports must be valid for at least three months beyond the time you intend to stay; returning home with an expired passport is illegal, and may result in a fine.

PHOTOCOPIES. Be sure to photocopy the page of your passport with your photo, passport number, and other identifying information, as well as any visas, travel insurance policies, plane tickets, and traveler's check serial numbers. Carry one set of copies in a safe place, apart from the originals, and leave another set at home. Consulates also recommend that you carry an expired passport or an official copy of your birth certificate in a part of your baggage separate from other documents.

LOST PASSPORTS. If you lose your passport, immediately notify the local police and the nearest embassy or consulate of your home government. To expedite its replacement, you will need to know all information previously recorded and show ID and proof of citizenship. In some cases, a replacement may take weeks to process, and it may be valid for only a limited time. Any visas stamped in your old passport will be irretrievably lost. In an emergency, ask for immediate temporary traveling papers that will permit you to re-enter your home country. Since your passport is a public document belonging to your nation's government, you may have to surrender it to a foreign government official. If you don't get it back in a reasonable amount of time, inform the nearest mission of your home country.

NEW PASSPORTS. Citizens of Australia, Canada, Ireland, the United Kingdom, and the United States can apply for a passport at the nearest post office, passport office, or court of law. Citizens of South Africa can apply for a passport at the nearest office of Foreign Affairs. Any new passport or renewal applications must be filed well in advance of the departure date, although most passport offices offer rush services for a very steep fee. Citizens living abroad who need a passport or renewal services should contact their home country's nearest consular service.

Australia: ☎131 232; passports.australia@dfat.gov.au; www.passports.gov.au/index.html. Apply for a passport at a post office, passport office (in all state capitals and Newcastle), or overseas diplomatic mission. Passports AUS$132 (36-page) or AUS$198 (64-page); valid for 10 years. Children AUS$66 or AUS$99; valid for 5 years.

Canada: Canadian Passport Office, Department of Foreign Affairs and International Trade, **Ottawa,** ON K1A 0G3 (☎613-994-3500 or 800-567-6868; www.dfait-maeci.gc.ca/passport/menu.asp). Applications available at 29 regional passport offices, Canadian missions, and post offices. Passports CDN$60 (24-page) or CDN$62 (48-page); valid for 5 years.

Ireland: Pick up an application at a *Garda* station or post office, or request one from a passport office. Then apply by mail to the Department of Foreign Affairs, Passport Office, Setanta Centre, Molesworth St., **Dublin** 2 (☎01 671 1633; fax 671 1092; www.irlgov.ie/iveagh), or the Passport Office, Irish Life Building, 1A South Mall, **Cork** (☎021 27 25 25). Passports IR£55; valid for 10 years. Under 16 or over 65 IR£10; valid for 3 years.

South Africa: Department of Home Affairs. Passports are issued only in Pretoria, but all applications must still be submitted or forwarded to the nearest South African consulate. Processing time is 3 months or more. Passports around ZAR190; valid for 10 years. Under 16 around ZAR140; valid for five years. For more information, usaembassy.southafrica.net/VisaForms/Passport/Passport2000.html.

UK: ☎0870 521 0410; www.open.gov.uk/ukpass/ukpass.htm. Get an application from a passport office, main post office, travel agent, or online (for UK residents only) at www.ukpa.gov.uk/forms/f_app_pack.htm. Then apply by mail or in person at a passport office (call to find the closest office). Passports UK£28; valid for 10 years. Under-15 UK£14.80; valid for 5 years. The process takes about 4 weeks; faster service (by personal visit) costs an additional £12.

US: ☎888-362-8668; www.travel.state.gov/passport_services.html. Apply at any federal or state courthouse, authorized post office, or US Passport Agency (in most major cities); see the "US Government, State Department" section of the telephone book or a post office for addresses. Processing takes 3-4 weeks. New passports US$60; valid for 10 years. Under 18 US$40; valid for 5 years. Passports may be renewed by mail or in person for US$40. Add US$35 for 3-day expedited service.

VISAS AND WORK PERMITS

VISAS. Citizens of the US, Canada, Japan, Ireland, South Africa, the UK, and most European nations do not need a visa to enter New Zealand or Fiji. For those travelers who need them, visas are available at most embassies and consulates and are usually valid for three months in New Zealand and four months in Fiji.

Upon arrival, travelers not requiring visas are granted **visitor permits.** To qualify for a visitor permit, you must display your passport and a valid ticket to a country to which you have the right of entry; you may also need to display sufficient funds to support yourself during your stay (usually NZ$1000). Major credit cards and traveler's checks also constitute sufficient funds. The visitor permit allows you to visit New Zealand for three months (six months for UK citizens) and Fiji for four months; to extend your stay, you must reapply at an immigration office before your current permit expires.

Be sure to double-check on entrance requirements at the nearest embassy or consulate for up-to-date info before departure. US citizens can also consult www.pueblo.gsa.gov/cic_text/travel/foreign/foreignentryreqs.html.

WORK PERMITS. Admission as a visitor does not include the right to work, which is authorized only by a work permit. Australian citizens and residents with a current **Australian resident return visa** do not need a visa or permit to work in New Zealand. Citizens of Canada, the Republic of Ireland, and the UK aged 18-30 are eligible to apply for a place in a New Zealand working holiday scheme which provides a work permit for up to twelve months; contact the nearest New Zealand Immigration Service office for more details (www.immigration.govt.nz). For more information, see **Alternatives to Tourism** p. 50.

IDENTIFICATION

When you travel, always carry two or more forms of identification on your person, including at least one photo ID; a passport combined with a driver's license or birth certificate is usually adequate. Many establishments, especially banks, may require several IDs to cash traveler's checks. Never carry all your forms of ID together; split them up in case of theft or loss. It is useful to bring extra passport-size photos to affix to the various IDs or passes you may acquire along the way.

For more information on all the forms of identification listed below, contact the organization that provides the service, the **International Student Travel Confederation (ISTC),** Herengracht 479, 1017 BS Amsterdam, Netherlands (☎ 31 20 421 28 00; fax 421 28 10; istcinfo@istc.org; www.istc.org).

TEACHER & STUDENT IDENTIFICATION. The **International Student Identity Card (ISIC),** the most widely accepted form of student ID, provides discounts on sights, accommodations, food, and transport. The ISIC is preferable to an institution-specific card (such as a university ID) because it is more likely to be recognized (and honored) abroad. All cardholders have access to a 24-hour emergency helpline for medical, legal, and financial emergencies (in North America call 877-370-ISIC, elsewhere call US collect +1 715-345-0505, UK collect +44 20 8762 8110, or France collect +33 155 633 144), and holders of US-issued cards are also eligible for insurance benefits (see **Insurance** p. 25). Many student travel agencies issue ISICs, including STA Travel in Australia and New Zealand; Travel CUTS in Canada; usit in the Republic of Ireland and Northern Ireland; SASTS in South Africa; Campus Travel and STA Travel in the UK; Council Travel (www.counciltravel.com/idcards/default.asp) and STA Travel in the US (see **Budget & Student Travel Agencies** p. 38).

The card is valid from September of one year to December of the following year and costs US$22. Applicants must be degree-seeking students of a secondary or post-secondary school and must be of at least 12 years of age. Because of the proliferation of fake ISICs, some services (particularly airlines) require additional proof of student identity, such as a school ID or a letter attesting to your student status, signed by your registrar and stamped with your school seal. The **International Teacher Identity Card (ITIC)** offers the same insurance coverage as well as similar but limited discounts. The fee is AUS$13, UK£5, or US$22.

YOUTH IDENTIFICATION. The International Student Travel Confederation also issues a discount card to travelers who are 26 years old or under, but are not students. This one-year **International Youth Travel Card** (**IYTC;** formerly the **GO 25** Card) offers many of the same benefits as the ISIC. Most organizations that sell the ISIC also sell the IYTC (US$22).

ISICONNECT SERVICE. If you are an ISIC card carrier and want to avoid buying individual calling cards or wish to consolidate all your means of communication during your trip, you can activate your ISIC's ISIConnect service, a powerful new integrated communications service (powered by eKit.com). With ISIConnect, one toll-free access number (☎0800 114 478 in New Zealand, in Auckland only dial ☎09 912 8211 for cheaper access; ☎0800 7132 in Fiji) gives you access to several different methods of keeping in touch via the phone and Internet, including: a reduced-rate international calling plan that treats your ISIC card as a universal calling card; a personalized voicemail box accessible from payphones anywhere in the world or for free over the Internet; faxmail service for sending and receiving faxes via email, fax machines, or pay phones; various email capabilities, including a service that reads your email to you over the phone; an online "travel safe" for storing (and faxing) important documents and numbers; and a 24hr. emergency help line (via phone or email at ISIConnect@ekit.com) offering assistance and medical and legal referrals. To activate your ISIConnect account, visit the service's comprehensive website (www.isiconnect.ekit.com) or call the customer service number of your home country (which is also your home country's access number): in Australia 800 114 478; in Canada 877-635-3575; in Ireland 800 555 180 or 800 577 980; in New Zealand 0800 114 478; in the UK 0800 376 2366 or 0800 169 8646; in the US 800-706-1333; and in South Africa 0800 992 921 or 0800 997 285.

CUSTOMS

As island nations, New Zealand and Fiji are free from many pests and crop blights, and they'd like to keep it that way. Before leaving for your travels, find out what you can bring home, before you get stuck at the airport. Upon **entering** New Zealand or Fiji, you must declare all food, plant, and animal goods, dead or alive, so look out for the blue declaration of goods forms. Restricted goods may or may not be confiscated, but they must be declared. Camping equipment must also be declared. Customs officials will likely inspect your equipment and, in New Zealand, used equipment may be cleaned.

Upon **returning home,** you must declare all items you acquired abroad and pay a **duty** on the value of those articles that exceed the allowance set by your country's customs service. The Goods and Services Tax and Value Added Tax are not refundable upon leaving. Goods purchased at **duty-free** shops abroad are not exempt from duty or sales tax at your point of return; you must declare these as well. "Duty-free" merely means no tax in the country of purchase. Keeping receipts for purchases made abroad will help establish values when you return.

NEW ZEALAND. Personal effects and goods up to a total combined value of NZ$700 are admitted free of duty or **Goods and Services Tax** (**GST;** see **Taxes** p. 20). Anything beyond the allowance must be declared and is charged a duty in addition to the GST. Visitors over the age of 17 are also allowed to enter with the following concessions duty- and tax-free: 200 cigarettes, 50 cigars, or 250g of tobacco, or a mixture of all three not weighing more than 250g; 4.5L of wine (six 750mL bottles) or 4.5L of beer; and one bottle containing not more than 1125mL of liquor.

FIJI. Personal effects and goods not intended for sale are admitted free of duty or **Value Added Tax** (**VAT;** see **Taxes** p. 20). Dutiable goods (other than alcohol or tobacco) up to FJ$400 are admitted and charged accordingly. Visitors over 17 are also allowed to enter with the following concessions duty- and tax-free: 500 cigarettes or any combination of tobacco products not weighing more than 500g; 2L of liquor or 4L of wine/beer or any combination that does not exceed the prescribed limit for any one item.

ESSENTIALS

MONEY

COSTS

If you stay in hostels, prepare your own food, and stick mostly to the free and low-budget natural attractions, you could probably get by on NZ$40-50 per day in New Zealand, and FJ$35-45 in Fiji. Transportation, dining out, and high-adrenaline adventure activities will dramatically increase this figure. It is probably best to decide before leaving exactly how much you will budget for activities like skydiving, bungy jumping, and scuba diving. The single biggest cost of your trip will probably be your round-trip **airfare** to New Zealand and/or Fiji (see **Airfares** p. 36.) A bus pass (see **Buses** p. 41, p. 45), car rental (see **Cars** p. 42, p. 45), or island-hopping pass (see **Flights** p. 45) would be another major pre-departure expense. You should keep handy a larger amount of cash when you are traveling into more rural areas. Also, don't forget to budget for emergency reserve funds (at least US$200).

TIPS FOR STAYING ON A BUDGET

Considering that saving a few dollars a day over the course of your trip might pay for days or weeks of additional travel, the art of penny-pinching is worth learning. Learn to take advantage of freebies: in New Zealand and Fiji nature is often the best attraction in town. Bring a sleepsack (see **Sleepsack** p. 27) to save on linen charges, and do your laundry in the sink (unless explicitly prohibited from doing so). You can split **accommodations** costs (in hotels and some hostels) with trustworthy fellow travelers; multi-bed rooms almost always work out cheaper per person than singles. Happy hours can provide both food and drink at reduced prices and going early to bars and clubs, especially in a big city, can often reduce or eliminate cover charges. You can also buy food in **supermarkets** instead of eating out; you'd be surprised how tasty (and cheap) bread can be with cheese or a spread. And the ubiquitous New Zealand **takeaways,** while not providing the most healthy or original fare, sell meat pies and pre-made sandwiches at disturbingly low prices. With that said, don't go overboard with budget obsession. Though staying within your budget is important, don't do so at the expense of your sanity or health.

CURRENCY AND EXCHANGE

New Zealand's unit of currency is the **New Zealand Dollar (NZ$).** Coins come in denominations of 5, 10, 20, and 50 cents, $1, and $2; notes come in denominations of $5, $10, $20, $50, and $100. Fiji's unit of currency is the **Fiji Dollar (FJ$).** Coins come in denominations of 1, 2, 5, 10, 20, and 50 cents, and $1; notes come in denominations of $1, $2, $5, $10, $20, and $50. Carry considerably more small change in Fiji for transportation costs. **Unless otherwise specified, all prices in the text are either in New Zealand Dollars or Fiji Dollars (depending on region).** Typical bank hours in New Zealand are Monday through Friday 9am to 4:30pm and major banks include Bank of New Zealand (BNZ), Australia and New Zealand Banking Group (ANZ), and ASB Bank (ASB). Bank hours in Fiji are typically Monday through Thursday from 9:30am to 3pm, and 9:30am to 4pm on Fridays. Major banks in Fiji include ANZ, National Bank, Fiji Westpac, and Bank of Hawaii.

The currency charts below are based on August 2002 exchange rates between New Zealand and Fiji Dollars (NZ$ and FJ$) and Australian dollars (AUS$), Canadian dollars (CDN$), Irish pounds (IR£), South African Rands (ZAR), British pounds (UK£), US dollars (US$), and European Union Euros (EUR€). Check the currency converter on the *Let's Go* Homepage (www.letsgo.com/thumb) or a large newspaper for the latest exchange rates.

As a general rule, it's cheaper to convert money in New Zealand or Fiji than at home. However, you should bring enough foreign currency to last for the first 24 to 72 hours of a trip to avoid being penniless should you arrive after bank hours or on a holiday. Travelers from the US can get foreign currency from the comfort of home: **International Currency Express** (☎888-278-6628) delivers foreign currency or traveler's checks 2nd-day (US$12) at competitive exchange rates.

ATMs are widespread in New Zealand (see **Cash Cards** p. 18) and are often the best and easiest way to acquire New Zealand currency. While not as common in Fiji, there are still readily accessible ATMs in many larger towns and cities.

Try to go only to banks that have at most a 5% margin between their buy and sell prices. Since you lose money with every transaction, **convert large sums** (unless the currency is depreciating rapidly), **but no more than you'll need.**

If you use traveler's checks or bills, carry some in small denominations (the equivalent of US$50 or less) in case you are forced to exchange money at disadvantageous rates, but bring a range of denominations since charges may be levied per check cashed. Store your money in a variety of forms; ideally, you will always be carrying some cash, some traveler's checks, and an ATM and/or credit card.

NZ DOLLARS ($)		
AUS$1 = NZ$1.22	NZ$1 = AUS$0.82
CDN$1 = NZ$1.58	NZ$1 = CDN$0.63
FJ$1 = NZ$1.05	NZ$1 = FJ$0.95
IR£1 = NZ$2.69	NZ$1 = IR£0.37
ZAR1 = NZ$0.29	NZ$1 = ZAR3.40
US$1 = NZ$2.42	NZ$1 = US$0.41
UK£ 1= NZ$3.46	NZ$1= UK£0.29
EUR€1 = NZ$2.12	NZ$1 = EUR€0.47

FIJIAN DOLLARS ($)		
AUS$1 = FJ$1.17	FJ$1 = AUS$0.86
CDN$1 = FJ$1.51	FJ$1 = CDN$0.66
IR£1 = FJ$2.57	FJ$1 = IR£0.39
NZ$1 = FJ$0.95	FJ$1 = NZ$1.05
ZAR1 = FJ$0.28	FJ$1 = ZAR3.56
US$1 = FJ$2.31	FJ$1 = US$0.43
UK£1 = FJ$3.30	FJ$1 = UK£0.30
EUR€1 = FJ$2.02	FJ$1 = EUR€0.49

TRAVELER'S CHECKS

Traveler's checks (**American Express** and **Visa**) are the most recognized) are one of the safest and least troublesome means of carrying funds. Several agencies and banks sell them for a small commission. Each agency provides refunds if your checks are lost or stolen, and many provide additional services, such as toll-free refund hotlines abroad, emergency message services, and stolen credit card assistance. Buying traveler's checks in New Zealand and Fijian dollars can be difficult, as many major check companies do not yet offer them.

While traveling, keep check receipts and a record of which checks you've cashed separate from the checks themselves. Also leave a list of check numbers with someone at home. Always sign checks when you buy them, but never countersign checks until you're ready to cash them, and always bring your passport with you to cash them. If your checks are lost or stolen, immediately contact the refund center of the company that issued your checks to be reimbursed; they may require a police report verifying the loss or theft. Ask about toll-free refund hotlines and the location of refund centers when purchasing checks. Always carry emergency cash.

American Express: ☎800 251 902 in Australia; in New Zealand ☎0800 441 068; in the UK ☎0800 521 313; in the US and Canada ☎800-221-7282; in Fiji call Australia collect 61 292 718 689. Elsewhere call US collect +1 801-964-6665; www.aexp.com. *Cheques for Two* can be signed by either of 2 people traveling together.

Thomas Cook MasterCard: In the US and Canada ☎800-223-7373; in the UK ☎0800 62 21 01; elsewhere call UK collect +44 1733 31 89 50. Checks available in 13 currencies at 2% commission. Thomas Cook offices cash checks commission-free.

Visa: Call 800-227-6811 in the US; in the UK 0800 89 50 78; elsewhere call UK collect 020 7937 8091.

CREDIT CARDS

Credit cards are generally accepted in most New Zealand and urban Fijian establishments, and often offer superior exchange rates—up to 5% better than the retail rate used by banks and exchange services. Credit cards may additionally offer insurance or emergency help, and are sometimes required to reserve hotel rooms or rental cars. **MasterCard** and **Visa** are the most welcomed; **American Express** cards work at some ATMs and at AmEx offices and major airports.

Credit cards are also useful for **cash advances,** which allow you to withdraw money from associated banks and ATMs instantly. However, transaction fees for all credit card advances (up to US$10 per advance, plus 2-3% extra on foreign transactions after conversion) tend to make credit cards a more costly way of withdrawing cash than ATMs or traveler's checks. In an emergency, however, the transaction fee may prove worth the cost. To be eligible for an advance, you'll need to get a **Personal Identification Number (PIN)** from your credit card company (see **Cash Cards** below). If you already have a PIN, check with the company to make sure it will work abroad. Also, be sure to check with your credit card company before you leave home—in certain circumstances companies have started to charge a foreign transaction fee. This also ensures that they don't think your card has been stolen.

CREDIT CARD COMPANIES. Visa (US ☎ 800-336-8472) and **MasterCard** (US ☎ 800-307-7309) are issued in cooperation with banks and other organizations. **American Express** (US ☎ 800-843-2273) has an annual fee of up to US$55. AmEx cardholders may cash personal checks at AmEx offices abroad, access an emergency medical and legal assistance hotline (24hr.; in North America call 800-554-2639, elsewhere call US collect +1 715-343-7977), and enjoy American Express Travel Service benefits (including plane, hotel, and car rental reservation changes; baggage loss and flight insurance; mailgram and international cable services; and held mail). The **Discover Card** (in US call 800-347-2683, elsewhere call US +1 801-902-3100) offers cashback bonuses on most purchases, but may not be readily accepted.

CASH (ATM) CARDS

Cash cards—popularly called ATM cards—are widespread in New Zealand and urban Fiji. In fact, New Zealand has more ATMs (often called **cashpoint machines**) per capita than any other country in the world. Depending on your bank's system, using an ATM card may be the best option for getting money while in New Zealand. ATMs get the same wholesale exchange rate as credit cards, but there is often a limit on the amount of money you can withdraw per day (around US$500). There is typically also a fee of US$1-5 per withdrawal. Be sure to memorize your PIN code in numeric form since machines often don't have letters on their keys. Also, if your PIN is longer than four digits, ask your bank whether you need a new number.

The most common types of ATMs in New Zealand are those owned by **ANZ** and **BNZ.** Both carry the two major international money networks, **Cirrus** (US ☎ 800-424-7787) and **PLUS** (US ☎ 800-843-7587). Cirrus usually charges US$3-5 to withdraw overseas; check with your bank. The back of your ATM card will have the symbol of networks with which it is compatible. To locate ATMs in New Zealand, call the above numbers, or consult www.visa.com/pd/atm or www.mastercard.com/atm. Most ATMs charge a transaction fee that is paid to the bank that owns the ATM.

Visa TravelMoney (for customer assistance call NZ ☎ 0800 449 149) is a pre-paid system allowing you to access money from any Visa ATM, common throughout New Zealand. You deposit an amount before you travel (plus a small administration fee), and you can withdraw up to that sum. The cards, which gives you the same favorable exchange rate for withdrawals as a regular Visa, are especially useful if you plan to travel through many countries. Obtain a card either by visiting a nearby Thomas Cook or Citicorp office, by calling toll-free in the US 877-394-2247, or checking with your local bank to see if it issues TravelMoney cards. **Road Cash** (US ☎ 877-762-3227; www.roadcash.com) issues cards in the US with a minimum US$300 deposit.

EFTPOS

Eftpos (Electronic Funds Transfer at Point Of Sale) is an extremely common way for New Zealanders to pay for goods. ATM cards (from New Zealand banks only) swiped at the register work as debit cards, withdrawing money directly from your bank account. This means that people can carry less cash, without worrying about credit card bills. If you'll be in New Zealand for a couple of months or more, the convenience of this service may justify opening a New Zealand bank account. Two forms of identification are required; your home driver's license and your passport are the most sure-fire bets. Be sure to bring along home bank statements from the last three months; although you are allowed to open an account without them, they expedite the process enormously. You can also expect the bank to perform a routine check on your credit history. Accounts can be ready in as little as an hour if you provide bank statements from home. While some banks require a minimum 3-month stay in New Zealand, **ANZ** waives this requirement and demands no permanent address, but only a passport.

GETTING MONEY FROM HOME

AMERICAN EXPRESS. Cardholders can withdraw cash from their checking accounts at any of AmEx's major offices and many representative offices (up to US$1000 every 21 days; no service charge, no interest). AmEx **"Express Cash"** withdrawals from any AmEx ATM in New Zealand or Fiji are automatically debited from the cardholder's checking account or line of credit. Green card holders may withdraw up to US$1000 in any seven-day period (2% transaction fee; minimum US$2.50, maximum US$20). To enroll in Express Cash, cardmembers may call 800-227-4669 in the US. The AmEx national number in New Zealand is ☎ 09 367 4567 or ☎ 0800 656 660. The national number in Fiji is ☎ 302 333.

WESTERN UNION. Travelers from the US, Canada, and the UK can wire money abroad through Western Union's international money transfer services. In Canada call 800-235-0000; in Fiji, 314 812; in New Zealand, 0800 270 000; in the US 800-325-6000; in the UK, 0800 83 38 33. The rates for sending cash are generally US$10-11 cheaper than with a credit card, and the money is usually available at the place you're sending it to within an hour. To locate the nearest Western Union location, consult www.westernunion.com.

FEDERAL EXPRESS. Some people choose to send cash abroad via FedEx to avoid transmission fees and taxes. While FedEx is reasonably reliable, note that this method is **illegal.** In Canada and the US, FedEx can be reached by calling 800-463-3339; in Australia, 13 26 10; in Fiji, 722 933; in Ireland, 800 535 800; in New Zealand, 0800 733 339; in South Africa, 011 923 8000; and in the UK, 0800 12 38 00.

US STATE DEPARTMENT (US CITIZENS ONLY). In dire emergencies only, the US State Department will forward money within hours to the nearest consular office, which will then disburse it according to instructions for a US$15 fee. If you wish to use this service, you must contact the Overseas Citizens Service division of the US State Department (☎ 202-647-5225; nights, Sundays, and holidays ☎ 202-647-4000).

TAXES

NEW ZEALAND. A **departure tax** is levied at the airport. Prices depend on the airport, but are generally NZ$20 for those over 12. The fee, sometimes included in your flight price, must be paid in New Zealand dollars. A 12.5% **Goods and Services Tax (GST)** is applied to all goods for sale and is usually included in display prices (see **Customs** p. 15).

FIJI. A similar **departure tax** of FJ$20 is levied at the airport for those over 12. A uniform 10% **Value Added Tax (VAT)** is applied to all goods for sale (see **Customs** p. 15).

TIPPING

Tipping is neither customary nor expected in New Zealand and Fijian establishments. In restaurants gratuity is always included in the price of the meal. If the service provided is exceptional you may consider offering a small tip, but it is by no means necessary or even common.

SAFETY AND SECURITY

EMERGENCIES	The emergency number in all of **New Zealand** is ☎ 111. The emergency number in all of **Fiji** is ☎ 000.

PERSONAL SAFETY

NEW ZEALAND. With minimal crime, New Zealand enjoys its reputation as a warm and fuzzy tourist haven. As is true anywhere, however, tourists are probably more vulnerable to crime than most—they often carry large amounts of cash and are not as street savvy as locals. Because the friendliness of New Zealanders is so infectious, you may be tempted to trust someone more quickly than usual, but it is always best to retain a certain measure of caution. If you are traveling alone, be sure that someone at home knows your itinerary. Similarly, if you are tramping alone, take advantage of the **intentions book** available at the nearest DOC office.

Nightlife in New Zealand cities is rife with tourists and is probably safer than in many other countries. But if you are concerned, a good **self-defense course** can give you more concrete ways to react to aggression (see **Self Defense** below).

FIJI. While in general Fiji is a safe country for foreign travelers, the general concerns that usually arise in any developing nation should be noted. Common sense is your best defense; don't do anything that seems risky or makes you feel uncomfortable. It is important to stay abreast of political developments while in Fiji, given the turmoil that has accompanied the failed 2000 coup (see **Political Upheaval** p. 383). As of the date of publication of this book, the US State Department has issued a **Public Announcement** concerning travel to Fiji, which can be viewed along with the latest Consular Information Sheet at http://travel.state.gov/travel_warnings.html.

EXPLORING. Try to blend in as much as possible. Respect local customs by dressing more conservatively. Familiarize yourself with your surroundings before setting out, and carry yourself with confidence; if you must check a map on the street, duck into a shop. If you are traveling alone, be sure someone at home knows your itinerary, and never admit that you're traveling alone.

When walking at night, stick to busy, well-lit streets and avoid dark alleyways. Do not attempt to cross through parks, parking lots, or other large, deserted areas. Look for children playing, women walking in the open, and other signs of an active community. If you feel uncomfortable, leave as quickly and directly as you can, but don't allow fear of the unknown to turn you into a hermit. Careful, persistent exploration will build confidence and make your stay even more rewarding.

LEGAL SUGAR HIGH Recent legislation has changed traffic laws in Fiji such that trucks transporting sugar cane, the country's main agricultural product, are no longer required to obey minor traffic regulations. Perhaps the most disturbing of these are the laws concerning the **maximum size of cane cargoes;** it isn't rare to see small 4WDs loaded to twice their height with swaying stacks of cane secured only by twine careening around corners. Those who choose to rent cars should pay particular attention to these vehicles and the random stalks that may fly towards unwary windshields at any moment; going off the road in Fiji by any other name is not so sweet.

ESSENTIALS

SELF DEFENSE. There is no sure-fire way to avoid all the threatening situations you might encounter when you travel, but a good self-defense course will give you confidence to combat unwanted advances. **Impact, Prepare, and Model Mugging** can refer you to self-defense courses in the US (☎800-345-5425; www.prepareinc.com) and Vancouver (☎604-878-3838). Brief workshops start at US$50; full courses run US$350-500.

DRIVING. Some of the more dangerous situations in New Zealand and Fiji occur on the roads. Firstly, they drive on the left side of the road; even worse, **drunk driving** among New Zealanders is a major problem. As a result, police occasionally stop all traffic on certain roads in order to give each driver a quick breathalizer test. The speed limit is 100 kph (63 mph) on major roads. Speeding carries rather steep fines (up to NZD$630) and, in many cases, a suspension of license. Seatbelts are mandatory. Almost all roads are sealed and in good condition, though they may be more narrow than foreign travelers are accustomed to.

Driving in Fiji can be quite hazardous; loosely enforced regulations and speedy Fijian drivers combine to create numerous fatal accidents each year, with a large number occurring on the less well-maintained Kings Road. If you choose to drive in Fiji **exercise caution;** the beautiful beaches and views are hard to enjoy from a hospital bed or the morgue.

For long drives in desolate areas invest in a cellular phone and a roadside assistance program (see **Cars** p. 42). Be sure to park your vehicle in a garage or well-traveled area, and use a steering wheel locking device in larger cities. **Sleeping in your car** is one of the most dangerous (and often illegal) ways to get your rest.

For info on the perils of **hitchhiking** see p. 44.

TRAVEL ADVISORIES. The following government offices provide travel information and advisories by telephone, by fax, or via the web:

Australian Department of Foreign Affairs and Trade: ☎02 6261 1111; www.dfat.gov.au.

Canadian Department of Foreign Affairs and International Trade (DFAIT): In Canada call 800-267-8316, elsewhere call +1 613-944-4000; www.dfait-maeci.gc.ca. Call for their free booklet, *Bon Voyage...But.*

Fiji Ministry of Foreign Affairs: http://fiji.gov.fj.

New Zealand Ministry of Foreign Affairs: ☎04 494 8500; fax 494 8506; www.mft.govt.nz/trav.html.

United Kingdom Foreign and Commonwealth Office: ☎020 7008 0232; fax 7008 0155; www.fco.gov.uk.

US Department of State: ☎202-647-5225, automatic faxback 647-3000; http://travel.state.gov. For *A Safe Trip Abroad,* call 512-1800.

FINANCIAL SECURITY

PROTECTING YOUR VALUABLES

While traveling, *you* may be your worst enemy. Travelers often find within a few days of arrival they are so enamored of the friendly and mellow Kiwis and Fijians that their eternal vigilance begins to fade. Contrary to appearances, theft, while uncommon in New Zealand, does occur, and the number of reported thefts in Fiji has increased recently. There are a few steps you can take to minimize your risk. First, **bring as little with you as possible.** Leave expensive watches, jewelry, cameras, and electronic equipment (like your Discman) at home; chances are you'd break them, lose them, or get sick of lugging them around anyway. Second, buy a few combination **padlocks** to secure your belongings either in your pack—which you should **never leave unattended**—or in a hostel or train station locker. Third, **carry as little cash as possible;** instead carry traveler's checks and ATM/credit cards, keeping them in a **money belt** along with your passport and ID cards. Fourth, **keep a small cash reserve separate from your primary stash.** This should entail about US$50 sewn into or stored in the depths of your pack, along with your traveler's check numbers and important photocopies. You may also want to keep a reserve credit card tucked away as well.

Never leave your belongings unattended; crime occurs in even the most demure-looking accommodations. In hostel shares, don't tempt your roommates by leaving a wallet or purse unattended. Bring your own padlock for hostel lockers, and don't ever store valuables in any locker. Be aware of the location of your belongings when traveling by bus or train. If you do elect to hitchhike (see **Hitchhiking** p. 44 for more on the dangers of doing so) always keep your belongings in the car with you. Baggage left in the trunk is easily stolen; after stepping out of the vehicle you may suddenly find yourself eating dust and watching your pack speed away.

DRUGS AND ALCOHOL

Remember that you are subject to the laws of the country in which you travel, not to those of your home country, and it is your responsibility to familiarize yourself with these laws before leaving. The legal **drinking age** in both New Zealand and Fiji is 18. First-time drunk-driving offenders in New Zealand can receive three months imprisonment, a NZ$4500 fine, and a six-month license suspension. Illegal drugs are, well, illegal. Possession of marijuana in New Zealand can result in a three-month imprisonment and a NZ$1000 fine, while selling is punishable with a maximum sentence of eight years. Possession of harder drugs can result in a $1000 fine and a six-month imprisonment; selling them can put you in jail for life. Fiji enforces similarly harsh drug laws, and in some situations penalties exceed those in New Zealand. If you carry **prescription drugs** while you travel, it is vital to have a copy of the prescriptions themselves and a note from a doctor, both readily accessible at country borders.

HEALTH

EMERGENCIES	The emergency number in all of **New Zealand** is ☎ 111. The emergency number in all of **Fiji** is ☎ 000.

In New Zealand and Fiji common sense is the simplest prescription for good health. Travelers complain most often about their feet and their gut: drink lots of fluids to prevent dehydration, wear sturdy, broken-in shoes and clean socks, and use talcum powder to keep your feet dry.

NEW ZEALAND. New Zealand offers a high standard of medical facilities, both public and private. However, these are not free; it is important to know that doctors often expect to be paid in cash right away for their services. A foreigner's office visit to most medical treatment centers costs about NZ$35. If your regular **insurance** policy does not cover travel abroad, you may wish to purchase additional coverage, although be sure you understand the coverage provided for New Zealand visitors by the **Accident Compensation Corporation** (**ACC**; see **Insurance** p. 25). Except for Medicare, most American health insurance plans cover members' medical emergencies during trips abroad; check with your insurance carrier to be sure.

It is common for pharmacies in a New Zealand town to take turns being the town's **late-night pharmacy;** call the local hospital to get the number.

FIJI. The health care system in Fiji is often inadequate by Western standards. While the many state health centers and hospitals are generally fine for minor injuries, anything serious should be dealt with at the **Suva Private Hospital** (☎303 404; see **Suva: Practical Information** p. 412), a first-rate 24hr. facility with well-trained doctors. If it is impossible or impractical to get to Suva, numerous **private clinics** (generally found only in more urban areas) are a better bet than state hospitals;

usually staffed by just one or two professionals and only open during normal business hours, clinics accept cash and often travelers insurance. If you are seriously injured anywhere in Fiji, **Island Hoppers** (☎720 410) provides emergency **helicopter airlifts** to the Suva Private Hospital.

BEFORE YOU GO

Preparation can help minimize the likelihood of becoming ill and maximize the chances of receiving effective health care in the event of an emergency. Although medical supplies are readily available in New Zealand, and most larger cities in Fiji have a pharmacy, it is often best to carry a few essential items from home. For tips on packing a basic **first-aid kit** and other health essentials, see **First-Aid Kit** p. 27.

In your **passport,** write the names of any people you wish to be contacted in case of a medical emergency, and also list any allergies or medical conditions of which you would want doctors to be aware. Carry up-to-date, legible prescriptions or a statement from your doctor stating the medication's trade name, manufacturer, chemical name, and dosage. While traveling, be sure to keep all medication with you in your carry-on luggage.

Travel to New Zealand or Fiji does not require vaccination against infectious diseases. Travelers over two years old should be sure that the following vaccines are up to date: MMR (for measles, mumps, and rubella); DTaP or Td (for diptheria, tetanus, and pertussis); OPV (for polio); HbCV (for haemophilus influenza B); and HBV (for hepatitus B). Those with medical conditions (diabetes, allergies to antibiotics, epilepsy, heart conditions) may want to obtain a stainless-steel **Medic Alert** ID tag (first-year US$35, $15 annually thereafter), which identifies the condition and gives a 24-hour collect-call number. Contact the Medic Alert Foundation, 2323 Colorado Ave, Turlock, CA 95382 (US ☎800-825-3785; www.medicalert.org).

ON THE ROAD

JET LAG. Many travelers to New Zealand and Fiji will arrive after a flight of over 12 hours and suffer from severe jet lag. While it may be tempting to sleep, some say it is best to force yourself to make it through at least to early evening. On long flights, search for and claim open rows of seats for better sleep. Despite preparation, however, most travelers will not be able to thwart jet drag. Expect to spend a few days adjusting to your new time zone and plan your trip accordingly.

HOT AND COLD. The most dangerous safety hazards in a country like New Zealand and Fiji are often the most obvious ones. **Heat exhaustion,** characterized by **dehydration** and salt deficiency, can lead to fatigue, headaches, and wooziness. Avoid heat exhaustion by drinking plenty of clear fluids, eating salty foods, and avoiding diuretics such as alcohol or caffeinated beverages. Wear a hat, sunglasses, and a lightweight longsleeve shirt in the hot sun. Continuous heat stress can eventually lead to **heatstroke,** characterized by rising body temperature, severe headache, and cessation of sweating. Heatstroke is rare but serious, and victims must be cooled off with wet towels and taken to a doctor as soon as possible.

Depleted ozone levels and unpolluted air make New Zealand and Fiji high risk areas for **sunburn,** especially on the beach, water, or on the slopes. Apply sunscreen liberally. Protect your eyes with good sunglasses. If you become sunburned, drink more fluids than usual and apply Calamine or an aloe-based lotion.

In some areas of New Zealand during the winter, travelers are at risk of **hypothermia** and **frostbite.** A rapid drop in body temperature is the clearest warning sign of overexposure to cold. Victims may also shiver, feel exhausted, have poor coordination or slurred speech, hallucinate, or suffer amnesia. **Do not let hypothermia victims fall asleep** or their body temperature will continue to drop and they may die. To avoid hypothermia, keep dry, wear layers of synthetics or wool (no cotton!), and stay out of the wind. When the temperature is below freezing, watch for frostbite. If a region of skin turns white, waxy, and cold, **do not rub the area.** Drink warm beverages, get dry, and slowly warm the area with dry fabric or steady body contact, until a doctor can be found.

INSECT-BORNE DISEASES. Many diseases are transmitted by insects—mainly mosquitoes, fleas, and lice. For precautions against **mosquitoes**, see **Wilderness Safety** p. 356. Both New Zealand and Fiji are virtually free from **ticks.**

FOOD- AND WATER-BORNE DISEASES. New Zealand and Fiji have few dangerous diseases that travelers should worry about. You can minimize the chances of becoming ill while traveling by taking a few precautionary measures. When spending time in the outdoors, never drink water from outdoor sources that you have not purified by boiling or treating with iodine tablets. Despite any reassurances from locals or the Visitors Bureau, **be very skeptical of most water sources in Fiji.** Although most visitors do not have problems with tap water in developed areas, bottled water is readily available and presents a much safer option.

Parasites (tapeworms, etc.) hide in unsafe water and food. **Giardia,** for example, is a major concern for outdoor enthusiasts, acquired by drinking untreated water. It can stay with you for years. General symptoms of parasitic infections include swollen glands or lymph nodes, fever, rashes or itchiness, digestive problems, eye problems, and anemia. Iodine may not be sufficient alone to treat water for giardia. As a general rule of thumb, boil your water, wear shoes, avoid bugs, and eat cooked food. **Amoebic Meningitis,** while rare, is a another serious infection, acquired by putting one's head under the hot, stagnant water in water holes. Symptoms include headaches, a stiff neck, extreme sensitivity to light, and a coma.

If you are concerned about disease in New Zealand and Fiji, or if you will be continuing your travels to other areas of the South Pacific, consult the US **Centers for Disease Control and Prevention (CDC)** (US ☎ 888-232-3299; www.cdc.gov), an excellent source of information for travelers.

AIDS, HIV, STDS

New Zealand and Fiji do not screen incoming travelers for the HIV virus; however, restrictions may apply to those staying longer to work or study in New Zealand (contact your nearest consulate). For detailed information on **Acquired Immune Deficiency Syndrome (AIDS)** in New Zealand, call the **US Centers for Disease Control's** 24-hour hotline (US ☎ 800-342-2437). The Council on International Educational Exchange's pamphlet, *Travel Safe: AIDS and International Travel*, is posted on their website (www.ciee.org/Isp/safety/travelsafe.htm), along with links to other online and phone resources. For more information once in New Zealand, you can contact the **AIDS National Hotline** (☎ 09 358 0099, 0800 802 437), a 24-hour hotline that offers AIDS counseling and information. The hotline is sponsored by the **New Zealand AIDS Foundation,** P.O. Box 6663, Wellesley St., Auckland (☎ 09 303 3124; http://nzaf.org.nz).

Sexually transmitted diseases (STDs) such as gonorrhea, chlamydia, genital warts, syphilis, herpes, and hepatitis B and C can be just as deadly as HIV. Though condoms may protect you from some STDs, oral or even tactile contact can lead to transmission. Warning signs include swelling, sores, bumps, or blisters on sex organs, the rectum, or the mouth; burning and pain during urination and bowel movements; itching around sex organs; swelling or redness of the throat; and flu-like symptoms. If these symptoms develop, see a doctor immediately.

INSURANCE

Visitors who suffer personal injury by accident in New Zealand are covered by the local **Accident Compensation Corporation** (known locally as ACC), which entitles them to a claim, irrespective of fault. ACC does not cover illnesses and even accidents covered by ACC require that the traveler pay some of the cost of treatment. Additionally, while some medical and hospital expenses are included in its benefits, ACC does not cover lost wages outside of New Zealand. For more information, or to request helpful ACC publications such as *"Visitors to New Zealand"*, visit the ACC website, www.acc.co.nz.

In spite of this free coverage, and for travelers to Fiji, it is often a good idea to have individual travel insurance as well. Such insurance generally covers four basic areas: medical/health problems, property loss, trip cancellation/interruption, and emergency evacuation. Although your regular insurance policies may extend to travel-related accidents, you may consider purchasing travel insurance if the cost of potential trip cancellation/interruption is greater than you can absorb. Prices for travel insurance purchased separately generally run about US$50 per week for full coverage, while trip cancellation/interruption may be purchased separately at a rate of about US$5.50 per US$100 of coverage.

Medical insurance (especially university policies) often covers costs incurred abroad; check with your provider. **US Medicare** does not cover foreign travel. **Canadians** are protected by their home province's health insurance plan for up to 90 days after leaving the country; check with the provincial Ministry of Health or Health Plan Headquarters for details. **Australians** traveling in New Zealand are entitled to many of the services that they would receive at home as part of the Reciprocal Health Care Agreement. **Homeowners' insurance** (or your family's coverage) often covers theft during travel and loss of travel documents (passport, plane ticket, etc.) up to US$500.

ISIC and **ITIC** (see **Identification** p. 14) provide basic insurance benefits to US citizens, including US$100 per day of in-hospital sickness for up to 60 days, US$3000 of accident-related medical reimbursement, and US$25,000 for emergency medical transport. Cardholders can access a toll-free 24-hour helpline for medical, legal, and financial emergencies overseas (US and Canada ☎ 800-626-2427, elsewhere call US collect 713-267-2525).

American Express cardholders, please note that American Express does not cover the required Collision and Damage Waiver in New Zealand, as it does automatically in most other countries.

INSURANCE PROVIDERS. Council and **STA** (see **Budget & Student Travel Agencies** p. 38) offer a range of plans that can supplement your basic coverage. Other private insurance providers in the US and Canada include: **Access America** (☎ 800-284-8300); **Berkely Group/Carefree Travel Insurance** (☎ 800-323-3149; www.berkely.com); **Globalcare Travel Insurance** (☎ 800-821-2488; www.globalcare-cocco.com); and **Travel Assistance International** (☎ 800-821-2828; www.worldwide-assistance.com). Providers in the **UK** include **Campus Travel** (☎ 018 6525 8000) and **Columbus Travel Insurance** (☎ 020 7375 0011). In **Australia**, try **CIC Insurance** (☎ 9202 8000).

PACKING

PACK LIGHTLY. Lay out only what you absolutely need, then take half the clothes and twice the money. The less you have, the less you have to lose (or store, or carry). Any extra space will be useful for souvenirs or items you might pick up along the way. If you plan to hike a lot, also see **Camping and Hiking Equipment** p. 355.

IMPORTANT DOCUMENTS. Don't forget your passport, traveler's checks, ATM and/or credit cards, and adequate ID (see **Identification** p. 14). Also check that you have any of the following that might apply to you: a hostelling membership card (see **Hostelling International** p. 29); driver's license (see **Cars** p. 42); travel insurance forms; and/or bus pass (see **Buses** p. 41).

LUGGAGE. If you plan to cover most of your itinerary by foot, a sturdy **frame backpack** is unbeatable. While staying in one city, toting a **suitcase** or **trunk** is fine, but it is a very bad idea if you're going to be tramping the Great Walks or exploring multiple islands. For the basics on buying a pack, see **What to Buy...** p. 355.

In addition to your main vessel, a small backpack, rucksack, or courier bag may be useful as a **daypack** for sightseeing; it doubles as an airplane **carry-on.** Once abroad you can fill your luggage with purchases and keep your dirty clothes in a lightweight duffel.

CLOTHING. Due to New Zealand's unpredictable weather patterns and occasionally fierce winds, a rain jacket and heavy sweater are absolute necessities. Gore-Tex® is a miracle fabric that's both waterproof and breathable. No matter when you are traveling, it's a good idea to bring a **warm jacket**, sturdy shoes or **hiking boots**, and thick socks. Remember that wool will keep you warm even when soaked through, whereas wet cotton is colder than wearing nothing at all. **Flip-flops** or other waterproof sandals can also be used as shower shoes.

Whereas clothing for New Zealand will generally be geared toward keeping warm, travelers to Fiji will want lots of cool, breathable wear such as **shorts** and **T-shirts**. Keep in mind, however, that the weather can become slightly chilly in the higher interior mountain ranges, and always avoid skimpy outfits when visiting small villages so as not to offend locals. A sulu (sarong) is an appropriate and traditional outfit for both men and women at any time.

If you are planning on enjoying the nightlife in New Zealand or Fiji, you should add one outfit beyond the jeans and t-shirt uniform. While bars and pubs are often fairly casual, nightclubs and some bars require neat dress including pants other than jeans and **formal shoes** (not sneakers).

SLEEPSACK. Some hostels require that you either provide your own linen or rent sheets from them. Save cash by making your own sleepsack: fold a full-size sheet in half the long way, then sew it closed along the long side and one of the short sides. If you are traveling to New Zealand in the winter (roughly Apr.-Sept.) you should bring a warm sleeping bag, as most hostels will not have central heating.

CONVERTERS AND ADAPTERS. In both New Zealand and Fiji electricity is 220/240 volts AC, enough to fry any 110V North American appliance. **Americans** and **Canadians** should buy an **adapter** (which changes the shape of the plug) and a **converter** (which changes the voltage; US$20). Don't make the mistake of using only an adapter (unless appliance instructions explicitly state otherwise). **South Africans** (who use 220V at home) won't need a converter, but will need a set of adapters to use anything electrical.

TOILETRIES. Toothbrushes, towels, soap, deodorant, razors, tampons, and condoms are widely available in New Zealand and Fiji, but slightly more expensive than those brought from home. **Contact lenses** may be difficult to find and expensive, so bring enough extra pairs and solution for your entire trip. Also, bring your glasses and a copy of your prescription in case you need emergency replacements.

FIRST-AID KIT. For a basic first-aid kit, pack bandages, aspirin or other painkiller, antibiotic cream, a thermometer, a Swiss Army knife, tweezers, moleskin, decongestant, motion-sickness remedy, diarrhea or upset-stomach medication (Pepto Bismol or Immodium), an antihistamine, insect repellent, and burn ointment.

FILM. Film and developing in New Zealand are reasonable (about NZ$6-10 to purchase a roll of 24 color exposures and an additional NZ$10 to have them developed), but are slightly more expensive in Fiji. Most travelers bring along enough film for their entire trip and develop it back at home. Despite disclaimers, airport security X-rays *can* fog film, so buy a lead-lined pouch at a camera store or ask security to hand inspect it. Always pack it in your carry-on luggage, since higher-intensity X-rays are used on checked luggage. Less serious photographers may want to bring a **disposable camera** rather than an expensive permanent one.

OTHER USEFUL ITEMS. For safety purposes, you should bring a **money belt** and small **padlock**. Basic **outdoors equipment** (plastic water bottle, iodine tablets, compass, waterproof matches, pocketknife, sunglasses, sunscreen, hat) may also prove useful. **Quick repairs** of torn garments can be done on the road with a needle and thread or electrical tape. Doing your **laundry** by hand (where it is allowed) is cheaper than doing it at a laundromat—bring detergent, a small rubber ball to stop up the sink, and string for a makeshift clothes line. **Other things** you're liable to forget: sealable **plastic bags** (for damp clothes, soap, food, shampoo, and other spillables); an **alarm clock;** safety pins; rubber bands; a flashlight; earplugs; garbage bags; and a small **calculator.**

ACCOMMODATIONS

Accommodation and restaurant listings are ranked in descending order according to our researchers' preferences. Campgrounds are generally listed last regardless of quality. Unless we state otherwise, you can expect that every establishment in New Zealand has **free hot showers** and **free linen**; amenities in Fiji vary greatly from hostel to hostel, and even the most basic services should never be expected.

When there is a linen charge in New Zealand, it is usually charged once per stay. Most offer **laundry** for a standard fee ($1-3), but rarely have dryers. **Central heating** is also rare in New Zealand and is listed wherever found. In our listings, a **twin** contains two single beds; a **double** has one double bed. **Seasonal fares** are flexible, and some accommodations vary fares at their own discretion. **Booking ahead** is a must in summer and on major holidays.

Budget-conscious travelers will benefit from the variety of accommodation networks in New Zealand and Fiji. Those who plan on traveling by RV in New Zealand (see **Motor Parks** p. 30) or doing a lot of camping, for example, may choose to join a network like the **Top 10 Holiday Parks** (www.topparks.co.nz; membership fee $20 for 2 years) to reap consistent 10% discounts at member parks.

HOSTELS

For tight budgets and those lonesome traveling blues, **backpackers** (the Kiwi term for "hostel") can't be beat. Backpackers are generally dorm-style accommodations, in large, co-ed or single-sex (especially common in YHA backpackers) rooms with bunk beds, although some backpackers do have private rooms for families and couples. In New Zealand they frequently offer bike hire, shuttle bus connections, a central lounge space and storage areas; most have central kitchens and laundry facilities. Almost all are also happy to book local activities and transport and many will offer a bed for the night in exchange for chores. Fees range from NZ$15-25 per night for a dorm bed. Since the quality of accommodations in Fiji varies so greatly, experiences are unpredictable and prices range from FJ$8-25. Many Fijian accommodations recognizable as hostels call themselves "hotels."

Since the backpackers network in New Zealand is so remarkable, it is vital to book ahead in high season (summer for most towns, and winter in ski areas). For large festivals and over the Christmas holiday, bookings should be made at least a few weeks in advance. Actually checking in at backpackers in New Zealand can be a remarkably laid-back process; after hours, you may sign in on a self-check blackboard, or you may be allowed to check the listings to see which beds are open and plunk yourself down for the night, making payment in the morning.

Backpackers associated with one of the large hostel associations (HI-YHA, VIP, NOMADS, etc.) often have lower rates for members. Check out the **Internet Guide to Hostelling** (http://hostels.com), which includes backpackers in New Zealand and Fiji and oodles of info about hosteling and backpacking worldwide. The following are the major hostel networks in New Zealand (HI-YHAs and NOMADS can be found scattered throughout Fiji as well).

Budget Backpacker Hostels: (bbh@backpack.co.nz; www.backpack.co.nz). Includes over 280 of the New Zealand's independent backpackers. Once a year, BBH surveys guests of all BBH backpackers and then compiles a free guide which lists its members and provides satisfaction ratings. This ubiquitous blue and green guide is very helpful and its rankings are reliable. Available at the Auckland and Christchurch airports, Visitor Information Network offices, participating backpackers, or via email. In addition, you can purchase a BBH Backpackers card for NZ$20 (including NZ$20 of pre-paid phone calls) good for various discounts on transport. Average overnight fee NZ$14-16. Reservations recommended, especially in peak season. Book directly to the backpackers.

Hostelling International-Youth Hostels Association of New Zealand (HI-YHANZ): National Office, 193 Cashel St., 3rd fl.Union House, P.O. Box 436, Christchurch (☎03 379 9970; fax 365 4476; info@yha.org.nz; www.iyhf.org); **National Reservations**

Centre, P.O. Box 436 Christchurch (☎03 379 9808; fax 379 4415; book@yha.org.nz; www.yha.org.nz). Because YHANZ is linked to the HI network, your **Hostelling International card** from home (see below) is recognized at all YHANZ backpackers and at most other establishments that give discounts for YHA membership. Or, you can purchase an annual membership fee once in New Zealand for NZ$40. Average overnight fee NZ$15-20. HI-YHA backpackers are inspected annually for quality and service standards; look in the HI-YHANZ Accommodation Guide to see a hostel's quality rating. The privately owned YHA Associate hostels, on the other hand, meet YHA standards, but offer the same rates to all guests. Reservations can be made in advance on the web at www.yha.org.nz. You must book at least 48 hours in advance, however, and your reservations are accompanied by a NZ$1 booking fee per hostel. Most student travel agencies (see **Budget & Student Travel Agencies** p. 38) sell HI cards, as do the national hosteling organizations listed below.

VIP Backpackers Resorts: Like HI-YHA cards, a VIP card obtains discounts at the 70 VIP backpackers and many other establishments in New Zealand. Annual membership fee NZ$35. Average overnight fee NZ$14-20. Book directly with backpackers (have credit card handy). VIP cards can be obtained from many visitors centers or VIP backpackers. In New Zealand, contact VIP Backpackers Resorts, P.O. Box 80021, Greenbay, Auckland (☎09 827 6016; fax 827 6013; www.vip.co.nz).

NOMADS World: NOMADS Hostels can be found in all major backpacker destinations and offers the NOMADS Adventure Card for an annual fee of AUS$25, which entitles the card-holder to hundreds of privileges such as discounts on accommodations, transport, attractions, phone calls with special international rates, and email. All Hostels within the NOMADS group operate under standard procedures, therefore travelers will find quality accommodations with linen, beds, self-cook kitchens and common rooms at every NOMADS hostel. Average overnight fee NZ$13-20, FJ$10-25; stay for six days and get the seventh free. Contact NOMADS headquarters in Australia at NOMADS World Pty Ltd., 43 The Parade West, Kent Town, South Australia 5067 (☎08 8363 7633; fax 8363 7968; info@nomadsworld.com; www.nomadsworld.com).

HOSTELLING INTERNATIONAL

Joining the youth hostel association in your own country (listed below) automatically grants you membership privileges in **Hostelling International (HI),** a federation of national hostelling associations. HI hostels are scattered throughout New Zealand and Fiji, and seven of the hostels in Auckland, Christchurch, Queenstown, Rotorua and Wellington accept reservations via the **International Booking Network** (Australia ☎02 9261 1111; Canada ☎800-663-5777; England and Wales ☎1629 581 418; Republic of Ireland ☎01 830 1766; NZ ☎09 379 4224; Northern Ireland ☎1232 324 733; Scotland ☎541 553 255; US ☎800-909-4776; www.hostelbooking.com). Check out www.iyhf.org and www.hostels.com for more info.

Most HI hostels also honor **guest memberships**—you get a blank card with space for six validation stamps. Each night you'll pay a nonmember supplement (one-sixth the membership fee) and earn one guest stamp; get six stamps, and you're a member. Most student travel agencies (see **Budget & Student Travel Agencies** p. 38) sell HI cards, as do all of the national hosteling organizations listed below. All prices listed below are valid for **one-year memberships** unless otherwise noted.

Australian Youth Hostels Association (AYHA), 422 Kent St., **Sydney** NSW 2000 (☎02 9261 1111; fax 9261 1969; www.yha.org.au). AUS$52, under 18 AUS$16.

Hostelling International-Canada (HI-C), 400-205 Catherine St., **Ottawa** ON K2P 1C3 (☎800-663-5777 or 613-237-7884; fax 237-7868; info@hostellingintl.ca; www.hostellingintl.ca). CDN$35, under 18 free.

An Óige (Irish Youth Hostel Association), 61 Mountjoy St., **Dublin** 7 (☎01 830 4555; fax 830 5808; mailbox@anoige.ie; www.irelandyha.org). IR£12, under 18 IR£6.

Hostels Association of South Africa, 73 St. George's St. Mall, 3rd fl., P.O. Box 4402, **Cape Town** 8000 (☎021 424 2511; fax 424 4119; info@hisa.org.za; www.hisa.org.za). ZAR55, under 18 ZAR30, lifetime ZAR250.

Scottish Youth Hostels Association (SYHA), 7 Glebe Crescent, **Stirling** FK8 2JA (☎01786 891 400; fax 891 333; info@syha.org.uk; www.syha.org.uk). UK£6, under 18 UK£2.50.

Youth Hostels Association (England and Wales) Ltd., Trevelyan House, 8 St. Stephen's Hill, St. Albans, **Hertfordshire** AL1 2DY (☎08708 708 808; fax 01727 844 126; www.yha.org.uk). UK£12.50, under 18 UK£6.25, families UK£25.

Hostelling International Northern Ireland (HINI), 22-32 Donegall Rd., **Belfast** BT12 5JN, Northern Ireland (☎01232 324 733; fax 439 699; info@hini.org.uk; www.hini.org.uk). UK£10, under 18 UK£6, families UK£20.

Hostelling International-American Youth Hostels (HI-AYH), 733 15th St. NW, #840, **Washington, D.C.** 20005 (☎202-783-6161; fax ☎202-783-6171; members@hiayh.org; www.hiayh.org). US$25, seniors US$15, under 18 free.

MOTOR PARKS AND CAMPS

Known as **holiday parks,** these accommodations complexes vary in size from sprawling compounds to grassy plots, all offering a range of options for the budget traveler. Motor parks and camps usually feature tent sites (from NZ$10) and caravan (RV or camper) sites (from NZ$20). Powerpoints are what Kiwis call on-site power hook-ups. Some also feature on-site caravans for rent, often with kitchen, sometimes with toilet. Most parks charge for tent and caravan sites per person. Many also offer cabins or flats with singles (from NZ$20), doubles (from NZ$30), and bunk rooms (from NZ$15) with varying amenities (kitchens, linens, etc.).

Renting a **campervan (RV)** will always be more expensive than camping or hosteling, but the costs compare favorably with the price of renting a car and staying in hotels. Rates vary widely by region, season (summers months are the most expensive), and type of campervan. A no-frills, two-berth campervan can cost as low as NZ$50 per day in low-season (NZ$100 in high-season), whereas a luxury 6-berth camper will run closer to NZ$70 per day (NZ$150 in high-season). In New Zealand, caravan sites cost around NZ$10 per person per night. To arrange a campervan rental, check with your local Automobile Association, contact a major international firm, such as Avis, Budget, or Hertz, or select one of the options below. In any case, it always pays to contact several different companies to compare vehicles, amenities, and prices.

Auto Europe (US ☎800-223-5555; UK ☎0800 899 893) rents campervans in NZ.

Maui Rentals: New Zealand, 36 Richard Pearse Dr., Mangere, **Auckland** (☎09 255 0620; fax 275 9690; nzinfo@maui-rentals.com; www.maui-rentals.com). Rents campervans in all shapes and sizes.

Newmans, P.O. Box 14069, **Christchurch** (☎03 358 1314; fax 353 5808; reservations@coachline.co.nz; www.newmans.com) rents a wide range of 2-6 berth vehicles.

BED AND BREAKFASTS (B&BS)

For a cozy alternative to impersonal New Zealand hotel rooms, B&Bs (private homes with rooms available to travelers) range from the acceptable to the sublime. Hosts will sometimes go out of their way to be accommodating by accepting travelers with pets, giving personalized tours, or offering home-cooked meals. On the other hand, many B&Bs do not provide phones, TVs, or private bathrooms and often discourage visits of children under 15. Rooms in B&Bs generally cost NZ$60 for a double. For more info on B&Bs, see **Nerd World's Bed and Breakfasts by Region** (www.nerdworld.com/users/dstein/nw854), or try **Bed & Breakfast Central Information (BBCI),** P.O. Box 38279, Colorado Springs, CO 80937 (US fax 719-471-4740; bbci@bbonline.com; www.bbonline.com/bbci). For a further resource on B&Bs in New Zealand, J. J. Thomas' **New Zealand Bed and Breakfast Book** (Pelican Publishing, US$18) is a recent updated reference book including contact information, prices, illustrations of and directions to over 1000 businesses in New Zealand.

HOMESTAYS AND FARMSTAYS

An intensely memorable experience, homestays and farmstays involve staying on a real working farm or orchard, often alone or with a few other guests. Such experiences are usually arranged through the nearest town's tourist office, although some companies also specialize in booking home- and farmstays. In New Zealand, prices start around NZ$100 per person and include participation in farm activities (more available in winter) and fresh, home-cooked meals; a few backpackers also provide some aspects of a "farmstay" experience, especially in more rural areas. **Rural Tours "Stay in a Country Home" Farmstays** books farmstays throughout New Zealand. Its central booking office is at 92 Victoria St., Cambridge (☎07 827 8055; fax 827 7154; www.ruraltours.co.nz). **American International Homestays,** P.O. Box 1754, Nederland, CO 80466 (US ☎800-876-2048 or 303-258-3234; fax 258-3264; ash@igc.apc.org; www.aihtravel.com), also arranges lodgings with host families.

HOME EXCHANGES AND HOME RENTALS

Home exchange offers the traveler various types of homes (houses, apartments, condominiums, etc.), plus the opportunity to live like a native and to cut down on accommodation fees. For more information, contact **HomeExchange.Com** (US ☎805-898-9660; www.homeexchange.com), **Intervac International Home Exchange** (NZ ☎04 934 4258; kettydavid@paradise.net.nz; www.intervac.com), or **The Invented City: International Home Exchange** (US ☎800-788-CITY, elsewhere call US +1 415-252-1141; info@invented-city.com; www.invented-city.com) **Home rentals** are more expensive than exchanges, but they can be cheaper than comparably-serviced hotels. Both home exchanges and rentals are ideal for families with children, or travelers with special dietary needs; you often get your own kitchen, maid service, TV, and telephones.

VILLAGE STAYS

An opportunity unique to Fiji, visitors can often arrange to spend a night in one of the many small Fijian villages throughout the islands—while this oftentimes requires an acquaintance who lives within the village, several locations in Viti Levu including **Navala** (p. 407), **Bukuya** (p. 408), and **Abaca** (p. 409) have capitalized on the process as a means of generating income. For more information on the niceties of visiting a village see **Fijian Village Etiquette** p. 385.

KEEPING IN TOUCH

SENDING MAIL TO NEW ZEALAND & FIJI

Mark envelopes "air mail" or "par avion" to avoid having letters sent by sea. In addition to the standard postage system whose rates are listed below, **Federal Express** (Australia ☎132 610; US and Canada ☎800-247-4747; Ireland ☎1800 535 800; UK ☎0800 123 800; www.fedex.com) handles express mail services from most home countries to New Zealand and Fiji; for example, they can get a letter from New York to Auckland in two business days for US$31.98, and from London to Auckland in two business days for UK£38.70.

> **Australia:** Allow 3-5 business days for regular airmail to New Zealand or Fiji. Postcards and letters up to 50g cost AUS$1; packages up to 0.5kg AUS$7.50, up to 2kg AUS$22.50. **EMS** can get a letter to New Zealand in 2-3 business days for AUS$26. www.auspost.com.au/pac.

> **Canada:** Allow 7-12 days for regular airmail to New Zealand or Fiji. Postcards and letters up to 20g cost CDN$1.05; packages up to 0.5kg CDN$10.20, up to 2kg CDN$38.55. www.canadapost.ca/CPC2/common/rates/ratesgen.html#international.

ESSENTIALS

First Aid for homesickness.
TalkPlus prepaid calling card. No contracts, no bills.

TalkPlus prepaid calling card lets you call family and friends from almost any touch tone phone in NZ. No contracts. No phone bills.

TalkPlus has great national and international rates, so you can avoid expensive payphone and motel phone charges.

TalkPlus

TalkPlus includes your own private voicemail box, so people can leave messages for you - wherever you may be.

Your **TalkPlus** card can be easily recharged over the phone using your credit card.

Available from stores throughout New Zealand - phone toll free **0508 888 800** or visit **www.clear.co.nz/products/talk-plus** to find the store nearest you.

Ireland: Allow 6-10 days for regular airmail to New Zealand or Fiji. Postcards and letters up to 25g cost IR£0.45. Add IR£2.60 for Swiftpost International. www.anpost.ie.

UK: Allow 4-8 days for airmail to New Zealand or Fiji. Letters up to 20g cost UK£0.65; packages up to 0.5kg UK£10.73, up to 2kg UK£42.23. UK Swiftair delivers letters a day faster for UK£2.85 more. www.royalmail.co.uk/calculator.

US: Allow 4-7 days for regular airmail to New Zealand or Fiji. Postcards/aerogrammes cost US$0.70; letters under 1 oz. US$0.80. Packages under 1 lb. cost US$12.50; larger packages cost a variable amount. **US Global Express Mail** takes 2-3 business days and costs US$17/21.50 (0.5/1 lb.). **US Global Priority Mail** (New Zealand only) delivers small/large flat-rate envelopes in 3-5 business days for US$5/9. http://ircalc.usps.gov.

RECEIVING MAIL IN NZ AND FIJI

There are several ways to arrange pick-up of letters sent to you by friends and relatives while you are abroad.

General Delivery: Mail can be sent via **Poste Restante** (General Delivery) to almost any city or town in New Zealand or Fiji with a post office. Address Poste Restante letters as in the following example: Chris FLING, Poste Restante, CPO, City, Country. No zip or area code is necessary. The mail will go to a special desk in the central post office, unless you specify a post office by street address or postal code. As a rule, it is best to use the largest post office in the area; this is especially true in Fiji. When possible, it is usually safer and quicker to send mail express or registered. When picking up mail, bring a form of photo ID, preferably a passport. *Let's Go* lists post offices in the **Practical Information** section for each city and most towns.

American Express: AmEx's travel offices throughout the world offer a free **Client Letter Service** (mail held up to 30 days and forwarding upon request) for cardholders who contact them in advance. Address the letter in the same way shown above. Some offices will offer these services to non-cardholders (especially AmEx Traveler's Cheque holders), but call ahead to make sure. *Let's Go* lists AmEx office locations for most large cities in **Practical Information** sections; for a complete, free list, call US ☎ 800-528-4800.

POST OFFICES IN FIJI. Note that **Post Fiji** (www.postfiji.com.fj), the official postal service, operates offices in the following locations only; send mail elsewhere at your package's peril: Ba, Dreketi, Government Buildings (Suva), Korolevu, Korovou, Labasa, Lakeba Village, Lami, Laucala Beach, Lautoka, Levuka, Lomivuna, Lomaloma, Nadi, Nadi Airport, Nakasi, Nasinu, Natewa, Nausori, Navua, Nayavu, Pacific Harbour, Rabi, Raiwaqa, Rakiraki, Rotuma, Sebeto, Samabula, Savusavu, Seqaqa, Sigatoka, Suva, Tavua, Tukavesi, Vatukoula, Vunidawa, Wainikoro, and Waiyevo.

SENDING MAIL HOME FROM NZ

Although post office hours vary somewhat with town size, most are open weekdays from about 9am to 5pm, and Saturdays from about 9am to noon. **Airmail** is the best way to send mail home from New Zealand. **Aerogrammes,** printed sheets that fold into envelopes and travel via airmail, are available at post offices. They cost NZ$1.50 to send anywhere in the world. It helps to mark "airmail." Most post offices charge exorbitant fees or simply won't send aerogrammes with enclosures.

Surface mail is by far the cheapest and slowest way to send mail. It takes 10-15 days for packages to reach Australia; to North America, 18-25 days; to the UK, Ireland, and most other international destinations, 25-45 days. This might be a good for items you won't need to see for a while, such as souvenirs or other articles you've acquired along the way that are weighing down your pack.

ESSENTIALS

Australia: Allow 3-6 days for regular airmail home. Postcards/aerogrammes NZ$1.50. Letters up to 200g NZ$1.50; packages up to 0.5kg NZ$8.10, up to 2kg NZ$20.66.

Canada: Allow 4-10 days for regular airmail home. Postcards/aerogrammes NZ$1.50. Letters up to 200g NZ$2.00; packages up to 0.5kg NZ$12.81, up to 2kg NZ$40.12.

Ireland: Allow 6-12 days for regular airmail home. Postcards/aerogrammes NZ$1.50. Letters up to 200g NZ$2.00; packages up to 0.5kg NZ$13.94, up to 2kg NZ$44.72.

UK: Allow 6-12 days for regular airmail home. Postcards/aerogrammes NZ$1.50. Letters up to 200g NZ$2.00; packages up to 0.5kg NZ$13.94, up to 2kg NZ$44.72.

US: Allow 4-10 days for regular airmail home. Postcards/aerogrammes NZ$1.50. Letters up to 200g NZ$2.00; packages up to 0.5kg NZ$12.81, up to 2kg NZ$40.12.

SENDING MAIL HOME FROM FIJI

While **Post Fiji,** the Fijian mail system, generally works better than those of other developing countries, it is occasionally somewhat unreliable. If you are sending something extremely important, you would do well to use DHL (available in most sizeable towns), **FedEx** (the national agent is **Carpenters Shipping** ☎ 722 933; fax 720 056), or some other international courier service. Allow from 1-2 weeks for regular airmail to North America, the UK, Ireland, Europe, and South Africa. Generally, postage for letters or postcards is under FJ$1.00. Airmail to New Zealand and Australia usually arrives much sooner, often in a week, and postage is about FJ$0.50.

BY TELEPHONE

CALLING HOME FROM NEW ZEALAND AND FIJI

A **calling card** is probably your cheapest bet. Calls are billed collect or to your account. You can frequently call collect without even possessing a company's calling card just by calling their access number and following the instructions. **To obtain a calling card** from your national telecommunications service before leaving home, contact the appropriate company listed below (using the numbers in the first column). To **call home with a calling card,** contact the operator for your service provider in New Zealand or Fiji by dialing the appropriate toll-free access number (listed below in the second column).

COMPANY	TO OBTAIN A CARD:	TO CALL FROM NZ:	TO CALL FROM FIJI:
AT&T (US)	800-222-0300	000 911	004 890 100 1
British Telecom Direct	800 34 51 44	000 944	004 890 440 1
Canada Direct	800-668-6878	000 919	004 890 100 5
MCI (US)	800 444-3333	000 912	004 890 100 2
Sprint (US)	800 877-4646	000 999	004 890 100 3
Telkom South Africa	10 219	000 927	N/A
Telstra Australia	13 22 00	000 961	004 890 610 1

You can usually also make direct international calls from pay phones, but if you aren't using a calling card you may need to drop your coins as quickly as your words. Where available, prepaid phone cards (see **Calling Within New Zealand** below) and occasionally major credit cards can be used for direct international calls, but they are still less cost-efficient. (See **Placing International Calls** below for directions on how to place a direct international call.)

Placing a **collect call** through an international operator is even more expensive, but may be necessary in case of emergency. You can place collect calls through the service providers listed above even if you don't have one of their phone cards.

PLACING INTERNATIONAL CALLS. To call New Zealand or Fiji from home or to call home from New Zealand or Fiji, dial:

1. The **international dialing prefix**. To dial out of **Australia,** dial 0011; **Canada** or the **US,** 011; **Fiji,** 05; the **Republic of Ireland, New Zealand,** or the **UK,** 00; **Japan,** 001; **South Africa,** 09.

2. The **country code** of the country you want to call. To call **Australia,** dial 61; **Canada** or the **US,** 1; **Fiji,** 679; the **Republic of Ireland,** 353; **Japan,** 81; **New Zealand,** 64; **South Africa,** 27; the **UK,** 44.

3. The **city/area code.** *Let's Go* lists the city/area codes for cities and towns in New Zealand opposite the city or town name, next to a ☎. If the first digit is a zero (e.g., 09 for Auckland), omit the zero when calling from abroad (e.g., dial 011 64 9 from Canada to reach Auckland). There are **no area codes in Fiji.**

4. The **local number.**

CALLING WITHIN NEW ZEALAND

National directory assistance: ☎018.
National operator assistance: ☎010.
International directory assistance: ☎0172.
International operator assistance: ☎0170.

The **North Island** has several different area codes (see inside back cover). The **South Island** has a single area code of 03. Phone numbers that begin with 025 or 021 are cellular phone numbers and cost more than a standard local call. Phone numbers that begin with 0800 or 0508 are toll-free freephone calls. Phone rates tend to be highest in the morning, lower in the evening, and lowest on Sunday and late at night. Local calls from pay phones start at NZ$0.20 per minute; non-local calls start at NZ$0.30 per minute; calls to mobile phones are considerably more expensive (from NZ$1.20); international calls start at NZ$3 per minute. Calls from private phones are substantially cheaper than those from New Zealand's pay phones.

The three kinds of public **pay phones** are color-coded: **card phones** are green, **credit card phones** yellow, and **coin phones** blue. Coin phones are gradually being phased out, however, so don't count on being able to access them everywhere. **Prepaid phone cards,** sold by Telecom New Zealand and operating using a computer chip, are widely available and can be purchased at tourist offices, backpackers, convenience stores and post offices; just look inside any phone booth to see a listing of places nearby that sell phone cards. These cards are far and away the easiest and most economical way to make domestic calls, although they can only be used from explicit card phones. When you make a call, the computerized phone will tell you how much time, in units, you have left on your card (don't forget to retrieve your card!). Another kind of prepaid telephone card (such as NetTell and YABBA) comes with a Personal Identification Number (PIN) and a toll-free access number. Instead of inserting the card into the phone, call the access number and follow the directions on the card; they can be used from any telephone. These cards are preferable to make international rather than domestic calls. The YABBA card (available from Telecom New Zealand, www.tele-com.co.nz) can be purchased before you leave home over the internet and recharged while you are on the road. The YABBA card does not offer especially favorable rates on calls within New Zealand, but its international rates are attractive. Additionally, during off-peak hours (weekday evenings and weekends), calls of up to six hours can be made overseas for a fixed rate (NZ$10 to Australia and NZ$15 to Canada, Ireland, the UK and the US).

CALLING WITHIN FIJI

National directory assistance: ☎011.

National operator assistance: ☎010.

International directory assistance: ☎022.

International operator assistance: ☎012.

The Fijian phone system is quite small (one phone book covers the entire nation), and is therefore extremely easy to use. There are **no regional area codes,** so most numbers may be dialed with just six digits. Although infrequently encountered, all numbers beginning with 0800 are toll-free calls (as in New Zealand). While most of the areas covered in this book have regular phone service, some outlying islands and remote villages maintain contact through **radiophone.**

The majority of payphones in Fiji operate on a card system. Over 700 phones throughout the islands accept **Phonecard,** an automatic prepaid card available in denominations of FJ$3, $5, $10, $20, and $50. Simply insert the card into the phone and dial the number you are calling. The few phones that don't accept Phonecards generally accept **Telecard,** which is a PIN-based prepaid service. Dial ☎101 for English instructions, enter the PIN number on the back of your card, and then dial the number you are calling. Both Phonecards and Telecards are widely available at post shops and milk bars.

BY EMAIL AND BY INTERNET

It is best to set up a free, web-based email account before leaving home. There are a number of free providers, including Hotmail (www.hotmail.com), OperaMail (www.operamail.com), and Yahoo! Mail (www.yahoo.com). *Let's Go* lists internet access in **Practical Information** and **Accommodations** sections of cities and towns.

NEW ZEALAND. New Zealand is known for embracing new technologies, and the internet is no exception. Cybercafes and other sources for internet access are proliferating, though fees can be rather high (normally between NZ$8-12 per hour). Traditional cybershops are extremely common, especially in big cities, but sites everywhere from small-town backpackers to the ski slopes are increasingly being equipped with coin-operated internet stations (NZ$2 per 10min). These stations offer full web browsers but usually do not allow for use of other programs; grab a stack of coins and email away. Netcafe Guide (www.netcafeguide.com) can help you find cybercafes in specific New Zealand locations.

FIJI. All major cities in Fiji have cybercafes, although connection speeds can vary greatly as the number of local users fluctuates; late night and weekends are usually the best times to experience reasonably fast connections, while during the middle of the day on weekdays connections in Nadi sometimes are so slow they just drop out completely. Access is generally cheap, averaging FJ$6-10 per hr. Most of the outlying island groups and small to medium towns will have little to no internet access.

INTERNATIONAL FLIGHTS TO NEW ZEALAND AND FIJI

AIRFARES

When it comes to airfare, a little effort can save you a bundle. If your plans are flexible enough to deal with the restrictions, courier fares are the cheapest. Tickets bought from consolidators and standby seating are also good deals, but last-minute specials, airfare wars, and charter flights often beat these fares. The key is to hunt around, to be flexible, and to ask persistently about discounts. Students, seniors, and those under 26 should never pay full price for a ticket.

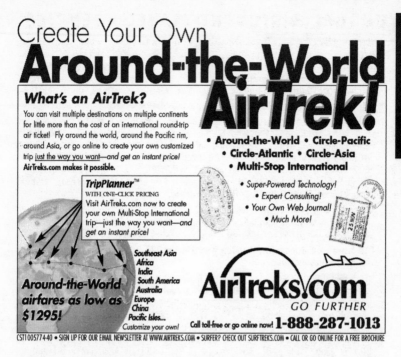
Timing: Airfares to New Zealand and Fiji peak between December and February; holidays are also expensive. Midweek (M-Th morning) round-trip flights run US$40-50 cheaper than weekend flights, but they are generally more crowded and less likely to permit frequent-flier upgrades. Traveling with an "open return" ticket is usually not an option for the budget traveler; return-date flexibility is more economically achieved by fixing a return date when buying the ticket and paying later to change it. If planning to stop in Fiji en route to New Zealand or Australia, **Air Pacific** (a Fijian airline) allows for one free stopover in Honolulu or Fiji.

Route: Round-trip flights are by far the cheapest; "open-jaw" (arriving in and departing from different cities, e.g. Los Angeles-Auckland and Christchurch-Los Angeles) tickets tend to be pricier. Patching one-way flights together is the most expensive way to travel.

Round-the-World (RTW): If New Zealand and/or Fiji are stops on a more extensive globe-hop, consider a RTW ticket. Tickets usually include at least 5 stops and are valid for about a year; prices range US$1200-5000. Try **Northwest Airlines/KLM** (US ☎800-447-4747; www.nwa.com) or **Star Alliance,** a consortium of 22 airlines including United Airlines and Air Canada (US ☎800-241-6522; www.star-alliance.com).

Gateway Cities: Flights between capitals or regional hubs will offer the cheapest fares. The cheapest gateway cities in New Zealand are typically Auckland and Christchurch, with very few international flights arriving into other cities. Almost all international flights to Fiji land in Nadi.

Boarding: Confirm international flights by phone within 72hr. of departure. Most airlines require that passengers arrive at the airport at least 2hr. before departure. One carry-on item and 2 checked bags is the norm for commercial flights.

Fares: Approximate **airfares** from Los Angeles to Auckland range from US$900-$1400, and from LA to Nadi US$850-1500, depending on the season.

BUDGET & STUDENT TRAVEL AGENCIES

While knowledgeable agents specializing in flights to New Zealand and Fiji can make your life easy and help you save, they may not spend the time to find you the lowest possible fare—they get paid on commission. Travelers holding **ISIC** and **IYTC cards** (see **Identification** p. 14) qualify for big discounts from student travel agencies. Most flights from budget agencies are on major airlines, but in peak season some may sell seats on less reliable chartered aircraft.

Usit world (www.usitworld.com). Over 48 **usit campus** branches in the UK (www.usitcampus.co.uk), including 52 Grosvenor Gardens, **London** SW1W 0AG (☎087 0240 1010); **Manchester** (☎016 1273 1880); and **Edinburgh** (☎013 1668 3303). Nearly 20 **usit NOW** offices in Ireland, including 19-21 Aston Quay, O'Connell Bridge, **Dublin** 2 (☎01 602 1600; www.usitnow.ie), and **Belfast** (☎02 890 327 111; www.usitnow.com). Offices also in **Athens, Auckland, Brussels, Frankfurt, Johannesburg, Lisbon, Luxembourg, Madrid, Paris, Sofia, and Warsaw.**

Council Travel (www.counciltravel.com). Countless US offices, including branches in **Atlanta, Boston, Chicago, L.A., New York, San Francisco, Seattle, and Washington, D.C.** Check the website or call 800-2-COUNCIL (226-8624) for the office nearest you.

CTS Travel, 44 Goodge St., **London** W1T 2AD (☎020 7636 0031; fax 7637 5328; ctsinfo@ctstravel.co.uk).

STA Travel, 7890 S. Hardy Dr., Ste. 110, Tempe AZ 85284 (24hr. reservations and info ☎800-777-0112; fax 480-592-0876; www.statravel.com). A student and youth travel organization with countless offices worldwide (check their website for a listing of all their offices), including US offices in **Boston, Chicago, L.A., New York, San Francisco, Seattle, and Washington, D.C.** Ticket booking, travel insurance, railpasses, and more. In the UK, walk-in office 11 Goodge St., **London** W1T 2PF or call 087 0160 6070. In New Zealand, 10 High St., **Auckland** (☎09 309 0458). In Australia, 366 Lygon St., **Melbourne,** Vic 3053 (☎03 9349 4344).

StudentUniverse, 545 Fifth Ave., Suite 640, New York, NY 10017 (toll-free customer service ☎800-272-9676, outside the US 212-986-8420; help@studentuniverse.com; www.studentuniverse.com), is an online student travel service offering discount ticket booking, travel insurance, railpasses, destination guides, and much more. Customer service line open M-F 9am-8pm and Sa noon-5pm EST.

Travel CUTS (Canadian Universities Travel Services Limited), 187 College St., **Toronto,** ON M5T 1P7 (☎416-979-2406; fax 979-8167; www.travelcuts.com). 60 offices across Canada. Also in the UK, 295-A Regent St., **London** W1R 7YA (☎020-7255-1944).

FLIGHT PLANNING ON THE INTERNET

Many airline sites offer special last-minute deals on the Web. The Internet is without a doubt one of the best places to look for travel bargains—it's fast, convenient, and you can spend as long as you like exploring options without driving your travel agent insane.

Commercial airlines' lowest regular offer is the **APEX** (Advance Purchase Excursion) fare, which provides confirmed reservations and allows "open-jaw" tickets. Generally, reservations must be made seven to 21 days ahead of departure, with seven- to 14-day minimum-stay and up to 90-day maximum-stay restrictions. These fares carry hefty cancellation and change penalties (fees rise in high season). Book peak-season APEX fares early; by October you may have a hard time getting your desired departure date. Use **Microsoft Expedia** (msn.expedia.com) or **Travelocity** (www.travelocity.com) to get an idea of the lowest published fares, then use the resources outlined here to try to beat them.

Popular carriers to New Zealand and Fiji include **Air New Zealand** (www.airnewzealand.co.nz), **Air Pacific** (www.airpacific.com), **Qantas** (www.qantas.com.au), and **United Airways** (www.united.com), most of which have daily nonstop flights from Los Angeles to Auckland. Other sites do the legwork and compile the deals for you—try www.bestfares.com, www.onetravel.com, www.lowestfare.com, and www.travelzoo.com.

■**StudentUniverse** (www.studentuniverse.com), **STA** (www.statravel.com), and **Council** (www.counciltravel.com) provide quotes on student tickets, while **Expedia** and **Travelocity** offer full travel services. **Priceline** (www.priceline.com) allows you to specify a price, and obligates you to buy any ticket that meets or beats it; be prepared for antisocial hours and odd routes. **Skyauction** (www.skyauction.com) allows you to bid on both last-minute and advance-purchase tickets.

An indispensable resource on the Internet is the *Air Traveler's Handbook* (www.cs.cmu.edu/afs/cs/user/mkant/Public/Travel/airfare.html), a comprehensive listing of links to everything you need to know before you board a plane.

Just one last note—to protect yourself, make sure that the site you use has a secure server before handing over any credit card details. Happy hunting!

NEW ZEALAND TRANSPORTATION

Transport in New Zealand is remarkably easy for tourists, particularly in high season, when local shuttles and backpacker buses come out in full force to supplement the main bus lines. **Booking ahead** on buses and trains will often get you significant fare reductions as well as a guaranteed seat. **Discounts** for students and YHA cardholders can be tremendous so be sure to ask. Transport can be booked by phone, at tourist offices and travel agencies, or at most backpackers.

FLIGHTS

While domestic flying is fast, it deprives travelers of spectacular road-level scenery—arguably one of the best (and least anticipated) parts of traveling New Zealand. The two major domestic airlines, **Air New Zealand** (NZ ☎0800 737 000; www.airnewzealand.co.nz) and **Ansett New Zealand** (US ☎+1 800-262-2468; www.ansett.co.nz), provide connections between major towns and cities. Air New Zealand covers the country comprehensively; a number of smaller companies are also grouped under Air New Zealand Link. "Flightseeing" is another option. Smaller local companies in each area provide beautiful views from the air for rates competitive to boat or ferry prices, starting at around NZ$90. See the **Sights and Activities** listings in each town for more details.

DISCOUNTED FARES. For travelers planning to visit Australia as well as New Zealand, it might be economical to explore multi-leg passes such as the **Boomerang Pass,** valid on Qantas, Ansett, or Air Pacific; inquire at your travel agent, or online at www.ansett.co.nz. The Boomerang provides open one-way tickets among a number of destinations in New Zealand, Australia, and the South Pacific. Within New Zealand trips are US$155; between New Zealand, Australia, and Fiji segments run US$190 (min. 2, max. 10 segments). Travelers who plan to stay within New Zealand for the duration of their trip may wish to consider Ansett's **New Zealand Airpass** instead (3 tickets, NZ$499) or the **Scenic Standby Airpass** (NZ$599, for 10 days of unlimited standby travel). Even if just buying a ticket within New Zealand, ask about the special economy fares available. Some Air New Zealand flights feature fares discounted up to 50%, while Ansett New Zealand flights offer discounts of 10-15%, depending on the season (restrictions apply). To get in on these deals, book as far in advance as possible.

TRAINS

TranzRail (NZ ☎0800 802 802, daily 7am-9pm; from overseas ☎04 498 3303; www.tranzrailtravel.co.nz) runs localized commuter trains as well as the phenomenal TranzScenic that runs between major cities and towns, providing its passen-

gers great views on the way. While train fares are generally more expensive than bus fares, TranzRail offers special discounted fares: for children aged four to 14 (40% off); travelers over 60 (30%); YHA and VIP members (30%); ISIC cardholders (20%); and those taking day excursions (30%). Minimum fare is $14 (children $9). There are also a limited number of Economy (15%), Saver (30%), and Super Saver (50%) discounted seats on each train. Some trains have a "no-frills carriage" for backpackers with less luxurious seating, smaller windows, and cheaper fares. This is a great way to meet your fellow travelers. Economy fares are offered regularly for travel at certain times of day, as well. Reserve all discounted fares well in advance, especially in peak season.

BUSES

Many budget travelers, especially backpackers, choose the bus (or coach, as the Kiwis say) as their transport of choice, especially in more remote areas. Remember that bus schedules can be somewhat flexible, and many buses will leave if you are not at the stop when they arrive. Always reserve at least one day in advance (earlier to take advantage of aggressive discount schemes), show up 15 minutes early, and do not be alarmed if buses are 20 to 40 minutes late. Visitors centers will have the most up-to-date information about bus schedules and fares, and many offer discounts if fares are booked through them. **InterCity** (☎ 09 913 6100; fax 913 6121; www.intercitycoach.co.nz), the major bus line, recently combined service with **Newmans** to form **Coachnet.** This combination service covers both islands extensively. InterCity also offers a series of TravelPasses, which allow for a certain number of days (5-22) of unlimited coach travel in a six month period as well as travel by ferry, rail, and domestic air (see website for details). All buses can be booked in advance by phone, at travel centers, or at most visitors centers. In addition, cyclists and snow bunnies will be happy to know that buses carry **bikes, skis,** or **snowboards** for a nominal fee.

DISCOUNTED FARES. YHA, BBH, and VIP membership along with possession of an ISIC card will get you 20% off fares for InterCity and Newmans. Children over five and under 16 travel for 60% off the full economy adult fare on major bus companies; travelers over 60 get 30% off. A limited number of Saver (30%) and Super Saver (50%) fares on each bus are also available by booking early (at least 5 days prior to travel for Saver and 10 days for Super Saver, with tickets purchased no later than 2 days prior to travel). During school holidays and peak season, these discounts sell out fast. All discounts are valid only on fares over NZ$20.

BACKPACKER BUSES. Many backpackers, with too little time to explore New Zealand on their own, opt to join up with one of the ubiquitous **backpackers buses.** Many travel agents try to sell these tickets before leaving your home country by making them slightly cheaper. Keep in mind that experiences greatly vary, refunds are forbidden, and tickets cannot be sold to other travelers. These tours have planned itineraries (including brief stops at sights and activities along their route) and always stop for the night at pre-arranged destinations. If you come to a place that seems particularly worthwhile, you can separate from the bus and stick around town. As each company has a fairly constant stream of buses running the same routes, you can join up with a new touring group when you're ready to move on again. The trade-off is that you lose the spontaneity that so many backpackers treasure, but in return, you meet a busload of starry-eyed young travelers and benefit from the knowledgeable tour guides. Trips range from whirlwind one week, one island loops to more leisurely whole country explorations. Accommodations are pre-booked by drivers with your input, but are not included in the overall price; food is also at your own cost. Many backpacker buses also reserve spaces with various adventure companies (like skydiving, kayak rentals, or glacier hiking outfits), offering decent discounts on activities along the route. Although travel is hop-on, hop-off flexible, reservations must be made at least a couple of days ahead of time and confirmed, especially in high season.

Kiwi Experience, 170 Parnell Rd. Parnell, **Auckland** (☎09 366 9830; fax 366 1374; enquiries@kiwiex.co.nz; www.kiwiexperience.com) is the most conspicuous of the backpacker buses, with over 20 green giants rolling through the country. Popular with North Americans and Europeans, especially Brits, Kiwi Experience caters to the party backpacker. Whether you're riding with them or not, you'll notice the significant impact that the Kiwi Experience buses have on the tourism industry, filling up certain hostels and showing up en masse at a bar. Kiwi Experience is good for travelers in their late teens and early twenties. Trip prices range widely depending on discounts and location booked, from one island loops at around US$150 and the whole country at around US$475. YHA/VIP 5% discount.

Magic Travellers Network, Union House 136-138 Quay St., **Auckland** (☎09 358 5600; fax 358 3471; info@magicbus.co.nz; www.magicbus.co.nz) provides a similar service, but a more subdued experience. While still providing energetic and friendly travels, Magic often shuttles slightly older backpackers. Again, trip prices and routes vary, but Magic tends to be slightly cheaper than Kiwi, with trips ranging from about US$140 to US$310. YHA 5% discount. Similarly, Magic has partnered with the New Zealand YHA to create **GoNZ** travel packages which include transport on the Magic bus as well as accommodation in YHA hostels (see www.yha.org.nz for more information).

SHUTTLE BUSES. Local shuttle buses often supplement the service of the major bus lines (and occasionally offer lower prices on mainstream runs). These services use vans, often collect travelers from their respective accommodations, and usually travel to small towns not serviced by the main coach lines. Companies include Atomic, Fiordland Travel, and Westcoaster. However, there is a high turnover in shuttle companies and they can be less reliable and comfortable. Local visitors centers will often have current info on prices and schedules and can do bookings. During winter and in more remote locations, make sure to call ahead.

CARS

INTERNATIONAL DRIVING PERMIT (IDP)

Even if you plan to drive a car while in New Zealand, you probably won't need an IDP, as long as you have a current license from your own country. A few car rental agencies do require the IDP, however (be sure to ask), and it can serve as an additional piece of ID in a tough situation. Your IDP, valid for one year, must be issued in your own country before you depart; AAA affiliates cannot issue IDPs valid in their own country. You must be 18 years old to receive an IDP. A valid driver's license from your home country must always accompany the IDP. An application usually needs to include one or two photos, a current local license, an additional form of identification, and a fee.

Australia: Contact your local Royal Automobile Club (RAC) or the National Royal Motorist Association (NRMA) if in NSW or the ACT (☎08 9421 4444; www.rac.com.au/travel). Permits AUS$15.

Canada: Contact any Canadian Automobile Association (CAA) branch or write to CAA, 1145 Hunt Club Rd., #200, K1V 0Y3. (☎613-247-0117 ext. 2025; www.caa.ca/CAAInternet/travelservices/internationaldocumentation/idptravel.htm). Permits CDN$10.

Ireland: Contact the nearest Automobile Association (AA) office. The Irish Automobile Association, 23 Suffolk St., **Dublin** (☎01 677 9988; www.aaireland.ie/home/index.asp), honors most foreign automobile memberships (24hr. breakdown and road service ☎800 667 788; toll-free in Ireland). Permits IR£4.

South Africa: Contact the Travel Services Department of the Automobile Association of South Africa at P.O. Box 596, 2000 **Johannesburg** (☎11 799 1000; fax 799 1960; www.aa.co.za). Permits ZAR28.50.

UK: To visit your local AA Shop, contact the AA Headquarters (☎0990 44 88 66), or write to: The Automobile Association, International Documents, Fanum House, Erskine, Renfrewshire PA8 6BW. To find the location nearest you that issues the IDP, call 0990 500 600 or 0990 448 866. For more info, see www.theaa.co.uk/motoringandtravel/idp/index.asp. Permits UK£4.

US: Visit any American Automobile Association (AAA) office or fill out the application online at www.ouraaa.com/index.html. You don't have to be a member to buy an IDP. Permits US$10. AAA Travel Related Services (☎800-222-4357) provides road maps, travel guides, emergency road services, travel services, and auto insurance.

CAR INSURANCE

Some credit cards cover standard insurance. If you rent, lease, or borrow a car, you will need the **"Green Card" (International Insurance Certificate)** to certify that you have liability insurance and that it applies abroad. Green Cards can be obtained at car rental agencies, car dealers, and some travel agents.

CAR RENTAL

Avis (NZ ☎09 526 2847; tollfree 0800 655 111; www.avis.com), **Budget** (NZ ☎09 976 2222, 0800 652 227; fax 976 2223; www.budget.com), and **Hertz** (NZ ☎03 358 6787; fax 358 6756; www.hertz.com) are the major car rental operators in New Zealand, and offer their services in all of the main cities and towns. Most agencies rent to those age 21 and over, although some agencies require drivers to be 25. Most cars in New Zealand are manual, so be sure to ask if you require an automatic. Rates vary according to season, as well as duration of rental and condition of car, and generally include unlimited mileage, loss damage waiver and GST. (**American Express** cardholders, please note that American Express does not cover the required Collision and Damage Waiver in New Zealand, as it does automatically in most other countries.) Expect to pay at least NZ$40 (NZ$60 in high season) a day for a month's rental from one of these companies; for cars of better condition and make, the price may skyrocket to as high as NZ$130 per day. **Darn Cheap Rentals** (☎0800 800 327) operates out of Auckland, Wellington, Christchurch, and Picton (NZ$35 per day for 7 days), though the cars are often very small. **Omega Rental Cars** (☎09 275 3265, 0800 525 210) has budget cars from NZ$39 per day and **Ace Rentals** operates out of Auckland, Wellington, Picton, and Christchurch (☎09 303 3112, 0800 502 277; info@acerentals.co.nz) rents from NZ$25 per day. Smaller operators often offer eye-poppingly low fares, but be cautious—look carefully into the reliability and reputation before committing.

Sometimes New Zealand rental companies also offer the opportunity of returning a rental car to its hub and only require you to pay for petrol. This arrangement allows travelers to cover long distances for minimal costs. Unfortunately, the opportunity is only found by searching bulletin boards in hostels. Often times travelers look for others to join the trip and split the petrol costs. Check the boards in city YHAs or larger dorm style hostels.

BUY-BACKS

Buying a car, then selling it upon departure, may be a smart option for longer stays. Buy-back outlets, such as the **New Zealand Guaranteed Buy-Back Vehicle Associates,** 825 Dominion Rd., Mt. Roskill, Auckland (☎09 620 6587), sell cars specifically for this purpose. Prices range from NZ$3000-7000; you must keep the car for a minimum of a month. At the end of your stay, the buy-back outlet in Auckland buys back the vehicle minus the depreciation rate.

If you prefer to strike out on your own car-buying spree, Auckland is definitely a hot spot for the best car deals: check out one of its car auctions or the used car section of *The New Zealand Herald* (especially on Wednesdays). The *Trade and Exchange*, another good place to look, comes out Mondays and Thursdays.

A car must have a V.I.C. (vehicle inspection certificate, sometimes called a W.O.F.), which ensures that it is road safe. Make sure that your potential car has received one within the past month. They are good for six months and cost NZ$25. A car must be **registered** (six months around NZ$100; one year NZ$200). Whenever there is a change of ownership, a **MR13A form** must be completed by the buyer and seller and turned in at a post shop. The buyer must also complete a **MR13B form** (NZ$9.20). Insurance is not necessary but highly recommended, as is membership in an Automobile Association (see above). The latter will get you emergency breakdown service, free service for simple problems, and free towing.

Before you buy your car, you should have it inspected. Vehicle inspection services can be found in the yellow pages under that heading and will do comprehensive pre-purchase checks for NZ$100. You may want to check out **car fairs** in Auckland; some are **Sell it Yourself,** 60 Wairau Rd., Glenfield (☎09 443 3800; open daily 7am-7pm); **Ellerslie Racecourse** (☎09 810 9212), off the Greenlane roundabout (open Sunday 9am-noon); and **Manukau City Park and Sell** (☎09 358 5000; open Sunday 9am-1pm). **Car auctions** in Auckland are another option. **Turners Car Auctions** (☎09 525 1920), corner of Leonard and Penrose Rd., Penrose, sells budget cars Wednesdays at noon and cars from $2000-8000 on Thursdays at 6pm. **Hammer Actions,** 830 Great South Rd., Penrose (☎09 579 2344), sells budget cars on weekdays at 6pm and at 10:30am on Saturday.

RULES OF THE ROAD

The Road Code of New Zealand (NZ$19.95), available at AA offices and bookstores, tells you all you need to know. First and foremost, Americans, join your Kiwi companions and drive on the left hand side of the road; many accidents arise from tourists who don't give themselves some extra practice driving time to adjust before heading out. Speed limits are strictly enforced; speed cameras are even set up at the traffic lights of many large towns to catch lead-footed offenders. Drunk driving laws are serious business in New Zealand and are strictly enforced. **Petrol** (gas) costs approximately NZ$1 per liter, although it is generally more expensive in smaller towns; when traveling, it can easily run NZ$15-20 per day. State highways are abbreviated SH; SH2 is in the process of being renamed the Pacific Coast Highway. Members of worldwide Automobile Associations (see **IDP** p. 42) can enjoy the reciprocal agreement with the **New Zealand Automobile Association (AA;** ☎0800 500 222) to obtain free maps and other services from AA offices in New Zealand. The AA **hotline** (☎0900 332 222) gives road reports for NZ$1 per minute.

HITCHHIKING

 LET'S GO DOES NOT RECOMMEND HITCHHIKING. *Let's Go* strongly urges you to seriously consider the risks before you choose to hitchhike. Although we try to report accurately on the availability of hitching opportunities in each area, we do not recommend it as a safe means of transport, and none of the information printed here is intended to do so.

Some visitors to New Zealand, particularly backpackers, rely on hitchhiking as a primary mode of transport, and express satisfaction with its safety and convenience. Others, however, report that hitchhiking is not as safe as it used to be, especially for women traveling alone. A man and a woman are a safer combination; two men will have a harder time finding a ride. No matter how safe or friendly New Zealanders may be, you should always think seriously before trusting your life to a stranger, as you risk suffering an accident, theft, assault, sexual harassment, or worse. Exercise caution if you elect to hitch: avoid getting into the back of a two-door car; when waiting for a ride, stand in a well-lit, public place; start early in the day; avoid hitchhiking at night; and avoid hitchhiking alone. Even at the risk of offending the driver, **do not put your backpack in the trunk;** you might not get it back. Trust your instincts—if you ever feel unsafe or threatened, do not hesitate to politely but firmly ask to be let off.

If you are planning on hitching, it is reported to be easiest just beyond the end of a town's residential area, but before the open highway. It is illegal on freeways. Hitching is not just a matter of luck. You can increase your chances if you choose a spot on the side of the road with ample space for a car to pull over. And no one wants to pick up a lazy backpacker sitting on his pack. Walk backwards with the traffic with your thumb out and try to make eye contact with the driver. Sometimes, drivers will pass and then turn around to pick you up. It is often easier to be picked up if you hold a sign indicating your desired destination; avoid accepting offers that will leave you in a small town, short of your ultimate goal.

FIJI TRANSPORTATION

Fiji has inexpensive and moderately reliable internal transportation. However, keep in mind that much of the country runs on **"Fiji Time"**—exact arrival and departure times can vary significantly, and it is best to remain as flexible as possible with travel plans.

DOMESTIC FLIGHTS

Domestic airlines are prevalent and reliable, often times flying tiny planes, which offer spectacular views. **Air Fiji** (☎722 521; fax 720 555; airfiji@is.com.fj) and **Sunflower Airlines** (☎723 016; fax 723 611; sunair@is.com.fj) offer service between major cities. Air Fiji provides the 30-day Discover Fiji Pass, with several itineraries from FJ$472 (sold only with the purchase of international airfare; inquire when buying your ticket to Fiji).

   Island Hoppers (☎720 410; fax 720 172; islandhoppers@is.com.fj) and **Turtle Airways** (☎721 888; fax 720 095; southseaturtle@is.com.fj) offer charter and scenic flights. See **Transportation** sections for specific destinations for further information.

BUSES

Most buses are hot, noisy, and smokey with tarpaulins pulled down to cover open windows during rain. Buses stop at stations in cities, but it is necessary to hail the bus in order to board in rural regions. When heading to rural areas be sure to check return times so as not to be stranded. **Fiji Holiday Connections** (☎720 977), **Pacific Transport Ltd.** (☎700 044), **Sunbeam Transport Ltd.** (☎662 822), and **United Touring Fiji** (☎722 811) run regular and express services along Queens Road. **PVV Tours** (☎700 600) and Sunbeam Transport travel along Kings Road.

CARS

Car rental in Fiji is expensive. Very few locals own cars, and as a result there are many cheap public transportation options serving virtually all locations. However, some areas, especially the Kings Road on Viti Levu (p. 399), are best explored by rental car. **Avis** (☎722 688, 722 233; freecall 008 003 005) and **Hertz** (☎380 981; fax 938 0758) are the major car rental outfits in Fiji. Check **Transportation** sections for car rental information in specific areas. Standard Fijian speed limits are **80kph** (about 50mph) on highways and **50kph** (about 30mph) otherwise. For more information on driving safety in Fiji see **Personal Safety: Driving** p. 22.

FERRIES

The most common way to travel between islands in Fiji is by ferry; services range from the reliable 42-passenger high-speed ferry operated by **South Sea Cruises** (☎750 500; see **The Yasawa Group: Interisland Transportation** p. 419) to small open boats with struggling outboards; make sure that any boat has adequate safety equipment (life jackets, radio, etc.) before you get onboard—*Let's Go* **does not recommend traveling in a boat without life jackets.**

HITCHHIKING

Again, *Let's Go* does not recommend hitchhiking as a means of transport. Fijians frown upon the practice as well, and almost never hitch. For more information on the dangers of hitchhiking, see the New Zealand **Hitchhiking** section p. 44.

ESSENTIALS

SPECIFIC CONCERNS

WOMEN TRAVELERS

Women exploring on their own inevitably face some additional safety concerns in Fiji, and even in a country as safe as New Zealand. As in most situations, it is best to trust your instincts and be more cautious than you think is necessary.

Stick to centrally located accommodations and avoid solitary late-night treks. When traveling, always carry extra money for a phone call, bus, or taxi. **Hitching** is never safe for lone women, or even for two women traveling together. Look as if you know where you're going (even when you don't). Watch out for persistent, too-friendly locals, especially when hitting the pub scene. Women traditionally posses a subservient role in Fijian culture, and female travelers sometimes encounter unpleasant attitudes and actions. A self-defense course will not only prepare you for a potential attack, but will raise your level of awareness of your surroundings as well as your confidence (see **Self Defense** p. 22).

Although **tampons, pads,** and reliable **contraceptive devices** are legal and easily accessible in New Zealand and Fijian cities, you may want to bring along your favorite brand, as type and quality vary (this is especially true for female travelers to more rural areas of Fiji). Women on the pill should bring enough to allow for possible loss or extended stays. Be sure to bring a prescription since forms of the pill vary. Women considering an **abortion** in New Zealand should contact the **New Zealand Family Planning Association (NZFPA)**, 6 Southmark House, 203-209 Willis Street, Wellington (☎ 04 384 4349; fpanz@globe.co.nz), for more information.

Let's Go: New Zealand lists specific emergency numbers and hotlines (such as **rape crisis lines**) in the Practical Information listings of most cities. The **general emergency numbers** in New Zealand and Fiji are: **New Zealand** ☎ 111, **Fiji** ☎ 000.

RESOURCES FOR WOMEN

Wander Women, P.O. Box 68058, Newton, Auckland 3 (☎ 09 360 7330; fax 360 7332; www.wanderwomen.co.nz; enquiries@wanderwomen.co.nz) offers guided sea kayaking and other outdoor trips for both women-only and mixed groups.

A Journey of One's Own: Uncommon Advice for the Independent Woman Traveler, Thalia Zepatos. Eighth Mountain Press (US$17). An inspiring collection of essays by women travelers in addition to practical travel information specific to women.

TRAVELING ALONE

There are many benefits to traveling alone, among them greater independence and challenge. Without distraction, you can write a great travel log in the grand tradition of Mark Twain, John Steinbeck, and Charles Kuralt. Traveling alone in New Zealand and Fiji is neither unwise nor uncommon. Many young solo travelers take advantage of backpacker buses like Kiwi Experience or Magic. While these have no Fijian counterparts, popular destinations like **Beachcomber Island** (p. 418) provide a comparable environment and social scene.

On the other hand, any solo traveler is a more vulnerable target of harassment and street theft. Lone travelers need to be well-organized and look confident at all times. If questioned, never admit that you are traveling alone. Maintain regular contact with someone at home who knows your itinerary.

For more tips, pick up *Traveling Solo* by Eleanor Berman (Globe Pequot, US$17) or subscribe to **Connecting: Solo Travel Network,** P.O. Box 29088, Delamont RPO, Vancouver, BC V6J 5C2 (☎/fax 604-737-7791; www.cstn.org; membership US$28), or the **Travel Companion Exchange,** P.O. Box 833, Amityville, NY 11701 (☎ 631-454-0880; or 800-392-1256; www.whytravelalone.com; US$48).

OLDER TRAVELERS

Many **senior citizens** discounts, especially on transport passes, only apply to local residents. For activities and accommodations, however, you may be able to finagle a special price if you ask nicely. Agencies for senior group travel are growing in popularity. A few organizations and publications are listed below.

ElderTreks, 597 Markham St., **Toronto,** ON M6G 2L7 (☎800-741-7956; or 416-588-5000; fax 588-9839; eldertreks@eldertreks.com; www.eldertreks.com). All-inclusive adventure travel programs for the 50+ traveler in New Zealand.

Elderhostel, 75 Federal St., **Boston,** MA 02110 (US ☎617-426-7788; or 877-426-2166; registration@elderhostel.org; www.elderhostel.org). Organizes 1- to 4-week "educational adventures" in New Zealand and Australia for those 55+.

The Mature Traveler, P.O. Box 50400, **Reno,** NV 89513 (US ☎775-786-7419, credit card orders 800-460-6676). Deals, discounts, and travel packages for the 50+ traveler. Sends trips that cover the North and South Island. Subscription $30.

BISEXUAL, GAY, & LESBIAN TRAVELERS

In 1993, discrimination of any kind became illegal in **New Zealand.** Intolerance does not need to be unduly feared in major New Zealand cities, many of which feature an active gay culture with gay-friendly bars, health centers, and bookstores. Auckland has an active, though partially segregated, gay and lesbian culture, while Wellington's gay and lesbian population is more integrated. More rural and remote areas are less accustomed to displays of homosexuality, however. They may be less friendly, but will not likely be openly or unpleasantly disapproving. Local organizations and particularly gay-friendly venues are listed throughout the book.

Although the constitution adopted in **Fiji** in 1998 established explicit official protection for homosexuals from discrimination (only the second nation in the world to do so), it has been abrogated in the wake of the 2000 coup, and gay and lesbian cultures still remain very quiet segments of life, especially compared to their Kiwi counterparts. Powerful and traditional conservative Christian elements of society are generally intolerant of public homosexuality. However, there are some friendly bars in Suva, and some resorts are quite gay-friendly. As always when traveling in developing and rural areas, the best course of action is to be discrete.

Listed below are some New Zealand contact organizations offering materials or services addressing some specific concerns; Fiji currently has little infrastructure in place to address BGLT issues. **Out and About** (www.planetout.com) offers a biweekly newsletter addressing travel concerns. The **International Gay and Lesbian Travel Association,** 4331 N. Federal Hwy., #304, Fort Lauderdale, FL 33308 (US ☎954-776-2626; fax 776-3303; www.iglta.com) is an organization of over 1350 companies serving gay and lesbian travelers worldwide. Their website provides links to a number of travel resources for gays and lesbians.

New Zealand Gay and Lesbian Tourism Association, Private Bag MBE P255, Auckland (☎0800 123 429; info@nzglta.org.nz; http://www.nzglta.org.nz). This professional, nonprofit organization provides an online travel planner to help gay travelers create a travel package which patronizes gay and gay-friendly establishments.

Gay Switchboard, P.O. Box 11-372, Wellington 6001 (☎04 473 7878; gayswitchboard@yahoo.com). Help and information for gay and lesbian individuals.

Travel Desk NZ Ltd., 45 Anzac Ave., Auckland (☎09 377 9031; out@nz.com). Open daily 8:30am-6pm.

Lesbian Line, Wellington (☎04 499 5567; open Tu, Th, and Sa 7:30-10pm).

FURTHER READING

Spartacus International Gay Guide. Bruno Gmunder Verlag (US$33).

The Gay Vacation Guide: The Best Trips and How to Plan Them, Mark Chesnut. Citadel Press (US$15).

ESSENTIALS

TRAVELERS WITH DISABILITIES

NEW ZEALAND. New Zealand is overall an accessible and welcoming country for the disabled. Law requires that every new motel and hotel provides a certain number of fully accessible rooms. In addition, a number of **tramps** and **walks** are wheelchair-accessible; always check with DOC. Main taxi companies in major cities and many towns have a **Total Mobility Taxi Service** offering transport for those with wheelchairs. With sufficient notice, some major car rental agencies will offer hand-controlled vehicles at select locations. The **Green Book** (http://members.nbci.com/thegreenbook/home.html) has a partial listing of disabled-access accommodations and sights in New Zealand.

Those with disabilities should inform airlines and hotels of their disabilities when making arrangements for travel; some time may be needed to prepare special accommodations. Call ahead to restaurants, hotels, parks, and other facilities to find out about the existence of ramps, the widths of doors, the dimensions of elevators, etc. **Guide dog owners** must apply for a **permit to import,** as well as provide appropriate documentation regarding the dog's health and qualifications. Applications for the permit should be made to the Chief Veterinary Officer, Ministry of Agriculture, P.O. Box 2526, Wellington. More information is provided at the Ministry of Agriculture and Forestry website (www.maf.govt.nz).

FIJI. While Fiji openly embraces all types of visitors, extremely little infrastructure has been developed for disabled travelers (especially those in wheelchairs)—this is less due to intolerance than to lack of understanding and public concern. While some upscale resorts may be wheelchair-accessible, the vast majority of Fijian accommodation and local transportation options are not extremely accessible to travelers with disabilities.

USEFUL ORGANIZATIONS

Mobility International USA (MIUSA), P.O. Box 10767, Eugene, OR 97440 (☎541-343-1284, voice and TDD; www.miusa.org). Sells *A World of Options: A Guide to International Educational Exchange, Community Service, and Travel for Persons with Disabilities* (US$35).

Society for the Advancement of Travel for the Handicapped (SATH), 347 Fifth Ave., #610, New York, NY 10016 (☎212-447-7284; www.sath.org). An advocacy group that publishes free online travel information and the travel magazine *OPEN WORLD* (US$18, free for members). Annual membership US$45, students and seniors US$30.

ORGANIZATIONS WITHIN NEW ZEALAND.

Deaf Emergency Telephone Number, ☎0800 161 616.

Disability Resource Center, P.O. Box 24-042, Royal Oak, Auckland 3 (☎09 625 8069; fax 624 1633).

Disabled Persons Assembly (DPA), Level 4, Tower Block, Wellington Trade Center, 175 Victoria St., Wellington (☎04 801 9100; fax 801 9565).

Enable New Zealand, 60 Bennett St., Palmerston North (☎06 952 0011, 0800 171 981; fax 952 0022; www.enable.co.nz). A wide variety of information, equipment, and referrals for the disabled and their families in New Zealand.

Taxi Companies for People with Disabilities: Cannons Total Mobility (☎09 836 4386); Co-op Taxis (☎09 300 3000); Independence Mobility (☎09 836 6761); North Harbor Taxis (☎09 443 1777); South Auckland Taxis (☎09 278 5678); Auckland Mobility (☎09 817 9442); United Taxis (☎09 298 1000).

Global Access (www.geocities.com/Paris/1502/disabilitylinks.html) has links for disabled travelers in New Zealand and details handicapped-accessible accommodations on the South Island.

MINORITY TRAVELERS

New Zealand's population is mainly of European descent; the largest minority group is Maori, followed by Polynesians and Asians (see **The People** p. 384). Race relations today between Maori and Pakeha (non-Maori peoples) appear to have reached some measure of stability, although tension remains. Debate, protest, and legal reform over the place of Maori culture, history, and land claims in New Zealand continues.

Fiji's population is mainly of Indian and native Fijian descent (see **The People** p. 384). Although there is much social and economic tension between these two main groups, visitors of all backgrounds experience little of the conflict personally.

Asian tourism, particularly Japanese and Korean, is becoming increasingly common in New Zealand and Fiji; prejudice against Asians in some areas is also growing. However, such prejudice rarely leads to violence. Visitors of Asian descent may possibly be at risk for theft, due to the stereotype of the wealthy Asian tourist. Other minorities may find that they stand out in a New Zealand crowd, but are more likely to invite curious looks than harassment or violence. Ironically, white travelers to Fiji generally stand out much more than any darker-skinned travelers.

As always, however, it is difficult to generalize about how minority travelers will be treated in a foreign country. *Let's Go* asks its researchers to exclude establishments that discriminate for any reason. If you experience discrimination in an establishment listed in this guide, please mail a letter to *Let's Go* stating the details of the incident (see **Helping *Let's Go*** at the beginning of the guide).

TRAVELERS WITH CHILDREN

New Zealand may be best known for its extreme adventure activities and hard-core tramping opportunities, but there is plenty to do for families who prefer a little less danger and a little more structure in their travel plans. From scenic flights to sailing tours, glass-blowing museums to glow-worm caves, and petrified forests to penguin colonies, there is plenty here to entertain parents and wear out even the most energetic of kids. The **Sights and Activities** sections of cities and towns offers a wide range of ways to get your thrills without risking life and limb.

Children's discounts abound in New Zealand. Restaurants often have children's menus, and virtually all museums and tourist attractions have a children's rate. Children under two generally fly for 10% of the adult airfare on international flights (this does not necessarily include a seat). International fares are usually discounted 25% for children ages two to eleven.

While some upscale resorts exclude children during certain times of the year, the majority of Fijian accommodations are very open to children. While probably a less exciting destination than New Zealand, there are still plenty of activities to keep children entertained.

When deciding where to stay, call ahead to inquire about family rooms and to make sure they allow children. If you rent a car, make sure the rental company provides a car seat for younger children. Be sure that your child carries a form of ID in case of an emergency or if he or she gets lost.

FURTHER READING

Backpacking with Babies and Small Children, Goldie Silverman. Wilderness Press (US$10).

Have Kid, Will Travel: 101 Survival Strategies for Vacationing With Babies and Young Children, Claire and Lucille Tristram. Andrews McMeel Publishing (US$9).

Trouble Free Travel with Children, Vicki Lansky. Book Peddlers (US$9).

DIETARY CONCERNS

Despite the culinary prevalence of lamb and meat pies, **vegetarians** should have relatively little problem finding suitable cuisine in New Zealand. Most restaurants have vegetarian selections on their menus, and some cater specifically to vegetarians. Ethnic restaurants, like Asian or Middle Eastern, are especially likely to have vegetarian entrees. Finding **vegan** fare will be a bit more challenging and will probably entail a good deal more self-catering. *Let's Go* often notes establishments with especially good vegetarian selections.

Vegetarians and vegans traveling in Fiji will have no problem fulfilling their dietary needs, so long as they like curry. The high percentage of establishments serving Indian food means that animal-free options are almost a guarantee.

The North American Vegetarian Society, P.O. Box 72, Dolgeville, NY 13329 (☎518-568-7970; www.navs-online.org), publishes information about vegetarian travel, including *Transformative Adventures: a Guide to Vacations and Retreats* (US$15).

Since the Jewish population in New Zealand is considerably smaller than one half of one percent, travelers who keep **kosher** should be prepared to receive some blank stares when inquiring after acceptable restaurants. The best bet may be to contact synagogues in larger cities for information on kosher establishments, or contact the **Israel Information Office**, P.O. Box 4315, Auckland (☎09 309 9444; fax 373 2283). Other New Zealand resources include **Jewish New Zealand**, available at http://webnz.com/israel/jnz.htm, or consult the more general **Jewish Travel Guide**, which lists synagogues, kosher restaurants, and Jewish institutions in over 100 countries. The guide is available in Europe from Vallentine Mitchell Publishers, Newbury House 890-900, Eastern Ave., Newbury Park, Ilford, Essex IG2 7HH (UK ☎020 8599 8866; fax 8599 0984) and in the US ($16.95 + $4 S&H) from ISBS, 5804 NE Hassallo St., Portland, OR 97213 (☎800-944-6190). Ultimately, however, if you are strict in your observance, you may have to prepare your own food on the road. This is especially true in Fiji, which has virtually no Jewish population.

ALTERNATIVES TO TOURISM

For an extensive listing of "off-the-beaten-track" and specialty travel opportunities, try the **Specialty Travel Index,** 305 San Anselmo Ave., #313, **San Anselmo, California** 94960 (☎888-624-4030 or 415-455-1643; www.specialtytravel.com; US$6). **Transitions Abroad** (www.transabroad.com) publishes a bimonthly on-line newsletter for work, study, and specialized travel abroad.

STUDYING ABROAD

A **student visa** is required for those intending to study in New Zealand for more than three months. The visa should be obtained from the nearest New Zealand embassy or high commission and requires an "offer of place," a letter confirming that you have been offered admission in a New Zealand educational institution. Exchange programs are available in Auckland, Christchurch, Wellington, Dunedin, and other smaller cities. Specific information about admissions requirements and course offerings should be obtained directly from a specific university.

In New Zealand, the academic year begins in March and is divided into three terms. The long vacation is from late November to early March and there are three week breaks between terms in May and in August.

There are eight separate state-funded universities in New Zealand, all of which welcome international students. University study in New Zealand is closer to a British than to an American system, as there is no equivalent of a "liberal arts" college. **New Zealand Education International**, P.O. Box 10-500, Wellington (☎04 472 0788; www.nzeil.co.nz) publishes a directory of universities, colleges of education

and polytechnics. Similarly, they can provide a list of secondary and English language institutions. American undergraduates can enroll in programs sponsored by US universities, although it may be cheaper to enroll in a local university directly.

Although Fiji's **University of the South Pacific** (p. 415) in Suva is the best university in the region, drawing students from hundreds of islands throughout the Pacific, it is generally not attended by any non-Pacific students.

American Field Service (AFS), 310 SW 4th Avenue, (Suite 630), Portland, OR 97204 (☎800-237-4636; fax 503-241-1653; afsinfo@afs.org; www.afs.org/usa). AFS offers summer-, semester-, and year-long homestay international exchange programs with New Zealand for US high school students and graduating high school seniors.

Association of Commonwealth Universities (ACU), John Foster House, 36 Gordon Sq., London WC1H OPF (☎020 7380 6700; www.acu.ac.uk). Publishes information about Commonwealth universities including the Universities of Auckland, Canterbury, Waikato, Otago, and Victoria University of Wellington.

Council on International Educational Exchange (CIEE), 205 East 42nd St., New York, NY 10017 (☎888-268-6245 or 800-407-8839; www.ciee.org/study) sponsors work, volunteer, academic, and internship programs in New Zealand.

School for International Training, College Semester Abroad, Admissions, Kipling Rd., P.O. Box 676, Brattleboro, VT 05302, USA (☎800-336-1616 or 802-258-3267; www.sit.edu). Semester- and year-long programs in New Zealand run US$10,600-13,700. Also runs the **Experiment in International Living** (☎800-345-2929; fax 802-258-3428; eil@worldlearning.org), 3- to 5-week summer programs that offer high-school students cross-cultural homestays, community service, and ecological adventure in New Zealand and cost US$1900-5000.

FURTHER READING AND RESOURCES

www.studyabroad.com

Academic Year Abroad 2000/2001. Institute of International Education Books (US$46.95).

Vacation Study Abroad 2000/2001. Institute of International Education Books (US$43).

Peterson's Study Abroad 2002. Peterson's (US$21).

WORKING & VOLUNTEERING

WORKING ABROAD

Officially, tourists and students cannot work legally in New Zealand or Fiji. Instead, foreigners can only hold a job with a **work visa** or **permit** (see **Visas and Work Permits** p. 13). To obtain these, you often need to be sponsored by an employer who can demonstrate that you have skills that locals lack—not the easiest of tasks. All visas must be obtained outside New Zealand and Fiji, so if you think you meet these criteria, call the nearest New Zealand or Fijian consulate or embassy to get more information.

However, despite these rather stringent requirements for obtaining a work permit, many backpackers have been known to support themselves in New Zealand (albeit illegally) in a number of ways—most notably, picking fruit or working as helpers in hostels (in exchange for free room and board). Such work is normally arranged, under the table, through hostel owners or other locals. These jobs, however, often do not pay particularly well and are either seasonal or short-term employment at best. Especially in areas heavy with seasonal employment (the Marlborough wine region, for example), many backpackers in New Zealand could aptly be termed "working hostels," for they are filled not with vacationers but with travelers and locals who have set up a temporary home near their jobs. Such hostels can sometimes be identified if they offer weekly rates for rooms, instead of only a nightly tariff. For full-time students at a US university, the simplest way to get a job abroad in New Zealand is through work permit programs run by **Council on International Educational Exchange** (p. 52). Potential jobs include fruit-picking, hotel staffing, or bartending, with weekly rages ranging from around US$300-400 a week. For a US$400 program fee, CIEE can procure three- to six-month work permits and a handbook to help you find work and housing. Unfortunately, it is basically impossible for travelers to find jobs, legal or otherwise, anywhere in Fiji.

VOLUNTEERING

New Zealand readily provides volunteer jobs, many of which provide room and board in exchange for labor. Contacting individual workcamps directly sometimes avoids high application fees. Jobs on organic farms arranged through **WWOOF** (where participants are called "wwoofers") are particularly popular. While Fiji has relatively few volunteer programs, Habitat for Humanity Fiji has several great programs, including one combining work with scuba diving for volunteers.

> **Earthwatch,** 3 Clocktower Pl., P.O. Box 75, **Maynard, MA** 01754 USA (☎800-776-0188 or 978-461-0081; www.earthwatch.org). Arranges 1- to 3-week programs in New Zealand to promote conservation of natural resources. Programs average US$1600.

> **Habitat for Humanity International,** 121 Habitat St., **Americus, GA** 31709 USA (☎800-422-4828; www.habitat.org). Offers opportunities to help build low-income housing in New Zealand. Cost US$2400-3000, including airfare from Los Angeles.

> **Habitat for Humanity Fiji,** P.O. Box 16154, **Suva,** Fiji (☎679 312 012; fax 300 836; hfhfiji@is.com.fj; www.fiji-online.com.fj/npo/hfhfiji). There is tremendous need for low-income housing in Fiji. The Suva affiliate was recently the recipient of the Asia/Pacific Award for Board Development. Unique hiking, rafting, and diving combo programs.

> **Willing Workers on Organic Farms (WWOOF),** P.O. Box 1172, **Nelson** NZ (☎/fax 03 544 9890; www.wwoof.co.nz). Distributes a list of names of over 500 farmers who offer room and board in exchange for help on the farm. Membership fee is NZ$30 from within the country; from overseas, AUS$35, UK£12, or US$20. Couples' discounts available.

FURTHER READING

> *International Jobs: Where they Are, How to Get Them,* Eric Koocher. Perseus Books (US$17).

> *International Directory of Voluntary Work,* Louise Whetter. Vacation Work Publications (US$16).

> *Teaching English Abroad,* Susan Griffin. Vacation Work (US$17).

OTHER RESOURCES

Let's Go tries to cover all aspects of budget travel, but we can't put *everything* in our guides. Listed below are websites that can serve as jumping off points for your own research.

TRAVEL PUBLISHERS & BOOKSTORES

> **Rand McNally,** 150 S. Wacker Dr., **Chicago, IL** 60606 (☎800-234-0679 or 312-332-2009; www.randmcnally.com). Publishes road atlases (each US$10).

> **Adventurous Traveler Bookstore,** 245 S. Champlain St., **Burlington, VT** 05401 (☎800-282-3963 or 802-860-6776; www.adventuroustraveler.com).

> **Bon Voyage!,** 2069 W. Bullard Ave., Fresno, CA 93711, USA (☎800-995-9716, from abroad 559-447-8441; www.bon-voyage-travel.com). They specialize in Europe but have titles pertaining to New Zealand. Free catalog.

> **Travel Books & Language Center, Inc.,** 4437 Wisconsin Ave. NW, Washington, D.C. 20016 (☎800-220-2665 or 202-237-1322; www.travelbks.com). Over 60,000 titles from around the world.

WORLD WIDE WEB

Almost every aspect of budget travel (with the most notable exception, of course, being experience) is accessible via the web. Within ten minutes at the keyboard, you can make a reservation at a hostel, get advice on travel hotspots from other travelers who have just returned from New Zealand, find out exactly how much a train from Auckland to Wellington costs, or make a reservation at a Fijian hostel.

Listed here are some budget travel sites to start off your surfing; other relevant web sites are listed throughout the book. Because website turnover is high, use search engines (such as www.google.com or the Australia/New Zealand specific au.yahoo.com) to strike out on your own. Remember, though, that most travel web sites exist simply to get your money.

THE ART OF BUDGET TRAVEL

How to See the World: www.artoftravel.com. A compendium of great travel tips, from cheap flights to self defense to interacting with local culture.

Rec. Travel Library: www.travel-library.com. A fantastic set of links for general information and personal travelogues.

Lycos: cityguide.lycos.com. General introductions to cities and regions throughout New Zealand, accompanied by links to applicable histories, news, and local tourism sites.

Travelog: www.travelog.net/default.htm. Thorough advice and links on budget travel.

INFORMATION ON NEW ZEALAND & FIJI

Fiji Government Online: www.fiji.gov.fj. The official government website has extensive (and usually biased) recent news briefs.

Fiji Visitors Bureau (FVB): www.bulafiji.com. Very slick and overly positive pages provide a great starting point for learning about Fiji.

Fijivillage.com: www.fijivillage.com. *Fiji Times* headlines, sports, and links to just about every Fiji site that exists.

Pipers New Zealand Web Pages: www.piperpat.co.nz/nz. Links to (almost) all the New Zealand web sites you will ever want.

New Zealand on the Web: www.nz.com. The award-winning site has resources for and about New Zealand; includes a guidebook, virtual tours, and online marketplace.

NZPages: www.nzpages.co.nz. A New Zealand website directory with links to government, tourism, and news sites.

Rob Kay's Fiji Guide: www.fijiguide.com. A personal, but relatively reputable, free guide to Fijian travel and culture. High-quality photo gallery collection.

TravelPage: www.travelpage.com. Links to official tourist office sites in New Zealand.

US Embassy to Fiji: www.amembassy-fiji.gov. Online registration for US citizens traveling in Fiji, as well as links to latest consular travel advisories.

World Travel Guide: www.travel-guides.com/navigate/world.asp. Helpful practical info.

AND OUR PERSONAL FAVORITE...

◼ *Let's Go:* www.letsgo.com. Our constantly expanding website features photos and streaming video, online ordering of all our titles, info about our books, a travel forum buzzing with stories and tips, and links that will help you find everything you ever wanted to know about New Zealand and Fiji.

NEW ZEALAND (AOTEAROA)

HISTORY AND CURRENT EVENTS

LEGENDARY PRE-HISTORY

According to Maori legend, at the beginning of time, Papa (the earth, clothed with animals, oceans, plants, and trees) and Rangi (the sky), clung together in darkness. However, since the loving couple nestled so close together, life on earth was a dark and cramped affair. To bring light into the world, their children (who were gods) schemed to separate the sky and the earth. The god Tane was finally able to drive a wedge between Papa and Rangi, and the world was flooded with light. Rangi and Papa cried due to their separation, and their tears are the rain, dew, and ever-present mist that blankets *Aotearoa* (New Zealand), the "land of the long white cloud."

Maori legend tells that New Zealand was created through the exploits of the irreverent and mischievous Maui, one of the most beloved demi-gods of Polynesian myth. One day he stowed away on a fishing trip and cast a hook (made from his grandmother's jawbone) with his own blood as bait. Almost instantly he hooked a fish which, when brought to the surface, extended in all directions. Magically making the fish lie still, Maui created *Te ika a Maui* (Maui's fish)—the North Island of New Zealand. Similarly, the South Island is known in legend as *Te waka a Maui* (Maui's canoe) and tiny Stewart Island is *Te punga o te waka a Maui* (Maui's anchor stone). At the tip of Ninety Mile Beach a large rock with a hole in it lies offshore. Maori believe this to be the eye of Maui's hook.

MAORI SETTLEMENT

The Maori believed that the forebears of New Zealand's first settlers had been living happily for many years in **Hawaiki,** the ancestral homeland, when **Kupe** the explorer set out on a scouting expedition to the east. In the course of his wanderings he discovered a lush, mist-covered stretch of land which he named Aotearoa. Years later, when intertribal dispute and strife forced the Maori ancestors to leave Hawaiki, they remembered Kupe's lavish praise of the paradise to the east. In seven mammoth canoes, the ancestors fled to Aotearoa.

Archaeological evidence tells a slightly different story. Currently, research indicates that the first settlers, the ancestors of the modern Maori, came to New Zealand from the eastern Polynesian Islands between 950-1300AD. Excavations demonstrate that these settlers made their living by hunting the flightless moa bird, fishing, and using stone and bone tools and by the 14th century were widely practicing horticulture. A staple of their diet, the *kumara* (sweet potato) is still grown today. While tribal life was highly communal, Maori were fiercely territorial

IMPORTANT EVENTS

C. 80,000,000 BC
New Zealand breaks off from Gondwanaland, isolating its flora and fauna

C. 26,000,000 BC
Southern Alps rise above the ocean

AD 186
A volcanic eruption, 100 times greater than the 1980 eruption of Mt. Saint Helens, creates Lake Taupo

C. AD 950-1300
Polynesian settlement

1642
Dutchman Abel Tasman makes the first European discovery of New Zealand

1733
The first sheep, thankfully a ram and a ewe, brought ashore by Captain Cook

and intertribal warfare was both brutal and common. Tribes kept close watch over their hunting, fishing, and burial lands, as attested by the widespread legacy of weapon artifacts and village *pa* (fortified hillsides) they left behind. This protective attitude toward their land was still in full force hundreds of years later, when they encountered the first Europeans.

1769 British explorer Captain James Cook circumnavigates New Zealand, bringing back geographical and botanical information

1806 The first European woman sets foot on New Zealand soil; a New Zealand ship enters Sydney with more than 60,000 seal skins in cargo, foreshadowing the seal trade that would devastate the native seal population

1814 Missionary Samuel Marsden preaches the first Christian sermon in New Zealand

1815 First European child born on New Zealand soil

1820-35 Musket Wars: inter-tribal conflict among Maori

1835 Naturalist Charles Darwin, on his famed voyage of the *Beagle*, spends Christmas in the Bay of Islands

1839 First brewery established at Thames

1840 Maori chiefs sign the Treaty of Waitangi; British claim sovereignty over the whole of New Zealand

THE EUROPEAN ARRIVAL

The first European to lay eyes on New Zealand was Dutch explorer **Abel Tasman.** In 1642, Tasman tried to land in what is now the South Island's Golden Bay, but never set foot on the islands, as he was met at sea by a hostile Maori tribe that killed several of his men. Several years later, a cartographer used Tasman's account to put the country on a world map for the first time, naming it *Nova Zeelandia* after a Dutch province.

The first group of Europeans to actually tread upon the uncharted land did not arrive until 1769, on the *Endeavour*, a British ship captained by the legendary explorer **James Cook.** During the many months of his travels, Cook circumnavigated the islands, gaining invaluable navigational and ecological information. In spite of a few early hostile encounters, Cook was able to establish friendly relations with many of the *tangata maori* ("the ordinary people," as they called themselves in order to distinguish themselves from the European explorers). Cook also sprinkled Anglicized place names left and right.

Given the glowing reports of virtually untouched natural splendor brought back by Cook and others, European settlement in New Zealand grew. **Sealers** and **whalers** were among the first to respond to the promise of pristine wilderness, arriving in droves in the early 1800s to make short work of New Zealand's then-abundant marine natural resources. The seal colonies were practically wiped clean by the 1820s, followed shortly by the whaling waters. **Missionaries** also made an early appearance, with Samuel Marsden preaching the first Anglican sermon on New Zealand soil on Christmas Day, 1814. Despite earnest efforts, Christianity did not spread quickly as Maori did not believe that it was a suitable religion for warriors. Heralding the start of heavier European settlement, independent **traders** were the next to arrive, seeking flax and novelty items (such as Maori-made trinkets, and even preserved heads) in exchange for firearms, metal tools, and other European goods.

This increase in interaction lead to cultural clashes; by 1840 both groups were inhabitants of an increasingly chaotic and unfamiliar world. The arrival of Christianity had undermined the tribal authority and *mana* (see p. 63) of the Maori chiefs and religious authorities, and fundamentally changed the organization of families and tribes. Traders brought the fatal gift of European disease, which killed an estimated 25% of the Maori population, while Western weapons escalated Maori intertribal violence and drastically increased fatalities. The culmination of this devastating warfare came in the form of the **Musket Wars** of 1820-35. Similarly, in a rush to settle the land as quickly and cheaply as possible, speculators cheated the Maori out of many acres of traditional tribal land. With relatively few European settlers (only about two thousand in 1838), settlers led a rough, brutish, and trying existence. Early settlers feared for the peace, safety, and stability of their settlements, and appealed to their governments for protection.

THE TREATY OF WAITANGI

By the late 1830s, the tensions between Maori and Europeans over land, government, and law had reached a breaking point. Both peoples were living in a lawless state, with Maori often duped and cheated by unscrupulous land speculators and Europeans fearful of the lack of established infrastructure. The New Zealand Company (a privately owned British settlement company), backed by Britain, brought boatloads of settlers to a sparsely populated and weakly ruled wilderness, further exacerbating the problem. It seemed, in late 1839, that the best and perhaps only solution to these problems was the creation of a system of British rule. To that end, in January 1840, the British Colonial Office sent **Captain William Hobson** to effect the transfer of sovereignty over the land and government from Maori chiefs to the British. With the help of British Resident **James Busby** among others, Hobson wrote the **Treaty of Waitangi**, and presented it to a gathering of more than two hundred Maori chiefs and leaders on February 5, 1840. The Treaty called for a complete cession of sovereignty by each Maori chief to the Queen of England, promised the Maori full rights of use and possession of their lands, and promised the Maori full rights of British citizens and the full extent of the Queen's protection. More than forty Maori leaders signed the treaty parchment, after which, Captain William Hobson shook each Maori's hand, proclaiming: *"He iwi tahi tatou"* ("Now we are one people").

Unfortunately, translation of this one phrase was more straightforward than missionary Henry William's translation of the Treaty itself. In fact, whether intentionally or not, crucial nuances of meaning were lost when the Treaty was translated from English to Maori. For example, in Article One, the English version boldly asked for all "rights and powers of sovereignty over the land," while the Maori translation understated the cession as control over *"kawanatanga"* (government or administration), presumably leaving ultimate sovereignty (perhaps better understood as *"mana"*) to Maori chiefs. Additionally, in Article Two, the Maori were ensured "exclusive and undisturbed possession of their lands" in the English version, while in the Maori version they were promised *"tino rangatiratanga"*: unrestrained exercise of chiefly authority over lands, villages, and natural treasures.

By the start of September 1840, when the last signature was added to the Treaty, more than 500 signatures had been gathered, although the Treaty still lacked the support of a number of powerful and influential chiefs. Despite this lack of unanimous acceptance of British authority, in May of 1840, Hobson proclaimed full sovereignty over New Zealand based on the acceptance of the Treaty of Waitangi on the North Island and a declared British right of discovery on the South.

CONFLICTS AND WARS

As European settlement increased after 1840, the relationship between Maori and settlers deteriorated. Although attempts were made to build a strong bi-racial community (including moving the capital city to Auckland, located between the areas of strong Maori and European presence), fundamental cultural differences divided the two New Zealand populations. While European settlers were inclined to cultivate all of the land that they occupied, Maori tradition dictated that only a small plot be culti-

NEW ZEALAND

1856
Britain declares New Zealand a self-governing colony

1858
Potatau Te Wherowhero proclaimed first Maori king

1860s
New Zealand Wars: conflict between British and Maori

1861
Gold discovered in Queenstown, starting a South Island gold rush

1862
First telegraph line built, between Christchurch and Lyttelton

1865
National capital moves from Auckland to Wellington as a concession to South Islanders

1867
Four Maori seats established in Parliament

1870
First rugby match played in New Zealand

1882
The refrigerated ship *Dunedin* sets sail for Britain with the first cargo of frozen meat, ushering in a new economic age

1886
Mt. Tarawera explodes over Rotorua, showering 500 cubic meters of ash over 15,000 square kilometers

1887
Kiwi featured on the uniforms of the Hastings Rifle Volunteers in one of the first uses of the bird as a symbol of New Zealand

1893
New Zealand becomes the first nation in the world to grant suffrage to women

1898
The first car imported, a Benz brought over from Paris, requiring an Act of Parliament before it could be driven

1903
Richard "Mad" Pearse makes several flights in a powered plane, beating the Wright Brothers as the first man in flight by months (see p. 313)

1907
New Zealand becomes a British dominion

1908
New Zealand native Sir Ernest Rutherford, the man who would split the atom, wins the Nobel Prize for Chemistry

1915
New Zealand troops land at Gallipoli to fight in the First World War

vated, while the rest of their vast territory be left as bush in which they could hunt and gather food. This cultural difference led Europeans to believe that Maori controlled more land than they needed, since they cultivated so little of their holdings. As a result, European settlers began to show increasing disregard for Maori property, and the support Governor Hobson had won among the Maori also disappeared.

Similarly, the British government that had been intended to bring greater peace and stability to the land lacked funding to perform even the most basic duties and the Maori, by virtue of their stronger position in trade and commerce, bore the brunt of the tax and tariff costs enacted to try to salvage it. Before long, the Maori began to suspect that they had given up more than they had intended by ceding some of their autonomy to the British and responded by rebelling against British authority. In 1844, **Hone Heke,** one of the first chiefs to sign the Treaty, cut down the flagpole at Kororareka near Russell (see p. 114), which he saw as a symbol of British oppression of the Maori. The government tried to re-erect the pole several times, finally giving up the fourth time Heke and his allies cut it down. The Russell incident marked the beginning of warfare between Heke's army and British-led forces, which lasted until 1846.

In 1852, the **Constitution Act** established a settler government with six provinces and a national parliament with a lower and an upper house. The Constitution Act also granted suffrage to men over 25 as long as they met a low property qualification. However, although the amount of property required was relatively low, Maori were almost entirely excluded because Maori land was often held under a communal, not individual, title. Once again, cultural differences between British and Maori undermined genuine attempts at cooperation. Under this system, New Zealand was not an equal bi-racial community. Instead, the Maori had effectively been disenfranchised.

The census of 1858 revealed that Maori had become a minority in their own land, with European settlers finally outnumbering non-Europeans on New Zealand soil. As British governmental influence grew, the Maori became increasingly disturbed to see the body that denied them representation taking shape and gaining power. Unscrupulous settlers often convinced Maori landowners to sell their lands at ridiculously cheap prices, promising governmental aid in the form of hospitals, schools, and land reserves in return. Savvy tribal leaders knew that as the Maori lost their land, they would lose whatever influence they may have had and encouraged a complete halt on land sales. They urged tribes to unite under one common leader and began the Maori **King Movement.** Supporters of this policy sought to centralize Maori resources, naming Te Wherowhero of Waikato their king in 1858 (see p. 136). The Maori king was not intended to be a military leader, but rather a cultural leader and land policy-maker. In spite of this peaceful intent, the British government refused to recognize the Maori king whom they viewed as a barrier to further settlement. When violent conflict erupted once again in the Taranaki region in 1860, **Governor George Grey** blamed the King Movement instead of addressing the recurrent problem of land ownership, deciding to strike at Waikato, the movement's primary stronghold. The **New Zealand Wars** (alternatively known as **The Maori Wars**) exploded across the North Island as a result, with British forces ultimately gaining victory around 1870. This narrow victory, however, came at great expense to Britain as the infighting between colonists and imperial troops alienated the ruling power from its people.

REFORMS

With the end of the New Zealand Wars, a modicum of order was restored as land disputes were settled through the courts. In 1865, the first **Native Lands Act** established a court to investigate Maori land ownership and distribute official land titles. Land titles in these disputes usually went to chiefs, making it even harder for individual Maori to hold onto land. In 1873, the second Native Lands Act split up the land title for a land block among its shared owners. Each individual's share had to then be passed on to all natural heirs, whittling down the size of the shares more and more with each generation and making it even harder for a tribe to hold onto communal blocks of land. In 1882, disillusioned with the colonial government, the Ngapuhi tribe sent the first delegation to England to personally petition Queen Victoria. Although they were never given audience, Maori continued to send representatives until the 1920s. By the end of the 19th century, an astounding 92% of New Zealand's land was out of Maori control. Even while Maori were struggling for their rights, the last decades of the 19th century were a period of dramatic **social reforms** for the non-Maori. Factory conditions improved, there were increasing conservation efforts, and, in 1893, New Zealand women were the first women in the world to gain the right to vote.

PROSPERITY AND WARS

In the 20th century, New Zealand, still forging its national identity, had to navigate increasingly complicated global relationships, conflicts, and markets. In 1907, New Zealand became a dominion of the British Empire, allowing it to determine its own foreign policy. By virtue of their relationship with Britain, in 1915, the **Australia and New Zealand Army Corps (ANZAC)** were enlisted to join troops in World War I. Chosen to join the infamous Dardanelles campaign, ANZAC fought at Gallipoli on April 25, attacking Turkish forces entrenched in the Dardanelles strait. The battle was a huge military failure, leading to massive casualties for Australia and New Zealand, but winning great respect for the soldiers' bravery. New Zealand suffered similar losses on the Western Front. Their reputation for courage was fostered by the grave and disproportionate casualties inflicted on New Zealand, as one in three men between the ages of 20 and 40 were wounded or killed in the war, the greatest per capita casualties of any combatant nation.

Like most of the western world, New Zealand suffered greatly during the Great Depression of the 1920s. However, the following decades were characterized by increasing prosperity. In 1935, the victory of the liberal Labour Party spurred the creation of the world's first universal social welfare system, including free health care and low-rent public housing. By the 1940s, New Zealand's main industries were booming and the country maintained one of the highest standards of living in the world. This prosperity came just in time to be disrupted by the **Second World War;** this time, with widespread fighting in the South Pacific, the disruption was much closer to home. Once again, when called to arms, New Zealand forces proved themselves to be tenacious and admirable soldiers. The **28th (Maori) Battalion,** in particular, won acclaim in battles fought from Crete to Africa and proved, not only to be fierce in battle, but creative and unorthodox in their

NEW ZEALAND

1918
Legislation passes forcing pubs to close at 6pm—these laws would stay on the books until 1967

1930s
New Zealand pioneers universal social welfare programs

1933
Elizabeth McCombs becomes the first woman elected to the House of Representatives

1936
Kiwi pilot Jean Batten makes the first-ever direct flight from England to New Zealand; government mandates the manufacturing work week be no longer than 40 hours

1937
First commercial planting of Chinese gooseberries (better known as kiwifruit)

1947
New Zealand becomes fully independent by adopting the Statute of Westminster

1950
Auckland hosts the British Empire Games

1953
Sir Edmund Hillary,
New Zealand
climbing god, and
Sherpa Norgay Ten-
zing become the
first men to summit
Mount Everest

1960
First television
broadcasts begin
in New Zealand;
the first computer
is installed, in the
Treasury in
Wellington

1970
Nga Tamatoa
forms, becoming
one of the largest
groups lobbying for
Maori cultural
identity and land
claims; New
Zealand bans the
pesticide DDT,
used in farming
since 1948

1975
Waitangi Tribunal
established to
investigate Maori
claims against the
government

1978
Kiwi Naomi Jones
becomes the first
woman to sail
single-handedly
around the world

1981
South African
rugby team makes
a controversial
tour of New
Zealand, in spite
of vigorous Maori
and Pakeha
opposition to the
South African
system of
apartheid

1982
First licensed FM
radio station in
New Zealand goes
on the air, in
Whakatane

tactics. As a result, an astonishing number were decorated for their service. In addition to the thousands of women who enlisted for active military duty, in 1942, all remaining New Zealand women between the ages of 18 and 30 were recruited to perform many types of essential domestic service, from mail delivery to industrial production.

Negotiations between Maori and non-Maori continued into the early 20th century. In 1909, the third **Native Lands Act** set aside funds specifically for Maori land development in order to aid Maori farmers. In an interesting paradox typical of the era, the same amount was also set aside to buy up Maori land. In 1922, in a landmark case, the government agreed to compensate the Te Arawa tribe for lost fishing and burial rights in the Rotorua lakes. Four years later, another agreement was made with the Ngati Tuwharetoa tribe concerning Lake Taupo. In 1935, the first **Labour Party** came into government, touting official recognition of the Treaty of Waitangi as part of their platform. They established connections with certain Maori political movements, but never incorporated the Treaty into official law.

POST-WWII

New Zealand was declared fully independent in 1947, but remained tied to a number of nations across the world, with economic, governmental, and military links proliferating following the end of WWII. The war had demonstrated New Zealand's dependence for military protection as US intervention protected New Zealand from possible Japanese hostilities. New Zealand aimed to secure its future by signing the **ANZUS Pact** (securing the mutual defense of Australia, New Zealand, and the US) and by independently harnessing its own energy resources. Maintaining strong ties to the greater community of nations, in 1945 New Zealand became one of the member states of the United Nations. Similarly, strong trade relationships were built with the United Kingdom, the US, and Australia.

Domestically, the government replicated its international spirit of cooperation, attempting to ease tensions with the Maori. By 1972, 65% of the Maori population had moved into urban areas, especially Auckland. Adherence to traditional beliefs among Maori declined dramatically, though the traditional tensions with the Pakeha (New Zealand residents of European descent) remained. In 1960, the **Waitangi Day Act** made February 6th a national "day of thanksgiving," in celebration of the bi-racial nature of the coalition created by the 1840 Treaty. Thirteen years later, it was declared an official public holiday. (Today, Waitangi Day is simultaneously a cause for celebration and a day of protest for those speaking out on perceived continued infringement of Maori rights.) The 1975 **Treaty of Waitangi Act** set up the Waitangi Tribunal to hear Maori claims against the Crown. Under the Act, the Tribunal had to consider both the Maori and English texts of the Treaty in its decisions—a revolutionary step for the government. However, this gesture did not ease all tensions. In the same year, the **Land March,** a protest against unfair land claim treatment, started at Te Hapua in Northland and ended at the Parliament building in Wellington.

New Zealand faced some difficult economic times in the late '70s and '80s, culminating in the 1987 stock market crash. The government sought to solve the nation's slow economic growth, caused partially by Britain's entrance into the European Economic Community, by deregulating the economy and opening up to free trade. In 1983, New Zealand and Australia established the **Closer Economic Relations Trade Agreement,** which allowed free and unrestricted trade between the two nations. During the mid-'80s, Labour's David Lange and his Finance Minister Roger Douglas cut spending on established national programs, increased privatization, and emphasized free enterprise in a movement known as "Rogernomics." New Zealand continued to nurse its economy back to health in the 1990s by instituting many free-market reforms; sheep husbandry is believed by some to have driven the recovery. New Zealand is the main global producer of lamb, responsible for a staggering 54% of world export trade.

With its foreign policy, New Zealand continued to retain its independent streak. In 1987, Labour Party Prime Minister David Lange committed New Zealand staunchly to the **anti-nuclear move- ment** by barring all nuclear-capable vessels from New Zealand harbors and stepping up pressure on the French government to stop nuclear testing at Mororua Atoll. His action was the culmination of a movement that was heightened by the 1985 bombing by French agents of the Greenpeace ship, *Rainbow Warrior* while it was in Auckland harbor (see p. 110). In 1995 New Zealand tried, unsuccessfully, to revive a case against French nuclear testing at the International Court of Justice.

NEW ZEALAND TODAY

GOVERNMENT

New Zealand is a parliamentary government with a popularly elected single chamber legislature, although it lacks a written constitution. In 1993, the majority of New Zealanders voted to establish a mixed-member proportional representation **(MMP)** system of government, similar to the German system. Under the system, a 120-seat Parliament was established, with a predetermined number of general electorate seats, party list seats (in which the elected party selects members), and Maori seats. New Zealand citizens are accorded two votes, one for the preferred ruling party and the second for a certain candidate to represent their electorate. Citizens of Maori descent may choose whether to register either on the general or Maori roll. Since the MMP is a representational system, it is difficult for one party to win a majority of the seats in the parliament. Instead, the ruling party controls only a plurality of the MPs and must carefully build coalitions in order to govern.

Because of the need for such coalitions, New Zealand politics in recent years has been defined by behind-the-scenes maneuvering, fragile power-sharing arrangements, and allegations of corruption. In November 1997, **Jenny Shipley** of the **National Party,** engineered a "coup" to seize party leadership. She was sworn in as New Zealand's first woman prime minister in December of that year. A primary focus of Shipley's government was to increase free-market competition and reduce government size. Shipley's term was thrown into disarray in August 1998. She inherited a fragile coalition between her own conservative National Party and the more liberal New Zealand First. During Shipley's tenure, she was often embroiled in controversy, a trait that may have led to her recent electoral loss.

In November 1999, parliamentary elections restored the center-left Labor Party, led by **Helen Clark,** to power after nine years in the opposition. Labor Party success was credited in part to its increased support from Maori citizens, following the erratic

NEW ZEALAND

1984
Labour Party wins election, leading to a new free-trade economy and privatization of industries

1985
Greenpeace vessel *Rainbow Warrior* is sunk in Auckland Harbour (see p. 110)

1987
New Zealand declared a nuclear-free zone; New Zealand wins the inaugural rugby World Cup; inventor of bungy, A.J. Hackett, bungy jumps off the Eiffel Tower; and the Maori Language Act establishes Maori as an official language, equal in standing to English for conducting New Zealand affairs

1990
New Zealand hosts both the Commonwealth Games and a visit from Queen Elizabeth II; mountaineers Gary Ball and Rob Hall summit the highest mountain on each of the 7 continents in just 7 months, shattering the previous record by 2 years

1992
Shortland Street, New Zealand's emergency room soap opera, debuts

changes in the previously Maori-dominated **New Zealand First** party. As Prime Minister, Clark has allied with the left-wing Alliance Party (10 seats) in coalition, but relies on support from the newly influential Green Party (7 seats). Early Labor policy has included a slight tax increase, relief for students with heavy loans, and a modest decrease in rents in government-owned low-income housing.

MAORI ISSUES

The recognition of **Maori land rights** continues to be an issue of heated governmental debate. Certain tribes in the Wellington area, for example, have made claims on land beneath the Parliament building and the National Museum, touching off a storm of controversy. While many non-Maori New Zealanders feel that they are not responsible for the past and that the country owes no debt to the Maori, the government has generally disagreed. The **Office of Treaty Settlement** is the government organization responsible for mediating between Maori claims and the New Zealand Crown. In one recent large settlement in November 1997, the New Zealand Crown admitted in the **Ngai Tahu Deed of Settlement** that it had acted unfairly and in violation of the 1840 Treaty of Waitangi. Many grievances have been filed and are still waiting to be addressed.

IN THE NEWS

ENVIRONMENT AND HEALTH. The DOC has recently published the Statement of Intent 2001-2004, which proclaims the conservation goals for the next ten years. It lists the priorities for the country and the strategies and financial plans for achieving those goals.

The DOC may add an item to their agenda with the recent discovery of oil at the Kauri field in Taranaki. Officials believe that the area may have enough oil to fill 200 million barrels. With a new source of energy, New Zealand may face fewer energy shortages due to fluctuations from hydropower resources.

Twenty cases of dengue fever have been reported in New Zealand in 2001. A viral infection that develops due to a bite from an infected mosquito, the fever is usually only found in the Pacific Islands. Twenty Kiwis returning from the Samoan Islands have reportedly been diagnosed with the fever.

WINE. A group of New Zealand scientists recently celebrated the discovery of Botry-Zen (a natural fungus), which controls the detrimental fungus botrytis, which drastically affects grape production for vineyards every year. The botrytis fungus normally costs the industry millions of dollars annually due to losses in grape productivity; with the new antidote bottled wine production could triple.

SPORTS. The **America's Cup 2003** may be some of the best racing yet as New Zealand gears up to defend the cup again. With technologies rapidly improving (New Zealand's ear piece communication systems was recently approved) and more teams being sponsored, the ferocity of the competition for the 2003 cup grows. American crew members have been studying the climactic records of the Hauraki Gulf for the past seven years, and with the recent announcement of the addition of Rob Waddell (2001 Olympic gold medalist in the single scull) to Team New Zealand, the excitement continues to boil in New Zealand. Sport fans are also anxiously anticipating the **New Zealand Open** on the Kapiti Coast in 2002. Tiger Woods being one of the athletes, tickets are already selling for as much as $500.

1995
New Zealand's *Black Magic* yachting squad wins the America's Cup, becoming only the second non-US team in the 144-year history of the competition to accomplish that feat

1997
Jenny Shipley becomes Prime Minister and the first female leader in New Zealand history

1998
The Museum of New Zealand Te Papa Tongarewa opens (see p. 227); a 9½ week power outage in Central Auckland; first edition of *Let's Go: New Zealand* goes to print

1999
New Zealand lowers the drinking age to 18

2000
Team New Zealand defends the America's Cup; US President Bill Clinton attends the APEC conference in Auckland, the first sitting US President to visit New Zealand

2001
DOC publishes goals and priorities for the environment; large oil fields discovered in Taranaki; World Champion Sculler, Rob Waddell joins Team New Zealand for the much anticipated America's Cup 2003

Christchurch resident Gary Endacott, who suffers from cerebral palsy, recently scaled Africa's highest peak, Mt. Kilimanjaro. Due to the extreme conditions and his physical limitations, Endacott crawled the final ten hours on his hands and knees before becoming the first climber with cerebral palsy to reach the summit. And though the Rugby Tri-Nations competition was not completed at the time of publishing, the All Blacks are looking good, very good. With a decisive victory over the South African Springboks in the series opener and a Springbok victory over the Australian Wallabies just one week later, the All Blacks will definitely put on a show when facing the Wallabies to take back the title. Unfortunately, New Zealand rugby officials have decided that the final game of the Tri-Nations series and the World Cup will indeed be the final games of that year, as they refuse to enter the All Blacks into a proposed Northern vs. Southern Hemisphere match for 2002.

THE CULTURE

THE PEOPLE

The total population of New Zealand is about 3.8 million, with three-quarters of the population living in the North Island (half in Auckland). Most of the population is **caucasian. Maori,** the largest minority ethnic group, make up 15% of the population; other **Pacific Islanders** are the next largest group at 6%. In fact, a greater concentration of non-Maori Polynesians live in the greater Auckland area than anywhere else in the world. **Asians** are also a fast-growing minority group, comprising 3% of the total population in 1996, a 74% increase from 1991.

Christianity is the predominant religion; Anglican, Presbyterian, and Catholic denominations are the most commonly practiced. Maori denominations of Christianity, such as the Ratana and Ringatu churches, were first developed during the missionary era of the late-19th and early-20th centuries in an effort to synthesize traditional Maori beliefs with the precepts of Christianity.

MAORI ARTS AND CULTURE

New Zealand society is largely bicultural, comprised primarily of **Pakeha,** the Maori word for people of European descent, and those of Maori descent. The word *"maori"* has an interesting origin in itself, as it was originally used not to denote a common background, but rather to distinguish the "ordinary people" from the extraordinary and strange European explorers. Similarly, **Maoritanga,** loosely translated as "the ways of the Maori," serves as an umbrella word for the communal, ceremonial, and cultural traditions and organization of Maori life. New Zealand has recently experienced a renaissance of *Maoritanga* as more Maori look to their rich heritage for security and identity. A growing movement today seeks to recover those *wahi ngaro* (lost aspects) of Maori tradition and culture like art forms and traditions. (See also the **Maori-English Dictionary** p. 438)

BASIC CONCEPTS

The most fundamental idea to Maori custom is the notion of **tapu** and its lesser known counterpart **noa.** *Tapu* indicates the presence of supernatural power (whether good or evil) and commands respect and attention. *Noa* underscores the absence of such power and thus deserves no special caution. But the two are complementary, similar to the Asian notions of yin and yang. For example, a man has the *tapu* responsibility in a tribe to oversee ceremonial duties and give speeches at a *marae* (see **Marae** below), but he cannot look respectable without the help of the female's *noa* duties of preparing food and singing songs.

Personal relationships within and between tribes also require an understanding of **mana.** Translated literally, the word means "prestige" or "respectability" but the true meaning is a supernatural essence that possesses and grants seniority to a worthy individual, especially an individual who respects the balance of *tapu* and *noa* in daily life. Traditionally, the amount of *mana* in an individual depends on his ancestry, experience, and seniority in a tribe. Nowadays, *mana* is often influenced more by one's success and achievements instead.

Above all, Maori traditionally look for balance and fairness personally and in a tribal community. When someone is made to feel inferior, he becomes **whakama**, either ashamed due to undue criticism, or actually guilty of a misdeed. In any case, Maori recognize the occurrence of *whakama* and either praise or punish the sufferer as appropriate to remedy the situation. Self-respect is just as crucial as the respect of others. One who is *whakaiti* (self-belittling) or, *whakahihi* (arrogant) lacks the composure and humility—the *mana*—to be a leader in a tribe.

MAORI TRIBAL STRUCTURE

In New Zealand, forty-two tribes are currently accorded the title of **iwi** since association with a tribe is not an official designation. Most Maori simply follow the membership of their parents in a tribe. Within the *iwi* exist smaller regional communities called **hapu**. These communities were originally descent groups that owned land within the tribe. In modern times, each *hapu* seldom owns more land than a *marae* reserve (see **Marae** below). For this reason, the *hapu* generally has more meaning to rural populations who live and work with other members of the same community; city-dwellers generally tend to identify less with their *hapu*. The smallest unit in tribal organization is the large-family whose members are directly related by blood, adoption, or marriage. Large-family and *hapu* are often used interchangeably. The prominence of cooperation and community within the tribe is a result of the extreme importance of and focus on common ancestry.

THE MARAE

The *marae* is the sacred grounds around a Maori *whare tupuna* (ancestral meetinghouse) and the site of the **powhiri** (or formal welcome) welcoming visitors into the community. The ceremony consists of four basic components. Upon arriving at the *marae*, a warrior from the village will greet your group with a *haka* (see **Dance** below), an elaborate set of prowling steps, body movements, and a tongue-protruding facial gesture (it's exceedingly uncouth to return such a gesture). The **wero** (challenge) ends when a **teka** (peace offering) is offered and accepted. After this step, a female elder will issue the **karanga**, a chant of welcome and mourning for the visitors' great ancestors. As your group crosses the *marae*, pause and bow in respect for the ancestors of the tribe before congregating in front of the *whare*. In his **whaikorero** (speech of welcoming), the chief of the tribe will welcome your group in Maori, and the designated chief of your group will deliver a brief speech in return (preferably in Maori as well, but protocol varies). To seal the bond of friendship, both chiefs press (but do not rub) noses together in the traditional greeting known as the **hongi**. After the *hongi*, the separate groups finally come together until called to dine in the *whare kai*. Shoes are not worn inside the *whare*, and pictures may not be permitted, depending on the tribe. After a **karakia** (prayer) is given, the dinner, **hangi**, is prepared by roasting sweet potatoes, meat, and other goodies in a pit of heated stones until they reach peak smoky delicacy.

SONG

Traditional Maori song and oratory are particularly important to ceremonial life. **Tau marae** orations are formal, stylized tributes to the dead performed at traditional funeral ceremonies for important chiefs. Another important type of oratory is **karakia** (chants), which were once strictly the property of **tohunga** (priests or specially learned men). *Karakia* imparted **mauri** (essence of its natural state) to objects, as in the Maori myth in which Tiki chants a *karakia* in order to bring his clay figurine to life. **Waiata** is the most common type of ceremonial song that is customarily performed at the conclusion of speeches of farewell at **tangi** (funerals) and those of welcoming at *powhiri*. In modern times, the two kinds of *waiata* that have survived—the *waiata tangi*, songs of mourning (often composed by women) and the *waiata aroha*, love songs (solely composed by women)—often dwell upon unrequited love, obstacles in love, and delinquent lovers. In all of these oral arts, tribes have nurtured their own traditions, creating specialized mythology and tribal historical accounts.

DANCE

Maori dance includes more than just fancy footwork; one's entire body, voice, and spirit are incorporated into what may be the most dramatic Maori art form. The vigorous arm-waving, chanting, foot-stomping **haka** is an all-male dance, once performed by armed warriors before battle as an invocation to the god of war. To see a modern *haka*, head to a *marae* (see below) or just check out the **All Blacks** (see p. 68) before every rugby match. **Taparahi,** on the other hand, are weaponless dances performed by both genders for a variety of reasons: to greet important guests, to honor the dead, or for sheer entertainment. In the **poi,** a dance now performed by women, balls on strings are twirled in elegant synchronicity. (It was originally designed to increase suppleness and flexibility in the wrists of warriors.)

CARVING

Carving is one early Maori art form still practiced today. The most common materials are bone, wood, and greenstone (*pounamu;* see also **A Jaded Perspective** p. 299). According to traditional Maori beliefs, it is the artist's responsibility to impart certain qualities such as fear, power, and authority to his or her pieces, in order to transform them from mere material objects to **taonga** (highly treasured, even sacred objects). Each object also accumulates its own body of **korero** (stories) with each successive owner. A design particular to a tribe is passed down from generation to generation, distinguishing itself by its repetition of certain stylistic features and motifs, such as **tiki** (human forms), **manaia** (bird men), and **taniwha** (sea spirits). Carvers create items large and small, decorating both towering meeting houses and tiny *tiki* pendants.

MOKO (FACIAL TATTOOING)

Moko has been one of the most famous Maori art forms since the days when 19th-century Europe was transfixed by portraits and photographs of New Zealand "savages" with full facial tattoos. While most tribes reserved the practice for males, *moko* sometimes served as a rite of passage for both males and females, as well as a marker of achievements and status. Men's *moko* began with a simple design for youths; more spiral flourishes were added as the wearer won prestige in battle. Thus, only older, highly distinguished warriors could sport full facial tattoos. Women's *moko* were more simple, usually surrounding only the lips and the tip of the nose, although some stout-hearted women elected to have their thighs and breasts tattooed as well.

Traditionally, *moko* was only executed by *tohunga ta moko*, experts trained extensively in using the sharp wooden adze and mallet or birdbone chisel to etch the design into the skin, then using a toothed chisel to fill in the ink dye (a mixture of burned kauri or totara resin and pigeon fat), all done in complete silence. The *tohunga ta moko* declared the recipient *tapu* (sacred) while the tattoo was healing, while leaves of the karaka tree were placed on the skin. During this time, sexual intimacy was prohibited and no one was permitted to view the *moko;* they believed it would fade if anyone saw it before it healed completely. Today, Maori continue to practice *moko*, though often using face paint to replicate this intricate art on occasions of ceremonial display.

VISUAL ARTS AND LITERATURE

A number of prominent and critically acclaimed artists have hailed from New Zealand in the last century. **Frances Hodgkins** (1869-1947) and **Colin McCahon** (1919-87) are two of the most famous 20th-century New Zealand painters. Hodgkins left New Zealand in 1913 for London, eventually becoming a leading figure in water-color figurative painting, then in oils. McCahon retained his base in New Zealand and is considered one of the most important influences on modern art there.

New Zealand has its share of literary stars as well. **Katherine Mansfield** (1888-1923), short story-writer, was another World War I expatriate to Britain. Her best-known short story collections are *The Garden Party* (1922) and before that,

Bliss (1920). Mansfield's childhood home in Wellington has been preserved as a museum (see p. 224). **Dame Ngaio Marsh** (1895-1982), most renowned for her mystery series featuring detective Roderick Alleyn, stayed firmly rooted in New Zealand as a member of the leading artistic group in Christchurch in the mid-1900s. Other notable New Zealand writers are poet **James K. Baxter** (1926-1972), renowned for his celebration of the New Zealand wilderness, and novelist **Janet Frame** (b. 1924), best known for *Owls Do Cry* (1957), *A State of Siege* (1966), and her autobiographical *An Angel at My Table* (1985), which was later adapted to film by Jane Campion.

Maori writers have surged onto the literary scene as well. For example, **Patricia Grace** (b. 1937), of Ngati Raukawa, Ngati Toa, and Te Ati Awa descent, is known for the bittersweet coming-of-age story *Mutuwhenua the moon sleeps* (1978), about a young Maori girl's love for a Pakeha (non-Maori). **Witi Ihimaera** (b. 1944) is best-known for *Tangi* (1973), an exploration of father-son relationships. Ihimaera's later works focus on issues of gay identity, in books like *Nights in the Gardens of Spain*. Perhaps the most well-known Maori author is **Keri Hulme** (b. 1947), a South Islander of Scottish, English, and Ngai Tahu descent, whose novel *The Bone People* won the 1985 Booker Prize. More recently, **Alan Duff** made a big splash in the fiction world with his hit *Once Were Warriors* (1992) and its sequel *What Becomes of the Broken-Hearted* (1997) about the trials of a Maori family in the modern world (see p. 66).

MUSIC

Geographic isolation hasn't disconnected New Zealand from music trends of the past. Kiwis had **punk** in the 1970s too, a phase that continued throughout the decade with the influential Christchurch label **Flying Nun.** In the 1980s, The **Split Enz** and its offshoot **Crowded House** enjoyed worldwide popularity as part of the **New Wave** movement. Alternative rock has also gained popularity, as with student band **Zed's** popular album *Silencer* and hits from **Th'Dudes'** like *Be Mine Tonight* and *That Look In Your Eyes.* Today, electronic music reigns supreme in the nightclubs, in a range of genres from house to drum 'n' bass.

Check out *The Fix*, a free glossy mag, for info on the Auckland scene. Down in Wellington, **Mu** demonstrates his skills on the vinyl, while **Manuel Bundy** crisscrosses the country with rhythmically centered beats. Perhaps of more interest to Top 40 fans, **OMC** (Otara Millionaires Club) laid claim to the hip-hop and dance music scene with their hit *How Bizarre* before breaking up a few years ago. Occasionally, big name pop stars like Robbie Williams and Ben Harper pass through New Zealand. **The Gathering** (http://www.gathering.co.nz) is a multi-day rave in the South Island, celebrating New Year's Eve and drawing an international crowd.

New Zealand's premier professional orchestra, the New Zealand Symphony Orchestra enjoys an excellent reputation which merits its traveling over 20,000 kilometers a year to perform. Internationally renowned opera star and New Zealand native **Dame Kiri Te Kanawa** also performs for audiences worldwide.

FILM

New Zealand's own film industry was not fully established until the 1970s. One notable figure from the New Zealand film scene was **Len Lye** (1901-80), kinetic sculptor and modern filmmaker of the '60s. Lye pioneered the technique of "direct filmmaking," in which images are etched or painted directly onto the film itself. Born in Christchurch, Lye left New Zealand for London in the early 1900s, joining fellow expatriate Frances Hodgkins (see p. 65) in London's artsy elite of the '20s and '30s, then moving to New York in 1944. Today his work is shown at the Govett-Brewster Art Gallery in New Plymouth (see p. 196).

The early '70s saw works mainly by independent filmmakers. A significant event in New Zealand film during this time, as well as a landmark work in Maori representation on the silver screen, was the release of **Tangata Whenua: The People of the Land** (1974), a six-part documentary series by Maori filmmaker Barry Barclay.

In 1978, the government created the New Zealand Film Commission, which encourages and financially supports the film industry. Since then, recent films made in New Zealand have become both popular and critical hits. One-sixth of the country viewed *Goodbye Pork Pie* (1981), directed by Geoff Murphy. A film every Kiwi will tell you to see is *Once Were Warriors* (adapted from Alan Duff's 1992 book of the same name), from prominent director Lee Tamahori. The film was critically acclaimed for its stark, honest appraisal of the plight of urban Maori today. Jane Campion's *The Piano* (1993), filmed in New Zealand, broke box office records and won two Cannes Film Festival awards and a Best Supporting Actress Oscar for teen star **Anna Paquin.** Kiwis love to claim the rough, tough and buff *Gladiator* **Russell Crowe** as a native; though born in Wellington, Crowe spent most of his life in nearby Australia. On the other hand, adoptive Kiwi **Sam Neill** wasn't born Down Under, but did grow up on the South Island before landing coveted roles in *The Hunt for Red October* (1990), *Jurassic Park* (1993), *Event Horizon* (1997), *Jurassic Park III* (2001), and as a cat burglar on an episode of *The Simpsons.* Proving that Kiwis exist on the other side of the camera as well, writer-director and Wellingtonian **Peter Jackson** is perhaps most famous for *Heavenly Creatures* (1992), based on the true story of two unhappy teenagers' unstable friendship and their escape into a fantasy world. However, it is the much-hyped release of his first installment of the *Lord of the Rings* trilogy (2001) that has geeks across the world drooling in anticipation; the film, of course, was filmed in New Zealand.

■**Lucy Lawless,** formerly known as **Xena,** continues to be New Zealand's pride and joy, as she moves onto bigger and (debatably) better things (the *X-Files*). You may still catch a glimpse of a rerun of *Xena, Warrior Princess* on late-night TV. And in case you are wondering, she prefers skimpy outfits "because they're better to fight in."

FOOD AND DRINK

In the tradition of the earliest inhabitants' dinners of roast moa and **kumara** (a sweet potato), New Zealanders still maintain a largely meat-and-potatoes diet. While **vegetarian** and vegan options are becoming increasingly trendy (**kosher** fare is still rare), traditional New Zealand food tends to run on the heavy, meaty side, with lamb, venison (called cervena when farm-raised), beef, and pork dominating the menus of traditional establishments. By far the national dish would have to be the hot **meat pies** loaded with lamb or beef and gravy in flaky pastry. Fresh **seafood** is always an abundant alternative; fresh fish, prawns (what Americans call jumbo shrimp), crayfish, shellfish, and more overrun coastal towns. Fruit-flavored **ice cream** loaded with chunks of real fruit is also consumed in vast quantities, although backpackers seem more likely to praise the **hokey pokey** variety, vanilla ice cream loaded with bits of toffee. New Zealand produces the ■**most ice cream per capita** in the world.

In small towns, the tendency toward the basic can be seen in the Main Street triumvirate of fish 'n' chips dives, cafes, and the ever-present Chinese restaurants, all serving fried and greasy goodies. Excellent foreign restaurants, such as Thai, Malaysian, and Indian, are no longer few and far between. Middle Eastern **kebab** joints, usually a good value, have proliferated recently. **BYO** (bring-your-own wine) restaurants without a license to sell liquor are widespread; some charge a corking fee. Keep in mind that ordering an **entree** will get you an appetizer or starter in New Zealand; main courses are listed as **mains. Tipping** is not expected, and closing hours tend to be flexible; many restaurants, especially in small towns, simply close their doors whenever business seems to have run dry.

With an average of 188 bottles per person annually, New Zealand ranks first in the world in **beer** drinking, consuming even more than their notorious guzzling neighbors, the Aussies. The Kiwis serve up a good brew, with various national lagers and draughts (such as Steinlager), regional beers (such as Speights and Tui), and specialty brews. The **wines** of the Marlborough and Hawke's Bay regions are world-famous, particularly the Sauvignon Blanc, Chardonnay, Riesling, Cabernet Sauvignon, and Pinot Noir varieties. New Zealand white wines are already challenging the French hold on the market, and red wines are improving yearly.

Hard liquor is less popular because import taxes make it more expensive. For non-alcoholic refreshment, try **Lemon and Paeroa (L&P),** a popular carbonated lemon drink that is "world-famous in New Zealand," as the advertisements tell you with a wink. For a more refined thirst-quencher, you can enjoy a British-style **Devonshire tea.** The late afternoon snack traditionally plies you with tea, scones with Devonshire cream or jam, crumpets, and other delectables. A lighter Kiwi treat, often served for dessert, is the **pavlova,** a tribute to egg whites and kiwifruit.

SPORTS

New Zealand loves sports like nobody's business. Almost half the population belongs to the New Zealand Sports Assembly, which represents 150 national sporting associations. In addition to the multitude of outdoor sports, including skiing, rafting, swimming, hiking, and jetboating, New Zealanders also hit the grass in organized sports like rugby, cricket, golf, tennis, and field hockey.

New Zealand keeps certain sporting heroes at the center of national pride. **Sir Edmund Hillary,** the first to climb Mt. Everest in 1953 is perhaps the most famous and is also on the $5 bill. New Zealand has also seen the rise of many prominent Olympians, especially in track and field events. **Jack Lovelock,** was a 1500m gold medalist in the 1936 Berlin Olympics. **Yvette Williams** was long jump champion in the 1952 Helsinki Olympics. And in the 1960 Rome Olympics, **Peter Snell** and **Murray Halberg** took home the gold in the 800m and 5000m respectively. Snell then went on to break records across five different events, including running a world record mile in 1962 and again in 1964. In recognition of his prodigious achievements, Peter Snell was celebrated throughout New Zealand in spring 2000 as the Alac "Sportsman of the Century."

Though New Zealand's performance in the 2001 Sydney Olympics seemed less than stellar, **Rob Waddell** brought home a gold medal in the single scull. A two time world champion in the single, a world record holder for 2000m at 6:36.38, and well over 220 pounds, Waddell was and is a force to be reckoned with. Waddell is the only athlete who has ever been voted the "Sportsman of the Year" twice: 1998 and 1999. Though presently retired, Waddell's next hardware may come from defending the title for the America's Cup in 2003 for Team New Zealand.

RUGBY. This active country also likes to sit on the sidelines, especially to watch rugby. Kiwi pride swells enormously for the **All Blacks,** the national team whose season usually runs from late May to September. When a crucial match like the **Bledisloe Cup Championships** is being televised, forget about going out to eat, changing money, or shopping—all the locals will be glued to their TVs, not running businesses. If anything, this craze became even worse following the All Black's 1987 victory in the rugby World Cup. Despite the All Blacks' widespread popularity, however, the team has encountered controversial moments in its history. In 1960, for example, the All Blacks made a vehemently protested national tour of South Africa in which Maori players were excluded. Then, in 1981, the South African Springboks made a tour of New Zealand, prompting many to claim that New Zealand was tacitly supporting apartheid.

Most people in New Zealand are die-hard **Rugby Union** fans. Historically, the Rugby Union organized amateur competition among teams. As players gained fame and prominence, the Rugby Union eventually became a professional sport. The **Super 12** tournament is a popular rugby event with the best players from Australia, South Africa, and New Zealand organized into 12 national (and regional) teams. In 2000, defending champions Canterbury Crusaders barely defeated the Canberra Brumbies. The highlight of the year is the **Tri-Nations Games** that takes place among the New Zealand, Australia, and South Africa teams from July to August; New Zealand will attempt to reclaim the title from Australia in 2001. This is the **All Blacks'** time to shine (see **All Black All Over** above).

ALL BLACK ALL OVER From hostel walls to the TV, from the daily paper to bathroom stalls, New Zealand's national rugby team, the All Blacks, are there. Protected with a fierce pride against such abominations as the padded wimpiness of American gridiron, rugby is a source of national unity and honor. Each player must be strong on both offense and defense, quick and powerful, fit enough to last the full grueling 80min, and most of all, tough. In 1986, Buck Shelford gave new meaning to the phrase "he's got balls" when he almost lost his in a test (international match) against France, leaving the game to receive emergency surgery. Although they lost to South Africa in the 1995 World Cup final, the team has consistently been one of the world's best. A loss by the All Blacks is so unexpected that tears from devastated fans mix with beer in pubs across the country. The marketing power of the team is so strong that every other national team is spun from their yarn; New Zealand fields the female Black Ferns in rugby, the All Whites in soccer, the Tall Blacks in basketball, the Black Sox in softball, and the Black Caps in cricket. While it may take Kiwi blood to fully understand the intricacies and meaning of the game, you don't have to jump in the middle of a scrum to appreciate the athletic prowess of popular star Jonah Lomu, the intensity of the Maori *haka* (war dance) challenge offered to opponents before each game, or the delirious passion of fans at the scoring of a try. Rugby is not merely sport, it is love.

Be sure not to confuse Rugby Union with the less popular, but no less exciting, **Rugby League** which features regional teams like the stalwart, ever-popular Auckland Warriors. The difference between the two can be confusing, but long ago the Rugby League split with Rugby Union over disagreement about the 'purity' of professional rugby play. While Rugby League sanctioned professional play, Rugby Union insisted on remaining amateur until turning professional a few decades ago.

CRICKET. There are two basic types of cricket competition. The first is **test-match cricket,** which takes place between two teams in a 6hr. match each day for five days. The second method of competition is **one-day cricket,** typically played, as the name suggests, as a one-day series between pairs of teams or round-robin competitions between teams. A World Cup one-day competition is played between all the Test nations—the nine nations officially recognized by the International Cricket Council. New Zealand has always been one of the top competitors among the World Cup nations. But the **Black Caps** suffered a shocking defeat to India in 2001, marking the fifth semi-final defeat in the seven World Cups.

SAILING. In 1995 the Kiwi sailing team **Black Magic** swiped the America's Cup from the United States, marking only the second time in 144 years that the cup was not won by an American team. The cup's subsequent mauling at the hands and sledgehammer of a Maori activist drew international headlines. Fully restored, the cup made several countrywide tours.

In March 2000, **Team New Zealand**, determined to protect the Kiwi hold on the Cup, masterfully trounced their Italian opponent Prada Challenge with innovative, and risky racing techniques. With this decisive victory, New Zealand cemented its reputation as a top yachting nation, becoming the first country other than the United States to successfully defend the Cup. With former Olympian and World Champion sculler, **Rob Waddell** (see p. 68) now on board, Team New Zealand's lookin' good for the 31st America's Cup on February 15, 2003.

THE LAND AND ENVIRONMENT

BEFORE HUMAN ARRIVAL

The ancient supercontinent of **Gondwanaland** was a fusion of modern-day South America, Africa, peninsular India, Antarctica, and Australia. When New Zealand split away from this landmass roughly 80 million years ago, it became an isolated biological time capsule. During the span of time before human arrival, the plants

ARE YOU SURE HE'S A HOOKER?

But he doesn't even know how to ruck... Some say rugby in New Zealand is a religion, others say obsession, still others say it's a way of life. The only thing that is certain is that rugby is never just a sport. And anyone visiting New Zealand in the winter can be lucky enough to witness the madness. It can be disconcerting, however, the first time you hear the announcer cry "The lock just blew past the number eight and looked to the try line, but when he was nabbed by the scrum half, the ball went into touch and they lost it to a line-out." Yes. It is English, but the previous sentence should warn you to leave any American football terms at home, you're on rugby turf now.

Despite its strange and colorful terminology, Rugby Union is not a difficult game to follow. Basically, 15 players from each team play on the **pitch** (field) at once, and attempt to outscore the opposing side. Play itself is fast and furious with high levels of athleticism and contact and relatively few penalties and play stoppages. There are no time-outs but substitutions are allowed, though relatively rare, during a typical 80 minute match. In the course of play the oval ball can either be passed (sideways or backwards but never forwards), kicked, or carried downfield. Penalties are awarded for such offenses as a high tackle or knocking the ball forward and result in either a kick or a **scrum** (which looks like two large masses of bodies hurling themselves at one another). If the ball goes **into touch** (out of bounds), it results in a **line-out,** in which the ball is thrown in a straight line and players are hoisted up to receive it (the opposing team attempts to intercept). Points are scored in three main ways—the ultimate success is achieved by carrying and grounding the ball across the opposing team's goal line, thereby scoring a **try,** worth 5 points. Following the try, the scoring team has the opportunity to kick a **conversion** through the uprights (2 points), with the position of the kicker depending on where along the try line the ball was grounded. The other way to score is through a **penalty,** when the ball is kicked through the uprights from the field (3 points).

Even if the finer points escape you, rugby can be the ultimate New Zealand cultural experience, whether in the stands or in the local pub. If in doubt, sit back, have a few pints, cheer for the home team, and never block the action. If your goal is just to get out and have a good time, these last rules may be the most important ones of all.

and animals on the islands evolved in new and unusual directions as they exploited food and habitat. With the absence of predators, New Zealand's birds evolved to occupy the niches that mammals took elsewhere in the world, gaining stronger legs, increasing dramatically in size, and sometimes even losing their wings. Two excellent examples of these unique birds—the **Haast eagle** *(Hapagornis)* and the **moa**—are now extinct. Though there are occasional reports of moa-sightings (see p. 278), it is fairly certain that none exist. The giant Haast eagle was the top carnivore in New Zealand; the world's largest eagle, it had a wing span of about 3 meters. The moa were the main grazers during this time. Some standing tall enough to look Big Bird in the eye, all 11 species of these flightless wonders were large; the smallest were the size of turkeys. The **kiwi,** a national emblem, is another flightless bird that flourished during this time and still exists today.

The flora of New Zealand, like the fauna, took several evolutionary turns since Gondwanaland. In the absence of large mammalian grazers and browsers, many plants never evolved toxic chemicals, tough leaves, or the spikes, thorns, and other defense mechanisms common in many other parts of the world.

INVASIONS

When the first settlers from Polynesia arrived over 1000 years ago with breeds of **dogs** *(kuri)* and **rats** *(kiore),* the pace of extinction rapidly increased due to the diseases they brought with them. The Maori and Europeans swiftly cleared forests for agriculture and hunted the moa to extinction. The two main culprits of species decline were wildlife habitat destruction due to industrialization and the introduction of non-native animals. Deer, goats, pigs, rabbits, and possums, brought to provide sporting opportunities, game, and fur, presented a fatal problem to the flightless birds and native animals that had not developed the defense mechanisms necessary for survival. **Wasps,** hidden in aircraft parts during World War II, entered the ecosystem and have reached epidemic proportions and threaten the food sources of birds and other insects. In another example of introductions gone awry, the stoats and weasels brought to the country to serve as predators of rabbits started feeding on hapless native birds when the local rabbit and possum supply diminished. In 2000, the honey bee industry was threatened by an infestation of **honey bee mites.** Since the mite can only live away from bees for a matter of hours, bees carrying the mite are believed to have been illegally smuggled into the country. The presence of the mite could have serious effects on both the ecosystem and the honey and farming industries. In addition to losing 43% of the frog fauna and over 40% of the bird fauna since humans first arrived, New Zealand now has over **600 endangered species.**

Non-native flora also disrupts the ecosystem, out-competing endemic flora for sunlight, space, and nutrients. Much flora introduced from harsher climates has a field day in New Zealand with the relatively mild year-round climate. The most famous pest in New Zealand is undoubtedly the climbing weed **old man's beard.** The plant has creamy white blossoms and gets its name from its characteristic yellow feathery seed heads. In the past few years, DOC has singled out **climbing spindleberry** as public enemy number one, trying to eradicate it before it can ravage the New Zealand environment, like it did in North America. **Asian kelp undaria,** better known as **Asian seaweed,** is considered the marine equivalent of old man's beard, strangling out native seaweeds and altering sea ecology. Unfortunately, it is considered a Japanese delicacy, and many people are looking to cash in on marine farming of the plant. With no native predators, and with introduced predators often feeding on indigenous plant life instead, the end result can be calamitous, disrupting the long-term stability of an ecosystem. Of the 20,000 non-native species introduced to the country, DOC reports that over 200 are now weeds.

FAUNA

Many species that evolved on the supercontinent never came into being in New Zealand; New Zealand has no snakes and no native land mammals. One immediately noticeable facet of New Zealand's wildlife, though, is the preponderance of strange and exotic birds. The four different species of **kiwi** display straight, thin, brown, or gray feathers and slender and probing beaks with external nostrils to help in scrounging for food on the forest floor. Solitary, nocturnal, flightless, tailless, and almost wingless, the kiwi is in a class of its own. The **kea,** the world's only alpine parrot, is one of the few birds to make its home in the peaks of the Southern Alps. Any visitor to the ski slopes or national parks of New Zealand will quickly realize that the kea is no ordinary polly, but rather a clever, destructive, and very bold menace (see **To Peck and Destroy,** p. 320). The **kereru** is the native pigeon, and the only bird able to disperse the larger seeds of some native plants. Fanciful names for New Zealand's amazing variety of birds abound: the **morepork** (*ruru*, the only native owl), the **muttonbird** (*titi*), and the **wrybill** (*ngutuparore*, with its slender and twisted beak), among others.

Unfortunately, many of New Zealand's beautiful birds are endangered today. Just 150 turkey-sized, blue-green, and strong-beaked **takahe** remain; the **black stilt** (*kaki*) are down to 70. Only 62 nocturnal **kakapo,** the world's heaviest parrot (males can weigh in at 4kg), are still in existence; DOC states that the kakapo "is, perhaps, the slowest-breeding bird on earth." Intensive conservation efforts are underway for all three species. Some of the most recognizable New Zealand bird species are its seven types of **penguins.** Among them the blue, yellow-eyed, and Fiordland crested are the most common. These interesting and potentially over-sexed species are often viewed by South Island tourists in Otago (see p. 328).

With over 1500 species of **land snails** (some of which are carnivorous), 11 species of the heaviest insect in the world (the ancient, mouse-sized, grasshopper-esque **weta**), teeming crayfish *(koura)*, pesky sandflies *(te namu)*, and the ethereal glowworms *(titiwai)*, there is no shortage of biological diversity. New Zealand also has the coastal **katipo spider,** a relative of the black widow. Another ancient relic found in New Zealand is the **tuatara,** a lizard-like creature old enough to have roamed with the dinosaurs 200 million years ago. An interesting feature of this reptile is its third eye, which helps to regulate its exposure to the sun.

Bats represent the only indigenous land mammals, though there are plenty of marine mammals. Orca, seals, and sea lions can be found in the waters off the South Island. New Zealand also boasts almost half of the world's whale, porpoise, and dolphin population. Species unique to New Zealand include **Hector's dolphin, beaked whales,** the **New Zealand fur seal,** and the **Hooker sea lion.** Today, climate changes and water pollution threaten these marine mammals, whose numbers reached drastic lows from the whaling and sealing trades earlier in the century.

FLORA

Before 1800, 70% of the landscape was covered in forest; today, only 15% of the original lowland forest and only 10% of the original wetlands remain. Ninety percent of the original **kauri** forests were harvested. Still, there are 2700 plants native to New Zealand (of which DOC reports that 80% are endemic). The most famous among these species are the towering kauri, whose forests are among the most ancient in the world, and whose value to today's tourist industry in Northland is inestimable (see p. 127). The kauri, however, are just one in a large family of **podocarps,** a broad class of conifers which includes other native trees such as totara, **rimu,** miro, and matai, and **kahikatea;** such podocarps dominate many of New Zealand's forested regions. **Beech forests** are also common; the *Nothofagus* is the most famous genus and can trace its roots to the Nothofagus forests that used to blanket Gondwanaland. There are 193 different species of fern in New Zealand, 88 of which are endemic. **Mamaku tree ferns** can grow up to 20m in height; the **ponga tree fern,** with its silver-underside fronds, is the national symbol.

The **pohutukawa,** often called "New Zealand's Christmas tree" for the bright crimson flowers that bloom in most varieties during late December, is another distinctive species found in the northern regions. Maori tradition holds that when these gnarled coastal trees bloom early there will be a long hot summer ahead. The **rata,** similar to the pohutukawa, adds a peachy-orangish cast to the landscape. The North Island rata begins life as a vine, and slowly strangles its host tree to death. Numerous other plant species besides trees are unique to the country as well (such as the world's largest buttercup, the Mt. Cook lily, and New Zealand's only native palm trees, the Nikau palms).

CONSERVATION

New Zealand is hailed worldwide as a leader in conservation efforts, both on land and at sea. About one-third of the country is set aside as protected land, and a massive international whale sanctuary established in 1994 includes more than 11 million square miles. The country is covered with 13 national parks, plus numerous other forest parks, groves, and wildlife reserves. The first national park, **Tongariro National Park,** was created in 1887 as a result of the foresight and efforts of Te Heuheu Tukino IV, the high chief of the Ngati Tuwharetoa Maori tribe. He offered the area as a gift to the New Zealand government on the condition that it be kept *tapu* (sacred). The other national parks see an equal share of visitors, many of whom come to tramp one of New Zealand's nine **Great Walks** (see p. 145). Unique to New Zealand, the Great Walks are designated multi-day hikes equipped with extensive overnight huts and camping facilities.

POSSUM PROBLEMS Although New Zealand's reputation of having several times more sheep than people still holds true, the fact is that there are now more possums than sheep. By some estimates, over 70 million of the marsupials are chewing tender leaves and damaging the flowers of New Zealand's native trees, carrying diseases, out-competing native birds for food, and steadily consuming much of the country's remaining native bush. If you visit the rare areas of the country where possums have not struck, such as Great Barrier Island, the damage wreaked by the animals in the rest of the country will become painfully evident. DOC's response has ranged from poison-trapping to offering head bounties, but in the wake of each subsequent ineffective attempt more and more radical approaches have been tried. The latest is the use of aerial poison bombs. A supposedly natural, biodegradable toxin known as "1080" is being dropped in many of the country's most rugged and intractable forests. DOC insists that studies overwhelmingly attest to 1080's safety, but they do warn surrounding areas before carrying out their aerial missions of eradication.

DOC is involved in many projects to maintain the country's natural beauty (www.doc.govt.nz/cons/cons.htm). In addition to protecting 30% of the land and working with other specialized groups in conservation efforts, DOC currently oversees 13 marine reserves and regulates the dolphin and whalewatching industries. It plays an active role in habitat protection, predator control programs, relocation of species to safer areas, and conducts surveys and research on the current status of endangered wildlife. A new project involving six "mainland island habitats" (isolated areas on the mainland of New Zealand) allows DOC to restore endangered species' habitats by managing introduced pests. DOC strives to protect the endemic and endangered animals of New Zealand in a variety of ways: it regulates the fishing industry, tracks flight patterns, cares for breeding sites of the albatross, rescues beached whales, relocates and cares for kiwi eggs (the kiwi is now vanishing at an annual rate of almost 6%), creates reserves for and curbs illegal poaching of the keruru, and educates New Zealanders on the importance of wildlife preservation.

NEW ZEALAND

AUCKLAND

| PHONE CODE | The phone code for Auckland is ☎09 |

Squeezed onto a narrow isthmus between sparkling Waitemata and Manukau Harbours, the inhabitants of New Zealand's largest and most cosmopolitan city are never far from the sea. Possessing more boats per capita than anywhere else in the world, Auckland clearly deserves its nickname, "City of Sails." Still fresh from victory in the America's Cup 2000 competition, the city's sleek waterfront landscape bubbles with excitement as the Kiwis prepare to defend their title in 2003.

Auckland's urban sprawl creates a number of thriving neighborhoods, each with its own distinct flavor and attitude. In the heart of it all, Central Auckland's downtown streets throb with power suits, corporate logos, and buzzing cellphones. On the periphery, the surrounding areas of Ponsonby, Parnell, and Mt. Eden cater to a calmer cappuccino crowd. Tranquil ferry rides away, the islands of the Waitemata Harbour dazzle with their unique charm and beauty.

Originally settled by the Maori over 650 years ago, today Auckland is home to over one million Kiwis. Combining the largest Polynesian population in the world with 150 years of European settlement and recent Asian immigration, the city is a multicultural mecca. A main arrival point for international visitors, Auckland is often viewed as a necessary stop before tackling the rest of New Zealand; those who linger enjoy Kiwi hospitality, hip cafes, active sports, and a vibrant nightlife.

▓AUCKLAND HIGHLIGHTS

2000 WAS A GREAT YEAR for the Waterfront, renovated to host the America's Cup; boats, restaurants, and a hopping nightlife still thrive 3 years after victory (see p. 92).

BUT ANYTIME IS A GOOD TIME on Auckland's K Road and High Street (p. 88) where the party lasts all night.

PICK YOUR URBAN POISON in Ponsonby, Parnell, or Mt. Eden, three character-laden neighborhoods with magnetic charm (see p. 94).

OR ESCAPE IT ALL on **Great Barrier Island,** a time warp to an isolated wilderness, or **Waiheke Island,** for wine tasting in paradise (see p. 101 and p. 98).

✈ INTERCITY TRANSPORTATION

Flights: Auckland International Airport (AKL), a 50min. drive from Central Auckland, is the port of entry for about 80% of New Zealand's overseas visitors. **Super Shuttle** (freephone in the *Visitor Information* concourse upon exiting the International Terminal, ☎66; 306 3960, fax 306 3959) may be the best option. **Airbus** (☎0508 247 287) runs every 20min. and makes many stops, including the YHA backpackers, Sky City bus station, Downtown Airline Terminal, and other transfer points. $13, $22 return; children $6/$12; YHA, VIP and seniors $11/$18. From the airport, a **taxi** downtown costs about $50. For **international flights, Air New Zealand** flies to Australian cities as well as to Pacific Islands: **Brisbane** (3½hr., 3 per day, $474); **Fiji** (3hr., daily, $794); **Melbourne** (4hr., 3 per day, $474); **Rarotonga** (3¾hr., 5 per week, $980); and **Sydney** (3½hr., 4 per day, $449), among others. For domestic flights, Air New Zealand (☎357 3000, nationwide 0800 737 000) flies to: **Christchurch** (1¼hr., 1-2 per hr., from $390); **Queenstown** (direct 1½hr., or via **Christchurch** 3¾hr., 4-5 per day, from $595); **Rotorua** (45min., 5-11 per day, from $192); and **Wellington** (1hr., every hour, from $294). Backpackers and students receive discounts (see **Flights** p. 39).

Trains: TranzRail (☎0800 802 802; fax 0800 101 525; www.tranzrailtravel.co.nz) leaves from the **Auckland Railway Station** (☎270 5209) which is located just a bit

North Island

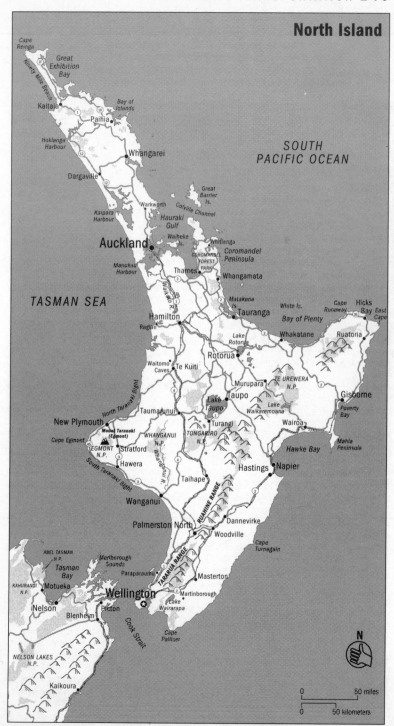

SOUTH
PACIFIC OCEAN

Cape
Reinga

Great
Exhibition
Bay

Ninety Mile Beach

Kaitaia

Bay of
Islands

Paihia

Hoklanga
Harbour

Whangarei

Dargaville

Kaipara
Harbour

Warkworth

Great
Barrier
Is.

Colville Channel

Hauraki
Gulf

Waiheke
Is.

Whitianga

Coromandel
Peninsula

CROMANDEL
FOREST
PARK

Auckland

Manukau
Harbour

Thames

Whangamata

TASMAN SEA

Matakana
Is.

Tauranga

White Is.

Bay of Plenty

Cape
Runaway

Hicks
Bay

East
Cape

Hamilton

Raglan

Whakatane

Ruatoria

Lake
Rotorua

Rotorua

TE UREWERA
N.P.

Waitomo
Caves

Te Kuiti

Murupara

Taupo

Gisborne

North Taranaki Bight

Taumarunui

Lake
Taupo

Lake
Waikaremoana

Poverty
Bay

New Plymouth

WHANGANUI
N.P.

Turangi

TONGARIRO
N.P.

Wairoa

Mahia
Peninsula

Cape Egmont

Mount Taranaki
(Egmont)

EGMONT
N.P.

Stratford

Hawera

South Taranaki Bight

Whanganui R.

Taihape

Hastings

Napier

Hawke Bay

RUAHINE RANGE

Wanganui

Palmerston North

Dannevirke

Woodville

Cape
Turnagain

ABEL TASMAN
N.P.

Marlborough
Sounds

Tasman
Bay

Paraparaumu

TARARUA RANGE

Masterton

KAHURANGI
N.P.

Motueka

Nelson

Blenheim

Picton

Wellington

Martinborough

Lake
Wairarapa

Cook Strait

Cape
Palliser

NELSON LAKES
N.P.

Kaikoura

N

0   50 miles

0   50 kilometers

inland off Beach Rd. (take Custom St. E past Anzac Ave.) between Central Auckland and Parnell. Open M-F 7:30am-6pm, Sa-Su 7:30am-1pm. Trains head daily to: **Hamilton** (2hr., $37); **Palmerston North** (8¾hr., $110), and **Wellington** (11hr., 1 per day for $145). Cheaper fares available by booking ahead (see **Trains** p. 39).

Buses: InterCity (☎913 6100; fax 914 0546; www.intercitycoach.co.nz) arrives at the travel center of **Sky City**, at Hobson and Victoria St. in Central Auckland. Service runs north to **Paihia** in the Bay of Islands (4hr., 3 per day, $44) via **Whangarei** (2¾hr., 3 per day, $32) and **Dargaville** (3hr., $41). Southbound runs include: **Napier** (7hr., 4 per day, $78); **New Plymouth** (6hr., 3 per day, $71); **Palmerston North** (9-10hr., 4 per day, $72); **Rotorua** (3½-5hr., 4 per day, $32) via **Hamilton** (2hr., 12 per day, $18); **Tauranga** (3½hr., 5 per day, $38); **Wanganui** (8hr., 3 daily, $71); and **Wellington** (11hr.; 3 per day; $97, night train $67) via **Taupo** (4½-5hr., 5 per day, $51). Special discounts can be obtained by booking 2 weeks ahead (see **Buses** p. 41).

Cars: SH1 is the main route into and out of Auckland. Toward the south, it's called the **Auckland-Hamilton Motorway,** with on-ramps at the top of Hobson St., Symonds St., and Khyber Pass Rd. Toward the north, it's called the **Northern Motorway,** with an on-ramp at Beaumont St. by Victoria Park.

Hitchhiking: While *Let's Go* does not recommend it, the collective wisdom of Auckland's backpackers says that the best **hitchhiking** can be found by taking a bus to the outlying suburbs and asking locals for current advice. To head north, hitchers reportedly catch the **Stagecoach** Hibiscus Coast Bus, from the downtown terminal to Orewa. (☎366 6400. $7.90.) To head south, hitchers take the 471 to Pahurere and switch to the 475 to Drury ($6.70). It is **illegal** to hitch on the freeway; hitchers recommend thumbing near on-ramps where cars can pull over. For more info see **Hitchhiking** p. 44.)

✠ ORIENTATION

Auckland and the city environs stretch across a narrow isthmus that connects Northland to the main landmass of the North Island. **Waitemata Harbour** and the Pacific Ocean lie to the east of the city, while **Manukau Harbour** stretches southward with the Tasman Sea in the west. **SH1** (the Southern Motorway) pumps traffic up from the south, becoming the Northern Motorway north of the city and converging with **SH16,** which stretches west to the Waitakeres and north to Ninety Mile Beach. While the greater metropolitan area is low-density suburbia, many of the attractive sights and neighborhoods are fairly centralized and only a walk—or a short bus ride—away from downtown.

The **Waterfront** is at the bottom of Queen St. by Waitemata Harbour. The **American Express New Zealand Cup Village,** the slick marina built for the America's Cup 2000 regatta, sprawls around **Viaduct Basin** near Hobson Wharf along the waterfront. **Quay Street** (key) also runs along the water, while **Customs St.** is parallel and one block inland. The **Ferry Building** is right off Quay St., across from **QE II Sq.** Inland to the east, in a different corner of town, stands the **Railway Station** off Beach Rd.; take Custom St. E past Anzac Ave. On the top of Queen St. past **Aotea Square** lies **Karangahape Rd.** (universally known as **K Rd.**), the gritty site of fashionable clubs, cafes, and some bars. Just west of Central Auckland, K Rd. leads to the trendy neighborhood of **Ponsonby,** filled with the hippest cafes and a substantial part of the city's gay and lesbian community. To the east of the city center is the fashionable area of **Parnell,** the site of old-money estates, historic buildings, and pricey boutiques and cafes. Just south of Parnell, Auckland residents go to **Newmarket** to do their shopping. Two kilometers south of the city center the charming suburb of **Mt. Eden** lies on a hill overlooking the metropolis. Home to a large number of artists and various artsy cafes, Mt. Eden is yet another gem on the outskirts of Auckland proper. Running east of Central Auckland, Quay St. turns into **Tamaki Drive,** which then swoops along the stunning coast. Take a look out at **Orakei Basin,** off **Hobson Bay, Bastion Point,** along the ocean, or at **Mission and St. Heliers Bays,** hits for summer sunbathing or an afternoon of boutique shopping.

▣ LOCAL TRANSPORTATION

Public Transportation: The **Link Bus** makes a complete loop through the central city in 1hr., ($1). The white-and-blue buses make both clockwise and counterclockwise ("anti-clockwise") loops through Queen St., Sky City, Victoria Park, Ponsonby, K Rd., Auckland University, the Auckland Domain, the Auckland Museum, Newmarket, Parnell, the Railway Station, and QE II Sq every 10min. on weekdays from 6am-5pm, and every 20min. on weekends. The **Explorer Bus** (☎0800 439 756) offers hop-on, hop-off service connecting the Ferry Building, Mission Bay, Kelly Tarlton's, Holy Trinity Cathedral, Auckland Museum, Parnell Village, Downtown Airline Terminal, Sky City, Victoria Park Market, and the American Express NZ Cup Village. An additional **satellite bus** operates Oct.-Apr. and stops at Auckland Museum, Mt. Eden, St. Luke's shopping center, Auckland Zoo, Museum of Transport and Technology, Force Entertainment Centre, and Auckland Art Gallery. Buses depart from the **Ferry Building.** Oct.-Apr. buses depart every 30min., 9am-4pm; May-Sept. every hour 10am-4pm. $25, children $15.) Ordinary city buses run by **Stagecoach** are a bit more challenging to negotiate because of their numerous and labyrinthine routes: **Rideline** (☎366 6400) gives advice. Open M-Sa 6:30am-9:30pm, Su 8am-6:30pm. Fares are calculated by the number of stages traveled, and range from Stage 1 ($1.20, children $0.70) to Stage 8 ($7.90, children $4.70). Or, eschew the stage system altogether and purchase a pass for unlimited travel. These buses are concentrated at the **Downtown Bus Centre** (not a place to be at night), or across from **QE II Sq.**, both on Customs St.

Ferries: Ferries leave from **Prince's Wharf** behind the Ferry Building, across from QE II Sq.; contact **Fullers** (☎367 9111) for schedules. The islands of **Rangitoto** (return $20, children $10; see p. 98) and **Waiheke** (return $23.60, 11.60; see p. 98) are accessible, as is **Devonport** (return $8, children $4; see p. 97). The ferry provides service to the unspoiled **Great Barrier Island**, departing from Mechanic's Bay during the summer (return $92, See p. 101). In summer, **Ship 'n' Shore** offers full-day excursions from the Viaduct Basin to **Coromandel**. (☎478 1462. $28. See p. 128.)

Taxis: Alert Taxis (☎309 2000), **Auckland Co-op Taxis** (☎300 3000), and **Discount Taxis** (☎529 1000) can be found at Victoria St. E and Queen St., and on K Rd.

Car Resources: The **Automobile Association,** 99 Albert St. (☎377 4660) is in Central Auckland on the corner of Victoria and Albert St. Open M-F 8:30am-5pm. *The Road Code of New Zealand* ($24.95) is a worthwhile investment for drivers. Similarly, drivers in Auckland might appreciate the *Driver's Guide* brochure, which indicates all of Central Auckland's one-way streets and parking areas. The *Minimap* series is quite comprehensive and available from the visitors center on Queen St. ($3.20-25). Alternatively, **Specialty Maps,** 46 Albert St. (☎307 2217) can provide some handy maps of the country. Open M-F 8:30am-5:30pm, Sa 10am-1pm.

Car Rental: Ace Rentals, 39-43 The Strand (☎303 3112) in Parnell, rents economy cars from $34 per day for up to 20 days and $25 per day for 20 days or more (includes unlimited km, insurance, 24hr. AA coverage, and tax). **Omega Rental Cars,** at the airport (☎275 3265) or 75 Beach Rd. (☎377 5573; 0800 525 210), starts its budget cars at $39 (min. 4 days; includes insurance, AA service, and unlimited km). One-way rentals to joint offices in Wellington, Christchurch, Nelson, Picton, and Queenstown are also available. **Maui Rentals,** 36 Richard Pearse Dr. (☎0800 651 080), 2km from the airport, rents campers with showers and kitchens from $115 (summer) and $70 (winter) per day. The worldwide chains **Avis** (☎526 2847; 0800 655 111), **Budget** (☎375 2222; 0800 652 227), and **Hertz** (☎0800 654 321) have offices at the airport.

Car Buying and Selling: If you'll be in New Zealand for an extended period of time, you may want to consider buying a car, and will probably be inundated with ways to do it. Most **backpackers** have postings on bulletin boards, with the most extensive at **Auckland Central Backpackers. Car auctions** are one option; **Turners Car Auctions** (☎525 1920; www.turners.co.nz), corner of Leonard and Penrose Rd. in Penrose, sells budget cars at noon on Wednesdays, and cars from $2000-8000 at 6pm on Thursdays.

Auckland see map pp. 80-81

🏠 **ACCOMMODATIONS**
Albert Park Backpackers, 17
Auckland Central Backpackers, 4
Auckland City YHA, 28
Auckland International YHA, 25
Bamber House, 66
The Brown Kiwi, 55
Central City Backpackers, 19
City Backpackers Hotel, 5
City Garden Lodge, 46
Downtown Constitution Hill
  Backpackers, 54
Georgia Parkside Backpackers, 42
International Backpackers, 52
Kiwi Backpackers, 24
Lantana Lodge, 47
Oaklands Lodge, 67
Posonby Backpackers, 61

🍎 **FOOD**
The Bog, 49
Café Cezanne, 56
Café Hasan Baba, 26
Circus Circus, 68
Diva, 69
Fusion, 57
Kebab Kid, 44
Khmer Satay Noodle House, 8
Mexican Café Bar & Grill, 16
Mt. Eden Bakery & Deli, 70

Otto Woo, 63
PASTArage, 43
Pizza Pizza, 20
Rasoi Vegetarian Restaurant, 31
Tanuki Sushi & Sake Bar, 22
Wolf Bagelry & Café, 15

🎵 **ENTERTAINMENT & CLUBS**
The Angle, 38
Cause Celebre/The Box, 13
The Classic Comedy & Bar, 21
Factory, 12
Galatos, 40
G.A.Y., 7
Java Jive, 58
Jones, 36
The Kiss Club & Bar, 34
Staircase, 37
The Supper Club, 33
Surrender Dorothy, 59
Temple, 27
Urge, 35
Wunder Bar, 9

🍺 **BARS**
The Carlton Tavern, 74
The Claddagh, 75
Crow Bar, 11
Deschlers Bar, 14

The Dog's Bollix, 41
Garagebar, 62
Khuja Lounge, 29
Kiwi Tavern, 6
Komodo, 51
Leftfield, 2
Margarita's, 18
The Nag's Head Tavern, 53
Papa Jack's Voodoo Lounge, 10
S.P.Q.R., 64
Spy, 1
Tabac, 3

☕ **CAFÉS**
Alleluya, 30
Atlas Power Cafe, 60
Atomic Cafe, 65
Barista, 48
Brazil, 39
City Cake Company, 71
Frasers, 72
The Live Poets Cafe, 32
The Other Side, 45
Raw Power Cafe, 8
Strawberry Alarm Clock, 50
Tea Total Cafe, 73

Hammer Auctions, 830 Great South Rd. (☎579 2344), also in Penrose, sells cars Monday through Friday at 6pm and Saturday at 10:30am. Car fairs are another way to buy or sell a car; Sell it Yourself, 60 Wairau Rd., Glenfield (☎443 3800; open daily 7am-7pm, in winter 8am-6:30pm) and 1106 Great South Rd., Westfield (☎270 3666, open daily 8am-6pm) and Manukau City Park and Sell (☎358 5000; open Su 9am-1pm), at the Manukau City Center, are two among many choices. Or, try Guarantee Buy Back Services such as Budget Car Sales, 10 Mt. Eden Rd., Mt. Eden (☎379 4120; open daily 8am-7pm) or Used Cars, 825 Dominion Rd., Mt. Roskill (☎620 6587; open daily 8am-6pm) and save the hassle of trying to sell your car later. For more information on short-term car purchase, see Car: Buybacks p. 43.

Bike and Motorcycle Rental: Adventure Cycles, 4 Quay St. (☎309 5566; 0800 335 566) hires mountain bikes from $25 per day and $90 per week. Touring and racing bikes roll from $18 per day and $70 per week. Open daily 7am-7pm. New Zealand Motorcycle Rentals, 31 Beach Rd. (☎377 2005; fax 377 2006; www.nzbike.com) offers motorcycles and scooters with rentals from $39 per day, include unlimited km, insurance, and 24hr. service. Open M-Sa 9am-5:30pm, Su 10am-3pm.

⁊ PRACTICAL INFORMATION

TOURIST AND FINANCIAL SERVICES

Visitors Center: Auckland Visitor Centre, 287 Queen St. (☎366 6888; airport branch ☎256 8480; fax 366 6893), in Central Auckland. The headquarters of New Zealand's extraordinary Visitor Information Network (VIN) offers a complete domestic booking system and every existing brochure and map about New Zealand. Open daily 9am-5pm. Another option is the New Zealand Visitor Centre (☎979 7005; fax 979 7010), corner of Quay and Hobson St., in the American Express New Zealand Cup Village. Open daily 9:30am-5:30pm.

Department Of Conservation (DOC): (☎379 6476; fax 376 3609), on Quay St. in the Ferry Building. Open M-F 10am-6pm, Sa 10am-3pm; Nov.-Feb. also Su 10am-3pm.

Budget Travel: STA travel, 10 High St. (☎309 0458; www.statravel.co.nz) has 4 branches in Central Auckland. Open M-F 9am-5:30pm, Sa 10:30am-2pm. usit Beyond, 18 Shortland St. (☎379 4224; fax 366 6275; www.usitbeyond.co.nz), is another option. Open M 9:30am-5:30pm, Tu-F 9am-5:30pm, Sa 10am-3pm. Otherwise, try the in-house travel centers at Auckland Central Backpackers (☎358 4875), or the Auckland City YHA (☎309 2802)—both open to non-guests. The Flight Centre (☎0800 354 448), has offices at: 350 Queen St. (☎358 4310) and 2 Fort St. (☎377 4655) in Central Auckland, and Broadway Plaza (☎529 2400) in Newmarket.

Consulates: Australia, 132-138 Quay St., 7th fl., (☎303 2429); Canada, all inquiries should be directed to the Wellington Office at 61 Molesworth St., 3rd fl., Phorndon (☎309 8516, 04 473 9577); Ireland, 87 Queen St., 2nd fl., Dingwall Bldg. (☎302 2867); US, 29 Shortland St., General Building, 4th fl. (☎303 2724); and UK, 151 Queen St., 17th fl. NZI House (☎303 2973). There is no South Africa consulate, but there is an honorary consulate (☎443 9700, ext. 9581) available at the Albany Campus of Massey University.

Currency Exchange: Interforex, 99 Quay St. (☎302 3066) in the Ferry Building, has the best hours. Open daily 8am-8pm. The National Bank, 205 Queen St. (☎359 9813) takes no commission on traveler's checks or foreign currency. Open M-F 9am-4:30pm.

ATM: They're all over Queen St., Ponsonby Rd., Parnell Rd., and Broadway.

American Express: 105 Queen St. (☎379 8286; fax 379 8280). The office changes foreign currency or traveler's checks without commission. Member mail held for up to 1 month. Open M-F 9am-4:30pm.

AUCKLAND

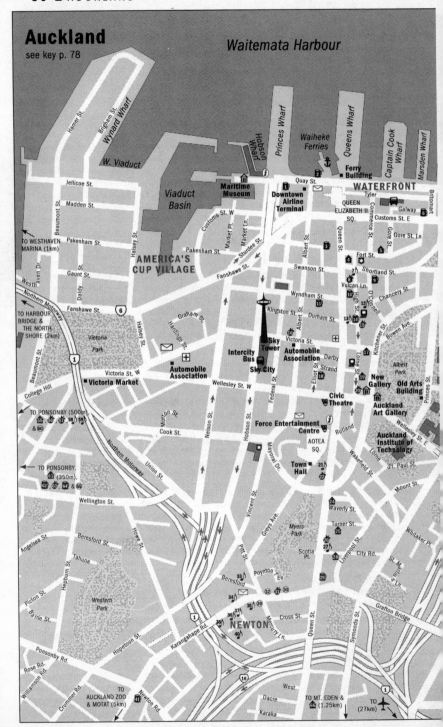

Auckland
see key p. 78

Waitemata Harbour

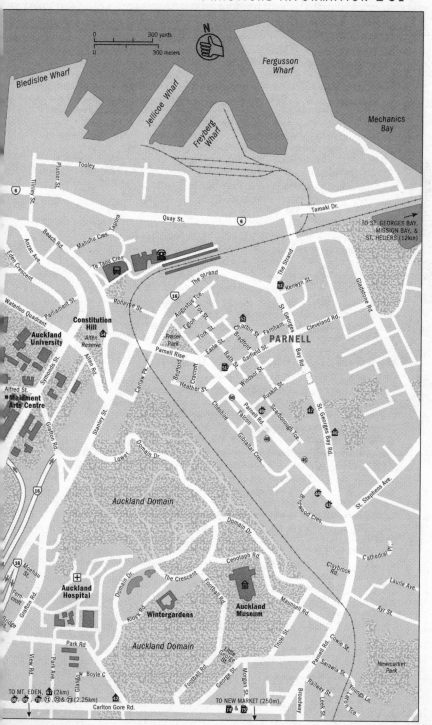

LOCAL SERVICES

Luggage Storage: National Mini Storage LTD, 68 Cook St. (☎356 7020) stores luggage for $0.50 per piece per day. Open daily 8am-6pm.

Bookstores: Whitcoull's (☎356 5400) on the corner of Queen and Victoria St., has 3 glorious floors and a cafe. Open M-Th 8am-6pm, F 8am-9pm, Sa 9am-6pm, Su 10am-5pm. For pre-loved books, **The Dead Poets Bookshop,** 238 K Rd. (☎303 0555; open M-F 9am-6pm, Sa 9am-5:30pm, Su 10am-4pm; Sa 2-4pm) and **Rare Books,** 6 High St. (☎379 0379; open M-F 9:30am-5:30pm, Sa 10am-2pm) have a wide range of titles.

Women's Organizations: Auckland Women's Centre, 4 Warnock St. (☎376 3227), in *Grey* Lynn, offers counseling and other services for women. Open M-F 9am-4pm, Sa 10am-1pm. **Wanderwomen** (☎360 7330) coordinates trips for women, including kay-aking and climbing. Weekend trips $260, 5-day $615. Based out of Waipu, **www.wom-entravel.co.nz** is a resource for women traveling in New Zealand (☎432 1234).

Gay-Bi-Lesbian Organizations: The **Gay and Lesbian Line** (☎303 3584; 0800 802 437; aglw@xtra.co.nz) provides info, support, counseling, and referrals. Open M-F 10am-10pm, Sa-Su 5-10pm. **The Pride Centre,** 281 K Rd. (☎302 0590), gives away informa-tion, referrals, and an events calendar. Open M-F 10am-5pm, Sa 10am-3pm.

Ticket Agency: Ticketek (☎307 5000) sells tickets for music, theater, and sporting events; book over the phone or at the **Countrywide Bank box office** in the **Aotea Cen-tre.** $6 surcharge for all advance tickets. Open daily 9am-5:30pm or later.

Weather Conditions: MetPhone (24hr. ☎0900 999 09) $1.15 per min. or **MetFax** (☎0900 779 99) $5.40 for the first min. and $0.99 per min. thereafter.

Publications: The Auckland-based **New Zealand Herald** is the country's most compre-hensive daily newspaper. **Metro** magazine has the pulse of Auckland's pop culture and politics, while **express** is the gay and lesbian paper. **The Fix** and **Infusion** have the dope on Auckland's dance clubs, while **pulp** lists headliner events nation-wide.

EMERGENCY, MEDICAL, AND COMMUNICATIONS

Emergency: Dial ☎**111** throughout New Zealand.

Police: Auckland Central Police Station (☎379 4240), on the corner of Cook and Vin-cent St. The **Downtown Station** (☎379 4500) is on the corner of Jean Batten Pl. and Fort St. Other stations include **Airport International Terminal** (☎275 9046), the **Karan-gahape Road Community Constable,** 281 K Rd. (☎309 8177), and the **Devonport Community Constable,** 19 Anzac St. (☎489 4008).

Hotlines: Lifeline (☎522 2808) provides counseling by appointment and support (☎522 2999). The **Auckland Help Foundation** (☎623 1700) aids victims of sexual assault. For STD concerns, call the **AIDS Hotline** (☎0800 802 437). All hotlines **24hr.**

Medical Services: Urgent Pharmacy, 60 Broadway (☎520 6634), in Newmarket. Open M-F 6am-1am, Sa-Su 9am-1am. The **Auckland Hospital** (☎379 7440) sits on the edge of the Auckland Domain on Park St. in Grafton. For less dire cases, **Travelcare,** 87 Queen St., 5th fl. (☎373 4621), in Central Auckland, will immunize, vaccinate, heal, and soothe. Open M-F 9am-5pm. **Ponsonby Accident and Medical Clinic,** 202 Pon-sonby Rd. (☎376 5555), has its own **pharmacy** (☎378 6075). Clinic open daily 7:30am-10pm; pharmacy 8am-9:30pm. For pharmaceuticals in Central Auckland, **Cammell the Chemist,** 104 Queen St. (☎303 4253) has the best hours around. Open M-Th 8am-6pm, F 8am-8pm, Sa 9:30am-5pm, Su 11am-4pm.

Internet Access: Prices are always changing. Many internet shops have cheap rates for calling overseas. **Netzone,** 4 Fort St. (☎377 3906) has speedy $5 per hr. connections. Open M-Sa 8:30am-11pm. **e-xile Internet Lounge,** 327 Queen St. (☎309 2101), also charges $5, but throws in free coffee. Open M-Sa 9am-9pm. Possibly the cheapest, **high-net,** 48 High St. (☎3379 7736), charges $3 per hr. Open daily 8am-7pm.

Post Office: Wellesley Street Post Shop (CPO), Bledisloe Building, 24 Wellesley St. (☎379 6710) holds Poste Restante. Open M-F 7:30am-5:30pm, Sa 9am-noon.

⌐ ACCOMMODATIONS

The accommodations in **Central Auckland** are all conveniently located in the heart of the metropolis; easy access to the city's offerings comes at the price of rowdy young crowds, urban fumes, and an impersonal feel. Older travelers, families, or those simply seeking a city location with a country feel should think outside the box and choose a neighborhood instead—**Ponsonby, Parnell,** and **Mt. Eden** all have backpackers and are only a short bus ride away from the city center. **Check-out time** is 10am, **key deposit** is $10, and **laundry** is $4, unless otherwise noted.

CENTRAL AUCKLAND

Albert Park Backpackers (VIP), 27-31 Victoria St. E (☎309 0336; fax 309 9474; bakpak@albertpark.co.nz). Brimming with twenty-somethings, the kitchen and lounge area feature a pool table, a view of downtown, and premium television. Free bike and luggage storage. Reception 7am-11pm, in winter 7am-10pm. 10-12-bunk dorms $19; 4-6-bed dorms $20; singles $40; doubles $50. 1 night free per week.

Auckland International YHA, 1235 Turner St. (☎302 8200; fax 302 8205; yhaakint@yha.org.nz), just off Queen St. The long colorful hallways, huge kitchen, and downstairs lounges will dazzle you with their spotlessness. Internet. 8-bed dorms $19; 4-bed dorms $20; twins and doubles $52, with bathroom $69. Non-members add $5.

Auckland City YHA (☎309 2802; fax 373 5083; yhaauck@yha.org.nz), at the corner of City Rd. and Liverpool St. In contrast to the International YHA just down the hill, this older brother attracts a younger crowd. On-site **Tommy's Bistro** (open M-Sa 6:30-11am, Su 7-11am, and daily 4:30-7:30pm) has cheap and easy eats. Internet. Reception 24hr. Dorms $19; singles $40; twins and doubles $48. Nonmembers add $5 per night.

Downtown Constitution Hill Backpackers (VIP), 6 Constitution Hill (☎303 4768; 0800 366 1444). Hidden down on a hill on the other side of Albert Park and the Railway Station. This petite, quiet, and fresh cottage is choice. Free luggage storage. Internet. Dorms $16; doubles $36, with bath $42. VIP $1 off. Cash only.

City Backpackers Hotel (NOMADS), 38 Fort St. (☎307 0181; 0800 220 198, booking code 110; fax 307 0182). This hostel treats backpackers to shared apartment-like complexes, complete with telephone (incoming only), living room, TV, bathroom, and slick kitchenette. Free breakfasts M-F. Key and linen deposit $20. Dorms $20; singles $40; twins $45; doubles $45-65; studio apartments for 4-6 people $140.

Auckland Central Backpackers (VIP), 9 Fort St. (☎358 4877; fax 358 4872; backpackers@acb.co.nz, www.acb.co.nz). With an unannounced new location, its 383 beds are more a place to dump your pack before heading upstairs to the **bar** (open daily 2pm-3am) than a spot to de-jetlag and unwind. Internet. Key deposit $20. Reception 24hr. Reservations recommended. Dorms $15-17; singles $32; twins and doubles $41.

Central City Backpackers (VIP), 26 Lorne St. (☎358 5685; fax 358 4716; ccbnz@xtra.co.nz). The CCB caters to a young crowd—with the noise, smoke, and constant craziness to prove it. The free beer with check-in is just a prelude to the debauchery ahead. Check out Happy Hour (6-9pm) at **Embargo,** in the basement (☎309 1850; open M-Su 5pm-3am). Storage $5 per item per week. Key deposit $20. Reception 24hr. Internet. 6-10-bed dorms $19; 1-4-bed dorms $21; singles $38; twins and doubles $48. Weekly: 6-10-bed dorms $108; 1-4-bed dorms $120 (credit card necessary to hold after 4pm).

Kiwi Backpackers, 430 Queen St. (☎/fax 358 3999). The rock-bottom prices at this backpackers often seduce budget-conscious travelers, but the scarcity of windows are a big trade-off for the saved coin. Key deposit $20. Parking available. Reception and bar open 8am-midnight. Internet. 4-6-bed dorms $15; twins and doubles $40.

PONSONBY

▧ **The Brown Kiwi,** 7 Prosford St. (☎/fax 378 0191). The Brown Kiwi puts you where you want to be—trendy Ponsonby—in one of the hippest backpackers in Aotearoa. This 2-story home is a serene masterpiece, with adult-sized bunkbeds, an elegant garden, and 2 Japanese-style fish ponds. They're even eco-conscious: "Save water, shower with a friend." Free local calls. Free storage. Internet. Laundry $3. Gay-friendly. 8-bed dorms $18; 4-bed dorms $20; doubles $48.

Ponsonby Backpackers, 2 Franklin Rd. (☎360 1311; 0800 476 676; fax 360 1365). The jumbled lounge is warmed by cushy couches and a fireplace. Internet. Reception 8am-8pm. Check-in as late as 11pm. Dorms $18; singles $25-30; doubles $45; tent sites $12.

PARNELL

Lantana Lodge (VIP), 60 St. George's Bay Rd. (☎373 4546). Guarded by a large banana palm tree, this Victorian home charms with a gingerbread porch and flower garden. Small, simple, and with a helpful staff, every square inch is compulsively clean. Free storage. Reception 8am-10pm. Dorms $18; twins and doubles from $44.

City Garden Lodge, 25 St. George's Bay Rd. (☎302 0880; fax 309 8998; city.garden@compuweb.co.nz). Quiet and set on a ½-acre of land, this backpackers was once owned by the Queen of Tonga. Free storage. Internet. Reception 8am-noon and 3pm-late. 8-bed dorms $18; 3- to 4-bed dorms $19; twins $40-44; doubles $46.

International Backpackers (Alan's Place), 2 Churton St. (☎/fax 358 4584; International.bp@xtra.co.nz). The 2-story brick building is complete with a walk-in fridge and a quiet backyard. Free storage. Internet. Reception 7am-10pm. Dorms $19; twins and doubles $46. YHA/VIP $1 off.

MT. EDEN

▧ **Bamber House,** 22 View Rd. (☎/fax 623 4267; bamber@ihug.co.nz). This white-painted colonial home has a comfortable feel with a luxurious living room. Take a dip in the outdoor pool or find your inner child in the backyard doll house. Internet. Laundry $3. Off-street parking. Dorms from $18; twins and doubles from $45. Family rooms available.

Oaklands Lodge, 5a Oaklands Rd. (☎/fax 638 6545; 0800 222 725) just off Mt. Eden Rd. Around the corner from Mt. Eden's cafes, this lodge relaxes even the most cramped of airplane muscles. Free on-street parking. Internet. Laundry $3. 10-bed dorm $18; 4-bed dorms $20; singles $35; doubles from $45. Family rooms available.

GRAFTON

Georgia Parkside Backpackers, 189 Park Rd. (☎/fax 309 8999; bacpacgeorgia@xtra.co.nz). The only backpackers in the neighborhood and close to Newmarket's shopping. Internet. Reception M-F 7am-8pm, Sa-Su 9am-1pm and 5-7pm. 12-bed dorm $18; 6-bed dorm $19; twins $40; doubles $42. Prices slightly lower in winter.

◪ FOOD

Auckland offers a mind-boggling selection of dining options, including authentic foods from all corners of the globe. Takeaways and food courts dot the city center, but supermarkets tend to be concentrated in **Newmarket** and **Ponsonby,** the most central being the **New World,** 2 College Hill near Victoria Park; the Link Bus stops right outside. (☎307 8400. Open M-Sa 8am-10pm, Su 8am-6pm.) For good value in **Central Auckland,** it's best to venture to the top of Queen St. or along K Rd. The neighborhoods of Ponsonby and **Mt. Eden** feature restaurants with a funkier feel and affordable prices, while those in **Parnell** cater to an upmarket crowd. See the **Cafes** section (p. 86) for more dining options.

CENTRAL AUCKLAND

Pizza Pizza, 57 Lorne St. (☎309 3333), tucked behind Queen St. to the East, on the second floor of an orange building. This funky, laid-back pad is placed on a pizza pedestal by students (who just happen to receive a 20% discount on smalls and larges). Free toppings and free delivery to Central City (min. order $12.95). Open M-F 10:30am-10:30pm, Sa-Su 4:30-10:30pm.

Khmer Satay Noodle House, 10 Vulcan Lane (☎366 4419). The address says swank, but the food screams delicious and affordable. Chicken or beef satay ($7) cooked before your very eyes. Seats are perfect for people-watching. Open daily 10am-9pm.

Tanuki Sushi and Sake Bar, 319 Queen St. (☎379 5353). Delectable Japanese mains ($5-16). In the darker depths below, **Tanuki's Cave** (☎379 5151; open Tu-Th and Sa-Su 6pm-midnight, F 5:30pm-1am) serves skewers of *yakitori* ($2-7.50) and over 35 different kinds of *sake*. Open Su-Th 5:30pm-11pm, F-Sa 5:30pm-midnight.

Café Hasan Baba, 466 Queen St. (☎358 5308). Those who enter this unassuming eatery will discover a taste of Turkey at bargain prices. A sit-down meal of char grilled chicken ($12.50) will delight. YHA discount 10%. Open daily noon-11pm.

Wolf Bagelry and Café, 54 High St. (☎366 7359). Bagel lovers can enjoy creative bagel-wiches like the vegetarian V-bagel ($7). Bagels $1.20 each, $16 per dozen. Open M-F 7am-5pm, Sa-Su 7:30am-5pm.

Mexican Café Bar & Grill, 67 Victoria St. W (☎373 2311). The pricey mains satisfy burrito cravings ($15-20). While Happy Hour (5-7pm) means cheap starters, the bar tap sees the most action. Open M-F noon-2:30pm and 5pm-late, Sa-Su 5pm-late.

Rasoi Vegetarian Restaurant, 211 K Rd. (☎377 7780), is an unusual all-veggie, all-the-time eatery. The Deluxe Thai platter, complete with rice and your choice of curry ($9.50) will fill you nicely. Open M-Sa 11am-9pm. Cash only.

PONSONBY

One Red Dog, 151 Ponsonby Rd. (☎360 1068). Try the beef and bernaise or sweet chili Thai pizza. Pastas $14.50. Unwind afterwards at the bar down the steps with the handless wall clock (beer tap $4, bottle $5.50-6). Open M-F 11am-1am, Sa-Su 10am-1am.

Café Cézanne, 296 Ponsonby Rd. (☎376 3338). A colorful menu of big breakfasts (gigantic muffins $2.50), pastas, and salads ($8-12) feeds the equally colorful crowd. Open Su-Th 9am-midnight, F-Sa 8am-2am.

Food for Life, 153 Ponsonby Rd. (☎376 5878). Vegetarians find nirvana in this dream world of all organic home-grown nourishment. Soups $5-7.50, pies $3.20, salads $7.50, casseroles $12.50. The bar in the rear offers a great view over Auckland from the deck. Open daily 7am-10pm (bar open till 1am).

Fusion, 32 Jervois Rd. (☎378 4573), just off Ponsonby Rd. is a bright blue slice of the Pacific with pictures by Gauguin on the wall. Open M-Sa 7:30am-6pm, Su 8am-6pm.

Ponsonby Fresh Fish and Chips, 127 Ponsonby Rd. (☎378 7885). "Best Fish & Chips in Auckland" (*Metro Readers Poll 2000*), the raw fish on street window display metamorphosize into cajun-style fish burgers ($5.20) and spicy grilled fish fries ($2.90). Open Tu-Sa 11am-9:30pm, Su-M 5-9:30pm.

Otto Woo, 47 Ponsonby Rd. (☎360 1989). A beacon in the land of takeaways, this restaurant serves Asian food packaged to perfection without pretension. The rice balls (5 for $4.50) will melt in your mouth. Open daily 5-10pm, and M-F noon-2:30pm.

PARNELL

The Bog, 196 Parnell Rd. (☎377 1510). Other than the pipe organ, the likes of Joyce, Shaw, and Wilde adorn the walls. The "Brendan behan" ($16.50) and kilo-of-mussels ($16) deliver more than kitsch Irish. Guinness and Kilkenny $6 a pint. Open daily 10:30am-late (usually 1am).

AUCKLAND

Kebab Kid, 363 Parnell Rd. (☎373 4290). Middle Eastern fast food may seem foreign to most, but the Kid has your favorite kebab ($8.50). Open Su-M 11am-10pm, Tu-Th and Sa noon-11pm, F noon-2am.

PASTArage, 381 Parnell Rd. (☎379 3719). This modern, black and white eatery is fresh, and so is the pasta—you can watch it come straight from the machine (M-Sa 9:30am-noon). Open M-F 9:30am-7pm, Sa 9:30am-3pm.

MT. EDEN

▓ **Circus Circus,** 447 Mt. Eden Rd. (☎623 3833). Step right up to see the "greatest cafe on earth." Filled with vintage circus posters, assorted clown paraphernalia, hanging trapeze figures, and even a red tent for smokers, this eatery is a 3-ring utopia (sandwiches $2.50-7.50). Show in progress daily 7am-4:30pm.

Mt. Eden Bakery and Deli, 464 Mt. Eden Rd. (☎630 1426). A day in Mt. Eden isn't complete without a visit to this local bakery. Inside the big green exterior, travelers and hordes of locals simply can't resist the heavenly sandwiches, quiches, pies, or cakes ($1.20-4.75), all brown-bagged at bargain-basement prices. Open M-F 7am-6:30pm, Sa-Su 7am-5:30pm.

Diva, 305 Dominion Rd. (☎623 2855). Representative of the many ethnic eateries on Mt. Eden's 2nd main road, Diva serves delicious Indian food (mains $8-17.50). Open daily 5-10pm (or late).

▐ CAFES

Auckland's vibrant cafe scene is an integral part of the social fabric of the city, coolly filtering out the espresso-ignorant. In **Central Auckland,** the narrow streets of High and Lorne as well as Vulcan Ln. and nearby K Rd. are brimming with coffee sippers; likewise, the main roads in **Parnell** and **Mt. Eden** feature a wide selection of java joints. However, stylish **Ponsonby** wins the caffeine crown for the highest concentration of cafes. In addition to the universal love of the coffee bean, most serve light meals and alcohol, and some feature occasional live music.

CENTRAL AUCKLAND

▓ **Brazil,** 256 K Rd. (☎302 2677). Electronica hangs in the air along with the distinct fragrance of roasting beans. Upstairs, resident DJs spin and scratch. Breakfast around $11. Internet. Open M-Tu 8am-8pm, W-Th 8am-midnight, F 8am-1am, Sa 9am-1am, Su 9am-8pm. Kitchen closes at 3pm.

Alleluya, 179-183 K Rd. (☎377 8424) in St. Kevin's Arcade. Situated on the oldest cafe site in Auckland, Alleluya is a spiritual caffeine-induced experience. Selection of salads and sandwiches around $10; come early on weekends if you want a seat for brunch. Open M-Tu 9am-5pm, W-Sa 9am-midnight, Su 9am-4pm.

Raw Power Cafe, 10 Vulcan Lane (☎303 3624). Follow the carrot and tomato sign to this haven of organic vegetarian delights. A mouth-watering salad bar ($7.50) and fresh fruit juices—come packed with nutrients travelers may lack. Open M-F 7:30am-4pm.

The Live Poets Cafe, 238 K Rd. (☎359 9936), adjacent to The Dead Poets Bookshop. The staff at this lively spot are well versed in coffee. Folk, jazz, and poetry performances Sa 2-4pm. Open Sa-Th 9am-6:30pm, F 10am-11pm.

Net Central Cybercafe, 5 Lorne St. (☎373 5186). Net Central pleases the speedy by combining access ($9 per hr.) with many forms of caffeine. Open daily 8:30am-10pm.

PONSONBY

Atomic Cafe, 121 Ponsonby Rd. (☎376 4954). All ages can find deep meaning in the Dr. Seuss books. Large breakfasts $7-13. Open M-W and F 7am-6pm, Th 7am-11pm, Sa 8am-5pm, Su 8am-4:30pm. Kitchen closes M-F at 2:30pm Sa-Su at 3pm.

Atlas Power Cafe, 285 Ponsonby Rd. (☎360 1295). Freshly roasted everyday, Atlas' coffee might not give you the strength of a Greek god, but it will certainly lift your spirits. Open daily 7am-6pm.

Turkish Cafe, 294 Ponsonby Rd. (☎360 0468). Sitting next to a wall carpet and paintings of ancient monuments, the Turks-at-heart sip Turkicino ($5.50; a strong Turkish coffee) or Sahlep ($4.50) and Tulasey ($4.75), while listening to tunes by Mustafa Sandhal or belly dance songs. The restaurant makes falafel ($14.50) and choban salata ($11.50). Open M-Th 11am-midnight, F-Sa 11am-2am.

Box.house, 286 Ponsonby Rd. (☎376 6538). The coffees ($2.50) and teas ($2.50) will clear your mind until late night. The restaurant serves mainly European/Chinese fare ($16.50-18.50). Open daily 7am-late (usually till 2am).

PARNELL

■ **Strawberry Alarm Clock,** 119 Parnell Rd. (☎377 6959). Once a fruit and vegetable shop, today this colorful cafe mellows even the most stressed of suits. While you savor the serenity, take a hint from the writing on the wall— "No Smoking" is inscribed in every imaginable language! Open M-F 7:30am-5pm, Sa 8:30am-4:30pm, Su 9am-4pm.

The Other Side, 320 Parnell Rd. (☎366 4426). Its location on the even side of the street with a gigantic tree on the premises is just one way that this cafe dares to be different. Try "The Works" breakfast ($10) with your joe for guaranteed full-day functionality. Open M-F 7am-10pm, Sa-Su 8am-10pm.

Barista, 193 Parnell Rd. (☎303 4050), hosts a young, modern crowd that spills out onto metal sidewalk seats. Enjoy a cuppa (from $2.50). Open daily 8am-5pm.

MT. EDEN

Frasers, 434 Mt. Eden Rd. (☎630 6825). Popular with locals, this corner cafe serves beverages and food morning, noon, and night. Chat with a friend over the homemade quiche ($7) and a cappuccino ($2.50). Open M-F 7am-11pm, Sa-Su 8am-11pm.

Tea Total Cafe, 442 Mt. Eden Rd. (☎623 4919). Follow the wooden monkey with teapot in tow into the home of New Zealand's foremost tea specialists. If the 126 tea selection overwhelms, try sencha lime, a popular leaf for locals (pot $3). Open daily 8am-5pm.

City Cake Company, 426 Mt. Eden Rd. (☎638 6499). Trendy, 30-something financiers turn their cell phones to vibrate to fully appreciate the bliss of chocolate cake ($6) and muffins ($3.50). Open daily 9am-6pm.

♫ ENTERTAINMENT

Living up to its cosmopolitan status, Auckland has a wide range of entertainment choices. From adult entertainment to the more classy opera, theatre, music, and dance options scattered along parts of K Rd., diversions abound.

MUSIC

Live music is a regular treat that livens up many local joints throughout the week (see also the **Cafes, Bars,** and **Nightclubs** sections). One establishment that makes its living by providing live acts is **Temple,** 486 Queen St. This intimate venue has nightly offerings that cover all musical tastes. Monday is open Mic jam night and Tuesdays offers up jazz, poetry, or comedy. Their daily Happy Hour (5-8pm) serves two spirits or NZ beers for just $5. (☎377 4866; www.temple.co.nz. Cover varies. Open daily 5pm-2am.) Filling more of a niche, but still providing nightly live tunes, is **Java Jive,** corner of Ponsonby Rd. and Pompallier Terrace in Ponsonby. Drop in at this subterranean blues/jazz/rock club for plenty of atmosphere and low-altitude attitude. Grab a seat by the piano-painted bar or beneath the smiling visages of blues greats. (☎376 5870. Open Tu-Su 6pm-3am, restaurant from 6pm.)

On the rare occasions that they pass through Auckland, big name bands generally play at the **Powerstation,** 33 Mt. Eden Rd. (☎377 3488) or the **North Shore Event Centre** (☎443 8199). Check at **Real Groovy,** 438 Queen St., for schedule and ticket information. (☎302 3940. Open Sa-W 9am-7pm, Th-F 9am-9pm.)

PERFORMING ARTS

The highbrow highlights of Auckland's entertainment scene cluster around the centrally-located Aotea Square (ow-TAY-ah); known as the **Edge** (☎309 2677; www.the-edge.co.nz), the complex includes the Aotea Center, the Civic, Auckland Town Hall, and the Force Entertainment Centre, all listed separately below. In the Aotea Center, the 2256-seat **ASB Theatre** is the majestic home to the **New Zealand Royal Ballet,** the **New Zealand** and **Auckland Philharmonics,** and world-class productions for limited engagements; the 186-seat **Herald Theater** and the **Ticketek** box office are also on site. Opposite Aotea Centre, classical music emanates from the recently renovated **Auckland Town Hall Concert Chamber,** which has great acoustics and is home to the **International Chamber Music Festival** (☎445 1863) in July. Just next door, the **Civic** (☎307 5700) hosts music and theater functions, including a range of classic films; the recently renovated and opulent interior seems like a rock-hewn Indian temple and is itself worth a peek. Theater, dance, and music performances are always on at the **Maidment Arts Centre,** 8 Alfred St., opposite the Auckland University Library. (☎308 2383. Tickets $15-45, students $15-29.) The **Auckland Theater Company** does drama there, at the Herald and at the Sky City Theater, usually 10 two-three-week runs; their **Second Unit** has up and coming playwrights and directors read their work once a month for free at the **Rdyge Hotel.** (☎309 3395. Tickets $18-41.)

At the other end of the theater spectrum stands the **SILO,** on Lower Greys Ave., behind Town Hall. Managed and staffed by art students, this underground experimental theater features a wide range of performances. (☎373 5151; www.silo.co.nz. Tickets $10-18. Reserve by phone or 1hr. before the show.)

The Classic Comedy & Bar, 321 Queen St. serves up good laughs. The wide variety of performances range from amateur open Mic (M, $5) to the humorous musings of seasoned pros later in the week. Happy Hour is M-F 6:30-7:30pm. Shows start at 8pm. (☎373 4321. Open M-Th 6:30pm-midnight, F-Sa 6:30pm-2am. Cover varies.) The agents at the **Covert Theater,** 84 K Rd. (☎366 6637) do improv at 8 and 10pm W-Su; catch the show from the cafe (open 10am-late) or bar (open 6pm-late).

CINEMA AND SPORT

In mid-July, the **Auckland International Film Festival** captures the attention of movie buffs with two weeks of screenings from all over the world. (☎307 5000. Tickets $11, senior citizens $6.) Year-round, standard-issue Hollywood films are shown in the flashy new **Force Entertainment Centre,** 291-297 Queen St. (☎979 2405), a complex which houses the **IMAX** screen (☎979 2400; tickets $15, student $13, Tu for $11), conventional cinemas, restaurants, and bars.

For a more active evening of entertainment, **Sky City** has casinos for all levels of gamblers. (☎912 6000. Free gaming lessons available.) Across the street is the **Palace,** 73-75 Victoria St. (☎366 0200), the only bar in Auckland that matches the casino by staying open **24hr.** For those who prefer games of skill to games of chance, the **Ponsonby Snooker Centre,** 106 Ponsonby Rd., is the classiest pool hall in Auckland, with three full-size snooker tables. (☎360 2356. $10 per hr., $12 per hr. after 6pm. Open daily 11am-1am. Reservations necessary at night.)

◪ NIGHTLIFE

BARS

Auckland's bars range from traditional Irish pubs to mellow lounges, but domestic beers are the drink of choice in almost every locale. Tap beers like Steinlager, Speight's, Lion Red, DB, and Export Gold are almost invariably higher in quality (and cheaper) than bottled imports. Spirits and cocktails have recently been gaining in popularity, especially with the Ponsonby jet-set. Also frequently sipped are sweet fruity drinks, such as KGB, Stolchinaya, and Tattoo, which have the alcohol content of beer and the tang of lemon or cranberry. Prices run $3-4 for a pint of beer, $5 for double spirits and premium spirits. Specialty cocktails and fancy shooters cost as much as $6-7 a shot, and a cocktail shaker costs around $20-25.

Along the **Waterfront** colossal bars cater to huge crowds and provide excellent harbor views free of charge. The rest of **Central Auckland** is host to traditional pubs, funky lounges, and backpacker havens alike. The surrounding neighborhoods, although often pigeonholed as cafe spots, do have some choice bars, frequented predominantly as pre-clubbing spots. **Ponsonby** packs black-clad yuppies, **Parnell** is home to the old money crowd, and **Newmarket** has some relaxed watering holes.

CENTRAL AUCKLAND

▨ **Khuja Lounge** (☎377 3711) corner of K Rd. and Queen St. Lebanese for "melting pot," Khuja draws a multicultural crowd, and the DJ mixes everything from soul to drum'n'bass nightly. Take the old-fashioned elevator up to this ultra-funky lounge. W is *Brisa Luca* with samba and basa nova. Cover usually $5. Open Tu-Sa 8pm-late.

▨ **Margarita's,** 18 Elliot St. (☎302 2764). Backpackers rush here for the cheap booze (M, Th, and Sa the first 100 patrons get a whopping 8 beers for $5) and the youthful vibe. Luckily, this spacious wood-floored watering hole with automobile decorations, pool tables, and a packed dance floor entertains with ease. Upstairs, **Chili Lounge** has a more elegant feel. Handles $3 daily 5-7pm and 9-10pm. Open daily 4pm-3am.

Leftfield, Shed 19 Princes Wharf (☎307 9500). Built for the America's Cup and pumping ever since, this colossal sports bar features three bars, stadium seating, a lounge, a restaurant, and excellent views of the harbor. Look behind you in line for the men's room—that may just be an ▨ All-Black (it would be wise to let him pass). W at 8:30pm the TV show "Lion Red Sportscafe" tapes here live. Handles $5. Open daily 10am-late.

Crow Bar, 26 Wyndham St. (☎366 0398). Bartenders, James Bond-style beautiful, quench the delicate thirsts of the posh clientele. Melt into the comfy couches with a beer ($5.50) or peer into the goldfish bowls upstairs. Open daily 7:30pm-late.

The Dog's Bollix (☎376 4600), at the corner of K and Newton Rd., proves Dublin is alive and well in Auckland. Su is locals' night with Irish dancing and spontaneous eruptions of the best Irish, English, and American folk in a free-for-all jam session (6:30pm). Live music W-Sa. Handles $4.50. Open M-Sa 8:30am-midnight, Su noon-midnight.

Papa Jack's Voodoo Lounge (☎358 4847), on Vulcan Ln. This 2nd fl. lounge provides all the ingredients for a devilish evening—from the bats and scorpions embedded in the bar to potent potions like $6 shots of "dragon's blood." The main alternative venue, Jack's features a range of live music Th 10pm. F cover $2. Open Tu-Sa 7pm-late.

Tabac, 6 Mills Lane (☎366 6067), just off Albert St. on a secluded side street. Enter to drown in a mellow sea of black, gossip over cocktails, or listen to the live music and DJs (nightly 9pm). On W owner Neil Finn of Crowded House often makes musical appearance. Rockstars—is there anything they can't do? Open Tu-Sa 4pm-late.

Deschlers Bar, 17 High St. (☎379 6811). Affectionately dubbed the "jazz version of Cheers," regulars return for the saxophone beer taps, posh dark surrounds, and live jazz 4 nights a week (M 8pm, F 9:30pm, Sa 10pm, Su 9pm). If you come often enough, perhaps they will come to know your name as well. Open M-Th and Su noon-3am, F noon-6am, Sa 3pm-3am.

Kiwi Tavern, 3 Britomart Pl. (☎307 1717), east of QE II Sq. along Customs St. opposite the Oriental Markets. You can't backpack in Auckland without hearing about this place. Tu, the 5 draft beers for $8 is a budget dream in a multi-level venue. House band plays W with $2 cover and $2 off draft beer and spirits. Downstairs, the **Kiwi Bar** complements with a more accessible space and creative, rustic aesthetic. Happy Hour daily 5-7pm (pints, wine $3). Tu DJ 8pm-late. Open Su-Th 11am-3am, F-Sa 11am-4am.

Spy, 204 Quay St. (☎377 7811), is a members-only champagne bar. To mingle with the poshest of the posh, dress like it, or the bouncer won't let you in. Open Tu-Sa 9am-5pm.

PONSONBY

S.P.Q.R., 150 Ponsonby Rd. (☎360 1710). S.P.Q.R. stands for *Senatus populus que Romanus* (The Senate and the Roman people), which harkens back to a unified and open-minded Roman republic. This cafe and bar, lit by candles and glowing orbs, attracts a mixed crowd. Pizzas and pastas $15.50-19.50. Gay-friendly. Open M-F 11am-2am, Sa-Su 10am-2am.

Garagebar, 152 Ponsonby Rd. (☎378 8237). The Ponsonby crowd steadily funnels in for the mellow vibe. Beer $6. House DJs W-Sa 9pm-2am. Open M-Sa 5pm-2amm.

PARNELL

The Nags Head Tavern, 117 St. George's Bay Rd. (☎309 3586), off the Strand. Right down the hill from Parnell's stretch of hostels, a down-to-earth crowd packs in for the English pub feel and beer to match (handles $4). Tu Happy Hour 5-6:30pm (a pint $2.50). Open daily 11am-late.

Komodo, 106b Parnell Rd. (☎309 3161), entrance on Garfield St. DJs keep the crowd going with uplifting trance while "Big Wednesdays" offer $3 drink specials (spirits 2 for $5). Open Tu-Sa 5pm-1am.

MT. EDEN

De Post Belgian Beer Cafe, 466 Mt. Eden Rd. (☎630 9330). Elegant Brussels Old World charm comes with a polished wooden bar counter and all the Belgian beer brands on tap ($5.50-8). Outdoor patio with seating upstairs. Open M-F 7am-1am, Sa-Su 8am-1am.

NEWMARKET

The Claddagh, 372 Broadway (☎522 4410). Celtic signs, mahogany walls, and draught Guinness—could it be anything but Irish? Live Irish music (daily 8pm) provokes a rollicking crowd. Enjoy a handle ($4.50) with the after-workers. Open daily 11am-midnight.

The Carlton Tavern, 489 Khyber Pass (☎529 0050), at corner of Broadway and Khyber Pass. Live DJs (Th from 9pm) and 2 shakers for a wee $12. Live music keeps the place rocking (F-Sa from 9pm). Handles $5. Open M-W 11am-midnight, Th-Sa 11am-3am, Su noon-midnight.

NIGHTCLUBS

During the week the nightlife in Auckland centers around venues with special club events. On weekends the city comes alive with the hottest DJs storming the scene and young urbanites clubhopping between hotspots. Although Auckland's surrounding neighborhoods light up with lively bars, **Central Auckland** dances til dawn. The downtown clubs are generally more relaxed about dress code and attract a younger crowd. Up on **K Road,** style reigns supreme as everyone dons his or her favorite shade of black and joins the queue. Adding color to the scene are drag queens, who come out at night and stay until the next day.

The two magic numbers in Auckland are 5 (the standard cover charge) and 20 (the standard age of admission) if you want to get in most clubs. Carding is strict, so bring your ID or passport; otherwise, you will be turned away. For the skinny on events, the glossy mag *The Fix* can't be beat, especially since it's free. Pick it up, as well as special events flyers, at **Beat Merchant,** on Albert St., **CyberCulture,** 151 K Rd., and the mother of all record stores, **Real Groovy,** 438 K Rd.

Cause Celebre and **The Box,** 33 High St. (☎303 1336). Auckland's longest running nightclub throbs with young dancing machines who circulate through the two related venues. W night is Retrorama with '80s and other flashback tunes, Th features live bands at Cause Celebre, and weekends are a sweaty, drum'n'bass- and house-induced haze in both clubs. Cover $10. Open W-Th 11pm-6am, F-Sa 5pm-10am.

The Kiss Club and Bar downstairs and **Bacio** upstairs, 309 K Rd. (☎303 2726) steal a huge percent of the K Rd. clubbers with seductive interiors. A funk beat fills the dance floor while a queue forms outside and waits. Cover $7 F-Sa. Open W-Sa 10pm-7am.

Galatos, 17 Galatos St. (☎303 1928), just behind K Rd. Attracting more mellow crowds than K Rd., Galatos lets aspiring DJs hire out the huge dance floor for the right to play their favorites, charging $5 and up for cover. The upstairs lounge is free—if the bouncer thinks you're cool enough to get in. Open W-Th 9pm-3am, F-Sa 9pm-6am.

The Angle, 258 K Rd. (☎307 0890). The seas of posh, teen pool sharks here are a distraction when it comes to billiards; the real game, however, is angling for a date (and there's lots of fresh catch). Sa fire dancers and jugglers liven things up. Cover $5. Open F-Sa 9pm-6am.

Jones, 350 K Rd. (☎377 0033). This upstairs drink-a-teria provides an intimate way to try to keep up with the Joneses. French house and uplifting funk keep the place pulsing all the time. DJs Th-Sa from 11pm. Cover $7 F-Sa after midnight. Triphop jazz Su from 10pm. Open Th 10pm-5am, F-Sa 10pm-7am, Su 9pm-4am.

Factory, 17 O'Connell St. (☎366 1616). Drum'n'bass and hip-hop rhythms keep the upstairs shaking while the second floor's swanky lounge chills. Tu aspiring DJs can spin their grooves on the open deck. W live bands. Cover $5. Open Tu-Sa 10pm-late.

Staircase, 340 K Rd. (☎374 4278). A string of black couches in the front bar leads to a rear dance floor dominated by a massive aluminum staircase. Cover $5 after 12am. Gay-friendly. Open W-Sa 10pm-6am, Su 10pm-2am.

The Supper Club, 2 Beresford St. (☎300 5040), just behind K Rd. Once the home of Auckland's public toilets, it is now the destination of choice for pre- and post-clubbing clubbing. Cover Sa $1-5. Open M-Th 11am-1am, F 11am-Sa 1pm, Sa 6pm-Su 1pm.

Wyndham Bowling Club, 18 Wyndham St. (☎373 3433). In an unassuming spot downtown, the WBC and their *Allstars* are making a name for themselves as one of the new hotspots. DJ's spin for a 20-something crowd on the big dance floor, while the cafe up front is decidedly more chill. Open W-Th 5pm-2am, F-Sa 11-7am.

GAY AND LESBIAN NIGHTLIFE

Ironically, Queen St. is *not* the center of queer activity in Auckland—instead **Ponsonby** takes the cake. Many gay-run bars and brasseries line Ponsonby Rd., promising numerous opportunities for a fabulous night out. Gay nightlife is well-integrated into the Auckland scene, and **K Road** clubs around the corner, are often gay-friendly, if not explicitly catering to the gay set (nightclub listings above note gay-friendly clubs). Downtown, **High St.** and **Vulcan Lane** host some choice gay nightspots. Scope out the *express* newspaper ($2.50 at newsstands, or free at Surrender Dorothy or Urge) for the most current listings.

Taking over Auckland for two weeks, the **HERO Gay and Lesbian Festival** (Feb. 8-25, 2002) is a carnivalesque celebration of theater performances, film screenings, and outdoor events culminating in a parade and lively all-night dance party. Check *express* or find HERO on the web at www.hero.org.nz for a peek at the schedule.

G.A.Y., 5 High St. (☎336 1101), in the basement. The subtle name says it all—this is Auckland's hottest gay dance club. Cages, platforms, and disco balls keep the crowd bumping. F-Sa drag queens come out at 11pm. Cover $5. Open W-Sa 9pm-4am.

Surrender Dorothy, 3/175 Ponsonby Rd. (☎376 4460), in Ponsonby. At the sign with the hairy legs and ruby slippers, you'll find an unpretentious and fun watering hole. Mixed but predominantly male couples; lesbian couples and friends of "friends of Dorothy" are more than welcome. Drag queens strut their stuff Sa at 10pm. Open "for joy and fabulousity" Tu-Sa 5pm-12:30am.

Wunder Bar, 5 O'Connell St. in the Administrator House, starts where *Queen's Ferry* left off: red velvet and gold tassels, stiff drinks and hard house, a popular scene and posh surrounds all make for lush life and lavishness at this (very camp, very *handbag*) club. Open daily 4pm-3am.

Urge, 490 K Rd. (☎307 2155). The heavy black curtain at the entrance is only the start of this environment, where heavy cruising is the norm for the mostly gay-male scene. F DJ party "Grind." Open M-Sa 8pm-late, Su 6pm-late; in winter Th-Su from 8pm.

◉ SIGHTS

VANTAGE POINTS

Auckland offers many ways to get your bearings before venturing into its urban sprawl. Volcanic hills rise up around the city and provide keen lookouts, though man has made a fair attempt at offering concrete alternatives as well.

AUCKLAND

MT. EDEN AND ONE TREE HILL. These two peaks offer the more famous natural vantage points from which to take in the city and harbor. Although many visitors head to Mt. Eden to partake of its artistic side, its parks provide a bird's eye (or at least a giraffe's eye) view of Auckland. Another fine lookout, One Tree Hill also houses the **Stardome Observatory** at its base, which offers a planetarium show. After shows, you can take a peak at the cosmos through the EWB 50cm telescope. *(Mt. Eden: Take bus #274, 275, or 277 from Commerce St. near Fort St. Observatory: Take bus #30 or 31 from the corner of Victoria and Queen St. Observatory ☎ 624 1246. 2-6 shows per day, W-Su. $10, children $5. Telescope $5, $3 children, bookings essential.)*

SKY TOWER. The most dominating feature of the city skyline rises above the steel and glass of Central Auckland. The 328m Sky Tower is 8m taller, and a lot brighter, than the Eiffel Tower (take that, France). The **observation deck** has a 360° view; the **Sky Deck** is 34m higher and offers almost the same views, but without all the mayhem; you can even step onto the glass in the outer ring or eat at **Orbit,** its requisite rotating restaurant. *(In the middle of Hobson, Wellesley, Federal, and Victoria St. Open Su-Th 8:30am-11pm, F-Sa 8:30am-midnight; last elevator 30min. before closing. $15, children $7.50, seniors $13.50. Sky Deck $3 more. Discount tickets available at the Auckland visitors center.)*

CENTRAL AUCKLAND

It won't take you long to discover that downtown Auckland is dominated by high-powered execs and bumbling tourists stocking up on Kiwi souvenirs. Teeming with modern buildings, banks, and suits, **Central Auckland** is the commercial heart of the city. **Queen St.**, the main strip in Auckland, runs north-south toward the water where it meets **Queen Elizabeth II Square** (known as **QE II Sq.**). **Victoria St.**, another major thoroughfare, crosses Queen St. and goes east-west starting from Victoria Park (on the west side of town) to Albert Park (east side).

ART GALLERIES. Next to Albert Park sits the prim white **Auckland Art Gallery.** Peruse the standing collection of 19th-century Maori portraits on the ground floor, or visit the rest of the gallery to see one of the traveling shows. Its sister gallery is the **New Gallery,** which focuses on contemporary art; the steel and glass space houses traveling shows. *(Auckland: at the corner of Wellesley and Kitchener St. ☎ 307 7700. Open daily 10am-5pm. Standing collection admission free; exhibit admission varies. New Gallery: a block down on the corner of Wellesley and Lorne St. ☎ 307 4540. Open daily 10am-5pm. $4, students and seniors $2.)*

AUCKLAND UNIVERSITY. As you traverse Albert Park it is impossible to miss the handsome tower of the **Old Arts Building,** 22 Princes St. Built in 1926, the 54m tower was inspired by that of Christ Church College, Oxford in England. The building is the symbol of **Auckland University,** the largest of New Zealand's eight public universities. The school itself sits on the other side of Albert Park, occupying the better part of four large blocks centered on Symonds St. The campus **library** is on the corner of Princes St. (the east edge of Albert Park) and Alfred St. The view from the top floor will distract anyone from Katherine Mansfield's books. *(University operator ☎ 373 7599. Open to the public M-Th 9am-9pm, F-Sa 9am-6pm, Su 10am-8pm.)*

PARKS. To escape from the city's chaos, **Victoria Park** to the west of Queen St. and **Albert Park** to the east will provide a welcome dose of nature. Across from Victoria Park, the aptly named **Victoria Park Market,** 210 Victoria St. W bustles with crafts, clothes, cafes, and weekend flea-markets. *(☎ 309 6911. Open daily 9am-6pm.)*

THE WATERFRONT

The **Waterfront** is at the bottom of Queen St. by Waitemata Harbour. **Quay** ("kee") **Street** runs along the water, while **Customs St.** runs parallel one block inland. The **Harbour Information Office,** a kiosk near the water, can answer most questions about the waterfront. *(☎ 357 6366. Open daily 9am-6:30pm; in winter 9am-6pm.)*

AMERICAN EXPRESS NEW ZEALAND CUP VILLAGE. Head to the bottom of Albert St. to find **Waitemata Harbour,** the site of the year 2000 America's Cup. Once there, turn left on Quay St. and continue to Viaduct Harbor to reach the American Express New Zealand Cup Village, home to numerous restaurants, bars, apartments, and hotels. Although the races are over, they certainly left a mark of modernity on Auckland. *(Viaduct Harbour is just west of QE II Square.)*

NEW ZEALAND NATIONAL MARITIME MUSEUM. This waterside museum has meticulously crafted exhibits on New Zealand's love-affair with the sea, all enhanced by true-to-life settings and sounds; a beacon for history-buffs, real sea-lovers will be beckoned away from the museum and *outside*. *(At the base of Hobson Wharf. ☎ 373 0800. Open daily 9am-6pm; in winter 9am-5pm. $12, students $6.)*

FERRY BUILDING. The beautiful 1912 Ferry Building is another important waterfront landmark and home of Fullers ferries, which has service to the islands of Waiheke (see p. 98), Rangitoto (see p. 98), and Great Barrier Island (see p. 101), as well as across to the North Shore community of Devonport (see below). See **Auckland: Transportation** for schedules and prices. Fullers also runs **harbor cruises,** the cheapest being the **Coffee Cruise** which circles the basin. *(Ferry building, 99 Quay St. Fullers ☎ 367 9111. Coffee Cruise 2hr., 3 per day, $30, $15 children.)*

COAST TO COAST WALK. The Ferry Building (see above) is the start of one of Auckland's most popular activities, the Coast to Coast Walk. The walk travels through the city from Waitemata Harbor to Onehunga Beach, the first European settlements in Auckland, and hits the Auckland Domain, Mt. Eden Domain, and One Tree Hill on the way; the path is marked every kilometer by blue and yellow signs. *(One way 16km., 4-6hr.)*

WESTHAVEN MARINA. Parking lot for Auckland's well-to-do, Westhaven is the largest man-made marina in the Southern Hemisphere. Further down Westhaven Dr., along the Rolex-wearing arm of the Marina, are the upper-crust **yacht clubs,** where crews return from civilized competition to enjoy a civilized drink (or six). The **Royal New Zealand Yacht Squadron,** established in 1859 at the end closest to the city and water, is one of the oldest and most posh. Back along Westhaven Dr. toward Central Auckland, the helpful staff at **Sea Tours** on **Pier Z** can answer questions about charter sailings. *(To reach Westhaven Marina, take Westhaven Dr. out of Auckland, along Gaunt St. from the American Express New Zealand Cup Village. Sea Tours ☎ 378 9088; www.seatours.co.nz.)*

THE BAYS

Running east of Central Auckland, Quay St. turns into **Tamaki Drive,** which then swoops along the stunning coast through **Orakei, Mission Bay, Kohimarama,** and **St. Heliers.** Skirting subtropical waters and cream-colored sands, it becomes a prime in-line skating, kayaking, and parading venue in the summer months. *(Buses #765 and 769 run past both Mission Bay and St. Heliers Bay; call Rideline ☎ 366 6400.)*

ACTIVITIES. If you have a car but want a different set of wheels, head to **Ferg's Kayaks** for **in-line skates.** Fit romantics might enjoy Ferg's **moonlight kayak trip** to Rangitoto Island. *(12 Tamaki Dr. ☎ 529 2230. Open daily 8am-6pm; in winter 8am-5pm. In-line skates 1hr. $10, $5 each additional hr., $25 per day. Kayaks $9 per hr. Kayak trip 6-11pm, $60. Bookings essential.)*

ORAKEI BASIN. The yacht-filled **Orakei Basin** is the sailing grounds of the rich of **Paritai Drive,** Auckland's wealthiest street in a gated community of million-dollar mansions. Take a longing look from Orakei Rd., which abuts **Hobson Bay** east of Central Auckland, to view frequent rainbows, hundreds of pleasure yachts, and Auckland's most expensive real estate.

KELLY TARLTONS UNDERWATER WORLD. Deep beneath Tamaki Dr. lurk stingrays, eels, and sharks in possibly the most ingenious use ever of converted sewage tanks. A dry-erase board at the entrance serves as a fishy tabloid of who's being fed, who's been born, and who's mating with whom. A moving walkway transports guests into the marine world of rays, sharks, and fish while a golf cart roller coaster transports passengers through the **Antarctic Encounter,** which features a colony of live King and Gentoo penguins; in both cases, seeing wildlife while moving through a plexiglass tube is slightly surreal. *(23 Tamaki Dr., 6km east of Central Auckland. ☎528 0603, 0800 805 050. Open Nov.-Feb. daily 9am-9pm, last entry 8pm; Mar.-Oct. 9am-6pm, last entry 5pm. $22, students and seniors $18, children $10.)*

ORAKEI MARAE. On a hill with great views, the **Orakei Marae** of the Ngati Whatua tribe is not really a tourist attraction; if you're interested in visiting, call ahead and be aware of *marae* protocol (see p. 64). In 1978, a Maori land claim was made here on Bastion Point, leading to escalating tensions and eventual military intervention by the New Zealand government. *(59b Kitemoana St., in Orakei. ☎521 0606.)*

MISSION BAY. Hiding around **Bastion Point** from Orakei is **Mission Bay,** a cool waterfront carousing and sunbathing outpost with an awesome stretch of lively bars and cafes. The golden sands wrap around to a series of small coves, including **Mission Bay,** named after an 1859 Anglican stone mission which is now an upscale French restaurant.

MICHAEL JOSEPH SAVAGE MEMORIAL GARDENS. This poppy-dotted park pays homage to New Zealand's first Labour Party Prime Minister—the view of Rangitoto and the Gulf is simply stunning. *(At the end of Hapimana Rd. just south of Bastion Point in Mission Bay, contact City Parks Office with questions ☎379 2020.)*

ST. HELIERS BAY. The restaurants, bars, and sands of Mission Bay are rivaled only in popularity and accessibility by **St. Heliers Bay.** Quiet throughout the winter, Tamaki Dr. and St. Heliers Bay Rd. throng with hordes of people in the summer. With white sand and a tiny shopping district, this Bay is prime ground to watch the *nouveau riche* wage elegant battles with the old money of **Paritai.**

AUCKLAND MUSEUM. Auckland's largest museum displays Polynesian, European, and natural history exhibits. Upstairs, the *Scars on the Heart* describes various New Zealand wars and may make you palpitate with patriotism; downstairs galleries feature Aotearoa's Maori heritage and house the **Hotuni whare,** a complete meeting-house on loan from the Tainui tribe of the Thames area. The *whare* is still considered a sacred space, so guests are asked to remove their shoes before entering. The museum is also the venue for the **Pounamu Maori Performance Group.** The blast of a conch shell announces the start of their amazing cultural show of music, dance, and weaponry. *(☎309 0443. Shows daily 11am and 1:30pm. $10, students and seniors $5. Museum open daily 10am-5pm. Donations requested.)*

INNER SUBURBS

PONSONBY. No visit to Auckland is complete without a day's jaunt to Ponsonby. This neighborhood has thankfully outgrown its reputation as the slum of Auckland and has become the affordable and cool place to live. While not exactly a historical district, the vibrant student and gay and lesbian populations give Ponsonby a more welcoming feel than Auckland's often sterile business district. Both sides of Ponsonby Rd. are lined with eateries, trendy cafes, and bars, with a healthy dose of second-hand and craft stores thrown in. Connecting Ponsonby to the top of the city, K Rd. still bears lingering signs of its adult entertainment industry (which threatens only one's aesthetic sensibility). The Link Bus will transport you to Ponsonby in minutes but if you happen to hike in that direction on a Saturday you will discover an open-air market on the bridge over the K Rd. motorway, with great bargains on second-hand clothing and funky garments made by aspiring fashion designers. *(Call K Rd. Business Association for more info. ☎377 5086. Open Sa 10am-4pm.)*

AUCKLAND DOMAIN. To the east of Central Auckland lies the vast expanse of grass and trees that is the Auckland Domain. The duck pond is in the center, and a nearby gazebo often hosts jazz bands that play free concerts on summer weekends. Amid the various attractions in the Domain are the free Wintergardens, a collection of glass houses around a lily pond. *(The park is best accessed from the Grafton Bridge, which extends across the motorway just a block from the Queen St. K Rd. intersection. Wintergardens open daily 9am-7:30pm; in winter 9am-4:30pm.)*

PARNELL AND NEWMARKET. On the far side of the Domain is the flashy, upscale neighborhood of Parnell, home to vast estates, historic buildings, and pricey boutique shopping. To sample Parnell, most stroll through the Domain or take the Link Bus. The most notable architecture is a group of Victorian homes-turned-boutiques, along the side of Parnell Rd., known as Parnell Heritage Village (look for the fleet of tour buses outside). At the top of the road on the opposite side sits Auckland's Anglican Cathedral of the Holy Trinity, which was moved completely intact in all of its 19th-century glory to make room for a larger church. The free and lovely Parnell Rose Gardens at the base of the hill bursts into bloom from November to March. Parnell Rd. leads straight into nearby Newmarket; take Carlton Gore Rd. when Parnell Rd. forks. A shopping mecca for Auckland residents, this tiny suburb bustles along Broadway St. The Link Bus will take you from Central Auckland to Newmarket and Parnell in minutes.

WESTERN SPRINGS

The residential suburb of Western Springs is home to two of Auckland's big name attractions: the **zoo** and **MOTAT**. To get to Western Springs, take the yellow bus #045 from Point Chevalier, across from QE II Sq. ($2.20).

AUCKLAND ZOO. Auckland's zoo features impressive *Rainforest* and *Pridelands* sections. The kiwi and tuatara exhibits are worth a look, as are the red pandas and the Wallaby Walkabout. *(On Motion Rd. ☎360 3819. Open daily 9:30am-5:30pm, last entry 4:15. $12, students $9, seniors $8, children under 15 $7, children under 5 free.)*

MUSEUM OF TECHNOLOGY AND TRANSPORT (MOTAT). A classic streetcar connects the zoo to its nerdy neighbor. Bring your science-bent young ones for the hands-on physics experiments; it's also appropriate for those who live and die for steam engines and antique cars. The entrance fee includes **MOTAT II,** a collection of classic aircraft and seaplanes in Sir Keith Park Memorial Airfield, 500m past the zoo on Motions Rd. *(805 Great North Rd. ☎846 7020. Open daily 10am-5pm. last entry 4:30. $10, children and senior citizens $5, children under 5 free, families $20.)*

🔼 OUTDOOR ACTIVITIES

As the primary gateway to the adventure-addicted New Zealand, Auckland has little choice but to sponsor its fair share of adrenaline. And though a plane jump may be cheaper in Taupo, and the dolphins more numerous in Kaikoura, the city does offer a convenient backdrop against which to experience your rush of choice. Of course, the area also excels at certain activities: **sailing** tops the list (and the price range), while **canyoning** (a mix of abseiling, swimming, climbing through caves, sliding down waterfalls, and leaping off minor cliffs) provides an adventure not found in other corners of the country. All prices are per person.

I LIKE MY KNICKERS DRY

Bungy Bobbing: So there's no jump off the Sky Tower, into the Mt. Eden Crater, or from the Harbour Bridge. There *is* something called the Sky Screamer (☎0800 932 8649), at Victoria St. and Albert St., which hurtles its 2 or 3 passengers 160km in 1½min. and then lets them bob up and down for another 5min. Open daily 11am-10pm. $35.

Cycling: Auckland Adventures (☎379 4545, mobile 025 855 856) leads full-day area tours, some of which include several hours of mountain biking, often downhill ($89, under 12 $44.50). **Adventure Cycles,** 1 Fort Ln. (☎649 309 5566, 0800 335 566), rents mountain bikes ($25-35 per day, $90-140 per week), touring bikes ($18 per day, $70 per week), and tandem touring bikes ($25 per day, $90 per week).

Motorbiking: 4 Track Adventures (☎420 8104, 0800 487 225), 30min. north of the city ($20 pick-up available), guides 4-wheel motorbike "safaris" through Woodhill Forest and nearby beaches (1hr. trip $95, 2hr. $155, 3hr. $195).

Rock Climbing: Birkenhead Indoor Climbing Wall, (☎418 4109), on. Onewa Rd. near Birkenhead War Memorial Park; take any North Shore-bound bus from Queen St. 10m high, with a 6m overhang. Open daily 10am-10pm. $13; shoe rental $5.

Skydiving: Mercer Skydiving Centre (☎373 5778, 0800 865 867), 35min. south of the city (return shuttle $20). Tandem jump from 12,000 ft. $250, from 10,000 ft. $220. 10% student discount.

I'D PREFER THEM WET

Canyoning: AWOL Adventures (☎630 7100) runs 6hr. tours that involve 3hr. exploring the canyons around Kitekite Falls ($125). **Canyonz** (☎636 7209, mobile 025 294 7724) runs full-day trips that include 3hr. in the Blue Canyons ($135, under 15 $105).

Jet Skiing: Jet Ski Tours (☎486 1886, mobile 025 711 145). 1½hr. $100.

Kayaking: Auckland Wilderness (☎813 3399, mobile 025 582 409) leads full-day trips to Rangitoto Island ($85) as well as 5hr. evening excursions ($75). **The Little Adventure Company** (☎ 0508 529 257, mobile 021 631 376) also runs guided tours in the Auckland Harbor and Hauraki Gulf (half-day $55, full-day $80).

Sailing: The sails in the City of Sails don't cater to those living on the cheap—most tourist boats cost hundreds of dollars a day. Sailing in Auckland is always expensive, but the following options do offer somewhat less pricey chances for visitors to come aboard. Designed to sail in the 1995 America's Cup (but not finished in time), the *NZL 40*, operated by **Viking Cruises** (☎ 0800 724 569), now makes several 2hr. outings daily ($75, under 14 $65). **H₂O Adventures** (☎mobile 021 132 1434) offers a more intimate, charter-esque experience on the *Alacalufe* for a min. of 2 and a max. of 6 people (4hr. $40, 7hr. $80, overnight $100). **LOGAN Ponsonby Sailing School** (☎376 0245) conducts 20hr. dinghy-sailing courses, primarily on weekends ($250).

Swimming: The 60m salt-water pool at Parnell Baths (☎373 3561), on Judges Bay Rd. overlooking the harbor in Parnell, has the most pleasant location. Open Nov.-Mar. M-F 6am-8pm, Sa-Su 8am-8pm. $4.50, under 17 $2.

Swimming with Dolphins: Operating in conjunction with research projects, **Dolphin Explorer** (☎237 1466) runs daily 4-5hr. trips through the Hauraki Gulf Maritime Park ($90, under 15 $45); if the boat doesn't encounter any dolphins or whales, you can take another trip for free.

Vineyard Touring: Who knew that there were almost 20 wineries in the mainland Auckland area? **Aotearoa Van Coach Tours** (☎834 5363, mobile 025 764 759) conducts half-day trips to 4 of them ($59). **Auckland Wine Trail Tours** (☎630 1540, mobile 025 227 4924) also does 4-vineyard trips ($65) as well as full-day tours that visit 6 ($95).

🖫 DAYTRIPS

NORTH SHORE

To the north of Auckland proper lies the North Shore, home to family beaches, suburban shopping centers, and vast numbers of commuters. The area was quickly populated after the completion of the Harbour Bridge in 1959. As the suburbs spread, the bridge soon became so clogged with traffic that the city contracted a Japanese company to come and install extensions on either side of the bridge, expanding the meager four lanes to eight. Today, Devonport's Victorian charm and Takapuna's stunning natural beauty deserve a day's visit. To Takapuna and beyond, the coast is characterized by curving sandy beaches separated into little bays by outcroppings of basaltic tuft. Some bays are protected areas, and huge fines (up to $5000) for pocketing shellfish are enforced; check the posted signs.

DEVONPORT. This small town with salty sea air and multi-colored Victorian rooftops feels miles away from urban Auckland, yet it's only a 12min. ferry ride away. Keep in mind, however, that although Devonport is a wallet-friendly daytrip, accommodation prices are astronomical; backpackers had best catch the last ferry back to Auckland—or face the pricey consequences. Most of Devonport's charming restaurants and cafes sit on Victoria Rd., the main street leading from the ferry wharf. Available to answer queries and direct the aimless, the chummy info hive of the **Devonport Visitor Information Centre** stands in the shade of "Albert," the Moreton Bay fig tree. A jaunt to any of the three extinct volcanoes in town promises an unparalleled sight; especially stunning panoramic 360° views can be seen from **Mt. Victoria,** accessible by foot or car. (Info center: Victoria Rd., only 1min. from the ferry, adjacent to the library. ☎446 0677; fax 446 0698. Open daily 9am-5pm. Devonport accessible by Fullers ferry ☎367 9111. Departs daily 6:15am-11pm, F-Sa until 1am. $8, $4 children.)

BEACHES. Just north of North Head, **Cheltenham Beach** (a protected area), and **Torpedo Bay,** closer to Devonport, are swimmable two hours before and after high tide, when swimmers are able to see (and avoid) the dangerous rocks. For a pleasant swim at any tide, head to **Narrow Neck Beach,** around the Takapuna Head, or **Devonport Beach,** near town. Also at Narrow Neck Beach is the recently restored **Fort Takapuna Historic Reserve,** home to a group of old military buildings and a beautiful park. Both Narrow Neck Beach and the summit of North Head afford milliondollar views of the **Hauraki Gulf** and the coastline. **St. Leonard's Beach,** which slides into **Takapuna Beach's** black sand, creates an immense playground for all. A coastal walk from Takapuna north through **Thorne Bay** to **Milford Beach** features awesome volcanic rock formations and the manmade Algie's Castle with battlements from the 1920s. Nearby **Long Bay** is a regional park and marine reserve. Jutting off into the open seas from the top of Long Bay is the lofty **Whangaparaoa Peninsula,** where you can bask in the beautiful views of Gulf Harbour.

OTHER NORTH SHORE ACTIVITIES. Town tours in Devonport are popular, particularly the **Devonport Explorer Bus,** that provides a reasonable, if not unique, mode of transport. You can also see Devonport for 45min. with **Tuk-Tuk Tours**—you'll know the Thai three-wheeler when you see it. Windsurfing is also popular on the North Shore, especially in the volcanic crater of **Lake Pupuke,** a clear blue lake with a reedy shoreline. (Explorer: ☎357 6366, 0800 868 774. Departs from the wharf daily every hr. 10:25am-3:25pm; $22, including ferry return. Tuk-Tuk: ☎0800 428 858. $15.)

THE WAITAKERE RANGES

Gorgeous and undertouristed, the Waitakeres await those exhausted by Auckland's wild nightspots, harbors, and shops. Lying between **Manukau Harbour** and the **Tasman Sea,** hundreds of acres can be explored on over 250km of walking and tramping tracks. The **Arataki Visitor Centre** on Scenic Dr. can help you plan your route. Getting there without a car is difficult, though buses from the city go to Titirangi, 6km down the road. Hitchhiking in these parts is also a dim prospect. (☎817 8470; fax 817 5656. Open daily 9am-5pm; Jul.-Aug. M-F 10am-4pm, Sa-Su 9am-5pm.)

BEACHES. If you have a car, driving along the coastline offers access to some amazing beaches. **Karekare,** the setting for the film *The Piano* (see **Film** p. 66), is the most scenic; a great waterfall is accessible by a short walk from the carpark on the approach to the beach. A bit farther north, the black-sanded **Piha** offers excellent surf but is often more crowded. At the southern tip right at the entrance to Manukau Harbor from the ocean is **Whatipu,** which has great fishing and cool caves accessible from the beach. Farther inland along the harbor, **Cornwallis** provides calmer waters well suited for swimming and a beach perfect for picnics. **Muriwai Beach** and its famed gannet bird colony are another nearby favorite (see below).

TOURS. Seven-hundred birds—they're staying at **Muriwai Beach. Auckland Adventures** organizes trips to Muriwai Beach—including the rare **gannet** bird colony—and Mt. Eden at a relaxed pace. Trekking options include the afternoon or wilderness adventure, while the mountain bike adventure covers more ground. (☎379 4545; mobile 025 855 856. Treks 5-8hr., $60-89. Mountain biking 8hr., $89.)

AUCKLAND

HAURAKI GULF ☎ 09

A sparkling antidote to urban exhaustion, the Hauraki Gulf has 57 islands of varying terrain and degrees of settlement. These islands distinguish themselves from Auckland in scenery and in attitude. Volcanic Rangitoto makes an educational daytrip, while Waiheke harbors an artsy vacation community, both ringed by long stretches of sand. Great Barrier Island lacks electricity, traffic, and crowds—even its stunning beaches lie empty. Another island worth a look is **Tiritiri Matangi,** an uninhabited bird and plant sanctuary that flaunts the many reasons the gulf has been protected as a marine park since February 2000. **Fullers Auckland** runs round-trip boats from Auckland that allow for a day on Tiritiri. (☎367 9102. 1¼hr.; Th-Su 9am, boats depart Tiritiri 3:30pm; $45, under 15 $23.) DOC administers a **bunkhouse** on the island, which is often booked months in advance. (☎476 0010. $20, under 15 $15.) Of course, if it's the gulf itself that interests you, **Fullers** runs a "Coffee Cruise Harbour Explorer," which stops at Rangitoto Island and Devonport. (☎367 9102. 1¾hr.; 3 per day; $30, under 15 $15.)

RANGITOTO ISLAND

Te Rangi i totongia a Tamatekapua ("The Day the Blood of Tamatekapua was Shed") is a long name for a little volcano, so the mount off Auckland's coast is known simply as Rangitoto. Since 1854, when the Crown grudgingly shelled out £15 for what seemed a mere lump of rock, it's been a premier picnic spot for Auckland daytrippers. Beyond picnics, the island's most popular activity is the **Summit Walk** (return 2hr.), which winds through lunar-like fields of volcanic rock and arboreal glens. During hot summers walking the track is akin to hiking on charcoal briquettes, so be sure to wear solid shoes and a hat. At the top you can take a peek into the perfectly inverted cone of the **crater.** The **lava caves** are a side trail option (return 20min.); bring a flashlight and wear durable clothes if you plan to explore these jagged passageways formed by hot lava flowing through cooling volcanic rock. **Fullers** runs a **Volcanic Explorer Tour** for those who don't want to walk the whole track; the narrated 4WD tram ride drops passengers at the base of the 900m boardwalk that leads to the summit. (2hr.; 2-3 per day, when the ferries from Auckland come in; $59, under 15 $30, including round-trip ferry journey.) Cruise and volcanic explorer packages are available ($49, children $25). Another worthwhile walk, the stroll down from the summit to **Islington Bay** yields secluded swimming beaches. The Auckland **DOC office,** in the ferry building at Quay St. and Queen St., has information on local tracks. (☎379 6476. Open M-F 10am-6pm, Sa 10am-3pm.)

Some folks **kayak** to Rangitoto (see **Auckland: Activities** p. 95), but most take the ferry. **Fullers** runs to Rangitoto Wharf from Auckland's Pier 3. (☎367 9102. 45min.; 2-3 daily; return $20, under 15 $10.) The area's only **campground** is located at Home Bay on adjacent Motutapu Island. Rudimentary facilities there include toilets, running water, and barbecue sites ($5 per night, children $2; book with the DOC).

WAIHEKE ISLAND

Waiheke's population of 6800 artists, retirees, and commuters more than quadruples in peak seasons. With a gorgeous coastline, an internationally renowned Easter jazz festival, rolling hills (home to almost 30 top-notch vineyards), a happening art scene, and a vital community spirit, Waiheke offers something for everyone.

▮ TRANSPORTATION

Ferries: Fullers Auckland (☎367 9102) departs Auckland's Pier 2 or Waiheke's Matiatia Bay (35min.; 9-15 per day; return $23, under 15 $11); their **Link Ferry** travels between **Auckland's ferry building** and **Matiatia Bay** via **Devonport** (40min.; 2-4 per day; return $17). **Pacific Ferries** (☎303 1741) departs Pier 2 or Matiatia Bay (35min.; Nov.-Jan. daily, Feb.-Oct. Sa-Su, every 2hr. 8am-9pm; return $17, under 15 $10).

Public Transportation: Fullers Waiheke Bus Co. (☎372 8823) meets all ferries and loops around the island. $1-3, all-day pass $7 or $5 with ferry ticket; under 15 half price. Fullers also offers an Island Explorer Tour, which includes return ferry, a 1½hr. island tour, and an all-day bus pass good on any island bus (daily 10am; $45, under 15 $21.50).

Taxis: Waiheke Taxi (☎372 8038) and **24hr. Dial-a-Cab** (☎372 9666).

Car and Scooter Rental: Waiheke Rental Cars (☎372 8635), at Matiatia Wharf car park. Cars $45 per day plus $0.50 per km. Scooters $40 per day. Open daily 8am-5pm. **Waiheke Auto Rentals** (☎372 8998), also at the wharf carpark. Cars $45 per day plus $0.50 per km. Open daily 8am-5pm.

Bike Rental: Wharf Rats Bike Hire (☎372 7937), at Matiatia Wharf. Half-day $15, full-day $25. Open daily dawn-dusk. **Attitude Rentals** (☎372 8767; mobile 025 728 767) rents "motor-assisted" bikes. Half-day $35, full-day $40. Open daily dawn-dusk.

Hitchhiking: Though *Let's Go* does not recommend it, Waiheke islanders are a charitable bunch, though winding roads can make it hard to find a good spot to stop.

✴🛈 ORIENTATION AND PRACTICAL INFORMATION

The passenger ferry docks at **Matiatia Bay,** from where it is a 1km uphill walk (or a 5min. bus ride; see **Public Transportation,** above) to **Oneroa,** the island's main town and the only one with an interesting strip of shops and cafes (along Oceanview Rd.). Other island centers include **Surfdale** and **Ostend** (both southeast of Oneroa, roughly 2 and 4km, respectively), **Onetangi** (7km directly east), and **Palm Beach** (4km northeast). All of these towns inhabit the western half of the 92 sq. km island; east of Onetangi, settlement drops off dramatically.

Visitors Center: Waiheke Island Visitor Information Centre, 2 Korora Rd. (☎372 9999; fax 372 9919), in the Artworks Centre in Oneroa. **Island maps** $1. **Luggage storage** $2 per bag. Open daily 9am-5pm.

Currency Exchange: BNZ, 110C Oceanview Rd. (☎372 1056), in Oneroa. **ATM.** Open M, Th-F 9am-4:30pm, Tu-W 9:30am-4:30pm.

Police: (☎372 8777), on Waikare Rd. in Oneroa. **Emergency** ☎111.

Medical Services: Centers in **Ostend** (☎372 5005) and **Oneroa** (☎372 8756).

Internet Access: Surfdale.com (☎372 5010), in the Surfdale Arcade on Miami Ave. in Surfdale. $7 per hr. Open M-Sa 9am-9pm. **The Lazy Lounge Cafe** (see **Food,** p. 100).

🛏🏕 ACCOMMODATIONS AND CAMPING

All of the following are long (40min.-2hr.), hilly walks from the ferry docks. Luckily, island bus service (see **Transportation: Public Transportation,** above) is cheap and comprehensive; ask bus drivers when to get off. **Campers** can head out to the little-visited **Whakanewha Regional Park** campground on the southeastern corner. (Reservations required; call Parksline at ☎303 1530. $5 per person, under 18 $2.)

◪ **Hekerua Lodge,** 11 Hekerua Rd. (☎/fax 372 8990; hekerua@ihug.co.nz), in Little Oneroa. This cabin house is tucked into an acre of native bush, just 15min. from the beach. Its sleek decks and adjacent stone swimming pool define relaxation. Occasional BBQ breakfast $10. Linen $5; laundry $3; Internet. Spa $5 per 30min. Dorms $18; singles $30; great doubles from $55; tent sites $15. Discounts on long stays.

Palm Beach Backpackers, 54 Palm Rd. (☎372 8662), is close enough to hear the surf break. The expansive lawn, bright kitchen, and well-stocked game room have more than enough space for the fully grown. Kayaks, boogie boards, and snorkeling gear for rent. Linen $5. Key deposit $10. Dorms $16-20; doubles $40-49; tent sites $12-15, depending on demand.

Waiheke Island Youth Hostel YHA (☎/fax 372 8971; robb.meg@bigfoot.com) on Seaview Rd. in Onetangi, a steep 4min. climb up from the beach. Nothing could beat the view from the picnic tables outside. Check yourself in if nobody's there. Mountain bikes. 2-person dorms $18, $15 during stays of 4 or more nights; doubles from $40.

⬛ FOOD

Ostend's **Woolworths** can take the sting out of Waiheke's pricey restaurant scene (☎372 2103; open daily 7am-9pm); there are also small general stores in every town center.

Pizzeria and Caffe da Stephano (☎372 5309), at the corner of Miami Ave. and Hamilton Rd. in Surfdale. Stephano used to work at a tire shop before he started selling pizzas, on the side. More popular than the tires, the pizzas remain—some islanders describe Stephano's as "the only place to eat on Waiheke." Pizza $12-20. Pasta $12-17. Open Dec.-Apr. daily 10am-2:30pm and 5:30-9, May-Nov. Tu-Su 5:30-9.

The Lazy Lounge Cafe, 139 Oceanview Rd. (☎372 5132), in Oneroa. Chill restaurant by day, Waiheke's only dance club by (weekend) night. Brief but eclectic menu includes nachos ($12), burgers ($11), and spicy Thai chicken salad ($14). **Internet access** $10 per hr. Open daily 8am-10pm (at least).

Vino Vino, 153 Oceanview Rd. (☎372 9888), behind Oneroa Delicatessen in Oneroa. Sweeping views from the terrace in summer and an open fire in winter lend an atmosphere worth paying for. Mains $18-24. Open daily noon-9pm (until 11 when busy).

Oneroa Delicatessen, 153 Oceanview Rd. (☎372 7659), in Oneroa. This tiny streetside spot serves a rotating menu of salads, sandwiches, soups, and pastas, all chock full of fresh vegetables ($6-12). Cakes $4.50. Open M-Sa 8am-5pm.

⬛⬛ SIGHTS AND ACTIVITIES

The **Waiheke Island Jazz Festival** (☎ 0800 529 933; www.waihekejazz.co.nz) takes the island by storm every Easter weekend. Now in its 11th year, the festival features the best of Kiwi jazz as well as big names from Europe and, especially, New Orleans. With five days and 22 venues, it's usually possible to get tickets to something, though true aficionados may want to plan several months in advance to get tickets ($25-35) for the best shows—not to mention to book a bed. Less internationally renowned though no less popular on the island, the **Ostend Market** reappears every week at the corner of Ostend Rd. and Belgium St. in Ostend. Local vendors hawk pottery, organic foods, massages, books, and tarot card readings (among other things), and some of proceeds go to the Waiheke Community Childcare Centre. (Open Sa. 8am-1pm.) Meanwhile, one night out of every 28, a group of islanders gathers at Palm Beach for **Full Moon Drumming,** a celebration of music, the moon, and an island of people who appreciate them.

BEACHES. Beaches surround Waiheke, but only those on the island's northern side are white sand. Just downhill from the town of the same name, **Oneroa Beach** is undeniably convenient; a bit farther east, playground-adjacent Little Oneroa Beach is popular with families. Between them lie two lovely **isolated coves,** beach-accessible at low tide (at high tide, follow the paths over the rocks). **Palm Beach** is another well-loved spot, though it's **Onetangi Beach,** the island's largest stretch of sand, that draws the most sunbathers. Flout tanlines at the western (to the left if you're facing the water), "clothing optional" ends of both of these beaches.

THE ARTS. Waiheke's creative nerve center is the **Artworks Centre,** 2 Korora Rd. in Oneroa, home to the Waiheke Community Art Gallery (☎372 9907; open daily 10am-4pm), which displays the varied works of New Zealand artists, and the Waiheke Community Theatre (☎372 2941), which brings the best of the West End and Broadway to the Hauraki Gulf. *Art on Waiheke* a free brochure available at the visitors center, includes a map of the island's two dozen other galleries. **Ananda Tours** visits the artist in his natural habitat—his studio. The $50 tour price includes a glass of Waiheke wine. (☎372 7530 or 021 471 355. Tour 4hr.)

KAYAKING. Gulf Adventures has bred at least one champion (the owners' son is one of New Zealand's top two) and now offers guided trips and freedom rentals, in single kayaks only. (☎372 7262, mobile 021 667 262. Rentals $45 per day, including all transport so you needn't double back. 1-3hr. tours $35-55, depending on number of people. $5 backpacker discount.) **Ross Adventures** runs guided tours at all hours. (☎372 5550. Half-day $60, full-day $110, 3hr. night trip $60.)

HORSEBACK RIDING. Shepherd's Point Riding Centre conducts rides and lessons for all experience levels. (☎372 8104. 2hr. beach ride $60, full-day trip $100.) **Club Waiheke** runs tours aimed at beginners—their $49 Scenic Circle Tour includes a lesson and a 1hr. ride, at a walk only. (☎372 6565, 0800 800 6565.)

WINE TASTINGS AND TOURS. There are 26 vineyards on Waiheke Island; several regularly open to the public for tours and tastings: **Camana Farm** (☎372 7257; tastings Dec.-Jan. W-Su 11am-4pm, Feb.-Nov. Sa-Su 11am-4pm, $5 for 2 wines), **Stonyridge Vineyard** (☎372 8822; 45min. tours Sa-Su 11:30am, $10), and **Te Whau Vineyard** (☎372 7191; tastings Nov.-Mar. W-M 11am-5pm, Apr.-Sept. Sa-Su 11am-4:30pm, $3 per wine); call for directions. **Fullers' Vineyard Explorer tour** visits three vineyards. (☎367 9102. 3hr.; Nov.-Mar. daily, Apr.-Oct. Sa-Su. $65, includes return ferry.) **Waiheke Tours** visits two to four wineries in its half-day tours. (☎372 7262, mobile 021 667 262. $25-50, depending on number of people.) **Jaguar Tours** tours to your choice of one, two, or three vineyards. (☎372 7312. 1 vineyard $18, 2 $24, 3 $34.)

WALKS. Two free visitors center pamphlets outline walking routes on Waiheke; *Whakanewha Regional Park Visitors Guide* includes a map of 270 hectares in the southeastern part of the island, while *Waiheke Island Walkways* describes paths elsewhere on Waiheke. History buffs will appreciate the hike to **Stony Batter** (return 3hr.), a reserve at the remote northeast end of the island that served as a fortress during WWII, described in *Stony Batter*, yet another free pamphlet available at the visitors center.

GREAT BARRIER ISLAND

The largest and most remote of the Hauraki Gulf islands, Great Barrier (pop. 1200) maintains few connections with the modern technology. The island is its own isolated world—one that lacks electricity and banks and possesses a decidedly unique weather pattern. It is also a a nature lover's dream, with deep forests and marshlands covering the terrain, silky white beaches breaking up the rocky coast, and blissful quiet blanketing each night.

▐ TRANSPORTATION

Getting to Great Barrier is no problem, but getting around Great Barrier is generally rather costly (bussing, renting a car) or rather slow (hitching, walking).

Flights: Great Barrier Airlines (☎256 6500, 0800 900 600) from Claris Airport to: **Auckland** (30min.; 3-5 per day; $99, return $189); **Whangarei** (30min.; F, Su; $99, return $189); and **Whitianga** (30min.; F, Su; $99, return $189). **Great Barrier Xpress** (☎0800 222 123) flies to **Auckland** (35min.; at least 3 per day; $99, $169 return).

Ferries: Subritzky Line (☎373 4036) operates the *M.V. Sealink* between **Auckland's Wynyard Wharf** and **Tryphena** (3½hr.; Su-M and W-F; return $75, students $45). **Fullers Auckland** (☎367 9102) runs between **Auckland's Pier 2** and **Tryphena, Whangaparapara**, and/or **Port Fitzroy** (2½hr.; F and Su; return $99, under 15 $49.50). The Stray Possum Lodge (see **Accommodations** below) offers a number of fly-ferry-bus **combination passes** ($155-235), a good value for those also traveling to Northland and/or the Coromandel; all originate in Auckland and can be used in either direction.

Taxis and Shuttles: Bob's Island Tours (☎429 0988) offers a shuttle service that meets all ferries ($5 to Tryphena town, $15 to Claris) and a **24hr.** taxi service ($30 from Tryphena wharf to Claris, $100 from the wharf to Port Fitzroy). The Stray Possum Lodge's

Stray Bus Service travels from Tryphena to Claris ($10) and back again 5-6 times per day; their Possum Pursuits Activities Passes (see **Accommodations** p. 102) allow for unlimited rides (1 day $25, 3 days $45).

Car Rental: Better Bargain Rentals (☎ 429 0092). $75 per day.

Bike Rental: Available as part of The Stray Possum Lodge's Possum Pursuits Activities Pass (see **Accommodations** below).

Hitchhiking: Though *Let's Go* does not recommend it, when there's traffic, it often stops to pick up hitchers—when there's traffic being the operative part of the sentence.

◆ ⚡ ORIENTATION AND PRACTICAL INFORMATION

Large and with few roads, Great Barrier is not difficult to navigate. Port Fitzroy in the north is the island's biggest settlement, but most backpacker activity takes place on the southern half of the island, around **Claris** (home to the airfield) and, farther south, **Tryphena** (home to the ferry docks). Tryphena encompasses the subtowns of Mulberry Grove and Pa Beach. Northwest of Claris, **Whangaparapara** is the island's other significant outpost. There is very little electricity (almost none after 10pm), so bring a **flashlight** and/or **candles.**

Visitors Centers: Great Barrier Island Visitor Centre (☎ 429 0033), near the Claris airfield. Open Sept.-Mar. M-F 9am-4pm, Sa-Su 9:30am-2pm, Apr.-Aug. M-F 10am-3pm, Sa 10am-noon. **Fullers Information Office** (☎ 429 0004), in Pa Beach. Open daily Christmas-Easter 8am-5pm. **DOC Field Centre** (☎ 429 0044), at Akapoua Bay in Port Fitzroy. Open M-F 9am-5pm.

Laundromat: Sunset Lodge (☎ 429 0051), in Mulberry Grove. Open Tu-Su 8am-2pm.

Police: (☎ 429 0343), on Kaitoki-Awana Rd. in Claris.

Pharmacy: Great Barrier Pharmacy (☎ 429 0006), just outside Claris. Open Nov.-Mar. M-Sa 9am-1pm, Apr.-Oct. M-F 9-noon.

Medical Services: Community Health Centre (☎ 429 0356), in Claris by the airfield.

Internet Access: Email Internet Cafe, 59 Blackwell Dr. (☎ 429 0551), in Tryphena. $10 per hr. Open daily 9am-5pm.

Post Office: (☎ 429 0242), on Hector Sanderson Rd. in Claris. Open Nov.-Mar. daily 8:30am-4pm, Apr.-Oct. M-Sa 9am-1pm.

🏠 🏚 ACCOMMODATIONS AND CAMPING

Only December and January draw hostel-filling crowds. Accommodations can arrange transport from the ferry docks or airport. **DOC** maintains six **campsites** ($7, under 15 $3.50), a backcountry hut ($10, under 15 $5), and an eight-person **cottage** (Oct.-Apr. $50 for 2, May-Sept. $30; each extra person $10) near Port Fitzroy.

Pohutukawa Lodge (☎ 429 0211; PLodge@xtra.co.nz), in Pa Beach. Sweet country-style rooms beside a sunny garden. Near shops. (Good) musicians can sing or play at the **Currach Irish Pub**—owned by the same Irish-Kiwi couple—next door for a free stay. Dorms $17; triples or quads with bath $95.

The Stray Possum Lodge (VIP) (☎ 429 0109, 0800 767 786; info@straypossum.co.nz), in Tryphena. Free transfer from wharf. Its **Possum Pursuits Activities Pass,** also available to non-guests, includes bus transport around the island and use of mountain bikes, boogie boards, and snorkeling equipment. Bar open nightly 6-10:30pm. Dorms $18 ($17 VIP); doubles $52; private unit $99; tent sites $12.

The Crossroads Backpackers and Internet Cafe (☎ 429 0889; xroads@ihug.co.nz.), in Claris. Food and hot springs are within walking distance; the owners shuttle people to the beach. Free linen. Internet. Dorms $17-20; singles $30; doubles $40.

Medlands Beach Backpackers (☎ 429 0320; tim-mbb@ihug.co.nz), between Claris and Tryphena. Medlands Beach is just a 5min. walk away. Free boogie boards, bicycles, and Internet. Dorms $20; doubles $50-70 depending on demand; tent sites $10.

FOOD

There are small, **groceries** in Mulberry Grove, Pa Beach, Claris, Whangaparapara, and Port Fitzroy; they cost significantly more than in Auckland.

Claris Texas Cafe (☎ 429 0811). The island's most inventive fare, dishes such as beef in black bean sauce with egg fried rice ($10) are hearty but not Texan. Mains $7-12. Open daily at least 9am-4pm (and as long as 8am-8pm in the busiest weeks).

The Currach Irish Pub (☎ 429 0221), in Pa Beach. A pub with an emphasis on food, it occupies one of the original homesteads in Tryphena. Th night jam sessions are a great local event. Burgers $6.50-10.50. Mains $12-20. Open Tu-Su 4pm-closing.

The Cruisy Cafe (☎ 429 0997), in Pa Beach. Standard bakery treats. Sausage roll $1.90. Vegetable sandwich $4. Small apple pie $3. Open Aug.-June Tu-Sa 10am-5pm.

◐ 🜲 SIGHTS AND ACTIVITIES

The Barrier's main draws are its gorgeous beaches and untrammeled nature—more than half the island's land belongs to DOC. With its graceful dunes, sapphire sea, and blissful breezes, **Medlands Beach** is the island's most popular (which means 20 people in the height of summer), though **Kaitoke, Awana, Haratonga,** and **Whangapoua Beaches** are just as lovely and secluded. All of these lie along the east coast and are noted for their surf. The west coast beaches are calmer, more mundane, and popular among yachts. Those in **Tryphena Harbour**—at Puriri Bay, Pa Beach, and Mulberry Grove—are good for snorkeling. **Aotea Kayak Adventures** runs a variety of guided kayak tours and freedom rentals. (☎ 429 0664. 2hr. trip $30; 4-5hr. trip with snorkeling $55; 6hr. trip with fishing $75; night trip $50. Rental $35 per day.) **GBI Adventure Horsetreks** leads riding trips. (☎ 429 0274. 1hr. farm ride $30; 2hr. beach ride $50.) Great Barrier's network of rugged roads also makes for great **mountain biking;** the well-graded Forest Rd., which runs between Whangaparapara and Kaiarara and is closed to all non-DOC vehicles, is one route of note. (See **Transportation** p. 101.) The easy **Kaitoke Hot Springs Track** (return 1½hr.) leads to a set of bathing pools. The main one is formed by a dam at the junction of two rivers, while smaller pools of varying temperatures lie up the left-hand stream. Mmm-mm, smell that sulphur. The **Te Ahumata Track** (return 1½hr.), also known as the "White Cliffs Walk" for the quartz crystals in stream beds along the way, climbs gradually to a 398m summit that offers expansive views of the ocean, Mt. Hobson, and the Coromandel. Significantly more challenging, the **Kaiarara** and **Palmers Tracks** (return 5hr. in conjunction) ascend steeply through untouched subalpine forest to the island's highest point, the 621m **Mt. Hobson (Hirakimata).** The visitors center and DOC office can provide **directions,** as well as a listing of the Barrier's tracks.

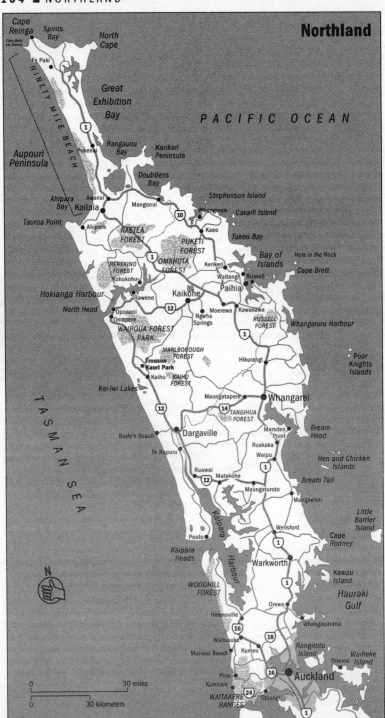

Northland

NORTHLAND

Northland is an enchanting, semi-subtropical world of dramatic cliffs, and lengthy beaches. Home to the first landings of legendary explorers Kupe and Captain Cook, this area is rich with the history of New Zealand's European and Maori cultures. The hauntingly empty beaches of the Aupouri Peninsula and Cape Reinga, the sheltered beauty of the Kaipara and Hokianga Harbours, and the isolated interior are greatly free from tourism, and provide a much needed respite from the long-toothed trappings of predictability and convenience.

⧉ NORTHLAND HIGHLIGHTS

OVER the heads of tourists, ancient kauri tower in **Waipoua Forest Park** (see p. 120).

IN romantic **Russell,** pack a picnic and enjoy a quiet day on the bay (see p. 113).

AROUND the **Bay of Islands,** a marine paradise tempts visitors to swim with its dolphins, kayak among its mangroves, and sail between its isles (see p. 108).

▆ TRANSPORTATION IN NORTHLAND

Rent a car if you have the means; it will give you the freedom to explore the **Twin Coast Discovery Highway** (SH1, SH10, and SH12) at your own pace, especially the Western and interior regions which tend to be hard to access. Keep an eye on fuel levels, as **petrol pumps are few and far between** when away from tourist towns. If you travel by bus, strongly consider buying a pass that lets you travel at your discretion. Although *Let's Go* doesn't recommend thumbing, **hitchhikers** on the east coast north of the Bay of Islands encounter sparse traffic and, consequently, long waits; on the west coast, SH12 is the road less traveled, but the locals are more accommodating. Campers should note that backcountry hut passes do not apply in Northland; you must book in advance for all huts and lodges (though empty beds in winter make reservations less essential).

WHANGAREI   ☎ 09

The journey to Whangarei, a 2hr. drive north of Auckland, is a spectacular escape into lush hills. Loosely translated from Maori, Whangarei (FAHNG-a-ray) means "cherished harbor," a name honoring the local waters that have brought food, recreation, and profit to the region for years. Whangarei (pop. 47,000) has a charm all its own. In addition to numerous parks, helpful local services, and world-class activities, Whangarei has a lively nightlife that is best described as diversion without debauchery.

▆ TRANSPORTATION

Buses: Coaches roll into the **bus stop** at **Northland Coach and Travel,** 11 Rose St. Open M-F 8am-5pm, Sa-Su 8:30am-2:30pm. **Northliner** (☎438 3206) and **InterCity** (☎439 2653) head to **Auckland** (2hr., 4 per day, $32) and **Kaitaia** (3½hr., 1 per day, $40) via **Paihia** (1hr., 2 per day, $19).

Car Rental: Budget (☎438 7292) and **Hertz** (☎438 9790) have offices on Water St. **Rent-a-Cheepy,** 69 Otaika Rd. (☎438 7373) and **Pegasus Rentals,** 54 Maunu Rd. (☎438 2962; fax 438 8384) offer economy rentals from $35 per day.

Taxis: For a cab, call **Kiwi Carlton Cabs (24hr. ☎438 2299).**

Hitchhiking: Though *Let's Go* doesn't recommend it, hitching to Auckland is reputed to be easiest from the Visitors Bureau in Tarewa Park; those heading to the Bay of Islands often park it on SH1 (Western Hills Rd.) before traffic picks up to 70kph.

▲♬ ORIENTATION AND PRACTICAL INFORMATION

Whangarei wraps around **Whangarei Harbour**, 167km north of Auckland up **SH1** on the east coast. The main drag, **Bank St.**, intersects **Cameron St.** at a pedestrian mall that buzzes during business hours; the surrounding four blocks contain the majority of restaurants and bars. **Hatea Dr.** stretches north from the Basin. Tourists and yachties gravitate toward the **Town Basin** development along the harbor.

Visitors Center: Whangarei Visitor Bureau, 92 Otaika Rd. (☎438 1079; fax 438 2943), in Tarewa Park, at the southern entrance to the city. The **DOC Visitor Centre** (☎/fax 430 2007), inside the Visitor Bureau. Open M-F 8:30am-5pm, Sa-Su 9:30am-4:30pm; Dec. 27 to Jan. 31 daily 8:30am-6:30pm.

Police: (☎430 4500), on Lower Cameron St.

Medical Services: White Cross Accident & Medical Clinic, 121 Bank St. (☎430 0046). Open daily 8am-10pm. **White Cross Pharmacy** (☎/fax 0800 438 7767) is in the same building. Open daily 9am-1:30pm and 2:30-9pm.

Internet Access: At the **library** on Rust Ave. $5 for access card, then $5 per 30min. Open M-F 9am-6pm, Sa 9am-5:30pm.

Post Office: (☎430 2761), on Robert St. Open M-F 8:30am-5pm, Sa 9am-1pm.

♠♠ ACCOMMODATIONS AND CAMPING

Bunkdown Lodge, 23 Otaika Rd. (☎438 8886; fax 438 8826). Super-friendly owners cater to budget guests' every interest from diving to caving. Free pick-up. Two kitchens. Fancy mountain bikes. Internet. Laundry $5. Dorms $17; twins $40; doubles $45.

Whangarei YHA Hostel, 52 Punga Grove Ave. (☎/fax 438 8954; fax 438 9526), off Riverside Dr. in a quiet residential area. An arduous 20min. hike up the hill from the bus station. Large dorms and a spacious lounge. Off-street parking. Reception 8-10am and 5-7pm. Internet. Dorms $16; twins and doubles $36; $3 extra for nonmembers. MC/V.

Central (Hatea) Hostel, 67 Hatea Dr. (☎437 6174; fax 437 6141; centralback@xtra.co.nz). A manageable 10min. walk up Hatea Dr. A tiny hostel with mini-kitchens in the cabins and a lovely garden view. Free pick-up. Kayak rental. Internet. Duvet $2. Laundry $4. Dorms $16; singles $33; doubles $38; double cabin $45. Cash only.

Whangarei Holiday Park, 24 Mair St. (☎437 6856; fax 437 5897), a 25min. walk up Bank St. The clean, basic cabins with outhouse baths are easily overshadowed by their beautiful location. Showers $0.20 per min. Bunks $15; cabins $36; tent sites $10.

♠ FOOD

The **Pak 'N Save**, at the Walton St. Plaza, is cheap and central, making self-catering easy. (☎438 1488. Open M-F 8:30am-8pm, Sa-Su 8:30am-7pm.)

Taste Spud, 3 Water St. (☎/fax 438 1164). This simple joint hits the spot with cheap but filling stuffed potatoes and burritos ($5-6). Open M 9am-8pm, Tu-Th 9am-8:30pm, F 9am-9pm, Sa 11am-2:30pm and 4:30-8:30pm.

Bogarts, 84 Cameron St. (☎438 3088), on the corner of Walton St. Small Uncle Scrooge gourmet pizza ($9) comes with tomato, cheese, and one topping. Open M-Tu 5-10pm, W-Su 12-3:30pm and 5 until late, usually around midnight.

Rin Chin Chilla, 6 Vine St. (☎438 5882). Super nachos for 2 ($9.50); lamb kebab ($6.50). Delivery $3.50. Open M-Su noon-3:30pm, Su-Th 5-9pm, F-Sa 5-10:30pm.

♠ NIGHTLIFE

Although several restaurants and cafes have active bars and weekend dance floors (try **Bank St.**), both **Powder Hound** and **Sound Factory** on Vine St. and **Insomniachs** at Bank and Cameron St. are full-time nightclubs.

Kaos, 21 Bank St. (☎430 0770). The *sub*-woofers at this raw red-walled klub pump *sub*-par electronica, making it more *sub*-urban than its rough city feel would suggest; young-bloods dance like there are no rules. $4 pints. Open M-Th noon-1am, F-Sa noon-3am.

Planet Earth B.C., 27 Bank St. (☎430 8000). Planet Earth is a good spot for couch lounging and some recreational boozing (pint $4). F-Sa nights the usually chill venue turns into a dancefest, which kicks off around 10pm. Pool $1. Bar meals $5-11. Happy Hour M-F 5-6pm and 9-11pm. Open M-Th 11:30am-midnight, F-Sa 11:30am-3am.

Metro Bar, 31 Bank St. (☎430 0446). A great spot for a late-night snack (fries $3.50) to the sounds of your rock 'n' roll favorites. DJs enhance the scene F-Sa 9:30pm-1am, when a younger crowd emerges. Open M 11:30am-7:30pm, Tu-Th 11:30am-late, F 11am-late, Sa 5:30pm-late.

👁 🔖 SIGHTS AND ACTIVITIES

Whangarei's tourist zone is the waterfront area, lovingly known as the **Town Basin,** where eccentric museums and pricey cafes connect via paved walkways. The **Clapham Clock Museum,** begun in 1900, has become a 1600-piece tribute to time-keeping. (☎/fax 438 3993. Open daily 9am-5pm. $5.) Pop into **Di's Dolls,** a 2,000-strong salute to dolls and dollmaking. (☎438 5181. Open M-Sa 9am-4:30pm, Su 10am-4:30pm. $3.50, children $1.50.) A 10min. walk from Bank St. on Rust St. (which turns into Selwyn Ave.) leads to the **Craft Quarry,** a collection of open art studios. (☎438 4125. Quarry open daily 8:15-5pm. Co-op store open daily 10am-5pm; in winter 10am-4pm.)

Leisure Craft Hire (☎437 2509), at the Town Basin, rents rollerblades ($10 per hr.), mountain bikes ($20 per half-day), and the "Orka Aqa Cykl," a self-pro-pelled bike-boat ($15 per hr.). The **Fernery,** at the end of First Ave., is an amaz-ing collection of the world's most peculiar plants. (Open daily 10am-4pm. Free.) The pleasant landscaped grounds in **Cafler Park** and the **Rose Gardens,** next to the Fernery on Water St., make a good spot for picnicking or sunning. For more athletic exploration, numerous 1hr. **walking tracks** wind through the hills that embrace the town; it's best to leave from Mair Park, on Rurumoki St. off Hatea Dr. (pick up the great map from the visitors center). No visitor should miss the 26m **Whangarei Falls,** located only 5km from town off Kiripaka Rd. on the way to Tutukaka. Maori boys have jumped off the dangerous cliff for hundreds of years as a rite of passage.

Those interested in spelunking should contact their hostel host, who can make affordable arrangements to explore the **Abbey Caves.** Or, for a thrilling (if more dear) combo, connect with the folks at **The Bushwacka Experience** for two tours of varying intensity. Both end at the **farm base,** where you can milk cows and shear sheep. (☎434 7839; mobile 025 578 240. 2hr. tour $55. Free pick-up with 1-day notice.) Those who want to venture farther (and have the wheels to take them) should explore the **Whangarei Heads** (a 30-40min. drive from Whan-garei). **Ocean Beach** offers great surf and rocky coastline. Just south, the **Bream Head Scenic Reserve** challenges the fit with a 10hr. walk around the entire 415-hectare reserve or a slightly more manageable 90min. walk to Peach Cove from near Ocean Beach; contact the visitors center for information on the **Whangarei Tramping Club's** 8-bed hut at Peach Cove. **Mount Manaia,** a 1hr. summit hike, dishes out a 360° view; the five "figures" represent legendary Manaia and his family, including his unfaithful wife turning her head away in shame; access from the **Early Settlers Memorial** just past McLeod's Bay.

POOR KNIGHT'S ISLANDS   ☎09

Eleven million years ago, eruptions off the coast of Northland gave birth to a string of islands, including the Poor Knight's Islands 24km off the east coast from Tutukaka. Although the Ngatiwai tribe had long inhabited these islands (calling them the Tawhiti Rahi and Aorangi Islands), a string of invasions and deaths in the early 1800s led the tribe to declare the islands *tapu* (forbidden). Today, landing on the islands without a permit is also *tapu*, but by decree of DOC, not the Maori. Thanks to a dearth of human interference, the islands are a haven for rare creatures, including prehistoric tuatara lizards and giant cat-sized weta grasshoppers.

Today the biggest human draw is world-class **scuba diving; Jacques Cousteau** rated the island area one of the ten best sites in the world. Special mooring buoys off the coast serve as landing points for the scores of scuba, snorkel, and kayak trips run out of Whangarei and the coastal town of **Tutukaka** (30km and 30 min. east of Whangarei). Sea caves both above and below water encourage the proliferation of marine life, making for awesome kayaking and snorkeling among moray eels, stingrays, and subtropical reef fish. There are also two newly sunk dive wrecks. **Dive Tutukaka** runs three boats from the Marina Complex. Dive guides brief divers on the topography of each dive site and where the resident fish like to gather. Free shuttles to and from your accommodations in Whangarei leave at the crack of dawn, so be sure to buy food for breakfast and lunch the day before. (☎ 0800 288 882. Guided dive $160; just tanks and weights $140. Free kayak use.)

BAY OF ISLANDS

The most celebrated visitor, Captain Cook, dropped anchor in 1769, befriended the local Maori, and sent word back to England to set the wheels in motion for permanent European settlement. Not particularly creative, he named the region after the 144 islands that now create little pockets of tranquility and keep local pocketbooks full from tourism. To best appreciate the Bay of Islands, follow Cook's lead—board a boat and discover the spectacular coast for yourself.

PAIHIA ☎ 09

Paihia, the center of commerce in the Bay of Islands, is a lesson in contrasts with an inlet full of green isles abutting a strip full of packed motels. In summer, the low-season population of 3000 skyrockets to nearly 40,000, consuming the bay. Agents around every corner try to entice visitors to cruise, fish, sail, dive, and even zorb, while the friendly and relaxed locals patiently watch the annual feeding frenzy. In spite of the camera-toting hordes, away from the crowd-covered wharf, near-deserted walks along miles of coastline beckon the budget traveler.

⬛ TRANSPORTATION

Buses: Buses arrive at the **Maritime Building.** Both **Northliner Coaches** (☎ 402 7857) and **InterCity** (☎ 357 8400) contract through **Westcoaster,** and run daily to: **Auckland** (3¼hr., 2-3 per day, $42) via **Whangarei** (1¼hr., $18); **Auckland** via **Waipoua,** (7hr., 3 per week, $58); and **Kaitaia** (2¼hr., $28) via **Kerikeri** (30min.,$8).

Ferries: Fullers Passenger Ferry (☎ 402 7421) departs daily for **Russell** (15min., on the half hour, $5). Buy tickets on board or at the Fullers desk in the **Maritime Building.** The **vehicle ferry** departs from Opua (about 10km south of Paihia) for Okiato, (about 8 km south of Russell) every 20min. in summer and every 30min. in winter (5min.; 6:50am-10pm; cars $8, campervans $12, motorcycles $3.50).

Taxis: Haruru Cabs (☎ 402 6292) or **Paihia Taxis and Tours** (☎ 402 5064).

Hitchhiking: Although *Let's Go* doesn't recommend it, hitchhiking to Kerikeri or points north is reportedly best attempted near the rotary at the end of Marsden Rd. To head south, wait at Paihia Rd. at the edge of town.

⚡ 🤚 ORIENTATION AND
PRACTICAL INFORMATION

Marsden Rd. runs along the waterfront and is Paihia's main artery. **Paihia Wharf** is roughly in the middle of town beside the **Maritime Building** and opposite the commercial center of **Paihia Mall. Williams Rd.** and **Bayview Rd.** border the mall, perpendicular to Marsden Rd.

Visitors Center: Information Bay of Islands (☎ 402 7345; fax 402 7314), in the white octagonal pavilion to the left of Paihia Wharf. **Internet** $7 per hr. **24hr. ATM.** Open daily 8am-8pm; in winter 8am-5pm.

Banks: Banks with 24hr. **ATMs** cluster around the Paihia Mall. Open M-F 9am-4:30pm.

Medical Services: Bay View Medical Centre, 7 Bay View Rd. (☎ 402 7132). Open by appointment M-F 9am-5pm. After-hours, the on-duty doctor (☎ 404 0328). **Paihia Pharmacy,** 2 Williams Rd. (☎ 402 7034; fax 402 7342) is open M-Su 8:30am-5pm.

Post Office, 2 Williams Rd. (☎ 402 7800). Open M-F 9am-5pm.

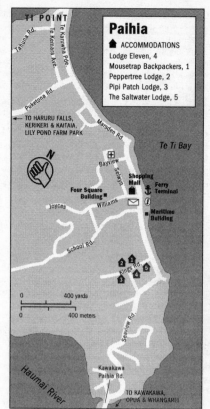

Paihia

🏠 ACCOMMODATIONS
Lodge Eleven, 4
Mousetrap Backpackers, 1
Peppertree Lodge, 2
Pipi Patch Lodge, 3
The Saltwater Lodge, 5

🏠 ACCOMMODATIONS

The number of beds in Paihia has been steadily increasing as a new backpackers springs up almost every summer. In peak season, reservations are essential. Most places lie mere yards apart on **Kings Rd.**, just minutes from the bus station.

▧ **Mousetrap Backpackers (VIP),** 11 Kings Rd. (☎/fax 402 8182), is just a crazy place. The ocean view transforms the otherwise standard porch into the soul of the hostel. Internet. Bike rentals $10. Laundry $4. Reception 8am-9pm. Dorms $16; twins and doubles $40. Discounts in winter.

Peppertree Lodge, 15 Kings Rd. (☎/fax 402 6122; peppertree.lodge@xtra.co.nz). With rooms so sanitary you would swear it was a hotel. Free use of owner's kayaks and tennis rackets. Duvets $1. Laundry $5. Internet. 6- to 8-bed dorms $18 year-round; 4-bed dorms with bath $20, in winter $18; twins and doubles $55/$49; studios $85/$60.

Saltwater Lodge, 14 Kings Rd. (☎ 402 7075, 0800 002 266; fax 402 7240). Superbly clean with a large TV, gym, carpark, free kayaks, tennis racquets, and bikes. Internet. Laundry $4.50. Dorms $19-21; rooms with bunks and king size bed or 2 doubles $100 for 2 in summer, $55 in winter; $110/$75 for 3; $130/$80 for 4.

Pipi Patch Lodge (VIP), 18 Kings Rd. (☎ 402 7111; fax 402 8300). If the giant green Kiwi Experience bus parked in front doesn't tip you of—the **bar** rocks until midnight. Key deposit $20. Internet. Reception 7:30am-8pm, in winter 7:30am-7:30pm. Dorms $19; singles, twins, and doubles $45-55. Discounts in winter.

Lodge Eleven YHA (☎/fax 402 7487; lodgeeleven@hotmail.com), at Kings and MacMurray Rd. Motel-style units are well-maintained by a friendly staff. Laundry $4. Key deposit $10. Internet. Reception 8am-8pm. Check-out 9:30am. Dorms $18; 4-bed dorms $22; singles $40; twins and doubles $55, in winter from $40.

▶ FOOD

Paihia's mall has eating opportunities around every corner. The **Four Square supermarket** is on Williams Rd. (☎402 8002. Open daily 7am-7pm.)

▧ **Kelly Tarlton's Tui Bistro and Cafe** (☎402 7018), next to the Waitangi Rd. bridge. A converted 3-masted sailing ship houses Tarlton's collection of shipwreck artifacts. Dine on deck surrounded by beautiful bay views. Mains $16-35. Open daily 10am-10pm, dinner from 6pm. The museum charges $7 for non-diners, children $2.50.

Poco Loco (☎402 8388), in the mall on Marsden Rd. across from the Wharf. $8 blueberry pancakes and other breakfast treats all day. Splurge on the $17.50 mexican chicken breast. Open daily 8-midnight.

The Swiss Cafe and Grille, 48 Marsden Rd. (☎402 6701) is known for excellent service and vegetarian options. Mains are pricey but tasty ($16-24). Open daily 5:30-10pm, in winter M-Sa 5:30-10pm. Closed mid-June to late July.

Cafe Over the Bay (☎402 8147), in the mall on Marsden Rd. across from the wharf. Friendly service and mellow tunes complement the light menu. Open daily 8am-3:30pm, with extended evening hours in summer.

▣ NIGHTLIFE

Follow the noise and plant yourself at the **Pipi Patch Bar** in the Kings St. hostel of the same name. (Open daily 3-11:30pm. Happy Hour 6:30-7:30pm.) After the staff uproots you at midnight, migrate to the **Lighthouse Black Boat Bar,** on Marsden Rd. in the mall. (☎402 8324. DJ daily from 9:30pm. Pints $3.80. Open daily noon-2am.) The cheapest beers ($2 specials) are at the bar next door, **The Swordfish Club,** in the mall on Marsden Rd. across from the wharf. (☎402 7773. Open daily 4pm-late.)

▣▶ SIGHTS AND ACTIVITIES

The **Maritime Building** by the wharf is the meeting point for many trips and the booking agents who hock them. (Open daily 6:30am-9pm; in winter 7am-7pm.) The visitors center books for all companies thereby achieving relative impartiality, but, consequently, prices are sometimes higher. In summer, expect hordes of fellow tourists—advance booking is key, especially on cruises around the bay or to Cape Reinga. In winter, you may encounter the opposite—fewer trips and many activities with minimum numbers required. Whatever the season, inquire about backpackers' discounts. Many of the trips listed will also pick you up in Russell.

RAINBOW WARRIOR The battered hull of Greenpeace's *Rainbow Warrior* rests offshore in Matauri Bay. After the French resumed nuclear testing in the South Pacific, Greenpeace dispatched the *Rainbow Warrior* to carry out a mission of protest. The French Secret Service got wind of the highly publicized endeavor and, on July 10, 1985, bombed the ship in Auckland Harbour. The event became instant international news. A bird reserve near Thames (see p. 125) was established in memory of Fernando Pereira, the on-board photographer who was killed, and the episode remains a sticking point in Kiwi-Franco relations. The sabotaged ship was moved to the Bay of Islands in 1987 and re-sunk in Matauri Bay, where it has become a playground for subtropical fish and world-class divers alike as part of an eco-friendly maritime park—an unexpected, but not altogether unfitting, end for the environmentalist vessel.

CRUISES. The **Hole in the Rock,** an island at the extreme end of the bay through which boats pass, is the one sight you are almost guaranteed to see. Aside from that, trips offered by different companies vary significantly; don't let price and duration be the sole criteria for your decision. **Fullers,** the ubiquitous ferry company, is the only operator to dock at **Urupukapuka Island,** which has hiking trails not overrun by mainland tourists. Hopping off the morning cruise and back on the afternoon one provides enough time for a hike and a picnic. (*☎ 402 7421. Return 4 hr. Sept.-May 2 per day, June-Aug. daily. $58, children $29.)* Fullers also offers a tame "undersea adventure" with the **Nautilus,** a semi-submersible boat that puts eye level below sea level. (*$12, children $8.)* The **Cream Trip Supercruise** meanders in and out of the smaller bays, delivering mail to the islands as part of one of the few official Royal Mail runs left in New Zealand. (*6½hr. $75, children $38. Sept.-May only.)* **Kings** offers a **Day in the Bay** cruise which includes the Hole in the Rock, an island stop, and a dolphin swim, and a shorter trip which has a wharf-side *powhiri* (see p. 64) and a retelling of Maori myth. (*☎ 402 8288. 6hr. $83, children $45. 3hr. $55/$25.)* **Darryl's Mini Cruises** runs an entertaining evening cruise, with a scrumptious steak dinner included, although they don't make it to the Hole in the Rock. (*☎ 402 7848 or 402 7730. 2½hr. $45. BYO.)* The **Rock** Overnight Eco-Adventure Cruise is an all-in-one, food, cruise, sleep, trek, swim, play, with a 24hr. stay on the floating *Mothership* (*☎ 402 7796 or 0800 762 527. $88.)*

ADVENTURE CRUISES. For those who seek the rush of shooting across the waves, several faster cruising options are available. The **Excitor** travels to the Hole in the Rock at up to 35 knots. (*☎ 402 7020. Return 1½hr. 4 per day 10:30am-6pm; in winter 2 per day. $60, children $30.)* **Mack Attack** is an open air boat that hits up to 45 knots, making the individual seats with belts a necessity. (*☎ 402 8288, 0800 622 528. 1½hr., 4-5 per day, $60. YHA, VIP and ISIC 10% discount.)* **Dolphin Discovery** runs the **Tornado,** which claims its the fastest at over 50 or even 100 knots, which goes all the way out to Cape Brett. (*☎ 402 8234. 1½hr., up to 4 per day. $60.)*

SWIMMING WITH DOLPHINS. Dolphin Discoveries, in the NZ Post Building at the corner of Marsden and Williams St., has been spotting dolphins since 1991 and has the highest success rate. (*☎ 402 8234. $85, children $45.)* Not wanting to miss out on any of the action, **Fullers** has a **Dolphin Encounters** trip. (*☎ 402 7421. 4hr. $85, children $45.)* **Kings** (*☎ 402 8288)* offers dolphin swimming as part of its **Day in the Bay** (see **Cruises** above). For a more personal touch, **Carino** is a 40-foot catamaran and the only yacht licensed to swim with dolphins. Its trip is a steal, offering a full day of sailing, sunning, fishing, bushwalking, and swimming with dolphins for $60. (*☎ 402 8040; mobile 025 933 827. $5 BBQ lunch and on-board bar.)*

SAILING. She's A Lady Charters, which can take you on a day of sailing, snorkeling, and knee-boarding, is a bit of a misnomer, since it's run by the decidedly masculine Caulton brothers. (*☎ 402 8119; mobile 025 964 010. 7-8hr. $65, including lunch.)* **Fullers** operates the **R. Tucker Thompson,** a majestic tall ship that replicates the Captain Cook experience, minus the hardtack and scurvy. (*☎ 402 7421. 7hr. Nov.-Apr. daily $85, children $45, including tea and lunch.)*

FISHING. The good folk at **Charter Pier** are familiar with every fishing operator, handle all the bookings, and will match you with a boat and guide. Generally, trips are 4-6hr. long, and snapper fishing is the most economical. You can also hire self-drive boats. (*Halfway down the wharf on the left. ☎ 402 7127. Around $65 for small boats.)*

KAYAKING. The oft-seen trademark logo of a woman drifting serenely through mangroves belongs to **Coastal Kayakers.** They offer independent kayak rentals, guided kayak tours, package tours, and hard-core wilderness expeditions. **Bay Beach Hire** rents both individual and tandem kayaks. They also have catamarans, windsurfers, and fishing tackle. **Island Kayaks,** based out of the Pipi Patch, offers half-day tours topped off by afternoon tea. (*☎ 402 8105. Kayaks: $10 per hr., half-day $28, full-day $40. Expeditions 2-3 days; Nov.-May; from $110. Bay Beach: On Marsden Rd., opposite the Edgewater Motel. ☎ 402 6078. Kayaks $10 per hr., half-day $25-35. Guided tours $45. Island Kayaks: ☎ 402 7111. 4hr., 1-2 per day, $49.)*

NORTHLAND

FLYING. Salt Air offers a 30min. flight around the Hole and a longer Bay Discovery tour. They also run a pricey tour to Cape Reinga, which catches the Cape before the lunchtime arrival of tour buses. *(Located in a kiosk just to the south of the Maritime Building. ☎ 402 8338, 0800 472 582. Trips $95, $145, and $285 respectively.)* **Flying Kiwi Parasailing** floats the fearless high above the bay, attached to the back of a speed-boat. The highlight of the trip is a simulated free-fall. *(☎ 402 6078. 400m tether $50, 800m tether $60. Book with Bay Beach Rentals.)*

SKYDIVING. SkyHi Tandem Skydive Ltd. go on the highway to the danger zone. Departing from Watea Airfield, they pick-up from accommodations, and from wherever you land, too. *(☎ 402 6744; mobile 025 756 758. 3000m $185, 4000m $235.)*

DIVING. Paihia Dive, on Williams Rd., offers dives to the *Rainbow Warrior*, and the Bay of Islands and Cape Brett reefs. *(☎ 402 7551; fax 402 7110. 2 dives $150, includes full equipment.)*

ON THE GROUND. Bay Beach Hire rents brand-spankin' new mountain bikes to explore the inland hills. *(☎ 402 6078. Half-day $15, full-day $20.)* For a completely unique Paihia experience, visit the **Lily Pond Farm Park.** Activities include horse and pony rides, feeding the animals, milking the cow at noon, a swimming hole, and a bush walk to a small waterfall. *(On Puketona Rd. on the way to Kerikeri. ☎ 402 6099. Open daily from 10am. Closed mid-July-mid-Sept. $5, children $3.)* Slightly less pastoral is **Zorb,** in which screaming loonies can roll down hills in a giant plastic ball. *(On Puketona Rd. 1.5km west of Paihia. ☎ 208 1319. $35.)*

TREKS. At the end of School Rd., 700m west of Pahia, the **Oromahoe Road Traverse** is a 2½hr. loop through regenerating forest to the **Opua Coastal Walk,** which returns to Pahia (another 2hr.). Alternatively, the **Opua Forest Lookout Track** starts at School Rd. and veers off to elevated forest and ocean views (30min. one-way).

FESTIVALS. The **Bay of Islands Jazz & Blues Festival** usually takes place over three days in early August, and features internationally acclaimed musicians as well as local talent. The **Bay of Islands Country Rock Festival** in May attracts thousands.

WAITANGI   ☎ 09

On February 6, 1840, more than 500 Maori, settlers, traders, dignitaries, and missionaries came ashore on the pebbled beach of Waitangi to witness the signing of the most important document in New Zealand's history—the **Treaty of Waitangi** (see p. 57). Today, the Treaty is the focal point of vigorously debated Maori land grievances. The **Waitangi National Reserve** is a remarkably serene and verdant place. (☎ 402 7437. Admission $8, children free. Open daily 8am-5pm.) To reach the reserve from Paihia, follow Marsden Rd. over the Waitangi Bridge, and then head up the rise (30min.). Alternatively, if you have a car, you can take the scenic route and check out **Haruru Falls** on Puketona Rd. on the way. The falls can also be reached via the **Waitangi National Trust Mangrove Walk,** a beautiful 2½hr. stroll from the visitors center. Waitangi's grounds include the **Treaty House,** one of the first architectural results of a British presence in New Zealand. From 1832 to 1844, it was home to watchdog "British Resident," **James Busby** (see p. 57); today it is a museum. To the left of its lush lawn is the **Whare Runanga,** a Maori meeting house for all tribes, constructed in 1940 to celebrate the Treaty's centennial. The world's largest war canoe, *Ngatokimatawhaorua* (35m) is hauled out by 80 warriors and paddled around the bay every February 6th (Waitangi Day).

See the bits and pieces of less fortunate voyages at **Kelly Tarlton's Museum of Shipwrecks,** which floats at the mouth of the Waitangi River by the bridge. The assembly of over 1000 artifacts was salvaged from the watery graves of 20 wrecks (☎ 402 7018. Open 10am-10pm. $7, children $2.50.) Eat there, or at the **Waikokopu Cafe** (☎ 402 6275) on the Treaty Grounds; the beautifully simple glass and wood eatery serves up saucy-named specials like Country Pumpkin Salad ($13.50). Open daily 8am-5pm, plus evenings for dinner in summer.

RUSSELL

☎ 09

On a sunny afternoon in Russell, it's hard to believe that the town was once known as the "Hell Hole of the Pacific," and was notorious for a thriving brothel industry, seedy sailor activity, and Maori-Pakeha clashes. Today, Russell's romantic, small-town charm is a welcome relief (and a short ferry ride) from the hubbub of Paihia.

TRANSPORTATION. Several companies provided identical **passenger ferry** service to Russell. **Fullers Passenger Ferry** is the largest and departs for **Paihia** daily on the hour. (☎402 7421. 15min.; 9am-6pm; in winter 7am-7pm. One-way $5, children $2.50.) Buy tickets on board, or at the Fullers' desk in the **Maritime Building** in Paihia. Rental cars are not allowed on the dirt road around the Bay to and from Paihia; the **vehicle ferry,** faster than the 20km trek, departs from Okiato (about 8km south of Russell) for **Opua** (about 10km south of Paihia) every 20min. in summer and every 30min. in winter (5min.; 6:40am-9:50pm; cars $8, campervans $12, motorcycles $3.50, passengers $1).

ORIENTATION AND PRACTICAL INFORMATION. Matauwhi Rd. dumps cars into town onto **York St.,** parallel to the **Strand,** which runs along the water from the **Russell Wharf.** All the shops are within two blocks of each other on these two streets, just east of a residential area, and south of **Long Beach Rd.,** which leads over a hill to (you guessed it) **Long Beach.** The privately run **Russell Information & Booking Centre** is in a kiosk on the wharf. (☎/fax 403 8020. Open in summer daily 8am-6pm, in winter 8am-4pm.) The **Bay of Islands Maritime and Historic Park Visitor Centre** on the Strand is also the main **DOC office** for the Bay of Islands. (☎403 7685; fax 403 764. Open daily 9am-5pm; in winter 10am-4:30pm.) Other services include: **BNZ** on York St. (open M-F 10:10am-2pm) and **Westpac Bank** on Cass St. near the Strand (open M-F 10am-1:45pm; extended hours in summer); **Russell Medical Services,** in the Traders Mall between York and Church St. (☎403 7690; open M-F 9am-4:30pm); **Russell Pharmacy,** 21 York St. (☎403 7835; open M-F 9am-5pm, Sa 9am-noon); **Internet access,** available at **Enterprise Russell** (☎403 8843; $10 per hr.; open M-F 8am-5pm), and a **post shop,** in the Russell Bookshop (☎403 7674, open daily 8:30am-5:15pm), both in the Traders Mall on York St. There are **laundry** and shower facilities at **Little Fresh Fruit & Vegetables** (☎403 8021) on Matauwhi Bay Rd.

ACCOMMODATIONS AND CAMPING. Run to the nearest phone and book one of only six beds at **The End of the Road,** 24 Brind Rd., at the top of Robertson Rd. and down the hill to the end of Brind. (☎403 7632. Dorms $18, in winter $17; twins $40; doubles $36.) Just up the road, **Pukeko Cottage,** 14 Brind Rd., can show you an amazing sunset from the dining room. (☎403 8498; barrymp@xtra.co.nz. Dorms $20, in winter $18; double in the cool converted caravan out back $35.) Flowering plants and trees abound at **Russell Holiday Park,** at James St. and Long Beach Rd. A popular choice with families; small children are often underfoot. (☎403 7826; fax 403 7221. Dorm rates in cabins when available $20; powered and tent sites $11-13; cabins, flats and motel units $32-150.)

FOOD. **Waterfront Cafe** on the Strand, 1 block south of the Wharf, has a beautiful beachfront view from the bar and an outdoor courtyard in back. Huge vegetarian nachos ($8) and bottomless coffee ($2) are patrons' favorites. (☎403 7589. Open daily 7am-4:30pm; in winter Tu-Su 7:30am-4pm.) **York St. Cafe** in the Traders Mall is a simple place that serves fresh, cheap food—an easy recipe for popularity. (☎403 7360. Open daily 10am-10pm.) The **General Store** across from the Wharf, has groceries. (☎403 7819. Open daily 8am-7pm.)

SIGHTS AND ACTIVITIES. The best collection of local historical treasures is housed at the **Russell Museum,** 2 York St. Displays range from the historical (a functional scaled replica of Cook's *Endeavor*) to the ridiculous (softball-sized cow hairballs and swordfish eye sockets). (☎403 7701. Open daily 10am-4pm; until

5pm in Jan. $3, children $0.50.) The Anglican **Christ Church,** on the corner of Baker and Robertson Rd., is the oldest still standing in New Zealand. Illustrious worshippers have included Charles Darwin, who attended services here while the *HMS Beagle* was anchored in the bay. Not to be outdone by the Protestants, Bishop Pompallier arrived in 1838, and his Catholic missionaries soon followed suit. The 1841 **Pompallier,** on the esplanade at the end of the Strand, is the only mission building that remains, and is now an award-winning *working* museum, continuing to tan leather and bind books in the Marist tradition. (☎ 403 9015. Open in summer daily 10am-5pm; open in winter for tours only 10:15am, 11:15, 1:15pm, 2:15 and 3:15. $5, students $2, children free.)

On the opposite side of the Russell waterfront is **Flagstaff Hill.** A short walking track ascends to the site where **Hone Heke,** the man who felled the symbol of British rule (the flagpole) four times in 1844-45, displayed his axe-wielding skills (see p. 57). When the tide is out, the hill can be approached along the beach at the north end of the Strand; otherwise take the signposted route off Flagstaff Rd. Lovely **Long Beach** of Oneroa Bay lies just over the hill at the end of Wellington St. and offers plenty of opportunities to sun and swim. Rent kayaks and paddle boats in the summer outside the **DOC office** by the waterfront (from $25 per day).

Trekkers come from all over to walk the medium-grade **Cape Brett Lighthouse Track** (return 16hr.). The old lighthouse keeper's house has been turned into a hut with a gas cooker, running water, and toilets, but no utensils. ($8 per person, children $4.) Book ahead at the DOC office in Russell, where you also pay the track fee ($8, children $4). The start of the track is a 1hr. drive from Russell and guides are usually available to introduce you to the history of the region (prices negotiable). One popular option is to be dropped off at the lighthouse by sea, and then hike back, enjoying the coast and saving a day; contact DOC for more information. They can also tell you about the **campsite** on the island of **Urupukapuka,** right at the beach, which has running water and cold showers, but no toilets; digging a hole is not allowed, meaning visitors must bring a chemical toilet, available for rent in Whangarei—ask the DOC for recommendations. ($6 per person, children $3.)

KERIKERI   ☎ 09

Kerikeri, strategically placed at the head of an inlet, was home to the marauding Maori chief Hongi Hika and a group of English missionaries under his protection, making the town an economic center for Christians throughout the bay. Meaning "dig, dig," quiet Kerikeri is where the first English plow cut into New Zealand soil. Budget travelers now reap the fruit of colonial labors—literally. Temporary agricultural employment attracts thin-walleted backpackers to Kerikeri year round, although the biggest wave hits in May at the start of the kiwifruit season.

◨ TRANSPORTATION. InterCity (☎ 913 6100) buses run to **Kaitia** (1½hr., 2 per day, $20) and **Paihia** (25min., 2 per day, $8). Never far from the tourists, **Fullers** tours Kerikeri from Paihia and hits history, horticulture, and shopping all in three hours. (☎ 407 7421. Daily 1:15pm; $45, children $25.)

◨◪ ORIENTATION AND PRACTICAL INFORMATION. Kerikeri Rd. is the main street, leading 5km east from **SH10** through town to the water and Rewa's Village. Most of the services are clustered within the triangle it forms with **Hobson Ave.** and **Cobham Rd.** in the center of town. The **Visitor Centre** in Paihia handles most Kerikeri queries, though info can be found in the office at Rewa's Village (☎ 407 6454), or at the **library** on Cobham Rd. in the center of town. (☎ 407 9297. Open M-F 9am-5pm, Sa 10am-12pm.) The **DOC** office (☎ 407 8474) is on Landing Rd. north of Rewa's Village. Other services include: the **Kerikeri Medical Centre** (☎ 407 7777), on Homestead Rd.; **Unichem Kerikeri Pharmacy** (☎ 407 8003, fax 407 8016; open M-F 8:30am-5:30pm, Sa 9am-1pm); **ANZ** (☎ 0800 269 296), on Kerikeri Rd.; **internet access** at **Kerikeri Computers,** 88 Kerikeri Rd. for $1 for first 5min., $0.15 for each additional min. (☎ 407 7941; open M W F 9am-5pm, Tu,Th 9am-7:30pm, Sa 9am-1pm); and the **post office** on Hobson Ave. (☎ 407 9721; open M-F 8:30am-5pm, Sa 9am-1pm).

⌐⌐ ACCOMMODATIONS AND FOOD. Hostels in Kerikeri are geared toward working backpackers and offer good weekly rates. Farms or orchards in search of seasonal workers usually contact the hostels first, who then post the job listings. The best times to find work in the area are early June, late March, and late December. Call ahead to see if there is a demand for workers.

The closest hostel to town is the **Kerikeri YHA,** 144 Kerikeri Rd., just past the edge of town toward the water. Like the rest of the budget accommodations, it is a rustic hostel—reminiscent of summer camp. (☎407 9391; fax 407 9328; yhakeri@yha.org.nz. Internet. Dorms $17; twins-doubles $40-42; self-contained cottage for 2 $70, $10 per additional adult.) To get to the **Hone Heke Lodge (VIP),** 65 Hone Heke Rd., turn off Kerikeri Rd. and then go left up the hill at the sign of the backpacking orange. This motel-style structure features a well-worn TV lounge, recreation room with pool and ping-pong tables. (☎/fax 407 8170; honehekelodge@hotmail.com. Bike hire. Free pick-up from bus stop. Shuttle to orchards $1. Laundry $6. Dorms $15/$77 per week; single $27.50/100; double $36/180; single w/ bath $37.50/150, double w/ bath $22/100.)

The **Fishbone Cafe,** 88 Kerikeri Rd., smack in the center of town, has reasonably priced food and an impressive wine list in a trendy dark wood and chrome atmosphere. (☎407 6065. Open M-W 8:30am-4pm, Th-Sa 8:30am-9pm; in winter same hours except Th closed at 4pm.) The award-winning **Rocket Cafe,** on Kerikeri Rd. 500m from SH10, has a veggie-friendly menu with tasty breakfast muffins ($2.50). (☎407 3100. Open M-F 8:30am-5pm, Sa-Su 9am-4:30pm.) Seek staples at the **New World** supermarket, at Homestead Rd. and Fairway Dr. (☎407 7440. Open Sa-Tu 8am-6pm, W-F 8am-8pm.)

◑◔ SIGHTS AND ACTIVITIES. Kerikeri is rich in Maori and European history. Stroll to the **Kerikeri Basin,** a 20min. walk down Kerikeri Rd. toward the water, to view a trinity of Anglican missionary power: **St. James Church,** the graceful white **Kemp House** (which claims to be the oldest standing wooden European building in the country), and **Stone Store,** constructed in 1832-36 to house supplies for the Church Missionary Society. (☎407 9236. Open 10am-5pm; in winter 10am-4pm. Stone Store and Mission House $6, students and children $2.50.) Cross the footbridge over the **Kerikeri River** and you will find yourself falling back in time at **Rewa's Village,** a replica pre-European Maori fishing village providing a glimpse into the age of chiefs Hongi Hika and Rewa. (☎407 6454. Open daily 9am-5pm; in winter 9:30am-4:30pm. $2.50, children $0.50.)

The area near the SH10 rotary yields kauri shops, ceramics, wineries, and a number of eccentric boutiques. Other (free) activities include swimming in the **Fairy Pools,** magical rock holes by the Kerikeri River. To reach the **Rainbow Falls,** start from the DOC parking lot and picnic area just past Rewa's Village (when coming from town), and walk along the river 2km; alternatively, drive along Waipapa Rd. 2½km east of SH10. There are a number of walking tracks in the **Puketi and Omahuta Forests** approx. 20km west of Kerikeri; access the park from Puketi (where there is DOC camping) off Puketotara Rd., or from Mangamuka off SH1; check with Kerikeri or Tarewa Park DOC for information.

THE FAR NORTH

KAITAIA   ☎09

A mostly working-class population of 5000 inhabits this small, functional town in which gas stations and warehouse buildings hide the majestic hills and dairy farms of the surrounding landscape; the town is best used as a stop-off or transfer point to more beautiful destinations. The scenic walkways of Kaitaia and its ocean-facing neighbor **Ahipara** are windows into the kauri industry of yesteryear; the **Kaitaia Walkway** (45min.) is expandable into a 9km track suitable for experienced trampers. The Ahipara **Gumfields** spread over most of the peninsula out to **Tauroa Point,** southwest of Kaitaia, and are littered with remnants of 19th-century gum digging (trenches, dams, and an old gum diggers' shack). Back in town at night, the **Scandals** nightclub, 15-33 Commerce St., upstairs at the Kaitaia Hotel, has a DJ spinning eclectic dance music. (Open Sept.-Jan. F-Sa 9pm-2am.)

Carless visitors to Kaitaia normally arrive on **InterCity** and leave the same way. Coaches head south daily to **Auckland** (7hr., 10:30am, $64) via **Whangarei** (4hr., $38) and **Paihia** (2hr., $28). For answers to all Cape queries, or $8 per hr. **Internet,** seek out the **Far North Information Centre,** in Jaycee Park on South Rd. (☎408 0879. Open daily 8:30am-5pm; in winter M-F 8:30am-5pm, Sa-Su 9am-1pm.) To overnight here, try **Main Street Backpackers YHA,** 235 Commerce St., on the edge of town. This dark and well-worn hostel is notable for its huge new *Whare Wanange,* where visitors can learn to carve bone ($20), among other handicraft activities, from local artisans. (☎408 1275; mainstreet@xtra.co.nz. Key deposit $5. Laundry $6. Dorms $13-16; singles $30; twins and doubles $34; tent sites $10. Weekly dorms $70.) **The Bluehouse Cafe,** 14 Commerce St., is a quiet, quality place, serving $6 paninis, like roasted pumpkin, or dinner like $16.50 lamb and vegetables. (☎408 4935. Open M-W 8am-3pm, Th-F 8am-8:30pm, Sa-Su 8:30am-8:30pm. AmEx/MC/V.) **Michaelangelo's,** 26 Commerce St., has basic filling foods, like $12 medium pizzas, but no masterpieces. (☎408 2001. Open M-W 10am-6pm and Th-F 10am-7pm. Cash only.) The **Pak 'N Save,** on Commerce St., is a giant warehouse of grocery items. (☎408 6222. Open M-W 8:30am-7pm, Sa-Tu 8:30am-6pm.)

AROUND KAITAIA

For more extensive trails, head to the **Karikari Peninsula,** 20km northeast of Kaitaia between **Rangaunu** and **Doubtless Bays.** The **Lake Ohia Gumholes** showcase the fossilized remains of a kauri forest amid rare ferns and orchids. The **Ancient Kauri Kingdom Ltd.,** on SH1 in Awanui, digs up kauri logs that were felled in the swamp 30,000-50,000 years ago, and carves the perfectly preserved wood into high-quality crafts and furniture. The massive spiral staircase in the center of the shop carved from a single log is very cool. Farther east along the base of the Karikari peninsula, **Coopers Beach** offers sunbathing and good surfcasting in Doubtless Bay. Farther north along the peninsula is a popular **DOC campground** at **Maitai Bay.** Facilities include cold showers, running water, and toilets. (Tent sites $6, children $3. Reserve through DOC in Kaitaia.) Pushing farther east along SH10, halfway between Kaitaia and Kerikeri on SH10, is the fabulous ◪**Kahoe Farms Hostel,** a dazzling 114-year-old family farm that spreads from the roadside eastward for acres, eventually to the coast. The immaculate wood floors and antique furniture lend the restored kauri villa a simple beauty, while Stefan the Chef's gourmet pizzas (around $15) are simply *bella.* (☎405 1804, kahoefarms@xtra.co.nz. Kayak rental. Internet. Free bikes. Dorms $17; twin $45; camping $10. Reservations essential.)

Further southeast lies **Whangaroa Bay,** a narrow inlet with a snaking coastline. On the eastern shore is the town of **Whangaroa,** home to the **Sunseeker Lodge** on Old Hospital Rd. A steep hill brings you to this small accommodation and its brilliant views of the bay, which is perfect for kayaking. Call for free pick-up from the bus station in Kaeo. (☎405 0496; sunseekerlodge@xtra.co.nz. Kayak hire. Internet. Spa $5 per person. Dorms $17; private double $40; motel units for 2 $70-95.) **Northland Sea Kayaking,** based 10km east of Whangaroa, does $60 per day kayak trips in Orua Bay, with accommodation available. (☎09 405 0381. Cash only.)

AUPOURI PENINSULA & CAPE REINGA   ☎03

The finger of the Aupouri Peninsula extends up from the northern coast. The Maori believe spirits of the dead travel over this land to Cape Reinga and dive into the ocean to return to the mythical homeland of Hawaiki.

◪🛈 ORIENTATION AND PRACTICAL INFORMATION

The path to the afterlife is gilded on the west by the golden sands of **Ninety Mile Beach,** a name more poetic than "ninety-kilometer beach" or "fifty-six mile beach," both of which would be more accurate. Near the top of the beach, the sands are

DRIVING CAN BE HAZARDOUS TO YOUR HEALTH! The route along SH1 has some treacherous unsealed roads frequented by top-speed tour buses. Resist the urge to keep pace with them—each season dozens of cars spin out on the curves and end up in the bush with a totaled car and a ruined holiday. Second, if you have a car, don't try to jaunt down the beach—although the beach is considered a road, in all likelihood you will get stuck. Guided trips pass the rusting automobiles of adventurous yet substantially less-skilled drivers who stopped on sandy Ninety Mile Beach. The buses parked along the sand are built for the terrain and helmed by drivers who have been navigating the changing sands for years. If you ignore this precaution, at least stay well away from the surf. Imagine you and a few chums (chumps?) watching helplessly as your car sinks out of sight. Though rental companies explicitly forbid driving on the beach, they know you are tourists, and tourists are stupid. The Houhora Tavern (☎ 409 8501) runs a towing company that will remove cars.

interrupted by the **Te Paki Stream,** which empties into the ocean. This is part of the **Te Paki Reserves,** administered by the **Te Paki DOC Field Centre** (☎ 409 7521), off SH1. With many walking tracks, the reserves offer a meditative serenity punctured in the summer by the screams of thrill-seekers coasting on their boards down the 100m high sand dunes. Don't venture out to the very tip of the beach, which is sacred and protected Maori land. On the opposite side of the peninsula, boarders boogie in the ocean waters of **Tapotupotu** and **Spirits Bay,** while landlubbers lie on graceful curves of sand. Slightly south along the side of the peninsula is **Great Exhibition Bay,** which, despite the name, entertains more anglers than nude bathers. The bluff is capped with a lighthouse that perches over the churning waters where the Pacific and the Tasman meet. **Cape Maria van Diemen** to the west and the **North Cape** to the east have equally breathtaking, if less celebrated, scenery.

ACCOMMODATIONS

Travelers with the blessing of an automobile should steer toward **Pukenui** (pop. 1000), a tiny and charming coastal town with New Zealand's northernmost backpacker accommodations. One of Northland's best hostels, **Northwind Lodge Backpackers,** 6km down Otaipango Rd., is 9km north of Pukenui in Henderson Bay. The beautiful and remote site offers a convivial cooking space and a cozy sleeping area. Basic groceries, Internet, and free boogie boards available. (☎/fax 409 8515; northwindlodge@xtra.co.nz. 4-bed dorm $16; twins $34) The **Pukenui Lodge (YHA),** on the corner of SH1 and Wharf Rd., has a cozy backpacker cabin adjacent to its motel accommodation; both come with pool access and a mind-blowing view of the bay. (☎ 409 8837; pukenui@igrin.co.nz. Dorms $15.50; singles $35; twins and doubles $40.) A short walk down Lamb Rd., backpackers set up next to trailers at the **Pukenui Holiday Camp.** Perks include a bountiful fruit garden in back and internet access. (☎ 409 8803; fax 409 8802. Communal kitchen and bathrooms. Dorms $15; great tent sites $10; basic cabins for 2 $35-60; tourist cabins with kitchen for 2 $50; flats with bathroom and kitchen for 2 $55.)

For more rustic accommodations, DOC maintains two **campsites** in the area of the Te Paki Reserve—they are only available in summer. One is **Tapotupotu Bay,** south of the Cape region, which has sheltered golden sands accessible by a posted turn-off 3km before the end of the road to the Cape. (Camping $6, children $3.) The other is at **Kapowairu,** along the east coast of Spirits Bay. (200 sites. $5, children $2.50.) Both are first-come, first-camped. DOC maintains a third campsite approximately in the middle of the Aupouri Peninsula at **Rarawa.** Sites can be found amid pine trees, a stone's throw from the white-sand beaches of Great Exhibition Bay. Follow the signs 1km north of Ngataki on SH1. (Open Labour Day-Easter. Sites $6, children $3.) All three feature DOC hallmarks of minimalism: cold showers, running water, and toilets. Call DOC at the Te Paki field center (☎ 409 7521) or in Kaitaia (☎ 408 6014).

NORTHLAND

DOLPHIN-CIDE? Opo was a lonely one-year-old when she first swam into the waters of Opononi in 1955. The young dolphin—whose companion Jack was mistaken for a shark and killed by locals—appeared almost daily to escort boats and soon became famous with huge crowds flocking to play with her. The town finally passed a law protecting her from harm, but on the same day, Opo disappeared. When Opo washed up on shore, it didn't take long for rumors to start spreading. Was there foul play? Poison? No one has ever ascertained the cause of death. Rumors these days suggest that Opo swam inland pining for Jack, eventually dying of a broken heart. Or, more realistically, Opo spent too much time making merry with tourists and not enough time hunting—slowly dying of starvation over two years.

🗺 🎣 SIGHTS AND ACTIVITIES

Most people elect to take a **guided day tour** in a specially designed sand-and-surf-worthy craft out of Paihia or Kaitaia. It makes for a long day, but it's a safer option for navigating the changing sands of an extremely remote region. Choose your tour carefully—many trips are designed with young people in mind and may not be appropriate for less-adventurous travelers.

Departing from Paihia, one good bet is ◼**Northern Exposure Tours** (☎402 8644, 0800 573 875), a "small bus with attitude" that makes a hugging stop at the kauri in Puketi. Dig for *toheroa* on Ninety Mile Beach, get sandblasted tobogganing on the dunes at Te Paki, and get spiritual at Cape Reinga, all in an 11hr., $69 day. The **4x4 Dune Rider,** also of Paihia, runs a similar tour in a rugged, air-conditioned Mercedes Benz bus with air-brushed cartoons of passengers on the side. (☎402 8681. Free pick-up daily from Paihia at 7:30am and Kerikeri at 8:15am; $75, children $55. Backpackers and AA 10% discount.) For an even livelier experience join the party-hard crowd onboard **Awesome Adventures,** which caters exclusively to backpackers. Unlike most tours lunch is not included. (☎402 6985. Departs Paihia 7:30am, $75.) With larger buses and an older crowd, **Kings** (☎402 8288) and **Fullers** (☎402 7421) are not as backpacker friendly (tours $60-80).

Some tours may stop at the **Wagener Museum** (☎409 8850), 40km north of Kaitaia on SH1 in Houhora, to check out the historic homestead ($3) or, better yet, the museum of natural and technological curiosities ($6).

HOKIANGA REGION ☎09

Every summer refugees from the full-blown commercialism of the Bay of Islands escape to the obscurity of the Hokianga region. In the constellation of tiny towns that sit on the Hokianga Harbour, adventure activities give way to bushwalking, fishing, swimming, and sand dune surfing. Hokianga is hailed as the last spot the great Maori navigator Kupe landed before departing home to Hawaiki. Long-standing Maori tradition holds that Kupe (as well as everyone else who pays a visit) will one day return to this area, known for its treacherous access to the Tasman Sea.

▤ TRANSPORTATION IN HOKIANGA

Limited **bus service** among the Hokianga towns means that either a car or patience is necessary to explore the area. The **Northland Wanderer pass** ($80-85, children $54-57, available through InterCity) may be the best antidote for fighting sporadic and expensive bus schedules. **Northliner** (Auckland ☎307 5873; Northland ☎438 3206) and **InterCity** (☎0800 401 500) contract out to **Westcoaster** in the region. Service is inconsistent at times, particularly in the winter, and runs on "Hokianga time,"—reservations are necessary even if you have a pass. From Paihia, buses run to **Kaikohe** (30min.; daily in summer 9am, in winter M, W, F and Su only; $9) and through the **Hokianga region** (2hr., about $25), to the **Waipoua Forest** (3¼hr., $35) and eventually on to **Auckland** (8¼hr., $50). Buses from Auckland arrive in **Omapere** by 2:00pm. Although *Let's Go* does not recommend it, many **hitchers** bum a ride by standing on the straightaways or approaching drivers at markets and post offices; those heading north or south take the Rawene-Kohukohu ferry and find a ride from drivers on board.

⑦ PRACTICAL INFORMATION

The **Hokianga Visitor Information Centre,** by Omapere on SH12, 450m out of "town," has a 1950s newsreels about town icon Opo the Dolphin in the "museum" upstairs. For more information on Opo's untimely demise, see **Dolphin-cide** below. (☎405 8869; fax 405 8317. Internet $10 per hr. Open daily 8:30am-5pm. Museum open daily 9:30am-4:30pm.) There are **no banks, ATMs, or cash advances** in the Hokianga, so bring EFTPOS or an adequate supply of cash. For medical assistance, **Hokianga Health** (☎405 7709) is located on SH12 just outside of Rawene. Call before coming.

OMAPERE ☎09

Keeping watch over the dangerous waters at the mouth of the Hokianga Harbour, Omapere (pop. 1300) is a breathtaking spot to stop before heading south to Waipoua or eastward to Kaikohe and the Bay of Islands. A short drive from Omapere along Waiotemarama Gorge Rd. leads to the **Labyrinth Woodworks,** which sells local crafts. (☎405 4581. Open daily 9am-6pm; maze open only in summer. $3.)

If you choose to stay in Omapere, **Globetrekkers (VIP),** off SH12, makes a good home. The backpackers cottage has a water view, comfortable beds, and a deck with picnic tables and rose bushes. (☎/fax 405 8183. Free pick-up from the visitors center. Laundry $7.50. Dorms $16; singles $25; doubles $40; double with bath $50.) **Calypso's Cafe,** just south of town on SH12, is bright with light pouring in its huge windows; $4.50 chicken burger and $17.50 chargrilled catch are equally refreshing. (☎405 8708. Open daily 9am-10pm-ish; in winter W-M 9:30am-4pm.) The **Omapere Restaurant and Takeaway,** on SH12, has simple fare and a super view. It serves fresh bread, a $2.50 cereal breakfast, and $4.50 toasted sandwiches. (☎405 8607. Open M-F 8am-5:30pm, Sa-Su 9am-4pm.) Next door is the **Four Square** which has a **post shop** inside. (☎405 8892. Open daily 7:30am-6pm.)

OPONONI ☎09

In the 1950s, a friendly dolphin in the nearby waters, nicknamed Opo the Dolphin, captured the affection of the town and the attention of the region. In the four decades since Opo put it on the map, **Opononi** has progressed about four years. It is still a small fun-in-the-sun resort town with sand, sea, and simple food. **Kupe's monument,** an anchor stone and commemorative plaque, sits at the top of a hill on the harbor side of SH12 between Opononi and Rawene. The grave of **Opo the Dolphin** (see Dolphin-CIDE p. 118), who turned belly-up one day, is located in front of the South Hokianga War Memorial. **Hokianga Express** offers water taxi service across the harbor to the dunes which lure sand surfers keen on sliding down the duneface and into the saltwater. They will even loan you boards and pick them up at the end of the day. (☎405 8872. $18.)

Opononi is a scant 3km up from Omapere on **SH12** and 23km from Rawene. Its wharf ties it to the harbor. If you're planning on spending the night, head up the hill from town to the epitome of Hokianga serenity at the **House of Harmony.** (☎/fax 405 8778; harmony@igrin.co.nz. Laundry $4. Haircuts on site. Dorms $16; twins and doubles $33; tent sites $10 per person.) For accommodations right on the waterfront, bask in the faded luxury of the **Opononi Resort Hotel.** In addition to the institutional, motel-style backpackers, the hotel features two bars. (☎405 8858.

NORTHLAND

Laundry $4. Dorms $15; singles $25; twins $40; doubles $50. Bars open 8am-midnight, or even later. AmEx/MC/V.) For a quick bite, stop in at the **Opo Takeaway** and try a dolphin-safe Opo Burger—fish, cheese, and tartar sauce for only $3.80. (☎405 8065. Open daily 11am-8pm; in winter 10am-9pm.) The **Four Square** has a **post shop** inside and **Internet** for $5 per 50min. (☎405 8838. Open daily 7:30am-8pm.)

RAWENE   ☎09

Rawene's centrality made it vital to the kauri shipping industry of yore. Today ferries, rather than cargo ships, dominate the area, carrying passengers and vehicles to **Kohukohu** on the opposite shore. **Ferries** depart on the half-hour. (15min., 7:30am-7:30pm, $2, cars $14 one-way or $19 return.) If all your travel has worn you out, Rawene has the perfect place for a sit (or a squat). Just past the service station on the waterfront are the much-celebrated **musical loos** of Hokianga. The fully automated, self-cleaning toilets play lovely piano music and feature mechanical toilet paper dispensers. Don't get too comfortable, though; the doors fly open after 10min. (Luckily there is a 1min. countdown).

The **Far North District Council,** on upper Parnell Rd., can answer travel queries. (☎405 7829. Open M-F 8am-4:30pm.) **The Boat Shed Cafe** on the water, up a bit from the ferry landing, makes a gorgeous espresso (flat white $2.50) to match its views and wood interior. The connected craft shop sells quality souvenirs without the kitsch. (☎405 7728. Open daily 9am-5pm.) Next door to the Boat Shed, **Hokianga Wholefoods** dispenses crunchy veggies and advice on the evils of genetically engineered foods. (☎405 7759. Open M-Sa 10:15am-5:15pm.) **The Wharf House** next door makes cheap, meaty burgers for $3. (☎405 7713. Open M-Th 7am-4:30pm, F-Su 7am-6pm.) The **Four Square** at the Waterfront) has a **post shop.** (☎405 7848. Open M-F 7:30am-5:30pm, Sa-Su 8:30am-4:30pm.)

KOHUKOHU   ☎09

Most commonly known as the other end of the Hokianga ferry (which departs for Rawene daily at 7:45am, 8:30am, 9am and then every hour on the hour until 8pm; $1.50), Kohukohu is known among budget travelers for its unique accommodations. ▧**The Tree House** is a sprawling wooden-planked network of decks and rooms in a 17-acre forest 3km from town. Easily one of the best backpackers in the country; many visitors find it hard to convince themselves to leave. A small shop at the front desk sells basic food and phone cards. Reservations are essential for everything (even tent sites). Call from Rawene for free pick-up from the ferry landing, or from town if you arrive from points north. (☎405 5855; fax 405 5857; tree.house@xtra.co.nz. Internet. Sheets $2. Duvets $2.50. Dorms $18; singles $29; twins $40; doubles $42; tent sites $11.) The **Bagend,** on Yarborough St. up the hill from town, is a brand-new hostel in a 12-year-old mud-brick house. (☎405 5806; bjcrooks@hotmail.com. Kayak rental. 4-bed dorm $18; $40 twin; $44 double.)

To explore farther upstream, you'll need the aid of **The Alma,** a 1902 kauri ship that swapped its twin masts for twin diesel motors and now tours up the harbor in the summer from Rawene. Meals are available ($5-15) if you book the day before, including fresh crayfish. (☎405 7704; mobile 025 997 450. $25, children $12.50.)

WAIPOUA FOREST PARK

Waipoua (north of Dargaville on Northland's western coast) is New Zealand's least-logged and best example of primary kauri forest. Remoteness and inaccessibility protected the virgin woods of the Waipoua region from 19th-century axe blades. The 1940s demand for shipbuilding timber stirred up controversy that resulted in Waipoua's being declared a sanctuary by 1952.

Everyone who visits the forest wants to see "the big tree" in northern Waipoua, and most buses (including InterCity) stop for at least a snapshot. A brief trek from the carpark off SH12 leads through dense, dripping bush to the 1200-year-old, 52m high, 14m wide **Tane Mahuta.** Nicknamed "Lord of the Forest," it is the **world's larg-**

est living kauri and **New Zealand's largest tree** of any kind. The boardwalk keeps admirers at a respectful distance to protect the Lord's shallow root system.

Waipoua's other "big trees" are accessible via walking tracks from the labeled carpark a few kilometers south of Tane Mahuta on SH12. A 20min. walk leads to the "diminutive" 30m **Te Matua Ngahere,** "Father of the Forest," the second largest living kauri; a 10min. walk takes you to the close-knit **Four Sisters,** four trees side-by-side; a 30min. walk goes to the **Yakas Kauri.** Although the Maori began the tradition of naming individual trees, not all bear Maori monikers: witness **Darby and Joan,** flanking either side of the bridge on SH12 north of the visitors center. For those with time to explore, the 3hr. **Yakas Track** connects the campground and visitors center to Yakas Kauri Carpark, winding through all sorts of trees and fording the Waipoua River. The 6hr. **Waiotemarama Walk** begins off Waiotemarama Gorge Rd. near Omapere, reaching a spectacular waterfall within 15min. and ending at the base of Mountain Rd. At its steepest point, halfway through, the walk connects with the **Waima Main Range Route.** This is a serious 3-4 day tramp passing over the highest point in Northland (often through low-lying clouds); trampers should possess good wilderness skills and be well equipped for foul weather. A less taxing walk along mostly flat beach is the 2-3 day **Waipoua Coastal Walkway,** linking Hokianga Harbour to the **Kai Iwi Lakes.**

Along with the kauri giants, Waipoua is home to the **Waipoua Forest Visitor Centre,** several walking tracks, and a **campground.** Self-register at the communal kitchen/shower/toilet building. Obtain cabin keys from the visitors center or, after-hours, check in with the caretaker. (Visitor Centre ☎ 439 3011; fax 439 3016. Open in summer daily 8:30am-6pm; in winter until 4:30pm. Campground tent and powered sites $7, children $3.50; cabins for 2 $28; cabins for 4 $40.)

DARGAVILLE ☎ 09

This riverside town (pop. 4600) is well-suited for stocking up on provisions—gas, food, batteries. While a handful of amusements and proximity to the kauri forests beg travelers to stay awhile, the absence of a seaside location should bump Dargaville down on many tourists' priority lists.

⊏ TRANSPORTATION. As in the rest of Northland, **InterCity** contracts out to **Westcoaster** to reach **Auckland** (3½hr.; M, Th, F 8:30am; $39) and **Paihia** (4¼hr.; in summer daily, in winter 3 per week; $32) via the **Waipoua Forest Park** (1¼hr., $15). They also service the Hokianga towns of **Omapere, Opononi,** and **Rawene** (2½-3hr., $17-25). **Hitchers** find that traffic along the Waipoua Forest Rd. in either direction is fairly regular and tend to wait at the edge of town past the Mangawhare Bridge, although *Let's Go* does not recommend thumbing.

◼◪ ORIENTATION AND PRACTICAL INFORMATION. Dargaville borders the **Northern Wairoa River,** 187km north of Auckland on the west coast. **Normanby St.** is the main road by which **SH12** traffic passes through town. One street over toward the river is **Victoria St.,** home to most of the shops. For information, try the **Kauri Coast Information Center,** corner of Poto and Normanby St., where there is also **internet access** for $7 per hr. (☎ 439 8360, 0800 528 744. Open daily 8:30am-6pm; in winter M-F 8:30am-5pm, Sa-Su 9:30am-4:30pm.) If you do nothing else in town, get plenty of money here, as there are no banks farther north in the Hokianga; **banks** with **ATMs** line Victoria St. Other services include: the **police,** on Portland St. (☎ 439 3400); the **Kaipara Unichem Pharmacy,** on the corner of Hokianga Rd. and Parenga St. (☎ 439 8325; open M-F 8am-6pm, Sa 9am-1pm, Su 9:30am-12:30pm); the **Dargaville Medical Centre,** on Awakino St. off of Hokianga Rd. (☎ 439 6015, after-hours ☎ 439 8079; open M-F 8am-5pm, Sa 9am-noon); and the **post office,** 80 Victoria St., in the Terartz Stationary Shop (☎ 430 6051; open M-Tu and Th 8am-5pm, W and F 8am-6pm, Sa 8am-7pm).

◪◪ ACCOMMODATIONS AND CAMPING. Just 33km north of town beyond Kaihu on SH12 is the **Kaihu Farm Backpackers,** a motel-clean hostel with at-home style. The owner drops off visitors at nearby lakes and forest walks for a small fee, and prepares home made freezer-meals ready for de-thaw dinner time. (☎439 4004. Bike rental. Dorm $16; double/twin $38.) The **Northern Wairoa Hotel,** on the corner of Hokianga Rd. and Victoria St., offers shocking value in the form of clean, well-kept single rooms. The rollicking pub downstairs features bands and karaoke on Thursday and Friday, with occasional "win-a-keg" competitions. (☎439 8923; fax 439 8925; northernwairoahotel@win.co.nz. Singles with plush linen and wash basin $20, with bath $40; doubles with bath $60; triples with bath $90.) **The Greenhouse (YHA/VIP),** 13 Portland St., has a dorm room—a large, spotless, mural-decorated sleeping hangar—with beds separated by shoulder-high dividers, providing more privacy than usual. (☎439 6342; fax 439 6327. Laundry $5. Dorms $16; singles $25; twins and doubles $38; negotiable weekly rates.) The **Baylys Beach Motor Camp,** 22 Seaview Rd., provides adorable cabins on a *pohutukawa*-edged green, which positively teem with families when the weather warms. (☎/fax 439 6349. Tent and powered sites $10; basic double cabins $20, extra person $10; double cabins with bath $33/$12.) Another camping option, the **Kai Iwi Lakes Camp** is on Kai Iwi Lakes Rd. Divided into two parts, the larger **Pine Beach Camping Ground,** on Lake Taharoa, accommodates up to 500 campers with rudimentary blocks of showers, toilets, and basins, no electricity, and coin operated gas BBQs. The second site, **Promenade Point** (100 sites), has only drop-toilets and basins. (☎439 8360. Water taps. No power for caravans. Both sites $8 per person, children $4.)

▢ FOOD. For prepared meals, the **Blah Blah Blah Cafe & Bar,** 101 Victoria St., has an eclectic cafe menu that changes every six weeks, though the prices are fairly stable (lunch $8.50, dinner from $12). (☎439 6300. Open M-Sa 9am-midnight, later F-Sa, Su 9am-4pm. YHA and VIP 10% discount.) The **Country Flair Cafe,** 75 Victoria St., is a local's lunchtime favorite, with fresh muffins ($1.20), and sandwich bagels ($3.30). (☎439 0393, 439 6175. Open M-F 7:15am-5pm, Sa 8am-3pm.) **Woolworth's** grocery is on Victoria St. at Gladstone St. (☎439 3035. Open daily 7am-10pm.)

◉◪ SIGHTS AND ACTIVITIES. The ▧**Kai Iwi Lakes** are rimmed with pure white silica sand and are a summertime mecca for water enthusiasts of all sorts. **Lake Taharoa** is the largest of the three and the best bet for swimming. Waterskiing is the sport of choice on **Lake Waikere.** The smallest and most serene is **Lake Kai Iwi** itself, trafficked solely by sails and dinghies and offering excellent fishing. **Buses** make it to the turn-off on Omamari Rd., 24km north of Dargaville on SH12, but you'll have to be resourceful to cover the remaining 11km to the first of the lakes; most travelers hitchhike. Closer waters lap the expanse of **Baylys Beach** (also known as Dargaville Ocean Beach or Ripiro Beach), which, at 100km, is New Zealand's longest. Astonishing in breadth as well as length, its vanishing point is often obscured by mist, as are the tops of nearby cliffs. Perhaps more remarkably, the beach is officially a public highway. Road rules apply; it's best to have a 4WD vehicle and a knowledge of conditions (see **Driving can be Hazardous to your Health** p. 117).

A more sedate pursuit, the **Kauri Museum,** on SH12 45km south of Dargaville in Matakohe, has exhibits about the mighty tree, but the gum display downstairs is the real star. An Intercity shuttle runs past the museum from Dargaville to Auckland Monday through Saturday, leaving town at 9am and 2pm; prebook to return at 11am and 4:05pm (return $16), otherwise the bus won't stop. (☎431 7417. Open Nov.-Apr. daily 9:30am-5:30pm; May-Oct. 9am-5pm. $9, children $2.50.)

Quad Safari can transfer passengers by boat or bus to the Pouto sand dunes for an individual 4WD adventure. (☎439 6554. Prices from $45.) For an excellent trek, the volcano **TokaToka** offers panoramic views of the region from its summit, 17km south of Dargaville. The track's steep 30min. ascent begins behind the TokaToka Tavern, a 15min. drive south along SH12. In town, and intended to "keep the kids of the streets" more than to entertain tourists, is the **Shed** on Logan St., an all-in-one indoor recreation center, with $2 rollerblade and skateboard rentals, skateboard ramps, table tennis, pool tables, indoor cricket, netball, and other juvenile diversions. (☎439 6093. $2 entry. Open M-F noon-9pm, Sa-Su 9am-10pm, though hours change frequently.) For a throwback, go see the Monday **animal auctions** on the corner of Kings Court and River Rd. at 1pm, just south of Victoria St.

COROMANDEL PENINSULA

Remote, if not entirely removed from the tourist loop, this charming peninsula harbors untouched natural beauty. Towns arose out of the dust of 19th-century gold mining and kauri logging, and the artists and potters of recent decades seem to have changed little. From Thames the Firth gently curves up to artisan Coromandel. The coastal road continues to the wild Coromandel Walkway, but the main road cuts inland, occasionally turning to gravel and passing several tramping trailheads before reaching the beach town of Whitianga. At Hot Water Beach, Hahei, and Opoutere, life is even simpler; Coromandel time seems to stand still. While the peninsula gets crowded during Kiwi holidays (avoid it altogether right after Christmas), there are no tour buses, crowds, traffic lights, or worries in the low season.

⚑ COROMANDEL PENINSULA HIGHLIGHTS

UNDER-APPRECIATED Where else but **Hot Water Beach** can you gleefully dig a grave and lie in it (see p. 133)?

UNDER-TOURISTED Often passed over by the typical tourist loop, **Coromandel town** offers tranquility and unique local crafts (see p. 128).

REMOTE Way off the beaten path, the **Northern Tip** and its Coromandel Walkway present unmitigated natural beauty (see p. 130).

⌐ TRANSPORTATION IN THE COROMANDEL

Flights: Air Coromandel (☎0800 900 600) flies to **Auckland** (2 per day, $90) from **Whitianga**, and to **Great Barrier Island** from both these locations ($89, return $169).

Buses: Bus transport on the Coromandel's narrow roads can be infrequent, especially in winter, consider buying a **Coromandel Busplan** from **InterCity,** which allows travel from **Auckland** to **Thames** and a circuit of the peninsula in a clockwise direction (Thames to Coromandel town to Whitianga to Thames) and a final leg to either **Auckland** or **Rotorua** ($89). **The Loop Pass** ($49), an abbreviated version, begins and ends in Thames. The **Pacific Coast Highway Traveler Pass** covers **Auckland,** the **Coromandel loop, Tauranga, Rotorua, Whakatane, Gisborne,** and **Napier,** and continues to **Palmerston North** and **Wellington.** Contrary to the name, the pass conveniently skips 8hr. of East Cape coastline and sets you back $149. (Loop runs daily Oct.-Apr.; in winter Su-F. Book each leg the day before.) For direct service from **Coromandel town** to **Thames,** InterCity contracts out to **Turley Murphy Buses** (1hr., M-F 7:30am, $12).

Shuttles: Go Kiwi Shuttles, 32 Moewai Park Rd. (☎07 866 5555; mobile 025 220 1519; fax 866 0337) services the eastern peninsula to and from **Auckland city** and **airport.** The Auckland service ($99) leaves **Whitianga** at 8am and **Thames** at 9:30am arriving in downtown **Auckland** at 11:45am. The return begins in **Auckland** at 1-1:30pm (depending on your pickup point). **Coromandel Bus Service,** based in Coromandel town, crosses to **Whitianga** and **Fletcher's Bay.** (☎866 8598. $15-17.) **Turley Murphy Buses** run between **Hot Water Beach** and **Hahei** among other destinations.

Cars and Car Rental: The Coromandel begs to be explored by car. Most roads are sealed and in good repair but have narrow shoulders, steep drop-offs, and hairpin turns. Take the **unsealed roads** up to Fletcher Bay and across the Peninsula on 309 Rd. slowly. Be sure to check your **rental agreement** for fine print concerning driving in the Coromandel. The

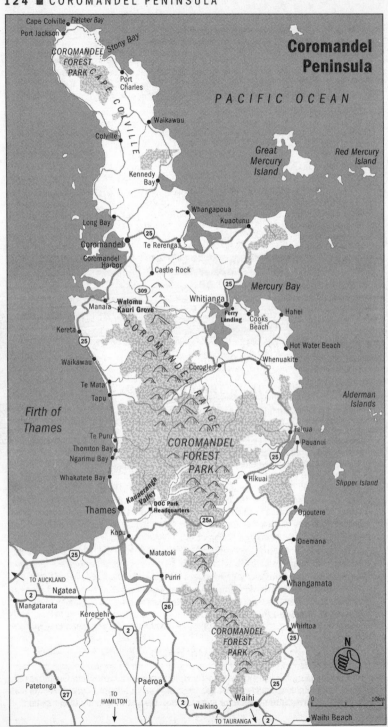

Coromandel Peninsula

last petrol station along the route to the tip is in **Colville**. Thames **Rent-a-Dent,** 733 Pollen St. (at Wiseman's Auto Workshop), starts at $36 per day plus $0.20 per km. (☎868 8838, 0800 736 822). Three years of driving experience required.

Biking: Bike touring is popular, if you've got the legs—many roads are hilly, unsealed, and winding. The ride to Coromandel town from Thames is a solid 4-5hr. with additional 2-3hr. segments up to Colville and Fletcher Bay. **Price and Richards,** 430 Pollen St. in Thames, rents 21-speed bikes with all necessary gear. (☎868 6157). $20 per day.

Hitchhiking: Although *Let's Go* does not recommend it, hitching between the major towns is reportedly fairly easy. Posting notices in hostels increases chances of a sure ride to Fletcher Bay or into the Coromandel Forest Park. Thumbers report long waits from some of the smaller towns (Hahei, Opoutere); arranging a ride back is advisable.

THAMES   ☎07

Arriving in this small, sunny town (pop. 6500), you'd never guess that it was briefly the country's largest city. In the 1870s, more than 100 hotels and bars poured whiskey for over 18,000 inhabitants, among them streams of hopeful gold miners. No longer marching with the pounding of stamper batteries or the miners' drunken revelries, the town is better known today as the gateway to (and the last shopping outpost of) the peninsula. Before passing through Thames, visitors should dig up some cash of their own; the town has one of the last ATMs on the peninsula.

▐ TRANSPORTATION

InterCity departs the visitors center for: **Tauranga** (2hr., $26) via **Auckland** (M-Sa 2 per day, Su 3 per day; $21); **Coromandel town** (1¼hr., M-F 3:50pm, $16); and **Whitianga** on a non-loop run (1¾hr., 3:35pm, $35). **Thames Gold Cabs** (☎868 6037) runs M-Th 8am-late, F-Sa 8am-2am. Although *Let's Go* does not recommend it, thumbers report it's easy to get to Coromandel town on Pollen or Queen St.

▟▐ ORIENTATION AND PRACTICAL INFORMATION

From Auckland, **SH25 (the Pacific Coast Highway)** wraps around the **Firth of Thames** before heading around the tip. Thames itself lies on a flat between the Firth and the upsweep of the gold-mine riddled Coromandel Range. Most of Thames' shops stretch along **Pollen St.** Parallel is **Queen St.,** the in-town name of SH25.

Visitors Center: The **Thames Information Centre,** 206 Pollen St. (☎868 7284). Open M-F 8:30am-5pm, Sa-Su 9am-4pm. **Kauaeranga Valley Visitors Centre (DOC)** (☎867 9080), 13km out of town (see **Coromandel Forest Park** p. 127). Open daily 8am-4pm.

Banks: BNZ (☎868 5811) at Sealey and Pollen St. There are only three or four other **ATMs** farther up the peninsula. Open M, Th-F 9am-4:30pm, Tu-W 9:30am-4:30pm.

Police: (24hr. ☎868 6040), on Queen St. across from the Mall.

Medical Services: A **pharmacy** (☎868 9095) is in Goldfields Mall. Open M-Th 8:30am-5:30pm, F 8:30am-8pm, Sa-Su 9am-4:30pm. **Thames Medical Centre** (☎868 9444) is on Rolleston St., just down from the hospital's side entrance. Open M-F 8:30am-5pm. The **Thames Hospital** (☎868 6550) is on MacKay St., parallel to Pollen St.

Internet: $2.50 per 15min. at the visitors center. Just a few blocks north on Pollen St., **United Video** (☎868 8999) charges $3 per 15-min., $9 per hr.

Post Office: (☎868 7850), on Pollen St. Open M-F 8:30am-5pm, Sa 9am-12:30pm.

▐▟ ACCOMMODATIONS AND CAMPING

Several motor camps lie along the coastal road between Thames and Coromandel, and DOC runs eight **campgrounds** in the Kauaeranga Valley (see **Coromandel Forest Park,** p. 127). During summer, make sure to book budget lodgings far, far ahead.

Sunkist Lodge (VIP), 506 Brown St. (☎868 8808, 0800 767 786; sunkist@xtra.co.nz). About 4 blocks up Brown St., off Queen St. at the Mall. This former gold rush hotel comes with sturdy bunks, spacious rooms, a sun-kissed 2nd-floor deck, and its own resident ghost. Free internet. Large dorms $16; 4-bed shares $18; twins and doubles $37.

Adventure Backpackers Coromandel, 476 Pollen St. (☎/fax 868 6200). Formerly the old Imperial Hotel, this hostel in the center of town offers a bit of history with an overnight stay. Free laundry. Dorms $14; singles $24; doubles with bath and TV $44.

Dickson Holiday Park YHA (☎868 7308; fax 868 7319), on Victoria St. 3km north of town off SH25. Free bikes, pick-up, a game room, solar-heated pool, and kitchen. Metered showers (20¢ per 5min.). Dorms $16; tourist cabins and on-site caravans with kitchenette for 2 $38-41; bush hut $34; tourist flats $62; tent sites $11 per person.

🌀 FOOD

Dining out in Thames is not terribly exciting; pinch pennies at the **Pak 'N Save,** in the Goldfields Mall. (☎868 9565. Open M-W 8:30am-7pm, Th-F 8:30am-8pm, Sa 9am-4pm, Su 10am-3pm.) Thames' takeaways and cafes line **Pollen St.**

Sealey Cafe, 109 Sealey St. (☎868 8641), is an all-day solid feed. Jazz photos on the brick and plaster walls add class. Place your order at the bar next to a bust of Satchmo himself. Most mains $9.50-12.50, others up to $25.50. Open daily 10am-late.

Food for Thought/Second Thought, 574-576 Pollen St. (☎868 6065), stocks healthy vegetarian fare, ensuring that your breakfast or lunch is incomparably fresh. Small veggie pizza ($3). Open M-F 6:30am-4:00pm, Second Thought also open Sa 6:30am-1pm.

The Udder Bar, downstairs from the Adventure Backpackers. A popular cafe/restaurant that hosts a mellow, sit-down crowd. Mains $12-20. Open daily 7pm-late.

The Krazy Cow Bar, downstairs from Adventure, isn't really known for its food. This weekend joint encourages rowdy crowds to dance on the tables in the glow of the biggest projection screen in town. Open F-Sa 8pm-2am, party gets going around 10pm.

👁 🔧 SIGHTS AND ACTIVITIES

An impressive memorial to the 19th-century gold industry is the **Gold Mine and Stamper Battery,** on SH25 at the north end of town. Thunderous demos of rock crushing and sifting will leave you with a pounding headache and no illusions about the glamour of gold mining. (☎868 8514. Open daily 10am-4pm. $8, children $4.) Illuminated at night, the **WWI Peace Memorial,** located atop Monument Hill up Waiotahi Rd. at the north end of town, gives a wide view of both the town and the Firth. The **Karaka Bird Hide,** built with French compensation funds for the bombing of the *Rainbow Warrior* (see p. 110), stands just past Goldfields Mall.

The best area walk is **Rocky's Goldmine Trail** (return 3hr.), which starts and ends at the Dickson Holiday Park. Beware that the area is riddled with old and dangerous mine shafts; stay on the path, as some are hidden. The track emerges on Tararu Creek Rd. From there, turn left to leave or right to reach a well-kept secret—the 3m **Black Hole Waterfall,** sliding into a deep pool below (about 2.6km up Tararu Creek Rd. from the entrance to Dickson; ask there for more specific directions). Also at the Holiday Park is the **Butterfly & Orchid Garden,** with 400 of the colorful insects fluttering around a climate-controlled greenhouse. (☎868 8080. Open daily 10am-4pm; in winter 11am-3pm. $8, students $7, children $4.)

The winding 55km scenic drive to Coromandel town, with rocky inlets and bays fading from the muddy brown of Thames to the jewel blue of the northern Peninsula, is arguably the loveliest drive on the North Island. When the road turns inland, the views over **Coromandel Harbour** will undoubtedly bowl you over (at which point you should pull over). Along the way, the **Waiomu Kauri Grove,** one of the finest old-growth stands, contains towering kauri. Turn right off of SH25 at the sign for Waiomu Bay Holiday Park. and walk 1hr. through farmland and bush from the end of Waiomu Creek Rd., 15km from Thames. About 5km farther is the turn-off for the **Tapu-Coroglen Rd.,** which cuts across the peninsula to rejoin SH25. Follow it for about

FALLEN GIANTS As stunningly scenic as it may be, the Coromandel is in many ways a case study in human greed—its very name is taken from a Royal Navy vessel that collected massive kauri logs from the peninsula in 1820. The knot-free wood and huge, straight trunks of these noble trees were coveted for ship masts and buildings. By the 1870s, the logging moved into the area's mountainous ridges, where elaborate innovations were used in tree removal. Logs were dragged, trammed, or rolled into streambeds behind dams. As water built up, loggers tripped the dams, releasing floods of trees that crashed down the valleys in a wasteful process that damaged the logs and gouged out the stream bed. Between logging and burning the land for farming, less than 1% of the region's forest survived the short-sighted exploitation. Although today you can see more of the original kauri wood in San Francisco and Auckland buildings than in the forest, much of the irreparably altered (but regenerating) landscape on the peninsula is now part of the Coromandel Forest Park.

9½km and look for the sign marking a steep 10min. walk through native bush to the 2500-year-old "square kauri tree." It's worth the quick detour.

COROMANDEL FOREST PARK   ☎07

The hills of the 72,000-hectare Coromandel Forest Park are tangled with regenerating bush, crawling with creepers, and sluiced by high waterfalls and small, fern-lined creeks. Deep within the hills that stretch up the peninsula's volcanic backbone, old kauri dams and mine shafts are interspersed with the few remaining patches of original forest. Active replanting efforts of native species are underway, as are rigorous pest management techniques (especially in the north, where possums have not fully infiltrated). You'll find plenty of walks in the Kauaeranga Valley east of Thames, as well as some remote walkways in the peninsular fingertip. Getting to Kauaeranga Valley without your own transport is a mild pain, especially at non-peak times. **The Sunkist Lodge** (see p. 126) occasionally runs a shuttle service (return $20, but negotiable). In a pinch, **Thames Gold Cabs** can take you for a heady $36 one-way fare. Although *Let's Go* does not recommend hitchhiking, the road to Kauaeranga is fairly hitchable on weekends (daily in summer), but finding a ride at other times is dodgy. Most thumbers arrange a return ride or run the risk of getting stuck. The **Kauaeranga Visitors Centre** is 13km up Kauaeranga Valley Rd., a winding half-paved road that branches off at the BP station at the south end of Thames. Stop in before heading to the trails to fill out help forms detailing your party. (☎867 9080. Open daily 8am-4pm.) **DOC campgrounds** are liberally scattered in the park, with eight off the road to Kauaeranga Valley and four at its tip; the **Kauaeranga** sites are cheap and basic ($7, children $2). The only hut in the park is the **Pinnacles Hut**, a rugged Ritz with views, a year-round warden, wood stove, gas cooking (bring your own utensils), 80 mattresses with fitted sheets, solar lighting, and toilets. It's about a 3hr. climb from the road end. ($15, children $7.50. Book in advance at the visitors center; annual or other hut passes not applicable.)

Numerous trails criss-cross the Coromandel, and signs of human influence are everywhere, making much of the park historically as well as naturally attractive. The **Kauaeranga Valley** is the most hiked spot, with walks heading off the road. A 5min. hop from the visitors center leads to an old intact kauri dam and the bludgeoned stream bed it helped carve out. A trip from the **Wainora campground** (return 2-3hr.) leads to two of the valley's only surviving large kauri. **The Kauaeranga Kauri Trail** heads up to Pinnacles Hut and the sheer jagged bluffs of the **Pinnacles** themselves, arching out of emerald water like fins. It's well worth the swing bridges and 1000-plus stairs through fern-laden bush. Atop the Pinnacles, 1hr. from the hut, the views across the peninsula will take away any breath you have left. The **Kauaeranga River,** running along the road up the valley, sports tons of swimming holes. Find your own, or check out **Hoffman's Pool,** a 2min. walk down the Nature Walk. For a tour of the best spots in the Coromandel Peninsula, including Waiau Falls and Hot Water Beach, **Driver Jim** departs Thames to give the grand tour. (☎0800 454 678. In summer M-Sa 10:15am, winter M,T,Th-Sa. $69 return).

COROMANDEL ☎ 07

The peaceful town of Coromandel (pop. 1200) unites artisans, individualists, and country bumpkins in a common love of the mesmerizingly blue waters of Coromandel Harbour and the deep greens of the hills sweeping above town. Visitors are both visually stimulated by the environs and aesthetically pleased by all the little craft shops. A short bike ride to some of the areas main attractions (e.g., railway, waterworks) will provide a dose of eccentric ingenuity in which to marvel.

▐ TRANSPORTATION

As in most of the Peninsula, transport services change rapidly and vary considerably by season—check with the visitors center for up-to-date schedules. The **Inter-City Coromandel Busplan** passes through to **Whitianga** (1hr.; 11:05am daily in summer, Su-F in winter), continuing to **Thames** (3hr.). You can go directly to **Thames** with **Turley Murphy** (1hr., M-F 7:30am, $12-16) or via **Whitianga** for the same price on the same day. **Coromandel Bus Service** (☎866 8045) goes to **Fletcher's Bay** and the **Coromandel Walkway** (pick-up after walk at Stony Bay) daily in the summer and on the weekends in winter (numbers permitting; $65; 9am departure, returning about 5:30pm). **Biking** is another good option; Whitianga is a 2½hr. ride, Colville is a 3½hr. pedal, and Fletcher Bay is 7hr. away. Although *Let's Go* does not recommend it, **hitchhiking** is reportedly easy to Thames and only slightly more difficult to Whitianga. The SH 25 road that turns off just past the fire station on Tiki Rd. is considered a better spot than the 309 Rd. Hitching northward in winter is difficult.

▐ PRACTICAL INFORMATION

The **Coromandel Information Centre** lies on Kapanga Rd. across the creek. (☎866 8598. Open daily 9am-5pm; in winter M-F 9am-5pm, Sa-Su 11am-3pm.) The **DOC office** is in the same building. Other services include: **BNZ**, at Tiki and Kapanga Rd. (open M-F 10am-3pm; with **ATM**); **police station** (☎866 8777), next to the visitors center; and the **post office**, 190 Kapanga Rd. (☎866 8865; open M-F 9am-5pm).

▐ ▐ ACCOMMODATIONS AND CAMPING

Bring cash; few of the hostels have credit card or Eftpos capabilities. Homestays spring up in the holiday season. However, if you decide to camp in peak months, be prepared to deal with crowds. Book ahead in January and February.

▩ **The Lion's Den**, 126 Te Tiki Rd. (☎866 8157). This laid back backpackers beats its competition by a country kilometer with friendly hosts. Free vegetables from the organic garden. Excellent home-cooked meals on request (picnic lunch $5, dinner $10). Dorms $16; doubles $32; tent sites $12. Cash only.

▩ **Celadon Motel** (☎866 8058), up a steep little hill on Alfred St., off Rings Rd., 1km from the town center. You'll never want to leave these self-contained cottages glowing with shiny wood, original artwork, and unbeatable views. Hospitable and conversational owner Ray Morley gives pottery lessons ($15 per hr.). Cottages $80-110, extra person $10; private B&B units in main house $90, without breakfast $70. $5 off with *Let's Go*.

White House Backpackers VIP (☎866 8468; whitehos@wave.co.nz), 1km north of the visitors center, at the corner of Rings Rd. and Frederick St. Owner Donatus works from his 3 airy white cottages to provide clean digs and free advice about local attractions. Free bikes. Internet. Free pick-up. 4-bed dorms $18; doubles $40. Cash only.

Tui Lodge, 60 Whangapoua Rd. (☎866 8237). From Kapanga/Wharf Rd. turn onto Tiki Rd. by the BNZ, and left onto Whangapoua Rd. The lodge is 500m on the right, down a gravel drive. With sheep grazing in the front pasture and an orchard in back, adjustment to Coromandel time is made easy. In-season fruit, trampoline, and free laundry. Dorms $16; twins and doubles $34; tent sites $8.

Tidewater Tourist Park (YHA), 270 Tiki Rd. (☎866 8888, fax 866 7231, tidewatr@world-net.co.nz). Explore on a mountain bike ($10 per day) or kick back in a throne facing the bay. Private sauna $5 for 30 min. Book far ahead for Dec.-Mar., though there's generally a bit of tenting room on the grass. Free laundry. Compact shares $15; twins and doubles $38; tent sites $9 per person. Nonmembers $1 more.

Long Bay Motor Camp (☎866 8720), 3km from town on Wharf/Long Bay Rd. You and your buddies in the tent next door will have beautiful views of blue waters. Metered showers. 2-person units $30; tent sites $9 per person, powered sites $2 extra per site.

◗ FOOD

For veggie options or more affordable dinners, head to ▨**The Success Cafe,** 104 Kapanga Rd. A hefty plate of steamers is $9—we don't know their secret, but we like their style. (☎866 7100. Open daily 10am-late.) **The Pepper Tree Restaurant and Bar,** on Kapanga Rd. in the town center, specializes in fresh seafood. You'll have to shell out a few clams (the pub menu is less expensive), but the food is memorable. (☎866 8211. Open daily in summer from 8am; in winter from 11am.) Dine in the brightly decorated **Assay House Café.** (☎866 7397. Open Tu-Su 9am-5pm in winter; daily in summer with extended hours.) The **Castle Rock Restaurant 'N Bar** offers several specialty pizzas ($10-19.50). (☎866 8618. Open noon-3:30pm and 6pm-late.) If bread is all you need, the **Bakehouse** on Wharf Rd. has a full range of cheap rolls, loaves and pastries. (Open daily 7:30am-4pm.) **Price Cutter,** on Kapanga Rd. just before the bridge, sells groceries year-round. (☎866 8669. Open M-F 7:30am-6pm, Sa 7:30am-6pm, Su 8am-6pm.)

◎ ▨ SIGHTS AND ACTIVITIES

Coromandel exudes artistic spirit from nearly every corner, and the pottery, weaving, embroidery, sculpture, and woodwork of local artisans dot the town and landscape. The **Weta Design Studio,** on Kapanga Rd., is the best of the local shops, offering quality over quantity with local and national art, crafts, and sculpture in the delightful outdoor courtyard. (☎866 8823. Open daily 10am-5pm.) Aside from crafts, Coromandel's biggest attraction is the **Driving Creek Railway,** 3km north of town. Begun as a pet project in 1975 to extract clay and kiln fuel from the hills, the narrow-gauge railroad has become the 20yr. passion of owner and potter Barry Brickell. The ever-growing track snakes through glowing forest and tunnels, around spirals, and over bridges. (☎/fax 866 8703. $12; children $6.) Eat dinner on the BBQ train ($38), which includes a scenic meal and an after-dark ride through colonies of glow worms. Also just north of town, visitors can pan for their own gold at the **Coromandel Gold Stamper Battery** while learning about the gold-mining industry that was once the backbone of the peninsula. (☎866 8758, mobile 021 257 8942. Open daily 10am-4pm. $6, children $3.) Owner Ashley also provides guided geological tours of the area. (☎866 8758. $30, children $15.)

The **309 Road,** branching off 4km south of the town of Coromandel and ending in Whitianga, is not so much horrifically narrow ("We're working on it," says one local) as it is winding and unpaved. It is worth traveling for its many attractions—just go slow around the bends and keep to your side of the road. The most eccentric attraction in the Peninsula is the **Waiau Waterworks,** 9km from Coromandel town. The Waterworks is a collection of whimsically and brilliantly engineered kinetic sculptures powered by—you guessed it—water. (☎866 7191. Open Sept.-June 9am-5pm; generally closed July-Aug. but worth checking; $8.) One hundred meters past Waiau Waterworks, the **Castle Rock** trail (return 2hr.), the best and steepest tramp in town, is an exposed vertebra of the peninsula's backbone yielding 360° views of the peninsula. Driving down 309 Rd. to the trailhead is best, but a rigorous 2hr. bike trip (much of it uphill) will get you there if you can take the workout. The **Waiau Falls,** set in a bush glade just off the road 7.3km from Coromandel, is a good place to cool off after a dusty ride. Be sure to stop at the **Waiau Kauri Grove** about 15km from Coromandel. Walk for 10min. to join other gape-mouthed visitors in the cathedral of soaring trees that once covered the peninsula. If you have no transport, try **Carter Tours,** which runs trips to just about wherever. (☎866 8045; mobile 025 937 259.)

THE NORTHERN TIP   ☎07

North of Coromandel, travelers are on their own. Comfy lodgings are far and few between, and there is only one cafe (this is the wilderness indeed). Jumbled green hills, deserted crescents of bays, twisting, gnarled trees that would make Van Gogh proud, and a wild coastline are broken up only by sheep placidly grazing on undulating farmland. The spectacular **Coromandel Walkway,** between Fletcher Bay and Stony Bay, is worth any effort it takes to get there.

▛ **TRANSPORTATION.** The quality of roads in the region is inversely proportional to the "gasp" factor—if the scenery is beautiful, the drive is probably harrowing. The narrow gravel roads do add charm, though they have a tendency to flood out in rain. One road winds up the west side to **Fletcher Bay** at the top of the Tip; another branches off just past **Colville** (28km north of Coromandel) and finds its way to Stony Bay. The well-stocked **Colville General Store** is the northernmost opportunity to fill up on **petrol** (and groceries) on the Tip. (☎ 866 6805. Open daily 8:30am-6:30pm; in winter M-Th 8:30am-5pm, F 8:30am-6pm, Sa 9am-5pm, Su 9am-4:30pm.) Before heading out in your rental car, make sure there's no fine print in your rental agreement about this area. Public transport is slim. Mountain biking is a great, but strenuous, way to circuit the Tip along the track connecting Fletcher and Stony Bay. *Let's Go* does not recommend **hitchhiking,** which is all but impossible up north in winter, though some succeed in summer (once past Colville thumbers usually only accept rides going all the way).

▛▛ **ACCOMMODATIONS AND FOOD. Colville Farm Backpackers** offers good, clean, rural fun (horses, glowworm walks, cow milking) in addition to tidy accommodations. The tourist flats are spiffier and have a price to match. (☎/fax 866 6820. Dorms $14; singles $15-17; self-contained huts $50-65 or $14 per person; self-contained houses for 2 $70-75). Just down the road is the **Colville Cafe,** an ideal place to mellow out before tackling the road ahead. (Open in summer daily 8am-8:30pm, winter daily 8am-4pm with dinner F-Su until about 8:30pm. Cash only.) **Fletcher Bay Backpackers,** next to the Coromandel Walkway trailhead is a base for tramps into the bush or along the coast. Owned by DOC, Fletcher's has just 16 beds, making bookings essential. (☎ 866 6712. Dorms $13.) In addition, DOC manages five basic **campgrounds** in the northern region.

▛ **ACTIVITIES.** The peninsula's crowning track, the 10.7km **Coromandel Walkway** (3hr. one-way), explores lonely bays and coves, passes turquoise waters along the coast between Fletcher and Stony Bay, and dips into inlets and bushy valleys. Other than a few short stiff climbs, it's not difficult, though it can be a bit hairy in winter before it's cleared for the summer season (it quickly becomes overgrown and can be really muddy). **Carter Tours** will do drop-offs and pick-ups in summer. (☎ 866 8045; mobile 025 937 259. $65, min. 3 people.) If you have to return to a parked car but don't want to hike for 6hr., start from the eastern Stony Bay side, walk for 1-2hr. and turn around; many regard this half as the best part of the hike. Another great tramp goes up the peninsula's tallest mountain, the 892m **Mt. Moehau.** As the top is private Maori land, you're requested to turn back just as you get tantalizingly close. Approachable from several points, the peak is perhaps most accessible from **Te Hope Stream,** 12km north of Colville (return 5hr.). The more strenuous **Stony Bay** route follows an exposed ridge (taking most of a day).

WHITIANGA   ☎07

Moving east across the peninsula, the coastline softens from mud and rocks into sandy beach. Among the dunes, Whitianga (fit-ee-ANG-guh), a small town born of timber (over 500 million feet of kauri were cut in 60 years), has become the Coromandel's main resort town. Whitianga loses a bit of its relaxed vibe during the summer, when it seems like every frenzied angler, boater, and sun worshiper from Auckland descends to plumb the rich, deep-sea fishing waters, explore the nearby marine reserve, or hit one of the many surrounding beaches.

TRANSPORTATION. The InterCity **Coromandel Busplan** buses leave the visitors center for **Auckland** (2 per day, 7:45am and 1:15pm) with a connection to **Thames** via **Whenuakite, Tairua,** and **Hikuai** ($24). To get to **Whangamata,** take the bus to Hikuai to be picked up by InterCity affiliate **Whangamata Tours.** (☎866 4397. 1½hr., 2:15pm, $29.) **Guthreys Express** leaves for **Tauranga** and **Mt. Maunganui** at 12:40pm ($30). **Mercury Bay Taxis** (☎866 5643) will also do a run to **Coromandel** for about $50 per van (fits 10). Book bus transport at the **Information Centre** (see below) or through **Travel Options** (☎866 4397; open M-F 9am-5pm, Sa 10am-noon). The visitors center also rents out bicycles ($25 per day, $15 per 1/2 day).

⊠ PRACTICAL INFORMATION. Whitianga sits where **Mercury Bay's** beach meets the waters of **Whitianga Harbour.** The route to **Hahei, Hot Water Beach,** and beyond is a lengthy detour around the harbor. **SH25** runs along the beach as **Buffalo Beach Rd.** and turns south to become **Albert St.,** the main drag. The **Whitianga Information Centre,** 66 Albert St., is run under the umbrella of the Business Association (Destination Mercury Bay)—be sure to ask the staff about *all* of your accommodation options, because the brochures only list members of the association. The visitors center also offers internet access at $3 for 15 min. (☎866 5555; fax 866 2205. Open Dec.-Mar. daily 8am-6pm; Apr.-Nov. M-F 9am-5pm, Sa-Su 9am-4pm.) The **Westpac Trust Bank,** on Albert St. by Monk St., has a **24hr. ATM.** (☎866 2701. Open M-Tu and Th-F 9am-4:30pm, W 9:30am-4:30pm.) Other services include: the **police** (24hr. ☎866 4000), on Campbell St.; **Mercury Bay Medical Centre** (☎866 5911), at Albert and Owen St.; and the **post office** (open M-F 8:30am-5pm).

⊼⊼ ACCOMMODATIONS AND CAMPING. In a sea-green converted motel about 1km from downtown, the **⊠Coromandel Backpacker's Lodge,** 46 Buffalo Beach Rd., is the independent traveler's best choice. Enthusiastic owners, a courtesy van, and a miniature visitors center with internet are welcome amenities. Free kayaks, boogey boards, fishing rods, and shovels for Hot Water Beach. (☎/fax 866 5380. Bikes. Dorms $18; twins and doubles $44). A jaunt from the town center off Albert St. lies **The Cat's Pyjamas Backpackers Lodge (NOMADS),** 4 Monk St. Ask Buster, the affable owner, about scenic flights in his Cessna. (☎/fax 866 4663, catspjs@ihug.co.nz. Flights $22 per person. Dorms $18; twins and doubles $40; tent sites $12.) Those wishing to escape the bustle of the summer season may wish to try the **309 River Lodge,** occupying an old country schoolhouse 12km from town on the 309 Road. Free pick-up is provided and bush walks, a swimming hole, organic produce, and farm animals contribute to the country feel. (☎866 5151; fax 866 5137; colin.megan@paradise.net.nz. Dorms $15; $45 for a whole room; tent sites $10 per person.) Catering almost exclusively to the busloads of Kiwi Experience bar hoppers, **Buffalo Peaks Lodge,** 12 Albert St., shows none of the wear and tear you might expect. (☎866 2933. Dorms $18; doubles $45.) **The Mercury Bay Motor Camp,** 121 Albert St., is 500m south of the town center with standard motor camp facilities, though showers are metered. (☎866 5579. Tourist flat singles $40; doubles $60, in peak season $120; tent and caravan sites $10-13.)

◻ FOOD. A diamond in the rough, **Cafe Nina** is on Victoria St. at the back side of the park. The muffins melt in your mouth and lunches ($6-9) have some veggie options. (☎866 5440. Open in summer daily 8am-5:30pm; winter hours vary.) For dinner, **Smitty's Bar and Grille,** 37 Albert St., has good fried fare. Burgers and a double-decker BLT are under $8. Smitty's is also a popular place to meet for drinks late at night or during televised rugby games. (☎866 4647. Open M-F 11am-1am, Su from 5pm.) **Four Square,** on Albert St. by the visitors center, has groceries. (☎866 5777. Open M-F 7am-8pm, Sa 7am-8pm; in winter M-F 7am-6pm, Sa 8am-6pm.)

⊙⊘ SIGHTS AND ACTIVITIES. The greatest joys in Whitianga are outdoors. Cross the river on the ferry and take the path to the small **Scenic Reserve** on the right. Follow the water's edge up to the 24m bluff of **Whitianga Rock,** an old Maori *pa*, from which stone for the old ferry landing wharf was taken. The walk from **Ferry Landing** up to the **Shakespeare Lookout** is worth the hour (you can also drive). Named for a resemblance to the Bard in its rocky profile, it's a jaunt along **Front Beach** to the crescent of **Flaxmill Bay**, and a steep hike up from the sign on the pohutukawa at the far end. The expansive view from the top includes a clear view of **Lonely Bay** below—the only legal nude beach on the Coromandel (bring your binoculars). Isolated from unsightly buildings and roads, the cove's golden sands and turquoise surf are accessible only by boat or by the steep footpath down from Shakespeare Lookout. The next beach over is **Cooks Beach,** a shallow 3km stretch of swimming area. **Buffalo Beach,** directly on the shores of Whitianga, is named for the HMS *Buffalo* which wrecked in 1840 while collecting kauri for England.

It's that blue water that draws most people to the Mercury Bay area. With **Cathedral Cove Marine Reserve** nearby and the Mercury Bay Islands off the coast, every kind of water activity from snorkeling to banana boating can be found here. Whitianga has some of New Zealand's best big-game **fishing** from December to March.

Bay Carving, on the Esplanade opposite the wharf beside the museum, will help you choose from an array of designs or create your own. The metamorphosis from paper to polished pendant in 3hr. is amazingly satisfying. (☎866 4021. Designs and tutelage from $35. Open daily 9am-9pm.) The **Mercury Bay District Museum** next door details Maori history starting with Kupe's landing and displays shipwreck artifacts. (Open daily 10am-4pm; in winter Tu, Th, and Su 11am-2pm. $2.)

Twin Oaks, 9km north of town on the road to Kuaotunu, takes riders of any skill through farmland and to dramatic views of the peninsula. Transport is possible if you call ahead. (☎866 5388. 2hr.; 3 per day, in winter 2 per day; $30.) **Purangi Winery** is favorably situated on the main road between Ferry Landing and the Hahei and Hot Water Beach area. The organic winery makes 23 varieties of fruit wines, ports, and liqueurs that you can taste in succession; try the passion fruit liquor and boysenberry port. (☎866 3724. Open for tastings daily 9am-9pm; in winter 9am-5pm.)

HAHEI ☎07

The name Hahei (HA-hey) stems from Chief Hei of the Arawa canoe that docked somewhere off the coast around AD 1350. A tiny town, most visitors will come for the pristine waters, the hot water beach, and the nearby, stunning Cathedral Cove Marine Reserve.

▐ TRANSPORTATION. **Guthreys Express** departs for **Auckland** via **Thames** daily at 12:45pm ($30). **Hot Water Beach ConXtions** has great service to and through these parts, making a circuit between **Ferry Landing, Hahei, Hot Water Beach,** and **Cooks Beach**. (☎866 2478. In summer 2-3 per day, 7:30am-5:30pm.) ConXtions also meets the **InterCity** bus from **Whitianga** to **Thames** into **Hahei** or **Hot Water Beach** (return $16). The **Explorer Bus Pass** ($25) lets you on and off all day, or you can travel each segment independently (ferry to Hahei $10, return $14).

▐▌ ACCOMMODATIONS AND FOOD. ▓**Tatahi Lodge** on Grange Road is reason enough to consider a stay in Hahei instead of Whitianga. Its lovely wood lodge, lounge, and window seats, are perfect for post-beach bliss. (☎866 3992; fax 866 3993; tatahi_lodge@xtra.co.nz. Bike hire. Internet. Dorms $18; twins and doubles $45. Motel units also available.) Not quite as spiffy is **Hahei Holiday Resort** and the accompanying **Cathedral Cove Backpackers Lodge (VIP),** at the end of Harsant Ave. off the town's main road. Sliding Japanese screens lend slight privacy from the corridor. Located just over the dune from the beach. (☎866 3889; fax 866 3098; info@haheiholidays.co.nz. Dorms $16; doubles and twins $38; tent sites $10, powered sites $11; campervan sites $11; tourist flats for 2 $49. Prices for non-backpacker units jump in the high season.)

The **Hahei Store,** on Beach Rd., sells groceries and snacks. (☎866 3855. Open daily 8:30am-6pm, with extended hours in summer.) **Luna Cafe** (☎866 3016), around the corner from the Hahei Store and next to the Tatahi Lodge, has a fresh and often inspired rotating menu with salads and light meals under $15.

◪ **ACTIVITIES.** Hahei's **beach,** sheltered by offshore islands, is great for swimming but bad for surfing. Many surfers instead head to **Hot Water Beach** (see p. 133) where the surfing is better, but swimming can be dangerous. To the south of Hahei rises the dramatic bluff of **Hereheretaura Point,** an ideal spot for an old Maori *pa;* cross the creek at the beach's end and follow the path (return 1hr.) for 360° views. To the north, around a green hill, gaze out at the small islands speckling the ocean and amble down to the Coromandel's poster child (literally): the **Cathedral Cove Marine Reserve (Te Whanganui-a-Hei).** To reach the majestic rock formations over the cove, you can either walk from the beach or turn left past the general store to reach the 1hr. track to the cove (45min. from the carpark atop the hill). The track passes through pastures and hundreds of descending steps, winding through bush toward the jewels that make the track one the most visited in New Zealand. The white sands and lapping turquoise waters of **Gemstone Bay** and **Stingray Bay**— though they beg you to go for a wade or snorkel—are merely preludes to neighboring **Mare's Leg Cove** and the famous **Cathedral Cove.** With a pristine beach and arching rocks, this idyllic expanse of subtropical water hemmed by high white bluffs is only accessible through a stone archway carved out by the sea (which can fill to the waist at high tide). To enjoy the many splendors, you can swim out to the warped stone formations, standing like forgotten sculptures in the shallows, or feel the freshwater falls trickling over the white cliffs.

Nigel and his **Hahei Explorer** provide spectacular scenic trips at any time of year (1hr., $40) to explore the local islands, hidden caves and archways, and a spectacular 30m blowhole. (☎866 3910. 4 per day; in winter usually on demand.) He also rents mountain bikes and snorkel gear (both $30 per day).

HOT WATER BEACH   ☎07

Imagine a beach where you could take a little shovel, dig a little hole, and watch the hot water fill in to create your own ocean-side thermal pool. Well imagine no more—it's real. Proving once again that Mother Nature can outdo the resort industry, the 30-50m golden crescent of steaming sands is a free spa, percolating with water as hot as 65°C. Rent a cheap shovel from the beachfront store (open daily 9am-5pm), and for 2hr. on either side of low tide you can soak in your own hollowed series of pools while watching dolphins or surfers offshore. Although cyclones in 1997 removed meters of sand, letting the tide come in too far to dig pools in the beach, the Coromandel's best activity is growing again. That said, the pools don't always work; locals say Mother Nature cooperates 60-70% of the year. Chances are better in summer, though you probably won't have the only set of legs poking out of the sand; on occasion up to 1500 people simultaneously try to dig pools in the limited space. The beach is beautiful, but the rips, reefs, and sandbars that bring good surfing breaks also make for treacherous swimming.

Hot Water Beach ConXtions (☎866 2478) runs by the beach several times daily on its circuit (Explorer pass $25), and also picks up from the holiday park to meet **InterCity** at Dalmeny Corner (1-2 per day, return $15) on its way to **Thames.** While aboard, you may as well rent a $2 shovel. Call dibs on the best plots at the beachfront at **Hot Water Beach Holiday Park,** a small and tree-lined park that can cram up to 400 people in its tent, caravan, and campervan sites. (☎866 3735. Caravans and campervan sites $12, in winter $8-10; tourist flats (max. 8 people) $80-100.)

OPOUTERE   ☎07

Stay by the tides for a day or three to experience the sound of silence, punctuated only by the shrieks of shorebirds, the chortles of tui and bellbirds, and the wash of surf along one of the last undeveloped beaches in the Coromandel. Lying on a harbor estuary at the mouth of the Wharekawa River, Opoutere (oh-POH-tury) isn't a town—it's just a place, home to an idyllic hostel, motorcamp, and little else but 5km of perfect, lonesome beach. In fact, the only lights between the YHA and the phone down the road are the constellations of glowworms in the banks, shining diamonds in the sky, and sparkling phosphorescence in the water.

COROMANDEL

To reach this magical nowhere, a mere 15min. drive north of Whangamata, **Whangamata Tours** (☎ 863 8627, mobile 025 727 708) runs through to connect with the InterCity bus. Capitalizing on this oasis from civilization is the appropriately peaceful ▧**Opoutere YHA Hostel,** 4km from the Opoutere turn-off from SH25 (follow the light of the glowworms). Housed in a group of old school buildings, this backpackers is a communal oasis unto itself—a vacation from a vacation, really. The office sells basic groceries and spectacular homemade yogurt ($2 for a big serving). (☎ 865 9072. 12-bed dorms $14; smaller shares $16; twins and doubles $19-22; tent sites $10. Nonmembers $3 more.) About 1km down the road at the far end of the estuary is the **Opoutere Park Beach Resort.** Tent and caravan sites are afforded a bit of privacy by pine plantings; tourist flats and chalets are set near massive old pohutukawas just 200m from the beach. The office has few groceries, so buy before you come. (☎ 865 9152. Open Sept.-May. Tent and caravan sites about $9.50; tourist flats about $48; chalets about $66.)

The **Wharekawa Harbour Sandspit Wildlife Reserve** is one of New Zealand's few remaining nesting places for the scarce oystercatcher, a large black bird with shockingly pink extremities, and for the similarly threatened New Zealand dotterel (30-50 of the remaining 1200-odd individuals make their home here). During the nesting season (Oct.-Feb.), DOC tries to fence off and guard the exposed sand where these claustrophobic birds nest (they require an almost 360° view of their surroundings.) At low tide you can cross the sand bar and head up the shelly beach to watch kingfishers dart above herons stalking their prey, digging with the oystercatchers for pockets of clam-like pipis to supplement dinner. However, at high tide, the sandbar floods and birdwatchers must take the bridge and footpath to the nesting site (10min.). **Ocean Beach,** on the opposite side of the sandspit from the estuary, is a great spot to study the incoming waves and the jagged line of the **Alderman Islands** far offshore. Diving into the bush will scare up flighty fantails (small sparrow-like birds that the Maori believed brought death when they entered a home), as well as the other numerous native birds that constantly clamor around Opoutere on their way to the summit of **Maungaruawahine pa.**

WHANGAMATA   ☎ 07

Whangamata's 4km of white sand encircling an island-studded bay are known as one of the North Island's top surf spots. Outside the summer crunch of surfers and vacationers, small Whangamata (Fahn-ga-mah-TAH) is sleepily residential and full of easy-going locals mingling among the surf shops, cafes, and takeaways lining the main drag. You're always within a board's length of beach and bush.

▣ TRANSPORTATION. No major bus lines come directly to Whangamata; local shuttles carry passengers out to meet them. Make arrangements with **Whangamata Travel and Services,** 640 Port St. (☎ 865 8776. Open M-F 9am-4:30pm, Sa 10am-1pm.) **Whangamata Tours** offers a shuttle to **Waihi** for InterCity connections to **Tauranga.** (☎ 863 8627; mobile 025 727 708. 30min.; 2-3 per day; $18, students and seniors $15.) For the same price, they also run out to the bump in the road that is **Hikuai** to meet the **InterCity** bus running from **Whitianga** to **Thames.** (30min., leaves at 1:35pm to meet the 2:15 bus.) Both shuttles swing by **Opoutere.** To get to **Whitianga** you must wait two hours at Hikuai for the 4:05pm bus from Thames.

▨ PRACTICAL INFORMATION. Snug against the beach at the mouth of **Whangamata Harbour,** the town is a maze of residential streets. Any action centers on **Port Rd.,** the main street that runs into SH25 at either end. **Whangamata Information Centre,** a low-key, largely volunteer establishment, is moored at 616 Port St. (☎ 865 8340. Open M-Sa 9am-5pm, Su 10am-4pm; in winter open only until 2 on Sun.) Other services include: **Westpac Trust Bank,** on Port St. (☎ 865 9771; open M-Tu and Th-F 9am-4:30pm, W 9:30am-4:30pm); **Internet access** at **Bartley Internet & Graphics,** 706 Port Rd. (☎ 865 8832; open M-F 9am-8pm, in winter until 5pm); and a **post shop,** on Port Rd. by the bank (☎ 865 8230; open M-F 8:30am-5pm, Sa 9am-noon).

ACCOMMODATIONS AND CAMPING. Dude, local surfers often bunk in their car (price: free), or even someone else's (price: depends on the surfer). For more traditional accommodations, prices skyrocket in the summer. The rooms at the **Garden Lodge,** 500m from the town center on Port Rd., are clean, comfortable, and overpriced in the summer—borrow a free bodyboard to feel better. (☎0800 659 580. Shares from $23, in winter $18; doubles from $55; motel units from $80.) By the beach at 227 Beverly Terrace (turn off of Port Rd. onto Ocean Rd. heading SE, turn left onto Short Rd., turn right onto Beverly, and go to the corner of Lowe St.) you'll find the **Whangamata Backpackers Hostel.** You won't be afraid to toss a wetsuit over the mismatched chairs in this comfy house just a minute from the ocean. (☎865 8323. All beds $15.) Park your tent across the fence from sheep at the **Pinefield Holiday Park,** a little less than 1km south on Port Rd. to enjoy standard communal facilities and a pool. (☎/fax 865 8791. Caravan and tent sites $12; basic cabin shares $18; cabins for 2 with kitchen from $55; chalet doubles start at $75.)

FOOD. At **Ginger's Health Foods and Cafe,** 601 Port Rd., you can get vegan wheat products. (☎865 7265. Open daily 7am-5pm; in winter closes at 3pm on weekends.) Several cafes cater to the coffee and wine crowd. **Vibes Cafe** in the center of town spreads good ones with great espresso, cheap vegetarian melts, and sandwiches under $5. (☎865 7121. Open daily 9am-5pm.) For live music, check out **Cafe 101** on Casement Rd., where owner Gary tickles the ivories. (☎865 6301. Open M-F 10am-late, Sa-Su 9am-late.) Get fresh food at **Quarry Orchards,** next to the post office. (☎865 8282. Open M-F 7am-5:30pm, Sa 7am-4:30pm.)

ACTIVITIES. Most come to Whangamata to marinate in the sun and surf or take low-tide wades out to **Hauturu Island.** The best waves are near the harbor mouth. **Whangamata Surf Shop,** 634 Port Rd. is owned by a long-time surfer who rents surfing accessories at fair prices (surf boots, wet suits $10). (☎865 8252. Half-day board rental $18, full-day $25. Open daily 9am-5pm.) **Windsurfing Whangamata** has been teaching people to windsurf since 1982; board hire is $20 per hr., but $30 gets you a lesson as well. (☎865 8186; mobile 025 264 9463. Open 3hr. either side of high tide during summer school holidays.)

Good hiking and biking trails abound in 11,500-hectare **Tairua Forest,** north of town. **Wentworth Valley,** on the turn-off 3km south of town on SH25, is the center for outdoor activities in Whangamata. The river valley's walks are strewn with mine shafts and relics from turn-of-the-century days. A 1hr. walk leaves the campground (sites $6) and heads up to **Wentworth Falls.** At low tide, the sea tunnel at **Pokohino Beach** leads to a rocky cove with isolated white sand. A short, steep walk leads to the beach from a carpark at the end of Pokohino Rd., a forest road that branches off Onemana Rd. 6km north of Whangamata on SH25. **Whangamata Mowers and Cycles** on Port Rd., can provide mountain bikes. (☎865 8096. $100 deposit, $7.50 per hr., $25 per ½day.)

COROMANDEL

THE WAIKATO AND KING COUNTRY

Today tranquility settles over the lush pastureland and lazy streams of the Waikato and King Country, but life in these parts was not always so easy. In the 1840s and '50s, the Maori tribes of the Waikato banded together to resist the encroaching European settlement, proclaiming Potatau Te Wherowhero the first Maori king in 1858. The king's signature white top hat was passed on to his son, King Tawhiao, who used it during the Waikato War (1863-64) to make a legendary gesture of defiance, casting his "crown" onto a map of the North Island and proclaiming

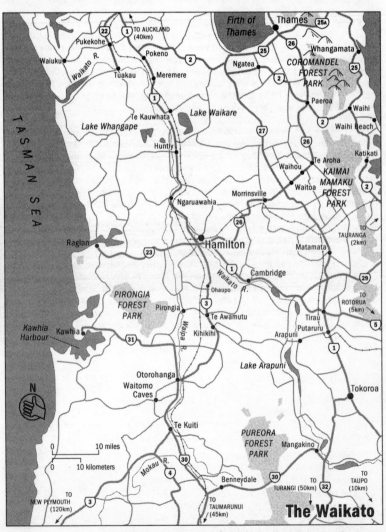

The Waikato

grandly, "There, I rule!" As a result, his people called the region *Rohe Potae*, "the brim of the hat." To the European settlers, however, it was simply "King Country," in grudging deference to the Maori dominance that lasted until the 1880s. Modern times brought a different kind of power to the region: the Waikato River churns out 50% of the North Island's electricity. The longest river in New Zealand, it is also the defining geographical feature of the region.

WAIKATO HIGHLIGHTS

UNDERGROUND CAVES in **Waitomo** allow curious spelunkers and adventuresome adrenaline-philes to explore New Zealand's mysterious underworld (see p. 145).

UNDERGROUND CULTURE of a different color defines the world-class surfing out post of **Raglan.** This town is the epitome of "cruisy" (see p. 141).

HAMILTON ☎07

As the home of Waikato University, Hamilton has a reputation as a lively town, and the extraordinary number of bars are testament to the youthful exuberance. Hamilton is the fifth-largest city overall. Other than the scenic Waikato River and many pea-soup-fog nights, Hamilton has few astounding geographical features and instead offers a central location. Half of the North Island and its terrestrial wonders are a few hours' drive away, making Hamilton a transport hub.

▐ TRANSPORTATION

Trains: TranzScenic (☎0800 802 802) heads daily to: **Auckland** (2hr., 4 per day, $35-43); **Rotorua** (2hr., 10:20am, $43); **Tauranga** (1½hr., 10:27am, $35); and **Wellington** (9hr., 2 per day, $105-116) via **Palmerston North** (6½hr., $79-89).

Buses: InterCity and **Newmans** head daily to: **Auckland** (2hr., 20 per day, $20); **Gisborne** (7hr., noon, $70); **Rotorua** (2½hr., 7 per day, $26); **Palmerston North** (9hr., 10am); and **Wellington** (9hr., 4 per day, $77). **Guthreys** (☎0800 759 999) runs to **Auckland** (2hr., 5 per day, $20) and **Rotorua** (2½hr., 4per day, $20). **Dalroy Express** (☎06 755 009, 0508 46 56 22) runs to **Auckland** (2hr., 10:45am, 12:45pm, $18) and **Hawera** (5hr., 3:20, 5:20pm, $55), with stops along the way. **Pavlovich buses** (☎856 4579) depart from the Transport Centre for **Raglan** (1hr., M-F 3 per day, $5).

Taxis: Red Cabs (☎839 0500) and **Hamilton Taxis** (☎847 7477) are abundant, especially at the corner of Victoria and Collingwood St.

Car Rental: Rent-a-Dent, 383 Anglesea St. (☎839 1049; 0800 736 822). Cars with unlimited mileage $49 per day.

Hitchhiking: Although *Let's Go* does not recommend it, hitching to Raglan is reportedly easiest along SH23. North to Auckland, many try from SH1 past the junction of Te Rapa St. and Avalon Dr., though they say it's best to take a city bus to the outskirts of town and hitch from there.

✳▐ ORIENTATION AND PRACTICAL INFORMATION

Hamilton lies off **SH1** and is bisected by the **Waikato River.** Most commercial activity and nightlife is on the west bank. **Victoria St.** is the main drag, with the stretch between **Ward St.** and **Hood St.** prime for daytime shopping and nighttime carousing. **East Hamilton** is more residential, housing **Waikato University** and many cafes.

Visitors Center: Visitor Information Centre (☎839 3580; fax 839 3127), in Transport Centre at Bryce and Anglesea St. Open M-F 8:30am-5pm, Sa 9am-4pm, Su 10am-4pm.

Currency Exchange: BNZ, across Victoria St. from Garden Pl.

Police: (☎ 858 6200), on Bridge St.

Medical Services: Hamilton Pharmacy, 750 Victoria St. (☎834 3444). Open daily 8am-10pm. **Anglesea Clinic** (☎858 0800), at the corner of Thackeray and Anglesea St. Open 24hr. **Waikato Hospital** (☎839 8899), on Pembroke St.

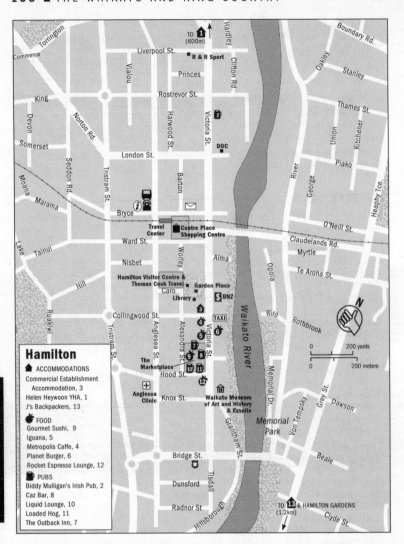

Hamilton

■ ACCOMMODATIONS
Commercial Establishment
Accommodation, 3
Helen Heywoon YHA, 1
J's Backpackers, 13

🍎 FOOD
Gourmet Sushi, 9
Iguana, 5
Metropolis Caffe, 4
Planet Burger, 6
Rocket Espresso Lounge, 12

🍺 PUBS
Biddy Mulligan's Irish Pub, 2
Caz Bar, 8
Liquid Lounge, 10
Loaded Hog, 11
The Outback Inn, 7

Internet Access: The **library** (☎838 6826) has connections. $6 for the first 30min., $4 each additional 30min. Open M-F 9am-8:30pm, Sa 9am-4pm, Su noon-3:30pm. The **Visitors Information Centre** also offers internet access at $3 per min., $8 per hr.

Post Office: 346 Victoria St. (☎838 2233). Open M-F 8:30am-5pm.

▟ ACCOMMODATIONS

Accommodations in Hamilton are spread out, so call ahead and arrange a ride. During **National Fieldays** (see p. 9) in June prior bookings are essential.

J's Backpackers, 8 Grey St. (☎856 8934; bookme@jsbackpackers.co.nz), in residential East Hamilton. A petite house with a sunken kitchen/lounge and impeccable bathrooms. Internet. Bikes free with 2-night stay, otherwise $5. Free pick-up. Laundry $4. Dorms $17; twins $40.

Helen Heywood YHA Hostel, 1190 Victoria St. (☎838 0009; fax 838 0837). As you head north up Victoria St.; it's on the right. Quiet, and reserved this utilitarian 24-bed YHA has a riverside location. Laundry $4. Reception 8-10am and 4-8pm. Internet. Dorms $16; singles $26; twins and doubles $38. Nonmembers $4 more.

Awesome Lodge Backpackers, 24 Bridge St. (☎838 2461; fax 834 3342; awesome_lodge@hotmail.com). Located just across the river bridge from Victoria St., in back of the Parklands City Motel, it's just a 5min. walk to late-night party central (the Marketplace). Laundry $5. Free pick-up. Backpackers $20-$25. Motel options as well.

Commercial Establishment Accommodation, 287 Victoria St. (☎839 4993; fax 834 2389). The renovated vintage hotel has private rooms along a long, dim corridor, 2 neighborhood bars (one right around the corner from the rooms), and a restaurant. Lounge has Sky TV. Laundry $4. Singles $45; doubles $60. VIP discounts.

▣ FOOD

Universities mean students, and students mean cheap food. Multicultural restaurants run along Victoria St., mostly between Hood St. and Garden Pl. **Food Town** (☎838 2739), on the corner of Bryce and Tristram St., is the most central market.

▣ Planet Burger, 206 Victoria St. (☎839 1444). Portions are huge: a basic Comet Burger ($5) and order of fries ($3) can easily feed 2 people, a deal on any planet. 20% student discount M-W. Open M-W noon-2pm and 5-late, Th-Su noon-late.

Iguana, 203 Victoria St. (☎834 2280). One of Hamilton's hippest places. Pricey meals aren't so costly if you share the heaping portion with a pal. The pizza ($16.50-$22.50) and salads ($10-16) are less bank-breaking. Open M-F 10am-late, Sa-Su 9am-late.

Gourmet Sushi (☎838 3500), in the Marketplace on Hood St. Vegetarian rolls under $1, inventive tofu-wrapped rice pieces $1.50. Open M-Sa 10:30am-4:30pm.

Metropolis Cafe, 211 Victoria St. (☎834 2081). Recently voted the country's best cafe, It serves mostly wine and coffee, but delivers items like mussels steamed in a lime, Riesling, and butter broth ($9). Open M-F 10am-midnight, Sa-Su 9:30am-midnight.

Rocket Espresso Lounge (☎839 6422), on the corner of Victoria and Hood St. Potent espresso ($3) bests inertia, heavenly muffins ($2.50) go fast, and panini ($6) complete your mission. Open daily 7:30am-4pm.

♪▣ ENTERTAINMENT AND NIGHTLIFE

Hamilton is home to numerous theaters, many affiliated with Waikato University. The most dynamic and impressive is the **Meteor,** 1 Victoria St. (☎834 2472) a versatile space for performances, raves, and other community events. With live music bars, university bars, Irish pubs, and two movie theaters to choose from, there's plenty to do at night in Hamilton…on the weekend. When in doubt, tap into the scene with *City Happenings*, available at the visitors center.

Caz Bar (☎838 0990), in the Marketplace on Hood St. Cafe by day, but the slick bar gets young revelers on weekends and a mature audience during the week. Live music 5 nights a week at 11pm. Open Tu-Sa 10am-3am, Su-M 10am-midnight.

The Outback Inn, 141 Victoria St. (☎839 6354). Waikato U's students try to memorize all 102 shooters ($5 each). Vegetarians beware: on weekends this is a beefy meat market. Open Su noon-11pm, M 5-11pm, Tu-Sa noon-3am.

Liquid Lounge, 21-23 Hood St. (☎ 838 0909). A small, trendy bar with modern decor and a luminescent fish tank. Jazz music. Open W-Sa from 5pm, closed Su-Tu.

The Loaded Hog, 27 Hood St. (☎839 2727). DJs spin tunes that spill out into the street from this hog heaven. Open M-F 10:30-late, Sa 10am-late, Su 9am-late.

Biddy Mulligan's Irish Pub, 742 Victoria St. (☎839 0306). Th DJs play '60s-'80s hits. F nights Irish band. Open Tu and Su 11am-11pm, W 11am-midnight, Th-Sa 11am-2am.

MMMM... SHEEP The National Fieldays are a huge deal. From June 12-15, 2002, 120,000 people will descend on tiny Mystery Creek (situated between Hamilton and Cambridge) for the Southern Hemisphere's largest A&P (agricultural and pastoral) show. With chainsaw demonstrations, head-to-head tractor pulls, and a fashion show of recycled farm material clothing, any stereotype of the simple farmer will surely be shaken. Come get a taste of real, rural Godzone. (☎843 4499 for more information. $12, children $6. Book hostels at least 1 month in advance.)

👁 🖪 SIGHTS AND ACTIVITIES

A walk through the **Hamilton Gardens** is definitely a highlight of the many cerebral diversions in town. Its historically-themed gardens are more than green; the enlightening and enlivening Japanese tea garden has a pleasant picnic pavilion, and, in the Modernist Garden, Marilyn Monroe's shining visage looks down upon strollers. (☎856 3200. Grounds open 7:30am-sunset.) At the **Waikato Museum of Art and History,** at the corner of Victoria and Grantham St., you can admire towering Maori carvings, an epic Kauri wood canoe, and rotating exhibits. (☎838 6606. Open daily 10am-4:30pm. Admission by donation.)

Not surprisingly, much of the recreation in Hamilton happens around the river. Paths on each side are ideal for joggers and cyclists to race with the canoers and kayakers in the middle. The paddle-wheel replica **M.V. Waipa Delta,** launches three trips per day, Thursday to Sunday. The luncheon cruise (12:30-2pm, $35) and afternoon tea trip (3-4pm, $20) are cheaper, although the dinner trip (7-10pm, $49) features live entertainment. (☎854 7813; 0800 472 335. Book ahead on weekends.)

Balloons Over Waikato, an awe-inspiring hot-air festival, takes place around early April (☎0800 2255 6669). For info on this and other events in the area contact **Events Hamilton** (☎838 6945, www.hamilton.events.co.nz).

CAMBRIDGE   ☎07

Cambridge (pop. 13,000) is the genteel neighbor of Hamilton and Raglan. In the middle of thoroughbred country, Cambridge admires the polished civility (and old money) of its English ancestry. Priding itself upon its reputation as the "town of trees," Cambridge roots itself firmly by the banks of the Waikato River, and then branches out into farms that speckle the surrounding volcanic hills.

🚌 **TRANSPORTATION. InterCity** runs daily to: **Auckland** (2½hr., 16 per day, $32) via **Hamilton** (30min., $10); **Rotorua** (1hr., 7 per day, $23); **Taupo** (2½hr., 8 per day, $27); and **Wellington** (8½hr., 3 per day, $72). Bookings can be made at **Cambridge Travel,** 74 Victoria St. (☎827 5096). **Guthreys** (☎0800 759 999) runs to: **Rotorua** (2hr., 8 per day, $20); **Auckland** (2½hr., 4 per day, $20); and **Taupo** (2hr., 12:55pm, $26). **Cambridge Taxis** operate **24hr.** (☎827 5999). **Four Seasons Mowers and Cycles,** 42 Victoria St. (☎/fax 827 6763), hires bikes for $30 per day. Although *Let's Go* does not recommend it, many **hitchhikers** headed to Hamilton walk along Hamilton Rd. (which becomes SH1) and stick their thumbs out before the 50km sign.

🖪🗐 **ORIENTATION AND PRACTICAL INFORMATION.** Cambridge is 24km east of Hamilton on **SH1.** The **Waikato River** runs through town, and **Te Kouto Lake** is a short walk from the **village green.** The **bus station** is on Lake St., behind the **visitors information center** under a green and tan awning. The **Cambridge Information Centre** (☎823 3456) is on the corner of Victoria and Queen St. Other services include: **BNZ,** 51-53 Victoria St. (open M-F 9am-4:30pm); **Bubbles Laundrette,** in the Hub Shopping Mall at the corner of Anzac and Alpha St. (open M-F 8:30am-5:30pm, Sa-Su 9am-2pm); **police,** 18 Dick St. (☎827 5531), across from the town square; **Boyce's Pharmacy** (☎827 7358; open M-Th 8:30am-5:30pm, F 8:30am-6pm, Sa 9am-noon); **Waikato Hospital** (☎839 8899), on Pembroke St; **Leamington Health and Medical Center,** 127 Shakespeare St. (☎827 5959), has a forwarding service to the **24hr.** on-call doctor; **internet access** ($10 per hr.) at the **library,** 23 Wilson St. (☎827 5403; open M and Th 9am-5pm, Tu 9:30am-5pm, W and F 9am-8pm, Sa 9:30am-noon); and a **post office,** 43 Victoria St. (open M-F 9am-5pm, Sa 9am-noon).

☕ ACCOMMODATIONS. You can taste rural life on a backpacker budget in the midst of a 5-acre hobby farm at the **Cambridge Country Lodge,** 20 Peake Rd., 2km north of Cambridge on SH1. The low-lying lodge is a series of adjacent units converted from stables into rooms with very comfy beds. (☎ 827 8373. Free pick-up and drop-off. 2- to 4-bed dorms with sheets $18; self-contained units for 2 $60, extra person $15.) The other cheap option in town, the **National Hotel,** is just around the corner from the bus station, at the corner of Lake and Alpha St. Pressed tin ceilings and intricate woodwork accent the 14 rooms; some have pleasant balconies overlooking Victoria St. It has a bar and casino, but limited cooking facilities. (☎ 827 6731; fax 827 3450. Singles $35; twins and doubles $60.)

◘ FOOD. Nothing beats a picnic on the shores of Lake Te Koutu. **Countdown Foods,** on the corner of Kirkwood and Lake St., is the place to stock up on groceries. (Open Sa-W 8:30am-7pm, Th-F 8:30am-8pm.) **Pumpkin Planet,** on Victoria St. between Queen St. and Hamilton Rd., has bountiful produce. (Open M-F 8am-6pm, Sa-Su 8am-5pm.) **Fran's Cafe,** 62c Victoria St., has antique tea pots and country crafts on display. You might fall in love with Fran's vegetarian lasagna ($4) or the sumptuous desserts. (☎ 827 3946. Open M-F 7am-5pm, Sa 7am-3pm.) **Prince Albert English Pub,** 75 Victoria St., in the Victoria Plaza, has more substantial fare. In the evenings, those who come out to play in Cambridge play here. (☎ 827 7900. Pints $4.50. Pool tables. Open daily 10:30am-midnight. Bar meals daily 11am-2pm and 5-9pm.)

◙▨ SIGHTS AND ACTIVITIES. Cambridge is well-known for being a stud area. Hold your horses, folks..."stud area" means it's a district for thoroughbred horse breeding. Add the antiquing and artisanry, and it's not surprising that this area has a reputation for being on its high horse; such pastimes regularly attract the moneyed elite of Auckland and the Waikato for weekends of indulgence.

Equine sports lie a bit afield; a walk or bike ride down **Racecourse Road** in Cambridge will take you past many stud, deer, and other hobby farms. Those 18 and over can slap money down on the pony of their choice at the renowned **Cambridge Raceway,** 47 Taylor St., about a 6min. drive from town. (☎ 827 5506. Races run M-Sa 6:15-10:30pm, Su noon-5pm. Closed in July. Basic stand ticket $4.) **Cambridge Thoroughbred Lodge,** on SH1 6km south of Cambridge, offers special horse shows that encourage audience participation. Many famous New Zealand race and show horses are quartered here. (☎ 827 8118. Open daily 10am-4pm for casual tours. Show runs Tu-Su at 10:30am. Tickets $12, children $5, families $25.) To ogle the studs working out, head to **Matamata Raceway** (☎ 888 4442), 35min. by car outside of Cambridge, New Zealand's largest thoroughbred training center. Eat breakfast while watching jockeys train the horses and amateurs ride before work.

Closer to town, the **Cambridge Country Store,** 92 Victoria St., has a selection of all things Kiwi within its 1898 church frame. The **All Saints Cafe** upstairs sells muffins and scones ($2.30), or light lunch items ($4-5). (☎ 827 8715. Internet. Open daily 8:30am-5:30pm; in winter M-Sa 8:30am-5pm, Su 9am-5pm.) **Tribal Art Collectors & Traders,** 89 Victoria St., may feel like a museum, but everything is for sale. (☎ 827 8848. Open M-F 10am-5pm, Sa 10am-1pm.) Saturday afternoons from October to May, **cricket matches** cover the lawn in the town square.

The nickname "Town of Trees" pays homage to the arboreal splendor cultivated by locals since Cambridge's inception. The **Cambridge Tree Trust** maintains the many "Tree Trails" around Lake Te Koutu. **Walking tracks,** accessible from the Victoria St. bridge, dart between riverbank and residential road on both sides of the water. To observe the green canopy from above, climb to the top of **Sanitarium Hill.**

RAGLAN
☎ 07

The inhabitants of the tiny coastal town of Raglan (pop. 3100), take relaxation and the "no worries" way of life seriously. The left-handed break at Manu Bay is considered one of the world's finest, and short of experiencing it first-hand, it is best appreciated in its full splendor in the classic 1966 film *The Endless Summer.* Join the surfers from around the world that cruise here each summer.

⌐ TRANSPORTATION

The only **public transport** service to Raglan are the **Pavlovich buses,** with a departure schedule designed primarily for those who live on the coast but work or study in Hamilton. Buses head to **Hamilton** from West Raglan, pausing right in front of the visitors center about 10min. later. There is no weekend service, but a weekend in Raglan might be just what you need if you're *that* concerned about strict schedules. (☎856 4579. M-F 3-4 per day) Although *Let's Go* does not recommend it, **hitchhiking** is practiced regularly along SH23, at the edge of town before the traffic picks up to 100kph. The favorite spots are the top end of Bow St. by the water tower (look for the giant surfing mural) and at the Te Uku outpost dairy.

✳❓ ORIENTATION AND PRACTICAL INFORMATION

Forty-eight kilometers of mountain road **(SH23)** winding around extinct volcanoes separate Raglan from Hamilton. The town sits back in the harbor, 6km from the coastline and the good surfing points. The **Raglan Visitor Information Centre** is at 4 Wallis St., near the intersection with Bow St. Call for weather and road conditions, as well as high tide information. (☎825 0556; fax 825 0557. Open M-F 10am-5pm, Sa-Su 10am-4pm. Go next door to the council office if no one is there.) Currency can be exchanged at **WestPac Trust Bank,** at the top of Bow St., where the palm trees start. (☎825 8579. **ATM.** Open M-Tu and Th-F 9am-4:30pm, W from 9:30am.) The **Raglan Surf Co.,** 3 Wainui Rd., rents surfboards for $30-35 per day and wetsuits for $20 per day. (☎825 8988. Open daily 9:30am-5pm.) For **daily surf conditions,** call Raglan Surf Co. or listen to "The Rock" 93 FM. Other services include: the **police** (☎825 8200), in a little clapboard house on Nero St.; **Raglan Pharmacy and Lotto,** for medicine or millions of dollars (☎825 8164; open M-F 9am-5pm, Sa 9am-7pm); **After-Hours Doctors** (☎825 0007); **Raglan Medical Centre,** 2 Wallis St. (☎825 8822); **West Coast Health** (☎825 0114); **internet access** at **Tongue and Groove** (see **Food** below), **Raglan Video** 9a Bow St. (☎/fax 825 0008) charges $5 per 30min. (open daily 10am-8:30pm) or the **library,** across from the visitors center ($5 per 45min.); and the **post office,** 39 Bow St., next to the town hall (open M-F 9am-5pm).

⌂🏕 ACCOMMODATIONS AND CAMPING

Raglan's wee population increases by 50% during the summer. In the winter, expect to find a number of visitors who came for a weekend and stayed for the season, as the surf is good year-round.

▨ **Raglan Backpackers and Waterfront Lodge,** 6 Nero St. (☎825 0515). Sharp rooms open onto an airy inner courtyard with hammock, flowers, and surfers lazing in the sun. Free surfing lessons, kayaks, and bikes. Surfboards $10 per day. Drop-off to beaches and walking tracks available. Mixed dorms $15; twins and doubles $36. Cash only.

Raglan Wagon Cabins, 161 Wainui Rd. (☎825 8268), outside of Raglan West. With the raging surf of Manu Bay only 2km away it's a favorite with surfers. Great views of the bay and of Raglan. Bunks from $20; self-contained cottages $80 for 2; tent sites $9.

The Raglan Kopua Holiday Park (☎825 8283; fax 825 8284), over the footbridge on Marine Parade, next to the Aerodrome and airstrip. The vast area can accommodate 2000. Kitchen has no utensils, but the ablution blocks have showers and toilets. Tent sites $8, in winter $7; powered sites $9, $8; 4-person chalets $10 each, min. $20.

◖🍴 FOOD AND NIGHTLIFE

▨**Molasses,** on Bow St., offers Green Eggs and Ham ($12) for your inner child and a Hangover Cure (priceless) for your remorseful adult. (☎825 7229. Open daily 8am-late.) Farmers and surfers chow down at the **Tongue and Groove,** on the corner of Bow St. and Wainui Rd. The veggie-friendly menu includes breakfast served until 2pm ($5-10) and dinner mains beginning at 6pm ($15). On weekend nights, the Tongue occasionally grooves to live music or DJs. (☎825 0027. Open M-F 9am-late, Sa-Su 8am-late.) Helpings of fresh fish for eat-in or takeaway can be found near the water at **Seagull's Seafoods** (☎825 8022), around the corner from the visitors center. Open daily 8am-late, live jazz grooves the place. In 1847, scores of prefab kauri wood cottages were deposited in Raglan in anticipation of a crush of immigrants. The only one remaining was retro-fitted a few years back to become **Vinnie's,** 7 Wainui Rd. The building has progressed from church, to school, to town hall, to a pizza pad and smoothie bar. Now the menu covers all manner of tastes (venison burger with apricot sauce $6.50) listed on several blackboards. (☎825 7273. Open M-F from 11am, Sa-Su from 8:30am; in winter Tu-Su only.) Raglan's only bar, **The Harborview Hotel** adjacent to the hotel of the same name in the center of town, is a favorite local hangout. (☎825 8010. Open daily 7pm-1am.) **Petchells Four Square,** 16-18 Bow St., is a market, auto supply, and sundry shop all in one. (☎825 8300. Open M-F 7:30am-5pm, Sa-Su 7:30am-4pm.)

👁🌀 SIGHTS AND ACTIVITIES

Whether you're seeking an "endless summer" or the dead quiet of winter, Raglan's black-sand beaches are worth the trip. Catching a ride to the coast is easy with one of the many beach-bound vehicles in town. If you have a car, make sure you lock it while you are at the beach; **theft** has been a problem in recent years.

Of the many choices for beach fun, **Te Kopua Beach,** the most accessible, can be reached via the footbridge at the base of Bow St. Accessibility has its price, though, as the beach is overrun with families and screaming children in the summer. Te Kopua also occupies a perfect harbor location for windsurfing. The less crowded **Cox's Bay** and **Puriri Park (Aro Aro Bay),** to the east of the town center, are ideal for children, picnics, or both. Walk along Wallis St. away from the visitors center to reach them. Find more space and swimming at **Ocean Beach (Ngaranui Beach);** the strong gusts also allow good windsurfing. Watch out for strong undertows; only the west end of the beach is patrolled by lifeguards.

Hard-core surfers head to **Manu Bay (Waireke).** Farther down the coast is **Whale Bay (Whaanga),** where green surf and rocky shore are accessible by a walking path from the cul-de-sac at the end of Calvert Rd. that goes over volcanic rocks to the black-sand beach. The surfing here is awesome in autumn, and in April and May there are often professional surfing competitions. If you're in search of a holy grail (or a red herring), somewhere between Manu Bay and Ocean Beach the elusive **Tattooed Rocks** can be found. Years ago, an unknown artist chiseled his way to local fame by sculpting two large rocks on the beach. They are only accessible at low tide, and some locals have searched for years without success. Today, the tattoos can be hard to see even when you stumble upon them. Farther down the coast, **Ruapuke Beach** offers rugged coastline and good surfcasting.

Although surfers might lead you to believe otherwise, Raglan has more to offer than the ocean. If you can't catch a wave, capture a spot on the slower (in fact, totally inactive) volcanoes of **Mt. Karioi** and **Mt. Pirongia** in **Pirongia Forest Park.** One glance at Mt. Karioi's curvaceous silhouette and it's no wonder that in Maori legend it is referred to as "the sleeping lady" (look SW from town in order to see her). With curves in all of the right places, Mt. Karioi's **Whaanga Road** wraps around the mountain's coastal side, making for terrific mountain biking. Refrain from careening around curves during the week—the one-lane road carries a considerable amount of traffic, and vehicles seem to be perpetually going over the edge. **Mt. Pirongia** is farther away, but is larger and has more trails. Another great ocean-view landmark, **Te Toto Gorge** has become the chasm where stolen cars are left.

Freshwater wonders also await. The locals are mighty proud of **Bridal Veil Falls** and the fact that it is higher than its Niagara counterpart. Its thin, delicate spray is best photographed from the lookout, a 20min. walk from the carpark on Kawhia Rd. The hike to the base is a steep one, but the pool is swimmable. Instead soak out many of life's aches and pains at the **Waingoro Hot Springs,** north of Raglan on

WAIKATO

SH22. (☎825 4761. Open 9am-9pm F-Su. $6.) With the proper DOC permits you can also hunt wild pigs or fly-fish for rainbow trout in the **Kaniwhaniwha Stream.** For those enamored with the surfer culture pervading the town, **Raglan Surfing School** offers 2hr. surfing lessons for $70 (equipment provided; 10am and 2:30pm). They also rent out surfboards, boogie boards, swimming flippers, and wet suits by the hour (☎825 6555. Open 10am-6pm daily.)

If it rains, rent *The Endless Summer* and cry in self-pity, or contact the secretary of the **Raglan Museum** on Wainui Rd. to see the photographic chronicle of the town's surfing legacy. (☎825 8129. Open Sa-Su 1-3:30pm or by appointment. Free.)

OTOROHANGA ☎07

The literal meaning of the town's name, "food for the long journey," originates with the legend of a great Maori chief who paused in his journey to multiply his few supplies, with a few magical incantations, into enough to sustain his trek. Otorohanga (pop. 2600) is known for its first-rate bird house (and Wiki, the kiwi welcoming committee) and a feisty town spirit.

▐ TRANSPORTATION. The **train station** is at one end of Wahanui Crescent. **TranzScenic** (☎0800 802 802) stops here on its way to **Auckland** (2½hr., 2 per day, $40-45) via **Hamilton** (1hr., $19-21), and **Wellington** (8hr., 2 per day, $95-106) via **Palmerston North** (6hr., $68-77). Like the train, **InterCity** also heads to **Auckland** (3hr., 2-3 per day) via **Hamilton** (1hr.) and **Wellington** (8hr., Su-F 12:05pm) via **Wanganui** (5hr.). **Dalroy Express** runs service to **Auckland** (2½hr.; M-Sa 9:55am, Su 11:55am; $33), and to **Hawera** (3½hr.; M-Sa 4:20pm, Su 6:20pm; $45). To get to **Waitomo,** take Bill Millar's **Waitomo Shuttle** from the visitors center or any accommodation. The shuttle drop-offs at accommodations. (☎0800 808 279. 5 per day, $7.) Bill also operates **Otorohanga Taxis** for your other local transport needs. (☎0800 808 279. Runs Su-Th 8am-11pm, F-Sa 8am-1am.) Although *Let's Go* does not recommend it, **hitchhiking** opportunities are said to be best from the bypass road north of town.

▚▐ ORIENTATION AND PRACTICAL INFORMATION. Maniapoto St. is the central road in town where most business takes place. The **bus station** is at the other end of Wahanui Crescent, at Maniapoto St. The **Visitor Information Centre,** 57 Maniapoto St., is located at the intersection with **Wahanui Crescent.** Keep an eye out for Wiki, the giant kiwi who greets visitors. (☎873 8951; fax 873 8398. Open M-F 9am-5:30pm, Sa-Su 10am-4pm.) **WestPac Trust Bank** on Maniapoto St. has an **ATM.** Fill up at one of the **petrol stations** in town, as there is no petrol station in Waitomo. The **police station** (☎873 7175) is located at 4 Ballance St. The **doctor on call** (☎873 8399) can be reached all day. **Internet access** is available for $0.20 per min. at **Corrugationz Souvenir Shop** on Maniapoto St. (☎873 8946; open M-F 10am-4pm, Sa 10am-1:30pm), at the **visitors center** ($2.50 for ¼hr.), and the **public library,** in the middle of the main street across from the ANZ bank for $10 per hr. (☎873 7175; open M-Th 10am-5pm, F 10am-6pm, Sa 10am-noon). The **post office** is inside King's Paper Plus, on Maniapoto St. (☎873 8816. Open M-F 8:30am-5pm, Sa 9am-7pm.)

▐▚ ACCOMMODATIONS AND FOOD. At the **Oto-Kiwi Lodge,** 1 Sangro Crescent, the energetic hosts welcome "backpackers, globetrotters, and musicians" to their compound at the end of the cul-de-sac. (☎873 6022; fax 873 6066; otokiwi@xtra.co.nz. *Let's Go* discount. Internet. Bikes and kayak rental. Laundry. Dorms $17; doubles $40; beds in recording studio $12; tent sites $8.50.) For hotel lodgings, try the brown splendor of the **Royal Hotel's** backpacker rooms with TVs, at the corner of Turongo and Te Kanawa St. Check in at the bar and pick up some cheap grub. (☎873 8129; fax 873 8744. Free laundry. Twins $45; doubles $60.) Slightly north of town, on Domain Drive and adjacent to the town's famous Kiwi House, is the **Kiwi Town Caravan Holiday Park and Motor Camp.** To contact the proprietor, the ubiquitous Bill of Waitomo Shuttle, use the phone in the communal kitchen. The shuttle travels to Waitomo at 9, 11:30am, and 2:30pm. Simple, clean facilities include a kitchen, toilets, showers, and laundry. (☎0800 808 279. Caravans for 2 $27; caravan sites for 2 $16, extra person $8; tent sites $7.)

Stop at **Tonis,** 13 Maniapoto St., for tons of tempting homemade goodies to top off your tasty $3 sandwich. (☎873 6611. Open M-F 8am-4pm, Sa 9am-3pm.) **Regent Cafe & Bar,** across the street from and slightly north of the visitors center, offers a large array of sandwiches, all under $3. (☎873 7370. Open daily 6:30am-5pm, with light meals F-Sa 5pm-9pm and Su from 6pm.) **Price Cutter,** at the south end of Maniapoto St., is the market of choice; it isn't tough when you're the only game in town. (☎873 7364. Open M-Th 8am-6pm, F 8am-7pm, Sa 9am-3pm, Su 10am-2pm.)

◙ SIGHTS. Let nobody tell you differently—Otorohanga is for the birds, but that's not necessarily a bad thing. As Wiki would tell you if he could speak, no stop in Otorohanga is complete without a visit to the **Otorohanga Kiwi House and Native Bird Park,** on Alex Telfer Dr. Although the birds are only awake in the day for 4hr., a sighting in the "moonlit" kiwi house is guaranteed; kiwis stay awake in shifts throughout the day. New Zealand's original walk-through aviary houses tuataras, geckos, and cave wetas. Don't look up. (☎873 7391. Open Sept.-May daily 9am-5pm, June-Aug. 9am-4pm. Last entry 30min. before closing. $8. Kiwi feeding 1:30, 3pm daily.) The Kiwi House operates a nightly **Kiwi Watch** where off-duty kiwis rest. Bookings before 7pm are essential and group size is restricted. (Allow 1½-2hr. Group size 2-6 people only. $15, children $6.)

WAITOMO   ☎07

Back in 1887, Maori chief Tane Tinorau and European surveyor Fred Mace chose to leave Maori legend behind and explore the depths of the local river cave. Although no gods were found that day, the two spelunkers were treated to an otherworldly display of bioluminescent blue, courtesy of thousands of glowworms. Within a year, Tinorau opened the cave to visitors to experience the ethereal wonder. One hundred years later, the glowworm population has remained stable, but the number of tourists has soared to nearly 500,000, putting this minuscule hamlet (pop. 250 on a good day) squarely on the map. Every day, over 50 tour buses roll into the village of Waitomo. After a few hours—and several million glowworms later—the buses cruise right on out again. While most visitors come for the "light show," nearly one-tenth are now attracted by the spectacular adventure caving industry, which offers trips of varying degrees of difficulty, low degrees of water temperature, and high degrees of pleasure.

WAIKATO

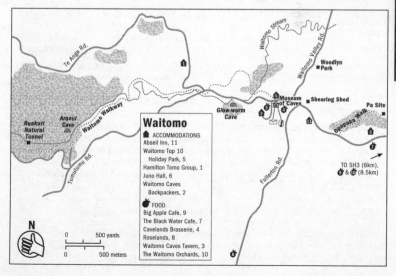

Waitomo

🏠 ACCOMMODATIONS
Abseil Inn, 11
Waitomo Top 10
  Holiday Park, 5
Hamilton Tomo Group, 1
Juno Hall, 6
Waitomo Caves
  Backpackers, 2

🍎 FOOD
Big Apple Cafe, 9
The Black Water Cafe, 7
Cavelands Brasserie, 4
Roselands, 8
Waitomo Caves Tavern, 3
The Waitomo Orchards, 10

⌸ TRANSPORTATION

Nearly 70% of visitors to the caves arrive by coach, and most transportation schedules accommodate same-day arrival and departure. **InterCity** runs daytrips from **Auckland** (4hr., 9am, $45) and **Rotorua** (4hr., 9am, $38); the bus returning to Rotorua departs Waitomo at 2pm, return to Auckland leaves Waitomo at 12:30pm. **Guthreys** runs service between Waitomo and **Auckland** (4 hr., 2-3 per day, $38), to and from **Rotorua** (2½hr., 2 per day, $38), and to **Wellington** (8hr., 11:15am, $99). The **Waitomo Wanderer** offers service between **Rotorua** (departs 7:15am) and Waitomo (departs 4pm). (☎873 7559. 2hr. one-way $25, return $45, children $15.) The **Waitomo Adventure Shuttle** (☎0800 924 866) runs Friday to Tuesday between **Auckland** (departs 7:30am) and Waitomo (3hr., departs 4pm, $31). The **Waitomo Shuttle** (☎0800 808 279; fax 873 8214) is the best option for those making **InterCity** or **TranzScenic** connections in Otorohanga. Pick-up from any Waitomo hostel is included (10min., 5 per day, $7; trips by arrangement $18). Although *Let's Go* does not recommend it, **hitchhiking** from Waitomo is reportedly best accomplished by standing at the junction of Waitomo Caves Rd. and SH3.

⊠ PRACTICAL INFORMATION

The Museum of Caves Information Centre is inside the entrance to the Museum of Caves in Waitomo village. Aside from booking any cave-related activity you could ever desire, the helpful staff can give detailed firsthand accounts of just how wet you'll get and how many glowworms you'll see. The **post office** and a shop offering the village's lowest prices on **groceries** and **souvenirs** are inside. **Card phones** are outside, as are **public toilets**. (☎878 7640; fax 878 6184. Open daily 8:15am-5pm; Jan.-Feb. 8am-8pm.) There are **no banks or ATMs** in Waitomo, so take out enough money for your trip and then some, before arrival. For medical help call the **Otorohanga on-call doctor** (☎873 8399). There is **internet access** at the Museum ($1.50 for 15min. or $6 per hr.) or the Black Water Cafe ($5 per hr.).

⌂⌂ ACCOMMODATIONS AND CAMPING

Despite Waitomo's popularity as a daytrip, accommodations fill up rapidly in the summer. Bookings are essential if you plan on spending the night.

Hamilton Tomo Group (☎878 7442), 2km past the village, is undeniably the coolest place to stay in Waitomo. Run by a local spelunking club, it offers very basic accommodations. The owner will take you on free caving and glowworm trips. Free laundry. Dorms $12 for the first night, $10 thereafter. Special rates for and spelunking club members.

Juno Hall (☎/fax 878 7649), on Waitomo Caves Rd., 1km from the visitors center and across the road from the Black Water Rafting headquarters. Perched on a hill just outside the village proper, Juno feels more isolated than it really is. Free pick-up and drop-off. Laundry $5. Dorms $17; doubles $42, extra person $12; suites with TV, shower, toilet $52, extra person $10; tent sites $10 per person.

Waitomo Caves Backpackers (☎878 8204; fax 878 8205), behind the Waitomo Caves Hotel in Waitomo village, is a surreal experience. The absence of any apparent staff gives the place an isolated feel. Check-out 10am. Dorms with basin and fresh linen $20, twins with bath $50, triples with bath $25/person.

Abseil Inn Bed & Breakfast (☎878 7815), at the other end of the price spectrum, offers bed and breakfast accommodations. Hosts Kimba and Brett work as adventure tour guides for the local caves, so ask all the questions you want. Twin rooms $90; queen rooms $100 for 2, $80 for 1. 5% *Let's Go* bookholder discount.

Waitomo Top 10 Holiday Park (☎/fax 878 7639; 0508 498 666; stay@waitomopark.co.nz), across the street from the Museum of Caves. Discount vouchers for Waitomo Caves. Linen $3. Laundry $4. Budget beds $16; cabins for 2 $35; self-contained units $70 for 2, extra adult $12; tent or powered sites $10 per adult.

📷 FOOD

Given the limited selection of overpriced groceries in the village, stock up at the markets of Otorohanga, Hamilton, or Rotorua, or at least in the visitors shop.

The Black Water Cafe (☎878 7361), 1km east of the village in the main Black Water Rafting building, has the best prepared food around, from large breakfasts ($5-13.50) to fresh-made lunch items ($3-6). The cafe has pleasantly cheap internet access ($5 per hr.), but be prepared to shimmy out of that wetsuit in record time or face the queue. Open June-Aug. daily 8:30am-4pm; Sept.-May daily 7:30am-8:30pm.

Roselands (☎878 7611), on Fullerton Rd. between Black Water Rafting and the village. Ironically, the best lunch in town is 5km out of it; the bountiful barbecue buffet ($22) is more than enough for you and a few tour buses. Buffet served daily 11am-2pm.

Waitomo Caves Tavern (☎878 8448), below the Waitomo Caves Hotel. *The* watering hole for all of Waitomo, and the only place in the village that serves dinner (read: pub grub) during the winter months. In summer, open for dining daily noon-2:30pm and 6-9pm, Su 6-8pm; in winter daily 6-8pm.

Cavelands Brasserie and Bar and General Store (☎878 7700) is the building next to the Museum of Caves. For those stranded in Waitomo village, this may be the only option for breakfast and lunch.Open daily 7:30am-7pm; in winter 8am-5pm.

The Big Apple Cafe and **Waitomo Orchards** (☎873 8753), are next to each other on SH3, 1 km north of the intersection with Waitomo Caves Rd. Besides free coffee for drivers, the Cafe has a freakishly huge hollow apple structure which visitors can climb for views of the countryside. Open daily 8am-8pm.

👁 SIGHTS

The holes dotting the green pastures around Waitomo are gateways to a mystical world where neither time nor temperature seem to exist—centuries are measured by centimeters of change, and the caves stay dark and cool regardless of conditions top-side. New adventure trips are constantly springing up to satisfy growing demand, and some advertise only in Waitomo. Given the labyrinthine array of caving possibilities (climbing, canoeing, strolling, and glowworm watching), it is best to book ahead and to check with the visitors center for the latest and greatest.

WAITOMO CAVES. If you are curious to see where all of those tour buses are headed, visit the cave everyone keeps talking about. Stroll along the stage-like boardwalk beside dramatically lit formations for a theatrical experience. **"The Cathedral"** has served as a venue for the likes of Kenny Rogers, the Vienna Boys' Choir, and Kiwi opera diva Dame Kiri Te Kanawa. The Disney-esque boat ride at the end is breathtaking, and probably the only time you'll find silence anywhere in the tourist-filled cave. Hear only the drip of water as the boat slips under a mantle of glowing stars. Take a midday trip and you will likely be consumed by a large coach tour. One of the most spectacular sights, the **Organ Loft** is so poorly ventilated that it is off-limits from roughly 10am to 2pm due to carbon dioxide levels. *(500m around the bend west of Waitomo village on Waitomo Caves Rd. Tours every 30min. 9am-5:30pm; in winter 9am-5pm. $22, children $11, families $20 for adults and $10 for children.)*

ARANUI CAVE. This cave holds a treasure trove of rock formations, and you don't even have to get your feet wet to see them. *(Tours run daily 10am-3pm on the hour. $22, children $11. Combination trip with the Waitomo Caves $35 adults, children $10.)*

MUSEUM OF CAVES. Any visit to Waitomo should include a trip to this revamped shrine to all things cavey. Inside, learn about how the caves were formed, contemplate the resident wildlife, and take in a multimedia spelunking experience in the small theater. Black Water Rafting provides a complimentary museum pass as part of their adventure, and Waitomo Down Under and Long Tomo Rafting will provide one on request. *(☎878 7640. Open daily 8:30am-5pm. $5, children under 18 free.)*

◪◪ ADVENTURE CAVING AND UNDERWATER RAFTING

Always go caving with a guide; **never cave solo,** even if you consider yourself an experienced spelunker. Virtually all caves are privately owned, and trespassing can be risky. Before you suit up, you may want to consider testing yourself for claustrophobia—head to the Museum of Caves and try the cave "crawl-through."

OPERATORS

▨ Waitomo Adventures (☎878 7788, 0800 924 866; bookings@waitomo.co.nz; www.waitomo.co.nz), next door to the visitors center, has the greatest variety of adventure caving trips ($65-300). Book from the Auckland Central Backpackers; substantial discounts are available. Office open in summer daily 8am-8pm; in winter 8am-6pm.

Black Water Rafting (☎878 6219, 0800 228 464; fax 878 5190; bwr@blackwaterrafting.co.nz; www.blackwaterrafting.co.nz). Founded in 1987, BWR is the oldest caving operator. Phenomenally experienced guides are sometimes called away from leading tourists to perform cave rescues all over New Zealand. Office open in summer 8am-8pm, winter daily 8:30am-5:30pm.

Waitomo Down Under (☎878 6577, 0800 102 605; wdu@xtra.co.nz). WDU offers 4 tours, frequently guided by direct descendants of Tane Tinorau. Trips depart from the WDU building next to the museum. Pick-up and drop-off available from. Students, YHA and VIP members, and groups of 6 or more 10% discount.

Waitomo Wilderness Tours (☎878 7640), an independent operator which runs **Long Tomo Rafting,** offers a less commercial approach and is the best value for limited budgets. Small group size (max. 6) allows trips to be tailored to the individual (e.g., the tubing to caving ratio). Activities include tubing, abseiling, and also the unique cave canoeing. Tours daily at 9am and 2pm; 11am and 3pm in summer. Call for details.

TRIPS

Fortunately, adventure tours in Waitomo cater to all levels of experience and enthusiasm. Each trip or tour has its own personality and pace—there is no absolute "best." Standard protocol for "adventure caving" involves slapping on a wetsuit and some coveralls (or just the coveralls if it's a "dry" trip), a hard hat with a head lamp, and gumboots. Check to see if you need to bring swimwear, a towel, and shower supplies. Trips that emphasize tubing or rafting are generally tamer than their spelunking brethren. Minimum age, height, and sometimes weight requirements apply to the trips, though exceptions are usually made for mature and fit younger children. Caving trips in Waitomo fall under three main categories, from short, sweet, and tame to wet, wild, and woolly; the most important thing is to decide how intense you are, and how much you are willing to spend.

I AM SCARED OF MY OWN SHADOW

These trips are, first and foremost, beautiful. While you will undoubtedly gasp, it will be from amazement, and not from lack of oxygen.

BLACK WATER I. The granddaddy of all underwater tubing tours in Waitomo, this trip involves a gentle float and the obligatory glowworm sighting. *(BWR. Allow 3hr., mostly for the ritualistic dressing procedure and post-rafting snack. 5-10 per day. $65.)*

TUMU TUMU TOOBING. Generally only available in the dry summer months, this trip features more caving and is the most adventurous of the gentle trips. Optional jumps and small rapids spice up the float. *(Waitomo Adventures. 4hr., 4 per day, $65. Book directly with Waitomo Adventures.)*

ADVENTURE I. This trip does provide the standard glowworm float, but a number of artificial structures (ladders, walkways and a water slide) mar the natural beauty of the cave. *(WDU. 3hr., about 5 per day, $65. Book at least one day in advance.)*

STARRY NIGHT Over the eons, humans have looked heavenward in search of inspiration and answers. Standing inside a glowworm cave, however, the answers might not be what you'd expect. The glowworm (*Arachnocampa luminosa*; in Maori *titiwai*), is actually not a worm at all, but the larva of a fly. After hatching, the baby flies secrete sticky threads (sometimes as many as 70, 1-50cm long) each with a drop of shiny stuff—the worm's waste product, lit up by the light of the bioluminescent larva itself (with the brightness of one-billionth of a watt). After months of trolling with poo, the glowworm undergoes metamorphosis and becomes a fly. Unfortunately, evolution was so busy figuring out how to make the glowworm's stool shine that it forgot to develop a mouth. After only a day or two of adult life—flying, mating, and laying eggs—the fly dies of starvation (or from being oversexed). The next time you gaze up in awe at the bluish stars in the nighttime sky of a cave's ceiling, remember that the speck of light is a maggot fishing for lunch with a glob of excrement. Ain't nature grand?

I AM ALLERGIC TO WATER

If you hear someone calling these trips "dry," rest assured they are not talking about their excitement level. More akin to true spelunking, perhaps, than rafting, these trips are a nice compromise between cave walks and full-on, no-holds-barred adrenaline.

ADVENTURE 2. Abseiling 50m into an absolutely stunning cave known as the "Baby Grand" gives real adventurers a little extra bang for their buck—you can choose to lock off your ropes and then swing, flip, and dangle in mid-air. Don't wear jeans or tight clothes. *(WDU. 2hr., about 4-5 per day, $65.)*

NIGHT ECOTOUR. Basically, it's Adventure 2 under the cover of darkness. Once you reach the free hang, the lights are turned out for a space walk in a galaxy of glowworms. Again, no jeans or tight clothes. *(WDU. 2hr., 1 per day, start time depends on daylight hours, $65.)*

ADVENTURE 3. A spelunking extravaganza where guests squeeze, climb, and get grubby with a smile. Bring a towel and soap. *(WDU. 2hr., min. 2 people per trip, $50.)*

BLACK WATER DRY. A family-friendly tour bringing visitors on a rafting journey beneath a canopy of glowworms. *(2½ hr.; 3 per day; $35, children $25.)*

I AM A BAD ASS

The next level of cave tours is a cross between Indiana Jones and being flushed down the loo on a string requiring basic fitness and comfort with tight spaces.

HAGGAS HONKING HOLES. Not for the faint of heart, and about as close to genuine caving as you're likely to get in a commercial operation. With "The Honk," participants explore caves on Farmer Haggas' property. The action includes three waterfall abseils, plenty of climbing and squeezing, and admirable formations all at a tearing clip. Prepare to get wet, dirty, and exhilarated. *(Waitomo Adventures. 4hr., about 2hr. underground; bring swimwear and shower supplies, 2 per day; $125.)*

BLACK WATER II. In October 1999, while Daddy was attending the APEX conference in Auckland, Chelsea Clinton and her buddy for the day, the daughter of NZ's Prime Minister, slapped on wetsuits to conquer these abseils, waterfalls, rock climbs, and flying fox. BWII spends two to three hours underground, but quite a bit of that is in view of unsightly artificial structures. *(BWR. 5hr., 2-3 per day, $125.)*

LONG TOMO RAFTING. This trip is arguably the best value for the money. With a dry abseil, tubing, and glowworming in a natural cave, the comparably low price-tag can't be beat. *(Waitomo Wilderness Tours. 5hr., 2-4 per day, $65.)*

LOST WORLD TRIPS. To say the Lost World Cave is just another cave is like saying that Notre Dame is just another church. In 1906, an awestruck reporter from the *King Country Chronicle* dubbed it "a fairyland without the fairies." **The Lost World Four Hour** is a 100m freehanging abseil into an ethereal world of mist and miniature ferns, not entirely unlike the land of Spielberg's dinosaurs. Don't wear jeans or tight pants—100m is a long time to endure a wedgie. The most daunting part of the trip is the 30m ladder climb back to civilization. *(Waitomo Adventures. 4hr., 2 per day, $195.)* If you've got the cash, spend it on the **Lost World All Day Epic Adventure.** The 7hr. odyssey begins with the 100m abseil, but skips the ladder in favor of swimming, wading, and walking a few kilometers upstream, passing spectacular formations along the way. *(Waitomo Adventures. Daily; 7hr.; $300, includes lunch.)*

AGRICULTURAL AND OTHER ACTIVITIES

Amazingly enough, there *are* activities in Waitomo that manage to entertain and astound despite a lack of wetsuits or worms.

◼ **THE SHEARING SHED.** It's actually not what you think. Each day visitors are treated to a free and unique experience—a shearing show that involves not sheep, but Angora rabbits. The fuzzy bunnies are denuded right before your eyes, but don't feel too sorry for them—they would overheat and die without the regular haircut. *(☎878 8371. On Waitomo Caves Rd. 12:45pm. Free.)*

WOODLYN PARK. Farmer, historian, and globe-trotting sheepshearer Barry Woods puts on an entertaining and authentic **Pioneer Show**, detailing Waitomo's colonial history. Expect animal antics, audience participation, and general agricultural hijinks. *(☎878 6666. Turn-off along Waitomo Caves Rd. toward Waitomo village. Daily in summer 1:30pm; in winter book ahead. About $10, children about $5, families about $30.)*

BARRY'S U-DRIVE JETBOAT. Although travelers inexperienced at piloting a jet-boat might rename this activity "U-Crash," safety equipment is in place, and the sloping walls of the water course are lined with tires. *(Also at Woodlyn Park. ☎878 6666. Open daily 9am-5pm; in summer also 6:30-8pm. 8 laps $35. Book ahead.)*

WorldPhone. Worldwide.

MCI℠ gives you the freedom of worldwide communications whenever you're away from home. It's easy to call to and from over 70 countries with your MCI Calling Card:

1. Dial the WorldPhone® access number of the country you're calling from.
2. Dial or give the operator your MCI Calling Card number.
3. Dial or give the number you're calling.

- New Zealand   0800-99-77-44 Clear Communications
                  000-912 Telecom NZ

Sign up today!

Ask your local operator to place a collect call
(reverse charge) to MCI in the U.S. at:

1-712-943-6839

For additional access codes or to sign up, visit us at www.mci.com/worldphone.

www.mci.com/worldphone

It's Your World...

www.mci.com/worldphone

BAY OF PLENTY

At the junction of natural wonders, cultural spectacles, and excessive cashflow, the Bay of Plenty is one of the North Island's most popular regions for travelers. Land of lakes, geysers, and hot springs, the inland tourist mecca of Rotorua captivates visitors with its pungent sulfuric smell and its wealth of Maori culture. Along the coast Mt. Maunganui rests on sun-warmed beaches while neighboring Tauranga pulses with nightlife. At the eastern end of the bay, the rough-edged Opotiki opens onto the remote, uncompromising East Cape and its intense natural beauty.

🖾 BAY OF PLENTY HIGHLIGHTS

FOR SKIN CARE geysers spray, ponds glow, and thermal spas and gurgling mud pools relax, reinvigorate, and exfoliate in **Rotorua's** thermal expanse (see p. 155).

FOR SUSTENANCE a **Maori *hangi*** is a tasty and cultural experience (see p. 158).

FOR SANCTUARY White Island, hidden in a perpetual cloud, is an eerie escape from the mainland (see p. 165).

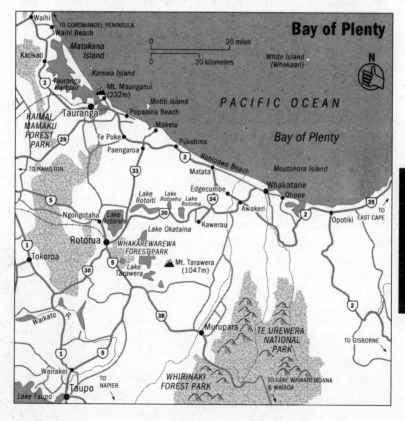

ROTORUA ☎ 07

You'll know when you've hit Rotorua. The smell of sulfur in the air, the threads of steam rising from the pavement, and the constant hum of tour buses will alert all of your senses. Named Roto- (lake) rua (two) upon the Maori discovery of the second (of 15) lakes in the region, the town is the North Island's most popular destination. Rotorua's energetic thermal activity and enlightening Maori offerings attract nearly a million visitors annually. Although tourism here is most definitely an industry, you'll undoubtedly find that the beauty justifies the hype.

▛ TRANSPORTATION

Flights: The **Rotorua Airport** is off SH30, around the east side of Lake Rotorua. **Air New Zealand,** 1103 Hinemoa St. (☎343 1100), and **Ansett,** 1200 Hinemoa St. (☎349 0146), both have 3-4 flights per day to: **Auckland** (45min., $97-225); **Christchurch** (1¼hr., $214-393); **Queenstown** (2½hr., $369-669); and **Wellington** (1hr., $138-256). **Super Shuttle** (☎349 3444. $10, 2 for $12) runs an airport shuttle to town.

Trains: TranzScenic's tracks end a few kilometers from the city center off Lake Rd. Trains leave daily for **Auckland** (4hr., 1pm, $63) via **Hamilton** (2¼hr., $40). **Super Shuttle** (☎349 4333) will take you from the visitors center to the train station (12:10pm, $3).

Buses: All buses come and go from the visitors center. **Newmans** and **InterCity,** both accessible at the **bus depot** (☎349 0590), depart daily for: **Auckland** (4hr., 4-7 per day, $34-43) via **Hamilton** (1½hr., $19-24); **Napier** (4½hr., 3 per day, $50-53); and **Wellington** (7¼hr., 3 per day, $60-75) via **Taupo** (1hr., $16-20). **Waitomo Wanderer** (☎873 7559) goes to **Waitomo** (7:15am and 6:15pm, in winter 7:45am and 6:15pm; $30, return $55), with pick-up and drop-off. **Guthrey's** (☎0800 759 999) departs 3 times daily for **Auckland International Airport** (4¼hr., $45) via **Hamilton** (1½hr., $20); and **Auckland** proper (4hr., $35).

Public Transportation: Rotorua City Buses (☎349 2994 ext. 2902) are cheap and run M-F 7am-5:15pm, Sa 8-11:20am. Routes are divided into sections; 1 section costs $1.60, 2 cost $2.20. The main stop is Pukuatua St. between Tutanekai and Amohia St. The green Ngongataha route goes to Rainbow Springs, the blue to Whakarewarewa.

Taxis: Fastaxis (☎348 2444) and **Rotorua Taxis** (☎348 1111) operate **24hr.**

Car Rental: Link Rentals, 1222 Fenton St., (☎349 1629) has "super saver" cars for $25 per day plus $0.18 per km. Open M-F 8am-5pm, Sa-Su 8am-noon. **Rent-A-Dent,** 14 Ti St., (☎349 3993) off Fenton St. past Big Fresh, has $49 per day rentals with 100km free. Open daily 7am-5:30pm.

Bicycle Rentals: Lady Jane's Ice Cream Parlour (☎347 9340) at Tutanekai and Whakaue St. Open M-F 10am-6:30pm, Sa-Su 10am-8pm. $10 per hr., $30 per day.

Hitchhiking: Although *Let's Go* does not recommend it, there's always hitchable traffic leaving Rotorua. Heading south toward Taupo, many hitchers start past Amohau St. and work toward Whakarewarewa. Amohau St. is also the branching point for SH5 north and SH30 east; many thumbers head a few blocks away from Pak 'N Save to go east. Catching a ride north is reportedly easier before Rainbow Springs.

✳❼ ORIENTATION AND PRACTICAL INFORMATION

Rotorua lies at the southern end of **Lake Rotorua,** but many geothermal and recreational attractions are spread along **SH5** and **SH30.** Downtown is a rectangular grid, delineated by **Fenton, Arawa, Ranolf,** and **Amohau Streets,** with the crossroads of **Tutanekai** and **Hinemoa St.** serving as a city center with stores, cafes, and banks.

Visitors Center: Tourism Rotorua, 1167 Fenton St. (☎348 5179; fax 348 6044), between Arawa and Haupapa St. A cafe and **currency exchange,** as well as accommodation, tour, and travel bookings. Open daily 8am-6pm; in winter 8am-5:30pm.

DOC: Most DOC services are provided by the **Map and Track Shop,** 1225 Fenton St. (☎349 1845). Open daily 9am-6pm; in winter 9am-5:30pm.

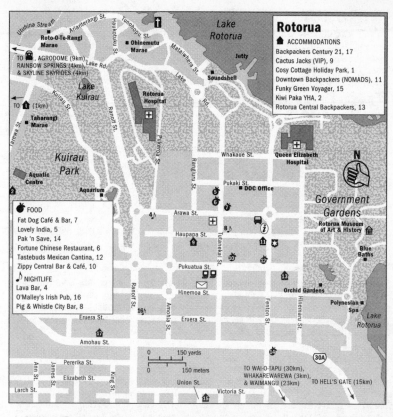

Rotorua

🏠 ACCOMMODATIONS
Backpackers Century 21, 17
Cactus Jacks (VIP), 9
Cosy Cottage Holiday Park, 1
Downtown Backpackers (NOMADS), 11
Funky Green Voyager, 15
Kiwi Paka YHA, 2
Rotorua Central Backpackers, 13

🍎 FOOD
Fat Dog Café & Bar, 7
Lovely India, 5
Pak 'n Save, 14
Fortune Chinese Restaurant, 6
Tastebuds Mexican Cantina, 12
Zippy Central Bar & Café, 10

♪ NIGHTLIFE
Lava Bar, 4
O'Malley's Irish Pub, 16
Pig & Whistle City Bar, 8

Currency Exchange: Banks with **ATMs** line Hinemoa St. Open M-F 9 or 9:30am-4:30pm.

American Express: Galaxy Travel, 1315 Tutanekai St. (☎347 9444) won't cash checks, but will hold mail for AmEx members. Open M-F 8:30am-5pm.

Medical Services: Lakes PrimeCare Pharmacy (☎348 4385), under the big turquoise sign at Arawa and Tutanekai St. Open daily 8:30am-9:30pm. **Lakeland Health Centre** (☎348 1199), Rotorua's public hospital, is on Pukeroa St. off Arawa St. at the northeast corner of the city center. **Lakes PrimeCare** (☎348 1000), next to the Lakes Care Pharmacy, has a doctor on call **24hr.** Open daily 8am-11pm.

Police: Diagonally across Fenton St. from the visitors center (**24hr.** ☎348 0099).

Internet Access: Vegas Cyber Cafe (☎348 5899), above Iconix at Pukuatua and Tutanekai St., plugs you in for $7 per hr. Open daily 9am-11pm; in winter 9am-6pm.

Post Office: 1189 Hinemoa St. (☎349 2397), near Tutanekai St. Open M-F 7:30am-5:30pm, Sa 8:30am-4pm, Su 9am-3pm.

🏠🏠 ACCOMMODATIONS AND CAMPING

Rotorua has no shortage of beds, though it may feel that way if you neglect to call ahead. Some good budget places line **Ranolf St.,** while the strip of motels along **SH5,** both at **Fenton St.** and the northeast side of town, give Rotorua its nickname: "Roto-Vegas." If you're desperate for a room contact Tourism Rotorua.

Funky Green Voyager, 4 Union St. (☎346 1754; fax 350 1100). Walk down Fenton St. to Victoria St. and turn right; Union St. is 2 blocks down. Staying in this environmentally-conscious hostel is a truly funky experience. Key deposit $10. 6-bed dorms $16; 4-bed dorms $17; twins and doubles $39; double with bath $43. Cash only.

Kiwi Paka YHA, 60 Tarewa Rd. (☎347 0931; fax 346 3167; stay@kiwipaka-yah.co.nz), 1km from town center. Walk west on Pukuatua St. past Kuirau Park, turn right on Tarewa Rd. An upbeat spirit reigns in this quasi-resort YHA. Free shuttle service to bus stop and hitchhikers' points. Key deposit $10. Dorms $18; singles $26; twins and doubles $42, with bath $49; triples and quads with bath $66-$88; tent sites $9; powered sites $10.50.

Rotorua Central Backpackers, 1076 Pukuatua St. (☎/fax 349 3285; rotorua.central.bp@clear.net.nz). From the bus station, turn right down Fenton St. and left on Pukuatua St. Managers help you conquer Rotorua with ease. Internet. Off-street parking. Bike rental $5-8. Key deposit $10. Dorms $16; twins $36-38; doubles $40.

Cactus Jacks (VIP), 1210 Haupapa St. (☎/fax 348 3121, 0800 422 288; isabella.pavlova@xtra.co.nz). Small personalized bedrooms Bike rental. Key deposit $10. Dorms $15.50; singles $33-35; twins $38; doubles $43.

Downtown Backpackers (NOMADS), 1193 Fenton St. (☎/fax 346 2831; downtownrotorua@xtra.co.nz), next to Tourism Rotorua. Quiet atmosphere suit its older crowd. Internet. Dorms $17-18; twins and doubles $42, in winter $40.

Backpackers Century 21, 105 Amohau St. (☎348 3001, 0800 100 656; fax 348 3006; backpackers.rotorua@voyager.co.nz). This backpackers was reincarnated for travelers seeking a little privacy. Spa pool, BBQ, laundry, parking, and game room. Internet. Dorms $16; twins and doubles $40; studio $50; family units $60-90.

Cosy Cottage International Holiday Park, 67 Whittaker Rd. (☎348 3793; fax 347 9634; cosycottage@xtra.co.nz), 2km from town, off Lake Rd. Thermally-heated sites and a private sand beach make up for the tired feel of communal facilities. Bike rental. Double flats with kitchenette $48, extra person $11; cabins for 2 with kitchenettes $44, extra person $11; tourist flats $65; tent sites $10; powered sites $11, for 2 $20.

◖ FOOD

A unique alternative to the droves of standard restaurants is the delicious and entertaining Maori *hangi*. Although the meals (which include a cultural show and/or concert) are above the normal backpacker allowance, they shouldn't be missed (see **A Maori Evening** p. 158). If you must self-cater in order to save up, **Pak 'N Save** is located at the corner of Fenton and Amohau St. (☎347 8440. Open daily 8am-9pm.)

▨ **Tastebuds Mexican Cantina,** 1213 Fenton St. (☎349 0591), under a "Mexican Food" sign. The cantina is always full of patrons bumping elbows to dig into plates of burritos, enchiladas, and tacos (all $5-9; choice of mild, hot, extra hot, or super hot salsa). Open M-W 10am-9pm, Th-Su 10am-10pm; in winter M-Sa 10am-9pm, Su 11am-8pm.

Fat Dog Café and Bar, 1161 Arawa St. (☎347 7586). This cafe shines with a playful atmosphere and colorful decor. $6 lunches and $9 dinners will surely coax a smile. Nice outdoor garden bar in the rear. Open M-F 8:30am-late, Sa-Su 8am-late.

Zippy Central Bar and Café, 1153 Pukuatua St. (☎348 8288). With an ever-changing menu, the tuna melt bagels ($6) are one of the tasty constants. For a few bucks more, dinner mains share the tables with candles. Open Su-Th 9am-9:30pm, F-Sa 9am-11pm.

Fortune Chinese Restaurant, 1129 Tutanekai St. (☎346 0523) 2 doors from Lovely India. Fortune smiles on those entering this Cathay made easy for Western tastebuds. Appetizers $5-7.50; mains $9-19.50. Open daily noon-2pm, 5-10pm.

Lovely India, 1123 Tutanekai St. (☎348 4088). A friendly staff brings a fresh slice of India (on a bed of basmati rice) to hungry locals. $10.90 lunch/dinner specials M-W. Open Tu-Su 11:30am-2:30pm, daily 5:30pm-late.

◖ NIGHTLIFE

Rowdy tourists are the sustenance of Rotorua nightlife. Even after a long day of mud and *marae*, travelers manage to hit the bars and beers with gusto.

Lava Bar, 1286 Arawa St. (☎348 8618), next to Hot Rock Backpackers. Green-bused backpackers crowd this mixer nightly, grinding to Top 40 dance music and pounding Lava's special shooters ($3). Happy Hour daily 4:30-6pm. Open daily 4:30pm-late.

Pig and Whistle City Bar (☎347 3025), at the corner of Tutanekai and Haupapa St. Weekends with live bands can still get downright felonious at this former police station. Weekend cover $2. Handles $4.50. Pub food until 9:30pm. Open daily 11:30am-late.

O'Malley's Irish Pub (☎347 6416) on Eruera St. by Ranolf St. The round pool table and live bands (F) attract a sprightly crowd. Happy Hour 5-7pm. Open M-W 11am-midnight, Th-Sa 11am-2am, Su 11am-10pm.

👁 SIGHTS

GEOTHERMAL WONDERS

Rotorua's thermal activity is caused by a volcanic fault line running from White Island (see p. 165), 50km offshore from Whakatane, to Mt. Ruapehu in Tongariro National Park (see p. 190). Colliding tectonic plates created the spectacular mountains, the bizarre landscape of the major geothermal parks, and innumerable steaming pools, craters, and vents—that's life on the geological edge for you.

▨ **WAI-O-TAPU.** This unbelievably beautiful "Thermal Wonderland" is the most colorful (and probably the finest) geothermal spot in the nation. Leased from DOC by private operators, the reserve is explored by self-guided tour, weaving among boiling mud pools, an expansive silicate terrace, brilliantly hued pools, craters, and (you are in Rotorua) crowds of tourists. While frustratingly veiled in steam all too often, the stunning ochre and turquoise colors of the bubbling **Champagne Pool** make the celebratory beverage pale in comparison. Erupting up to 21m each day at precisely 10:15am, **Lady Knox Geyser** is another Wai-O-Tapu attraction. Mother Nature isn't really that regular—the geyser gets a liberal dose of soap every morning to disperse the upper level of water and relieve surface tension. Prisoners discovered this handy trick in 1896 while washing clothes. *(Just 30km south of Rotorua on SH5. ☎366 6333; www.geyserland.co.nz. Open daily 8:30am-5pm. $14, children $4.)*

THE NEW ZEALAND MAORI ARTS AND CRAFTS INSTITUTE. Containing the Te Whakarewarewa Thermal Reserve and Maori Cultural Centre, this attraction, commonly called **Whaka,** is the source of a billowing cloud of steam, boiling mud pools, a kiwi house, and demonstrations on carving, weaving, and crafts. Along the reserve's walking tour, New Zealand's largest and most famous geyser, **Pohutu,** spurts daily up to 30m. *(3km south of town, accessible by Sala St. off Fenton St. ☎348 9047. Open daily 8am-6pm; in winter 8am-5pm. Free guided tours every hr. from 9am-4pm. Daily 30-min. cultural performance 12:15pm. $18.)*

PROPHET OF DOOM The events of May 31, 1886 were troubling to the Maori living under Mt. Tarawera. Sophia Hinerangi witnessed a vision: a spectral war canoe, its warrior paddlers wearing ominous symbols on their heads, emerged from a bend in the lake and then disappeared. Consulted for interpretation, the old priest Tuhoto said these natural and supernatural signs foretold something cataclysmic. He had warned his people in Te Wairoa that their departure from the ancestral ways—their gradual adoption of the white man's greed—would lead to punishment by his ancestor, the spirit Tamahoi, buried within the mountain. The night of terror came on June 10, 1886, when the three domes on the now flat-topped volcano blew and rent the mountain asunder, ripping a 17km wound of red, white, and black scoria-lined craters. The largest eruption in 500 years, it blasted away the bed of Lake Rotomahana, burying Te Wairoa and other nearby villages in mud, rock, and ash; roars were heard as far as Christchurch and Auckland. When the search parties finally uncovered Tuhoto's house, days later, they found the old man still alive. Tamahoi had protected his prophet. The Rotorua Museum of Art and History (see **Other Sights** below) screens a great dramatized version of this story.

WAIMANGU VOLCANIC VALLEY. This southern end of the rift created by Tarawera's 1886 eruption hosts several hot geothermal phenomena. Along its trail, the **Echo Crater** is home to the world's largest hot springs, where dancing steam creates fanciful patterns on the gleaming water. The ice-blue, and extremely acidic **Inferno Crater Lake** is actually a geyser, living on a 38-day cycle. The path also passes the site of **Waimangu**, once the world's largest geyser; the white cross nearby marks the site where four overzealous tourists were killed in 1903. Take a 1hr. guided boat cruise to the former sites of the **Pink and White Terraces** and steaming cliffs and exercise your powers of imagination. *(23km from Rotorua off the Taupo Hwy. ☎ 366 6137. Open daily 8:30am-5pm. Valley $16, with boat ride $36; boat ride alone $20.)*

HELL'S GATE. In addition to admiring 10 hectares of seething mud, pools, and the largest steaming hot waterfall in the Southern Hemisphere, you can pretend to be a Maori warrior salving his battle wounds in New Zealand's only "mud bath" complex. There is recuperation even in hell. *(15km east of Rotorua on SH30. ☎ 345 3151. Open daily 9am-5pm. Park entry $12, children $6; spa only $10, children $6; mud bath $25.)*

TOURS

THERMAL AND CULTURAL SHUTTLE. These friendly and informed drivers make runs to Wai-O-Tapu, Waimangu, Tamaki Maori Village, and Waikite Hot Pools from the visitors center and most accommodations. *(☎ 0800 287 2968. Daily 7:55am-4:15pm. Day pass $25 including entry to Wai-O-Tapu.)*

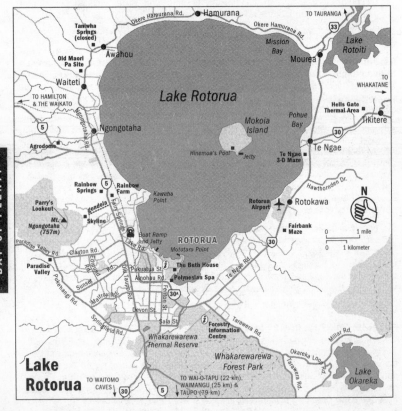

CAREY'S SIGHTSEEING TOURS. This operation offers a wide array of half-, three-quarter, and full-day tours including pick-up and in-coach commentary. A full-day tour, covers the geothermal wonders of Wai-O-Tapu, Waimangu, and Whakarewarewa as well as Rainbow Trout Springs and Farm Show. *(Office 1108 Haupapa St. ☎ 347 1197, 0800 222 739. Adults $65-145, children $33-80.)*

TE KIRI TREK. As advertised—rough, tough, wet, and wild. After a walk through Wai-O-Tapu and a thermal river swim, 4WDer Roger—sporting his daily uniform of gumboots, camouflage jacket, and buzzcut—takes you up to Tarawera Falls and down through Rotoiti Forest, with an all-you-can-eat lunch along the way. *(☎ 345 5016, mobile 025 391 288. Pick-up at 8:30am with drop-off around 6:30pm; $120.)*

MT. TARAWERA. The volcanic Mt. Tarawera (1111m), the cause of the 1886 commotion, towers over all Rotorua backpackers. While getting up Tarawera by foot is possible, the access point from Ash Pit Rd. near Lake Rerewhakaaitu south of town is nearly impossible to reach without your own transport. *Day pass for walking or hiking $23; 4WD shuttle service $80.* **Mt Tarawera NZ** *(☎ 349 3714; www.mt-tarawera.co.nz),* which issues the day pass and runs the shuttle service, also operates half-day 4WD tours and helicopter trips. The former features a guided walk around the crater and free tea and cookies *(departs 8am and 1:30pm; $110)* and the latter includes a landing on Mt. Tarawera (Flight time approx. 45min; $270 per person).

AGRICULTURAL DIVERSIONS

■**AGRODOME.** Entertaining busloads of tourists daily with amusing shows, the Agrodome's resident "farmer" shears sheep, performs a mock auction, leads sheepdog trials, and coaxes the camera-happy crowd to milk cows and pet baby lambs. You can also tour the working farm. *(10km north of town on SH5. ☎ 357 1050, 0800 339 400. Both activities run 3 times per day. $13 each, or $20 for both.)*

RAINBOW SPRINGS. For an agricultural experience that is almost identical to the aforementioned Agrodome (but with only 15 breeds of sheep), the **Rainbow Farm Show** gives visitors five chances a day to see its ovine extravaganza. A ticket gets you access to the show and a 40min. walk among animals and springs across the highway. *(On SH5, 5km north of town, opposite the Skyline Gondola. ☎ 347 9301. $18.)*

MAORITANGA

OHINEMUTU. A visit to this lakefront Maori village of the Ngati Whakaue tribe rewards visitors with a patient introduction to Maori culture. Of the compound's buildings, the **Tamatekapua Meeting House** is the most symbolically important. The interior is closed to the public, except for nightly concerts (see **A Maori Evening** p. 158), and showcases a smattering of paua shells and rich, red carvings with a maze of figures. *(Off Lake Rd., down Tutanekai St. ☎ 349 3949.)*

ST. FAITH'S ANGLICAN CHURCH. Across from Ohinemutu, this church has an incongruous Tudor exterior and Maori interior. The pulpit is supported by carved figures of five Maori ancestors, while an etched window panel shows Christ clad in the cloak of a Maori chief—from a certain angle, he appears to be walking on Lake Rotorua. A potent focus of cultural history, the church continues to hold services (the original St. Faith's held Rotorua's first Christian service in 1831).

OTHER SIGHTS

ROTORUA MUSEUM OF ART AND HISTORY/TE WHARE TAONGA O TE ARAWA.
To gain a greater appreciation for just about everything in Rotorua, give yourself 1½hr. in this outstanding locale. A former luxury spa, it houses permanent exhibitions on the eruption of 1886, the Te Arawa people, area geology, and the former spa itself. The various films featuring Rotorua stories are must-see exhibits. *(In the neo-Tudor Bath House, just to the right of the public Government Gardens at the end of Hinemaru St. ☎ 349 4350. Open daily 9:30am-6pm; in winter 9:30am-5pm. $7.50, students $6.)*

THE BLUE BATHS. Begun as the first unisex pool in the country, today the original site houses a museum about the baths, an elegant outdoor hot pool, and a charming cafe that serves tea and tiered cakes on antique trolleys. *(Next door to the Rotorua Museum. ☎ 350 2119. Cafe closes at 4:30pm; in winter at 4pm. Museum open daily 10am-5pm; in winter 10am-4pm. $5. Pools open daily 10am-9pm; in winter 10am-6pm. $7.)*

◤ ACTIVITIES

A MAORI EVENING: THE HANGI

The best way (in the best place) to learn about Maori community is through participation in a Maori *hangi*, or feast. Some emphasize learning about Maori history and traditions, while others consist solely of song and dance. Some *hangi* are held on real *marae*, some in specifically built commercial locations, and some in plush motel restaurants; be prepared, many evening commercial packages tread a delicate line between education and exoticization. The package you choose, and the attitude the sponsoring company displays, can significantly alter your *hangi* experience. Although the camera flashing can be disconcerting, this may be your best chance to move beyond postcard images of tongue-protruding tattooed Maori warriors to get a glimpse of the beauty, power, and richness of the Maori tradition. The *hangi* is also a damn good meal (see p. 158). Full evening tours by the several Maori-owned operators usually include an introductory communication protocol, challenge and welcome ceremony, concert, and *hangi*—all with transport from any accommodation (book directly or through the visitors center).

■ **TAMAKI TOURS.** Rotorua's most popular and polished Maori experience begins by choosing a chief from each of the several busloads of spectators who will represent his canoe (tour bus) for the remainder of the evening. After the welcome, groups walk through a model *pa* built to showcase age-old customs performed by Maori. Then, there is a engrossing group concert and festive *hangi*. *(☎ 346 2823; fax 347 2913. Evening $65, children $30; advance bookings essential. Dress warmly in winter.)*

MAI ORA. At a pre-European village overlooking the **Whakarewarewa Thermal Reserve,** this *hangi* is prepared by the underground heat of the water. Whakarewarewa also offers daytime concerts. *(☎ 348 9047. $65, children $35. Summer only.)*

ROTOITI TOURS. Run by the Ngati Rongamai tribe, Rotoiti Tours stages more authentic evenings in the Rakeiao *marae*, on the shores of scenic Lake Rotoiti. Groups average 80-100 people on summer evenings. Winter groups may be under 20, but performances are sporadic, so call. Overnights are also possible, but mainly for groups of more than 10. *(☎ 348 8969. 6:30pm. $55, under 12 half-price. Overnights from $60, based on group size. Includes bedding, kitchen, and breakfast; summer only.)*

WATER ACTIVITIES

POLYNESIAN SPA. Where else can you don your swimsuit, soak in ecstasy, and comfortably chat with travelers from around the globe? The **Radium** and **Priest Springs** ($10), filled with acidic water that reaches 33-43°C, are famed for their supposed healing powers. The luxurious **Lake Spa,** a landscaped terrace of caves and waterfalls, has a steep $25 price tag, commensurate with its stunning scenery. *(At the Government Gardens end of Hinemoa St. ☎ 348 1328; www.polynesianspa.co.nz. Open daily 6:30am-11pm, last ticket sales at 10:15pm. $10.)*

FISHING. With all its lakes (and purportedly more trout per capita than even Lake Taupo), Rotorua is an angler's paradise. Lakes Rotorua and Okareka are open year-round; other fishable lakes are open October through June. *(Fly guides begin at $70 per hour; contact Tourism Rotorua for a listing of operators and to get a $13 1-day license.)*

KAYAKING. To travel along the azure lakes that gave the city its name, **Adventure Kayaking** provides the transport. Conditions are especially good on Lake Tarawera and Lake Rotoiti. *(☎ 348 9451. Kayaks $35 per day, tandem $80 per day. Full-day guided trip $70, half-day $60. Twilight paddles $60.)*

ADVENTURE ACTIVITIES

AGRODOME ADVENTURE CENTER. With four original attractions immune to the "been there, done that" brag, this adrenaline mecca draws the bold and the beautiful. You can **bungy jump** off a 43m tower, zips around a small rubber-banked pond in a tiny 450-horsepower jetboat on the **Agrojet,** or roll down a hill in a **zorb.** The **Swoop** raises one, two, or three people linked in padded sleeping-bag-like-sacs to a height of 40m, and then lets you pull a rip-cord and fall at 130kph. (☎357 1050; www.agrodome.co.nz. Bungy $80; Agrojet $35, children $25; wet or dry Zorb $40; Swoop $35-45. All of the adventure rides operate 9am-6:30pm; in winter 9am-5pm.)

SKYDIVING. One of the cheaper options for skydiving in New Zealand, **Tandem Skydiving Rotorua** offers a 9,500 ft. or 12,000 ft. drop over spectacular Lake District scenery. (☎345 7520. $180 and $205. Book ahead.)

SKYLINE SKYRIDES. Rotorua is the semi-official luge capital of the country (not that there was much competition) thanks to **Skyline.** After ascending in a scenic gondola ride ($13), the luge hurls you back down on a three-wheeled plastic cart. Other attractions at the top include a sidewinder toboggan, a shooting gallery, a skyline ride, and mountain biking. (4-5km from the city center, next to Rainbow Springs on SH5. ☎347 0027. Open Su-Th 9am-5pm, F-Sa 9am-9pm. Luge rides $4.50 each, $16 for a 5-pass.)

WHITEWATER RAFTING. Adrenaline junkies twitching for their next fix will rush to the short but sweet Kaituna River, with the 7m Okere Falls drop, spilling out onto Lake Rotoiti. Trips to other area rivers, including the Rangitaiki, Wairoa, and Tongariro, are offered by many different companies, but are subject to good weather and safe water levels. The original company, with strong local endorsement, is **Kaituna Cascades.** (☎357 5032, 0800 524 8862. 50min. $65.)

OTHER ACTIVITIES

WHAKAREWAREWA FOREST PARK. It may not be native bush, but the 5667-hectare exotic pine plantation draws visitors with awesome mountain biking trails. For walking or riding, get maps and permits from **Fletcher Challenge Forest Visitor Centre.** (On Long Mile Rd., a short drive or bike from the city center off the road to the airport. ☎346 2082. Open M-F 8:30am-6pm, Sa-Su 10am-4pm; in winter M-F 8:30am-5pm, Sa-Su 10am-4pm.)

TAURANGA ☎07

Tauranga's warm weather and commercial conveniences have made it one of New Zealand's fastest growing cities; many come to Tauranga for the jobs in the kiwifruit industry in Te Puke, but vacationers also flock to the nearby beaches.

▆ TRANSPORTATION

Trains: The Station is on the Strand in the City Center. **TranzScenic** (☎0800 802 802) heads daily to **Auckland** (3½hr., 1:05pm, $58) via **Hamilton** (1½hr., $35).

Buses: Station at the **Visitor and Information Centre** on Wharf and Willow St. **InterCity** and **Newmans** head daily to: **Auckland** (4hr., 1:20pm, $39); **Hamilton** (2hr., 4:15pm $25); and **Rotorua** (1hr., 4 per day, $22-24). Transfers from Rotorua for **Whakatane** and points in **East Cape. Guthreys** (☎0800 759 999) runs to **Auckland** via the **Coromandel Peninsula** (3½hr., 3 per day, $30). **Supa Travel** (☎571 0583) runs additional service to **Auckland.**

Ferries: (☎578 5381) from **Coronation Pier** to Mt. Maunganui (summer 1 per hr., $4).

Public Transportation: City Travel (☎544 5494) runs buses along Cameron Rd. to nearby suburbs (M-F).

Taxis: Tauranga Taxis (☎578 6086), **Bay City Cabs** (☎577 0999), and **Coastline Taxis** (☎571 8333) are all available **24hr.**

Hitchhiking: Although Let's Go does not recommend it, hitchhikers heading to Auckland or the Coromandel Peninsula suggest trying **Waihi Rd. (SH2),** past Jonathon St. about 500m beyond the Otumoetai Rd. roundabout. Thumbers to Whakatane or Rotorua often start on **Dive Crescent** before the bridge and head east via Mt. Maunganui.

✦ 🔢 ORIENTATION AND PRACTICAL INFORMATION

Downtown Tauranga is located on a narrow northern peninsula in **Tauranga Harbor**. With the thickest concentration of attractions on **the Strand**, a strip of cafes and clubs along the eastern coast of Waipu Bay, the commercial area spreads west to **Cameron St.** and south to **Elizabeth St.** Cross-streets south of Elizabeth St. are numbered in a southward ascending order. 15th Ave. is the continuation of SH2.

Tauranga

▲ ACCOMMODATIONS
Bell Lodge, 9
Just the Ducks Nuts (VIP), 1
YHA Hostel, 8

🍴 FOOD
Fish Crazee, 7
Shiraz Cafe, 5
Sunrise Natural Cafe, 6

Visitors Center: Visitor and Information Centre, 91 Willow St. (☎578 8103; fax 578 7020). Open M-F 7am-5:30pm, Sa-Su 8am-4pm.

DOC: 253 Chadwick Rd. (☎/fax 578 7677), in West Greerton. Open M-F 8am-4:30pm.

Currency Exchange: BNZ (☎578 8009), on Willow St. and **ANZ** (☎578 2049), at the corner of Spring and Grey St. are both open M-F 9am-4:30pm.

Police: (☎577 4300), on the corner of Willow and Monmouth St.

Medical Services: John's Photo Pharmacy (☎578 3566), on the corner of Cameron Rd. and 2nd Ave., operates evenings. Open daily 8am-9pm. For after-hours only, try **Baycare Medical Services** (☎578 8111), on Tenth St. and Edgecumbe Rd. Open daily 5pm-8am. The **hospital** (☎579 8000) is on Cameron Rd. between 17th and 18th Ave.

Internet: Cybersurf (☎578 0140), in the Picadilly Arcade between Devonport Rd. and Grey St. $9.60 per hr. Open M-F 9am-6pm, Sa 10am-4pm, Su 11am-4pm.

Post Office: 17 Grey St., inside **Books & More**. Open M-F 8:30am-5pm, Sa 9am-noon.

▲ NIGHTLIFE
Lone Star, 2
Crown and Badger, 4
Bahama Hut, 3

🔢 ACCOMMODATIONS

While those without vehicles will stay downtown, more mobile visitors will find an array of motorparks and motels along **Waihi Rd.** (coming from Auckland) or **Turret Rd./15th Ave.** Kiwifruit contractors rely upon hostels to supply labor, which runs from mid-Apr.-May, with packing and pruning lasting into June.

Just the Ducks Nuts (VIP), 6 Vale St. (☎576 1366), in Otumoetai. Take Chapel St. from Tauranga. A free pick-up whisks you to a suburban hostel with a glassed-in conservatory, fireplace, and pool table. Free bikes. Dorms $18; twins or doubles $38; tent sites $10. Weekly singles $90.

YHA Hostel, 171 Elizabeth St. (☎/fax 578 5064), a convenient 10min. walk from the Strand. Employment help and discounts for area activities. Reception 8-10am and 5-10:30pm; in winter 5-8:30pm. Dorms $19; doubles $40; tent sites $10 per person.

Bell Lodge, 39 Bell St. (☎578 6344; fax 578 6342; bell.lodge@host.co.nz), near the Otumoetai Rd. roundabout off Waihi Rd. (or SH2). It offers modern rooms overlooking a patio. Internet. Reception from 8am. Dorms $15-16; twins and doubles with bath $36, with TV $42; tent sites $9; ensuites $70. Weekly dorms $80; discount with *Let's Go*.

FOOD

Shiraz Cafe, 12 Wharf St. (☎577 0059). The cream of Tauranga's cafe crop, Shiraz offers Mideast bang for your buck (hummus $6). Outdoor seating and pleasant courtyard. Open M-Sa 11am-2:30pm and 5-10pm (closing time varies).

The Sunrise Natural Cafe, 10 Wharf St. (☎578 9302). Vegetarian sandwiches and tantalizing desserts (all $2-4) offer a respite from the deep-fried delights of typical Kiwi cuisine. Shares outdoor seating with Shiraz. Open M-F 8am-3:30pm, Sa 9am-2pm.

Fish Crazee, 85 the Strand (☎577 9375). A friendly local fish'n'chipper decorated with bronzed fish poised to take revenge on humanity for frying their brethren in hot oil (fish'n'chips under $5). Go nuts there or have your crazee delivered ($3.50 extra). Open M-Tu 4pm-late, W-F 11am-late, Sa-Su 8am-late.

NIGHTLIFE

The Crown & Badger, 91 the Strand (☎571 3038), at the corner of the Strand and Wharf St. Dim lighting, background music, and ample space turn this tavern into the new watering hole of the moment. Snacks $3-8. Meals served noon-2:30pm and 6-9:30pm ($8.50-14.50). Open daily 10am-2am.

Bahama Hut, 19 Wharf St. (☎571 0839). Two pool tables, a big-screen projection TV, surfboards, and glowing torches complete the party picture. In winter open Su-Th 4pm-3am, F-Sa noon-3am. Open earlier in summer.

Lone Star, 51 the Strand (☎571 4111). Longhorns on the wall, an open hearth fire, and an American flag over the entrance to the bathrooms should help wayward cowpokes feel at home. Beers $3.50-4.

SIGHTS

Although Tauranga has a notable history, don't expect to spend the day marveling at architecture or museums—people come here for the beach and bars. Activities and adventure options abound in Tauranga.

If the line at the **Bungee Rocket** (see **Adventure Activities** below) is too long, at the end of the Strand sits **Te Awanui,** an intricately carved replica Maori canoe. The small greenhouse and rose gardens of **Robbins Park** have a view of the harbor and the less-than-picturesque shipping industry. Up Cliff Rd. and left on Mission St., the beautiful grounds of the **Elms Mission Station** were established in 1835 as Tauranga's first mission. Walk the small path through the tranquil grounds where ripe kiwifruit and tangerines hang down by the chapel in late fall. A bit farther off the beaten track, is the Mission's cemetery on a mound, just to the right of Dive Crescent's intersection with Marsh St. (☎578 4011. Building open Su. 2-3:30pm. Grounds open anytime.) At the **Mills Reef Winery,** 143 Moffat Rd., off Waihi Rd. on the way out of town, has free tastings of both kiwifruit and grape wine. (☎576 8800. Open daily 10am-5pm. Tastings 10am-5pm.)

ADVENTURE ACTIVITIES

For the restless and reckless, there is skydiving, gliding, and, in a bizarre manifestation of the Kiwi obsession with all things bungy, the **Bungee Rocket.** Situated on the Strand right on the waterfront, this unique expression of human creativity shoots its hapless passenger 50m into the air at speeds up to 160kph. (☎578 3057. Open M-W, Su 10am-8pm, Th 10am-10pm, F-Sa 10am-1am. $35.) **Papamoa Adventure Park** in Papamoa off Welcome Bay Rd., provides horse-trekking, grass-skiing, target shooting, and 160 acres of pastoral land with superb vistas for picnics. If these attractions and the community of farm animals don't justify the 15min. drive from town, the death-defying dirt luge track certainly will. (☎542 0972. $10.)

Tauranga is not far from the **Wairoa River** and its gut-wrenching Class V rapids. However, the river is only raftable 26 days a year from Jan.-Mar. when the dam on its upper reaches is opened. In that brief window, **Wet 'n' Wild Adventure** runs one-hour jaunts down the Wairoa. (☎348 3191, 0800 462 7238. $80, double run for $130.) Whether it's deep-sea fishing or reefer-game, most trips are booked at, and leave from, the **Fishing and Boat Charters office** (☎577 9100) on Coronation Pier. A full-day excursion with shaggy-bearded Butler and **Gemini Galaxsea Charters** will take you onto the open seas to swim with the dolphins and explore off-shore islands and seal colonies. (Evening/winter ☎578 3197, mobile 025 272 8353; www.swimwithdolphins.co.nz. $90, gear provided.) For those with an aversion to water, there are other fish in the proverbial sea of activities. You can act out your death wish in a 2500m fall with **Tandem Skydiving.** (☎576 7990, $190.) Slightly less precipitous for both body and budget, the **Tauranga Gliding Club** offers varying height levels of flights on weekends and Wed. afternoons. (☎575 6768, $50-75.)

▨ DAYTRIPS AND WALKS

Thirty-five kilometers offshore lies **Mayor Island,** an isolated and undeveloped volcanic region under Maori ownership. Snorkeling and diving areas abound, but the island has no amenities beyond a rugged campground, and you must obtain permission to land beforehand. **MV Manutere** makes seasonal runs to the island—more information can be found at **Coronation Pier.** Even fewer people make it out to the 24km of beaches at nearby **Matakana Island.** However, stretching across the entrance to Tauranga Harbour and absorbing the blows of the Pacific, the island makes for one of the Bay of Plenty's best surf spots.

The **McLaren Falls Park tracks,** a 15min. drive down SH29 toward Hamilton, is a pleasantly pastoral area hike. For more mobile travelers, the **Kaimai Mamaku Forest Park,** stretching to the west of town, provides 37,140 hectares of forests and rivers laced with trails. It's basically an extension of the **Coromandel Forest Park,** but houses fewer crowds. Otherwise, you'll have to duke it out with the joggers on the boardwalks around the popular **Waikareao Estuary.**

MT. MAUNGANUI   ☎07

An extinct volcanic cone visible from kilometers away, Mt. Maunganui rises from the mists of Tauranga Harbour. Attracting tourists from all over New Zealand and abroad, "the Mount" explodes with activity in the summer months. Formerly a Maori residence and stronghold, the mountain now reigns over the seasonal town that bears its name.

▐ **TRANSPORTATION.** Local **buses, InterCity,** and **Newmans** (☎571 3211) run daily to **Tauranga** (15min., several times a day), with stops at the Hot Pools, Bayfair Shopping Center (3km from town), and the McDonald's on Maunganui Rd. Depending on the bus you catch, service may continue to **Thames, Auckland, Hamilton,** or **Hastings.** Guthreys (☎0800 759 999) also runs service to **Auckland** via **Tauranga** three times a day (leaving at 8:30am, 10:30am, and 12:45pm). In the summer, take the **ferry** to **Tauranga** from Salisbury Wharf. (Every hr. 9am-5pm, $6.)

▨▐ **ORIENTATION AND PRACTICAL INFORMATION.** The town's main drag is **Maunganui Rd.,** and the center of town is almost directly below the Mount. **Marine Parade/Ocean Beach Rd.** runs along the ocean and toward the fine sands of **Papamoa Beach Reserve. The Mall** runs on the harbor side of downtown. The **Information Centre** is on Salisbury Ave. (☎575 5099. Open M-F 9am-5pm, Sa-Su 9am-4pm. Extended hours in summer.) Other services include the **Post Shop and Copy Centre,** 155 Maunganui Rd. (☎575 8180. Open M-F 9am-5pm, Sa 9:30am-noon.)

▐▨ **ACCOMMODATIONS AND FOOD. Mount Backpackers,** 87 Maunganui Rd., is in the town center. Space is tight throughout, but the hosts are helpful, and it's a stone's throw from the beach and the bars in town. (☎/fax 575 0860. Dorms $16-18; doubles $45. Weekly dorms in winter $95.) Bright blue **Pacific Coast Lodge (NOMADS),** 432 Maunganui Rd., has plenty of space with comfy mattresses and a quiet atmosphere. (☎574 9601. Key deposit $10. Dorms $16-18; twins and doubles $20-25 per person; singles $35.) At the very base of the mountain is **Maunganui Domain Motor Camp**, 1 Adams Ave., with 274 powered tent or caravan sites stretching from the harborside to the beachfront, and a tourist cabin with a kitchenette. (☎575 4471; fax 575 4476. $15 deposit per night. Tent sites from about $10; vehicles or caravans from about $10 per person, children under 15 $5.)

Crush, 107 Maunganui Rd., offers the funkiest, freshest grub in town. Specializing in vegetarian and seafood fare, this laid back cafe serves generous portions. (☎/fax 575 0096. Open daily 8am-10pm, closes early on Mon.) For the most chow for your New Zealand buck, **Kwang Chow,** 241 Maunganui Rd., next to the town's multiplex cinema, offers an all-you-can-eat smorgasbord of standard, but bountiful Chinese food. Reservations are suggested. (☎575 5063. Open 11:30am-late.) **Price Cutters,** at the corner of Pacific Ave. and Maunganui Rd., has beach snacks. (Open M-Sa 7:30am-6pm, Su 7:30am-5pm.)

◐◪ SIGHTS AND ACTIVITIES. It doesn't take a rocket scientist to find the attraction in the Mount—it sticks out like, well, an **extinct volcano** rising 232m out of the sea. Follow Adams Ave. or the Mall to where they peter out into a paved lot and well-maintained track around the base of the volcano. The track is an easy and dramatic 45min. walk with fantastically warped rocks and crashing surf on one side and grazing sheep and tangled forest on the other. Routes go up the mountain at several spots off the base track, each offering a strenuous 35min. ascent and a knee-knocking 20min. descent. There's also a short jaunt out onto the oddly peninsular **Moturiki Island** that juts into the main beach, and the nearby **Blow Hole**.

The Mount's other major draw (beaches not withstanding) is the **hot saltwater pools,** located at the base of the mountain. A more tepid lap pool, private pools, storage lockers, and multi-trip passes are all available. (☎575 0868. Open M-Sa 6am-10pm, Su 8am-10pm. $2.50, children $1.50. Private pools $3.50 per 30min.) The prime surfing **beach** is next to the mountain, but white sand stretches for miles to the east, and sheltered waters wait across the peninsula in **Pilot Bay. Ocean Sports,** 96 Maunganui Rd. rents surfboards, bodyboards, and wetsuits. (☎575 9133. Surfboards $30 per day; wetsuits $10 per day; lessons $25 per hr.)

WHAKATANE   ☎07

The town of Whakatane (FAH-ka-tah-nee) boasts some trendy cafes and shops in addition to the wealth of its natural surroundings. Visitors come mainly for the beaches, the climate, and White Island, the ominously smoking volcanic island 50km offshore and the town's single largest draw. As transport options are limited, it's a good idea to rent a car out of Whakatane (pop. 14,400) to reach surrounding attractions—in some cases hiring a taxi might come out cheaper.

▐ TRANSPORTATION. InterCity departs from the Whakatane Information Centre (☎308 6058) on Boon St. for **Gisborne** once daily (3hr., $48) via **Opotiki** (45min., $16); **Tauranga** ($25) via **Rotorua** (1hr., 1 per day, $25); and **Auckland** (6hr;, 1 per day M-Sa, 2 per day Su; $56). For **Wellington,** catch the InterCity bus to Rotorua and connect from there. For **taxis,** call **Dial-a-Cab** (☎0800 342 522). **Hertz,** 105 Commerce St. (☎308 6155) is the most accessible rental company from downtown. Although *Let's Go* doesn't recommend it, **hitchers** often head immediately across the Whakatane River Bridge. The roundabout where Gorge Rd. branches off Commerce St. towards Ohope is considered by many to be the best spot for those going east.

▣▐ ORIENTATION AND PRACTICAL INFORMATION. Whakatane lies on drained wetlands between high bluffs and the final bend of the Whakatane River. The commercial center is pushed up against the bluffs along **the Strand,** with **Boon St.** and **Richardson St.** branching off. **Landing/Domain Rd.,** the western entrance of SH2, and **Commerce St.** against the bluffs are the main routes in and out of town. The **Whakatane Information Centre** is on Boon St. (☎308 6058. Open M-F 9am-5pm,

Sa-Su 9:30am-3:30pm; in Dec.-Jan. daily 7am-7pm. Scheduled to move to a new location on the corner of Kakahoroa St. and Quay St. by March, 2002.) Other services include: **WestpacTrust Bank** with **ATM**, on the Strand between Boon and Commerce St. (open M-Tu and Th-F 9am-4:30pm, W 9:30am-4:30pm); **police** (24hr. ☎308 5255); **hospital** (☎307 8999), west on Domain St., left on King St., and right on Stewart St; **internet access** at **Artex** across from the visitors center ($12 per hr.; open M-F 8:30am-5pm); and a **post office,** on Commerce St. at the Strand (☎307 1155; open M-F 8:30am-5pm, Sa 9am-noon).

█▐ ACCOMMODATIONS AND FOOD. For beachfront views at comparable prices, those with transport should head 7km over the hill to the **campground** or motels at Ohope Beach (see p. 165). In town, **Karibu Backpackers,** 13 Landing Rd. near the corner with King St., is a good bet with nice new facilities, free transfers to/from the bus stop and off-street parking. (☎/fax 307 8276. Free bikes. Dorms $16; doubles/twins $40; camping $12 per person.) **The Whakatane Hotel,** at George St. and the Strand, is clean and centrally located with a kitchen and lounge area. (☎307 1670; fax 307 1679. Dorm $16; singles $30; twins and doubles $55.) The **Whakatane Motor Camp and Caravan Park** pulls no punches. Follow Beach Rd. to the end of McGarvey Rd. 1km from the town center to find typical facilities with a game room. (☎308 8694; fax 308 2070. Tent sites, caravans, and vehicles $10 per person; austere cabins $20 per person; tourist cabins with TV, kitchen, and fridge $40, extra person $10.) Grab a bite at the **Why Not Cafe and Bar,** 76 The Strand, next door to the Whakatane Hotel. With all-day omelettes ($8), Thai chicken ($13.50), and specialty coffees ($6.50). (☎308 8138. Open daily 11am-late.)

▟ OUTDOOR ACTIVITIES. The two biggest attractions in the area are trips to **White Island** (see below) and dolphin swimming with **Dolphins Down Under,** on the wharf at the end of the Strand. They provide equipment, instruction, refreshments, and even hot showers for the 3-4hr. trip. Depending on the tides and weather, there can be as many as five trips per day during the summer. (☎308 4636. Direct booking $100, under 12 about $50.) For a more predatory interaction with Whakatane marine life, join **M.V. Charmaine** on a fishing trip. (☎308 6871. $30.)

There are three **scenic reserves** in the small area around Whakatane, providing a number of fine bush walks: **Kohi Point,** atop the hill over Whakatane, has panoramic views; **Ohope Scenic Reserve** is home to one of New Zealand's largest remaining pohutukawa forests; and **Mokorua Bush Scenic Reserve** is a recovering pasture land. The walk around the hill between Whakatane and nearby Ohope Beach is breathtaking without leaving you gasping for air. The walk to the **Tauwhare Pa** (1hr.), built several hundred years ago, and the **Mt. Tarawera Crater Walk** (2hr.), a difficult but rewarding walk up a dormant volcano (see **Rotorua: Geothermal Wonders** p. 155), are also worth a try. Access may be restricted during the summer due to the danger of fires. A long walk, the **Nga Tapuwae o Toi** (the Footprints of Toi) connects the three reserves; while the more than 20km trail can be covered in one day, it may be more enjoyable to split it into three shorter segments. The **Information Centre** on Boon St. has more information including departure points.

MONEY DOESN'T GROW ON TREES Alternately backpacking and picking one's way across the North Island may sound appealing, but the job is far from glamorous. Kiwifruit contractors assemble groups of 9 to 15 pickers, who earn about $12.50 for each bin they pick. Depending on the speed of their team, pickers can earn anywhere from $60-100 a day. Because picking is a group effort, one slacker can ruin both the speed and paycheck of an entire team. Workers must wear gloves and days are 9hr. Although grueling, the teamwork and bonding under stress create a distinct culture; backpackers from all around the world often converge on the kiwi farms to earn extra cash and enjoy the fruits of their labors.

WHITE ISLAND ☎ 07

Fifty kilometers off the coast of the Bay of Plenty, Whakaari, "that which can be made visible, uplifted to view," and its vapor sheath are visible from Whakatane on most sunny days. Captain Cook, in his circuit around New Zealand, called it White Island because of the steam cloud perpetually hanging above its volcanic peaks. Composed of three distinct cones, of which two are now extinct, White Island is a landscape of lunar dimensions, with craters and steaming vents, boiling sulfuric acid pools, and sinuous flows of solid rock. The still active volcano now and then does get more active, occasionally spewing out ashes that are carried by wind as far as Whakatane, giving the town a thin white coating. Even in such an inhospitable environment, ever-resourceful humans attempted to eke out profit with a sulfur mine that operated intermittently throughout the late 1800s and early 1900s. This evidently did not please the gods; a violent explosion and landslide killed 10 men in 1914. Today, mining for gold in tourists' purses has become the popular way to exploit White Island. For a price, anyone can strap on a gas mask, brave the noxious sulfur fumes, and make their own offering to the volcano.

The most affordable approach is by boat. **PeeJay Charters** was named "guardian" of White Island—perhaps the reason behind their slightly higher prices. (☎308 9588, 0800 PEEJAY. 5-6hr. trip $110, includes lunch. Weather and tide dependent.) **Blue Sky Tours** runs daily trips in the summer and weekend trips in the winter. (☎323 7829; mobile 025 988 748. $95, lunch included.) **Scott Air** (☎308 9558) and **East Bay Flight Centre** (☎308 8446) offer trips over White Island. (Return 50min.; $135 per person, min. 2 people.) For a touch-down on the cratered surface and a fly-over, a trip with **Vulcan Helicopters** (☎0800 804 354; www.vulcanheli.co.nz) costs $375 per person. Both planes and helicopters depart from the airport on Aerodrome Rd., about a 10min. drive from Whakatane town center.

OHOPE BEACH ☎ 07

Ohope Beach is just that—11km of unbroken beach blessed with rolling azure waves and views of the rugged East Cape. Visitors come to marinate in sun and sand or to tramp around Mokorua, the hill between Ohope and Whakatane. A 2hr. journey by sand allows travelers to traverse the length of Ohope's narrow strip of land, from the steep bluffs of Mokorua, where surfers struggle to ride small waves, to the entrance of Ohiwa Harbour, a historically rich shellfishery and current resting place for wayward golf balls from the Ohope Beach Golf Course.

The schizophrenic main road, branching off at the end of the highway, is West End Rd., becoming Pohutakawa Rd. as you move east, which changes to Harbour Rd. The **Whakatane Information Centre** staffs a beachfront **hut** off West End Rd. (Dec.-Feb.). **Buses** on the way to Opotiki stop across from the Mobil Station on Pohutakawa Rd., 300m down from the West End turn-off (daily around 3:45pm; book in Whakatane). Although *Let's Go* doesn't recommend it, thumbers who head to Ohope Beach report that **hitchhiking** prospects are fairly good. The **Ohope Beach Holiday Park** (☎/fax 312 4460), at the east side of the beach, offers spectacular views. There are 200 tent sites, 100 powered sites ($11-15), and tourist flats or cabins for two (from $40). Right next door on Harbour Rd. is **Surf & Sand Holiday Park.** Showers, toilet, kitchen, TV room, and laundry are all free. (☎312 4884. Open mid Dec.-early Feb. Powered sites $15 per person, children $7.50.)

OPOTIKI ☎ 07

A day in Opotiki (o-PO-tah-kee) often brings the sensation of isolation and wilderness, even within the town limits—but it's precisely that wildness and independence that draws most visitors. It is the last town of any size (pop. 4153) before the remote, rugged beauty and isolated Maori settlements of the East Coast.

▣ TRANSPORTATION. InterCity leaves from the **bus depot,** next to the Caltex station on the corner of Church St. and Bridge St. 1km from the visitors center for **Gisborne** (2hr., 1-2 per day, $28) and **Rotorua** (2hr., 1-2 per day, $40) via **Whakatane** (1hr., $16). Book tickets at the **Whakatane Information Centre** (☎308 6058).

⑦ PRACTICAL INFORMATION. The **Information Centre** is at St. John and Elliott St. (☎/fax 315 8484. Open daily 8:30am-5pm; in winter M-F 8:30am-5pm. Hours flexible.) Pick up the super-helpful *Opotiki and the East Cape* brochure. The **DOC** office is in the same building, but closes at 4:30pm. The **ANZ** on Church St. has a **24hr. ATM.** (☎315 1185. Open M-F 9am-4:30pm.) The **post office** is on Church St. in Paper Plus. (Open M, W-F 8:30am-5pm, Tu from 9:30am, Sa 9:30am-noon.)

▣▢ ACCOMMODATIONS AND FOOD. You can almost skip a rock across the surf from the porch of the **Opotiki Beach House Backpackers,** on Appelton Rd. at Waiotohi Beach 5km west of town on SH2. Sit on the deck (an informal cafe in summer) and watch White Island smoke, or borrow a free surf kayak or surfboard and hit the beach. (☎315 5117; slowry@paradise.net.nz. Free bikes. Dorms $15; doubles $35; tent sites $11. Cash only.) The inside of **Central Oasis Backpackers,** 30 King St., endears itself with a homey kitchen and relaxing lounge. (☎315 5165; centraloasis@hotmail.com. Dorms $12; twins and doubles $30; triple $42; tent sites $8.) The **Masonic Hotel,** at Elliott and Church St., has small rooms, but a popular restaurant below (mains $11-18; open daily 6pm-late). (☎315 6115. Singles $25; twins and doubles $45.) If you have seen Church St., you have seen your **food** options. But even without competition, the **Opotiki Hotel** restaurant, on Church St. opposite the museum, has delicious food. (☎315 6078. Open Tu-Sa 6pm-9pm.)

◪ SIGHTS. In a shocking parallel to Opotiki's culinary options, if you have seen the beach, you have pretty much seen the sights. On rainy days, entertain yourself at the **Opotiki Heritage and Agricultural Society Museum,** 123 Church St. (Open M-Sa 10am-3:30pm, Su 1:30-4pm. $2, children $0.50.) Head across the street to **Hiona St. Stephen's Anglican Church,** the site of the brutal 1865 murder of Rev. Karl Volkner, casualty of a Maori-Pakeha conflict (ask at the museum for a key). A popular attraction 7km from town is **Hukutaia Domain,** an 11-acre park with a great collection of New Zealand's native plant species. It's worth going, if only for the **Taketakerau,** a huge hollow puriri tree that was sacred to the local Whakatorea tribe.

EAST COAST & HAWKE'S BAY

The East Coast and Hawke's Bay is sun-drenched much of the year, from the flamboyant Art Deco Napier and Hastings to the self-proclaimed home of the world's first dawn, Gisborne's Mt. Hikurangi. The rays give rise to orchards and fields overrun with luscious produce and grapes, ripening the "Fruit Bowl of New Zealand." Wineries and award-winning Chardonnays draw visitors to both easterly Gisborne and cosmopolitan Napier. The stubborn streak of the East Coast's personality appears in the remote East Cape and the dense inland wilds of Te Urewera National Park and the North Island's largest remaining tract of native forest.

░ EAST COAST AND HAWKE'S BAY HIGHLIGHTS

NATURAL SPLENDOR abounds among the waterfalls and tramps of the virtually tourist-free **East Cape** (see p. 172).

NATURAL DIVERSITY flourishes in the isolation of the **Whirinaki Forest Park,** which supports a wide range of New Zealand's flora and fauna (see p. 175).

UNNATURAL ARCHITECTURE brightens the streets of **Napier** in joyfully garish Art Deco fashion (see p. 175).

EAST COAST

GISBORNE ☎ 06

Greeting the dawn has become an industry for Gisborne (pop. 30,000), which markets itself as the first city to see the sun each morning. Gisborne is also known as one of the top surf areas in New Zealand. The city's 50% Maori population, combined with its Polytech art classes, makes it New Zealand's largest center for contemporary Maori art. The site of Captain Cook's first landing in 1769, the city also has a vast history it won't let you forget, no matter how hard you may *Endeavour*.

▣ TRANSPORTATION

Flights: The **airport** is west of the city, at the end of Chalmers Rd. off Gladstone Rd. **Air New Zealand Link** (☎ 867 1608) has many daily flights to **Auckland** (1hr., $235) and **Wellington** (1hr., $250). Book direct or use the **ANZ** office, 37 Bright St. (☎ 868 2700; fax 868 2701). Taxis to the airport run around $10.

Buses: The **bus station** (☎ 868 6139) is at the visitors center. **InterCity** leaves daily for: **Auckland** (9hr., 8am, $82); **Napier** (4hr., 9am, $34); and **Rotorua** (4hr., 1 per day, $61) via **Whakatane** (3hr., $45). For transportation in the **East Cape** see p. 171.

Taxis: Gisborne Taxis (☎ 867 2222), **Sun City Taxis** (☎ 867 6767), and **Eastland Taxis** (☎ 868 1133) all run **24hr.**

Car Rental: Scottie's, 265 Grey St. (☎ 867 7947), next to the visitors center and part of Ray Scragg Motors, offers the cheapest rates. Standard economy vehicle from $35 per day, $0.19 per km; or $55 per day, unlimited mileage. Open daily M-F 7am-5pm. For weekend service, use **Budget** (☎ 0800 650 700) at the airport.

Bicycle/Surf Rental: Maintrax Cycle (☎ 867 4571), at the corner of Roebuck and Gladstone St., has bikes ($10 per day, deposit $50). **Sungate,** 55 Salisbury Rd. (☎ 868 1673), rents surfboards ($30 per day), body boards ($20), and kayaks ($35).

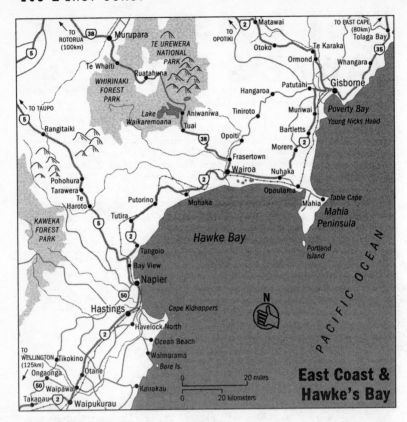

East Coast & Hawke's Bay

Hitchhiking: To head to the surf beaches at Wainui or Makorori, many hitchhikers start out along **Wainui Rd.** Hitchers going southwest toward Wairoa or north to Opotiki head to the end of **SH35/Gladstone Rd.** at Makaraka Rd., where the highway branches off to its respective destinations. *Let's Go* doesn't recommend hitchhiking.

✈ 🛈 ORIENTATION AND PRACTICAL INFORMATION

Gisborne is located where the **Taruheru** and the **Waimata Rivers** join to form the **Turanganui River** (one of the world's shortest rivers at 1200m). **Gladstone Rd.** (**SH35**, which turns into **Wainui Rd.** over the Turanganui Bridge) is the main drag; orient yourself by the **clock tower** at Gladstone and Grey St., alongside the mock-up of Captain Cook's Endeavour. The **Esplanade** runs along the Wainui Rd. side of the river, while **Awapuni** and **Salisbury Rd.** run parallel to the main beaches.

Visitors Center: Gisborne Information Centre, 209 Grey St. (☎868 6139; fax 868 6138), has East Cape tourism info. Open M-F 7:30am-5:30pm, Sa-Su 10am-5pm.

DOC: 63 Carnarvon St. (☎867 8531; fax 867 8015). Open M-F 8am-4:30pm.

Currency Exchange: Westpac (☎867 1359, 0800 400 600), at the corner of Gladstone Rd. and Peel St. Open M-Tu and Th-F 9am-4:30pm, W 9:30am-4:30pm.

Police: (☎867 9059), at the corner of Peel St. and Gladstone Rd.

Medical Services: Kaiti Road Medical Center (☎867 7411), at the corner of Turenne and De Lautour Rd., off Wainui Rd. Open M-F 8am-8pm, Sa-Su 9am-6pm. For **urgent care** only, look to the **hospital** (☎867 9099) on Ormond Rd.

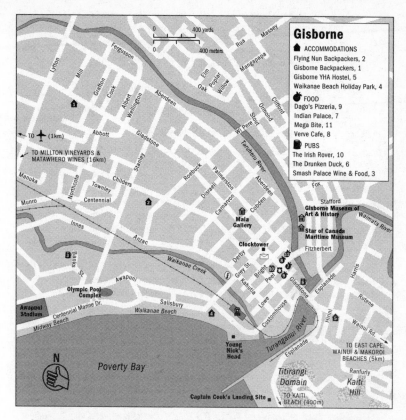

Gisborne

🏠 ACCOMMODATIONS
Flying Nun Backpackers, 2
Gisborne Backpackers, 1
Gisborne YHA Hostel, 5
Waikanae Beach Holiday Park, 4

🍴 FOOD
Dago's Pizzeria, 9
Indian Palace, 7
Mega Bite, 11
Verve Cafe, 8

🍺 PUBS
The Irish Rover, 10
The Drunken Duck, 6
Smash Palace Wine & Food, 3

Internet Access: Cyber-zone, 83 Gladstone Rd. (☎868 7138). $12 per hr. Open in summer M-Sa 10am-8pm, Su noon-6pm; in winter M and W 10am-8pm, Tu and Th-Sa 10am-5pm, closed Su.

Post Office: The Gisborne Post Shop, 166 Gladstone Rd. (☎867 8220), inside Books and More. Open M-F 8:30am-5:30pm, Sa 9am-4pm, Su 10am-3pm.

🏠🏕 ACCOMMODATIONS AND CAMPING

Beachfront accommodations often charge $10-20 more than those just across the street. In the off-season, hostels attract permanent boarders who rent out rooms for months at a time, creating a very different atmosphere from the summer.

Flying Nun Backpackers, 147 Roebuck St. (☎868 0461; fax 867 0067; yager@xtra.co.nz), off Gladstone Rd. at the corner of Childers and Roebuck Rd. Cheap rates and a rowdy summer atmosphere Key deposit $10. Dorms $15-17; singles $25; twins $40; doubles $40; tent sites $8. Cash only.

Gisborne YHA Hostel (☎867 3269; fax 867 3296; yha.gis@clear.net.nz), on the corner of Wainui Rd. and Harris St. A 5min. walk from downtown, this bright orange YHA attracts young and old alike with diverse rooms. Internet. Dorms $16; singles $26; twins and doubles $38; triples $57.

Gisborne Backpackers, 690 Gladstone Rd. (☎868 1000; fax 868 4000; gisbornebp@xtra.co.nz), 2km from downtown. Comfortable rooms with thick mattresses. Free pick-up. Linen $4. Dorms $16; singles $25; twins/doubles $40; deluxe twins $50.

Waikanae Beach Holiday Park (☎867 5634; fax 867 9765), end of Grey St. On the beach near downtown, this municipal property has excellent facilities. Tent sites are granted privacy by rows of pines. "Ranch house" accommodation (1-2 people) with vinyl mattresses $28; ensuite self-catering tourist flats $55, deluxe ones $60; tent sites $9 per person, powered sites $10. Prices rise $2-5 in summer.

◧ FOOD

Gisborne's nicer downtown cafes and restaurants, most on **Gladstone Rd.**, offer a respite from the usual artery-clogging budget cuisine. And there's always **Pak 'N Save,** a block up from the clock tower on Gladstone Rd.

■ **Dago's Famous Pizzeria and Thai Cuisine,** 50 Gladstone Rd. (☎868 7666; 867 0543), cooks up some of Gisborne's tastiest and most creative takeaway dishes. Meals include mini pizzas ($6), Thai mains ($12-15), sushi ($6), and pasta ($12). Delivery $4. Open daily 9:30am-9:30pm.

Mega Bite (☎867 5787), on Peel St. by Palmerston Rd. Backpackers from across the globe find home-cooking sanctuary here. Open daily 6:30am-5pm; later in summer.

Indian Palace, 55 Gladstone Rd. (☎863 0901). Try the mouth-melting butter chicken curry ($14.90). Curries $13.90-15.90. Open for lunch Tu-Su 11:30am-2:30pm, for dinner M-Su 5:30pm-late.

Verve Cafe, 121 Gladstone Rd. (☎868 9095). The airy Verve has local artwork on the walls, couches in the back, and limited internet access. Grilled sandwiches with a choice of meat ($8) and fulfilling fish dishes ($13). Open daily 8:30am-10pm.

◧ NIGHTLIFE

■ **Smash Palace Wine and Food Bar,** 24 Banks St. (☎867 7769). Take Awapuni Rd. west into the industrial district. Enjoy local $3.50 brews like Gisborne Gold. Open winter Su-Tu 3pm-late, W-Sa 1pm-late; in summer daily noon-late.

The Irish Rover (☎867 1112), on Peel St. Snag a Guinness ($5.50) in this popular barn-style pub. Weeknights are low-key, but weekends often feature live music (cover $3). Handles on tap $3.50. Open M-F 11am-3am, Sa 3pm-3am, Su 10am-10pm.

The Drunken Duck, 9 Gladstone Rd. (☎867 3199). Centrally located, this funkadelic pub is No. 1 with surfers. Collecting residual sand on F-Sa nights, the wooden floorboards resound with live music F-Su. Open M-F 11am-3am, Sa-Su 2pm-3am.

◧ SIGHTS

Titirangi Domain, also known as **Kaiti Hill,** is a good starting place for seeing Gisborne's sights. Once across the river, follow the signs from Hirini Rd. At the base of the hill sits **Te Poho-o-Rawiri,** the largest traditional *marae* built from modern materials in New Zealand. It is cavernous and stunningly crafted, with painted roof rafters, woven tukutuku reed panels, and intricately carved dark wood panels with iridescent paua shell eyes. The large panels, *pou pou,* chronicle Maori genealogy; each figure represents a specific ancestor. Be sure to ask permission at the office first, and remove your shoes before entering. Nearby sits **Toko Toru Tapu,** a small Maori church nestled on the hillside.

Continue up the hill—a steep one popular with masochistic joggers—for a series of phenomenal views across the city and Poverty Bay to the white cliffs of **Young Nick's Head,** named after Captain Cook's cabin boy Nicholas Young, who first sighted New Zealand from the *Endeavour.* Kaiti Hill can also be tackled via a path winding up from the base of the Cook Landing Site (accessible from the Esplanade along the river).

The **Tairawhiti Museum of Art and History** (☎867 3832), on Stout St., features rotating art galleries and several displays on natural and cultural history, with this year's focus on the sculpture of indigenous peoples. Just behind the Art and History museum on the riverbank sits the **Star of Canada Maritime Museum,** the transplanted bridgehouse of a British steamer that grounded on Kaiti Beach in 1912. (Both museums open M-F 10am-4pm, Sa-Su 1:30-4pm; in Jan. daily 10am-4pm. Free.) For contemporary art-in-progress, head to the **Maia Gallery,** on Cobden St. between Gladstone Rd. and Palmerston St. This airy showroom and workshop is a studio for students in the Toihoukura (Maori Visual Arts) course at the local Tairawhiti Polytechnic. (☎868 8068. Open M-F 8am-5pm. Free.)

The **Eastwoodhill Arboretum** is a popular attraction 35km northwest of the city on the Ngatapa-Rere Rd. Laid out by an obsessive collector, its 64 hectares grow some of the finest flora from the Southern Hemisphere (around 500 genera). (☎863 9800. Open daily 9am-5pm. Admission $5, children free.)

◪ ACTIVITIES

For the area's safest and most convenient waters, try **Waikanae Beach,** stretching from the end of Grey St.; it gets a bit crowded at peak times. The shore becomes **Midway Beach** a little farther along Poverty Bay, with soft sand and a prime surf spot at its western end. While the bay beaches have their golden wave moments, many surfers with more experience head north of the city to the coastal beaches at **Wainui,** about 6km out on SH35, and **Makorori,** another 4km along. These beaches are used for swimming as well, but have been known to have riptides. **Kaiti Beach,** at the base of Kaiti Hill, is rocky and unpatroled, but there are great gusts for windsurfing because of its exposed location. Or head one block inland from Waikane Beach to the **Gisborne Olympic Pool Complex,** on Centennial Marine Dr. (☎867 6220. Open daily 6am-8pm. Admission $2.50, children $1.50.)

Stop by the organic **Millton Vineyard** (☎862 8680), in Manutuke on Papatu Rd. off SH2 towards Wairoa, or the **Matawhero Wines** (☎868 8366) on Riverpoint Rd. For touring and tasting of a different spirit, clear your palate for the cider, scrumpy, and schnapper of **Bulmer Harvest,** on Customhouse St. by the water. (☎868 8300. Open daily 9am-5pm; in winter closed Sa-Su.) The **Sunshine Brewing Co.,** 109 Disraeli St. off Gladstone St., makes Gisborne Gold, Sundowner, Moonshine, and other naturally brewed beers. (☎867 7777. Open M-Sa 9am-6pm. Call ahead for free tour.) **Waimoana Horse Trekking,** based on Mysnar St. off Wainui Rd., offers an unforgettable trek over sheep-dotted bush and surf-crashing beach; all levels welcome. (☎868 8218. 1hr. $30; 2hr. $40. $5 *Let's Go* discount.).

If you're around in October, partake of the **Gisborne Wine and Food Festival;** the visitors center organizes the Festival and has information on winery bus routes.

THE EAST CAPE   ☎07/06

New Zealand's final frontier of tourism, the East Cape's stunning craggy coastline, draws travelers in search of the ever-elusive "untouched New Zealand." From Opotiki (see p. 165) to Gisborne (see p. 167), the Pacific Coast Highway (SH35) passes scores of sleepy seaside towns on its way around the rugged Raukumara Mountains of the interior. The vast majority of the people living here are Maori, and intricate traditional carvings adorn the many churches and *marae.*

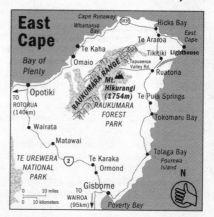

▐ TRANSPORTATION IN THE EAST CAPE

Buses: Slim's East Cape Escape (☎07 345 6645) is the only transport to circumscribe the region partners with Kiwi Experience, the legendary Slim runs a 3-day circuit letting passengers on and off as they please. Buses depart Rotorua M, W-F (M, W, F in winter), spend 1 night on the East Cape, 1 in Te Urewera National Park, and then loop back to Rotorua. $220, not including meals or accommodations, which Slim's can arrange.

Courier Transport: These mini-vans deliver parcels and supplies from **Opotiki** and **Gisborne** to the various settlements and farms around the Cape, allowing passengers to see much that would be missed from the main highway. **Polly's Passenger Courier Service** (☎020 702 9621) runs between Whakatane and Hicks Bay (3½hr.; M-F departs Whakatane noon, Hicks Bay 7:30am; $30, $25 between Opotiki and Hicks Bay) and between Hicks Bay and Gisborne (3½hr.; M-F departs Hicks Bay 6:30am, Gisborne 1pm; $30). **Dick Cook Courier Service** (☎025 371 364) travels between Hicks Bay and Gisborne (4½hr.; M-Sa departs Hicks Bay 7:30am, Gisborne 2pm; $25) and can transport between Whakatane and Hicks Bay with a related courier (4½hr.; M-F departs Whakatane 1pm, Hicks Bay 6:30am; $30, $25 between Opotiki and Hicks Bay).

Hitching: Hitchhikers find friendly rides around the cape in summertime; late afternoon is peak traffic time as people return from Gisborne or Opotiki. In winter, increased rain and reduced traffic makes hitching a more dubious prospect, particularly on the less populated northern coast. However *Let's Go* does not recommend hitchhiking.

▐ ▐ ORIENTATION AND PRACTICAL INFORMATION

Well maintained and fully paved, **SH35** runs the Cape's 334km perimeter. Most towns along the way have at least one store, takeaway, gas station, and postal service, sometimes all in one.

Visitors Center: The visitors centers in **Opotiki, Gisborne,** and the **Te Puia Springs Service Centre** (☎06 864 6853) are the best bet for questions regarding the southern coast. Open M-F 8am-4:30pm. The comprehensive and free *Opotiki and East Cape*, available at all of the above, lists most travelers' resources, kilometer by kilometer.

Banks: Westpac (☎06 864 8443), in Ruatoria, is the only bank in the East Cape. Open M-Tu and Th-F 9am-4:30pm, W 9:30am-4:30pm. There are **no ATMs.**

Telephone Codes: ☎07 from Opotiki to Hicks Bay; ☎06 from Hicks Bay to Gisborne.

▐ ▐ ACCOMMODATIONS AND FOOD

The coastline between Gisborne and Hicks Bay contains several designated spots for **free camping** (between Labour Day and Easter), usually recognizable by a morass of caravans. Try **Pouawa Beach** (17km north of Gisborne), **Loisel's Beach** at Waihau Bay (50km), **Tokomaru Bay** (90km), **Waipiro Bay** (106km), or **Hicks Bay** (180km). The East Cape's northern shore tends to restrict tenting. As for **food,** the East Cape lacks restaurants and supermarkets alike. In a grave departure from *Let's Go* format, the following accommodations are listed in **geographical order** (following SH35 from Opotiki to Gisborne) rather than in order of preference.

House of the Rising Sun (☎06 864 5858), on Potae St. in **Tokomaru Bay,** less than a block from the beach. Free use of bicycles, boogie boards, and fresh vegetable garden. Internet $6 per hr. Dorms $15; doubles $34; tent sites $9.

Brian's Place (☎06 864 5870), up the hill from Potae St. in **Tokomaru Bay;** follow the sign. Super cool lofts, wicked views, and a porch studded with Central American hammocks define this tiny backpackers. Dorms $14; 1 double $36; tent sites $8.

SunRise Lodge and Beachcamp (☎0800 574 137), in **Te Araroa.** This windswept patch of land and its home-style accommodations are as peaceful as it gets. 2 backpacker beds $20 per person; B&B twin or double $75; tent sites $8.

Hicks Bay Backpackers Lodge (☎06 864 4731), a couple of km off the main road. Plain, simple, and next to a good swimming and surfing beach. Free use of videos, boogie boards, and kayaks. Dinner $10. Dorms $15; doubles $40; tent sites $9.

Maraehako Bay Retreat (☎07 325 2648), in **Maraehako Bay,** 50m past Rendezvous on the Coast. Tucked into a rocky cove, this hand-crafted Retreat boasts a ping-pong table next to a waterfall. Dorms $18; singles $25; doubles $45.

Rendezvous on the Coast Holiday Park (☎07 325 2899), in **Whanarua Bay.** A well kept campground with a pool, skateboard bowl, and a mini-golf course. Half-day bike tours $30. Half-day kayak rental $20. Dorms $12; tent sites $8, powered sites $10.

Robyn's Place (☎07 325 2904), in **Whanarua Bay.** There's music on the stereo and a batik thrown over the couch. Like a university apartment—except this one has views of the ocean. Free laundry and linen. Dorms $17; the double $40; tent sites $9.

Te Kaha Holiday Park and Motel (☎07 325 2894), at the northern end of **Te Kaha.** "Luxury" backpacker facilities (reading lamps, in-room kitchen) don't make up for squeaky beds. Dorms $15; tent sites $9, powered sites $10.

👁 🌊 SIGHTS AND ACTIVITIES

From Opotiki to Hicks Bay, the highway skirts the green lush coast and reveals the Cape's spectacular views, especially in December when the pohutukawa trees explode with red flowers. In **Whanarua Bay,** beneath the Rendezvous on the Coast roadside advertisement, a door marked "Track" leads down to a stunning and undeveloped section of rocky beach full of tidal pools. After Hick's Bay, the road moves inland. En route to Te Araroa it passes the Te Araroa Holiday Park, home to the **world's easternmost cinema.** (☎06 864 4873. $5, children $3.) Just down the road, the beachfront schoolyard in **Te Araroa** holds the **world's largest pohutukawa tree.** Te Araroa is also the gateway to the lonely **East Cape Lighthouse,** at the easternmost point in mainland New Zealand. **East Cape 4WD Sunrise Tours** does a morning run along the 20km road to the lighthouse. (☎06 864 4775. $25; min. 2 people.)

In **Tikitiki, St. Mary's Memorial Church** perches on a hill overlooking SH35. One of the most impressive Maori buildings in the region, the church's western exterior hides an ornately carved inner sanctuary. A turn-off from the main highway near **Ruatoria** leads to Pakihiroa Station, the trailhead for the track up **Mount Hikurangi** (1754m). Access to the peak is restricted, but eager hikers can usually obtain permission to stay in a hut 10km up the mountain ($5 per night) at the **Te Runanga o Ngati Porou** office (☎06 867 9960).

Brian of Brian's Place (see Accommodations, above) runs **horse treks** out of **Tokomaru Bay** (2hr. $30, full-day $70, overnight $130; longer trips available on demand). Another 36km toward Gisborne, **Tolaga Bay** harbors the longest wharf in the southern hemisphere, a deteriorating 600m testament to the days before highways, resting at the end of Wharf Road, 1.5km off SH35. Nearby is the **Cooks Cove Walkway,** an unchallenging trip to the site of one of Captain Cook's first landings in Aotearoa (5.8km, 2½hr. return, closed Aug.-Oct. for lambing season).

TE UREWERA NATIONAL PARK ☎06

Te Urewera National Park's misty ridges and untamed valleys shelter a proud history of, well, misty ridges and untamed valleys. The park's isolated bush has long been home to the Tuhoe (TOO-hoy) Maori, who resisted European intrusion with greater force and success than most other tribes. The beech and podocarp now stand in the largest national park on the North Island—and the only one in New Zealand named for a camping accident ("urewera" means "burnt penis," the ailment of a rather unfortunate Maori chief who rolled onto his fire one night).

EAST COAST

AT A GLANCE	
AREA: 212,672 hectares. **CLIMATE:** Warm weather Oct.-Mar. Cold and boggy in winter. **FEATURES:** Largest forested wilderness. Hunting, fishing. **HIGHLIGHTS:** Lake Waikaremoana.	**GATEWAYS:** Whakatane, Taneatua, Murupara, Ruatahuna, Wairoa. **CAMPING:** Fully serviced motor camp at Lake. Unserviced campsites. Backcountry huts. **FEES & RESERVATIONS:** Book well in advance in summer. Huts $14, camping $10.

TRANSPORTATION

Often unsealed, **SH38** cuts through the park on its way from Wairoa to SH5 (which leads north to Rotorua and south to Taupo). From Wairoa to Rotorua is a total of 170km. **Big Bush Holiday Park** (see **Camping** below) operates a **bus** between Rotorua and Lake Waikaremoana (3½hr., M and F, $60) and between Lake Waikaremoana and Wairoa (45min., daily, $25). **Slim's East Cape Escape** also drives the road's length as part of a several-day shuttle tour (see **East Cape: Transport** p. 172). **Hitchhiking** to and within the park can be a difficult proposition, as there is very little traffic, but, although *Let's Go* does not recommend it, those with patience report success.

ORIENTATION AND PRACTICAL INFORMATION

WHEN TO GO The park is best enjoyed in the summer (mid-Oct.–March) since the winter weather can be wet and cold; the walks are usable year-round with the right equipment. However be prepared for all weather conditions.

SH38 bisects Te Urewera just north of Lake Waikaremoana. Most visitors stay at one of the two holiday parks within the park's limits (see **Camping** below); both lie east of **DOC's Aniwaniwa Visitor Centre** on Lake Waikaremoana. (☎837 3803. Open daily 8am-4:45pm.) There are small **general stores** in Tuai and Murupara, and at the Waikaremoana Motor Camp (see **Camping** below), but supermarkets in Wairoa and Rotorua have better prices and an **ATM.** As for **parking,** the Waikaremoana Motor Camp's lot (free even for non-guests) is safer than the trailheads.

CAMPING

The central **Waikaremoana Motor Camp** occupies a gem of a location on the lake shore, with a small store and a petrol station. (☎/fax 837 3826. Dorms $16; 2-person cabins $40; tourist flats $60; tent sites $7.50 per person, powered sites $9. Store open daily 8am-5pm.) **Big Bush Holiday Park** lies 3km east of the lake and the Onepoto trailhead. (☎837 3777. Internet. Shuttle to Hopuruahine trailhead $25. Restaurant open evenings. Dorms $17; motel doubles $70.) There is also **free camping** around the lake, as long as tents are pitched more than 500m from all tracks and not on private land (clearly marked on most maps).

OUTDOOR ACTIVITIES

The Lake Waikaremoana Track (3-5 days, 48km) is in the heart of the remote and thickly forested park. This track climbs towering bluffs topped with gnarled beech trees around the lake (see p. 358). Among the most scenic day hikes, the well-graded **Lake Waikareiti Walk** (return 2hr.) travels through forest to island-dotted Waikareiti, improbably set on a lush green hilltop. The **Waipai-Ruapani-Waikareiti**

Walk (a 6hr. loop), visits the Waipai Swamp and Lake Ruapani as well as Lake Waikareiti. For a great view, hike up **Panekiri Bluff** (see **Lake Waikaremoana** p. 358). The less-traveled northern reaches of Te Urewera provide even more remote tramping experiences; the **Six Foot Track** (3 days) cuts through the Tauranga Valley and demands solid navigational skills, while the nearby **Whakatane Loop Track** (4-5 days) makes a full circuit through the Whakatane Valley.

Since all of the desirable fish and game in the park are introduced species, DOC smiles upon their slaughter. **Fishing licenses** are available at Waikaremoana Motor Camp ($28 per week, $13.50 per day), which also rents and sells gear (1-day rod rental $5). Noel Himona of **Waikaremoana Guided Tours** leads hunting trips and fishing forays. He also rents **kayaks** and **canoes**. (☎837 3729. Fishing and hunting $250 per day for 1 person, $300 for 2; kayaks $30-35 per day, canoes $45 per day.) Additionally, DOC rents rowboats ($30 per day).

WHIRINAKI FOREST PARK ☎07

Although not as dramatic as the neighboring Te Urewera National Park, 55,000-hectare Whirinaki Forest Park contains magnificent lowland rainforest. Soaring podocarp and tawa canopy shelter tree ferns and native birds like the tui and the kiwi. And although Whirinaki is accessible year-round (if somewhat drizzly in the winter), relatively few visitors make it this far into the sticks. The **Rangitaiki Area DOC Office,** on SH38 in Murupara 60km southeast of Rotorua, distributes information on park walks and weather conditions. (☎366 5641. Open M-F 8am-5pm.)

HAWKE'S BAY

In February, 1931, a massive earthquake (7.9 on the Richter scale) rattled much of Hawke's Bay into rubble. Though the history of the region didn't begin with the big bang, it certainly seemed to freeze there. Napier and Hastings were rebuilt in the flamboyant Art Deco and Spanish Mission styles popular at the time; the main attractions of the region are the anachronistic buildings and scenic wineries. Most tourists miss Hawke's Bay, leaving the region uncrowded and laid back. Shhh.

NAPIER ☎06

You know you've hit Napier when cafes outnumber takeaways, and even the McDonald's is McDeco. Design and architecture buffs will go wild in this Art Deco city. Napier also has the highest per capita rate of oddball attractions in New Zealand. A furry opossum mortuary selling souvenirs is just down the road from a sanctuary for disabled penguins and overweight sea lions.

▐ TRANSPORTATION

Flights: The Hawke's Bay **Airport** (☎835 1130), is north of Napier on SH2. The **ANZ Travel Centre** (☎833 5400), at corner of Hastings and Station St., books flights to **Auckland** (7 per day, around $243) and **Wellington** (5 per day, around $218). Open M-F 9am-5pm, Sa 9am-noon. The **Supershuttle** (☎844 7333) offers service to the **airport** ($9) and **Hastings** ($25 for min. 2 people). A taxi to the airport costs about $9.

Trains: Bay Express (☎0800 110 077), departs from Munroe St. daily for: **Wellington** (5hr., 2:05pm, $75) via **Hastings** (25min., $16); and **Palmerston North** (3hr., $47).

Buses: Intercity coaches leave from Napier Travel Centre (☎834 2720) at the train station on Munroe St. **Intercity/Newmans** departs for: **Wellington** (6hr., M-Th and Sa 2 per day, F and Su 3 per day, $60-62) via **Palmerston North** (3hr., $38-41); **Auckland** (7hr., 3 per day, $78) via **Rotorua** (3hr., $55-57) and **Taupo** (2hr., $35-37). InterCity goes to **Gisborne** (4hr., 1 per day, $34) via **Wairoa** (2hr., $21). **Nimbus** (☎877 8133) runs hourly M-F 7am-5:30pm to **Hastings** (45min, $5) and to **Havelock North** (1hr,

$5). Nimbus departs from the bus terminal on Dalton St. near Dickens St. To get to Hastings on weekends, catch an InterCity or Newmans bus heading south ($11).

Taxis: StarTaxis (☎835 5511) and **Napier Taxis** (☎835 7777, 0800 627 437).

Car Rental: Metro Rent-A-Car (☎835 0590, 0508 350 590), on Corunna Bay off Hyderabad Rd. Economy cars from $69 per day; min. age 21.

Bike Rental: Napier Kart and Cycle Center, at corner of Tennyson St. and Clive Sq. West (☎835 9528), rents in summer (Oct.-Apr.) for $25 per day with helmet and lock.

Hitchhiking: Although *Let's Go* doesn't recommend it, hitchhikers heading south recommend getting rides along Marine Parade; a bit past the Aquarium, it becomes SH2 and picks up more traffic. Heading north, the best spot is reputed to be across Pandora Rd. Bridge. Most traffic heads to Taupo; those going to Wairoa or Gisborne should ask to be let out where SH5 branches off.

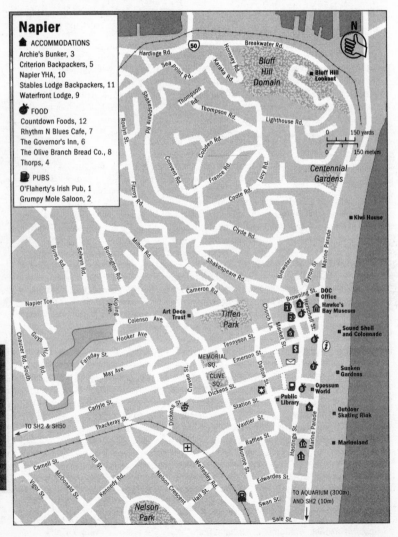

Napier

🛏 **ACCOMMODATIONS**
Archie's Bunker, 3
Criterion Backpackers, 5
Napier YHA, 10
Stables Lodge Backpackers, 11
Waterfront Lodge, 9

🍎 **FOOD**
Countdown Foods, 12
Rhythm N Blues Cafe, 7
The Governor's Inn, 6
The Olive Branch Bread Co., 8
Thorps, 4

🍺 **PUBS**
O'Flaherty's Irish Pub, 1
Grumpy Mole Saloon, 2

✦ ℹ ORIENTATION AND PRACTICAL INFORMATION

Marine Parade and **Hastings St.** run parallel to one another, stretching southward along the bay. Central Napier's streets lie up against the bluffs. Be careful about meandering through palm-lined **Emerson St.**—despite the misleading bricked landscaping, it's a main traffic thoroughfare. Tennyson and Dickens Streets run parallel to it on each side; the gardens of Clive Sq. mark the edge of the town center.

Visitors Center: Napier Information Centre, 100 Marine Parade (☎834 1911; fax 835 7219). Open M-F 8:30am-5pm, Sa-Su 9-5pm; later in summer.

DOC: 59 Marine Parade (☎834 3111). Open M-F 9am-4:15pm.

Currency Exchange: ASB, on Emerson St. Open M-F 9am-4:30pm. **BNZ,** 126 Hastings St. (☎0800 275 269). Open M and Th-F 9am-430pm; Tu-W 9:30am-4:30pm.

Bi-Gay-Lesbian Organizations: Gayline (☎843 3087) has info on current goings-on. Dances are hosted the third Sa of each month at the Bay City Club on Milton Rd., partway up Bluff Hill, off Tennyson St. Cover $5.

Police: (24hr. ☎835 4688), on Station St.

Medical Services: The Doctors, 30 Munroe St., (☎835 4696), has a **pharmacy.** Open daily 8am-9pm. **Napier Health Centre** is on Wellesly Rd. (24hr. ☎878 8109).

Internet Access: Stables Lodge Backpackers, 370 Hastings St. (☎835 6242). Available daily 8am-8pm. $7 per hr. **Cybershed,** 177 Hastings St. (☎834 3055), on the corner of Station St., charges $8 per hr. Open M-Th 9am-10:30pm, F-Su 9am-midnight.

Post Office: Corner of Dickens and Hastings St. Open M-F 8am-5pm, Sa 9am-noon.

▌ ACCOMMODATIONS

Most, smack dab in the center of town, provide convenient but often noisy stays, while those on the outskirt reward the commute with quiet seclusion.

Criterion Backpackers, 48 Emerson St. (☎835 2059; fax 835 2370; cribacpac@yahoo.com). Friendly staff and free transpo. Mountain bike hire. Key deposit $10. Dorms $16; singles $22; twins and doubles $38, with bath $50. Cash only.

Napier YHA, 277 Marine Parade (☎/fax 835 7039; yhanapr@yha.org.nz), at the corner of Vaultier St. Some rooms have an oceanview. Bike hire. Reception in summer 8am-8pm; in winter 8-10am, 1-7pm. Dorms $18; singles $25; twins and doubles $40. Nonmembers $3 extra.

Archie's Bunker, 14 Herschell St. (☎833 7990; fax 833 7995; archiesbunker@xtra.co.nz), opposite Hawke's Bay Museum. The specklessly clean facilities include an enormous upstairs lounge. Bike hire. Free bus/train pick-up/drop-off. Internet. Dorms $17; singles $20-25; twins $38-40; doubles $43-50.

Stables Lodge Backpackers, 370 Hastings St. (☎/fax 835 6242; stables@ihug.co.nz). With the lovable dog Max making the rounds, goodwill abounds at this environmentally-aware hostel. Comfy bunks, lockable storage, and free tea, blankets and use of bikes. Internet. Dorms $15; twins and doubles $36.

Waterfront Lodge (VIP), 217 Marine Parade (☎/fax 835 3429). Sip free tea or catch some Zs in the comfortable beds. Reception 8am-9pm. Bike hire. Free pick-up/drop-off. Dorms $17; singles $25; twins and doubles $40-55; family rooms $75; tents $10.

▐▌ FOOD AND CAFES

Countdown Foods, at the corner of Dickens and Station St. near Thackeray St., is one of the many supermarkets. (Open M-F 8am-9pm, Sa-Su 8am-8pm.)

Thorps, 40 Hastings St. (☎835 6699), by Tennyson St. With 7 breads, 7 meats (including salmon), and over 10 dressings, only the indecisive should dodge this coffee shop. Open M-F 7:30am-4:30pm, Sa 7:30am-2pm.

HAWKE'S BAY

The Olive Branch Bread Company (☎835 8375), on Hastings St. by Albion St., has ready-made sandwiches ($4.50) and sweets, but the real deals are the freshly-baked breads ($2-5)—perfect as a meal by themselves. Open M-F 8am-3pm, Sa 8am-2pm.

Rhythm N Blues Cafe, 131-33 Marine Parade (☎835 5438), opposite Sunken Gardens. Imbibe in the art studio-like vibe, people-watching and eating brunch ($4-10.50). Open M-F 7am-late, Sa-Su 8am-late.

The Governors Inn (☎835 0088), inside The Dome building on the corner of Emerson St. and Marine Parade. The bar/cafe serves brunch and light meals ($7.50-12), mains ($10-19), and coffee ($2.50-4.50). Open daily 10am-10pm (or until late).

🐱 NIGHTLIFE

Many clubs and bars are found near the intersection of Hastings and Tennyson St., or farther up Hastings St. on Shakespeare Rd. Follow your ears.

O'Flaherty's Irish Pub, 37 Hastings St. (☎834 1235), by Tennyson St., is an authentic tavern for both and veteran drinkers. Pints $2 during the daily 5-7pm Happy Hour. Live music every weekend and fresh homemade pies. Open daily 11am-late.

Grumpy Mole Saloon (☎835 5545), on the corner of Hastings and Tennyson St. The nightclub saloon, hot twenty-somethings, and American West decor, are an odd but popular hybrid for those who pass the "no-scruffiness" door test. Open Tu-Sa 4pm-3am. **Stogies Bar,** inside the same building and connected to Grumpy Mole through a door, is a jazzy, loungy bar serving Cuban cigars, late night coffee, and single malt whiskeys.

👁🐱 SIGHTS AND ACTIVITIES

TOURS
Tours in Napier come in two varieties: local architectural tours that pay tribute to the Deco-dent decoration of Napier and winery tours.

ART DECO NAPIER. The color-laden symmetry of the buildings is perhaps itself the main sight in Napier—even the manhole covers can't escape the craze. Tennyson St. has a row of classic structures; admire the Maori Deco of the **Antique Centre,** the Shamrock Deco of the **Munster Chambers,** and the Deco-overload of the **Daily Telegraph building.** Market St. has terrific glass windows; the peach and green **Countrywide Bank** building on Dalton and Emerson St. is impressive. And don't forget to check out the Greco Deco of the **Colonnade** and the **Sound Shell.** The **Tom Parker Fountain** in the gardens along Marine Parade gets **technicolor** light treatment from dusk until midnight. The most famous of all is **Rothmans Building** (built in 1933) at the corner of Bridge St. and Ossian St, combining elements of Art Deco, Art Nouveau and the Chicago School of architect Louis Sullivan. **The Art Deco Trust,** 163 Tennyson St., runs a 1.5km guided walking tour of Napier's Deco. (☎835 0022. Oct.-June twice daily; July-Sept. twice daily W, Sa, Su. 10am from Napier visitors center and 2pm from the Art Deco Trust. $8 per person.) The Trust's brochures (available at the Trust or the visitors center) provide those interested in a self-guided walk a middle ground between aimless wandering and the full-on tour.

GRAPIER NAPIER. Napier sits on the edge of the vineyard-studded Hawke's Bay plains, one of New Zealand's major wine-producing regions. Originally set up by priests for religious wine, **Mission Estate Winery** is New Zealand's oldest winery. (☎844 2259. Open M-Sa 8:30am-5:30pm, Su 11am-4pm. Tours M-Sa 10:30am and 2pm.) **Ngatarawa Wines** (☎879 7603) is a small winery in a restored stable on lovely grounds. The winery offers tastings of their wines daily 11am-5pm. Several tour operators offer short guided tours and tastings. **Vicky's Wine Tours** (☎843 9991), **Bay Tours and Charters** (☎843 6953), and **Vince's Vineyard Tours** (☎836 6705) offer 4-5hr. tours ranging $35-50 per person with free pick-up. Or try **Toast the Bay** if you're on a tighter schedule. (☎844 2375. 2½hr. tour. $30-35. Book at the visitors center.)

FESTIVALS

Napier shakes, rattles, and rocks in February with festivals. Dust off your zoot suit for the glam **Art Deco Weekend** and its endless series of stylish events from balls and cafe crawls to champagne breakfasts and country house tours. (☎835 1191; www.hb.co.nz/artdeco/weekend; 3rd weekend of Feb.) There's somewhat less to do if you're short on cash, but you can still check out the museum exhibitions, find some free jazz, and pack a hamper for Sunday's **Great Gatsby Picnic** on the beach. There's also the **Harvest Hawke's Bay Wine** and **Food Festival** (first weekend of February), a weekend of similarly upscale revelry, with several evening outdoor concerts. Local wineries are packed with shuttle tours and tasters all weekend long. The **International Mission Estate Concert** in January to March at the Mission Estate Winery is a big regional deal in a gorgeous setting. You don't have to wait for a festival; at any time of year, there might be impromptu jazz concerts at the wineries or other entertainment in the soundshell.

MUSEUMS AND AQUARIUMS

If you've begun to overdose on Deco, head to Marine Parade. Interspersed among manicured gardens, burbling fountains, and statues like Pania of the Reef (a distinctively toothy mermaid) there are some quirky sideshows.

HAWKE'S BAY MUSEUM. In addition to its garish and impossible-to-miss large colored cylinders, this museum has exhibits on the earthquake, the East Coast Ngati Kahungunu Maori, Hawke's Bay dinosaur fossils, and, of course, Art Deco. A video display on the lower level has some fascinating first-hand accounts from survivors of the earthquake. (65 Marine Parade. ☎835 7781. Open Dec.-Mar. 9am-6pm; Apr.-Nov. 10am-4:30pm. $5, children free.)

MARINELAND. Follow the sound of marine mammals to the mecca of undersea activities. Two of the largest, and oldest, attractions are Shona and Kelly, the two aged dolphins. To get a better look, Marineland offers a daily swim-with-the-dolphins program with advance booking. Those not keen on swimming can get a sensory behind-the-scenes tour of Marineland, petting and feeding the dolphins. (☎834 4027; fax 834 4037; www.marineland.co.nz. Dolphin shows daily at 10:30am and 2pm. $9, children $4.50. Dolphin swim $40, gear hire $10. Book at least a month ahead in summer. Behind-the-scenes tour daily 9am. $15, children $7.50. Book at least a day in advance. No sandals. Penguin workshops daily 1-1:45pm. Arrive 15min. early. $15. Advance booking required.)

NATIONAL AQUARIUM. While the aquarium is not yet operational, construction is expected to finish by the end of 2001. Plans include a walk-through bush exhibit and shark feedings. Qualified divers can call a day in advance to tempt sharks and fate itself during feeding time. (☎834 1404. Hours and prices to be determined.)

ODDBALL ANIMAL ATTRACTIONS

OPOSSUM WORLD. This bizarre shrine to all things rodent features a static display on opossum trapping and a boutique tannery that borders on fetish fascination. Odd, but can you really pass up a stuffed kiwi made of the hide of its predator? Now there's irony for you. (157 Marine Parade. ☎835 7697. $3, families $6.)

CLASSIC SHEEPSKINS. Gain insight into what really happens to 80,000 of those cute fluffy herbivores each year—a violent and painful, but profitable, death. The tour passes massive vats curing the hides on the way to a field of sheepskins drying in the sun. At the retail shop—don't miss the bins of "seconds" skins, available for as little as $21. (22 Thames St., off Pandora Rd. (SH2 North). A courtesy van picks up from the visitors center. ☎835 9662; www.classicsheepskins.co.nz. Shop hours M-F 7:30am-5pm, Sa-Su 9am-4pm. Free tours daily 11am and 2pm.)

HAWKE'S BAY

HASTINGS ☎06

Hastings has a more subdued atmosphere than wealthier Napier. Only 12km away, it fell victim to the same quake as Napier, but was partially rebuilt in Spanish Mission style. The architecture never reached the same gaudy heights as Napier, and little effort has been put into promoting the style further. There are many kiwifruit orchards in the area, and consequently fruit pickers come to town during the harvest season (Nov.-Apr.). Most visitors to Hastings visit the wineries, Cape Kidnappers, the beaches, Te Mata Peak, and the natural attractions of Hawke's Bay.

TRANSPORTATION. Napier and Hastings are about 30min. apart by bus or train. **InterCity, Newmans,** and **Bay Express** leave from the Hastings Travel Centre, at the beginning of Caroline Rd. (☎878 0213. Bookings M-F 7:45am-4pm.) Fares are generally $2-3 different from those from Napier (see **Transportation** p. 175). **The Nimbus** leaves from Eastbourne St. by the Russell St. corner, or from the Kmart by the visitors center. (Runs M-F 7am-5:30pm. For details see **Napier: Transportation** p. 175). **Car rental** is available from **Metro Rent-A-Car** (☎835 0590) in Napier. Although *Let's Go* does not recommend it, hitchhikers going south often head out just past the 30kph zone beyond the racecourse; those going to Napier usually thumb up Karamu Rd. North, while those heading to Taupo, Wairoa, or Gisborne take the route that bypasses central Napier by getting rides from Pakowhai Rd.

ORIENTATION AND PRACTICAL INFORMATION. Flat and orderly Hastings is perturbed only by the slant of the railway track slicing through the heart of the city center. **Heretaunga St.,** the main road, turns pedestrian for a block on either side of the railway (a herd of ceramic sheep flock at the Market St. end of this stretch). Streets are tagged west to one side of the railway and east to the other; south and north designations split at Heretaunga St. The **Visitors Information Centre** is on Russell St. North. opposite K-Mart. (☎873 5526; fax 873 5529. Open M-F 8:30am-5pm, Sa-Su 10am-3pm.) Other services include: a **BNZ,** on Heretaunga St. next to **Westpac Trust** (open M and Th-F 9am-4:30pm, Tu-W 9:30-4:30pm); **police** (24hr. ☎878 0870), on Railway Rd.; **The Doctors** (☎878 8123; open daily 8am-9pm) at 110 Russell St. with a **pharmacy; Internet World** 102 Queen St. East, with access for $12 per 1hr. (☎876 4876; open M-F 8:30am-6:30pm, Sa 9am-4pm, Su 10am-4pm); and the **post office** (☎878 9425), on Russell St. opposite the visitors center.

ACCOMMODATIONS AND CAMPING. Most backpackers accommodations help arrange work for fruit-picking travelers. **AJ's Backpackers,** 405 Southland Rd. just off Southhampton St., is a home away from home. Jackie and Alan still find time to be hospitable while looking after their two small daughters and friendly dogs. (☎878 2302. Free pick-up. Dorms $15, weekly $85 if you're employed locally.) At **Hastings Backpackers,** 505 Lyndon Rd. East between Hastings St. and Willow Park Rd., both work and play are available. (☎876 5888. Dorms $14, weekly $80; doubles $28; tents $12.) Almost nightly, summer BBQs fill the courtyard of picnic tables at **Travellers Lodge,** 606-608 St. Aubyn St. W. Turn right from the train station and follow signs. Spacious rooms complete with a roomy TV lounge, foosball table, and sauna. (☎878 7108. Free pick-up and bikes. Off-street parking. Key deposit $10. Internet. Dorms $15; singles $24; doubles $36. Weekly rates available.) The **Hastings Holiday Park,** 25min. from town by Splash Planet on Windsor Ave., has lots of green space, large trees, and a duck-filled creek. Basic plyboard sleeping cabins are outfitted with heaters. (☎878 6692; fax 878 6267; holidaypark@hastingstourism.co.nz. 3-bed dorms $40 per room; tourist doubles $65; motel doubles $80; power and tent sites $10-11 per person.)

FOOD AND NIGHTLIFE. A high point in the Hastings culinary experience is the rich fruity scoops at **Rush Munroe's Ice Cream Gardens,** 704 Heretaunga St. West. Their 74 years of experience has perfected flavors from classic vanilla to loads of luscious fruity flavors. (☎878 9634. Open in summer daily 10am-9pm; in winter 10am-5:30pm.) The **Corn Exchange**, at 118 Maraekakaho Rd., has an a-maize-ingly chic central fireplace. The menu features fringe meats like venison and bison, as well as steak, chicken, and vegetarian standards. Mains are pricey ($15-28), but meals like the wood-fired pizzas ($14-16) are filling, and the bar is well-stocked. (☎870 8333. Open M-Th 11:30am-11pm, F-Sa 10:30am-1am or until late, Su 10:30am-11pm.) **Robert Harris Coffee Shop**, 104 Russell St. South, is in the town center. Part of a larger coffee shop chain, it offers fresh sandwiches (under $4). (☎878 2931. Open M-F 8am-5pm, Sa-Su 8am-3pm.) **Countdown Foods** is the supermarket on Queen St. North. (☎878 5091. Open M-F 8am-9pm, Sa-Su 8am-8pm.) Nightlife in Hastings, more often than not, includes a pint of Steiny or cider under the dark pine beams lined with beer towels at the **Cat and Fiddle Ale House**, 502 Karamu Rd. North. (☎878 4111. Open Sa-W 11am-midnight, Th-F 11am-2am.) **Friends Bar & Cafe**, 131 Heretaunga St. on the corner with Karamu Rd., has a mellow feel inside the large interior. Bar food here is $3-12 and coffee $3. (☎878 6701. Open M-F 11am-late, Sa-Su 8am-late.)

◘◪ SIGHTS AND ACTIVITIES. Hastings shares many of its most compelling draws with Napier (p. 175), such as area **wineries, Cape Kidnappers,** and killer surfing beaches like **Ocean Beach** on the south side of the Cape and **Waimarama** farther south. However, there are a few attractions in Hastings that are worth a mention. For example, **Splash Planet** is New Zealand's only water theme park that offers both year-round (heated indoor pools, jeeps, mini golf course etc.) and summer attractions (water slides, etc.). The 6½-hectare park is a 5min. walk from downtown Hastings. (☎876 9856; www.splashplanet.co.nz. Open Sept.-Apr. daily 10am-6pm; May-Aug. Sa-Su and school holidays 10am-5pm. In summer $22, children under 15yrs. $16; in winter $11, children $8.) Or, one can sample over 85 different varieties of stone fruits (in season) at **Pernel Fruitworld**, on Pakowhai Rd. about a 5min. drive northwest of Hastings, with tours every hour from 9am to 4pm (☎878 3383. $8, children, $4). The **Hawke's Bay Exhibition Centre**, 201 Eastbourne St. East, has showings of local and national art and scientific displays. (☎/fax 876 2077. Open M-F 10am-4:30pm, Sa-Su 11am-4pm. Free.)

CAPE KIDNAPPERS

Thousands of birds nest on a remote cliffpoint in the Southern Pacific. From September to March they are home to the world's largest mainland nesting grounds of the **Australasian gannet.** Fifteen thousand of the large tawny-headed, white-and-black birds arrive en masse in early September and set up their nests in quasi-orderly rows at the three colony sites at the 13-hectare Cape Kidnappers Gannet Reserve. Chicks hatch in early November and mature through the summer before flying the coop on their ambitious maiden air voyage of 2800km across the Tasman Sea to Australia. In the meantime, it's a scene straight from Alfred Hitchcock: male gannets wheeling and bearing down like 747s toward the teeming colony, then stopping on a dime to drop nesting material to their Mrs. Gannet below.

The area is closed to the public between July and October, when the birds are in the early nesting stage. At other times you are free to visit the gannets (and gannet, ahem, residue). It's a stunning walk at any time of year, even in winter when the birds are gone. Check with the Napier Visitors Center for local tour operators and hiking trails among soaring stone and crashing surf. (Trips usually 4hr., $20-38.)

TAUPO AND TONGARIRO

With fire and brimstone bubbling beneath its surface and snow-capped peaks towering at its center, the and Tongariro region uneasily awaits further volcanic tantrums. If you can find a patch of surface undimpled by jet skis, kayaks, or sailboats, Lake Taupo reflects an impressive scene of adrenaline. The mighty trio of Mounts Ruapehu, Ngauruhoe, and Tongariro are home to the famed Tongariro Northern Circuit tramp (located in Tongariro National Park) and the popular Whakapapa and Turoa ski fields. Cast yourself into the scene before more underground rumbling changes the landscape again.

TAUPO   ☎07

The adrenaline capital of New Zealand. The relief after surviving a morning skydive and bungy jump combo and the residents of this sunny community (pop. 21,257) who preside over the largest lake in New Zealand (616 sq. km) and its population of fat trout make smiling easy. The town lies at the Waikato River and rides the same belt of smoking geothermal activity that powers Rotorua, harboring natural attractions that rival even its thrilling, and ubiquitous, adrenaline offerings.

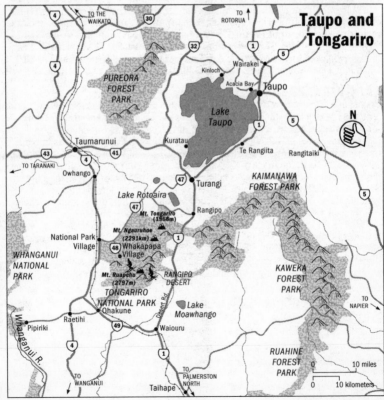

Taupo and Tongariro

◪TAUPO AND TONGARIRO HIGHLIGHTS

TRAMP the rugged volcanic terrain and steaming turquoise pools of the splendid **Tongariro Crossing,** oft-called the best day hike in New Zealand (see p. 360).

TRAIL the steady stream of backpackers who finally take the **skydiving** plunge in Taupo, partly because it gives a bird's-eye view of the region's splendor, and partly because it's nice to scream with a friend (see p. 187).

▬ TRANSPORTATION

Flights: Air New Zealand (Taupo airport ☎378 5428) 7km south on SH1, flies daily to: **Auckland** (55min., 3 per day; $196 one-way); **Wellington** (1hr., 3 per day, $230 one-way); **Christchurch** (2¼hr., 3 per day, $349 one-way); **Queenstown** (5hr., 2 per day, $558 one-way); and **Nelson** (2hr., 3 per day, $294 one-way). Taxis run from the airport (10min., door-to-door, $9 one-way).

Buses: InterCity/Newmans leave from Taupo Travel Centre (☎378 9032) on Gascoigne St. for: **Auckland** (5hr., 4 per day, $39-51); **Hamilton** (3hr., 4 per day, $25-33); **Napier** (2hr., 3 per day, $24-36); and **Rotorua** (1hr., 4 per day, $16-22); and **Wellington** (6hr., 4 per day, $53-68). InterCity connects daily with **Turangi's Alpine Scenic Tours** (☎378 7412; mobile 025 937 281) to reach **National Park** and **Whakapapa Villages** (2hr., 2:30pm, $29). During ski season, **Tongariro Expeditions** (☎377 0435, 0800 828 763; www.thetongarirocrossing.co.nz) runs daily from Pointons Ski Shop to the **Whakapapa ski field** (7:30am, return $30) and to/from **Tongariro Crossing** and **Northern Circuit** (departs Taupo 6:30am and Ketetahi Hut 4:30pm).

Taxis: TOP Cabs (☎378 9250) and **Taupo Taxis** (☎378 5100) have **24hr.** service.

Rentals: Rent-a-Bike (mobile ☎025 322 729) rents bikes (half-day $20, full-day $25) and front shock bikes (half-day $30, full-day $40) and delivers them right to your door. On Tongariro St., near the Lake Terrace Cross, **Pointons Ski Shop** (☎377 0087) has a ski, boots, and poles package for $25 or a snowboard and boots combo for $40. Open daily 7am-7pm. For fishing gear, **Taupo Rod 'n' Tackle,** 7 Tongariro St. (☎378 5337) rents out fly-fishing outfit for $35 per day ($20 half-day) and spin-fishing outfit for $20 per day ($10 half-day). Open in summer daily 8am-5:30pm; closed Su in winter.

Hitchhiking: Taupo is at the crossroads of the North Island; rides are easy, but getting far enough out of town (especially to go south on SH1) may not be. To head north on SH1, many thumbers cross the Waikato to the intersection of Norman Smith St. Note that *Let's Go* does not recommend hitchhiking.

✴❼ ORIENTATION AND PRACTICAL INFORMATION

Tucked into a corner created by the **Waikato River** as it gushes from the northeast bulge of **Lake Taupo,** the city radiates like a streaking comet. Its head, at **Tongariro St.,** aims at the visitors center and the Boat Harbor, and its outer tail angles away along **Lake Terrace, Spa Rd.,** and the river. Taupo's center lies between **Tongariro** and **Ruapehu St.** The wayward streaks of **SH1** and **SH5** exit across the Waikato to Rotorua and Auckland, or the other way to Turangi and Napier.

Visitors Center: Taupo Visitor Centre, 30 Tongariro St. (☎376 0027; fax 378 9003). Open daily 8:30am-5pm.

DOC: 115 Centennial Dr. (☎378 3885), off Spa Rd. Open M-F 8am-4:30pm.

Currency Exchange: Banks line Tongariro St. with **ASB Bank** (☎376 0063), at Tongariro and Horomatangi St. Open M-F 9am-4:30pm.

Police: (24hr. ☎378 6060), behind the visitors center in Story Pl.

Medical Services: Main St. Pharmacy (☎/fax 378 2636), corner of Tongariro and Heu Heu St. Open daily 9am-8:30pm. The **Taupo Health Centre,** 117 Heu Heu St. (☎378 7060). Open M-F 8:30am-5pm. The **hospital** (☎378 8100) is on Kotare St.

Internet Access: Central Plateau Reap (☎378 8106), at the corner of Heu Heu and Kaimanawa St., is the cheapest at $5 per hr. Open M-Th 9am-4:30pm, F 9am-3pm.

Post Office: At Horomatangi and Ruapehu St. Open M-F 8:30am-5:30pm, Sa 9am-noon.

ACCOMMODATIONS AND CAMPING

Older, cheaper places are clustered along the streets a few blocks east of the town center. Otherwise, the cheapest riverfront bed in town is the free camping on Reid's Farm Rd., a bit south of the Falls along Huka Falls Rd. (2km north of town off SH1). As always, never leave any of your possessions unattended here.

■ **Action Down Under YHA** (☎378 3311; fax 378 9612; yhataupo@xtra.co.nz), at the corner of Tamamutu and Kaimanawa St. Shiny and specklessly clean. Enjoy beautiful views of snow-capped peaks. Heated spa. On-site parking. Central heating. Rental bikes. Internet. Disabled rooms available. Dorms $15-17; singles $30; twins and doubles $40, $45 with bath; family rooms with bath $70; camping $10 per person.

Rainbow Lodge, 99 Titiraupenga Rd. (☎378 5754; fax 377 1548; rainbow@clear.net.nz), just off Spa Rd. The sunny patio is great for socializing. Free coffee. Sauna. Off-street parking. Mountain bike and fishing rod hire. Key deposit $10. Dorms $15-18; singles $30; twins and doubles $38; hotel-quality doubles with bath $44.

Burkes Lodge and Backpackers (NOMADS), 69 Spa Rd. (☎378 9292; fax 378 9092; burkesbp@ezysurf.co.nz). This renovated motel has private bathrooms and a pleasant central courtyard. Spa. Bike hire. Key deposit $10. Internet. Dorms $17; doubles $38, with bath $40. Family rooms available.

Go Global VIP (☎377 0044; fax 377 0059), at the corner of Tongariro and Tuwharetoa St. This large and centrally located backpackers clears a well-worn path for a lively young crowd. Key deposit $20. Internet. Dorms $19; twins $44; doubles $48.

Sunset Lodge, 5 Tremaine Ave. (☎378 5962; sunset@reap.org.nz), 3km from town. Turn off Lake Terrace onto Hawai St. Don't let the free bikes distract you from the homemade banana bread. Key deposit $10. Internet. Dorms $15-16; twins and doubles $36.

Berkenhoff (VIP), 75 Scannell St. (☎/fax 378 4909; bhoff@reap.org.nz), a 15min. walk from town center. With a $1000 palm tree, and a free spa and pool, this lodge attracts long-term residents. Free breakfast, pick-up, and drop-off. BBQ dinners $3.50-10. Dorms $17; twins and doubles $38, with bath $42.

Taupo Motor Camp, 15 Redoubt St. (☎/fax 377 3080; tpocamp@voyager.co.nz). Go up Tongariro St. about 100m past the visitors center, then turn left. Dorms $18, in winter $15; cinderblock cabin singles $40/$25; doubles $44; campsites $11 per person.

■ **Orakei Korako Geyserland** (☎378 3131; fax 378 0371; ok@reap.org.nz), 35km from Taupo. If you've got your own transport, this hidden lakeside lodge across the water from Taupo's best geothermal site is unbeatably scenic and peaceful. Bring bedding and food. Rustic communal lodge and bunks that were once trees $20; tourist flats with kitchenettes $80 (max. 4 people), each additional person (up to 6-7) $20.

FOOD

For the true Taupo experience, delight in some trout. While it can't be sold over the counter, many places around town will prepare your catch (for a fee). The **Pak 'N Save,** is at the corner of Ruapehu and Tamamutu St. (☎377 1155. Open Sa-Tu 8am-8pm, W-F 8am-8:30pm.)

Pasta Mia, 5 Horomatangi St. (☎377 2930). Enjoy delicious single servings of pasta for $7.50 (double $14.50). For around $13, you can transport enough uncooked pasta and sauce back to your hostel to feed you and a few friends. Open in summer daily 11am-10:30pm, Tu-Th 11am-5:30pm; in winter F-M 11am-9:30pm.

Replete Delicatessen and Cafe, 45 Heu Heu St. (☎378 0606). With items under $7, it's no wonder that lunchtime's crowded. Open M-F 9am-5pm, Sa-Su 8:45am-3:30pm.

Taupo

🏠 ACCOMMODATIONS
Action Down Under YHA, 5
Berkenhoff (VIP), 6
Burkes Lodge &
   Backpackers (NOMADS), 2
Go Global VIP, 8
Orakei Korako
   Geyserland, 15
Rainbow Lodge, 3
Sunset Lodge, 13
Taupo Motor Camp, 1

TO HUKA FALLS RD. (100m), HUKA
FALLS (4km), CRATERS OF THE MOON (6km),
WAIRAKEI (5km), ARATIATIA RAPIDS,
ORAKEI KORAKO (30km), AUCKLAND, ROTORUA,
REID'S FARM RD. (1.5km) & 🏠 (32km)

🍎 FOOD
The Dodgy Geezer, 14
Million Dollar View, 12
Pak 'N Save, 4
Pasta Mia, 7
Replete Delicatessan & Cafe, 9
♪ NIGHTLIFE
Axis/Finn MacCuhal's, 10
Holy Cow, 11

Waikato River

Tauponui-a-Tia
College

TO CENTENNIAL RD. (900m),
A.C. BATHS (1km), &
TAUPO BUNGY (1km)

Taupo
Domain

Municipal
Camping
Ground

Taupo District
Museum of
Art & History

Gallagher
St.

N

0   200 yards
0   200 meters

TO 🏠 (3km),
(6km), SH1 SOUTH, SH5

The Dodgy Geezer, 76-80 Lake Terrace (☎378 0457) between Rifle Range Rd. and Tui
St. With delicious mains ($8.50-22.50), and a choice lakefront location, this place is
an ideal dining spot. Open daily 10:30am-late.

The Million Dollar View, 5 Tongariro St. (☎378 8539). The name says it all; the view
through the large glass walls at this upstairs corner joint's prime lakefront location can't
be beaten. Excellent catch of the day ($16-26) as well as burgers ($12-13). Open daily
5:30pm-late (also open 11am-2pm in summer).

🎸 NIGHTLIFE

After a day packed with death-defying activities, visitors to Taupo can keep the
excitement pumping until the wee hours of the night.

Holy Cow, 11 Tongariro St. (☎378 0040). Every backpacker, her uncle, and the guy they
hitched in with head to the bar of Taupo. Tables are mounted fairly early in this rump-
shaking second-floor mixing bowl; it can get racy here! Belching DJs mix commercial
hits nightly. Handles $3.50. Happy Hour 7-9pm, handles $2.50. Open daily 7pm-3am.

Axis (☎377 4466), at the corner of Tongariro and Tuwharetoa St. This large corner bar
draws a lively young crowd downing beer (handles $4) and grooving to the beats of the
live DJ (Th-Sa). Th 10pm-midnight beer and spirits are half price, F 5-7pm everything is
$1 off. Open Su-W noon-midnight, Th-Sa noon-3am (closed Su and M in July-August).

Finn MacCuhal's (☎378 6165, ext. 3), at the corner of Tongariro and Tuwharetoa St.,
right below Go Global. With M quiz nights and live music 4 nights a week (W and F-Su),
a rollicking crowd keeps the Guinness flowing. $10 meals include free ale or wine. Han-
dles $3-4. Open daily 11am-3am.

TAUPO

👁 SIGHTS

GEOTHERMAL WONDERS
Though Taupo's geothermal wonders may not get as much press as those of Rotorua, they lie along the same belt of primeval geological action.

CRATERS OF THE MOON. A 1954 explosion in the thermal area, resulting from the drilling of a geothermal bore, created a steaming pockmarked landscape of craters and boiling mud pools so unique it is now managed by DOC. As small vents collapse and become blocked, minor eruptions can occur at any time. Whirling steam adds a ghostly otherworldly feel. *(A few kilometers north of town on SH1. Free.)*

ORAKEI KORAKO GEYSERLAND AND CAVE. Although it is far away (and inaccessible to those without transport), this dramatic and undeveloped private geothermal reserve is more mysterious for it. A shuttle boat crosses the idyllic lake during the day to reach a range of steamy wonders. On the far side lie pockets of glistening silica terraces, spurting geysers (including a fascinating horizontal geyser), colorful mineral crusts, and deep, scalding hot cyan pools. Don't miss the spectacular fern-lined amphitheater of Aladdin's Cave with its warm mineral pool. Jewelry can reportedly be naturally cleaned in the pool in 3min. while its owners gaze at the postcard view from the cave's mouth. *(Reached via a sign-posted road that winds through hills and deer farms off SH1 about 25min. north of Taupo. ☎ 378 3131. Open daily 8am-4:30pm; in winter 8am-4pm. Entrance fees and boat ride $17.)*

TAUPO VOLCANIC ACTIVITY CENTRE. The public side of the adjacent IGNS (Institute of Geological and Nuclear Sciences), the Centre has a crack team of researchers who monitor the Taupo volcanic zone. This attraction recently became more interactive with the introduction of a model geyser, a small earthquake simulator, and even a glass-encased tornado machine. Check out the seismograph readings of Ruapehu and recent eruption film footage. *(Take the Huka Falls Rd. turn-off from SH1. ☎ 374 3875. Open M-F 9am-5pm, Sa-Su 10am-4pm. $5, children $2.50.)*

TAUPO HOT SPRINGS. After a long day of touring, you may want to pay a visit to one of Taupo's bubbling pools of tranquility. Both public and private indoor or outdoor pools are available. *(On the Taupo/Napier Highway, only 5min. from town. ☎ 377 6502; www.taupohotsprings.com. Open daily 7:30am-9:30pm, last entry 9pm. Pools $8-9.)*

TOURS
You can approach the lake scenery with your own rented boat, or with relatively cheap narrated cruises. The western shores of Acacia Bay end at cliff and bush, with an undulating edge of rocky inlets and bays. Along part of the uninhabited coastline, a set of impressive (if not ancient) Maori carvings have been chiseled into the rock faces at Mine Bay, on private land accessible by boat only. Many cruises include the **carvings,** the **Western Bays, Hot Water Beach,** and much of the lake itself; contact the **Charter Office** (☎378 3444) at the harbor to book.

SUPERJET. The only way to see all the sights in a relatively short amount of time is on this speedy jetboat, which does a 2hr. comprehensive loop at up to 50 knots. Informative commentary, windsuits, and life jackets are provided. *(☎377 4855, 0800 278 737. 1hr. $29, children $15; 2hr. $59, children $29.)*

BARBARY. For a more active experience, this sexy 1920s sailing yacht, once owned by none other than **Errol Flynn,** is now captained by colorful Bill Dawson, who teaches you how to sail it yourself. *(☎378 3444. 2½hr., 2-3 per day, $25.)*

REPLICA STEAMBOAT CRUISES. Board a 1920s steamboat replica for informative and affordable 1 and 2hr. scenic tours to Hot Water Beach, the Maori rock carvings, Jerusalem Bay, Acacia Bay, and Two Mile Bay. *(☎378 3444; 378 6136. Written commentary also in French, German, Japanese, Chinese, Dutch and Korean; book ahead. Hot Water: Adults $22; under 15 $11. Two Mile: Oct.-Apr. Adults $11; children $6.)*

IT'S A BIRD, IT'S A PLANE, IT'S... Your one-stop potty shop, the **SuperLoo,** located on Tongariro St. next to the visitors center, was voted "the best loo in New Zealand" by Keep New Zealand Beautiful. The country is full of automated public toilets, but nothing compares to SuperLoo. Inside the stalls, exclamations of "this really *is* a super loo" can be heard.

Envisioning a new standard of sanitation in New Zealand, the makers of the SuperLoo set a lofty goal; some said it couldn't be done. But in October of 1993, when the SuperLoo first opened, Taupo knew it had something special. The opening celebration, was said to have been epic: toilet paper streamers and bobbing for apples in the fresh toilet water. Especially enthusiastic attendees vowed never to wipe again. Today, after eight years of operation, the SuperLoo hasn't lost its sheen. (Toilets $0.20. 4min. shower $1; towel hire $1, soap 30¢, shampoo 50¢. Lockers $1 per day. Open in summer daily 7:30am-9pm; in winter M-Th 7:30am-5:30pm, F-Su 7:30am-6:30pm.)

OTHER SIGHTS

WAIRAKEI PARK. The park combines a slightly bizarre amalgamation of sights, recreational activities, a geothermal power station, a geothermally heated prawn farm, shops, and lodgings. At its north end sits the world's first geothermal power station, the **Wairakei Geothermal Power Development** (built 1959-64). From the **Bore Lookout,** at the end of the road turn-off, a post-apocalyptic terrain of massive, steaming, stainless-steel tubes worm along the ground to feed Taupo's energy needs. *(Across the Waikato Bridge on SH1, less than 8km from town.)*

HUKA FALLS. Maori for "long white water," the Falls are a great place to watch nature fight reason—bus loads of camera toters flock each day to witness the 100m-wide, 4m-deep Waikato River force itself into a 15m-wide, 3m-deep rock chute. Spurting out of the bottleneck, the water rushes breathlessly below a footbridge over the channel, and ejects finally into a pool below. The cheapest and most aerobic way to capture the falls on your roll of film is via the Huka Falls Track. *(Leaves from Spa Thermal Park, off Spa Rd. Return 1hr.)*

⚑ ACTIVITIES

PLUMMETING OUT OF THE SKY

If you've been resisting peer pressure or sudden impulses, Taupo is the place to throw caution to the wind and hurtle out of a plane at 3000m or plummet toward water attached only to an elastic cord. For a deal on all three activities (bungy, skydiving, and Huka jet-boating), complete the **MaxBuzz Challenge** (www.maxbuzz.co.nz). To promote the area's adrenaline boosters, MaxBuzz offers a **free beer** at the **Holy Cow** for each activity completed, and a free T-shirt once you conquer all four activities (trip to Holy Cow included).

⚑ TAUPO TANDEM SKYDIVE. A tandem jump here is **cheaper** than anywhere else in the world (doubtless because of the sheer number of jumps—over 50,000), and the views on a clear day are spectacular, stretching from Ruapehu to Taranaki to Tarawera. This ultra-professional organization has been sending people up (and "escorting" them back down) since 1990. *(☎ 377 0428, 0800 275 934; fax 378 0468; www.skydive.net.nz. 12,000 ft. $199. 100kg weight limit. Call ahead.)*

TAUPO BUNGY. Since December 1991 more than 107,000 have ventured off the cantilever platform 47m above the hauntingly crystalline Waikato. For $99, you can hook up and ponder the sheer cliffs, the impending water, or the pickup raft below. Or, you can just close your eyes and take the plunge. A water touch is an option. Call ahead. *(202 Spa Road. ☎ 377 1135, 0800 888 408; fax 377 1136; www.taupobungy.com. Open daily 9am-7pm; in winter 9am-5pm; free shuttle within Taupo.)*

TAUPO

ROCK 'N ROPES. This adult playground has an arousing array of ropes and adventure exotica including the Chicken Walk, Criss Crotch, Floating Log, Vertical Playpen, and Giant Swing. Great value for money and a surefire confidence builder; many takers find these challenging highwires even scarier than the bungy or skydive. *(Located at Crazy Catz Adventure Park, off Highway 5 just north of Wairekai. ☎374 8111, 0800 244 508; fax 378 1351; www.rocknropes.co.nz. Swing $15; high beam, giant trapeze, and swing combo $35; half-day $59; free transport available.)*

ON THE WATER

Lake Taupo's blue waters fill the crater of the volcano responsible for some of the most disruptive eruptions the world has ever witnessed. Its final blast, 1809 years ago, ejected ash and pumice meters-thick over much of the North Island—the resulting blood-red skies were recorded in ancient Chinese and Roman literature.

FISHING. The world-famous Taupo trout, both brown and rainbow, were introduced from California in the late 1800s and continue to draw novice and experienced anglers from across the world. All legal details are printed on the back of the fishing license you have to purchase for any line you drop. The apex of fish phenomenon takes place around ANZAC Day (April 25, 2002), when the ECNZ International Trout Fishing Tournament takes over town with 500 anglers eager to take the biggest, prettiest, and feistiest trout of the lake. *(Charters $50-130 per hr. Spinning and fly-fishing permitted in Lake Taupo year-round; on rivers, only fly-fishing is allowed. 12 fish per day license $12.50; 26 per week license $27. Available from the visitors center, sports shops, or the offices at the harbor.) Check with the visitors center for options and outfitters.*

KAYAKING. Kayaking Kiwi offers half-day paddles to the carvings and other sights. *(☎/fax 378 5901; mobile 025 288 1137; www.kayaking-kiwi.co.nz. $49.)* **Zig Zag Fun Co.** runs kayaking trips past the Orakei Korako thermal park and then farther up the Waikato than other kayaking companies. *(☎377 0688; mobile 025 755 294. Free pickup. Half-day $45, full-day $75.)*

HUKA JET. Take this heart-racing jetboat blast down the Waikato, performing 360° turns for the Kodak-heavy crowds at **Huka Falls.** *(6km north of Taupo off SH 1. ☎374 8572, 0800 485 2538; www.hukajet.com. Boats run every 30min. Free shuttle from the visitors center. 30min. ride $59, children $30. Reservations essential.)*

TURANGI   ☎07

Renowned for its abundant rainbow and brown trout, the town really comes across best when the surrounding natural riches—the mountains of Tongariro, the remote Kaimanawa range, and the Tongariro River—speak for themselves.

⧉ TRANSPORTATION. InterCity/Newmans stops at the **Travel Centre** (☎386 8918) and heads daily to: **Auckland** (5½hr., 3-4 per day, about $62) via **Taupo** (45min., about $15) and **Hamilton** (3½hr., about $40); **Wellington** (5½hr., 3 per day, about $62) via **Palmerston North** (3hr.). **Starlighter** heads to **Auckland** daily at 1:10am and to **Wellington** daily at 1:45am. The laid-back folks of **Alpine Scenic Tours** (☎386 8918; mobile 025 937 281), also at the Travel Centre, run daily shuttles to **National Park Village** (1-2 per day, return about $20) and **Whakapapa Village** or straight to **Whaka-papa** (45min., 2-3 per day, return about $20). In summer, Alpine also travels to the endpoints of the Tongariro Crossing (return about $25). **The Bellbird Lodge** runs a shuttle to the Tongariro Crossing. (☎386 8281. Departs 6:30am, return $20.) **Extreme Backpackers** (see below) also runs shuttle service to the Crossing's endpoints, leaving Extreme at about 7:30am. **Tongariro Expeditions** (☎377 0435, 0800 828 763) runs shuttle service from Turangi to the endpoints of the **Tongariro Crossing** at 7:15am, leaving Ketetahi to return to Turangi at 4:30pm. Although *Let's Go* does not recommend it, **hitchhiking** to Taupo is reportedly not too difficult; those heading north on SH1 to wait at the corner of Pihanga Rd. near the visitors center or near the Shell station. Traffic is lighter going south.

▚▞ ORIENTATION AND PRACTICAL INFORMATION. Some 4km from Lake Taupo on **SH1**, Turangi has no lakefront view. SH1 continues both north around the lake to Taupo, and south (where it's known as the **Desert Rd.**). **Ohuanga Rd.** is the main road through town, and virtually all essential shops and services are in the **Town Centre** complex, a short diagonal walk from the bus stop. The **Turangi Visitor Centre** is just across from the Town Centre. Check here in winter to make sure the Desert Road is open before heading south. (☎386 8999; fax 386 0074. Open daily 8:30am-5pm.) For more park information, and before attempting any serious Tongariro walks, stop by the **DOC** office in Turanga Pl., at the south edge of town. (☎386 8607. Open M-F 8am-5pm.) Other services, all located in the Town Centre unless noted, include: a **bank** (open M-F 9am-4:30pm); the **police** (☎386 7709), at Ohuanga and Tautahanga Rd.; **Turangi Pharmacy** (☎386 8565; open M-F 8:30am-5:30pm, Sa 9am-1pm, Su 10:30am-noon); **Dr. Liaw** (☎386 8898) and **Dr. Leigh** (☎386 0680), Turangi's main general practitioners; **internet access** at the **visitors center** ($2 per 10min.) or **Civic Video** in the Lotto shop next to B & P (☎386 8811; open M-Sa 8:30am-8pm, Su noon-8pm; $0.15 per 1min., $10 per hr.); and the **post office** (☎386 7769; open M-F 9am-5pm) at Naylors Bookshop.

▐▞ ACCOMMODATIONS AND CAMPING. Well-organized and often providing shuttles, Turangi's accommodations will set you up with discounts for affiliated area outfitters. **▨Extreme Backpackers,** 26 Ngawaka Pl., is just around the corner from the bus depot. With an inner courtyard, state-of-the-art kitchen, and open log fire in the Sky TV lounge, this is even better than home. (☎386 8949; fax 386 8946. Off-street parking. Linen $3. Key deposit $5. Internet. 4-bed dorms $17; doubles with linen $40, with bath $48; family rooms $55; tent sites $10.) Quiet reigns in the four houses of the **Bellbird Lodge,** on the corner of Ohuanga and Rangipoia Rd. in the residential north end of town. Friendly owners bring free cake around nightly. Call for pick-up. (☎386 8281; fax 386 8283. Mountain bike hire. Dorms $16; twins and doubles $36; tent sites about $9.) The coolest thing about **Club Habitat (YHA/VIP),** 25 Ohuanga Rd., is the backpacker-oriented bar with internet, pool tables, and home-brewed beer. (☎386 7492; fax 386 0106. Key deposit $10. Sauna, spa, restaurant, and bar. Internet. Dorms $16; singles $23; twins $40; doubles $40, with bath $64; tent sites $8.) Try the **Turangi Cabins and Holiday Park,** off of Ohuanga Rd., just a little west of the town center. (☎/fax 386 8754. Cabins and chalets $16 per person; on-site caravans $40 for 2; tent sites $9 per person.)

◨ FOOD. The **Grand Central Fry,** 8 Ohuanga Rd., is a cut above the typical takeaway, with excellent burgers and fish 'n' chips, most under $7. (☎386 5344. Open daily 11:30am-9pm; phone in your order to avoid the wait.) **Baks Brasserie & Bar,** at the corner of Pihanga and Ohuanga, serves up good breakfast fare, and also operates a restaurant and bar with frequent karaoke nights. (Outdoor beer garden in summer. Open Tu-Su 9:30am-9pm; kitchen closes between 4:30-5:30.) Fortunately for insomniacs, Turangi is also blessed with the 24hr. **Turangi Truck Stop.** Just 1km west of the town center, on Atirau Rd., you can place your order at the counter, through phone, or by CB. (☎386 8760; grub $1.50-8.) For groceries, head to the **New World,** in the Town Centre. (☎386 8780. Open M-F 8:30am-6pm, Sa-Su 9am-5pm.)

◪▟ SIGHTS AND ACTIVITIES. The **Tongariro River** is ideal for three things: fishing up, kayaking/rafting down, and walking around. Knowing, perhaps, that they are Turangi's premier attraction, husky 1½-2kg **trout** are a sure-fire bite. (Fishing guides for the river and lake range from $40 to $65 per hour. Licenses cost $12 per day and are available at the visitors center, as well as several sports and fishing tackle shops.) Several operators raft down the Class III upper section, over 60-odd rapids closed in by walls of bush. **Rock 'n River** will take you rafting to a hidden waterfall and on a walk up the canyon. (☎386 0352, 0800 865 226. $85.) The **Tokaanu Thermal Pools** are off the main road of tiny Tokaanu Village down SH41 from Turangi. Immerse yourself in small, covered private pools ($6 per 20min., price includes public pool open daily 10am-9:30pm) or in the slightly cooler, and much less expensive, $4 public pool. (☎386 8575. Open daily 10am-9pm.)

Turangi's other big attractions are the nearby **Tongariro Crossing** (see p. 190), often hailed as the finest one-day trek in the world, and the rugged hills east of Tongariro that constitute part of the **Kaimanawa Forest Park.** Kaimanawa, primarily used for multiday hunting and tramping trips, is hard to access and not developed for visitors. The **Lake Rotopounamu walk,** which leaves from a signpost 11km up SH47, does an easy 5km loop through native fern forest around this small lake hidden at the base of **Pihanga** (the 1325m extinct volcano towering over Turangi).

TONGARIRO NATIONAL PARK

Three larger-than-life volcanoes tower over the roof of the North Island: massive Ruapehu (rue-uh-PIE-oo; 2797m), conical Ngauruhoe (nair-uh-HO-ee; 2291m), and Tongariro (1967m). These volcanoes—all still active—were once considered so sacred that all but the highest-born Maori shielded their eyes against their grandeur. An eerie, windswept land, it encompasses New Zealand's only desert (the desolate Rangipo), native forests of beech in its lower areas, hardy alpine shrublands across its lava-built slopes, and those famous gem-like crater lakes.

AT A GLANCE	
AREA: 78, 651 hectares.	**GATEWAYS:** Turangi, National Park, Ohakune. Whakapapa is in the park.
CLIMATE: Mild climate in summer, extreme conditions in winter.	
	CAMPING: Accommodations and camping in Whakapapa. Backcountry huts.
FEATURES: Craters, active volcanoes, herb fields, dessert.	
	FEES & RESERVATIONS: Camping $10-12, pass $14-18. Great Walks pass necessary in summer.
HIGHLIGHTS: Emerald Lakes, Tongariro Crossing.	

TRANSPORTATION

Highways encircle Tongariro National Park. To the east, **SH1**, also called the **Desert Road,** streaks through the **Rangipo Desert;** ice occasionally closes this road in winter. To the south, **SH49** splits off from SH1 at the army base town of **Waiouru** and then runs west until it hits **SH4,** which flanks the park's western side. **SH47** traces the park's northern edge between SH4 and SH1. **SH48** (also called Bruce Rd.) and **SH46** branch south from SH47 to Whakapapa and the Mangatepopo road end, respectively. **Hitchhiking** along any of these roads can be a slow process, but traffic is particularly sparse along SH48. Although *Let's Go* does not recommend it, those determined to get past Whakapapa Village start early to catch ski field employees and never wait until dark to try their luck going down. The same is true for those hitching along Ohakune Mountain Rd., which heads north from SH49. Most visitors to the park stay in **Turangi** (see p. 188), **National Park Village** (see p. 192), **Whakapapa Village** (see p. 193), or **Ohakune** (see p. 193). Whakapapa Village is the most convenient to the **Tongariro Northern Circuit** and the **Whakapapa ski fields,** while Ohakune provides the easiest access to the **Turoa ski fields.** Operators shuttle walkers to the **Tongariro Crossing** trailheads from Turangi, National Park Village, and Whakapapa Village.

 WHEN TO GO. Though the Tongariro National Park can be visited year round, extreme weather conditions and difficult tramping makes the winter dangerous. Trampers must be experienced and have appropriate gear, including crampons, an ice axe, and appropriate clothing.

◾🛈 ORIENTATION AND PRACTICAL INFORMATION

Tongariro National Park lies just southwest of Lake Taupo. The park's boundaries are relatively continuous. Start your exploration at **DOC's Whakapapa Visitor Centre,** with its high-tech audiovisual shows and displays on volcanism and the park's cultural history. Its **Tongariro Summer Programme** (late Dec.-early Jan.) features ranger-led activities from backcountry heli-hikes ($110) to free evening talks. (☎07 892 3729. Open Dec.-Mar. daily 8am-6pm, Apr.-Nov. 8am-5pm.) There are also smaller **DOC offices** in Turangi (☎07 386 8607; open M-F 8am-5pm) and Ohakune (☎06 385 0010; open M-F 8am-3pm). Turangi and Ohakune harbor **supermarkets,** where the food's more affordable, and have **ATMs**. **Secure parking** is available at the DOC lot beside the Whakapapa visitors center; vandalism and theft run rampant in many other area lots, particularly those at trailheads. The **telephone codes** for this region are 06 in Ohakune and 07 in all points further north.

🞖 OUTDOOR ACTIVITIES

Tongariro Northern Circuit (3-4 days, 51.5km) winds around the three great volcanoes and passes wild and unique lava formations, desolate moonscapes, and technicolor waterlets. The **Tongariro Crossing,** "the finest one-day walk in New Zealand," is part of the circuit (see p. 360). The less-crowded **Round-the-Mountain Track** (4-5 days) runs around Mt. Ruapehu, traversing windswept slopes, crossing a deep gorge, and passing along the edge of the forsaken Rangipo Desert (huts $10, camping $5). The track intersects the Northern Circuit at both Whakapapa Village and Waihohonu Hut; people often walk the two in conjunction—storing food for the second half of the journey in Whakapapa means a 10min. detour off the hike, but also a lot less pack weight in the initial days. Daywalks abound; many start right from Whakapapa Village. The relatively easy **Tama Lakes Walk** (return 5hr.), which follows an undulating, tussocky landscape past the Taranki Falls to the incongruous blue of the Tama Lakes, is one of the best of these. The unmarked climb to the active **Ruapehu Crater,** on the otherhand, is the most difficult (official) dayhike in the park. Ice, snow, and volcanic activity can make the trip a risky one, and several unprepared people have died doing it. Most begin the trek from the top of Bruce Rd. (SH48) near the base of the Whakapapa ski lifts (return 7hr.); others ride the lifts to their terminus (open daily 8:30am-3:30pm; return $15) and start from there (return 5hr.). Staff from the Mt. Ruapehu Ski Area conduct **guided walks** along this route. (☎07 892 3738. Dec.-Apr. daily 9:30am. $45, under 16 $20.)

⛷ SKIING AND SNOWBOARDING

Tongariro draws nearly half of its visitors in the winter months, thanks to the commercial ski slopes hugging Ruapehu's slopes. The **Mt. Ruapehu Ski Area** is the largest and most developed ski area in New Zealand. One pass provides access to lifts on both sides of the mountain, shuttles transport skiers from one to the other, and a traverse between the two (for intermediate and advanced skiers only) is in the works. Although Ruapehu attracts bad weather like a 2797m magnet (gale-force winds and storms often close the fields), the management offers a weather guarantee that allows refunds or credits if lifts have to close. (☎07 892 3738; snowphone 0900 99 333; www.mtruapehu.com. Open July-Oct.; lifts open daily 8:30am-4pm. Skis, boots, and poles $29, under 16 $18. Snowboard and boots $40. Lift pass $54, under 16 $27; half-day $30, under 16 $16; deals available on multi-day and beginners' equipment and lift passes.)

WHAKAPAPA. The Whakapapa side of the mountain has killer views of distant Mt. Taranaki on clear days. It includes six chairlifts, eight T-bars or platters, six rope tows, a beginner's area, plenty of groomed, patrolled trails, and good open terrain. Snowboarders are welcome, but most seem to prefer Turoa. (At the top of Bruce Rd. from Whakapapa Village.)

TUROA. With the country's longest vertical drop (720m) and 400 hectares of patrolled snow, Turoa is known for wide open terrain, long runs (4km is the longest), four chairlifts, three T-bars, four platter lifts (two in beginners' area), and one rope tow. Turoa also has some off-trail skiing; it's even possible to haul gear up to Crater Lake and ski down (always check with the Ski Patrol first). Another culture altogether, snowboarders love Turoa for the natural half-pipes in its gulleys and the lack of any major flats—almost half of the slope at any time is covered with bleach-blond, styled-out boarders. You can rent equipment on the mountain (see above), but there may be a better selection at one of Ohakune's shops, though prices are roughly equivalent. *(Accessible via Ohakune Mountain Rd.)*

NATIONAL PARK VILLAGE   ☎ 07

National Park Village is little more than a cluster of accommodations at the junction of SH4 and SH47; the Tongariro Crossing, Whakapapa ski fields, and Whanganui River Journey are all comfortably close to this one-horse, three-volcano town.

◪ **TRANSPORTATION.** The **train station** is on Railway Rd., at the end of Carroll St.; **buses** depart from the dairy near Carroll and Ward St. **TranzScenic** and **InterCity** head north to Auckland daily (5½hr., $39-49) via Hamilton (3½hr., $26-32); and south to Wellington (5½hr., $44-55) via Ohakune (30min., $11). TranzScenic also goes daily to Palmerston North (3½hr., $22-44), while InterCity heads to Wanganui (2½hr., $27); **Ski Haus** and **Howard's Lodge** (see below) handle bookings. **Howard's Lodge** runs an on-demand shuttle to Whakapapa Village ($6, return $10) and the ski fields ($10, return $15). **Alpine Scenic Tours** (☎ 386 8918; mobile 025 937 281) runs to Whakapapa Village for the same price, and includes Turangi (2-3 per day, $15).

⁊ **PRACTICAL INFORMATION.** Most accommodations hire a range of **gear** for all seasons. There are **no ATMs** in town. The little **police station** (☎ 892 2869) is on Buddo St., parallel to SH4. The **BP station** at the highway junction stocks basic groceries, and serves as a **post office.** (☎ 892 2879. Open M-Th 7:30am-7pm, F 7:30am-7pm, Sa-Su 7:30am-7pm; in winter M-Th 7:30am-7pm, F 7:30am-10:30pm, Sa 7am-8pm, Su 7am-7pm.) **Internet access** is available at **Howard's Lodge** ($12 per hr.).

⌂ **ACCOMMODATIONS.** The quality lodges of National Park Village are absolutely stuffed with skiers in winter, and the summer traffic of trampers is on the rise. **Howard's Lodge (NOMADS),** down Carroll St., serves travelers well with its extensive shuttle services. Particularly clean and hospitable, the free spa, train shuttle, and ski clothes for guests are added bonuses. Winter weekends demand bookings up to three weeks in advance. (☎/fax 892 2827; howards.nat.park@xtra.co.nz. Internet. Mountain bike hire $20. Dorms $18, in summer $15; twins and doubles $70, $40; rooms with bath $90, $60.) **Ski Haus,** across the road, has a restaurant and bar. Guests without bookings are welcome to roll off the night train straight into Room 16. (☎/fax 892 2854; www.skihaus.co.nz. Spa $2 per 30min. Key deposit $10. Dorms in winter $15-25, in summer $15; doubles in summer $40; tent sites $10; caravan sites $5, extra person $10.) **National Park Lodge and Motel,** two minutes up Carroll St., has clean and comfortable dorm rooms in the main lodge and self-contained motel rooms in the building next door, each with a TV lounge and a small kitchen. (☎ 892 2993; 0800 861 861; fax 892 2992; natparkodge@xtra.co.nz. Internet. Dorms in winter midweek $20, weekends $25, in summer $15; motel rooms $100-140, in summer $60 for 2.)

⌂ **FOOD.** Beyond lodge restaurants, there are two dining venues in National Park Village. **Eivin's Ski Shop Cafe,** at Carroll St. and SH4, serves delicious sandwiches ($5) and will dig out an awesome Ruapehu photo album for those who ask. (☎ 892 2844. Open daily 7am-late; in summer noon-late.) The **Schnapps Hotel,** at Findlay St. and SH4, rocks the ski season with bands every Saturday night (cover $5), and a bizarre grab bag of drinking games. Unwind with one of the mains ($12-18) and a cold beer. (☎ 892 2788. Open daily 11am-2am; in summer noon-2am.)

▲ ACTIVITIES. The **Tongariro Forest Conservation Area,** just north of town, is home to the **42 Traverse,** one of the country's most satisfying mountain bike trails. The organ-jiggling ride follows well-maintained old logging trails, with a stream crossing and a 570m descent (4-5hr.). Howard's Lodge (see above) runs a shuttle service to the starting and ending points ($20 per person for 2 people).

WHAKAPAPA VILLAGE   ☎ 07

This tiny clutch of establishments, the most prominent of which is the non-budget Grand Chateau, is the foundation of ski operations in Tongariro National Park, and is the most immediate base for skiing on the north side of Ruapehu.

▣ TRANSPORTATION. Alpine Scenic Tours (☎ 386 8918; mobile 025 937 281) leaves Whakapapa Village for **National Park Village** (2-3 per day, $10), the Tongariro Crossing endpoints at the **Ketetahi** and **Mangatepopo carparks** (on request), and **Turangi** ($15). Service can be rather flexible to accommodate transport dilemmas, but it must be booked in advance. **Whakapapa Shuttle** (☎/fax 892 3716; mobile 021 256 3109) provides service from the village up to the **ski field** ($6, return $10).

⑦ PRACTICAL INFORMATION. Whakapapa Visitor Centre, which also acts as the **DOC** office, presents two high-tech audiovisual shows ($3 adult, $1 children, discount for 2-show package). (☎ 892 3729; fax 892 3814. Open daily 8am-6pm; in winter 8am-5pm.) There are **no banks or ATMs.** Both **internet access** ($8 per hr.) and the **post office** are in **Fergusson's Cafe** (see **Food** below).

▐▜ ACCOMMODATIONS AND CAMPING. Grand Chateau, Grand Schmateau. The perky **Skotel** has, hands down, the finest view of any budget accommodation on the North Island. To get to this spot, turn left just before the visitors center and after the Grand Schmateau. Complete with all the ski-lodge amenities—internet, spa, sauna, drying room, cushy mattresses, and small communal kitchen—functional shares cost $20 in summer, but go up to $30 during winter. (☎ 892 3719, 0800 756 835; fax 892 3777; skotel@clear.net.nz.) Set beside a stream, the **Whakapapa Holiday Park,** just across the road from the visitors center, offers small but private tent and caravan sites carved out of the native bush, and good kitchen facilities. Spartan bunks populate the backpackers lodge. (☎ 892 3897; fax 892 3026. Key deposit $5. Dorms in summer only $12.50; cabins $35; tourist flats $55; tent sites $8; caravan sites $10.)

◘ FOOD. Refined, historic, and decidedly non-budget, the **Grand Chateau** hotel dominates the village both in size and in the number of eating establishments it owns. Aside from the in-house bar and restaurant at the Skotel, all of the food listings below run under the capable hands of the Chateau (☎ 892 3809; ask for the appropriate extension). The lodge-like **Fergusson's Cafe** does a brisk business with soups, hot quiches, sandwiches, and coffee. (☎ ext. 8435. Internet. Open daily 8am-5pm; in summer 8am-3pm.) Across the road, the elegant interior of **Pihanga Cafe** has surprisingly affordable mains, usually $11.50-18.50. (☎ ext. 8560. Open daily 11:30am-late; kitchen closes at 9pm.) When basic groceries are necessary, **Whakapapa Holiday Park** has a small supply.

OHAKUNE   ☎ 06

Ohakune (pop. 1500) sits wedged between Mt. Ruapehu and a giant carrot. Mt. Ruapehu, the active volcano that last blew its top in 1995-1996 now flows with skiers. And the carrot is not an arbitrary monument; when the snow melts and the ski lifts shut down, focus turns back to the rich volcanic soils, renowned for producing world-class carrots, sprouts, and potatoes.

▯ TRANSPORTATION

Trains: Since Ohakune is halfway between Auckland and Wellington, arrivals and departures are virtually all in the middle of the day or the middle of the night. **TranzScenic** (☎0800 802 802) runs daily to **Auckland** (6hr., 2 per day, $70-81), via **National Park** (30min, $16-18); and **Wellington** (5hr., 2 per day, $61-68), via **Palmerston North**.

Buses: InterCity runs Su-F to **Auckland** (6hr.) and **Wellington** (5hr.), with several stops along the way. **Guthreys** (☎0800 759 999) also runs service to **Auckland** via **Hamilton**, and to **Wellington** via **Palmerston North**. To get to **Taupo**, either take the train to Waiouru and catch a bus from Aldo's Restaurant, or catch a connection from Turangi.

Ski Shuttles: The **Snowliner Shuttles** (☎385 8573) run on demand to the ski-fields of **Turoa** ($8, return $15) and **Whakapapa** ($20, return $30; if Turoa is closed), and to trailheads during the summer. **Snow Express** runs on demand to Turoa (☎385 4022; $16, $9 one-way). **Tongariro National Park Shuttle Transport** (☎0800 825 825) also runs to **Turoa** (return $15), **Whakapapa** (return $20, min. 4 people), and in the summer to the **Tongariro Crossing** (return $25).

Hitchhiking: Although *Let's Go* does not recommend it, hitchhiking is reportedly not too hard between Ohakune and National Park or Waiouru. Hitching up the mountain is reportedly easier in the morning, but success depends on your amount of gear. Catching a ride is more difficult in the summer.

▦▯ ORIENTATION AND PRACTICAL INFORMATION

The south end of town, where **SH49** merges, has most services (like the grocery store and pharmacy) and is active year-round. The north end, known as the **Junction**, lies 3km up by the railroad tracks, and comes alive during the winter with seasonal chalets and jumping nightlife. It also marks the start of the **Ohakune Mountain Rd.**, leading up past the entrances to several scenic tramps, and the ski lifts of **Turoa**. **Goldfinch St./Mangawhero Terrace** (the road changes names) runs between the two (20-25min. by foot).

Visitors Center: Ohakune Visitor Centre, 54 Clyde St. (☎385 8427; fax 385 8527), has a relief map of Tongariro National Park. Open M-F 9am-5pm, Sa-Su 9am-3:30pm.

DOC: (☎385 0010; fax 385 0011), beyond the railroad tracks on Ohakune Mountain Rd. One of Tongariro's two field centers. Open M-F 8am-3pm.

Banks: A couple of banks line **Goldfinch St.** including **Westpac** (☎385 8154), next to New World. Open W-M 9am-4:30pm, Tu 9:30am-4:30pm.

Medical Services: Dr. Perera (☎385 8356), on Goldfinch St., is the town's one-man medical service. **Ohakune Photo Pharmacy** (☎385 8304) is open M-F 9am-5pm; in winter Sa also 9am-noon.

Internet Access: Snowbird Copy Centre, 92 Clyde St. (☎385 8756) costs $7.50 per hr. Open daily 9:30am-5pm, but open later in summer.

Post Office: 5 Goldfinch St. (☎385 8645) in Broadbents Bookshop. Open M-F 6:30am-6pm, Sa 6:30am-7pm, Su 8:30am-4pm.

▮▮ ACCOMMODATIONS AND CAMPING

Rimu Park Lodge and Chalets (VIP), 27 Rimu St. (☎/fax 385 9023; rimu-lodg@ihug.co.nz). Close to the nightlife, the lodge has an open fire. Free pick-up and breakfast in winter. 30min. free internet with 2-night stay, otherwise $5 per ½hr., $8 per hr. Bunks from $23 midweek, in summer $16; twins and doubles $35/$18.

Ohakune YHA, 15 Clyde St. (☎/fax 385 8724). Laid-back atmosphere and lack of TV fosters easy conversation among guests. Dorms $18 for 3-bed, $16 for 6-bed; twins $44; doubles with bath $26, $66 family room. Closed in summer.

Matai Lodge (☎385 9169; fax 385 9196; matai.lodge@xtra.co.nz), at the corner of Clyde and Rata St. A clean and spacious lodge, complete with central heating, a game room, and Internet. Dorms Su-Th $20, F-Sa $22; in summer $15.

Alpine Motel and Lodge, 7 Miro St. (☎/fax 385 8758; alpine.motel@xtra.co.nz), near the corner of Clyde St. and Raetihi Rd. Offers small bunk rooms plus all the motel freebies (spa, train pick-up, on-site restaurant). Key deposit $6. Bunks Su-Th $20, F-Sa $25; in summer $15. 2-day min. stay on weekends in peak season.

Ohakune Top 10 Holiday Park, 5 Moore St. (☎/fax 385 8561), off Clyde St. This park provides the basics with some extras. Tent sites $10, powered sites $10; tiny backpacker cabins $17, extra person $12; doubles with kitchens and showers $57.

█ FOOD

Utopia, 47 Clyde St., serves up tasty nibbles (read: nachos, paninis, soup) in a hip locale. During the ski season, Thursday nights feature $15 curries. (☎ 385 9120. Open daily 9am-2pm; in winter until 3pm and also Th-Sa 6pm-late.). Just a few doors down, **Mountain Kebabs Cafe,** 29 Clyde St., has filling meat and vegetarian kebabs (medium $7-7.50) in a newly renovated setting. (☎ 385 9047. Open daily about 10am-10pm; frequently closed in summer.) Up at the junction end of town, near the corner of Rimu and Thames, **Margarita's** serves up heaping Mexican mains ($14.50 and up) and a chill nightlife around a huge open fire. Sundays are super with $10 specials. (☎ 385 9222. Open in ski season daily 3pm-3am, closed Nov.-mid Apr.) **La Pizzeria,** 6 Thames St., next to the Turoa Ski Lodge, offers terrific gourmet pizzas for gourmet prices—at least $14 meal. (☎ 385 8558. Open in ski season daily 6pm-late; in the off-season F-Sa 6pm-late.) Stock up on groceries at **New World,** 12 Goldfinch St. (☎ 385 8587. Open M-W 8:30am-6pm, Th-F 8:30am-7pm, Sa 8:30am-5:30pm, Su 8:30am-4:30pm; in winter M-Sa 8am-6pm, Su 8:30am-5pm.)

█ NIGHTLIFE

Dry-docked snowboarders replace the families after dinner at ever-popular **Margarita's** (see **Food** above). On the corner of Ohakune Mountain Rd. and Thames St., the polished wood of the **Powderkeg Bar** explodes on weekends with DJ and drink specials providing the spark. (☎ 385 8888. Open daily 7am-late; hours vary in summer.) Upstairs, the party high continues at the **Matterhorn.** (☎ 385 8888. Open daily 5pm-3am during ski-season; in summer, hours alternate with those of Powederkeg). Follow your ski instructor to the bar at **Turoa Ski Lodge.** (☎ 385 8274. Open in winter daily 4pm-1am.)

█ OUTDOOR ACTIVITIES

Most people come to Ohakune to ski the fine slopes, but the area does have summer activities. The sealed 18km **Ohakune Mountain Rd.** makes for a exhilarating and scenic **mountain biking** when ski traffic is gone. Ron Rutherford's **Ride the Mountain** operation rents bikes and runs to the top. (☎ 385 8257. $30.) The **Powderhorn Shop and Ski Hire,** in the grand chalet rents bikes (half-day $25, full-day $35) and tramping equipment. (☎ 385 8888. Open daily 7:30am-6pm; in summer 9am-5pm.)

From October to April, Ohakune is a point of departure for **canoe trips** on the Whanganui River, a tranquil ride running through the heart of the wilderness (see p. 139). **Canoe Safaris** offers 2-5 day guided tours of the Whanganui, with 1-5 day tours down other routes (prices range from $75-725 per adult, $55-435 per child; prices include food and camping equipment).

TARANAKI & WANGANUI

The looming peak of Mt. Taranaki (Mt. Egmont), in the center of the North Island's westernmost extremity, defines the region's ancient mythology and contemporary tourism. Legend speaks of Taranaki as a restless, sorrowful place, and it is true that the mountain has the natural instability of a volcano. Year-round relaxation is afforded by Taranaki's balmy summer weather and gentle, wintry charm. The rugged green slopes nourish one of the richest dairylands in the world; Taranaki just might deserve its unofficial title as the "Udder of New Zealand." Although the region may lack extreme adventure, the unique mix of surf, snow, and river ensure that the region remains free from bucolic blandness.

▓ TARANAKI AND WANGANUI HIGHLIGHTS

BY LAND The diverse **Egmont National Park** has excellent opportunities for tramping and skiing (see p. 201).

BY SEA The **Whanganui River Journey** is the only Great Walk where you float to the finish line (see p. 362).

NEW PLYMOUTH ☎ 06

Residents of New Plymouth love to point out that surfing the Tasman and skiing the slopes of Taranaki are both within one hour's drive. While this is indeed an exciting proposition for sports enthusiasts, the city itself gets lost somewhere. Regardless, Taranaki's only city has managed to make some waves of its own. Featuring renowned parks and numerous walks, New Plymouth might capture your attention as more than just a break between the snow and the surf.

▐ TRANSPORTATION

Flights: Flight information (☎ 755 2250).

Buses: Depart from the **Travel Centre,** at the corner of King and Queen St. Free luggage storage for the day. **InterCity** (☎ 759 9039) departs for: **Auckland** (6¼hr., 2 per day, $70) via **Hamilton** (4hr., $48); and **Wellington** (6¾hr., 2-3 per day, $61) via **Stratford** (30min., $14), **Hawera** (1¼hr., $19), **Wanganui** (2½hr., $30), and **Palmerston North** (4hr., $41). **Dalroy Express** (☎ 755 0009) runs service to **Auckland** (5hr., 1 per day, $65) via **Hamilton** (3½hr., 1 per day, $42) and **Hawera** (1hr., $13) with stops along both routes. **White Star** (☎ 758 3338) also runs to and from **Wellington** (6¼hr., 1-2 per day, $43), and makes stops in **Stratford, Wanganui,** and **Palmerston North,** among other destinations.

Taxis: New Plymouth Taxis (☎ 757 5665), **Egmont City Cabs** (☎ 754 8801), and **Energy City Cabs** (☎ 757 5580) queue at corner of Brougham and Devon St.

Bike Rental: Raceway Cycles and Mowers, 207 Coronation Ave. (☎ 759 0391). Mountain bikes from $30 per day.

Hitchhiking: Although *Let's Go* doesn't recommend it, hitchhiking toward Wanganui around the east side of Egmont is reportedly easiest in the nebulous zone on the outskirts of town on SH3, before the traffic picks up to 70kph. More traffic usually heads this way than heads up SH3 toward Otorohanga, Hamilton, and Auckland.

🚺 PRACTICAL INFORMATION

Visitors Center: New Plymouth Information Centre (☎ 759 6080), at the corner of Leach and Liardet St. Open M-F 8:30am-6pm, Sa-Su 9am-5pm; in winter M-F 8:30am-5pm, Sa-Su 10am-3pm.

DOC: 220 Devon St. W (☎ 758 0433; emergency mobile 025 438 956; fax 758 0430). Bevy of brochures on Egmont National Park, North Taranaki Walks, and Sugarloaf Marine Park; fishing queries also answered. Open M-F 8am-4:30pm.

Currency Exchange: Thomas Cook, 55-57 Devon St. E (☎ 757 5459). **BNZ** on Brougham St. offers good exchange rates. Take your pick of the **ATMs** along Devon St.

Police: 89 Powderham St. (☎ 759 5500).

Medical Services: Care Chemist, 10 Egmont St. (☎ 757 4614), open daily 8:30am-9:30pm. **Accident and Medical Clinic** (☎ 759 8915), in Richmond Centre on Egmont St. Open daily 8am-10pm. **Taranaki Base Hospital** (☎ 753 6139), on David St.

Internet Access: New Plymouth Library (☎ 758 4544), on Brougham St. $8 per hr. Open M, W, and F 10am-8:30pm, Tu and Th 10am-5:30pm, Sa 10am-4pm, Su 1-5pm.

Post Office: (☎ 758 2110), on Currie St. Open M-F 7:30am-6pm, Sa 9am-1pm.

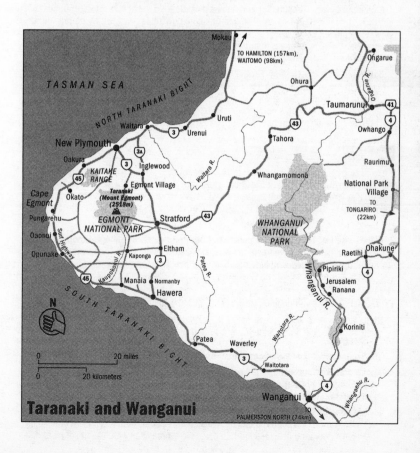

Taranaki and Wanganui

📷 ACCOMMODATIONS AND CAMPING

All of New Plymouth's accommodations encourage visitors to partake of Mt. Taranaki's splendor by providing shuttles to its base. However, after dark those without cars might find the hike from their beds to the nearest pitcher slightly more complicated.

Shoestring Backpackers (VIP), 48 Lemon St. (☎/fax 758 0404), a 5min. walk from town center in a residential neighborhood. Get to know potential mates at the large dining table or, better yet, in the sauna ($4). Free transport for bus station and hitchhikers' spots. Internet. Laundry $4. Dorms $16; singles $24; doubles $36, with TV $40.

Egmont Lodge (YHA), 12 Clawton St. (☎753 5720; fax 753 5782). Take Frankley Rd. at the Dawson St. fork and follow the signs, or call for pick-up. Nightly servings of mountain-shaped "Egmont Cake" and the TV-free lounge encourage conversation. Key deposit $10. Reception 8-10:30am, 5-9pm. Dorms $16; doubles $40; tent sites $10.

Central City Lodge, 104 Leach St. (☎758 0473; fax 758 6559; centralcity@xtra.co.nz). Although not quite as central as the name suggests, this lodge can accommodate everyone from the solo backpacker to traveling football teams. Heated indoor pool and spa $2 for your entire stay. Linen $5. Key deposit $5. Reception 7am-10pm. Dorms $15; singles $30; doubles $40. Also, B & B options: single $40, double $60.

Richmond Corner Backpacker and Accommodation, 25 Ariki St. (☎759 0050; fax 759 0051; jrsanders@xtra.co.nz). This establishment is smack in town. A barren lounge doesn't promote socializing, so strike up a conversation about the mural: "It's ok to eat the fish, they are dripping from the ceiling." Internet. Laundry $2. Reception 7:30am-9pm. Dorms $15; singles $30; twins and doubles $45, both with bath. Cash only.

Belt Road Seaside Holiday Park, 2 Belt Rd. (☎/fax 758 0228; info@beltroad.co.nz). Listen to the waves lap. The 25min. walk from town yields sweet rewards: an exquisite view of the Tasman Sea and proximity to the beach (just 1km away). Communal toilets and kitchen (use of pots and utensils $5). Linen $5. Backpackers cabins $25 for two, $18 for one; cabins with bath $30-55; tent and powered sites $9 per person.

🍴 FOOD

New Plymouth's main drag, **Devon St.,** is sprinkled with an assortment of takeaways featuring burgers, kebabs, pizza, and more. Gorge on these delectable goodies, or if inspiration strikes, build a meal of your own with food from **New World,** located on the block bounded by Leach, Courtenay, Liardet, and Gover St.—it's the closest market to the hostels. (☎759 9052. Open daily 8am-9pm.)

E.S.P.resso (☎759 9399), adjacent to the Govett-Brewster Art Gallery. Although food at a museum cafe may not strengthen your sixth sense, it will certainly satiate your tastebuds. The best cafe eating in New Plymouth. Open daily 8am-4pm.

El Condor, 170 Devon St. (☎757 5436). Renowned in New Plymouth for its delicious Argentinian cuisine, El Condor draws flocks of hungry diners nightly. Pasta dishes (mains $14.50) and gourmet pizzas ($10.50-23) available. Open Tu-Sa 5-10pm.

Steps Restaurant, 37 Gover St. (☎758 3393). Step up to gourmet Mediterranean cuisine at prices that won't lead you above and beyond your budget. The ever-changing menu features diverse lunch items ($9-17) and elegant dinners ($20-26). BYO. Open Tu-F noon-2pm, and Tu-Sa from 6pm.

Agra Indian Restaurant, 151 Devon St. E (☎758 0030). An open kitchen allows you to watch as the chefs prepare your tasty dishes (mains $10-20). Open M-Su 5:30pm-late, with mid-day lunches Th-F.

Simply Read Cafe and Bookshop, 2 Dawson St. (☎757 8667). Don't let the exquisite westward view of the ocean, the offbeat selection of books, or the exhibition of local art distract you from the delicious food. Delicate filos come filled with all sorts of meat and vegetable goodies ($7.50-8.50). Open M-Su 9am-4pm.

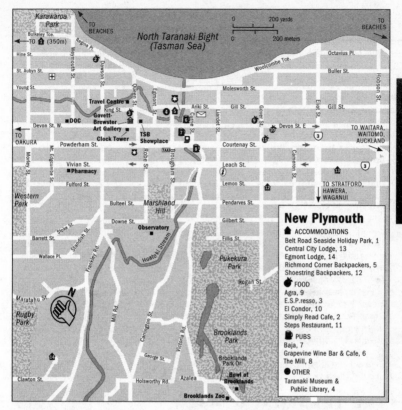

New Plymouth

🏠 ACCOMMODATIONS
Belt Road Seaside Holiday Park, 1
Central City Lodge, 13
Egmont Lodge, 14
Richmond Corner Backpackers, 5
Shoestring Backpackers, 12

🍴 FOOD
Agra, 9
E.S.P.resso, 3
El Condor, 10
Simply Read Cafe, 2
Steps Restaurant, 11

🍺 PUBS
Baja, 7
Grapevine Wine Bar & Cafe, 6
The Mill, 8

⚫ OTHER
Taranaki Museum &
   Public Library, 4

TARANAKI

🎭 NIGHTLIFE

Early in the week the nightlife in New Plymouth resembles that of Taranaki's rural towns—there's almost none. The weekends are another story as people emerge from the mountain and sea to party hard 'til the stroke of three.

The Mill, 2 Courtenay St. (☎ 758 1935), impossible to miss at the end of Currie St. Once a functioning flour mill, today the grinding at this local bar involves bodies rather than wheat stalks. Music pumps in the basement dance area dubbed **Underground** (open F-Sa 11pm-3am). Celebrity DJs throw dance parties monthly. Open M-Sa 11am-late.

Baja, 17-19 Devon St. W (☎757 8217). This Mexican cafe bar serves tasty meals ($6.50-17) and assorted drinks (beer $3.80). For a less taxing musical experience visit **The Beaten Path** at the back of the restaurant (open W-Sa 6pm-3am), where a live DJ spins the latest grooves nightly. Open Su-Tu 11am-11pm, W-Sa 11am-3am.

Grapevine Wine Bar & Cafe, 38C Currie St. (☎757 9355). Catering to a slightly more sophisticated set, this bar and cafe serves up more vintages than an antique show. Live music Th-Sa, with jazz Th. Open Tu-Sa from 5pm.

👁 🗝 SIGHTS AND ACTIVITIES

The best way to look at New Plymouth is from the outside in. Known for its parks and walkways, as well as its close proximity to excellent beaches and mountains, the city offers a variety of activities for the outdoor enthusiast. For a firsthand look at New Plymouth's pastoral splendors, head to the contained nature of **Pukekura Park** at the top of Liardet St. (no bicycles allowed), reportedly the most stunning park in New Zealand.

If the weather cooperates, visit the calla lilies in **Stainton Dell** or the green grandeur of the leg-stretching walk to **King Fern Gully.** No matter what the weather, the **Fernery** warmly awaits hushed footfalls on a carpet of cedar chips. (Fernery open daily 8:30am-4pm. Gates to Pukekura Park are open from 8:30am-6pm.) Adjacent to Pukekura Park is yet another confederation of structures and gardens, the **Brooklands,** which includes a **children's zoo.** (Open daily 8:30am-5pm. Free.) If you are in town anytime from the week before Christmas 2001 until February 6, 2002 (Waitangi Day), walk through and see the park illuminated for the **Festival of Lights.**

Once you have had your fill of man-made parks, point your hiking boots toward one of New Plymouth's many scenic walkways. Detailed guides are available at the visitors center. The **Te Henui Walkway** (return 4½hr.) is one of the best, following the Te Henuistream through 5.9km of natural splendor down to the sea. The **Coastal Walkway** offers dramatic views of the sea crashing against the rocky coastline (return 8hr.). Follow this path south past industrial areas and arrive at **Paritutu,** a prominent rock at the edge of the shore (in Maori, *pari* is "cliff" and *tutu* is "to stand erect"). Epic views of the coast and, on a clear day the mountain, are the reward for those brave enough to take the 154m trip (deservedly rated "hard").

With its proximity to the Tasman Sea, New Plymouth also offers a variety of aquatic options. Surfers and windsurfers can get their adrenaline fix year-round at **Fitzroy** and **East End** beaches. For those who prefer watching the surf to being immersed in it, let Dave Chadfield of **Happy Chaddy's Charters** take you for a cruise around the Sugar Loaf Islands where you can enjoy a visit to the seal colony. (☎ 758 9133. $20; children $10; fishing trips $10 per hr.)

For those rainy days (and there may be plenty), head to the town center to see why New Plymouth is the only real roost for Taranaki's culture vultures. A stroll down **Devon St.** reveals the city's 19th-century heritage, evidenced by artful moldings and dates embossed on the upper levels of the downtown shops. A few blocks away, the sleek exterior of the **Govett-Brewster Art Gallery** (☎ 758 5149), at the corner of King and Queen St., gives way to a collection of contemporary work of artists from New Zealand and abroad. The permanent collection features the work of **Len Lye** (see p. 65), and his kinetic sculptures are displayed frequently. (Open daily 10:30am-5pm. Free.)

THE TARANAKI COAST
☎ 06

Encouraging a laid-back lifestyle of catching rays on beaches and waves on year-round surf, the Taranaki coast from New Plymouth to Hawera is a surprisingly under-appreciated destination. Hitchhikers find success sporadic at best, and in winter frequent rains make the experience even more unpleasant. Generally it's better to hire a car or a guide. You can circumnavigate Mt. Taranaki (Egmont) and travel along the coast in two ways. For a scenic journey (1½hr.) with easy access to various bush walks and the best views of the Taranaki Bights and the Tasman Sea, take Carrington Rd. from New Plymouth to Okahu Rd. and then circle around. The coastal route (3½hr.) is best done on SH45, but unless you stop and walk to the shore expect only glimpses of the ocean (much of the view on this route is obscured by either hedges, great distance, or both).

OAKURA
☎ 06

A one-horse town (pop. 1500) with an awesome beach that is wide, flat, and family-filled in summer, the town of Oakura is representative of the population "centers" that dot the coast. Take "Surf Highway 45" between Okato and Opunake for a glimpse of killer waves that pound the coast; the region frequently hosts surfing and windsurfing competitions. In summer it is possible to camp in the area for free; be prepared for swarms of other tourists. The **Oakura Boardriders Club** provides free toilets/showers/changing rooms just off the beach, near the corner of Wairu Rd. and Tasman Parade. The point at the end of **Ahu Ahu Road** yields an amazing surf by the **Wavehaven Hostel,** near the corner of Ahu Ahu Road and SH45. Surfboard and kayak rentals (half-day $10, full-day $15) with wetsuits are available, and surfing lessons for novices can be arranged. There is also a climbing wall and volleyball court. (☎/fax 752 7800; wave.haven@taranaki.ac.nz. Laundry $4.

Dorms $15; singles $25; doubles $30; weekly dorms $75.) It is also home to **Deelush**, on Main South Rd., whose specialty is pizza; a gourmet pizza ($25) will feed you and three of your closest friends. (☎ 752 7303. Open Tu-Su 10am-late; in winter 6pm-late, with F-Su brunch from 10am.) Just next door, **Butler's Bar and Cafe**, the only bar in town, offers lunches and dinners from 11:30am. Chug a $3.40 handle over the 40-foot well in front of the fireplace (☎ 752 7765).

OPUNAKE   ☎ 06

The closest to a bustling metropolis, Opunake (pop. 1587) harbors both the dramatic cliffs of Middleton's Bay and the pleasantly swimmable Opunake Beach, with its teeming campground. For a good night's sleep, head to **Opunake Motel and Backpackers**, 36 Heaphy Rd., which contains a variety of rooms in all their rustic glory. (☎ 761 8330; fax 761 8340. Dorms $15; cottages $20 per person; motel units $55, for 2 $70, extra person $13.) Nab cheap supplies at **Beau's Supermarket**, 77-79 Tasman St. (☎ 761 8668. Open M-Th and Sa 7:30am-6pm, F 7:30am-8pm, Su 7:30am-5pm.) A little farther south on SH45 is the little town of **Manaia**, where **Yarrow's the Bakers**, on South Rd., tempts even the most frugal gourmet with six scrumptious croissants for just $2. (☎ 274 8195. Open M-F 7am-4pm.)

EGMONT NATIONAL PARK   ☎ 06

Rolling hills bow like green-robed disciples to their master and maker, majestic Mt. Taranaki (Egmont). Everything within a 10km radius of the nearly symmetrical volcanic peak was declared part of New Zealand's second national park in 1881, thankfully restraining the vigorous logging boom of the day and preserving area farmlands. With more than 300km of prime tracks ranging from primal first class (read: good condition) to backcountry adventure (read: mud), Egmont remains New Zealand's most accessible national park.

AT A GLANCE

AREA: 33,534 hectares.	**GATEWAYS:** New Plymouth, Stratford, and Opunake.
CLIMATE: Mild coastal climate and high rainfall. Dangerous in winter.	**CAMPING:** Permitted except at the summit. Back country huts.
FEATURES: Rapid weather changes.	**FEES & RESERVATIONS:** Hut ticket $5.
HIGHLIGHTS: Superb views	

⊏ TRANSPORTATION

Although there are no public buses to Egmont National Park, **Cruise New Zealand Tours** shuttles trampers. (☎ 758 3222; fax 758 3224. Daily from New Plymouth at 7:30am, returns daily 4:15pm.) Guided trips offer transportation as well (see **Activities** below).

◼✻⤵ ORIENTATION AND PRACTICAL INFORMATION

Three paved roads go into the park: **Egmont Road**, from New Plymouth through Egmont Village to the North Egmont Visitor Centre; **Pembroke Road**, from Stratford to the **Stratford Mountain House** and the **Manganui Ski Field**; and **Manaia Road**, from the Manaia/Hawera area to the Dawson Falls Visitor Centre. A fourth road, **Carrington Road**, bisects the park between the Pouakai and Kaitake Ranges. The **North Egmont Visitor Centre** will help with reservations. (☎ 756 0990; nevc@doc.govt.nz; open daily 8am-4:30pm, extended hours in summer.) A short drive from Egmont Village, is the port of entry for most of the park's visitors. Here, DOC officers point trampers in the right direction with the aid of color-coded walks, and visitors can take a 20min. audio/visual tour ($10, children $5). From the south, visitors can enter the park by means of Manaia Rd., 8km of pavement that leads to the **Dawson Falls Visitor Centre**, with easy access to ski fields and dozens of bush walks. (Mobile ☎ 025 430 248. Open daily 8am-4:30pm; in winter W-Su 8:30am-4:30pm.)

WHEN TO GO Climbing Mt. Taranaki (Egmont) is far more than a leisurely walk in the park. The mountain has already claimed the lives of 60 people, making it the most dangerous peak in New Zealand. The upper slopes are prone to dramatic and sudden weather changes, and chilling rain can fall at any elevation at any time of the year. Even during the summer months and when weather conditions are favorable, only physically fit people with a good level of outdoor experience and proper equipment can hike without the help of a guide. In winter, even the most hardened mountain climbers are strongly advised to take along a guide. DOC strongly advises trekkers to leave their plans with someone before the hike—either a family member, friend, or DOC officer. It is also imperative that climbers assemble proper gear and check the mountain forecast before setting out. If all of these requirements seem daunting, various services offer guides to assist in the ascent of Mt. Taranaki.

ACCOMMODATIONS AND CAMPING

In Egmont Village, just outside the park and east of New Plymouth on Egmont Rd., hop over to **Missing Leg Backpackers,** 1082 Junction Rd. The name comes not from a horrific tramping incident, but from the three-legged pooch that used to reside here. Reserve ahead to stay at the cozy mountain retreat with mountain bikes and camping gear for hire. Inquire at the visitors center about the $4 shuttle from New Plymouth to Inglewood. (☎/fax 752 2570. Oct.-Apr. dorms $14; doubles $35. May-Sept. dorms $12; doubles $30.)

Those planning to sleep in the park can purchase hut tickets $5, children $2.50.

NORTHERN EGMONT. DOC has reopened the **Camp House,** a budget accommodation only 50m from the visitors center. ($15, children $7.50; book at visitors center.) There are also three private huts on the mountain, each run by one of the three mountain clubs: the Tahurangi Lodge, the Manganui Lodge, and the Kapuni Lodge. The **Tahurangi Lodge,** owned and run by the Taranaki Alpine Club, offers kitchen facilities and a great location at 1520m ($15 per night). Prior booking is essential; inquire at the visitors center, or write P.O. Box 356, New Plymouth.

SOUTHERN AND EASTERN EGMONT AND DAWSON FALLS. For a night's rest try **Manganui Lodge,** the private hut run by the Stratford Mountain Club. Advance booking is required; contact the club officer (☎757 8586). DOC runs the somewhat bare **Konini Lodge** complete with an expansive kitchen and common room areas. (Mobile ☎025 430 248. $15 per person, children $7.50. Prior booking is required.) Also nearby is the **Kapuni Lodge,** which rounds out the trio of private huts on the mountain. Maintained by the Mt. Egmont Alpine Club of Hawera, the club offers gas cooking, running water, and 18 bunk beds ($10); book ahead of time by contacting Paul Adowd (☎/fax 278 4765) and arrange to collect a hut key in Hawera.

OUTDOOR ACTIVITIES

A quick summary of Mt. Taranaki's offerings: North—the safest and easiest side featuring good bush walks with the best vehicle access from New Plymouth; West—similarly good bush walks but the most remote with few people; East—the most challenging (pros only); South—the coldest (skiing when available). There are *endless* trail options in the park; visit the DOC office at Northern Egmont or Dawson Falls and make your own hiking plans. While camping is permitted in Egmont National Park, it is strongly discouraged on the summit out of respect for both the Maori and the environment. **Syme Hut** on Phantom's Peak (1900m) is arguably the best place to watch the sun rise or set; however, the hut's prime location also means that it is exposed to wind and ice. The **Mt. Taranaki Round-the-Mountain**

Track (4 days, 55km) traverses the upper slopes of the volcano, affording excellent views of the surrounding farmland and coast. It can begin from any of the several main entrances to the park. During the summer and in appropriate conditions, the trail can be shortened substantially by taking shorter routes at higher altitudes. In the spring, water runoff from the mountain and rains often cause rivers and streams to rise, making crossing difficult. In the interest of safety, hikers should wait for levels to subside, as the flows are fast and deceptively deep. Take heart, however; streams tend to go down quite quickly.

Chris Prudden's **Mountain Guides Mt. Egmont** (☎758 8261; mobile 025 474 510), out of New Plymouth, will guide one person for $300 and groups of two to four for $340. Ian McAltine's **MacAlpine Guides** provides similar service for $200 per person (max. 2 in winter, 5 in summer), and also leads tramping tours in Egmont National Park (☎751 3542, or 0800 866 486; alpineguidesmac@xtra.co.nz).

NORTHERN EGMONT. Well-prepared trampers might make the full-day trek to the **Ahukawaka Swamp,** home to unique lichen, mosses, and microbes.

For the less hardy, regional day hikes abound. One short-but-sweet walk, the **Connet Loop Track** (return 30min.), departs from the base of the North Egmont car park. Winding its way through the "Mountain Forest," the track showcases a world of fern and moss. Alternatively, the **Ngatoro Loop Track** (return 40min.) lets trampers navigate through stately cedars to the wing beats of native birds. For an 1½hr. pure bush experience, hit the **Veronica Loop Track. Bells Falls,** best reached from **Holly Hut,** is also worth checking out. The north side of the volcano offers great views of New Plymouth and beyond; the route to the **summit** from North Egmont is purportedly safer than that from the other entry points (return 1 day).

SOUTHERN AND EASTERN EGMONT AND DAWSON FALLS. Roughly 15% of park visitors enter the perimeter from the east, by way of Stratford and the **Stratford Mountain House,** with access to the Manganui ski fields in winter and several trails in other seasons. Trips to the summit can also be attempted from this side, but the route is longer (return 1 day) and more technically demanding.

From the visitors center, you can hike to the **Wilkies Pools** (return 3hr.), a series of plunge pools spilling into each other—remember that the water is ice-cold.

STRATFORD ☎06

Ah, Stratford... would a town by any other name smell as sweet? Perhaps, but in this small hamlet the moniker is half the character. One of 13 towns in the world christened after Shakespeare's British birthplace, Stratford has taken this connection to the extreme by naming most of its streets after the Bard's colorful characters and erecting a Glockenspiel (New Zealand's only) that thrice daily recites lines from *Romeo and Juliet*. The other half of Stratford's claim to fame, and the reason most visitors pass through this way, stems from the town's proximity to Mt. Taranaki. Occasionally referred to (in the first person, much of the time) as the "Gateway to the National Parks," Stratford offers easy access to one of New Zealand's most famous peaks. It is Taranaki's constant presence, more than any of the offerings within town, that lends a dose of drama to this locale.

▣ TRANSPORTATION. InterCity buses depart from the visitors center and head to **Auckland** (7hr., 1-2 per day, $71) via **New Plymouth** (35min., $13); and to **Wellington** (5½hr.; M-F 2 per day, Sa-Su 2 per day; $54) via **Hawera** (20min., $13), **Wanganui** (1½hr., $25), and **Palmerston North** (3hr., $37). **Dalroy Express** (☎755 0009, or 0508 465 622) passes through Stratford on its way to **Auckland** (6hr., 1 per day, $72) and **Hawera** (½hr., 1 per day, $6). **Central Cabs** (☎765 8395) and **Stratford Cabs** (☎765 5651) are available for local transportation needs. Although *Let's Go* does not recommend it, **hitchhikers** report that hitchhiking to New Plymouth and Wellington gets easier the farther along SH3 you get from the center of town.

⊠ PRACTICAL INFORMATION. Broadway (SH3) is the main drag. The **Information Centre** is on Broadway South (☎/fax 765 6708. Open M-F 8:30am-5pm, Sa-Su 10am-3pm; closed Sa-Su in winter). The **DOC office**, on Pembroke Rd., RD 21, provides information on Egmont National Park (☎765 5144; fax 765 6102. Open M-F 8am-4:30pm). Other local services include: **BNZ** on Broadway St. (☎765 7134; open M-F 9am-4:30pm); **police** (☎765 7145), on Miranda St.; **Stratford Medical Center**, on Miranda St. South, one block from the visitors center (☎765 5454; open M-W and F 8:30am-5pm, Th 8:30am-6pm); **24hr. on-call doctor** (☎765 5300); **post office** on Miranda St. at Prospero Pl. (☎765 6009; open M-F 8:30am-5pm); and **internet access** at the visitors center ($10 per hr.).

⊠⊠ ACCOMMODATIONS AND CAMPING. The **Stratford Top 10 Holiday Park**, 10 Page St., is a motel, backpackers, and campground all rolled into one. After a long day exploring on a bicycle ($5 per hr., $20 per day), visitors can soak in the $3 spa. (☎/fax 765 6440; stratfordholpark@hotmail.com. Internet. Linen $5. Laundry $2.50. Key deposit $10. Reception 8am-10pm. Bunks $16; cabins for 2 $35, extra person $12; tent sites $9, powered sites $10.) You certainly won't feel claustrophobic at the **Taranaki Accommodation Lodge**, 7 Romeo St. Renovated from a nurse's home, this lodge has the choice of 42 rooms (the others belong to permanent residents) and free use of the outdoor tennis courts. (☎/fax 765 5444. Communal kitchen, showers, and toilets. Linen $5. Singles $18; doubles $20. Cash only.)

⊠⊠ FOOD AND NIGHTLIFE. Broadway is brimming with cheap takeaways, but finding diverse fare is another matter. Those camping or graced with kitchens may want to shop for food at the **New World**, on the corner of Orlando and Regan St. (☎765 6422. Open daily 8am-8pm.) The little red-walled bistro, the **Backstage Cafe**, 234 Broadway St., is the exception to Stratford's general culinary mediocrity. Enter stage left (or, if heading north, stage right) for food that is right on cue. The inexpensive lunch options definitely merit applause. (☎765 7003. Open Tu-F 10am-late, Sa 10am-2pm and 6pm-late, Su 10am-2pm.) The **Axeman's Inn**, 305 Broadway St., pays tribute to the prolific logging industry in an appropriately rugged setting. Wash down standard pub food ($8-20) with a $3 pint of ale. (☎765 5707. Open daily 11am-3am. Live music Th.) When the weekend rolls around, **Hotshotz**, 295 Broadway St., is the place to be. The only (and therefore best) dance club in Stratford features a DJ and plenty of room to groove. (☎765 6525. Open F-Sa 5pm-3am.)

⊠⊠ SIGHTS AND ACTIVITIES. For a true taste of Taranaki, try **O'Neill's Brewing Company**, 4281 Mountain Rd. (☎764 8335), off SH3 toward Eltham. Brian and Helen O'Neill have converted an old service station into a microbrewery and cafe/bar that produces Ngaere Draught and Black Peat Lager. All beers are batch-brewed with natural ingredients; regulars swear the lack of preservatives, sugar, and chemicals results in hangover-free drinking. Cheers! (Open M-Sa 2-6pm. Reservations essential; call ahead for a free tour.) With **Mt. Egmont** looming in the background, it's little wonder that skiing is a major activity in the area—when there's snow. The **Manganui Ski Field** is the only field on the mountain and is open June through October. One T-bar and three rope tows offer access to several expert runs and two natural half-pipes for snowboarders. (Ski conditions ☎765 7669. Lift ticket $30, students $20, children $15, over 60 free; half-day rates available.) For rentals call the **Mountain House Motor Lodge**. (☎765 6100. Skis, boots, and poles around $30 per day.) Outdoor excitement continues with **Off the Beaten Track Adventures**. Adventurers Paddy and Margaret Gooch will help you put together a choose-your-own-adventure day or two. Activities include hunting, canoeing, bushwalking, camping, 4WD trips, and horsetrekking. (☎/fax 762 7885. $25 per hr.; half-day $50; full-day $85, lunch provided; 2-day trip $170, includes campout, tent, and meals.) For a brief jaunt through Stratford's past, head to the **Taranaki Pioneer Village**, just outside town on SH3. The 50 fully-restored turn-of-the-century buildings help celebrate Taranaki's pioneer history. (☎765 5399. Open daily 10am-4pm. $7, children $3.)

THE AXEMAN COMETH One of the most successful sportsmen in New Zealand history, axeman Ned Shrewry competed in a time when a wood chopper could become a national hero. Born in Stratford in 1889, Ned's career as a wood chopper lasted from 1910 to 1934, truly the glory days of the sport. He was the dominant chopper of the era, capturing three world titles and countless New Zealand and Australian crowns. His career was interrupted by World War I, where he was twice injured and won the Military Medal—in his opinion "because I kept the cookhouse supplied with kindling wood." In reality, the medal was granted for surviving a shell explosion that buried him alive, but simultaneously knocked his helmet off his head and over his face, keeping the dirt out and creating an air pocket that kept him alive until he could be saved. Shrewry died in 1962, but received immortality in 1996 when he was voted into the New Zealand Sports Hall of Fame.

TARANAKI

HAWERA ☎ 06

Hawera (pop. 8,500), which means "the burned place" in Maori, derives its name from a fire that consumed a nearby *pa* in Whareroa. Since its founding, the town has lived up to its name admirably, racking up four major fires since 1884; so many that steamed residents finally demanded the construction of a 150,000 gallon water tower as a preventative measure. The town bounced back from the devastation of the original fires. However, it is the heifer, not the phoenix, that has risen from the ashes, symbolizing the dairy industry that dominates the region. Today, Hawera's tourism industry continues to suckle at the teat of the omnipresent cow, offering farmstays and multimedia tours of the dairy center to travelers who soon find themselves adopting the early-to-bed, early-to-rise rural lifestyle.

⊏ TRANSPORTATION. The **bus station** is at the base of the water tower and is the point of departure for **InterCity** which leaves daily for **New Plymouth** (1hr., 3-4 per day, $18) and **Wanganui** (1hr.; M-F 4-5 per day, Sa-Su 3-4 per day; $20), with continuing service to **Palmerston North** (3hr., $30) or **Wellington** (5½hr., $50). **Dalroy Express** (☎ 755 0009, or 0508 46 56 22) heads to **Auckland** once per day (6½ hr., $78), with stops including **New Plymouth** (1hr., $13), **Otorohanga** (3½ hr., $45), and **Hamilton** (5hr., $55). The **White Star** (☎ 758 3338) bus service also stops in town en route between **New Plymouth** ($15) and **Wellington** ($35). **Southern Cabs** (24hr. ☎ 278 8888) has a stand on Victoria St. near High St, and **Hawera Taxis** (☎ 0800 278 7171) run **24hr.** Rent a used bicycle for $15 per day from **Seaver Cycles,** 18 Regent St. (☎ 278 6046. Open M-F 8am-5pm). Although *Let's Go* does not recommend it, **hitchhikers** often find a ride on High St. between Argyle and Albion St. or at the junction of SH3 and SH45 (South Rd. and Waihi Rd.). Most cars head to New Plymouth or Wanganui via SH3; hitchhiking to the coastal beach communities of western Taranaki along SH45 can be more difficult.

▪◪ ORIENTATION AND PRACTICAL INFORMATION. The main drag through town is **High St.** At the west end of High St., **Waihi Rd.** (SH3) is the primary northern route. **South Rd.** becomes the coastal route to New Plymouth (SH45) in one direction and to Wanganui (SH3) in the other. The **South Taranaki Visitor Information Centre,** 55 High St., is located at the base of the **water tower,** and sells DOC hut tickets. (☎ 278 8599; fax 278 6599. Open Nov.-Feb. M-F 8:30am-5pm, Sa-Su 10am-3pm; Mar.-Oct. M-F 8:30am-5pm, closed on weekends except during extended holiday weekends.) Other services include: **ATMs** along High St.; currency exchange at **BNZ** on Princes St. (open M-F 9am-4:30pm); **hospital** (☎ 278 7109) on Hunter St.; **police** (☎ 278 0260) on Princes St.; **post office,** 74 Princes St. (☎ 278 8680; open M-F 8:30am-5pm); and **internet access** at **Hawera Library,** 46 High St. ($1 per ¼hr.; open M, Tu, Th 9am-5:30pm, W 9:30am-5:30pm, F 9am-6pm, Sa 9am-noon) or **Bitworks,** 155 High St. (☎ 278 4927; $8 per hr.; open M-F 8:30am-5pm).

ACCOMMODATIONS AND CAMPING. Wheatly Downs Farmstay, 7km out of town on Ararata Rd., offers free pick-up with advance notice. Fifth-generation farmer Gary Ogle offers backpackers hands-on experience riding horses, herding cattle, and shearing sheep. Enjoy a perfect view of Mt. Taranaki (Egmont) from the living room couch or fly around the mountain in a plane that picks you up right in front of the farmhouse. It's $50 for a 40min. flight; ask Gary to arrange it. (☎278 6523; fax 278 6541; wheatlydowns@taranaki-bakpak.co.nz. Free laundry. Book in advance. Dorms $16; singles $25; doubles $36. Cash only.) For those travelers stuck in town, or for those not quite ready for an udder encounter, **King Edward Park Motor Camp**, 70 Waihi Rd., is located near the town center. Navigate your way through this land of communal showers, kitchens, and toilets. (☎/fax 278 8544; nikida@xtra.co.nz. Cabins to fit 4-5 and onsite caravans $28 for two people, extra person $10; tent sites $8, powered sites $9.)

FOOD. While the number of restaurants may be inversely proportional to the number of cows, those few in Hawera are quite good. Before perusing the made-to-order options, fill your basic grocery needs at **New World**, 307 High St. (☎278 8528; open daily 8am-8pm), or at **Price Chopper**, which, at the corner of Nelson and Victoria, is closer to town (☎278 0026; open daily 7am-10pm). If you would rather eat off the floor than cook your own food, then **Morrieson's Cafe and Bar**, 60 Victoria St. is the place for you. In fact, the tables of this establishment are actually former floorboards from the home of the late, local novelist Ronald Hugh Morrieson (1922-68). While perhaps not a literary masterpiece, the menu features a medley of delectable mains ($12-20) and traditional brews. (☎278 5647. Pints $5. Open M-Sa 11am-1am, Su 11am-10:30pm.) Though the name may conjure images of a smoky dive, **Rough Habits Sports Bar and Cafe**, 79-81 Regent St., actually has a well-vacuumed look. The bar and cafe share one large room with TV monitors ablaze. Share one of the sizeable starters among friends ($6-14) or dine solo on meaty mains ($17-20). Whichever option you prefer, wash it down with a $3.30 handle. (☎278 7333. Open M-Sa 11am-late, Su 11am-11pm, kitchen closes around 9:30pm.) For good, clean, G-rated fun, head to **Barry's Family Restaurant**, on Princes St., right next to the post office and near the corner of High St. The large and inexpensive portions should feed you, your loved ones, and then some. (☎278 4998. Mains $17-25. Open daily 11am-late.) For a quick bite, **Kreative Kebabs**, at 135 High St., offers above-average gourmet kebabs and burgers (☎278 5552. Open M 11am-2:30pm, Tu-F 11am-2:30pm and 4:30-8pm, Sa-Su 4:30-8pm).

SIGHTS AND ACTIVITIES. Climb the 215 steps of the **water tower** for a scenic view of the countryside or use it as a navigational beacon at night, when it is lit up with red neon. (Open Nov.-Feb. daily 8:30am-5pm; Mar.-Oct. M-F 8:30am-5pm, Sa-Su 10am-3pm. $2.) Nigel Ogle's **Tawhiti Museum**, near the corner of Ohangi Rd. and Tawhiti Rd., has been acclaimed as the best private museum in New Zealand, and it's easy to see why. With a subtle sense of humor (outhouse not withstanding) and the skill to craft stunningly realistic fiberglass figures, the former art teacher brings the regional history to life in a series of miniature and life-size dioramas. (☎/fax 278 6837. Open in summer Sa-M 10am-4pm and daily in Jan.; in winter open Su only. Adults $6.50.) Afterwards, stop in at adjoining **Mr. Badger's Cafe**, where visitors can dine among *Wind in the Willows* dioramas, and dinner guests are treated to fireside readings of the book. For a dose of regional history in person, travel a few kilometers out of town (up Turuturu Rd.) to view **Turuturu Mokai**, the remains of a 400-year old Maori fortress. Today only the large man-made mounds and a carved post remain, but this was once the setting of a bloody battle. The name comes from the Maori words for "the stakes" (Turuturu) and "dried heads" (Mokai). Fans of the King will rejoice at Kevin D. Wasley's garage-turned-**Elvis Presley Memorial Record Room**, 51 Argyle St. Although you won't see the King himself, you can feast your eyes on a collection of rare recordings, assorted memorabilia, and even Wasley's own Elvis-esque haircut. (☎278 7624; mobile 025 982 942. See

God Save the King above. Visits by appointment. Donation requested.) The staple of dairy county, **Dairyland**, at the corner of SH3 and Whareroa Rd. and guarded by the giant fiberglass cow, offers a million-and-one ways to get your calcium fix. Functioning as the visitors center for **Kiwi Cooperative Dairies,** the largest milk processing plant in the world, Dairyland features a kid-friendly exhibit and a revolving cafe. Moo-ve on in to learn about the multiple uses of milk, watch live footage from the dairy, and experience the vibrating pleasure of a **simulated milk tanker** with your animatronic driver Darryl. (☎ 278 4537. Exhibit and cafe open daily 9am-5pm; cafe also open for dinner W-Su 6pm-late. $3.) If adrenaline-inducing action is what you're after, try **Dam Dropping.** Darren Parata guides you as you plunge head-first on a boogie board over an 8m dam, followed by 3hr. of "white water sledding." (☎ mobile 021 461 110. $80 per person; groups from 2 to 10.)

WANGANUI ☎ 06

From December to March the streets of Wanganui are adorned with hanging baskets, but the downtown's picturesque character persists year round. Home to an art school, an opera house, and a regional museum, a bohemian laid-back mentality merges with historic appreciation as visitors soak in the most funky and cosmopolitan spirit in Taranaki. Slight tensions between Maori and European cultures may be best reflected in the grassroots movement among locals to restore the "h" to the town's name, which was "accidentally" Anglicized in the early 20th century. Regardless, Wanganui remains a pleasant stop for a stroll down the main street or tea by the river.

▌ TRANSPORTATION

Buses: InterCity stops at the **Wanganui Travel Centre,** 156 Ridgway St. (☎ 345 4433). Open M-F 8:15am-5:15pm. Buses leave for: **Auckland** (8hr., 1-3 per day, $70) via **Hamilton** (6hr., $51); **New Plymouth** (2½hr., 3-5 per day, $31); **Palmerston North** (1½hr.; M-F 3-4 per day); **Wellington** (4hr., 2-3 per day, $36).

Public Transportation: Tranzit CityLink (☎ 345 5566, www.horizons.govt.nz) handles all buses transport to **Castlecliff Beach,** and to the suburbs. All buses depart from Maria Pl. between Victoria Ave. and Hill St. and run until early evening ($2).

Taxis: River City Cabs (☎ 345 3333) and **Wanganui Taxis** (☎ 0800 500 000).

Car Rental: Rent-A-Dent, 26 Churton St. (☎ 345 1505). $40 per day plus $0.20 per km. Open M-F 7:30am-5pm, Sa 8am-5pm. **Affordable Rentals** (☎ 343 9288), corner of Anzac Parade and Jones St., from $45 per day. Open daily 6am-10pm.

Hitchhiking: Although *Let's Go* does not recommend it, many thumbers head to the outskirts of town where traffic flows at speeds less than 70kph. People going toward Taranaki do so by way of Great North Rd., toward Ruapehu by way of Anzac Parade, and toward Wellington by way of Main South Rd. Be sure to stay clear of Cobham Bridge, which is not accessible for pedestrians or cyclists.

▌▌ ORIENTATION AND PRACTICAL INFORMATION

Wanganui is located at the junction of SH3 and SH4; the latter is called **Anzac Parade** within the city limits and runs alongside the **Whanganui River** (Taupo Quay and Somme Parade follow a similar course). They meet at **Victoria Ave.,** which runs perpendicular to the river and is the main street in town.

Visitors Center: Wanganui Visitor Information Centre (☎ 349 0508; fax 349 0509), near the corner of Guyton and St. Hill St. next to the District Council. Open M-F 8:30am-5pm, Sa-Su 10am-3pm. Extended hours in summer.

DOC: (☎ 345 2402; fax 345 8712) at the corner of St. Hill St. and Ingestre St. Heaps of information on Whanganui National Park and more. Open M-F 8am-5pm.

Currency Exchange: Money ebbs and flows across Victoria Ave. at **BNZ, ANZ, Westpac Trust,** and **National Bank** (all with **ATMs**). Open M-F 9am-4:30pm.

Police: 10 Bell St. (☎ 349 0600).

Medical Services: Esquilant Unichem Pharmacy, 145 Victoria Ave. (☎345 7529), Open M-F 8:30am-5pm, Sa 9am-2pm, Su 10am-2pm. **Wanganui City Doctors,** 163 Wicksteed St. (☎348 8333). The **Wanganui Hospital** (☎348 1234) is on Heads Rd.

Post Office: 226 Victoria Ave. (☎345 4103). Open M-F 8:30am-5pm.

Internet Access: Available at the **library,** Queens Park (☎345 8195; open M-F 9am-8pm, Sa 9am-4:30pm) and the **visitors center** (see above) for $6 per hr.

🏠🏕 ACCOMMODATIONS AND CAMPING

Those staying in Wanganui may be charmed by riverside life; most of the hostels and backpackers are rooted on the riverbanks beside English oak trees.

▨ **The Tamara Backpackers Hostel,** 24 Somme Parade (☎347 6300; fax 345 8488; tamaralodge@paradise.net.nz). 5min. walk from center of town or call for free pick-up. Super-friendly hostel with heated rooms, river views, and lounges. Offers a guitar, piano, pool table, and dartboard. Internet. Linen $1. Laundry $4. Key deposit $10. Reception 8am-9pm. Dorms $16; singles $25; twins and doubles $36, with bath $23 per person.

Riverside Inn (YHA Associate), 2 Plymouth St. (☎/fax 347 2529), 5min. from the center of town. The B&B vibes of this century-old pink and mauve Victorian house spill over into the backpackers units in the rear. Laundry $5. Dorms (coed and women's) $16; doubles $36; B&B singles $50; B&B doubles $80; tent sites $10.

Aramoho Top 10 Holiday Park, 460 Somme Parade (☎0800 272 664; fax 343 8402; aramoho.holidaypark@xtra.co.nz). Bus stops at the gate. Sidle up to the river in this tranquil setting. Showers, kitchen, toilets. Spa $5 per 30min. Kayaks $5 per day. Cabins $25-30; tourist flats $50-55; motel units $65-70; powered sites $10-18;.

🍽 FOOD

Wanganui sticks with the basics and does them well. Eateries cluster around **Victoria Ave.** and its side streets from the river to **Guyton St.** Whip up your own dish after a stop at **Countdown,** at Taupo Quay and St. Hill St. (☎345 8720. Open daily 8am-9pm.) At the other end of Victoria Ave., **Woolworths** is open 24hr. (☎347 9840).

Amadeus Riverbank Cafe, 69 Taupo Quay (☎345 1538). Delicious burgers and sandwiches ($6.50-12.50), sweets from the Calorie Gallery ($2-5.50), and occasional live music make hordes of diners happy. Open winter M-W 8:30am-4pm, Th-F 8:30am-late, Sa 10am-late, Su 10am-4pm; extended hours in summer.

Royal Bengal Restaurant, 7 Victoria Ave. (☎348 7041). Across the street from the city cinema, the bright blue interior lends a cheerful atmosphere to the Indian cuisine. Curry dishes are $12-13, but $10 M-Tu or anytime with copy of *Let's Go.* Open daily 5:30pm-10:30; lunch W-Sa 11am-2pm.

Caffeine Fixx, 71 Liverpool St. (☎345 7557). Get a light meal and coffee buzz while surfing the web ($5 per hr.) at this trendy, laid-back joint. Suits mix with students amid bright colors and original art. Open M-F 8:30am-8pm, Sa-Su 9:30am-4:30pm.

🎵 NIGHTLIFE

While rather empty during the week, pubs are all the rage on the weekends.

The Fuel Shed (☎345 7278) corner of Victoria Ave. and Taupo Quay. The newest kid on the block is also the hottest. Burn the night away to the groove-mix of F-Sa DJs. Fill your tank with gourmet pizza ($13.95). Open M-Th 3:30pm-late, F-Su 11am-late.

The Red Lion Inn, 45 Anzac Parade (☎ 345 3831). Across the river from the main town, two separate rooms house different scenes. On the right, locals bet on horse races while "skulling" handles of the namesake brew ($3.70). The more clean-cut crowd in "Burton's Cafe" gaze at the river over a glass of wine ($4-6). Open daily 11am-3am.

The Slippery Saddle, 146 Victoria Ave (☎ 348 7566). On weeknights there may be more action in the rodeo murals than on the dance floor, but this cowboy-themed restaurant and bar sees life once the weekend moseys around. Have a saddle burger ($6.50) at a giant cactus table. DJ F-Sa. Open Th-Sa 11am-3am, Su-W 11am-10pm.

◎ 🔣 SIGHTS AND ACTIVITIES

Before heading out into the wilderness, get your bearings and survey the land from the top of the **Durie Hill Lookout Tower.** The journey begins from Anzac Parade at the base of Victoria Ave. where a long tunnel takes you 205m into the hill. Then an elevator whisks you 66m up *through* the hill, depositing you at the top. (Elevator runs M-F 7:30am-6pm, Sa 10am-6pm, Su 11am-5pm. One-way $1.) But why stop there? Climb the nearby 33.5m **Durie Hill Memorial Tower** for the ultimate view. If the murky waters of the Whanganui beckon, the **PS Waimarie** is at your service. Built in 1899, the restored paddle steamer (the last in New Zealand) chugs from the Whanganui Riverboat Centre 16km up the river. (☎ 347 1863. Return 2hr. $25, seniors $20.) The narrow and winding 79km **Whanganui River Road,** which begins 14 km north of the city, took 30 years to build and winds through scenic vistas, historic locales, and past several local *marae*. Drive it yourself, or catch a ride with the rural mail service. (Arranged through **Rivercity Tours.** ☎ 344 2554. $25, bring lunch.)

Get your fill of culture in **Queens Park,** just a block away from Victoria Ave. toward the river. Overlooking the green hills is the stunning white-domed exterior of **Sarjeant Gallery,** home to a collection of contemporary local art, as well as visiting shows. (☎ 349 0506. Open M-F 10:30am-4:30pm, Sa-Su 1-4:30pm. Free.) Just steps away, modernity gives way to Maori history at the **Whanganui Regional Museum.** Its Te Atihau forum (a place for all peoples to "anchor their canoes"), houses the largest surviving *waka taua* (war canoe) in the Wanganui area. (☎ 345 7443. Open M-Sa 10am-4:30pm, Su 1-4:30pm. $2.)

Sports enthusiasts, should circle **Cooks Gardens,** on Maria Pl., home to a rugby pitch, New Zealand's wooden cycling velodrome, and a running track that was the site of Peter Snell's world-record mile (see p. 68). For wet action, head to one of the local beaches for some killer waves. **Castlecliff Beach,** where the river meets the sea, is notable for black sand and good surf. To get there, take Quay St. W to Heads Rd. and continue another 9km. Alternatively, head for Maria Pl. in town and catch the #3 or #4 taxi bus. Farther up the coast, **Kai Iwi Beach** also has good swells and attracts locals who wish to avoid the crowds, but is less accessible by public transport. The uninitiated may want to hop into the **The Sportz Shed,** 63A Victoria Ave., for tips from local surfing mavens who can teach you the art of catching a wave. (☎ 347 6500. Open M-F 9am-5:30pm, Sa 9:30am-1:30pm.) Mountain bikers are also drawn to the region for the 3km of forested single tracks built by the **Wanganui Mountain Biking Club.** For maps or bikes, call Marray Ackeroyd ☎ 345-8086.

WHANGANUI NATIONAL PARK ☎ 06/07

According to legend, the great mountains Tongariro and Taranaki fought over a lovely summit named Pihanga. Defeated, Taranaki gouged a furrow in the earth on his way westward, a cleft that his wise rival filled with life-bestowing water. As a result, lush greenery surrounds the Whanganui (fang-gah-NEW-ee) River as it flows from the slopes of Tongariro down to the Tasman Sea—the longest navigable course (234km) in New Zealand. Maori *pa* (fortified villages) once stood in numbers atop these high ponga-lined bluffs, but that was before European missionaries and steamboats of the 19th century changed the river life. In recent year however, local Maori families have reestablished *marae* along the river, bringing vital community spirit and hospitality to those who journey downstream.

AT A GLANCE

AREA: 74,231 hectares.

CLIMATE: Unpredictable weather and mild summers.

FEATURES: Hills and valleys through lowland forests.

HIGHLIGHTS: Whanganui River, the longest navigable river in New Zealand.

GATEWAYS: Whanganui and Taumarunui.

CAMPING: Tents permitted. Back country huts available.

FEES & RESERVATIONS: Hut passes $4 each, more in summer.

TRANSPORTATION

Few roads penetrate the park's boundaries. The **River Road** (see p. 211) dips into the southern limits, while a road from Owhango heads to **Whakahoro Hut** (see p. 363). People who have **hitched,** report that flexibility is a necessity; however, *Let's Go* does not recommend hitchhiking. Most people planning a Whanganui excursion stay in **Taumarunui** (see p. 212), **National Park Village** (see p. 192), or **Ohakune** (see p. 193) and arrange transport with the operators who rent equipment for the River Journey (see **Gear** p. 362).

ORIENTATION AND PRACTICAL INFORMATION

WHEN TO GO The park is better enjoyed in the summer since its greatest attraction is the Wanganui River. Be sure to bring warm clothing for unpredictable weather and waterproof gear.

The Whanganui National Park boundaries encompass various small pockets and larger blocks west of SH4. Between the towns of Taumarunui in the north and Wanganui in the south, the biggest swaths of bush enclose the middle reaches of the Whanganui River. Despite its name, the city of **Wanganui** is not the best base for exploring the Whanganui River, though it does contain the park's main **DOC visitors center** (☎06 345 2402. Open M-F 8am-5pm). There are also sporadically open **DOC field centers** in Taumarunui (☎07 895 8201) and Pipiriki (☎06 385 4631), where you'll find **supermarkets** and **ATMs.** Most gear outfitters (see **Gear** p. 362) can provide secure **parking,** however there are no places to stay directly outside the park. The **telephone codes** for the region in Taumarunui, National Park Village, and points in between is 07; Ohakune and points farther south use 06.

TREKKING

The **Whanganui River Journey** (3-5 days by canoe, 145km) is the only Great Walk that requires a paddle; canoeists and kayakers battle small rapids beneath the sheer banks and brilliant greenery of the Whanganui River. The chance to stay at two Maori *marae* can make the trip a breathtaking cultural experience as well (see p. 362). The park holds some more isolated, less famous tracks (also less crowded) for those who'd rather walk than paddle. The **Mangapurua** and **Kaiwhakauka Tracks** combine to form a 40km (3-4 day) trip. Mangapurua takes off from **Mangapurua Landing** (see p. 362) on the river, then heads over the **Bridge to Nowhere,** through the Mangapurua Valley, and past vast sections of former farmland. The track climbs to the **Mangapurua Trig,** which offers panoramic views of Mt. Tongariro, Mt. Taranaki, and the junction with the Kaiwhakauka Track. Then it's down through farms and bush to the Kaiwhakauka Valley and the **Whakahoro Hut** ($10; see p. 363). This is the only hut along the whole track, though flat campsites are plentiful.

The park's other major trail is the **Matemateaonga Track,** which tempts die-hard hikers with 42km (3-4 days) of serpentine trail following an old Maori route into the

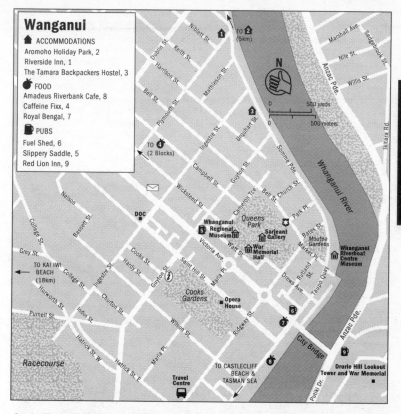

Wanganui

🏠 ACCOMMODATIONS
Aromoho Holiday Park, 2
Riverside Inn, 1
The Tamara Backpackers Hostel, 3

🍎 FOOD
Amadeus Riverbank Cafe, 8
Caffeine Fixx, 4
Royal Bengal, 7

🍺 PUBS
Fuel Shed, 6
Slippery Saddle, 5
Red Lion Inn, 9

WANGANUI

bush. The path leads from the **Kohi Saddle** on Upper Mangaehu Rd. east of **Stratford** (see p. 203) across to **Tieke Marae** (see p. 363) on the Whanganui River. There are three huts ($10 each) on the track, which is flatter than the Mangapurua/Kaiwhakauka. **Wades Landing Outdoors** does jetboat river pick-ups and drop-offs for trampers. (☎ 07 895 5995; mobile 025 797 238. $95.) A significantly shorter option, the **Atene Skyline Track** (6½hr.) leads to views of Mt. Ruapehu, Mt. Taranaki, and the Tasman Sea, almost forming a complete loop, and makes a good daytrip from Wanganui. The trailhead waits 36km north of Wanganui on **River Road** (see p. 211).

THE RIVER ROAD   ☎06

After a 30-year construction fraught with floods and mudslides, 1934 saw the opening of the aptly named **River Road.** Dancing a *pas de deux* with the bushy banks of the Whanganui River, the road allows the only automobile access to the settlements upstream from Wanganui. In fact, it was the completion of the road that signaled the end of the paddlewheel boat as a viable transport method by reducing a 10-hour boat ride between Wanganui and Pipiriki to a 1½-hour drive. The River Road parallels SH4, some 15km to the east, connecting Wanganui and **Pipiriki.** From Pipiriki, the road continues out of Whanganui National Park to meet up at **Raetihi** (27km), less than 15km from the ski town of **Ohakune** (see p. 193). The northern extremes of the park can be reached from **Whakahoro** via roads from **Owhango** (south of Taumarunui, p. 212) or **Raurimu** (just north of the town of National Park, p. 192), both on SH4. If you don't have your own car, riding along with the **mail run** is a great way to get into the heart of the river valley and meet locals at the same time. (Mobile 025 443 421.

Pick-up 7:15am from Wanganui with advance reservation; otherwise, show up early behind the post office, 60 Ridgway St.) The run returns to Wanganui around 2 or 3pm, or you can ask to be dropped off anywhere along the way and be picked up on a different day ($25).

Travelers heading up the road from Wanganui soon see the **Oyster Cliffs,** which take a large white bite out of the river—a reminder of a time when oceans enveloped this valley. A bit farther up, there's riverside camping at the **Otumarie Campsite.** Those who continue upstream arrive at one of the most wonderful homestays in New Zealand, ▧**The Flying Fox,** 44km up the River Rd. from Wanganui. Truly off the beaten track, The Flying Fox is accessible only by boating up the river or via an aerial cableway—a "flying fox" in Kiwispeak—suspended 20m above the river. En route travelers are also welcome to sip cool drinks in the shade of the English oaks. Stay the night in one of the two self-contained cottages—the brewhouse or James K. (named after the poet James K. Baxter and filled with his books and memorabilia). Self-proclaimed hippie proprietors Annette and John may feel personally insulted if you don't stop in for a homemade beer made entirely from forest ingredients. (☎/fax 342 8160; theflyingfox@paradise.net.nz. Free mountain bikes. Canoes $35 per day. Free laundry. Cabins for 2 $70; single rates negotiable; tent sites $8. Advance booking absolutely required.)

A trio of Maori villages stand farther upstream. **Koriniti** (Corinth) features the Opeiriki *pa* (never once taken in battle), a lovely *marae*, and the first Anglican church on the river (est. 1840). **Ranana** (London) is one of the bigger villages on the river, and retains traces of its past as a traditional center of agriculture. **Hiruharama** (Jerusalem) was home to a French Marist Mission and guards the grave of the poet James K. Baxter. Just before Hiruharama is **Moutoa Island** from which Maori followers of Hauhauism (a xenophobic religious sect) launched ritualized battles against the tribes of the lower river. Continuing upstream, find the cascading beauty of **Omorehu Waterfall.** A bookend of a town, **Pipiriki** is at the end of the River Rd. and is also the beginning for many jetboat rides and walking tracks. One especially lovely path, the **Pukehinau Walk** loops 1km to the Pukehinau crest, once a Hauhau outpost with strategic (and gorgeous) views of the river valley. **Wairua Hikoi Tours** is a unique tour with a spiritual emphasis on Maori culture that offers shorter one-day canoe trips to The Flying Fox. (☎345 3485. $45 unguided, $75 per person for a guided trip, food, and vehicle transfer.) You must find your own way to Hiruharama, though, perhaps by the mail run (see above).

TAUMARUNUI   ☎07

Although undeniably a small town (pop. 7668) with few offerings along its commercial strip, Taumarunui offers access to much of the surrounding region, thus living up to its reputation as the "Heart of the King Country." Situated at the confluence of the Ongarue and Whanganui Rivers, it is the logical starting point for expeditions down the Whanganui. Taumarunui also lies at the junction of SH4 and SH43 (the **Taumarunui-Stratford Heritage Trail**), serving as a crossroads for those traveling through the Taranaki and Ruapehu regions or to Whanganui and Tongariro National Parks. Regardless of your destination, this is a good place to resupply on the basics before hitting river, road, rail, or trail.

▮ **TRANSPORTATION. TranzScenic** heads to **Auckland** (4½hr., 3:11pm and 2:31am, $64) and **Wellington** (6½hr., 1:01pm and 1:08am, $72-84). **InterCity** also runs to **Auckland** (4¾hr., daily Su-F, $48) and **Wellington** (6hr., daily Su-F, $67). **Pioneer Jet Boat Tours Ltd.** (☎895 8528) buses to **Hamilton** (M-F 8am, $27) and leaves from the hospital or visitors center. Toward National Park, most **hitchhikers** (though *Let's Go* does not recommend it) try the area by the Hakiaha St. railyards, past the Main Trunk Cafe. Toward Te Kuiti, they park it on the Ongarue River Rd. (SH4). **Silver Cabs** (☎895 5444) will help you get around town.

⚡🏃 ORIENTATION AND PRACTICAL INFORMATION. Taumarunui sits along the **Main Trunk Railway** and **SH4** (called Hakiaha St. within the town limits), 43km north of the town of **National Park** (p. 192), 129km east of **Stratford** (p. 203), 82km south of **Te Kuiti,** and 65km west of **Turangi** (p. 188). The **Visitor Information Centre** is conveniently located in the railway station on Hakiaha St. (☎895 7494. Open M-F 9am-4:30pm, Sa-Su 10am-4pm.) Take a nature walk through Cherry Grove to get to the **DOC Field Centre.** (☎895 8201; after-hours mobile 025 946 650. Open M-F 8am-5pm.) Other services include: **banks** with **ATMs** on Hakiaha St. (open M-F 9am-4:30pm); the **hospital** (☎896 0020) on Kururau Rd.; **police** (☎895 8119), on Hakiaha St.; **internet access** at the public **library** in the center of town (☎895 7538; $3 per ¼hr., $5 per ½hr.; open M-F 10am-5pm, Sa 9am-noon); and a **post office** at 47-49 Miriama St. (☎895 8149; open M-F 9am-5pm).

🏠 ACCOMMODATIONS. Those planning a trip downriver can take advantage of off-street parking and close proximity to supply shops at **Taumarunui Family Inn,** 4 Marae St. (☎895 3478; fax 895 6072. In-house restaurant. Dorms $16; singles $20; doubles $48.) Further from town (4km south), but with fishing, swimming, and kayaking (kayaks $5 per ½hr.), is **Taumarunui Holiday Park,** on the Whanganui River, with standard facilities and free pick-up. (☎895 9345; fax 895 6345; taumarunui-holiday-park@xtra.co.nz. Tent sites $8 for 2, powered sites $9 for 2; cabins for 2 $29; self-contained tourist flat $45, plus $12 per person.)

🍴 FOOD. Though quality dining establishments are scarce in Taumarunui, the **Rivers II Cafe,** 43 Hakiaha St., stands out. Patrons can enjoy meals in a spacious, bright interior or at outside tables. The French toast with banana ($9) deserves special praise. (☎895 5822. Open daily 8am-5pm, F until 10:30pm.) **Ruddie's Place,** 93 Hakiaha St., is a welcome new addition to the culinary scene. A restaurant, bar, and cafe in one; each has a different menu and different hours. (☎/fax 896 7442. Cafe open M-Sa 9am-5pm, Su 10am-2pm; restaurant open W-Su 6-9pm; bar open W-Th, Su 5-10pm, F-Sa 5pm-midnight.) For a quick bite before you catch a bus, or to cure a case of the late-night munchies, the **Main Trunk Cafe,** on Hakiaha St., is your best bet. Look for the dormant red railway cars sitting next to the tracks. Also provides takeaways. (☎895 6544. Open W-Su 10am-10pm.) On weekdays a pub-like atmosphere reigns at the **Taumarunui Family Inn;** wrap your hand around a $3 handle. (Open daily 11am-2am.) The most comprehensive supermarket is the **New World,** at the northern end of Hakiaha St. (☎896 0070. Open daily 8am-7pm.)

📷🎿 SIGHTS AND ACTIVITIES. Many visitors are drawn to Taumarunui by the serpentine **Raurimu Spiral.** A mighty feat of engineering, this 1908 section of railway track loops and twists and at one point doubles back on itself as it climbs onto the central plateau. The best way to experience the stomach-churning glory of the spiral is to take a **scenic train ride,** which departs Taumarunui daily at 1pm, returning at 3pm ($28). Or just gaze upon its loopiness from the lookout 37km south on SH4 at Raurimu. The **Visitor Information Centre** also has a 3-dimensional model of the spiral on display. Drivers can also traverse the **Taumarunui-Stratford Heritage Trail,** a 150km stretch of SH43 established in 1990 to provide travelers with an introduction to regional history. Teal and yellow signs along the trail mark lookout points and historic sites. The **Manu Ariki Marae,** Okahukura Back Rd., 12km north of Taumarunui on SH4 offers tours of the *marae* ($10) and a miniature train ride ($5) on a 5km track. (☎896 6971. Open M-Sa 9am-5pm, Su 9am-noon. Call ahead.) Multi-day canoeing trips on the scenic Whanganui River are also a popular activity, and a few companies offer canoe rentals. **Blazing Paddles** (☎/fax 895 8074) offers 1-5 day canoe rentals for $55-134 and kayaks for $55-180 per person.

WELLINGTON
AND AROUND

WELLINGTON ☎ 04

Though it lies directly on a major earthquake fault and is one of the windiest cities on earth, the capital city of Wellington is a better place for catching your breath than losing it. Looking out on a gorgeous harbor near the North Island's southern tip, New Zealand's second-largest city abounds with cultural celebrations ranging from an impressive series of festivals to some of New Zealand's best theater and dance. The enormous $317 million Museum of New Zealand Te Papa Tongarewa, the gem in Wellington's cultural crown, is definitely worth a visit. When the sun sets over the city, scores of cafes, bars, and nightclubs keep the party going. Before passing through, take a refreshing dip into the cosmopolitan Kiwi capital.

> ### ⬛ WELLINGTON AND AROUND HIGHLIGHTS
>
> **EAT** a snack in Wellington, where the highest density of **cafes** in the Southern Hemisphere turn it up at night (see p. 220).
>
> **AND BE MERRY** at the Kiwi cultural mecca of **Te Papa Museum**, Wellington's pride and joy (see p. 223).
>
> **FOR TOMORROW WE DIE** although the good folk at **Kapiti Island** do their best to protect New Zealand's endangered species from suffering the same fate (see p. 227).

✈ INTERCITY TRANSPORTATION

Flights: The **Wellington International Airport** (☎385 5123) stretches across the narrowest portion of the Miramar Peninsula in the city's southeastern suburbs. The only international flights here are those from **Sydney, Brisbane, Melbourne, Fiji,** and **Western Samoa** on Qantas or **Air New Zealand (ANZ). ANZ** has an office at the corner of Lambton Quay and Grey St. and hits most domestic destinations (☎474 8950, 0800 737 000). **Freedom Air** (☎0800 600 500), a subsidiary of ANZ, is a "value-based" airline which flies to **Auckland** and **Christchurch;** its cheapest domestic fares are only available online. Frequent flights to **Auckland** start from $150 return (1hr., 1-2 per hr.); flights to **Christchurch** are slightly cheaper (¾hr., around 1 per hr., return from $139). With an **International Student Identification Card** (ISIC) or advance booking, fares drop dramatically. **Soundsair** (☎388 2594, 0800 505 005) flies to **Picton** (25min.; 6-8 per day; $68, backpackers $61, return $125). **Cityline** (☎569 2933) runs service every 30min. between the airport and Lower Hutt ($4.50). **Super Shuttle** (☎387 8787) runs one-way from the railway station to the **airport** (every hr. from 9am-4pm, every ½hr. from 7:30-9am and 4-6pm; $5) and does pre-booked door-to-door service ($10).

Trains: The **Railway Station,** on Bunny St. at Waterloo/Customhouse Quay, houses the train and bus depots. **TranzScenic** (☎0800 802 802) provides daily service to: **Auckland** (11hr.; day train 8:45am, overnight train 7:50pm; from $90) via **Palmerston North** (2hr., from $21) and **Hamilton** (9hr., from $74); and **Napier** (5½hr., 8am, from $53) via **Palmerston North** (2hr., from $23). A taxi between the Railway Station and downtown costs about $9. **TranzMetro** (☎498 3000, ext. 44933), a regional commuter line, leaves from the Railway Station. There are four regular lines with many stops on the way including **Paraparaumu** (1hr., $7.50). Limited service to **Palmerston North** is offered by **Capital Connection** (1½hr., M-F 5:17pm, $18).

Buses: Depart from the rail station. **InterCity/Newmans** (☎472 5111) goes daily to: **Auckland** (11hr., 3 per day, from $49) via **Hamilton** (9hr., from $39); **Napier** (5hr., from $30); **New Plymouth** (6hr., 3 per day, from $31) via **Wanganui** (4hr., from $18); **Palmerston North** (2hr., 1-6 per day, from $12); **Rotorua** (7½hr., 1-4 per day, from $39) via **Taupo** (6hr., from $34); **Tauranga** (8-8½hr., 4 per day, from $44).

Ferries: The Interislander ferry terminal is inconveniently located on **Aotea Quay,** north of town on SH1. There's a free shuttle from Platform 9 of the railway station 40min. before each scheduled departure, and back to the station upon ferry arrival. The **Interislander** (☎0800 802 802; fax 0800 101 525) runs daily to **Picton,** just across the Cook Strait on the South Island (3hr., 4-5 per day, from $24). Bookings are essential. Small car transport from $88.) Ask about 1-day and 3-night excursion fares. Also book a passage on the **Lynx,** to Picton, but it departs from Waterloo Quay in downtown Wellington (2¼hr., 2 per day, from $32).

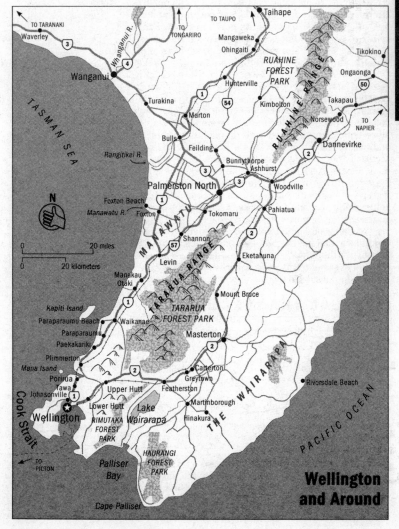

Wellington and Around

Hitchhiking: Although *Let's Go* does not recommend it, **hitchhikers** report that riding from Wellington is sometimes difficult, but a few pickup spots are worth a try. If Aotea Quay or the railway station aren't working, the old main road (where SH1 and SH2 branch a few kilometers north of the ferry station on Hutt Rd.) is known to be a successful spot. This branchpoint is a long walk, so some hitchers try their luck where the cars roll right off the boat at the ferry terminal. Also, some believe it's best to take the train to Paraparaumu (45km north on SH1) or Masterton (on SH2) and catch a ride there.

⚡ ORIENTATION

Wellington is remarkably compact, though its suburbs stretch around the harbor into nearby valleys and out onto the **Miramar Peninsula.** Its main downtown zone (most of the city's flat land) sits between the **Railway Station, Cambridge,** and **Kent Terraces** at the base of **Mt. Victoria,** and can be explored in the course of a day. **Lambton Quay,** home to hordes of suits, big shopping centers, and pricey restaurants, is the main artery. **Courtenay Place,** between Cambridge Terrace and **Taranaki St.,** hops with nightlife on the weekends, while **Cuba St.** between **Abel Smith** and **Manners St.** maintains a more bohemian air, filled with the haunts of students and twenty-somethings. At the Cuba and **Vivian St.** intersection is the "red light district," as the locals say. The **Civic Square** is both a conceptual and spatial bridge between downtown and the harbor, leading to the waterfront with its public parks, **Queens Wharf,** the colossal **Te Papa,** and **Oriental Bay's** flashy shops, cafes, and beach. In the northern part of the city is the historic area of **Thorndon,** home to old wooden houses, the **Railway Station,** and government buildings, such as the **Beehive** of Parliament. The little wooden houses, quiet residential streets, and backpackers of the Mt. Victoria area are in the southern edge of downtown.

⬛ LOCAL TRANSPORTATION

Wellington

⌂ ACCOMMODATIONS
Beethoven's, 35
Downtown Backpackers, 6
Top 10 Hutt Park Holiday Park (VIP), 1
Maple Lodge, 37
Moana Lodge, 3
Paekakariki Backpackers, 2
Rowena's (VIP), 36
Trekkers (NOMADS/VIP), 24
Wellington City YHA, 34
Wide World Backpackers, 14

🍎 FOOD
Big Thumb, 32
Daawat, 16
Kopi, 11
One Red Dog, 33
The Vegetarian Cafe, 25
Wellington Fish Supply, 4

🍺 BARS
Ballroom Billiards, 30
Bar Bodega, 22
The Malthouse, 9
Matterhorn, 18
Molly Malones, 28
Tupelo, 15
Zebos Bar/Southern Cross, 23

♪ NIGHTCLUBS
£, 26
Barney's/Bo Jangles, 17
The Grand, 31
Wellington Sports Cafe, 29

○ CAFÉS
Ed's Juice Bar, 10
Eva Dixon's Place, 27
Fidel's, 21
The Krazy Lounge, 19
Midnight Espresso, 20

● SERVICES
American Express, 7
Automobile Association, 8
Capital E, 12
DOC Office, 5
Michael Fowler Centre, 13

Public Transportation: The **Ridewell Service Centre** can answer any and all questions about fares, routes, and timetables for buses, trains, or the cable car. (☎801 7000, 0800 801 700. Open M-Sa 7:30am-8:30pm, Su 9am-3pm.) **Stagecoach** (☎387 8700) services the main city and most surrounding suburbs. Main line buses run daily from 6:30am-11pm, while some of the peripheral lines run approximately 7-9am and 3-6pm. Most backpackers use the line between the Railway Station and the Cambridge Terrace end of Courtenay Pl. ($1). Fares go up for longer distances. The #1 and 2 buses run between these points every 10-15min. during the day, and every 30-45min. during evenings and weekends. Most other buses cover this route: all but #7, 8, 10, 11—just check with the drivers. The **City Circular** (☎387 8700) runs every 10min. from all the major inner-city locations (single ride fare $1). Alternatively, there is a $5 Daytripper pass available that allows for unlimited downtown travel (from 9am M-F, from 6am weekends). **Cityline Hutt Valley** (☎569 2933) runs the #81 and 83 buses between Courtenay Pl. and the railway station and around the bay to Petone and Eastbourne every hour during the day (more in peak times, fewer in evenings).

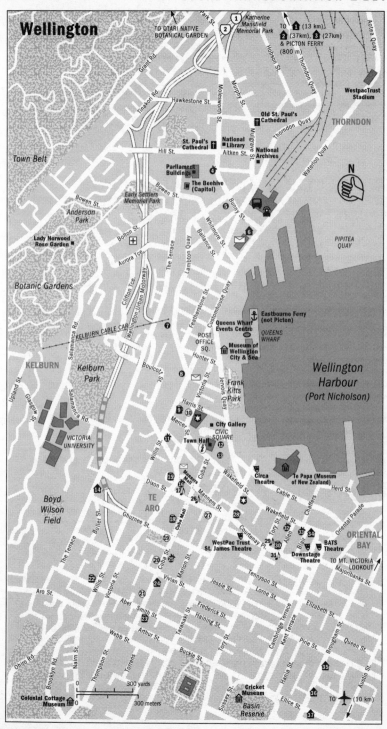

Wellington

TO OTARI NATIVE
BOTANICAL GARDEN

Katherine
Mansfield
Memorial Park

TO ⬆ (13 km),
2⃣ (37km), 3⃣ (27km)
& PICTON FERRY
(800 m)

WestpacTrust
Stadium

Town Belt

Hawkestone St.

Old St. Paul's
Cathedral

THORNDON

St. Paul's
Cathedral

National
Library

National
Archives

Parliament
Buildings

The Beehive
(Capitol)

Early Settlers
Memorial Park

Anderson
Park

PIPITEA
QUAY

Lady Norwood
Rose Garden

Botanic Gardens

Eastbourne Ferry
(not Picton)

Queens Wharf
Events Centre

QUEENS
WHARF

KELBURN

Kelburn
Park

POST
OFFICE
SQ.

Museum of
Wellington
City & Sea

Wellington
Harbour
(Port Nicholson)

VICTORIA
UNIVERSITY

Frank
Kitts
Park

City Gallery

CIVIC
SQUARE

Town Hall

Boyd
Wilson
Field

Circa
Theatre

Te Papa (Museum
of New Zealand)

TE
ARO

Cuba Mall

WestPac Trust
St. James Theatre

Downstage
Theatre

BATS
Theatre

ORIENTAL
BAY

TO MT. VICTORIA
LOOKOUT

Colonial Cottage
Museum

Cricket
Museum

Basin
Reserve

TO ✈ (10 km)

0   300 yards
0   300 meters

N

Taxis: Taxis frequent **Lambton Quay, Courtney Pl.,** and many other drags. If you need to call one, try **Wellington Combined Taxis** (☎384 4444) or **Safeway** (☎802 5111).

Car Rental: Avis (☎0800 374 832), **Budget** (☎0800 652 227), and **Hertz** (☎0800 654 321) are at the airport. You can often arrange to get the car at the ferry terminal. **Omega Rentals,** 96 Hutt Rd. (☎472 8465), has free pick-up and 24hr. AA breakdown help. Four-day unlimited mileage in a budget car is $39 per day; an economy car is $49 per day, and a touring car is $59 per day (min. bond $750). **AA,** 342-352 Lambton Quay (☎470 9999), has a **Travel Centre.** Open M-F 8:30am-5pm, Sa 9am-1pm.

Bike and In-Line Skate Rental: Penny Farthing Cycles, 89 Courtenay Pl. (☎385 2279), has a good selection. Open M-F 8am-6pm, Sa 9:30am-4pm, Su 10am-4pm. $35 per day, $100 per week. On weekends, the **Rollerblade Van** (mobile 025 540 747), parks by the wharf opposite New World grocery store at Cambridge Terrace $10 per hr.

◪ PRACTICAL INFORMATION

TOURIST AND FINANCIAL SERVICES

Visitors Center: The Wellington Information Centre, 101 Wakefield St. (☎802 4860), at the Civic Centre. Luggage $4. Open M-F 8:30am-5:30pm, Sa-Su 9:30am-4:30pm. **Airport branches** (☎385 5123) meet incoming flights. Open daily 7am-7pm.

DOC: (☎472 7356; fax 471 2075), in the Old Government Building across Lambton Quay from the Beehive. They sell backcountry hut passes and permits for Kapiti Island. Open M-F 9am-4:30pm, Sa-Su 10am-3pm.

Budget Travel: STA Travel, 37 Willis St. (☎472 8510), near the Lambton Quay end. Open M-F 9am-5:30pm, Sa 10am-1:30pm. **e-flights,** 18 Manners St. (☎0800 767 000), 3 blocks from the visitors center. Open M-F 9am-5:30pm, Sa 10am-4pm.

Embassies and High Commissions: Australia, 72 Hobson St. (☎473 6411), in Thorndon, north of the railway station. **Canada,** 61 Molesworth St., 3rd floor (☎473 9577; fax 471 2082). **UK,** 44 Hill St. (☎472 6049; fax 471 1974). **US,** 29 Fitzherbert Terrace (☎472 2068; fax 471 2380), in Thorndon. **Ireland** has its main consulate in Auckland.

Currency Exchange: In the main downtown areas, you're never more than a mad dash from an **ATM. Thomas Cook,** 358 Lambton Quay (☎472 2848), near Willis St. has Sa. hrs. Open M-F 9am-5:30pm, Sa 9:30am-1pm.

American Express: 280-292 Lambton Quay, P.O. Box 10182 (☎473 7766, 0800 801 122), in Books & More. They hold mail—no parcels—for members for up to 30 days. Open M-Tu and Th-F 9am-5pm, W 9:30am-5pm.

LOCAL SERVICES

Tramping Gear: Mainly Tramping, 39 Mercer St. (☎473 5353), provides a 10% YHA discount. Open M-Th 9am-5:30pm, F 9am-7pm, Sa 10am-4pm, Su 11am-3pm.

Bookstores: The Map Shop (☎385 1462), at Vivian and Victoria St., rocks your tramping world with a complete set of New Zealand park, city, and topographical maps. Open M-F 8:30am-5:30pm.

Bi-Gay-Lesbian Organizations: Gay Switchboard (☎473 7878) runs a hotline daily 7:30-10pm and provides support and info on the Wellington scene. It's also a contact point for other area groups like **Icebreakers,** a young gay/bi social group. **Out! Bookshop,** 15 Tory St. (☎385 4400), has a wide array of gay-oriented magazines and other items. Open M-Sa noon-11pm, Su noon-9pm. The **express** paper, available at Bo Jangles or the Wellington YHA, has info on Wellington's gay scene.

EMERGENCY AND COMMUNICATIONS

Emergency: Dial ☎111 throughout New Zealand.

Police: (☎381 2000), at the corner of Victoria and Harris St.

Hotlines: AIDS hotline (24hr. ☎0800 802 437). **Rape and Sexual Abuse Support Hotline** (24hr. ☎499 7532), run by the Help Foundation.

Medical Services: Unichem Pharmacy (☎499 1466), at the corner of Cuba and Manners St. Open M-Th 8:30am-6pm, F 8:30am-9pm, Sa 9:30am-6pm, Su 10am-6pm. **Wellington Accident and Urgent Medical Centre,** 17 Adelaide Rd. (☎384 4944), in Newtown by the Basin Reserve, has a doctor on duty **24hr.,** and a **pharmacy** (☎385 8810), next door. Open M-F 5-11pm, Sa-Su 9am-11pm. The **hospital** (☎385 5999) is in Newtown on Riddiford St.

Internet Access: United Video, 31 Courtenay Place (☎385 1470) has long hours and a screamer rate. $4 per hr. Open Su-Th 8am-1am, F-Sa 24hr.

Post Offices: Scattered throughout the city. Only the **Post Shop,** 43 Manners St. (☎473 5922), holds Poste Restante. Open M-F 8am-5:30pm, Sa 10am-1:30pm.

🏠🏕 ACCOMMODATIONS AND CAMPING

Central Wellington has several satisfactory backpackers, most south of Civic Square with a fair number along the quiet, tree-lined **Brougham St.** Consider heading a bit north along the coast for some truly outstanding seaside backpackers.

Wellington City YHA (☎801 7280; fax 801 7278; yhawgtn@yha.org.nz), at the corner of Cambridge Terrace and Wakefield St., a 25min. walk from the Railway Station. This hulking 6-story YHA is blessed with a stellar location. Laundry. Internet. 4-bed bunks $20; 6-bed dorms $18; twins and doubles $46; family rooms from $58. Nonmembers $3 more.

Wide World Backpackers, 291 The Terrace (☎802 5590; fax 802 5591; worldwide@paradise.co.nz). From town, go up Ghuznee St. and turn right. Board games, complimentary breakfast (7:45-9am), complimentary wine (7-7:30pm), free local calls, and free internet (5-9pm). Key deposit $10. Reception 7:45am-noon and 4:30-10pm. Dorms $19; singles $35; doubles and twins $45.

Maple Lodge, 52 Ellice St. (☎385 3771), around the corner from Brougham St., feels close to home and far from the bustle of the city. Off-street parking. Reception 8:30am-noon and after 5pm. Dorms $19; singles $25; twins $40; doubles $42.

Beethoven's, 89 Brougham St. (☎939 4678).This place isn't for everyone. Eccentric owner and a classy wake-up call before the 8am complimentary breakfast. Get to know fellow travelers through the shower room door (a sign encourages towel-drying in view of passers-by.) Internet. Dorms $16-18, weekly $108; doubles $42-44. Cash only.

Rowena's (VIP), 115 Brougham St. (☎385 7872, 0800 801 414; rowenas@iconz.co.nz), is a hilltop house with great balcony views. Breakfast $6. Key deposit $10. Free shuttle service to ferry, buses, trains, and hitchhikers' points. Off-street parking. Internet. Dorms $19; singles $26; doubles with sheets $46; tent sites $10.

Downtown Backpackers (VIP), 1 Bunny St. (☎473 8482; fax 471 1073; db@downtownbackpackers.co.nz), across from the Railway Station. While close to transport terminals, Wellington's largest hostel is far from the city's bars and restaurants. Key deposit $20. Reception 24hr. Free pick-up from ferry. Internet. Bunks $20; singles $38; twins $46; doubles with bath $50, with SkyTV $58.

Trekkers (NOMADS/VIP), 213 Cuba St. (☎385 2153; fax 382 8873; info@trekkers.co.nz). The views of fire escapes and the adjacent strip bar may not entice every trekker, but at least the hostel is near Cuba St. Key deposit $10. Reception 24hr. Bunks $20; singles $30; twins $44. Prices lower in winter.

Top 10 Hutt Park Holiday Park, 95 Hutt Park Rd. (☎568 5913, 0800 488 872; fax 568 5914), in Lower Hutt some 13km from Wellington. By far the closest holiday park, it's mostly a pass-through stay for ferry-catchers. Pohutukawa-lined tent sites for 2 $20, powered sites $22; small, basic cinderblock cabin units for 2 $32; nicer tourist cabins with kitchen $45, extra person $8-11.

NEARBY SEASIDE BACKPACKERS

■ **Moana Lodge,** 49 Moana Rd. (☎233 2010; fax 233 9465; moanalodge@ clear.net.nz), in Plimmerton. 20min. north of Wellington. With an idyllic seaside location, ultra-modern kitchen, and plush rooms, this is definitely one of the best backpackers in New Zealand . Free kayaks, mountain bikes, tea, and coffee. Call for pick-up, often even from Wellington. Internet. Singles $25; twins $40; doubles $40-44. Call ahead.

■ **Paekakariki Backpackers,** 11 Wellington Rd. (☎902 5967; fax 902 5969; paekakbp@voyager.co.nz), 40min. from Wellington on the Kapiti Coast. Just a block from the Paekakariki train station, a steep tiled path leads to this quiet seaside cottage with breathtaking views of wind-swept hills. Laid-back hosts Peter and Denise have a zoo of pets—4 cats, a friendly yellow dog, an axolott, and a cockateel. Internet. Dorms $15; twins and doubles $38, with bath $45; tent sites $10. Call ahead.

🍴 FOOD

Lambton Quay and **Willis St.** are full of lunch spots, but are rather dead at night. The fashionable length of **Courtenay Place** and its side streets are where Lambton Quay's young and coiffed migrate on evenings and weekends, while **Cuba St.** is populated by smaller, cheaper, ethnic restaurants and cafes. With a preponderance of Malaysian, Indian, Chinese, and Cambodian food, Wellington dining has a true Asian flavor. You can find groceries at **New World**, on Wakefield St. at the corner with Cambridge Terrace (open daily 7am-11pm), and fresh fruit and veggies across the street at **Mr. Chan's** (open M-W, Sa 8:30am-7:30pm, Th-F 8:30am-9pm, Su 8:30am-6pm). The very early Saturday morning **Porirua market** (5am-9am) offers everything Polynesian at dirt-cheap prices. Take the TranzMetro to Porirua, and you'll see it by the McDonald's.

■ **Daawat,** 88 Manners Mall (☎472 0060). *The* place in Wellington for curry provides the trinity of backpacker desires: low prices, great quality, and heaping portions. *Dal makhani* ($9; black lentils in spicy tomato puree) is truly divine. BYO wine. Open for lunch M-F 11:30am-2pm and for dinner daily 5:30pm-late.

■ **Kopi,** 103 Willis St. (☎499 5570). Manager James has a strong local following among those who know good food. Enjoy award-winning Malaysian dishes like the deliciously tender lamb *korma* ($15.50). Be early or be prepared to wait. Open daily 10am-late.

The Vegetarian Cafe, 179 Cuba St. (☎384 2713). A sarong-clad staff happily feeds diners wearing everything from suits to tongue studs. Massive bowls filled with vegetarian concoctions ($6-12) are enough to convert even the staunchest carnivore. Open M-Sa 9am-9pm, Su 9am-4pm.

One Red Dog, 9-11 Blair St. (☎384 9777), off Courtenay Pl. There's never a dull bite into these thick pizzas with trendy toppings (med. $16.50, large $24.90). The ridiculously overstuffed calzones, however, are a true steal ($14). Arrive early or be prepared for an almost interminable wait. Open Su-Th 10am-1am, F-Sa 10am-3am.

Big Thumb, 9 Allen St. (☎384 4878), off Courtenay Pl. Although there is no connection to the *Let's Go* thumb, a swollen neon digit marks the entrance to this popular Chinese eatery. Delicious *Sichuan* cuisine like the smoked beef with red chili ($14) will encourage you to pull a Siskel and Ebert of your own. Open daily 11am-2:30pm and 5pm-late.

Wellington Fish Supply, 40 Molesworth St. (☎472 4055), just across from Parliament. For 60 years, this shop has sustained a tradition of ruling class fish 'n' chips. A sizeable, fresh fish 'n' chips is $3.30. Open M-Th 9am-8pm, F 9am-9pm, Sa 9am-7:30pm.

🏠 CAFES

With the highest number of cafes per capita in the southern hemisphere and yet only two Starbucks, Wellington is certainly doing something right. **Courtenay Pl.** is lined with standard cafes, while funkier finds dot the bohemian stretch of ■**Cuba St.** Most cafes serve food and many keep the party going later with liquor licenses.

Fidel's, 234 Cuba St. (☎801 6868). Images of the dictator stare down at patrons inside, but a charming rear garden lets you sip your latte in peace. A delicious blackboard menu complements the full range of tea and coffee drinks ($3-4). Live jazz every Th at 8pm. Licensed. Open M-F 7:30am-midnight, Sa-Su 9am-midnight.

Midnight Espresso, 178 Cuba St. (☎384 7014). Time stands still in this funky cafe, fixed by the good music, laid-back patrons, and plaster monsters. A delicious selection of salads ($3-5) and cakes changes daily. Fill up on fresh juices from Lucky's Juice Joint ($2.50) so you don't miss the black-lit trip to the loo. Open daily 8am-3am.

The Krazy Lounge (☎801 6652), at the corner of Cuba and Ghuznee St., under the joker's cap. A great location lures a sizeable crowd, nodding to the beat of soft techno-trance rhythms over a frothy mug. Licensed. Open M-F 7:30am-late, Sa-Su 9am-late.

Eva Dixon's Place, 35 Dixon St. (☎384 1000). Entrance through alley, on the second floor at the corner of Eva and Dixon St. If you can find this delightful cafe, you'll be rewarded with wrap-around windows, comfy turquoise seats, and an all-day "brekkie" menu ($3-14). Open M-F 7am-7pm, Sa 8:30am-7pm, Su 9am-7pm.

Ed's Juice Bar, 95 Victoria St. (☎478 1769). Savor an irresistible smoothie ($2-7) or a steaming soups ($5). Great selection of vegetarian and vegan food. Ask Ed for "The Boris," jam-packed with secret fruity ingredients. Open daily 6:30am-6:30pm.

🎵 ENTERTAINMENT

With a wide variety of diversions, from high art to sport, Wellington has something for everyone. Prices vary widely; inquire at the visitors center to learn what will be taking place in the upcoming days and to inquire about rush tickets. Just down Wakefield St., **Ticketek** (☎384 3840) sells seats for most Wellington events.

MUSIC AND PERFORMING ARTS

Downstage (☎801 6946), at the corner of Courtenay Pl. and Cambridge Terrace. Wellington's oldest established professional theater puts on a wide range of productions from classic and modern drama to cabaret and comedy. Tickets $20-35, students $15.

Circa, 1 Taranaki St. (☎801 7992; www.circa.co.nz), next to Te Papa. Mainstage plays (tickets $30, students $24) and a studio with smaller, more experimental shows and cheaper seats (tickets $25, students $19). Ticket office open M-Sa 10am-4pm, Su 2-6pm; show nights also 4pm until 1hr. before showtime.

BATS, 1 Kent Terrace (☎802 4175; www.bats.co.nz), is the most experimental, on-the-fringe venue, putting on exclusively New Zealand productions—you won't stumble into any of the classics here. Tickets $15-20, students or unwaged $8-14.

The WestpacTrust St. James Theatre, 77 Courtenay Pl. (☎802 4060). Restored Edwardian lyric theater, home to the Royal Ballet, opera, and musicals. Prices often $45-55.

Wellington Festival and Convention Centre (☎801 4242; www.wcc.govt.nz) stages mostly lectures, classical, and chamber music concerts (including the New Zealand Symphony Orchestra) at the Michael Fowler Centre, Wellington Town Hall, and other venues. Book through **Ticketek** (see above).

CINEMA AND SPORT

Cinema: Paramount, 25 Courtenay Pl. (☎384 4080), dishes out arthouse cinema fare, as does **Rialto** (☎385 1864), at the corner of Cable St. and Jervois Quay. For a dose of Hollywood, check out **Embassy,** 10 Kent Terrace (☎384 7657); **Hoyt 5** (☎472 5182), at Manners Mall; or **Midcity** (☎384 3567), on Manners St. Showings change each Th.

WestpacTrust Stadium (☎473 3881), on Waterloo Quay. The shiny new stadium is jokingly called "The Cake Tin" for its metallic outer shell. But don't let that fool you—Wellington is mighty proud of its oversized tin can which hosts events like rugby, soccer, and large concerts. Prices vary, but rugby tickets usually cost $35-40.

Queens Wharf Events Centre (☎472 5021), at Queens Wharf, is the main venue for major indoor sporting events like international basketball and netball, as well as popular music concerts. Prices vary.

Basin Reserve, Kent Terrace (☎384 5227), just 20min. from downtown, has been home to Wellington cricket for more than 125 years and enjoys National Heritage status. Most matches take place between Nov. and Feb.

FESTIVALS

The annual competition between the months for best festival is always intense. This year, January and February combine their hands for the **Summer City Festival** (www.wcc.govt.nz), a brilliant parade of concerts, celebrations, and events like Sunday night jazz in the Botanic Gardens, mass walks up Mt. Victoria, and a Pacific Island festival. The **New Zealand Festival** (☎0900 33784825; 22 Feb.-17 Mar.), the country's biggest cultural celebration, is on in 2002. Bringing artists and performers from across the globe, this month-long party celebrates New Zealand's place in the world at the start of the new millennium. March's other ace is the **Fringe Festival** (www.fringe.org.nz), an annual theatrical event that celebrates alternative and experimental artistic shows. May plays the joker with the **TV2 International Laugh! Festival** (1-19 May, 2002; www.laugh.co.nz), showcasing comedians from inside and outside New Zealand. Always a high roller, July presents the Kings and Queens of the Silver Screen in the annual **New Zealand International Film Festival** (www.enzedff.co.nz). And, just when it looks like the game is up, October rushes in with the **Wellington Jazz Festival** (www.jazzfestival.co.nz).

◪ NIGHTLIFE

Wellington nightlife comes in a few flavours ranging from business chic to skater cool; the trick is finding your vibe. The **Courtenay Pl.** stretch is clogged with stylishly slick bars frequented by after-work suits and black-clad students; most are indistinguishable from one another. For those who aren't fond of rock remixes, the pubs on **Cuba St.** and the nearby blocks tend to be just as crowded but more relaxed. Since Wellington party life centers mainly around bars and pubs, the few nightclubs that do exist don't usually get going until late and often aren't truly packed until after 3am on weekends (when all the pubs close). However, there are a number of great bars which manage to pack their dance floors by 11pm, allowing patrons their groove and some time for beauty sleep. Be sure to carry appropriate identification as many bars will card patrons.

For the latest happenings, grab the free weekly *The Package, Capital Times,* or *City Voice* from newsstands or check cafes for fliers. While only two nightspots are listed as primarily gay and lesbian, some bars and clubs have designated gay nights. Scope out *express* for the most current listings.

BARS

▩ **Matterhorn,** 106 Cuba Mall (☎384 3359). Walk down a long dark hallway to enter the realm of Matterhorn. Mellow vibes circulate through the intimate lounge bar with $5 beers, $3.50 coffees, and a selection of munchies from $4. Early evenings are appropriately subdued but late-night DJs (Th-Su) get a funky crowd grooving in the rear courtyard. Open M-Sa 11am-3am, Su noon-2am.

▩ **The Malthouse,** 47 Willis St. (☎499 4355), on the second floor. While the post-work crowd often overwhelm the bar, the enclosed sun porch is a bright and toasty place to unwind. Like any great pub, The Malthouse takes its beer seriously—a separate menu describes each of their 30 draught beers in loving detail. While most are worth a go, the Roosters Dark ($4.50) is truly exquisite. Open M-Sa 11am-late.

Molly Malones (☎384 2896), on the corner of Courtenay Pl. and Taranaki St. Every hour is Happy Hour at this popular pub with live Irish and cover bands every night for no charge. Open daily 11am-late, Su until midnight.

Tupelo, 6 Edward St. (☎384 1152), off Victoria St. Not surprisingly, wine glasses far out-number handles in the manicured hands of Tupelo's trendy. A higher standard of dress applies. Open M-Tu 5pm-late, W-F noon-late, Sa 6pm-late.

Zebos Bar (Southern Cross Tavern), 35 Abel Smith St. (☎384 9085), toward the top end of Cuba St. Lots of space make it easy to migrate from the bar to the pool tables to the dance floor and back again. Nights overflow with buzzed Vic Uni students. Open daily 11:30am-3am.

Bar Bodega (☎384 8212), at the corner of Willis and Abel Smith St. This small space with sparse seating attracts an eclectic crowd and some of the best live music in town. Live bands Tu-Sa 10pm. Cover charge $5-10. Handles $4.50. Open daily 4pm-3am.

Ballroom Billiards, 68 Courtenay Pl. (☎801 7994). Dark, smoky, and brimming with pool tables, the Ballroom combines free-flowing alcohol and a sport that requires care-ful coordination. M-W until 6pm pool is $5 each all night. Tables regularly $10 per hr. Open M- Tu 11:30am-1am, W 11:30am-2am, Th-Sa 11:30am-3am, Su noon-midnight.

BARS WITH DANCE FLOORS

🎵**The Grand,** 69 Courtenay Pl. (☎801 7800). Cruise past the bouncers at the door and up the stairs to join the gyrating dance-house scene. Mostly top pop, the music keeps an all-ages crowd hopping until the wee hours. Open daily 11am-late.

Wellington Sports Cafe (☎801 5115), at the corner of Courtenay Pl. and Tory St. Part sports bar, part grind-fest. After the game of the moment ends, the tables are pushed aside and open season is declared on one of the wildest dance floors in town. Lines often form late. Open daily 11am-5am.

Barney's Place and **Bo Jangles,** 60 Dixon St. (☎384 8441), on the second floor. Bar-ney's is the '80s bar that the 1980's wishes they had created. Next door, Bo Jangles is all dance floor. A lively and gay-friendly crowd packs in at 11pm. Beer $4, spirits $5.50. Both open W-Sa 7pm-late.

GAY AND LESBIAN NIGHTLIFE

£ (☎384 6024), at Dixon St. on the second floor of the Oaks Complex. The latest (and second) addition to Wellington's gay nightlife scene draws a subdued after-work crowd with $4.50 pints. Later at night, migrate to the dance floor where DJs spin house and techno (W-Sa) and live entertainers take the stage (F-Sa). Free pool and Happy Hour on Su. Open W-Su 5pm-5am.

◎ SIGHTS

A visit to Wellington will quench any traveler's thirst for some pure, enlightening, adrenaline-free culture. The capital city's museums, government buildings, grandi-ose gardens, and stunning waterfront are guaranteed to put some wind in your sightseeing sails (if the day isn't breezy enough already).

MUSEUMS

▧**MUSEUM OF NEW ZEALAND TE PAPA TONGAREWA.** Like a massive father fig-ure encouraging your first stumbling steps as a tourist in Wellington, this enor-mous couple of informative and entertaining exhibits seems to bellow, "Come Te Papa." This enjoyable and educational behemoth is deservedly Wellington's pride and joy; the free admission is just a bonus. Standing exhibits explore New Zealand's land, history, culture, and art. Upstairs, Te Marae showcases a contem-porary interpretation of Maori iconography. Or, for slightly stiffer fees ($2-9), try the interactive exhibits including a virtual bungy jump, virtual sheep-shearing (complete with virtual blood if you do a bad job), a virtual ride into prehistoric moa-laden New Zealand, and more. It's virtual insanity. *(On the waterfront, just at the end of Taranaki St. on Cable St.* ☎*381 7000; www.tepapa.govt.nz. Open daily 10am-6pm, Th until 9pm. Free, but a helpful floor-map costs $2.)*

WELLINGTON

THE MUSEUM OF WELLINGTON CITY AND SEA. Constructed in 1891, this museum explores the unique relationship between Wellington residents and the sea. Probably not a comforting trip before heading to the South Island, as its extensive collection of ship models includes a re-creation of the sinking of the *Wahine* interisland ferry. *(At the corner of Queens Wharf and Jervois Quay. ☎472 8904. Open daily 9:30am-6pm; in winter 9:30am-5:30pm. $5, children $2.50.)*

KATHERINE MANSFIELD BIRTHPLACE. Home to the beloved short story writer for the first six years of her life, this painstakingly restored house is a haven for literature lovers. A narrated display explores Mansfield's private life as it influenced her work and an elaborate dollhouse based entirely on one of her stories has been carefully constructed; strong debate apparently raged over what shade "oily spinach green" should be. *(Up Molesworth St. at 25 Tinakori Rd., in Thorndon. ☎473 7268. Open daily 10am-4pm. $5, students and children $4. Call ahead to book a guided tour.)*

OTHER MUSEUMS. The **Dowse Art Museum** has one of the country's best collections of craftwork. *(Catch the #83 Eastbourne bus to Queensgate from Courtenay Pl. 35 Laings Rd., in Lower Hutt. ☎570 6500. Open M-F 10am-4pm, Sa-Su 11am-5pm. Free.)* If you miss the thwack of the national pastime, the **Cricket Museum** has more old bats than a bingo game in Boca. *(In the Basin Reserve grandstand. ☎385 6602. Open daily 10:30am-3:30pm; in winter Sa-Su 10:30am-3:30pm. $3, children $1.)*

CITY SIGHTS

PARLIAMENT. The top visual attractions (or distractions, as the case may be) in Wellington—the capital city since the government moved from Auckland in 1865—have prime national significance. Of the three buildings that make up the parliamentary complex, the most distinctive and well-known is the **Beehive.** Home to the offices of the Prime Minister and other bigwigs, this monstrosity of '70s architecture serves as a landmark for Parliament, but the interior is closed to the public. Next door, the Neoclassical **Parliament House** is home to the **Visitors Center** on the ground floor. From here, free hourly tours give a peek at parts of the buildings that would otherwise be off-limits. See the carefully designed Maori Affairs Select Committee Room and the huge art installation representing New Zealand's cultural traditions. The gorgeously ornate Victorian Gothic **Parliamentary Library,** restored from a 1992 fire, is part of the tour as well. You can even send a letter postmarked "Parliament" from here. To see the House in action, get a schedule in advance. *(Molesworth St., a few blocks from the Railway Station. ☎471 9503. Tours leave on the hour; groups of 10 or more call ahead. Open M-F 10am-4pm, Sa 10am-3pm, Su noon-3pm.)*

CIVIC SQUARE. The public buildings in Wellington's bricked **Civic Square** are the perfect place to people-watch on sunny weekends. At one side sits the elegant **City Gallery,** which showcases contemporary exhibitions with top caliber New Zealand and international artists. *(101 Wakefield St. ☎801 3021; www.city-gallery.org.nz. Open daily 10am-5pm. NZ exhibits free; international exhibits up to $10.)* In the far corner of Civic Square is the huge, circular **Michael Fowler Centre** *(☎801 4242),* an events and conference center which is home to the New Zealand Symphony Orchestra. Inside are the two towering modern Maori pillars, *Te Pou O Wi Tako* and *Te Pou o Taviwi*, dedicated to the people of the land and to visitors, respectively. Just under the base of the bridge sits **Capital E,** a children's center with a hands-on toy store, constantly changing exhibitions, and a theatre for the kids. *(☎384 8502. Open daily 10am-5pm. Exhibitions range from free to $8. Theatre $10.)* Cross the bridge to the waterfront and the green public space of **Frank Kitts Park.**

VANTAGE POINTS. Rising from the city's south end, **Mt. Victoria** can elevate you to new heights of long-range vision. If you're not up for the 30min. hike, you can drive or ride. *(M-F take bus #20.)* Some locals say that the view from the **ECNZ wind turbine** is even better. *(Take bus #7 from the Railway Station or Willis St. up to the shops on Brooklyn St.; there are signposts from there. It's a steep climb.)*

LIBRARIES AND CATHEDRALS

NATIONAL LIBRARY. Home to over 1.8 million books, including the **Cartoon Archives** and the **Gay and Lesbian Archives,** the National Library has an exhibition hall which showcases excellent temporary exhibits. Also inside, the **Alexander Turnbull Library** houses an extensive collection of early printed materials and photographic archives. *(58 Molesworth St. ☎ 474 3000. Open M-F 9am-5pm, Sa 9am-1pm for research and gallery only. Archives are available for viewing by arrangement.)*

NATIONAL ARCHIVES. A dimly lit, thick-walled vault towards the back of the archives building displays all of New Zealand's most important documents, including the original copy of the 1840 Treaty of Waitangi, the Statute of Westminster, and the petition for women's suffrage. *(Around the corner from the National Archives. 10 Mulgrave St. ☎ 499 5595. Open M-F 9am-5pm, Sa 9am-1pm.)*

OLD ST. PAUL'S CATHEDRAL. Constructed in 1866 from native timber, this small church might look simple from the outside, but the colonial Gothic interior has warm, rich color and superb stained-glass windows. *(Molesworth St., one block past the Archives. ☎ 473 6722. Open daily 10am-5pm.)*

ST. PAUL'S CATHEDRAL. Just next to Parliament towers Wellington's recently completed, Byzantine-style, salmon-colored St. Paul's. *(☎ 472 0286. Open M-F 7:30am-5pm, Sa 10am-5pm, Su 7:30am-4pm.)*

GARDENS AND TOURS

BOTANIC GARDENS. A trip to the gardens may call to mind similarities between Wellington and San Francisco, especially if you ride the Wellington Cable Car 610m up to the Kelburn Terminal. *(☎ 472 2199. Departs every 10min. from Cable Car Ln. on Lambton Quay. Open M-F 7am-10pm, Sa-Su 9am-10pm. $1.50, students and children $1.)* Relax in the 26-hectare public **Botanic Gardens** and follow one of the many paths that snake around from herb garden to planetarium with canopied views of the city and hills in the distance. One of the most spectacular spots is the **Lady Norwood Rose Garden,** with hundreds of different kinds of roses blossoming out from a central fountain. After you explore, walk down the lush length of the gardens and follow Bolton St. out to the Terrace and downtown. *(☎ 801 3073. Always open, though best visited during the day. Roses Nov.-May only.)* Anyone with a botanical bent should also visit the 80-hectare **Otari Native Botanic Garden,** which is dedicated solely to native plants. *(160 Wilton Rd. ☎ 475 3245. Take the #14 Wilton bus. Free.)*

WALLY HAMMOND'S WELLINGTON SCENIC TOURS. Though decidedly not a normal budget pursuit, these tours do showcase the superior Wellington sites in a user-friendly way. The running commentary is enjoyable and the views of the city through large, clear windows are unmatched. *(☎ 472 0869. 2½hr. city tour $25. Kapiti Coast tour $55. Wairarapa tour $110. Free pick-up.)*

THE ENORMOUS CROCODILE COMPANY. Every weekend, the waterfront is decorated with giggling green streaks—the trail of sparkling, speeding tour bikes rented out by the Crocodile Co. *(☎ 904 2762. 2-seater $15 per hr., 4-seater with 2 child baskets $25 per hr. Available Sa-Su 10am-sundown.)*

WELLINGTON ZOO. New Zealand's oldest zoo and a world leader in breeding programs for some of New Zealand's most famous species, the Wellington Zoo is a wild escape located just 10min. from town. Rare and exotic animals such as the Sumatran Tiger, the Malayan Sun Bear, and the Cotton Top Tamarin sun just a few minutes from such New Zealand favorites as the Brown Kiwi, the Tuatara, and the Giant Weta. The newly constructed Tropical River Trail is just one example of the Zoo's move toward constructing more natural habitats for its various tenants. *(☎ 381 6750. On Manchester St. in Newtown. Take the #10 or 23 Stagecoach bus to Newtown Park. Open daily 9:30am-5pm. $9.)*

WELLINGTON

⚠ ACTIVITIES

Although Wellington is better known for its culture, there are plenty of outdoor opportunities. This is New Zealand, after all.

WALKS. The **Northern, Southern,** and **Eastern Walkways,** detailed in leaflets from the visitors center or DOC office, are tame and accessible walks through the city's greenbelt and coastline. Alternatively, the **Red Rocks Coastal Walk** is a terrific 8km return trip along the jagged southern coastline, past the pillow lava formation of Red Rocks. The walk then heads out to the crashing surf of **Sinclair Head,** where, in winter, a colony of fat fur seals is sure to be lazing around. A 4WD ride from **Red Rocks Seal Tour** travels to the colony along rugged and otherwise inaccessible tracks. *(Book with the visitors center. 2½ hr. trip $50.)*

ADVENTURE ACTIVITIES. For more cardiovascular pursuits, **Fergs Rock 'n' Kayaks,** has **rock-climbing** trips and hires **sea kayaks, inline skates,** and **scooters.** *(At Queens Wharf. ☎ 499 8898. Rock-climbing from $12. Kayaks $12-15 per hr. Inline skates $10-15 per hr. Scooters $10 per hr.)* **HangDog** and **Top Adventures** specialize in caving, rafting, canyoning, and other high-adrenaline pursuits. Who said Wellington was all about culture? *(☎ 589 9181; www.topadventures.co.nz. Trips from $55.)* For off-road fun, **All Track Adventures** has a variety of 4WD rides over rugged hill country with stunning views of Cook Strait and the South Island. *(☎ 0800 494 335. $39-149.)*

◗ BEACHES

It's shocking that a city built along the sea has so few accessible beaches; if you have the time, Plimmerton and the Kapiti Coast (see p. 226) provide consistently better swimming and sunning. Walking distance from downtown, **Oriental Bay,** while popular with city dwellers, is less a beach than a grassy promenade overlooked by trendy cafes. Wellington's **surfing** is rather wind-dependent: winter southerlies cause stronger waves, but breaks are more consistent east of the Wairarapa towns of Martinborough and Masterton. Locals like **Lyall Bay,** which has a patrolled swimming stretch and relatively consistent breaks at the airport end.

The **Evening Post Ferry** is one cheap way to get out onto the harbor. Full of Wellingtonians escaping the city, it leaves from Queens Wharf and crosses to the little cafe-and-antique-shop community of **Day's Bay,** with its small but popular swimming beach. Past Day's Bay is the village of **Eastbourne,** similarly bedecked with cafes, blue penguins, and a pebbly beach. *(☎ 499 1282. M-F 9 return sailings per day, Sa-Su 5 per day; return $15.)* Some ferries also stop at **Matiu/Somes Island.** A former quarantine island and POW camp, the smallpox and rats now eradicated, it has become a bird sanctuary. For a good 3hr. getaway, bring a picnic lunch, wander the revegetating bush, and admire a 360° panorama including great views of Wellington. (Daily 10am, noon, 2:15pm; return $16.50.)

KAPITI COAST

Arcing 32km up the west coast, the Kapiti Coast is Wellington's scenic weekend getaway, a 40min. drive from the city. Stretching from Paekakariki to Otaki, small wildlife sanctuaries, a stunning coastline, and the wild, bird-filled Kapiti Island draw visitors to the region. While nearly every town has a public beach, Waikanae Beach is the region's finest, with a long stretch of often uncrowded sand.

◨ KAPITI COAST TRANSPORTATION

Several tour operators cover Kapiti; **Wally Hammond's** takes you through the natural attractions, stopping at all of the tourist spots as well. *(☎ 472 0869. 2 trips per day, $55. Free pick-up.)* **TranzScenic** stops hourly at **Paekakariki** (¾hr., $6) and **Para-**

paraumu (1hr., $7.50) on its way north from Wellington. An unlimited day pass will get you to both of these stops and back again for only $10 (travel must begin after 9am weekdays). Trains run weekdays from 6am to midnight, until 8pm on weekends; prices are 25% lower between 9am and 3pm. **Newmans/InterCity** buses stop along the **Kapiti Coast** as well, but booking is required. (☎472 5111. 9 per day, $11.) Also, there's a fair amount of regional traffic all the way from Otaki to Paekakariki, and although *Let's Go* does not recommend it, **hitchers** reportedly have a good chance of bumming a ride.

KAPITI AND MANA ISLANDS ☎04

Once the stronghold of Te Rauparaha and an anchorage for whalers, Kapiti Island has been cleansed of introduced mammals as part of a stunning experiment in floral and avian regeneration. A true bird-lovers paradise, Kapiti Island is one of the only wild and accessible places in New Zealand where you're practically guaranteed to see takahe and kaka, whole flocks of melodious tui, and perhaps one of the last saddlebacks or kokako.

Kapiti Island lies about 5km offshore from Paraparaumu Beach; the nature reserve contains toilets, a shelter, three tracks, and no other amenities. **DOC** limits access to the island to 50 people per day, and requires a permit ($9, children $4.50); book with the **Wellington Office** (☎472 7356; fax 471 2075). Spaces fill up far in advance, December to February, especially during the weekend slots, but there's often last-minute availability on weekdays; in winter, there can be too *few* visitors for the boats to run. **Kapiti Tours** (☎237 7965, 0800 527 484) and **Kapiti Marine Charter** (☎297 2585; mobile 025 424 850) both run daily from Paraparaumu Beach to the island (15-20min., 9am and 9:30am, return $30). From Wellington, only the 6:55am **TranzMetro** ($7.50) reaches Paraparaumu in time to catch the 7:55am **Mana Coach** (☎0800 801 700; 20min., $1.70) from the railroad station, which is the latest to arrive at Paraparaumu Beach before the 9am boats leave. Visitors are given a nature talk upon arrival, and must catch the boats back around 3pm.

To the south of Kapiti Island and 4km offshore from Titahi Bay near Porirua lies **Mana Island.** Once the site of Te Rauparaha's *whare* and the first sheep farm in New Zealand, today a massive DOC regeneration program has been started to bring the island back to its former glory. **Friends of Mana Island** (☎233 2010) run trips to the scientific reserve ($15-30) where visitors can help in the restoration of the island while exploring native bush, birds, lizards, and giant weta. The welcoming **Moana Lodge** (see p. 220) provides an easy jumping-off point for clean and green Mana Island excursions.

PAEKAKARIKI ☎04

Meaning "resting place of the green parakeet," Paekakariki has outgrown its name in more ways than one. First, its colorful namesake birds were driven out by European colonization, and, more recently, locals have informally shortened the town's unwieldy name to the more user-friendly "Paekak." The town's main street spans only a few blocks, but residential areas follow its long golden strip of shell-filled beach. Paekakariki's location at the southern point of the Kapiti Coast makes for breathtaking coastal views; if you have your own transport, take **Paekakariki Hill Rd.,** off SH1, in order to climb a hill that winds up through a blindingly green valley before turning the corner to a drop-dead view of the Tasman Sea and the entire curve of Kapiti Coast. **Kapiti Island** and the **Marlborough Sounds** float in the distance. A more recent craze in Paekakariki is yet another invention in the country's endless search for an adrenaline rush: the **Fly By Wire,** a patented, 12min. thrill ride in an open-air rocket-like contraption. Riders gain full pilot control of a high-speed tethered plane that can hit 140kph. (Mobile 025 300 366. Park at the BP station and walk up a steep dirt path. $99, including video. Open M-F 10:30am-4:30pm, Sa-Su 9:30am-5pm.) Off Highway 1 at Queen Elizabeth Park, is the **Wellington Tramway**

WELLINGTON

Museum, where you can take a train ride to the beach on one of Wellington's 19th-century tramcars. (☎202 8361. Open Sa-Su 11am-5pm. $4, children $2.) For accommodations, you can't beat the ▓**Paekakariki Backpackers** (see p. 220).

PARAPARAUMU   ☎04

Tiger's in Paraperam, oh my! Or at least he will be. The main town of the Kapiti, and home to a slew of retirees, Paraparaumu (or as locals call it, Paraperam or Pram) is all worked up over the planned visit of Tiger Woods. In preparation for hosting Tiger and the **New Zealand Open** in January 2002, Paraperam is turning its eagle eye inward, to ensure that everything from the illustrious **Coastlands Shopperworld** to the gleaming white **Our Lady of Lourdes statue** is up to par. While the narrow Paraparaumu Beach has a built-up shorefront and fine views, it's better suited to water activities than lounging in the sand. Along Highway 1, and the route of the #5 Mana Coach, are two worthy attractions. The first is the **Southward Car Museum,** with a collection of vintage autos and motorcycles. You can peek into Marlene Dietrich's custom-made Cadillac or check out the bullet holes in the gangster car. (☎297 1221. Open daily 9am-4:30pm. $5, children $2.) The second is the **Lindale Centre,** a sprawling country farm complex that will put a cherry on top of your day with outstanding homemade ice cream. Containing a dairy factory, honeybee shop, olive shop, and an enormous sculpture of Swiss cheese, it offers sheep shearing, cow milking, and baby animal feeding at 2pm on weekends. (☎297 0916. Ask for free samples. Show and farm walk $7.50, farm walk alone $5. Open daily 9am-5pm.) The #4 Mana Coach delivers you to the sweet smells of the **Nyco Chocolate Factory & Shop,** on the corner of Highway 1 and Raumati Rd. Put on a hairnet and take a tour through the small factory, complete with free chocolate tastings. (☎299 8098. Tours M-F 10:30am and 2:30pm, $1. Factory open daily 9am-5pm.)

The local bus, **Mana Coach** (☎0800 801 700), has #3 and 4 run to Paraparaumu Beach (15min., $1.70) and #5 to Waikanae (every hour M-Sa, $2). The **Coastlands** shopping complex, just across from the railroad station, contains a **post office, supermarket,** and **pharmacy.** The **Paraparaumu Information Centre** is an island in the Coastlands shopping complex. (☎298 8195. Open M-Sa 9am-4pm, Su 10am-3pm.) Motels stretch along Kapiti Rd. and down the beachfront, but **Barnacles Seaside Inn,** 3 Marine Parade, is seaside and cheap. Rooms are well-kept and private, with heaters, electric blankets, and shared showers. (☎902 5856; fax 902 5857. Singles $23, with linen $30; twins and doubles $36, with linen $40.)

OTAKI   ☎06

While not as popular as its southern Kapiti neighbors, Otaki acts as a regional mediator, with access to both the Kapiti Coast and the Manawatu region, to sandy coastline, and verdant native bush. Even the township itself acts as an access point to the nearby **Otaki Forks,** the main western entrance to the Tararua Forest Park (see p. 230); the Forks are located 19km inland from Otaki itself. While not regarded as the primary entrance to the Forest Park, Otaki Forks is the starting point for a number of lovely hikes, most of which showcase the pioneer history of the region. The **Arcus Loop** track meanders over the Waiotauru River swingbridge and crosses over streams and gullies before returning to the carpark (return 45min.). Also around the Otaki Forks area, the Waiotauru River has several safe swimming holes and the Otaki River (Class II) is popular for rafting and kayaking.

The park is accessible off SH1 along the often treacherous Otaki Gorge Road. The road itself is narrow, windy, and largely unsealed. Additionally, as the name suggests, it follows the **Otaki Gorge,** making for a potentially steep drop. To avoid making the drive on your own, contact **River Rock** (☎364 3110) to explore a number of adventure tour options. Either way, stop at one of the many fresh fruit and vegetable stands along the highway on either side of Otaki to prepare a cheap and healthy picnic. Campgrounds are available at the Schoolhouse Flat area (contact the Waikanae Field Centre ☎04 293 2191).

THE WAIRARAPA ☎ 06

In summer, the Wairarapa coast buzzes with daytrippers from Wellington and weekenders seeking the solace of its verdant gardents and award-winning wines. The newly-opened Martinborough Wine Centre (see p. 229) takes the sting out of winter. Divers, surfers, and others wild-at-heart all flock to the cold-water coast (though south of Riversdale to Tora is off-limits for surfing), while many tend to devote a day or few to exploring the area's natural offerings, such as the high and mighty Castle Rock (east of Masterton on Castlepoint Road), Palliser Bay's fur seal colony, and Tararua Forest Park. Regional transportation is a little pricey, since cars or tour buses are needed to access the coast from towns along SH2, but once you're there, attractions are easy on the wallet (if not on the liver). A copy of the helpful pamphlet *Wairarapa Events 2002* (http://wairarapanz.com) will allow you to cash in on dozens of concerts, horse shows, sporting events, and country fairs that liven up the towns.

MASTERTON ☎ 06

The main transport and tourist hub of the Wairarapa, Masterton (pop. 19,800) has grown out of its agricultural roots but still hosts the fantastically popular annual Golden Shears sheep-shearing competition (usually in March). Despite being the only sight in town, Masterton's 32-hectare **Queen Elizabeth Park** on Dixon St. is perfect for a picnic. Its suspension bridge, rose gardens, pedal-boat pond, and miniature railway exude tranquility. The new skate park does not. On the last weekend in February (February 23-24, 2002), things become a tad more frenzied as the park is transformed by the **Masterton Wine and Food Festival,** which celebrates the growing fame of the area's vineyards. A bit farther afield, 30km north of Masterton on SH2, the **Mt. Bruce National Wildlife Centre** lets you see a kiwi and a tuatara in the same day, a feat you may not be able to accomplish on your own—yet. With 15 different aviaries and outdoor reserves, Mt. Bruce is practically crowing with pride over its many successful captive breeding programs. The wildlife center has numerous displays on the management regimes for rearing threatened native birds. (☎375 8754. Open daily 9:30am-4pm. $8.)

TranzMetro (☎04 498 3000, ext. 44933) runs to **Wellington** more frequently than the bus (1½hr.; M-Th 4 per day, F 5 per day, Sa-Su 2 per day; $11.50). **Tranzit Coachlines** (☎377 1227) departs from the Queen St. terminal for: **Palmerston North** (2hr., 1-2 per day, $15) via **Mt. Bruce Wildlife Centre** (25min., $6); and **Wellington** (2½hr., 4:40pm, $13) via **Carterton** (15min., $2.20), **Greytown** (25min., $2.60), and **Featherston** (40min., $3). **Tranzit** also heads directly to **Carterton, Greytown,** and **Featherston** (M-F, 4 per day).

Queen St., which runs parallel to Chapel St. (SH2), is home to most of Masterton's cafes, stores, and restaurants. The **Tourism Wairarapa Head Office,** 5 Dixon St. is at the corner of Queen St. and Lincoln Rd. (☎378 7373; fax 378 7042. Open M-F 9-5pm, Sa-Su 10am-4pm.) Banks with **ATMs** (open M-F 9 or 9:30am-4:30pm) and a **post shop** (in Books&More; open M-F 8am-5pm, Sa 9am-1pm) are located on Queen St. The **Empire Lodge,** 94 Queen St., is centrally located; adequate rooms are sunny and cheaper than you'll find at area motels. Queen St. teems with cafes, takeaways, and other small eateries—**Food For Thought** is one of the best. Cafeteria-style dining makes service quick and the ample seating allows you to linger over lunch. Sandwiches and fresh muffins go for $2-5. (☎377 5195. Open M-F 7am-5pm, Sa 8am-3pm, Su 9am-2pm.) **Woolworth's** supermarket, near the end of Queen St., has an especially good produce section. (☎377 0050. Open daily 7am-10pm.)

MARTINBOROUGH ☎ 06

The major wine village of the Wairarapa, Martinborough (40km east of Masterton) pays homage to its British roots with streets laid out in the pattern of the Union Jack. High sunshine and low autumnal rainfall are the most important elements in cultivating choice vintages (you can't go wrong with a Pinot Noir) from the 20 area wineries. Most are within walking distance of each other; call

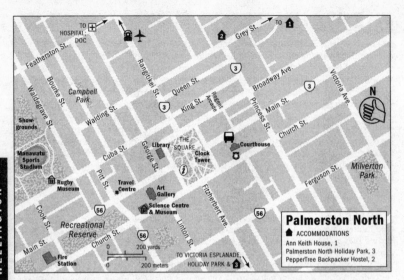

Palmerston North

⌂ ACCOMMODATIONS
Ann Keith House, 1
Palmerston North Holiday Park, 3
PepperTree Backpacker Hostel, 2

ahead before setting out in winter. Both the **Martinborough Information Centre,** on Kitchener St. (☎306 9043; fax 306 8033; open daily 10am-4pm), and the **Tourism Wairarapa Head Office** in Masterton can provide maps and information for your drinking pleasure. Some year-round wineries are the **Palliser Estate,** on Kitchener St. (☎306 9019), **Martinborough Vineyard,** on Princess St. (☎306 9955; tastings daily 11am-5pm), and **Te Kairanga Vineyard,** on Martins Rd. (☎306 9122; tours Sa-Su 2pm). The **Martinborough Country Fair** draws sizeable Wellington crowds (March 2, 2002), while **Toast Martinborough** (November, 2002; ☎306 9183) sells you the proverbial bottomless glass, providing an unparalleled opportunity to sample the region's best. If you are short on time or transport, the **Martinborough Wine Centre,** 6 Kitchener St. (☎306 9040) has amassed all of the best regional vintages in one central location. On Saturdays, a village market lures local growers with fresh farm produce to sell at bargain prices. To get there, **Wairarapa Coach Lines** (☎378 2911) connects to Masterton and meets the train in Featherston. Prior booking is essential.

TARARUA FOREST PARK   ☎06

There are some great hikes off the tourist radar in the Tararua Forest Park, though the weather can be harsh. Covering 117,225 hectares and 75% of the Tararua Range, it was the first forest park established in New Zealand. Marked tracks meander through beech forests, alpine grasslands, and even leatherwood shrublands. Severe wind and mist have made this region famous for capricious weather. The popular **Mt. Holdsworth Circuit** (20km, 2-3 days) begins at **Mt. Holdsworth Lodge,** 20min. west of Masterton, and climbs through bush to the mountain before winding back to the lodge (huts $4-8). The 15,000-year-old Class 2 **Waiohine River** runs through the Waiohine Gorge in the southeastern part of the Tararuas. A large swing bridge crosses the river by the carpark for the popular camping and recreation areas nearby, surrounded by rimu, beech, rata, and kahikatea trees. From there, the **Loop Track** (return 1½hr.) crosses through regenerating bush, while the **Cone Hut Track** (return 6hr.) climbs to a terrace of the **Tauherenikau River.** Get **hut tickets** from the **DOC** in Masterton (☎377 0700), the Holdsworth ranger (☎377 0022), local visitors centers, or various sports shops.

PALMERSTON NORTH ☎ 06

Around 40% of Palmerston North's 75,000 residents are involved with higher education in one way or another, giving credence to its nickname "Knowledge City." Home to Massey University, New Zealand's second-largest university, and a host of other schools, "Palmy" has more book-filled backpacks than traveling backpackers. More of a transport hub than a top destination, the city's two loves—movies and rugby—can occupy you during a day's stopover.

⊏ TRANSPORTATION

Trains: TranzScenic (☎0800 802 802) leaves from the railway station on Matthews Ave. off Tremaine Ave. (about a 20min. walk from The Square). Trains leave daily for: **Auckland** (8½hr.; 10:57am and 10:09pm; $104-116) via **Ohakune, National Park,** and **Hamilton; Napier** (3hr., 10:14am, $47); and **Wellington** (2hr., 3 per day, $30-33). **TranzMetro** (☎04 801 7000) runs to **Wellington** M-F via the **Kapiti Coast.**

Buses: InterCity/Newmans leave from the Travel Centre at Pitt and Main St. (☎355 5633) and **White Star** (☎0800 800 287) leaves from the courthouse on Main St. Both go daily to **New Plymouth** (4hr., 2-3 per day, $40) via **Wanganui** (1½hr., $17); and **Wellington** (2hr., several times per day, $27). InterCity/Newmans also heads daily to **Auckland** (8-10hr., 2-4 per day, $70); **Masterson** (1¾hr., 1-2 per day, $19); and **Rotorua** (5hr., 2 per day, $57) via **Taupo** (4hr., $44). **Guthreys** (☎0800 759 999) runs to **Auckland, Rotorua, Napier, Taupo,** and **Wellington. White Star** (☎758 3338) runs to **Wellington** ($18) and to **New Plymouth** ($30) via **Wanganui** and **Stratford.**

Taxis: Palmerston North Taxis (☎357 6076), **Gold & Black** (☎355 5059) run **24hr.**

Hitchhiking: Although *Let's Go* does not recommend it, thumbers report luck along any of the main roads. Rangitikei St. joins SH1 at Bulls, heading toward the volcanic heartland and Auckland. Napier Rd. (Main St. E.) heads to Napier. Pioneer Highway (further along Main St. W.) and Fitzherbert St. both head to Wellington.

✴ ? ORIENTATION AND PRACTICAL INFORMATION

The downtown is centered around The Square, Palmerston North's well-kept central green space. **Rangitikei St.** heads north, while **Fitzherbert Ave.** leads south toward the Manawatu River. **Main St.** heads east and west from The Square.

Visitors Center: Destination Manawatu Visitor Centre, Square Edge Building, The Square (☎354 6593). Open M-F 9am-5pm, Sa-Su 10am-3pm.

DOC: 717 Tremaine Ave. (☎350 9700; fax 350 9701), 1km from Rangitikei. Helpful with the Tararuas or Ruahines. Open M-F 8am-4:30pm.

Currency Exchange: BNZ (☎358 4149), at the corner of The Square and Rangitikei St. Open M and Th-F 9am-4:30pm, Tu-W 9:30am-4:30pm. **Thomas Cook** (☎356 2962), at the corner of Broadway and Princess St. Open M-F 9am-5pm.

Police: (☎351 3600), on Church St., off the McDonald's corner of The Square.

Medical Services: City Doctors, 22 Victoria Ave. (**24hr.** ☎355 3300). **City Health Pharmacy,** 22 Victoria Ave. (☎355 5287). Open daily 8am-10pm. **Palmerston North Hospital,** 50 Ruahine St. (☎356 9169).

Internet Access: The $13 million **library** (☎351 4100) on The Square has public showers and internet for $5 per hr. Open M-Tu and Th 10am-6pm, W and F 10am-8pm, Sa 10am-4pm, Su 1-4pm. **@Computers,** 25 Fitzherbert St. (☎357 1213), is another option. $10 per hr. Open daily 10am-late.

Post Office: 338 Church St. (☎353 6900) has Poste Restante. Open M-F 7:30am-6pm, Sa 9:30am-12:30pm.

WELLINGTON

🏠🏠 ACCOMMODATIONS AND CAMPING

Palmerston North's few budget accommodations and more common motels along Fitzherbert Ave. are far from the standard backpackers' circuit. For a true collegiate experience, you can spend a night in a dorm at **Massey University,** giving you access to cheap dorm food and, for a fee, the university gyms. (☎350 5056; fax 350 5675; k.l.macey@massey.ac.nz. Singles $28.)

PepperTree Backpacker Hostel (YHA), 121 Grey St. (☎355 4054; fax 355 4063; peppertreehostel@clear.net.nz), at the corner of Princess and Grey St. Host Cherie keeps up a standard of excellence that makes PepperTree the best and busiest in town. Off-street parking. Dorms $16; singles $30; twins and doubles $38; tent sites $8.

Ann Keith House, 146 Grey St. (☎358 6928; fax 355 0291; annkeithhouse@backpackersnbnb.co.nz). Comfortable mattresses in antique-furnished rooms provide a good night's sleep. Key deposit $5. Dorms $18.50; singles $30; twins and doubles $45.

Palmerston North Holiday Park, 133 Dittmer Dr. (☎/fax 358 0349). From Fitzherbert Ave. turn on Park Rd. towards the Esplanade, then left on Ruha St., and descend into the park. Park-like, without ever really letting you forget you're in the suburbs. Tent sites $8.50; powered sites for 2 $20; cabins for 2 $28-55.

🍴 FOOD

Knowledge City needs food for thought, and food it has. Anchored by its student population, Palmy has the usual takeaways and fast food chains. **George St.,** home to funky cafes with affordable price tags, is worth a wander. You can stock up at groceries at **Pak 'N Save,** 335 Ferguson St. (open daily 8am-midnight).

Barista, 77 George St. (☎357 2614). A gem on George Street's stretch of cool cafes. Start the day right with Barista's superb coffee ($2.50) and the "heart stopper" ($15), a smorgasbord of all your favorite breakfast goodies. Open daily 6:30am-midnight.

Aqaba, 186 Broadway Ave. (☎357 8922; fax 357 3648). Don't let the decor fool you; the menu holds no national allegiance. Suits, students, and families enjoy tasty dishes ($11-26) in the airy environs. Open M-F 7:30am-late, Sa-Su 9am-late.

Bella's, 2 The Square (☎357 8616). Plates gleam like the shiny floors after you finish with dinner. Affordable delights like Thai chicken curry ($15) and pasta ($10.50) keep Bella's packed with patrons. Open Tu-Sa 11:30am-3pm, also M-Sa 6-10pm.

George Street Deli (☎357 6663), corner of George and Main St. More of a cafe than a deli, squeeze between the colorful walls to witness a stream of hungry folks devouring quality eats. Open daily 6am-6pm.

🎵 NIGHTLIFE

Palmerston North nightlife can get lively during the school year, although "nightlife" is a variable term—on rugby Saturdays, drinking starts at 3pm.

High Flyers, corner of Main St. E and The Square (☎357 5155). At this bar, "where everybody is somebody," a savvy crowd boogies down to DJs Th-Sa. Sports bar and cafe as well. Open daily 11am-3am.

Fat Ladies Arms (☎358 8888), at the corner of Church and Linton St. Despite the rather unpleasant image the name inspires, this bar swarms with a lively university crowd who can't resist the W-Sa DJs or $3 Th drinks. Open Tu-F 4pm-3am, Sa 2pm-3am.

Diablos, 96 Fitzherbert Ave. (☎355 5571), serves a snazzy, well-dressed crowd who rock the Southwest-inspired bar on weekends. F are "Boogie Nights" with retro music plus $10 shakers. Drinks $2.50 Th 9-11pm. DJ Th-Sa. Open daily 11am-late.

Loaded Hog (☎356 5417), at the corner of George St. and Coleman Pl. You can dance, drink, or enjoy $5 breakfasts (Sa-Su 10am-noon) and $5 lunches (M-F 11am-noon). Open M-F 11am-late, Sa-Su 10am-late. Kitchen closes at 10pm.

The Cobb (☎357 8002), in the Empire Hotel at the corner of Princess and Main St. is 3 bars in one: sports, dancing, and chatting. W free pool and jukebox. Handles $3.50. Open M-Sa 8am-3am, Su 10am-late.

◉ 🔰 SIGHTS AND ACTIVITIES

The west side of downtown, beginning with the snazzy new library and cafe at The Square is touted as the cultural center—and nothing says Kiwi culture like sport. Paying homage to the pinnacle of sport, one block north and several west of The Square, is the **New Zealand Rugby Museum**, 87 Cuba St. Quite the shrine for die-hard fanatics of The Game, this two-room gallery is cluttered with uniform displays, trophies, and memorabilia from one of the world's oldest remaining jerseys to the intricate "All Black Stars" quilt made by an enthusiastic fan to commemorate the team's 1995 World Cup run. (☎/fax 358 6947; www.rugbymuseum.co.nz. Open M-Sa 10am-noon and 1:30-4pm, Su 1:30-4pm. $4.) On Saturdays in winter, you can watch the real thing in the **Showgrounds** next door. The beautiful **Victoria Esplanade** (walk down Fitzherbert Ave. and turn right on Manawaroa St.) is a pleasure. With a conservatory, rose garden, paddling pool, and miniature railway, there's something for everyone. (☎356 8199. Open daily 8am-9pm; in winter 8am-6pm.)

For more traditional highbrow pursuits, ignore the oversized bronze beetles creeping over the roof of the **Manawatu Art Gallery**, 398 Main St. W (☎358 8188), and venture inside to view contemporary works by New Zealand artists. Next door is the **Science Centre & Manawatu Museum** (☎355 5000). To gawk in the face of power, the **Tararua Wind Farm,** 11km east of downtown, is located on 700 hectares of private farmland. Wind turbines stand 40m high with blades more than 23m wide, generating all sorts of heat for Palmerstonians. **Explore Manawatu** provides tours of the windfarm daily by appointment. (☎0800 497 567. From $35 per person.) The same company will take you through effervescent **glowworm caves** for $45. **City Rock Adventures,** 55 Taonui St., has indoor **rock climbing** and will organize trips to go abseiling, caving, canyoning, kayaking, or even bridge-swinging. (☎/fax 357 4552. Climbing $8, students $7; other activities from $15. Open daily 10am-10pm.)

WELLINGTON

MARLBOROUGH
AND NELSON

Stretching from Farewell Spit to the tranquil Marlborough Sounds and from the
marine paradise of Kaikoura to the secluded Nelson Lakes, the "top of the south"
provides a variety of natural gems and endless ways to appreciate them. Whether
it's kayaking in the Sounds, soaking in a hot spring, tasting award-winning wine,
swimming with dolphins, or hiking through fern-filled forests, Marlborough won't
bore even the shortest attention spans. Take full advantage of the well-developed
tourism infrastructure, or escape it all in the majestic seclusion of the Sounds.

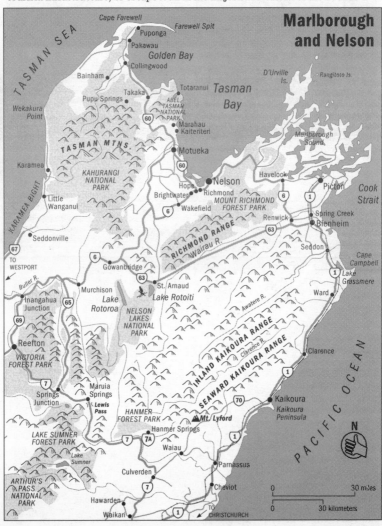

**Marlborough
and Nelson**

Cape Farewell
Puponga
Farewell Spit
Pakawau
Golden Bay
Collingwood

TASMAN SEA

D'Urville Is.
Rangitoto Is.

Bainham
Takaka
Totaranui
Tasman Bay
Pupu Springs
ABEL TASMAN NATIONAL PARK
60
Marahau
Kaiteriteri

Wekakura Point

TASMAN MTNS.
Motueka
60

Karamea
KAHURANGI NATIONAL PARK

Havelock
Marlborough Sound

Hope
Nelson
Brightwater
Richmond
Picton
Cook Strait

Little Wanganui
6
Wakefield
MOUNT RICHMOND FOREST PARK
6
1

KARAMEA BIGHT
Seddonville

Renwick
63
Spring Creek
Blenheim

RICHMOND RANGE
Wairau R.

67
TO WESTPORT

Seddon

Gowanbridge
6
63

Cape Campbell

Buller R.
St. Arnaud
Lake Rotoiti

1
Lake Grassmere

Inangahua Junction
65
Murchison
Lake Rotoroa
NELSON LAKES NATIONAL PARK

Ward
Awatere R.

69

INLAND KAIKOURA RANGE
Clarence R.

Reefton
VICTORIA FOREST PARK

SEAWARD KAIKOURA RANGE
Clarence

7
Maruia Springs
Lewis Pass
70
Kaikoura
Kaikoura Peninsula

Springs Junction

HANMER FOREST PARK
Mt. Lyford

PACIFIC OCEAN

LAKE SUMNER FOREST PARK
7
7A
Hanmer Springs

Lake Sumner
Waiau
1

ARTHUR'S PASS NATIONAL PARK

Culverden
7
Parnassus

N

Hawarden
Cheviot
0   30 miles

Waikari
1
TO CHRISTCHURCH
0   30 kilometers

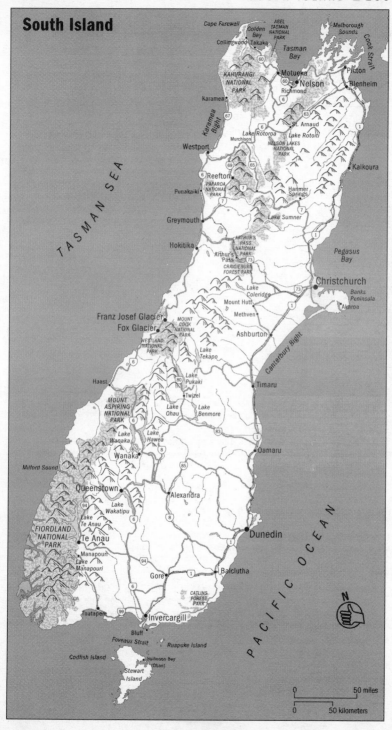

South Island

Cape Farewell

Golden Bay

ABEL TASMAN NATIONAL PARK

Collingwood Takaka

Malborough Sounds

Cook Strait

Tasman Bay

60

Motueka

KAHURANGI NATIONAL PARK

Picton

Nelson

Blenheim

Richmond

6

Karamea

63

St. Arnaud

1

67

Lake Rotoroa

Lake Rotoiti

Karamea Bight

Murchison

NELSON LAKES NATIONAL PARK

Westport

6

Kaikoura

69

6

Reefton

65

PAPAROA NATIONAL PARK

7

Hanmer Springs

Punakaiki

7

Greymouth

Lake Sumner

Hokitika

ARTHUR'S PASS NATIONAL PARK

Pegasus Bay

Arthur's Pass

73

CRAIGIEBURN FOREST PARK

Christchurch

Banks Peninsula

Lake Coleridge

Akaroa

Mount Hutt

73

Franz Josef Glacier

Methven

1

Fox Glacier

MOUNT COOK NATIONAL PARK

Ashburton

WESTLAND NATIONAL PARK

Lake Tekapo

6

80

Lake Pukaki

Timaru

Haast

Twizel

MOUNT ASPIRING NATIONAL PARK

Lake Ohau

Lake Benmore

6

Canterbury Bight

83

1

Lake Wanaka

Lake Hawea

Oamaru

8

Wanaka

85

Milford Sound

Queenstown

Alexandra

94

Lake Wakatipu

8

Lake Te Anau

6

FIORDLAND NATIONAL PARK

Te Anau

Dunedin

Manapouri

Lake Manapouri

94

Gore

Balclutha

1

6

CATLINS FOREST PARK

99

Tuatapere

Invercargill

N

Bluff

Foveaux Strait

Ruapuke Island

PACIFIC OCEAN

Codfish Island

Halfmoon Bay (Oban)

Stewart Island

TASMAN SEA

MARLBOROUGH

0   50 miles

0   50 kilometers

▨ MARLBOROUGH AND NELSON HIGHLIGHTS

IT'S ALL WET in **Kaikoura,** where visitors can swim with dolphins, frolic with seals, and search for surfacing whales (see p. 241).

IT'S ALL AFLOAT in the **Marlborough Sounds,** with many of the best hostels and lodges accessible only by water-taxi (see p. 239).

IT'S ALL ON YOUR BACK... along the **Abel Tasman Coastal Track,** with terrain ranging from verdant rain forest to golden beaches (see p. 363).

OR NOT... along the **Queen Charlotte Track,** where you can have all your bags carried for you (see p. 376).

MARLBOROUGH

PICTON   ☎03

Sitting at the head of the dramatic Queen Charlotte Sound, Picton is often a way station for travelers switching islands or switching gears between traveling and tramping. The first European descendent was born in Picton and it was here that sheep first stepped on kiwi soil. Today, starry-eyed travelers, arriving from Wellington on the Interislander ferry, tread their first path on the South Island.

▮ TRANSPORTATION

Flights: The **Koromiko airstrip** is about 9km away. **Sounds Air** (☎573 6184, 0800 505 005) has daily flights to **Wellington** (25min., up to 9 per day 8:30am-6:15pm; $68) and a free shuttle to and from the airstrip in Picton.

Trains: TranzScenic (☎573 8649, 0800 802 802) offers daily service from Auckland St. to **Christchurch** (5hr., 1:40pm, $77) via **Kaikoura** (2½hr., $42).

Buses: InterCity (☎573 7025) leaves from the ferry terminal for: **Christchurch** (5½hr., 5 times per day, $60) via **Blenheim** (30min., $10) and **Kaikoura** (2¼hr., $35); **Nelson** (2½hr., 4-5 times per day, $30).

Ferries: Interislander Ferry (☎04 498 3303, 0800 802 802) from the **Foreshore** for **Wellington** (3hr., 3-5 per day, $49). **The Lynx** takes just over 2hr. (2 per day, $63).

Taxis: Blenheim Taxi (☎578 0225).

Car Rental: Rent a car from any of the many companies located at the ferry terminal.

▰▰ ORIENTATION AND PRACTICAL INFORMATION

Home to the ferry terminal and other crucial transport links, the whole area lining the harbor is known as the **Foreshore. Auckland St.** is the hub of transport in Picton, while **High St.** is home to **Mariner's Mall** and many of the town's shops and cafes. Residential neighborhoods stretch up into the hills.

Visitors Center: Picton Visitor Information Centre (☎573 8857; fax 573 8858), inside the railway station on Auckland St. near the Foreshore. Open Jan.-Feb. daily 8:30am-8pm; Mar.-Apr. and Oct.-Dec. 8:30am-6pm; May-Sept. 8:30am-5pm. The **DOC office** (☎520 3007) is also inside. Open M-F 8:30am-4:30pm.

Currency Exchange and Banks: BNZ, 56-8 High St. with **ATM.** Open M, Th, and F 9am-4:30pm, Tu and W 9:30am-4:30pm. **Four Square supermarket,** 49 High St. (☎573 6443), will change money after hours. Open daily 7:30am-9pm.

Police: 36 Broadway St. (☎573 6439).

Pharmacy: Rob Roy's Pharmacy, 6 High St. (☎573 6420). Open M-F 9am-6pm, Sa 9am-2pm; extended hours in summer.

Medical Services: Picton Medical Center, 71 High St. (☎ 573 6092; after-hours ☎ 577 1941). Open M-F 8:30am-5:30pm, Sa 9am-noon.

Internet Access: United Video, 61 High St. (☎ 573 7466; open daily 9am-9pm) and the **library,** 67 High St. (☎ 520 3200; open M-Th 8am-5pm, F 8am-5:30pm, Sa 10am-noon) both offer connections for $6 per hr.

Post Office: (☎ 573 6900), Mariner's Mall on High St. Open Oct.-Apr. M-F 8:30am-5pm, Sa 9:30am-12:30pm; May-Sept. M-F 8:30am-5pm, Sa 10am-noon.

ACCOMMODATIONS AND CAMPING

■ **The Villa Backpackers Lodge,** 34 Auckland St. (☎/fax 573 6598), near the intersection with Dublin St. This restored villa goes from charming to stellar—free pick-up, free breakfast, free apple crumble with ice cream every night in the winter, and free use of bicycles and fishing gear. Internet. Spa $2. All you can eat veggie soup during the winter $2. Book in advance. Dorms $18; twins and doubles $46.

■ **Sequoia Lodge (NOMADS),** 3A Nelson Sq. (☎/fax 573 8399, 0800 222 257; stay@sequoialodge.co.nz). This comfortable hostel has recently been renovated. Fresh bread made nightly. Off-street parking. Internet. Free pick-up and delivery. Dorms $16; twins and doubles with bathroom $45.

The Juggler's Rest Backpackers, 8 Canterbury St. (☎/fax 573 5570, jugglersrest.co.nz). The owners (3 professional jugglers) give free workshops. Fire-eating lessons are offered. Free pick-up, tea and coffee, and use of bikes. Dorms $16, in winter $14; twins and doubles with linen $45. Juggle 5 balls and get a $1 discount, 6 balls for $2, 7 balls for $3, juggle 10 for a free night and dinner with the owners.

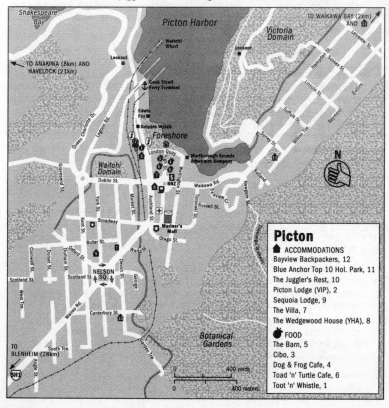

Picton

🏠 ACCOMMODATIONS
Bayview Backpackers, 12
Blue Anchor Top 10 Hol. Park, 11
The Juggler's Rest, 10
Picton Lodge (VIP), 2
Sequoia Lodge, 9
The Villa, 7
The Wedgewood House (YHA), 8

🍎 FOOD
The Barn, 5
Cibo, 3
Dog & Frog Cafe, 4
Toad 'n' Turtle Cafe, 6
Toot 'n' Whistle, 1

MARLBOROUGH

Bayview Backpackers and Lodge, 318 Waikawa Rd. (☎/fax 573 7668; bayview.back-packers@xtra.co.nz). A 4km trek from Picton, you won't find better views anywhere in town. Free kayaks, rowboat, fishing gear, and bread in winter. Free pick-up and delivery. Dorms $16-17; 3-4 person shares $18 per person, with bath from $45 for 2.

Picton Lodge (VIP), 9 Auckland St. (☎573 7788; fax 573 8418). The closest accommodation to the ferry, though it still offers free ferry transpo. Free use of bikes. Internet. Dorms $16; singles $28; twins and doubles $38. VIP $1 off. $1 *Let's Go* discount.

The Wedgewood House (YHA Associate), 10 Dublin St. (☎573 7797; fax 573 6426). The lodge has a large wooden porch and a minuscule kitchen. Free in-room lockers and duvets. Reception 8-10am, 1-2pm, 5-6:30pm, and 8-10pm. Dorms $17; twins $20.

Blue Anchor Top 10 Holiday Park, 78 Waikawa Rd. (☎/fax 573 7212, 0800 277 299, 2stay@blueanchor.co.nz). Clean and modern cabins offer more privacy and comfort. Standard cabins $35-40 for 2, kitchen cabins $48 for 2; units $60-80 for 2, extra adult $15; powered sites $11 per person ($15 for 1); tent village $10 per adult, $6 per child.

▐ FOOD

Picton is small enough to wander, with **High St.** acting as home to a variety of restaurants. **Supervalue** is in the **Mariner's Mall,** chock full of groceries. (☎573 0463. Open M-W 8am-6pm, Th 8am-7:30pm, F 8am-8:30pm, Sa 8am-7pm, Su 9am-5pm.)

Cibo, 33 High St. (☎/fax 573 7171). Sit at the funky carved table and enjoy a rotating menu, which includes tapas ($3.50-12), veggie options, and handmade chocolates. Mains ($12-20). Open daily 9am-8:30pm.

The Barn Cafe & Bar, High St. (☎/fax 573 7440). Country music completes the feel. Veggie options ($8.50-14.50). Open daily 4-10pm in winter, midday-late in summer.

The Dog and Frog Cafe, 22 High St. (☎573 5650), contains a scattering of amphibious statues and canine pictures to complement the all-day breakfast ($10), sweet treats ($5), or fish 'n' chips ($11), depending on your mood. Open daily 8am-8:30pm.

Toad 'n' Turtle Cafe (☎573 7748), on High St. A good place to sit, snack, and read. Serves normal takeaway fare and all-day breakfast. Open daily 7:30am-4pm in summer, until 3pm in winter.

Toot 'n' Whistle, 7 Auckland St. (☎573 6086), near the visitors center. A smoky diner and bar with a friendly, laid-back atmosphere, and a broad menu. All-day breakfast. Meals from $8. Open daily 7am-late; in winter from 9am.

◉ ▓ SIGHTS AND ACTIVITIES

Many visitors to Picton come to tramp the 71km **Queen Charlotte Track** (see p. 376). The trail heads are inaccessible from town by foot, but several transportation services cater to those wishing to approach by boat. **Endeavour Express** will take you to the start of the track and even transfer your pack between the many accommodations that line the trail. (☎579 8465. One-way transport $25, round-trip with 3 free pack transfers $45.) Picton also has some great day hikes which look out over the harbor, Pine Bay, and Waikawa Bay. Cross the parking lot and the footbridge to get to the walks from Wellington Street. The **Victoria Domain** (return 3hr.) leads up to the lookout over the Scenic Reserve and continues out to "The Snout" and the **Queen Charlotte Lookout** (return 4hr.). The **Pelorus Mail Boat** takes along passengers who want to catch a glimpse of everyday life along the rural Pelorus Sound. (☎0800 624 526. 10:15am departure; $58.) Picton retains vestiges of its dignified history all about town. The **Edwin Fox,** the oldest wooden merchant ship in the world, greets arrivals at the Foreshore. Built in 1853 in Calcutta, it transported tea to London, British immigrants to New Zealand, convicts to Australia, and troops to Europe during the Crimean War. Claiming a brief but well-deserved rest in dry dock, it is now an informative exhibit at the **Edwin Fox Maritime Centre** which chronicles the ship's history and details plans for its eventual restoration. (☎573 6868.

Open daily 8:45am-5pm. $5.) Wine connoisseurs can explore the Marlborough region's famous **wineries** by bus through **De Luxe Travel Lines** (☎578 5467, 0800 500 511; $45) or **The Sounds Connection** (☎573 8843, 0800 742 866; $45 half-day, $55 full-day). Or, for those who can hold their liquor, **Wine Tours by Bike** offers a unique two-wheeled perspective on the wine region from nearby Blenheim. (☎577 6954. $35 for half-day bike rental, $50 for full-day, with guide $120 per day.) Mountain bikes and kayaks can also be rented from **Marborough Sounds Adventure Company** at the Waterfront (☎573 6078, 0800 283 283).

MARLBOROUGH SOUNDS ☎03

A grand maze of waterways at the South Island's northeastern extremity, the Marlborough Sounds harbor ample sea life and green peaks amid thousands of beautiful coves. Day activities run from Picton, though the **Queen Charlotte Track** (see p. 376) is the most well-known and well-tramped attraction. Whether you actually backpack, or just relax in one of the lovely and secluded backpackers instead, you will not leave the Marlborough Sounds disappointed.

⊟ TRANSPORTATION. All transport departs from the **Picton Foreshore,** between Wellington St. and the footbridge. **Ferry** services provide the most transport around the Sounds. **The Cougar Line** (☎573 7925, 0800 504 090) departs the Picton town wharf two or three times daily and runs to: **Ship Cove** ($38); **Resolution Bay** ($33); **Endeavor Inlet** ($33); and **Torea Wharf** ($15). **West Bay Water Transport** (☎/fax. 573 5597) runs four times daily from the floating jetty by the ferry terminal to: **Torea Wharf** ($15); **Lochmara Lodge** ($12); **Te Mahia Resort** ($15); and **Anakiwa** ($20). **Endeavour Express** (☎579 8465) operates September to April, departing from the Picton town wharf three times daily to: **Ship Cove** ($30), **Resolution Bay** ($30), and **Endeavor Inlet** ($35, return $60). Some areas in the Sounds are also road-accessible; scenic and sealed 35km **Queen Charlotte Drive** connects Picton and Havelock. *Let's Go* does not recommend it, but **hitchhikers** report that the drive attracts a fair amount of through-traffic, though the same cannot be said of those north-bound routes.

⊞⊟ ORIENTATION AND PRACTICAL INFORMATION. Three distinct sounds and innumerable bays and islands make up the Marlborough Sounds region. Kayakers should keep in mind that some of the islands are private property and that others are human-free wildlife sanctuaries. New Zealand's fifth largest land mass, **D'Urville Island,** is the region's distinctive northern tip. To its south lies **Pelorus Sound,** the largest of the three sounds. It flows into the smallest, **Kenepuru Sound,** which **Havelock** overlooks. **Picton** sits on the easternmost, **Queen Charlotte Sound,** which the ferries navigate on the way to the North Island.

⊟⊟ ACCOMMODATIONS AND CAMPING. DOC maintains 40 **campsites** ($5, under 14 $2.50) throughout the Sounds. Some are near roads and tend to get crowded, while others are accessible only by boat and feel as though they're at the end of the earth. All have toilets and untreated water supplies. *The Marlborough Sounds: A guide to conservation areas* pamphlet ($1), available at area DOC offices, contains a complete listing. Many of the Sounds' best accommodations (**Lochmara Lodge, Noeline's,** and **Homestay Backpackers** among them) lie along the Queen Charlotte Track (see **Queen Charlotte** p. 376), but all are also accessible by water-taxi, road, or both.

One wonderful new exception is ▨**The Chill Inn,** 770 Queen Charlotte Dr., 8km toward Picton from Havelock. Games, guitars, and great music fill the lounge, and a hammock-speckled balcony provides great views over Kenepuru Sound, a 5min. walk away. (☎574 1299, mobile 025 606 2684; thechillinn@hotmail.com. Free shuttle from Havelock or Anakiwa. Internet. Spa. Kayaks. Bikes. Closed July-Aug. Breakfast included. Dorms $19; doubles with linen $50.)

▨ **OUTDOOR ACTIVITIES.** The **Queen Charlotte Track** (3-5 days, 67km) is a popular, mellow walk winding along shimmering inlets of the Sounds (see p. 239). Pampered trampers can stay in trackside hostels and have packs transported by boat (see p. 376). **Sea kayaking** allows the freedom to explore the curving coastline, tranquil inlets, and hidden accommodations, while **mountain biking** gives access to backcountry trails. **Marlborough Sounds Adventure Company** (☎573 6078, 0800 283 283), on the waterfront in Picton, rents single and double kayaks to a minimum of two people (1-day $50 per person, multi-day $35-40 per day per person) and mountain bikes ($50 per day). Their guided kayak trips range from one-day tours ($85, includes lunch) to all-inclusive three-night expeditions ($475). **Sea Kayaking Adventure Tours** (☎574 2765; SKATA@xtra.co.nz), based in Anakiwa, also rents kayaks ($40 per day, $35 per day after 3 days) and mountain bikes ($35 per day) and runs guided kayak trips (1-day $65, 3-day $280). **Sea Kayaking Wilderness Co.** (☎574 2610), based in Havelock, rents kayaks (1-day $50, multi-day $25-45) and conducts guided tours (1-day with lunch $75; multi-day self-catering $95 per day).

Diver's World (☎573 7323), across London Quay from the visitors center, organizes shore dives into the Queen Charlotte Sound ($59 with equipment), two-dive trips to the Mikhail Lermontov wreck ($135, gear hire $50), and Open Water certification courses ($399). **Dolphin Watch Marlborough**, next to the visitors center in Picton, runs ecotours to birdlife sanctuary **Motuara Island** and historic **Ship Cove**, encountering penguins and dolphins along the way. (☎573 8040. Daily 8:45am and 1:45pm; in winter 1:45pm. $65, under 18 $35.) Alternatively, contact **Beachcomber Cruises** (☎573 6175, 0800 624 526), on the Picton Foreshore, to see the Sounds along with the **mail runs** to Queen Charlotte (4hr.; M-Sa 1:30pm; $58, under 15 free) or Pelorus Sound (4-6hr.; Tu, Th, F mid-morning; $90, under 15 free).

BLENHEIM ☎03

Most tourists who flock to Blenheim come to indulge in the region's award-winning wines. Many wineries are open to the public and offer tastings in addition to exquisite food. More frugal travelers in need of work see these same vineyards as a gold mine, seeking vines in need of pruning and grapes in need of plucking. Vineyard work is plentiful, if often grueling; all but the most destitute should avoid working with the painful, prickly boysenberries.

▤ **TRANSPORTATION.** The **railway station**, which also serves as a **bus station**, is located across the river at the end of Alfred St. If you fancy the **train**, **TranzScenic** (☎0800 802 802) goes to **Christchurch** (5hr., 2:10pm, $29-67) and **Picton** (30min., 12:20pm, $14-19). **InterCity** (☎577 2890) heads daily to: **Christchurch** (4½hr., 1:45pm, $26-55) via **Kaikoura** (1¾hr., $15-30); **Nelson** (1¾hr., 1:25pm, $15-22); and **Picton** (30min., 2 per day, $6-8). **Kiwilink** (☎0800 802 300) and **Knightline** (☎547 4733) go to **Nelson** (1¾hr., 4 per day, $17) and **Picton** (30min., 4per day, $7). **Blenheim Taxis** (☎578 0225) provides in-town transport.

▨ **PRACTICAL INFORMATION.** The **Blenheim Information Centre**, 2 High St., can wet visitors' parched lips with a $2 map of the Marlborough wine region. (☎578 9904; fax 578 6084. Open daily 8:30am-6pm; in winter M-F 8:30am-5:30pm, Sa 9am-4pm, Su 9:30am-2:30pm.) Travelers in search of **employment** in Blenheim's busy fruit industry can talk to hostel owners or look in local newspapers. The **DOC field center** (☎572 9100) is on Gee St. in nearby Renwick. Other services include: the **medical center**, 24 George St. (☎578 2174); **police**, 8 Main St. (☎578 5279); and **internet access** at **Internet Direct**, 15 High St. across the street from the visitors center. (☎578 1100; $2.50 per 15min., $8 per hr; open M-F 8:15am-5:15pm). Although the **post office** is technically located at 2 Main Street, the **post shop** is around the corner on Scott St. (Open M-F 8:30am-5:15pm, Sa 9:30am-12:30pm.)

ACCOMMODATIONS AND CAMPING. A new coat of paint and a fresh crop of citrus fruit has left **Koanui Backpackers,** 33 Main St., looking and smelling fantastic. Long-term residents and a helpful owner have the skinny on the best employment opportunities going. (☎/fax 578 7487. Free pick-up and bike use. Reception 7:30am-9:30pm. Dorms $16; singles $30; twins and doubles $40.) To get to **The Grapevine Backpackers,** 29 Park Terrace, follow Main St. and take a left onto Park Terrace. Paddle the free canoes in the adjacent river, or ride a free bicycle to the local vineyards. A house across the street offers more private accommodations for long-term fruit pickers. (☎578 6062. Free pick-up and laundry. Internet. Dorms $15; twins and doubles $32-36; tent sites in summer $10 per person.) A recent addition to the Blenheim budget scene, **Traveller's Rest,** 144 High St., has all of the makings of a choice hostel just getting onto its feet. (☎578 7375. Free pick-up and breakfast. Dorms $18, $105 per week; doubles $50.) **Blenheim Bridge Top Ten Holiday Park,** 78 Grove Rd. (☎/fax 578 3667), has a range of choices for all inclinations and budgets, from completely self-contained tourists flats ($68 for 2; in winter $60), tourist cabins without bath ($50 for 2), standard cabins with communal facilities ($40), and tent sites ($9 per person; powered sites $10, children $5).

FOOD. If paid employment and frugality are the order of the day, Blenheim is a great place to cut back on eating out. The **Supervalue Plus,** on Queen St. in the **Forum,** is an inexpensive option for groceries. (Open M-Tu and Sa 8am-7pm, W-F 8am-8pm, Su 9am-6pm.) The sharp decor at **Tuscany's,** 36 Scott St., accompanies a menu of pasta, seafood, and an all-day breakfast. (☎577 5050. Kitchen open daily 10am-10pm; bar open later.) While the totem pole, scattered cacti, and faux adobe walls are intended to conjure images of the American Southwest, the menu at **Bar Navajo,** on the corner of Maxwell and Queen St., is decidedly Kiwi. All mains, including ribeye steak, hotpot, and local specialty Marlborough mussels, are under $15. (Open M-Th 11am-late, F-Sa 11am-2am.)

GETTING SLOSHED. The Wairau valley is the largest wine-producing region in New Zealand, making Blenheim a great spot to visit a vineyard by bike, car, or taxi, to learn about winemaking and, more importantly, to savor Marlborough in all of its red, white, and rosé splendor. **Wineries** abound, as do different tour and tasting options; the visitors center can help make concrete plans. **Cloudy Bay** (☎520 9140) and **Cairnbrae** (☎572 8018), up Jackson Rd., are two excellent nearby wineries; be sure to taste the award-winning Sauvignon Blanc of Cloudy Bay and the noble Riesling of Cairnbrae. For an organized coach trip, contact **DeLuxe Travel Line.** (☎0800 500 511. Departs 11am, returns 4:30pm. $40.)

KAIKOURA ☎03

Kaikoura's brilliant blue bay and snowcapped peaks are the dramatic setting for a a fully interactive ecological wonderland. Kaikoura (pop. 3,300) means "to eat crayfish" in Maori, and while these crunchy crustaceans can be found paddling beneath the waves, the offshore waters are also replete with fur seals, albatross, dusky dolphins, and whales. The views at dusk are breathtaking and the local tourism industry has worked out every way short of being swallowed by a whale to experience the unique ecology. The varied tours and accommodations fill up early during the summer, so book ahead; the winter scene is markedly more hushed.

TRANSPORTATION

TranzCoastal (☎0800 802 802) has daily train service to **Christchurch** (3hr., 4:05pm, $31-41) and **Picton** (2½hr., 10:25am, $29-42). Kaikoura handles all transport bookings in person at the **visitors center. InterCity** runs to: **Christchurch** (2½hr., 2-6 per day, from $15); **Picton** (2hr., 2-3 per day, from $15); **Nelson** (5hr., 1 per day). At least 4 bus and shuttle companies run daily to **Christchurch** (2½hr., $15-20) and **Picton** (2hr., $15-20). **Hanmer Connection** (☎0800 377 378) also heads to **Hanmer Springs** (2hr.; Tu, Th, and Sa 2:30pm; $30, one-way $25). For taxi service, call **Kaikoura Taxi** (☎319 6214) or **TJ Tours** (☎319 6803, mobile 025 211 8983).

⊞✶⁊ ORIENTATION AND PRACTICAL INFORMATION

Midway between Picton (154km away) and Christchurch (183km away), **SH1** becomes, at various points, **Churchill St., Beach Rd.,** and **Athelney Rd.** Bear right just before Beach Rd. onto the **Westend** (which turns into the **Esplanade** about 1km south), home to most of Kaikoura's shops and accommodations.

The **Kaikoura Visitor Information Centre,** located on the Westend, will store luggage ($1 per day), change money on the weekends, and help with transport and bookings. (☎319 5641; fax 319 6819. Open Sept.-May daily 8:30am-5:30pm; June-Aug. 9am-5pm.) Other services include: **BNZ,** with **ATM,** 42 Westend (open M, Th-F 9am-4:30pm, Tu-W 9:30am-4:30pm); the **police** (☎319 5038); a **hospital** (☎319 5027); a **pharmacy** on Westend (☎319 5035; open M-Th 8:30am-5:30pm, F 8:30am-6pm, Sa 9am-12:30; after hours ☎319 7067); **internet access** at **Kodak Express shop,** on Westend ($8 per hr.; open M-F 9am-6pm, Sa 9am-5pm, Su 9am-5pm, extended hours in summer), and at the **public library** ($8 per hr; open M-Th 9:30am-5:30pm, F 9:30am-7pm, Sa 10am-1pm); a **post office** at 41 Westend (open M-F 8:30am-5:30pm, but W until 6:30pm, Sa until 7pm; extended hours in summer).

⋔⋔ ACCOMMODATIONS AND CAMPING

Most accommodations are located along **Westend, Beach Rd.,** and the **Esplanade** along the beach, while a few others are on the hill overlooking the bay.

▨ **Dolphin Lodge,** 15 Deal St. (☎319 5842; dolphinlodge@xtra.co.nz). A lodge with a quiet and peaceful air. Free spa or hammock with incredible sea and mountain views. Free bicycles, book exchange, and Internet. Bunks $16; doubles $40, with bath $45.

▨ **Dusky Lodge,** 67 Beach Rd. (☎319 5959; fax 319 6929; duskyjack@hotmail.com). A pool table in the entrance area awaits challengers, and a brand-spanking-new deck with spa encourages mountain vista gawking. Free pick-up. Breakfast included in winter. Free bikes. Internet. Book ahead in summer. Dorms $17; twins and doubles $40.

Maui YHA, 270 the Esplanade (☎319 5931; fax 319 6921, yhakaikr@yha.org.nz). The pink, clean, motel-like interior, ocean views, and beguiling manager more than make up for the 20min. hike from town. Storage lockers and small hostel shop available. Dorms $16-18; twins and doubles $40.

Topspot Backpackers, 22 Deal St. (☎319 5540; fax 319 6587). From the visitors center, walk across the street and uphill on Lydia Washington Walkway to Deal St. Popular with 20-something partyers, the loft brings TV-watching to new heights. Free Internet and apple crumble in the winter. Dorms $17; doubles (some with bath) from $45.

Bad Jelly Backpackers, 11 Churchill St. (☎319 5538, fax 319 5539). This homey backpackers offers colorful rooms and a spa out the back. It's a good spot for couples to escape the swinging scenes found elsewhere. Twins/doubles $20 per person.

Adelphi Lodge, (☎319 5141, 0800 472 856; fax 319 6786), on Westend. Right in the middle of town, the lodge's budget accommodations are a little bare, but giant *Far Side* cartoons add a touch of gaiety. Parking, a spa pool, and hammocks out back. Internet. Dorms $16, in winter $12.50; twins and doubles with linen $45/$40.

Kaikoura Top 10 Holiday Park, 34 Beach Rd. (☎/fax 319 5362, 0800 363 638), provides camping facilities. Follow Beach Rd. away from the town center and cross under the railway overpass. Dorms $15; standard cabins for 2 $33, deluxe $40, $12 for extra adult; tourist cabins for 2 $45-48; tent sites $18 for 2, extra person $8.50; powered sites $20 for 2, extra person $10.

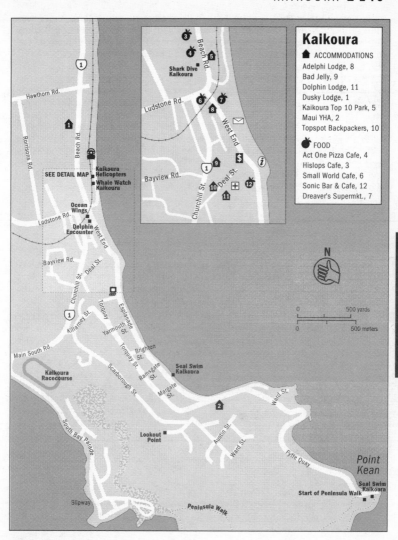

FOOD

Newly renovated, the **Small World Cafe** on Westend seats patrons at beautiful wood bars on swiveling iron chairs that will make your small world spin. Delight in the chicken, beef, lamb, or falafel souvlakis ($5.50-9) and the freshly baked bread and bagels ($2-5). The passionfruit smoothie ($3.50) wins rave reviews. (☎319 7070. Open daily 9am-late; in winter 10am-5pm.) The romantic, candlelit **Act One Pizza Cafe and Bar,** 25 Beach Rd., offers an array of creative gourmet pizzas for all tastes and appetites. Prices range from $11 to $30 for large, exotic pizzas. (☎319 6760. Open daily 5pm-midnight or later.) Pop into the award-winning **Hislops Cafe,** 33 Beach Rd., where all of the produce is organic. Although the main meals are quite pricey ($18.50-25), the sandwiches and pastas ($9.50-15) are more reasonable. (☎319 6971. Open daily 10am-

10pm; in winter Th-M 10am-8:30pm.) With a giant fish seemingly poised to cough Jonah up onto the patrons, **Sonic Bar and Cafe,** 93 Westend, caters to backpackers. Enjoy wallet-friendly pizzas ($8.50-17.50) amid misplaced urban chic. (☎319 6414. Open daily 11am-midnight.) **Dreaver's Supermarket** 31 Westend, has all your grocery needs. (☎319 5333. Open daily 8am-6pm.)

👁️ 🔷 SIGHTS AND ACTIVITIES

DOLPHINS. Weather permitting, ⬛**Dolphin Encounter** gets you into a wetsuit and plops you in the ocean, smack in the middle of a friendly and playful pod of dusky dolphins. The water can be chilly and the frolics exhausting, but the being circled and investigated by sleek dolphins is unmatched. Bring a towel and warm, wind-resistant clothes. *(58 Westend. ☎319 6777; 0800 733 365; www.dolphin.co.nz. $95, spectators $48. Book well in advance; waits can be as long as 2-4 weeks in the high season.)*

SEALS. A highlight of Kaikoura is the **Point Kean seal colony,** where visitors can literally walk among the seals. The reef off the coast is a major breeding site for fur seals and is busiest during the breeding season (Nov.-Feb.), although the seals are present year-round. The seals are relatively accustomed to humans, but stay at least 5m from them. After strolling among the seals, there is no better way to view the entirety of the colony and the beauty of the bay than the **Peninsula Walkway,** which explains the history of the peninsula along the way. If you elect to follow the cliff route, prepare for hurdling turnstiles and getting chummy with the local livestock (the route crosses private farmlands at times). If you want to travel the shoreline route, which allows you to see more seals and explore local tide pools on the limestone (be careful; the rocks are slippery), check the visitors center first; the walk is best enjoyed within 2hr. of low tide. *(Colony 1hr. walk down the Esplanade from the visitors center. Return 3hr.)* If you just can't get enough of the stinky bastards, **Ohau Point** is the main breeding site on the Kaikoura Coast. DOC has set up a viewing platform overlooking the scores of sunning fur seals. *(24km north of Kaikoura off the main highway.)* **Seal Swim Kaikoura** operates land-based seal snorkeling from November to April. *(☎319 6182; mobile 025 886 235. 2½ hr., $40.)* **New Zealand Sea Adventures** runs a similar trip by boat from September to May. *(85 Westend. ☎319 6622, 0800 728 223. $50, viewing $25.)* Other seal snorkeling tours include **Topspot Backpackers** with guided, up-close kayak encounters through **Seal Kayak Kaikoura** *(Topspot 2hr., daily Nov.-Apr., $40. Seal Kayak half-day trips available all year; leaves from visitors center; ☎319 5641, mobile 025 201 3298; $55.)*

SHARKS. If coming face to face with ocean life sounds like sissy stuff, try to catch a glimpse of a shark with **Shark Dive Kaikoura;** there's nothing like it. *(☎319 6888, 0800 225 297. 3hr., cage time 10min.; daily Nov.-Apr.; $110, with all equipment provided. No scuba experience necessary.)*

WHALES. Whale Watch Kaikoura conducts information-packed tours of waters filled with whales, seals, royal albatrosses, and gulls. They offer a refund of up to 80% if no whales are seen during the trip. In June and July, keep an eye out for humpback whales; in summer, look for orca instead. *(At the old "whaleway" station. ☎319 6767, 0800 655 121; www.whalewatch.co.nz. 3½hr. $99.50, ages 3-15 $60. No children under 3. Book 1-2 weeks ahead in summer, 3-4 days in winter. Anti-seasickness wristbands provided.)* **Wings Over Whales** operates year-round aerial whale-watching tours with a short lesson on the magnificent sperm whales before takeoff. The flight also provides a beautiful view of the coastline and mountains. *(☎319 6580, 0800 226 629. 30min. flights $99, children $60, children under 5 free. Transport to airfield $5.)* If you'd rather hover over the whales (which may make photo ops easier), **Kaikoura Helicopters** will help you do just that *(☎319 6609; after hours 319 6359; mobile 025 372 300; www.worldof-whales.co.nz. 30-40 min. trips; $150-$230.)*

SEABIRDS. Albatross Encounters combines with **Ocean Wings** to run a 2-3hr. boat trip to view Kaikoura's pelagic (ocean-going) bird life. Feathers unruffled by the presence of humans, small seabirds and giant albatross flock, squawk, and tustle within arm's reach over pieces of fish liver tossed overboard. More than 15 different species of bird, as well as dolphins and seals are sighted. *(☎319 6777, 0800 733 365; www.oceanwings.co.nz. $60, children $30. Book at Dolphin Encounter.)*

KAYAKING. Paddle away with **Sea Kayak Kaikoura** to float into sheltered bays with nearly 100% visibility, even when the rest of Kaikoura is overcast. *(Mobile ☎025 201 3298. 2 trips per day; half-day $55, children $35.)*

WALKS. The circular **Hinau Track** and **Fyffe-Palmer Track** are steep but manageable; you may see a black-eyed gecko or the world's heaviest insect, the giant weta. *(Hinau starts 15km from town, return 45min. Fyffe-Palmer starts 6km from town, return 2hr.)*

HORSE TREKS. If you prefer land-based mammals to sea-going ones, take a ride up through the foothills and over some farmland with **Fyffe View Horse Treks.** Trips are offered to the experienced and inexperienced alike, but riders must be over 12. *(☎319 5069; mobile 025 353 904. 2hr., $40.)* **Lake View Horse Treks** (☎319 5997) and **Ludley Horse Treks** (☎319 5978) offer treks over farmland and beach areas.

SKIING. For ski addicts, **Mt. Lyford** is a mere 60km from Kaikoura. Graham from Seal Swim can provide transportation to the ski-fields (☎319 6182). For a day excursion from Kaikoura including ski hire, field pass, and transport, inquire at the visitors center. *(☎315 6178. Open June-Oct. Day pass $40, university students $35, high school students $25. Ski hire $15-25, snowboard hire $40, combo package including transport, ski hire and lift pass $80.)*

HANMER SPRINGS
☎03

The rare combination of converging faultlines and connected underground fractures brings Hanmer Springs (pop. 600) to geothermal life. Frown lines melt away in the thermal springs at the center of this small resort town, where shivering skiers from the nearby slopes and bone-weary jetboaters flock to unwind in the steaming waters. After drying off, the relaxation therapy can continue with soothing walks through the gentle surrounding hills and shadowy peaks. Or, try one of the many adventure activities surrounding the area to recharge your adrenaline.

▐ TRANSPORTATION. Some coach transport does not enter Hanmer proper, but instead deposits riders at the **Hanmer Turnoff** (10km from the village); inquire before booking. Both the **Hanmer Connection** (☎315 7575, 0800 377 378) and **Lazerline** companies drive into the main town. Coming by **Southern Link** (☎358 8355) bus from the West Coast via Lewis Pass, you will probably be dropped off at the **Hanmer Turnoff**; arrange for a $5 pick-up on M, W, F, Su from **Hanmer Connection.** To get out of town, **Hanmer Connection** runs to **Christchurch** (2hr.; daily 5pm, extra service F and Su; $25 one-way) and **Kaikoura** (2hr.; Tu, Th, and Sa; $30 one-way) from their station on Amuri Ave. **Lazerline** (☎0800 220 001) runs to **Christchurch** ($19) and **Nelson** ($35) upon request.

▐▐ ORIENTATION AND PRACTICAL INFORMATION. Hanmer Springs is about 10km off SH7 and 136km north of Christchurch. The **Hurunui Visitor Information Centre,** 42 Amuri Ave., sits to the side of the thermal pools. (☎315 7128, 0800 442 663. Open daily 10am-5pm.) Other local services include: **BNZ** in the visitors center (☎314 7220; open M-F 10am-2pm); an **ATM** in the exit from the thermal pools (open daily 9am-9pm); the **Four Square supermarket,** in the Conical Hill Rd. shopping center, containing a small **post office** (☎315 7190; open M-F 8:30am-6pm, Sa 9am-5pm, Su 10am-4pm); the **Hanmer Springs Medical Centre** (☎315 7503; open M-F 9am-12:30pm and 2:30-4:30pm); the **ambulance** (☎0800 222 600); and **after hours medical help** (☎315 7503).

MARLBOROUGH

▐▌ ACCOMMODATIONS AND FOOD. Only a couple of budget accommodations are within walking distance of the pools. **Kakapo Backpackers,** 14 Amuri Ave., a clean, though somewhat bare hostel can snuggle 14 people, and a new addition is on the way. (☎/fax 315 7472; stay-kakapo@xtra.co.nz. Dorms $16, doubles/twins $40.) The lodge-like **Hanmer Backpackers,** 41 Conical Hill Rd., a 5min. walk past the thermal reserve on the right, houses guests in a loft and an insulated aluminum house out back. It's all in the family as the lounge and kitchen area are shared with the backpackers' owners. The backpackers lacks central heating, so be prepared for a chilly night. (☎ 315 7196. Dorms $15; doubles $36.) **Mountain View Top 10 Holiday Park,** on the corner of Bath St. and Hanmer Springs Rd., is the most conveniently located motor camp, about an 8min. walk out of town. (☎ 315 7113; fax 315 7118. Cabins with communal kitchen $35, extra person $12; tourist cabins for 2 with kitchens $45; tent sites for 2 $18; powered sites for 2 $20.) Best food options cluster around the small shopping center in town. **Jollie Jack's Cafe & Bar** is the standout among them, offering tasty meals for $13.50-22. (☎ 315 7388; fax 315 7381. Open daily 11am-11pm.)

▐▌ OUTDOOR ACTIVITIES. Hanmer's main attraction is never hard to find; if the smell of sulfur isn't enough, follow the plumes of steam to the ▨**Hanmer Springs Thermal Reserve,** on Amuri Ave. Prove your superhuman powers of endurance in the 42°C pool, or pull a Goldilocks and try each of the 14 different public pools until you find one that's just right; Baby Bear never had it this good. (☎ 315 7511. Open daily 10am-9pm. $8, return entry $11, waterslide $5 extra.) The **Hanmer Springs Health, Body, and Mind** center next to the pools provides the icing on the cake with indulgent package deals for facials, manicures, or massages. (☎ 315 7567, 0800 873 529. $30-95. Open 11am-7:30pm.)

Adventure options abound at **Rainbow Adventures** from canyoning (2hr., $42), to rafting (half-day $60, full-day $98), to paragliding ($135), as long as you hit Hanmer between October and May. (☎ 315 7401. Closed in winter.) For year-round thrills, **Thrillseekers Adventure Centre** (☎ 315 7046), at the Historic Ferry Bridge, takes advantage of the Waiau River's natural splendor by offering bungy jumping above it ($99), jetboat rides down it (30min., $69), and rafting through its steep-sided gorge ($69). Book directly by phone or at their office outside the town shops. Transport will be arranged. **Rainbow Horse Trekking** leads experienced and novice riders over the hills. (☎ 315 7444. 1-6hr., $35-150.)

Short walks, day-hikes, and serious traimps run directly out of, or near, Hanmer Springs. The **Woodland Walk** (45min.), **Forest Walk** (1hr.), **Conical Hill Walk** (1hr.), and **Waterfall Track** (3hr.) are the most popular; many treks can be combined for longer excursions. Checking in with the visitors center for track conditions and maps is strongly encouraged. To explore on a bike, **Dust-n-Dirt,** 20 Conical Hill Rd., hires mountain bikes and offers trail maps. (☎/fax 315 7233. Half-day $22, full-day $28.)

In winter, hit the slopes at the **Hanmer Springs Ski Area,** a 45min. drive (with $10 toll) from town. With some runs groomed for smooth skiing and others left untouched, it's hardly a surprise that its nickname is "the friendly field." (☎ 315 7233, after hours 025 221 1568. Tow fees $34, students $23, under 18 $17. Ski hire $20-30, snowboard and boots $45.) Call **Hanmer Springs Ski Field Transport** for a ride. (☎ 315 7401. Return $20.) A bit farther from town (75min.), **Mt. Lyford Ski Field** is but preferred by novice snowboarders. (☎ 315 6178. Tow fees $40, university student $35, high school student $25. Skis $25, snowboard and boots $40.)

NELSON ☎ 03

Home to the country's first game of rugby, the first 8hr. working day in the world, and the oldest New Zealand railway, Nelson (pop. 55,000) is the geographic center of the country and a popular domestic holiday destination. Nelson is surprisingly on top of modern social trends for a city its size, with a stylish movie theater, bustling coffee houses, and a wide range of dining, shopping, and activities. The clay in the area is particularly suited for pottery (traded throughout the South Pacific), making Nelson a haven for sculptors. Nelson's art scene reaches its zenith with the **Wearable Art Awards** every September, but the scores of artisan dens and studios maintain the creative spirit year-round.

TRANSPORTATION

Flights: The **airport** is located past the Tahunanui Beach area. **Air New Zealand Link** (☎0800 767 767) flies daily to **Christchurch** (50min., 2-5 per day, $79-285) and **Wellington** (35min., 8-12 per day, $64-219). **Origin Pacific** (☎0800 302 302) covers the same routes, often for less. Inquire about student fares.

Buses: All buses leave from the visitors center; inquire about hostel pick-ups. **InterCity** (☎548 1539) heads daily to **Fox Glacier** (11hr., 7:30am, $73-97) via **Westport** (4hr., $35-47), and to **Picton** (2hr., 10am, $20-27) via **Blenheim** (1½hr., $17-22). You can also take the bus to Blenheim and transfer to **Christchurch** (8½hr., $42-54). **Lazerline** (☎0800 220 001) and **White Star/Southern Link** (☎546 8687) also go daily to **Christchurch** (7½hr., 9 and 9:40am, $35-40) via **Springs Junction** (3½hr., $20-23). White Star makes it possible to transfer at Springs Junction for **Westport** (6hr., $27). **Atomic Shuttles** (☎573 7477) also goes to **Westport** (10am, $30). **Wadsworth Motors** (☎522 4248) is significantly cheaper but longer (3½hr.; M, W, and F 10am; $12) than Atomic Shuttles (10am, $20) to get to **St. Arnaud.** To get to **Abel Tasman National Park,** call **Abel Tasman Coachlines** (☎548 0285) or **Kahurangi Bus Service** (☎525 9434). Prices and times vary according to destination (1½-4hr., 3 per day, $13-29).

Taxis: Nelson City Taxis (☎548 8225, 0800 108 855) and Sun City Taxis (☎548 2666, 0800 422 666) run **24hr.**

Car Rental: Pegasus Rental Cars Nelson, 83 Haven Rd. (☎548 0884, 0800 803 580) or **Omega** (☎0800 277 447). Cars average $35-40 per day on rentals of 4+ days.

Bicycle Rental: Stewarts Cycle City, 114 Hardy St. (☎548 1666). Half-day $15, full-day $20. Open M-F 8am-5:30pm, Sa 9am-1pm. Open later in the summer.

NELSON

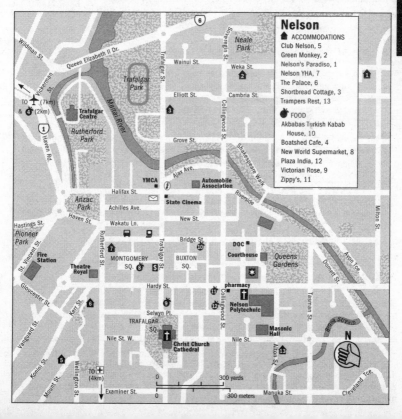

⚡ ORIENTATION

While the Nelson suburbs reach far into the hills, Nelson proper is very compact. **Christ Church Cathedral**, on Trafalgar St., dominates central Nelson and stands tall above its surrounding gardens. **Trafalgar, Bridge,** and **Hardy St.** comprise the main shopping district and enclose a plethora of shops, accommodations, and restaurants. From the bus depot, take a left onto Bridge St. and you'll hit Trafalgar St.

🛈 PRACTICAL INFORMATION

Visitors Center: Nelson Visitor Centre (☎548 2304; fax 546 7393), at the corner of Trafalgar and Halifax St., a 10min. walk on Trafalgar St. from the cathedral steps. Open daily 8:30am-5:30pm; in winter M-F 8:30am-5pm, Sa-Su 9am-5pm.

DOC: 186 Bridge St. (☎546 9335), in the Monro State Building. In the summer, DOC provides information at the visitors center. Open M-F 8am-4:30pm.

Currency Exchange: All major banks with **ATMs** on Trafalgar St.; open M-F 9am-4:30pm.

American Express: (☎548 9079). Travel service representative at 153 Trafalgar St.

Camping Equipment: Rollo's BBQ and Camping Centre, 12 Bridge St. (☎548 1975). Open M-F 8am-5:30pm, Sa 9am-1:30pm; Sa until 4pm in summer.

Police: (☎546 3840), on St. John St. in central Nelson.

Medical Services: Prices Pharmacy, 296 Hardy St. (☎548 3897), at Collingwood St. Open M-F 8:30am-8pm, Sa-Su 9am-8pm. **Nelson Hospital** (☎546 1800) on Tipahi St., open **24hr. City Care,** 202 Rutherford St. (☎546 8881), has a doctor on duty **24hr.**

Internet Access: Boots Off, 53 Bridge St. (☎546 8789), near the bus terminal, has a slew of terminals. $6 per hr. Open daily 9am-9pm; in winter daily 10am-7pm.

Post Office: 108 Trafalgar St. Open M-F 7:45am-5pm, Sa 9:30am-12:30pm.

🏠 ACCOMMODATIONS AND CAMPING

Maybe it's something in the water, but outstanding hostels just keep popping up in Nelson. As a general rule, the smaller hostels are lovely homestyle accommodations, whereas the larger backpackers compensate for their lack of intimacy with freebies and facilities. Some of Nelson's hostels close for part of the winter season, but are filled to overflowing during the summer.

■ **The Green Monkey,** 129 Milton St. (☎545 7421). Warm colors permeate the bedrooms and front and back gardens beg for summer BBQ. Thoughtful extras like individual reading lights in dorm rooms attest to the extensive budget travel experience of the owners themselves. Linens provided. Dorms $18; double with TV $46.

■ **Trampers Rest and Wheelpacker,** 31 Alton St. (☎545 7477; fax 548 7897), on one of Nelson's heritage streets. Book ahead to reserve one of six spots in one of the South Island's best hostels. Quiet and homey, the Rest offers fresh herbs for tea and a grand selection of music for the piano in the living room. Dorms $17; doubles $40.

Nelson's Paradiso, 42 Weka St. (☎546 6703; fax 546 7533). If a sauna, spa, swimming pool, and volleyball court sound like a smashing recipe for a good time, call the Paradiso for a free pick-up (it's a 15min. walk from town). Free breakfast and vegetable soup served in the winter. Internet. Dorms $17; twins and doubles $44.

Nelson YHA, 59 Rutherford St. (☎545 9988; fax 545 9989). Spotless rooms, real sheets, and a cheerful staff. A location that is ideal for exploring Nelson's nightlife. Internet. Reception 8-10am and 3-9:30pm. Dorms $20; singles $35; doubles and twins $50; doubles with bath $70. Nonmembers $3 more.

The Palace, 114 Rutherford St. (☎548 4691; fax 548 4658). Tops in Nelson in more ways than one, The Palace occupies a magnificent hilltop historic home and waylays travelers with its friendly vibe, city views, and 24hr. spa. Reception 8am-9pm. Internet. Dorms $17; doubles $34-40. Cash only.

Club Nelson, 18 Mount St. (☎ 548 3466), up the Wellington St. hill. Multiple lounges, clusters of citrus trees, a swimming pool, tennis courts, and even a basketball court make wonderful use of the backpackers' 4-acre grounds. Reception 8-11am and 2-8pm. Dorms $16; singles $32; twins $39; doubles $40; tent sites $12.

Shortbread Cottage, 33 Trafalgar St. (☎ 546 6681), is a worthwhile 4min. walk from the center of town. The bright cozy cottage is *actually* surrounded by a white picket fence. Fresh shortbread baked almost daily sweetens the already sweet deal. Free pickup. Dorms $18; doubles with TV $45. Call ahead, the 12 beds fill fast.

Tahuna Beach Holiday Park, 70 Beach Rd., Tahunanui (☎ 548 5159, 0800 500 501; fax 548 5294). With its own store, function center, mini-golf course and highway system, all this huge 54-acre facility is missing is its own government. Hundreds of tent and powered sites ($19-20) and an incredible variety of cabins and motels ($28-80, in winter $25-72) are often booked out in summer. Reception 8am-9:30pm.

▐ FOOD

Many of Nelson's restaurants, cafes, and takeaways are located on Trafalgar, Bridge, and Hardy St., though several seafood restaurants along the oceanfront, on Wakefield Quay, can be reached by taxi ($5), bus ($2), or car. If you're in a rush, a $5 falafel from the **kebab cart** which parks on the corner of Hardy and Trafalgar is ⸱ ;at meal on the run. Collect supplies at **New World,** Montgomery Sq. (☎ 548 ⸱ 1; open M-F 8am-9pm, Sa 8:30am-7pm, Su 9am-7pm).

Plaza India, 132 Collingwood St. (☎ 546 9344). The decor is unexciting but traditional Indian mains are reasonably priced ($11-13). Licensed. BYO wine. Open for lunch M-Sa 11am-2:30pm and for dinner daily 5:30pm-late.

Akbabas Turkish Kebab House, 130 Bridge St. (☎ 548 8825). A small restaurant and takeaway with low tables and floor pillows that make for social dining. Spicy chicken kebab in a pita $6.50, large $8.50; falafels $5, large $6.50. Open daily 11am-9:30pm; in winter until 8:30pm.

Boat Shed Cafe and Restaurant, 350 Wakefield Quay (☎ 546 9783), on the oceanfront (a taxi ride away). Highly recommended by locals, the old, converted boat shed practically sitting on the ocean is known for fresh seafood with a great view on the side, try the seafood chowder ($10). The meals can get expensive, but this is definitely the place to splurge. Licensed. Open daily 9am-2:30pm, dinner from 6pm.

Victorian Rose, 281 Trafalgar St. (☎ 548 7631). Probably the most recognized joint in town, many pub meals can be had for $9-13. The Sunday roast ($12.50) is an all-you-can-eat affair with soup and dessert included (from 5:30pm). Look for a coupon granting 10% off all meals. Kitchen open daily 11am-9:30pm.

▐ CAFES

Cafes in Nelson are really about two things: the sun and the scene. Luckily it is easy to soak up both without emptying your wallet.

▨ **Lambretta's,** 204 Hardy St. (☎ 545 8555). A classy slice of Italy, this cafe buzzes with the chatter of all ages. The menu is a mix of light counter meals and reasonably-priced mains (small pizza $10.50). Licensed. Open daily 9am-late; in winter closed Su.

Chez Eelco, 296 Trafalgar St. (☎ 548 7595). The mellow vibe spills out of this earthy cafe and onto its sunny patio, which is just far enough from downtown to be restful. Coffee $3-4; light snacks $5-8. Coin-operated Internet. Open daily 7am-7pm.

Zippy's, 276 Hardy St. (☎ 546 6348), between Hope and Collingwood St. The regular menu includes topped bagels (from $4.50), spirulina fruit smoothies ($3.50). Die-hard carnivores steer clear—nothing on Zippy's menu contains meat. Open M-Sa 9am-6pm, Su 10am-4pm. Cash only. BYO.

Broccoli Row Cafe, 5 Buxton Sq. (☎548 9621). For $9 you can get a full lunch in a garden setting. Savoury soups and hulking slices of quiche $6-9. Open M-Sa noon-7pm.

Penguino Ice Cream Cafe, 85 Montgomery Sq. (☎545 6450). Fresh Italian gelato is made daily on the premises of this vintage ice cream parlour. The 18 flavours change regularly. Open daily in summer.

♫ ▣ ENTERTAINMENT AND NIGHTLIFE

Nightlife in Nelson is really hit or miss—some nights you will have to fight your way into local bars, while others involve seemingly endless and unsuccessful scoping for the in-crowd. Local bars often have live bands, theme nights, or drink deals, especially on weekends; check the listings outside each establishment.

A definite party, every September, the **Montana New Zealand Wearable Art Awards,** in Nelson's Trafalgar Centre, churn out human spectacles. For judges, gawkers, and their own entertainment, contestants design themselves as everything from wispy, gauze dragonfly beauties and surreal spiked cyberpunks to jellyfish swathed in gyrating colors. Tickets sell out as early as six months in advance. Call **Everyman Records,** 249 Hardy St. (☎548 3083), to reserve yourself a slot.

If sobriety is the order of the day (or night), Nelson also offers a four-screen cinematic experience at the **State Cinemas** (☎548 8123), corner of Trafalgar and Halifax St., across from the visitors center. Tickets are $7 before 5pm (and all day Tuesday) and $10 in the evenings; student discounts are available on weeknight shows ($8.50). Buy your tickets in advance, especially on weekends. The **Suter Cinema** (☎548 0808) screens less mainstream movies; call for titles and showtimes.

Victorian Rose, 281 Trafalgar St. (☎548 7631). This popular restaurant (see **Food** above) also attracts a sizeable crowd to its bar, especially after work. Don't let the delicate English name fool you, crowds frequently gather to celebrate (or mourn) the outcome of the most recent rugby game. Open daily 11am-late.

Royal Hotel and O'Reilly's Bar, 152 Bridge St. (☎546 9279). So Irish, this pub even has green lighting. Irish jam nights are not to be missed (Tu 8pm). Handles $3-4. Open daily 11am-midnight, until 3am weekends.

Molly Maguire's Irish Bar, 123 Bridge St. (☎548 1457), acts as Nelson's favorite local; sooner or later the whole town seems to pass through. Molly's showcases the earthier side of Nelson. Open W-Sa 5pm-late.

Shark Club (☎546 6630), upstairs on the corner of Trafalgar and Hardy St. If pool tables and a nightclub appeal, cruise with the youngest crowd in town. Free pool daily 5-7pm. Backpacker drink deals and specials. Open M-Sa 3pm-late.

Artery (☎546 6918), on New St., under the funky sculpture. Hosts local concerts and raves; the schedule changes frequently. Prices vary from free on up.

◉ ▣ SIGHTS AND ACTIVITIES

The best way to groove with the many faces of Nelson is to wander among them at Nelson's weekly **flea market.** Held Saturday and Sunday mornings (8 or 9am-1pm) in the Montgomery Sq. carpark, the market offers local crafts, a wide selection of art, fresh produce, food vendors and much more (including a selection of the trendiest local activists).

ADVENTURE ACTIVITIES. Most backpackers to Nelson only have eyes for one thing—**Abel Tasman National Park** (see p. 254). In fact, it is quite easy to use the city as a base from which to take a variety of trips. If you came to sea kayak, both **Abel Tasman Kayaks** (☎0800 527 802) and **Ocean River** (☎527 8266, 0800 732 529) provide pick-up in Nelson for guided trips; many other companies will do the same. Additionally, transport from Nelson to various trailheads along the Coastal Track can be arranged (see **Essentials: Transportation** p. 39for full details).

Several different adventure options provide a look at Nelson's wild side without venturing so far north. **Stonehurst Farm Horse Treks** (☎542 4121) offers a variety of 1-4hr. adventures, including the Rambler Trail through scenic farmland (1hr., $30) and the longer RiverRide, which includes afternoon tea (half-day, 1:30pm, $69). New in 2002 is a **Skywire ride,** a zipline, which sends you and three of your nearest and dearest hurtling down the longest 1.6km of your life ($85). **Happy Valley 4x4 Motorbike Adventures** (☎545 0304) offers four-wheel motorbike excursions, such as the Farm Forest (1hr., $45) or the Bay-View Tour (2½hr., $75), both of which see Matai trees that are 40m tall and over 2000 years old. For the aquatically-minded, **Sail Tasman** can treat you to a Wednesday evening race cruise in the Nelson Harbour, or a 3-day excursion by boat to Abel Tasman. (☎548 2754. 3hr. cruise $40-45. 3-day trip $325, includes food, beach visits and short hikes. Book in advance.)

"Adrenaline dealers" **Natural High,** 52 Rutherford St., hire mountain bikes, guide bike tours, kayak trips to Abel Tasman, and rent tramping gear. (☎546 6936. Bikes half-day $15, tours from $36. Guided sea kayaking trips from $80.) See the scenery while paragliding with **Nelson Paragliding.** (☎544 1182. Tandem flight $110.) **Tandem Skydive Nelson** provides a more daring option, often taking the plunge over the Abel Tasman. (☎528 4091, 0800 422 899. From 3000m, $210; from 4000m, $260.)

TOURS. To get up close and personal with Nelson's various creators and producers, head out of town by car or tour bus (walking isn't really feasible). **JJ's Wine Tours** offers the full booze tour, hitting several local wineries, breweries, and distilleries. (☎544 7081. Half-day $50.) **Nelson Day Tours** covers a range of local highlights, including the city district and several wineries and craft centers. (☎548 4224. 3-4hr., $45.) They also run trips to Golden Bay (from $85) and Lake Rotoiti (from $65) on demand. Stop by **McCashin's Brewery,** 660 Main Rd. (☎547 0526), in Stoke, about 15min. outside Nelson. Tours run at 11am (and 2pm in summer) for a mere $5 fee. Their product, **Mac's Beer,** is a local favorite, made at the brewery without chemicals or preservatives in a distinctive bottle. Continuing on SH6, at the corner of the Richmond Bypass, you'll find **Craft Habitat** (☎/fax 544 7481). Watch the artisans at work, as some weave rich wool while perfect their jewelry or pottery. From SH6, turning right on Queen St. in Richmond then left on Lansdowne Rd. will bring you to the **Höglund Art Glassblowing Studio,** where two galleries display glass. (☎544 6500. Open daily from 9am to 5pm. Free.)

OTHER SIGHTS AND ACTIVITIES. If you have a hankering for a fowl-free picnic, head to **Anzac Memorial Park,** off Rutherford St., or to the **Miyazu Japanese Garden,** on Atawhai Dr. near the water. Otherwise, the Victorian **Queens Gardens** has plenty of bold birds guarding entrances on Hardy St. and Bridge St. **Suter Art Gallery,** next to Queens Gardens, on Bridge St., is a public art museum with a strong collection of New Zealand and local art, as well as a craft shop, cinema theater, and restaurant. (☎548 4699. Open daily 10:30am-4:30pm. $2, students $0.50.) A mixture of industrial and Gothic architecture, **Christ Church Cathedral** sits atop Church Hill on Trafalgar St.

The best guide to Nelson's natural history is *Walk Nelson*, a brochure which outlines 30 local walks ($4); the pamphlet is available from the Nelson City Council office, 110 Trafalgar St. (Open M-F 8am-4:30pm.) The steep **Centre of New Zealand Walk** will get you close, to the center of New Zealand. (Return 40min.; begins in the Botanic Gardens.) The **Maitai River Walkway** (return 4hr.) will take you along the river, past a wishing well into the countryside. The fine sands of **Tahunanui Beach** ("shifting sands") make it a popular holiday destination; it's accessible by bike down Wakefield Quay, which turns into Rocks Rd. (20-30min.).

NELSON

NELSON LAKES NATIONAL PARK ☎ 03

Pristine byways pass through evergreen beech forests, mountains, and tussock grasslands surrounding Lake Rotoiti and Lake Rotoroa. In winter, nearby slopes are a haven for skiers and the tracks draw visitors in the summer. The gateway to the park is the lakeshore village of **St. Arnaud,** which sits on the moraine of the glacier that originally formed Lake Rotoiti. Unfortunately, the main attractions of Nelson Lakes National Park are living on borrowed time. The harsh elements in the area are eroding the mountains and depositing the sediment into the lakes, dooming the region to one day be a vast flatland.

AT A GLANCE	
AREA: 102,000 hectares.	**GATEWAYS:** St. Arnaud.
CLIMATE: Temperate beech-forest.	**CAMPING:** Huts on the tracks, and several campgrounds at Lake Rotoiti.
FEATURES: Lakes Rotoiti and Rotoroa, Mt. Arnaud.	**FEES & RESERVATIONS:** Huts on first-come, first-served basis are $10 per night.
HIGHLIGHTS: The Travers-Sabine circuit, skiing on Mt. Arnaud.	

TRANSPORTATION. Sounds to Coast shuttle service (☎0800 802 225) drives to **Picton** (1¾hr.; M, W, F 4:30pm; $20) via **Blenheim** (1¼hr., $15). **Atomic Shuttles** (☎573 7477) runs to **Nelson** (12:30pm, $20). **Wadsworth Motors** (☎522 4248) makes the trip for less as part of a lengthy mailrun (2½hr.; M, W, F 1:10pm; $12). Coaches depart from the **Nelson Lakes Village Centre. Nelson Lakes Transport** (☎547 5912; fax 547 5914) and **JJ Ski Transport** (☎544 7081) offer daily transport to **Rainbow Ski Area** (45min.-1hr., 8-8:30am, $15-20) and **Nelson** (1½hr., 4 or 5pm, $20-30). Coaches depart from the **Nelson Lakes Village Centre.**

WHEN TO GO. Nelson Lakes National Park can get very cold in winter—be sure to bring adequate clothing and equipment if you plan on doing winter hiking. While the Park is gorgeous in summer, huts can quickly fill up.

PRACTICAL INFORMATION. The **DOC headquarters** in **St. Arnaud,** on View Rd. off SH63, also serves as the **Nelson Lakes sNational Park Visitors Centre.** (☎521 1806; fax 521 1896. Open daily 8am-4:30pm.) The **petrol station, post office,** and **general store** are all at the **Nelson Lakes Village Centre.** (☎521 1854. Open daily 8:30am-6:30pm.)

ACCOMMODATIONS AND CAMPING. Sleeping options are slim in St. Arnaud. The bright **Yellow House (YHA Associate),** 150m from the petrol station, is a good bet with a personable staff that can also act as resources for park info. Warm, clean rooms make for a relaxing stay. Internet, spa pool, and camping and hiking gear are available. (☎521 1887; fax 521 1882. Dorms $19; twins $44; doubles $46.) The **Alpine Chalet,** part of the Alpine Lodge, across the street from the petrol station, has cramped but clean budget accommodations. No one mans the chalet so visit the lodge to get your questions and concerns answered. (☎/fax 521 1869; reservations 0800 367 777. Shower $1. Dorms $16; doubles $45.) Lake Rotoiti has two **DOC campgrounds,** one at **Kerr Bay,** and another at **West Bay.** Both have tent sites, though West Bay is closed in winter. ($8, powered sites $9.)

OUTDOOR ACTIVITIES. The most well-known trail is the **Travers-Sabine Circuit,** a strenuous, 4-7 day hike that crosses the 1787m Travers Saddle. The huts in the Travers Valley are first-come, first-served, and often fill in summer; tickets can be purchased at DOC ($10 per night). Hikes begin in the Kerr Bay carpark and range in duration from 30min.-9hr. depending on your ambition; a pamphlet is available at the visitors center, or just follow the well-marked signs. Those crunched for time can do the **Honeydew Walk** (return 45min.), with a beautiful view especially at sunset, of Kerr Bay and the daunting mountains behind Lake Rotoiti.

The **Rotoiti Outdoor Education Centre** (☎521 1820) hires hiking gear year-round for all pursuits. For a bit more guidance, at **St. Arnaud Guiding Services** eco-tourism experts lead on- and off-track walking trips into the park, from nature tours to gold prospecting. (☎521 1028. Half-day $85, full-day $130.) Rafting trips on the Buller Rivers and horse trekking outside of St. Arnaud are alternatives to hiking.

The glaciers that carved out the Travers Valley were also responsible for creating **Lake Rotoiti**, 8km long, 80m at its deepest point, and jumping with brown trout. You can fish, canoe, jetboat, or waterski on the lake where Maori once fished for eels and mussels. **Rotoiti Water Taxis** can take you to the head of the lake among other spots. They also hire kayaks and canoes. (☎521 1894; mobile 021 702 278; fax 521 1897. $10 per 10min.; min. $40.) Lake Rotoiti's big sister, **Lake Rotoroa** (off SH6), was carved out by two glaciers that formed the Sabine and D'Urville Valleys (jetboating and waterskiing prohibited). Fishermen and birdwatchers can contact **Rotoroa Water Taxi** for a ride to the lakehead. (☎523 9199. $25 per person; min. $60.)

Wintertime revelers use **Mt. Arnaud** as a skiing and snowboarding base. The 350-hectare **Rainbow Ski Area** offers slopes for all levels of ability. (☎521 1861. Day lift pass $47, student $35; afternoon pass $35, $24. Skis, boots, and poles $33 per day; snowboard and boots $45 per day.) Rainbow also rents ski suits and runs a shuttle to and from the ski field (return $10). (snowphone ☎0900 47 669. $0.99 per min.) **Mt. Robert Ski Club** is a private club, but nonmembers are still welcome. Huts are available on the mountain for $15 per night but be sure to book ahead. Helicopter transport up the mountain is available for $40 per person plus an additional charge of $15 for skis; gear is not available for hire on the mountain. Bring warm clothes and sturdy boots as a 2hr. hike may be necessary to leave the mountain, depending on weather conditions. (☎548 8336. Pass $20, students $15; cash only.)

MOTUEKA
☎03

Motueka (pop. 10,000) sits at the mouth of the Motueka River on SH60. The entire area was once under water; today the land is unusually fertile, making it a choice location for fruit growing (the apple, pear, and kiwifruit orchards attract legions of fruit pickers each summer). Motueka's ample services and budget digs make it a comfortable place to start trips into Abel Tasman National Park—the Coast Track trailhead is 30min. north at Marahau—and the rest of Golden Bay.

TRANSPORTATION. Abel Tasman Coachlines (☎528 0285) runs to: **Marahau** (½hr., 2-3 per day, $7) via **Kaiteriteri Beach** (¼hr., $7); **Nelson** (50min., 1-2 per day, $9); **Takaka** (1hr., 1-2 per day, $15). **Kahurangi Bus Services** (☎525 9434) runs to: **Marahau** (½hr., Nov.-Apr. only, 3-4 per day, $7) via **Kaiteriteri Beach** (¼hr., $7); **Nelson** (50min., 1-4 per day, $9); **Takaka** (1hr., 1-2 per day, $15). **Mountain bike rental** is available at **Holidays Cycle Centre**, 277 High St. (☎528 9379. Open Dec.-Jan. daily 8:30am-5:30pm, Feb.-Nov. M-F 8:30am-5:30pm, Sa 9am-12:30pm. $35 per day.)

ORIENTATION AND PRACTICAL INFORMATION. SH60 is called **High St.** where it cuts through town. All shops and most backpackers lie on or just off High St.; building numbers increase as one heads south (toward Nelson). Buses drop-off at the **Motueka Visitors Centre** on Wallace St. (☎528 6543. Open Nov.-Feb. daily 8am-7pm; Mar.-Oct. M-F 8:30am-5pm, Sa-Su 9am-3:30pm.) The **DOC office**, on High St. at King Edward St., is 2km toward Nelson from the visitors center. (☎528 9117. Open M-F 8am-4:30pm.) **Coppins Great Outdoor Centre**, 225 High St., stocks tramping gear. (☎528 7296. Open Nov.-Jun. M-Th 8:30am-5:30pm, F 8:30am-6:30pm, Sa-Sa 9am-3pm; Jul.-Oct. M-F 8:30am-5:30pm, Sa 9am-2pm.) Other services include: **banks** with **ATMs** along High St. (most open M-F 9am-4:30pm); the **police**, 68 High St. (☎528 8800); **Healthcare Pharmacy**, 125 High St. (☎528 9080; open M 9am-5:30, T-Th 8:30m-5:30pm, F 8:30am-6pm, Sa 9am-1pm, Su 10am-noon); the **Motueka Emergency Duty Doctor Number** (☎528 8770); **Internet access** at **Cyberworld**, 15 Wallace St. (☎025 627 0419; open M-F 8:30am-7pm, Sa-Su 9am-5pm; $12 per hr.); and the **post office**, 207 High St. (☎528 6600; open M-F 8am-5:30pm, Sa-Su 9am-5pm).

NELSON

ACCOMMODATIONS AND CAMPING. The great **White Elephant (NOMADS)**, 55 Whakarea St., lies less than 1km off High St. From the visitors center, take a left onto High St., turn right at KFC, and continue down Whakarea; the hostel is on the left. This sunny Victorian house holds well-worn common spaces and comfortable beds. Equipment rented, but bikes are free. (☎528 6208; fax 528 0110. Bunks $17-18; twins and doubles, some with bath, $40; tent sites $10; $1 NOMADS discount.) The facilities at large **Bakers Lodge (YHA)**, 4 Poole St., are so shiny and antiseptic that the place still feels new. From the visitors center, take a right onto High St.; the hostel is two long blocks down on the right. (☎528 0102; bakers@motueka.co.nz. Internet. Dorms $17-20; twins and doubles $40, with shower $50-$55.) **Fearon's Bush Camp**, 10 Fearon St., just off High St. north of town center, allows tenters to pitch anywhere in its shady fields. (☎528 7189. Camping $10, under 15 $5; double cabins $35.)

FOOD. Bake House, across from the visitors center on Wallace St., serves delicious pizzas ($13-34) and pastas ($17-20) in a room dotted with fish tanks and pictures of Rome. (☎528 6111. Open daily 9am-9pm; in winter M-W 9am-3pm, Th-Su 9am-8:30pm.) Brightly muralled walls support the astronomical ceiling at **Hot Mama's Cafe**, 105 High St. Lunch (salads and sandwiches $6.50-12) in the mellow garden or sup (mains $16.50-18.50) at the indoor, Jackson Pollock-inspired tables. (☎528 7039. Open daily 8:30am-late. Closed July-Oct.) **The Swinging Sultan,** 172 High St., serves juicy lamb, chicken, and vegetarian kebabs ($6-9) to take away. (☎528 8909. Open daily 10am-8pm.) Self-caterers can choose between **Supervalue,** 108 High St. (☎528 7180; open M-W 8am-7pm, Th-F 8am-8pm, Sa 9am-7pm, Su 9am-6pm) and **New World,** 271 High St. (☎528 6245; open M-W 8am-7:30pm, Th-F 8am-8:30pm, Sa 8am-7pm, Su 9am-7pm).

SIGHTS AND ACTIVITIES. Relatively quiet **Kaiteriteri Beach** is just a 15min. drive (13km) north from town; buses stop en route to **Marahau** (see **Transportation,** above). **Takaka Hill** (791m), 20km from town, serves as a starting point for a multitude of short walks, including the recently opened **Takaka Hill Walk** (return 15min.) at the very top. Also at the top of Takaka Hill, the **Ngarua Caves** showcase moa bones and illuminated stalactites. (☎528 8093. Open Sept.-May daily 10am-4pm. $11, under 8 $4.) Back in town, the **Motueka District Museum**, 140 High St., has an assortment of Maori artifacts and an exhibit on the history of the area. (☎528 7660. Open M-F 10am-3pm. $2, under 15 $0.50.)

GOLDEN BAY

Abel Tasman's first sight of Aotearoa was Golden Bay; it was the setting for New Zealand's first gold rush and its first gold rush collapse a few years later. Today's Golden Bay is a seductive half-moon where international hippies settle and young Kiwis rave through the New Year (www.gathering.co.nz). Artsy Takaka and tiny Collingwood lie at the core of the region, the beaches of Abel Tasman National Park and wide wilderness of Kahurangi National Park sprawl on either side, and the shifting sands of Farewell Spit crown the area known as the north of the South.

ABEL TASMAN NATIONAL PARK   ☎03

Most of New Zealand's national parks were created in order to protect untouched nature from falling into developers' hands. Abel Tasman National Park, by contrast, was formed around existing settlements. In 1942, conservationist Pérrine Moncrieff used the 300-year anniversary of Abel Tasman's visit to these shores to convince the government that this habitation-speckled swath of coastal forest was worth protecting from the timber industry. With subtropical weather, turquoise waters, golden sands, and, farther inland, bizarre rock formations, New Zealand's smallest national park draws kayakers and trampers year-round.

NELSON

AT A GLANCE

AREA: 22,139 hectares.	**GATEWAYS:** Marahau and Totaranui.
CLIMATE: Subtropical.	**CAMPING:** Abel Tasman Track 4 huts. Inland Track has 4 huts and free camping.
FEATURES: Coastal track.	
HIGHLIGHTS: Golden beaches along turquoise water.	**FEES & RESERVATIONS:** Great Walks Pass required ($7-9). Coastal huts $14, inland $5. Reserve in summer.

TRANSPORTATION. Sandy Bay Rd. breaks off from SH60 between Motueka and Takaka Hill and terminates at **Marahau** (18km north of Motueka), the tiny tourist village at the southern end of the park that serves as its main water transport base. **Abel Tasman Dr.** heads east from Takaka to **Wainui carpark** (21km east of Takaka), **Totaranui campground** (32km east of Takaka), and **Awaroa Inlet** (31km east of Takaka), all near the park's northern end. **Abel Tasman Coachlines** (☎548 0285) and **Kahurangi Bus Services** (☎525 9434) run daily among these access points; see **Abel Tasman Coastal Track** (p. 363) and coverage of **Nelson** (p. 246), **Motueka** (p. 253), and **Takaka** (p. 256) for schedules. **Water taxis** travel along the coast to beaches and accommodations that are not road-accessible. Although *Let's Go* does not recommend it, **hitchhikers** report plenty of traffic in summer.

ORIENTATION AND PRACTICAL INFORMATION. Abel Tasman National Park lies east of SH60, on the peninsula that separates Golden Bay from Tasman Bay. The **Motueka DOC office** (☎528 1810) on High St. and the **Takaka DOC office**, 62 Commercial St. (☎525 8026) are the main contact centers for the park (both open M-F 8am-4pm). The **Motueka Visitor Centre** on Wallace St., also handles bookings and issues Great Walks passes. (☎528 6543. Open Nov.-Feb. daily 8am-7pm; Mar.-Oct. M-F 8:30am-5pm, Sa-Su 9am-3:30pm.) The nearest **supermarkets** and **ATMs** are in Motueka and Takaka. The best bet for **secure parking** is in backpackers' carparks; in Marahau, Old Macdonald's Farm (see **Accommodations and Food**, below) employs a guard dog to watch its cars ($3 per night for non-guests).

ACCOMMODATIONS AND FOOD. Just a stone's throw from the Coast Track's Marahau trailhead, **The Barn** offers a tranquil and cheerful range of accommodations—some with sea views, many in a refurbished barn. (☎527 8043. Free use of bikes. Small shop. Dorms $16; doubles in a truck or teepee $40; tent sites $9.) Just up the road, surrounded by the same lush hillside, the hundred-acre **Old Macdonald's Farm** has a bustling, clothing-optional caravan park and some rustic indoor rooms. (☎527 8288; oldmacs@xtra.co.nz. Swimming hole. Camping gear for hire: stove $5 per day, four-person tent $10 per day. Internet. Restaurant open Nov.-Mar. Small shop. Dorms from $15; doubles $40; tent sites $9, powered sites $20-24.) Marahau's sole proper restaurant, **The Park Cafe** serves burgers ($10), bagel sandwiches ($9), and other middle-of-nowhere gourmet fare. (☎527 8270. Open daily 8am-9pm. Closed May-Sept.) The DOC-run **Totaranui Campsite,** home to a harem of caravans and tents, lies along a gorgeous beach but is also road-accessible. (☎528 8083. Small shop. Dec. 20-Jan. 31 bookings must be made by July 1-5. Tent sites $8, children $4; $2 penalty if you don't check in on arrival.)

OUTDOOR ACTIVITIES. The Abel Tasman Coast Track (3-5 days, 51km) may be the most popular of the lot, with golden beaches and turquoise ocean views fringed by fern-filled forest (see p. 363). The less-traversed **Inland Track** (3-5 days) also connects Marahau and Wainui, but is considerably more challenging than the Coast Track. Added to the park in the '70s, it passes a variety of mixed forests, subalpine vegetation, and strange marble formations. The Inland Track has four huts ($5); camping is free. It is also possible to access the track at its midpoint via the 11km **Canaan Rd.,** which branches off SH60 midway between Takaka and Motueka. The end of Canaan Rd. is also the starting point for the walk to the stone splendor of **Harwood's Hole's** 183m vertical drop (return 1½hr.); numerous other **day hikes** begin from Totaranui campground and Wainui carpark.

Of course, many visitors bypass Abel Tasmans land-based activities in favor of wetter sports. Established in 1993, the **Tonga Island Marine Reserve** stretches one nautical mile into the sea between Awaroa and Bark Bay, and confers full protection to all the creatures that dwell there. **Abel Tasman Seal Swim and Water Taxi** gets visitors in the water with Tonga Island's sea lions without coercing or feeding the animals. (☎ 0800 527 8136. Nov.-Apr. daily 8:45am and 1pm. $65, watching only $55, child $55, with day at beach $83. See **Transportation** p. 363) **Windrider Sea Adventures,** near Kaiteriteri Beach, offers the chance to cruise Tasman Bay in your own kayak-cum-sailboat trimaran. (☎ 526 8749, 0508 732 238, mobile 021 702 237. 1-day trips $90-115, half-day $65.)

◖ **KAYAKING.** The park's clear waters, trackless beaches, and fine weather have inspired a sea kayaking explosion in recent years. Sea kayakers can visit beaches such as **Mosquito Bay** and **Observation** that the Coast Track doesn't reach, as well as numerous off-shore islands. The profusion of companies can be overwhelming at first, but most offer similar guided excursions, independent rentals (2-person minimum), kayak/tramp options, and kayak pick-up ($25-35) for independent paddlers who don't want to double back; all provide extensive instruction before sending anyone out. The trips and rentals listed below give any idea of each company's prices but do not by any means cover all the offerings.

Abel Tasman Kayaks (☎ 527 8022, 0800 527 8022), in Marahau. Probably the most popular backpacker option. Free transport from Nelson or Motueka. 1-day rental $60, $35-40 per subsequent day, 5th day free. 24hr. rental $75, $15-40 per subsequent 24hr. 1-day guided $99-130. 3-day guided $295 (BYO food) or $385 (including food).

Ocean River (☎ 527 8266, 0800 732 529), in Marahau. 2-day rental $99, $40 per subsequent day, 5th day free. No 1-day rental. 1-day guided $99-129. 3-day guided $495 (including food). Fancier lodge-based trips also available.

Marahau Beach Camp (☎ 527 8176, 0800 808 018), in Marahau. 1-day rental $50. Multi-day rental $50 1st day, $40 per subsequent day, 5th day free.

Southern Exposure Sea Kayaking (☎ 527 8424, 0800 695 292), near Marahau. Operates Nov.-May only. Free transport from Nelson or Motueka. 2-day rental $95, $35-40 per subsequent day, 5th day free. No 1-day rental. 1-day guided $80-114. 3-day guided $285 (BYO food) or $375 (food included).

Kaiteriteri Kayaks (☎ 527 8383, 0800 252 925), near Kaiteriteri Beach. Half-day rental $35. 2-day rental $95. No 1-day rental. Half-day guided $50. 1-day guided $80-95. 3½hr. guided sunset trip $45.

The Sea Kayaking Company, 506 High St. (☎ 528 7251, 0508 252 925), in Motueka. 2-day rental $90. 1-day guided $85. 2-day guided $230.

Golden Bay Kayaks (☎ 525 9095), in Pohara. The only operator by the northern side of the park. Operates Nov.-May only. Rental $40 per day. Half-day guided $50. **Windsurfers** $40 per day. **Snorkeling gear** $5 per day.

TAKAKA   ☎ 03

The mailboxes in Takaka (pop. 1500) are brightly hand-painted, and every third person on the street sports dreadlocks. With formidable populations of hippies both young and aging, Takaka may well be the only town in New Zealand where pottery studios abound. A convenient access point for Kahurangi and Abel Tasman National Parks, Takaka also has its own attractions: the famously clear Pupu Springs, the tame (but hungry) Anatoki eels, and the limestone Rawhiti Caves.

▐ **TRANSPORTATION.** Takaka is 58km north of Motueka, 8km west of Pohara, and 27km east of Collingwood. **Abel Tasman Coachlines** (☎ 548 0285) travels to **Nelson** (2½hr., 1-2 per day, $22) via **Motueka** ($1hr., $15), and **Totaranui** (1hr., 1-2 per day, $11) via the **Wainui carpark** (½hr., $7). From mid-October to mid-April, **Bickley Motors** (☎ 525 8352) heads to the **Heaphy Track** (1¼hr., 1 per day, $22) via **Colling-**

wood (½hr., $14). **Kahurangi Bus Services** (☎525 9434) runs to: **Nelson** (2hr., 1-4 per day, $22) via **Motueka** (1hr., $15); **Totaranui** (1hr., 1 per day, Nov.-Apr. only, $11) via the **Wainui carpark** (½hr., $8); and the **Heaphy Track** (1¼hr., 1 per day, $20) via **Collingwood** (½hr., $12). See **Sights and Activities** below for **bike rental.**

■◪ **ORIENTATION AND PRACTICAL INFORMATION.** Takaka's main—some might say only—drag is **Commercial St.**, which becomes Willow St. at its southern (Motueka-bound) extremity. **Motupipi St.** branches northeast where Commercial St. becomes Willow St. Buses stop at the **Golden Bay Visitor Information Centre,** on Willow St. (☎525 9136. Open daily 9am-5pm.) Trampers stop at the **Golden Bay Area DOC Office,** 62 Commercial St. (☎525 8026. Open M-F 8am-4pm.) Other services on Commercial St. include: **Westpac Trust Bank** (☎525 8950; open M-Tu and Th-F 9am-4:30pm, W 9:30am-4:30pm), with one of the area's rare **ATMs;** the **police** (☎525 9211); the **Golden Bay Pharmacy** (☎525 9490; open M-Th 8:30am-5:30pm, F 8:30am-6pm, Sa 9:30am-noon); the **Golden Bay Medical Centre** (☎525 9911); **Internet access** at **Baylink Communications,** 6 Commercial St. (☎525 8863; open M-F 9am-5pm, Sa 9:30am-noon; $10 per hr.); and the **post office** (☎525 9916; open M-F 8:30am-5:30pm, Sa 9:30am-12:30pm).

▐▐ **ACCOMMODATIONS AND FOOD.** Every form of accommodation in ◪**The Nook** is impeccably decorated, from the straw-bale cottage ($90 for 2) to the super-funky solar-powered house truck ($45 for 2). An 8min. drive away in nearby Pohara (turn right down Abel Tasman Dr. from Motupipi St.), The Nook isn't only a back-packers, it's a work of art. (☎525 8501. Free pick-up from visitors center. Bikes $5 per day. Dorms $17; twins and doubles $40-50; tent sites $11.) On the left on Motupipi St. as you walk away from Commercial St., **Annie's Backpackers** provides soft beds, free duvets, a garden common room, and a typically Takakan old-hippy atmosphere. (☎525 8766. Free bikes. Dorms $15; doubles $40.) Still thought of as the new kid in town though it's been around for a few years, **Golden Bay Backpackers,** 114 Commercial St., beds its guests in wooden bunks in clean pastel rooms. It also offers complimentary fruit, milk, fresh bread, use of bikes, visitors center pick-up, and transport to Pupu Springs. (☎525 7005, 0508 525 700; goldenbaybackpackers@clear.net.nz. Dorms $17; 1 tiny double $36.) About 3km out of town toward Pupu Springs stands the rambling **River Inn,** which has revived the tradition of renting out rooms over the pub. (☎525 9425; fax 525 8148, 0800 222 572; riverinn@xtra.co.nz. Free bikes. Internet. Beds $18, mainly in single and double rooms.) The **Wholemeal Cafe,** on Commercial St., combines a keen aesthetic with delicious variety. Choices rotate but often include curries (small $12.50, large $16), fresh pastas ($10-15), and $7 sandwiches. (☎525 9426. Open daily 9am-9pm.) **The Dangerous Kitchen,** 48 Commercial St., makes a potent pizza ($10-24), among other other daring dishes. (☎525 8686. Open Nov.-Mar. 8:30am-11pm; Apr.-Oct. 8:30am-6pm.) **Supervalue** is also on Commercial St. (☎525 9383. Open M-Th 8am-6pm, F 8am-6:30pm, Sa 9am-1pm.)

◪▐ **SIGHTS AND ACTIVITIES.** The bubbling **Te Waikoropupu Springs** ("Pupu Springs" for short), 7km northwest of Takaka, are New Zealand's largest freshwater springs system. Ages ago, underground streams carved out chambers and passages in the marble, which eventually filled with the rushing waters of a full-on subterranean river. Now among the clearest in the world, these crystalline depths have an underwater visibility of more than 70m. River Inn (see **Accommodations** above) organizes **"float and swim"** excursions that include transport to the springs, snorkeling gear and wetsuits. The **Rawhiti Caves,** a one-million-year-old hole (with a 60m-wide entrance) filled with thousands of naturally colorful stalactites, untainted by artificial lighting. The caves lie a rough 45min. bushwalk from the nearest road and thus are best visited with John Croxford of **Kahurangi Guided Walks** (☎525 7177) who runs informative 3hr. trips ($25).

The **Quiet Revolution Cycle Shop,** 7 Commercial St., rents mountain bikes and offers guided trips to area hot spots like Harwood's Hole (see **Abel Tasman National Park: Activities** p. 255) and Pupu Springs. (☎/fax 525 9555. Half-day rental $15, full-day $35, $25 when business is slow. Guided trips $30 per person, min. 2 people. Open M-F 9am-5pm, Sa-Su 10am-noon.) **Takaka Tandems** gets visitors involved (and aloft) in one of Golden Bay's pet pastimes: paragliding off Takaka Hill. (☎ 035 289 283, mobile 025 247 4402. 12-20min. flight $110, discounts for groups of 2 or more.)

The highlight of a trip to the **Bencarri Farm and Cafe,** on McCallum's Rd. 5km south of Takaka, is feeding the hungry but harmless native eels. Cool your hand in the river before touching their heat-sensitive skin, then put your trust in the adage about biting the hand that feeds you. (☎ 525 8261. Open Sept.-Apr. Th-M 10am-5:30pm; in winter on demand, usually 1:30pm. $8, children $4.) With its antiques, tools, geological specimens, and handful of Powellipanta shells, the **Golden Bay Museum,** in the old post office on Commercial St., represents the best of the small town collections that try to explain the history of the Abel Tasman. (☎ 525 9990. Open daily 10am-4pm; in winter closed Su. $2.)

COLLINGWOOD AND FAREWELL SPIT   ☎ 03

In 1856, New Zealand's first big gold rush made a boom town of Collingwood, where 4000 residents clamored to name it the capital city. Three major fires and one depleted gold supply later, modern-day Collingwood (pop. 300) may be a shadow of its former self, but that doesn't affect its prime location. Full of swamp, scrub, mudflats, and 60ft. sand dunes, the country's largest sandspit (33km at low tide) can change from just 1km wide in high water to 7km wide when the tide goes out. The most interesting time to visit is from September to mid-March, when flocks of up to 90 different species of bird swoop in from as far away as Siberia.

█ TRANSPORTATION. Bickley Motors runs to Takaka October to April. (☎ 525 8352. 30min., 1:10pm, $15.) **Kahurangi Bus Services** does the same in the morning. (☎ 525 9434. Noon, $12.) **There is no bus to Collingwood November to March.** Although *Let's Go* doesn't recommend it, hitching in Golden Bay is reportedly easy.

█ PRACTICAL INFORMATION. Collingwood lies at the terminus of **SH60,** 27km north of Takaka and 23km south of **Puponga,** the settlement at the base of Farewell Spit. As SH60 enters Collingwood from the west, the first street on the left is **Tasman St.,** the town's one-block-long main thoroughfare. One block farther east, **Beach Rd.** runs parallel to Tasman St. and, on its other side, the beach. **Farewell Spit Cafe and Visitor Centre** in Puponga is the only info outlet in the area. The cafe has spectacular views of the spit. (☎ 524 8454. Open Jan.-Feb. daily 9am-5pm; Mar.-June and Sept.-Dec. 10am-4pm. Closed mid-July-Aug. Lunch $5-10.) The area has **no ATMs.** Communication services include **internet access** at Farewell Spit Nature Tours on Tasman St. (☎ 524 8188, $10 per hr.) and the **post office** on Tasman St. (☎ 524 8916. Open M-F 8:30am-5:30pm, Sa 9am-12pm.)

█ ACCOMMODATIONS AND FOOD. The best places to stay in the area are outside town but easily reached by car or thumb. Serene, environmentally-conscious ⬛**Shambhala Guesthouse,** 9km out of Collingwood toward Takaka, boasts private beach access and rooms with water views. Call for pick-up from the Mussel Inn. (☎ 525 8463. Bikes $5-10 per day. Dorms from $16; twins and doubles $38. Closed June-Sept.) ⬛**The Innlet,** 11km out of Collingwood toward Farewell Spit, is an equally lovely and eco-friendly spot with several kilometers of marked bushwalks in the surrounding woods. (☎ 524 8040; theinnlet@goldenbayindex.co.nz. Internet. Bikes. Guided rainforest kayaking $75. Dorms $17.50; twins and doubles $42; self-contained cottages $110. Closed July-Aug.) The **World's End Backpacker Lodge** in Puponga may exaggerate its place in the world, but its comfortably shabby furniture and good selection of board games certainly occupy the last backpacker at the top of the South Island. (☎ 524 8112. Dorms $15; doubles $36.) **The Courthouse Inn and Cafe,** at the corner where SH60 turns into Tasman St., provides small rooms in Collingwood proper. There are no cooking facilities, but the adjacent cafe serves tempting gourmet fare. (☎ 524 8566. Lunch $6-12. Dinner mains $19-23. Dorms open Dec.-Apr. only, $15.) **Collingwood Motor Camp,** at the far end of Tasman St., has tent sites overlooking the water and aging indoor acommo-dations. (☎524 8149. Canoes $5 per few hours. Bunks $18; cabins for 2 $50, extra person $10, under 14 $7; tent sites $9, under 14 $5.)

Great grub awaits at the **Mussel Inn** on SH60, 200m toward Collingwood from the turn-off to Shambhala Guesthouse. Bohemian offerings include strangely-named local brews, a mean veggie lasagna ($13), and live music. (☎525 9241. Open daily 11am-late; in winter Th-Sa 5pm-late.) **Rosy Glow Chocolates** on Beach Rd. produces treats so sweet that they're already the stuff of local legend. From the Courthouse Cafe, head a block down Elizabeth St. and take a right on Beach; Rosy's is a 5min. walk on the right. (☎524 8348. Chocolates $2.50-3 per piece. Open Sa-Th 10am-5pm.) For more prosaic needs, stock up at the **Collingwood General Store.** (☎524 8221. Open M-F 8am-5:30pm, Sa-Su 9am-3pm; in winter closed Sa-Su.)

◪▨ SIGHTS AND ACTIVITIES. There are two ways for visitors to explore Farewell Spit. They can walk 4km out onto the sand peninsula, stopping first at the visitors center for directions, or take a tour with one of two companies licensed to drive the Spit's west coast (most of the east coast belongs strictly to the birds) and get all the way to the lighthouse near the tip. Tour structure and departure times change with the tides but run daily most of the year. **Farewell Spit Tours** has been running 4WD trips along the Spit since the mid-1940s. (☎524 8257, 0800 808 257. 5½hr. trip $58. 6½hr. trip to a gannet colony $70. 10hr. trip to experience high tide on the Spit $200.) **Farewell Spit Nature Tours** has cushy vehicles and usually makes some stops in Puponga Farm Park before or after exploring the Spit. (☎524 8188, 0800 250 500; info@farewell.spit.co.nz. 6½hr., $65 including lunch.)

At the Spit's base, **Puponga Farm Park** serves as an environmental buffer for the unique sand habitat. 30km of walking trails allow visitors to roam through a patch-work of native plants and bleating livestock. The park's under-touristed **Wharariki Beach** is also definitely worth a visit. Low tide reveals fascinating caves and arches that beg exploration. The nearest carpark lies at the end of Wharariki Rd., 6km west of Puponga town; from there, it's a 20min. walk through sand dunes to the beach. **Cape Farewell Horse Treks** leads trips through the area for riders of all levels. (☎524 8031. 3½hr. ride on Wharariki Beach $55. Pick-up from Collingwood $10.) Meanwhile, many locals consider the **Te Anaroa Caves,** 9km southeast of Colling-wood in Rockville, to be the Golden Bay's most stunning cave system. (☎524 8131. Jan. 4 tours per day; Feb.-Dec. by appointment. $15, under 15 $6.)

KAHURANGI NATIONAL PARK ☎03

The vast wilderness that dominates the northwest corner of the South Island finds protection in 451,494-hectare Kahurangi National Park. The country's youngest and second-largest national park, Kahurangi accommodates snowcapped peaks, rolling tussock, verdant valleys, and palm-lined coasts that defy attempts to cate-gorize the area's landscape. Yet this wide range of habitats supports an astounding degree of biodiversity; over half of New Zealand's native plant species grow here (67 of them live nowhere else in the world). While experienced kayakers can brave the Class 5 Karamea River, most people experience this great and wild land on Kahurangi's network of challenging and well-benched tramping tracks.

AT A GLANCE

AREA: 452,000 hectares.

CLIMATE: Temperate forest.

FEATURES: Rivers, high plateaus, coastal forest, alpine herbfields.

HIGHLIGHTS: Trout fishing and over 570km of walking track.

GATEWAYS: Motueka, Takaka, Karamea, Murchison.

CAMPING: Backcountry huts.

FEES & RESERVATIONS: Inform DOC of any plans and for possible hut passes.

 TRANSPORTATION. **Aorere Valley Rd.** and **Karamea-Kohaihai Rd.** head south-west from Collingwood and north from Karamea, respectively, to the Heaphy Track's two trailheads. See **Heaphy Track** p. 367 for information on bus transport to these points. Additionally, **Cobb Valley Rd.** heads 27km from Upper Takaka to the Cobb Reservoir. **Hitchhikers** report long waits, and *Let's Go* doesn't recommend it.

 PRACTICAL INFORMATION. Kahurangi stretches from the west coast east to SH60 and from the base of Farewell Spit south to SH6. The park's sprawl trans-lates to highly decentralized information and access. The **DOC offices** in Nelson (see p. 246), Motueka (see p. 253), Takaka (see. p. 256), Karamea (see p. 260), and Westport (see p. 286) all sell hut passes and have information on the park. There are **supermarkets** and **ATMs** in Takaka and Westport; Collingwood and Karamea have smaller food shops. Although most of the trailhead car parks don't have trou-bled histories, it's still safer to **park** in a hostel lot in one of the nearby towns.

 WHEN TO GO. Kahurangi is beautiful year-round. Most visitors come between December and February; March and April tend to be the mildest.

 ACCOMMODATIONS. Almost all convenient accommodations are in the out-lying towns. **Heaphy Backpackers**, 3km toward Collingwood from the Heaphy Track's northern trailhead, is a notable exception. This hostel has incredible views of the Aorere River valley; its Swiss-artist owner provides free transport to and from the trailhead. (☎524 8252. Closed in winter. Bunks $16; doubles $40.)

 OUTDOOR ACTIVITIES. The **Heaphy Track** (4-6 days, 82km; see p. 367) passes through lofty beech forest, wind-swept alpine meadows, lowland podocarp forest, and wild palm-lined beaches. The **Wangapeka Track** (3-5 days) is the most popular tramp in the southern half of the park. It forms a loop with the Heaphy, so some people walk the two in conjunction (though the Wangapeka is significantly more rugged than the Heaphy). Its eastern trailhead lies 30km west of **Tapawera** (which is 62km west of Nelson); from there, the track follows several rivers through beech-green valleys to a carpark 23km from **Karamea**. Ten huts ($5-10) provide shelter along the way. Other tramping options include intensive backcountry grunts like the **Leslie-Karamea Track** (6-9 days) to the many sub-alpine dayhikes around **Mt. Arthur** and the **Cobb Valley**. A steep and narrow track to the incredible viewpoint of **Parapara Peak** (1249m; 9hr. return) begins just 2km off SH60 between Takaka and Collingwood at the Ward-Holmes Rd. end.

Ultimate Descents runs **rafting** trips on the **Karamea River** and can organize **kayak** rental. (☎523 9899, 0800 748 377. 5-day hike in, raft out journey $825. 3-day heli-journey $795. 1-day heli-journey $275. Kayaks $35 per day.) **Buller Adventure Tours** conducts heli-rafting trips (☎789 7286, 0800 697 286; full-day $245), as does Karamea's **Last Resort** (full-day $239; see below). Last Resort also runs rafting and canoe trips on mellower parts of the river (2½hr., $30).

KARAMEA ☎03

Karamea is a small town in the shadow of big wilderness. Best known as the end-point of the **Heaphy Track** (see p. 367) the village also hosts visitors to the nearby **Oparara Basin**, famous for its huge limestone arches and delicate Honeycomb Cave system. From the carpark on Oparara Rd. (a well-marked 1hr. drive north of town), the **Oparara (Big) Arch trail** (return 45min.) leads to that 43m-high, 219m-long arch, while the **Moria Gate trail** (return 1½hr.) heads to Little Arch. Last Resort offers **transport** (return $30) as well as **tours** through the area; their 5½hr. Honey-comb Cave tour ($60) takes in several caves and Big Arch and is a worthwhile option for would-be spelunkers, as **it is not possible to visit the Honeycomb Caves except as part of a tour.** There are numerous other short hikes near town as well, though most require a drive—hitchhikers say locals are receptive to outstretched thumbs, but even in summer there's little traffic; *Let's Go* does not recommend thumbing. The **Fenian Track** (return 5hr.) gives trampers a taste of the rainforest. The walk to **Scott's Beach** (return 1½hr.) begins at the Heaphy Track trailhead.

Karamea sits at the northern end of SH67. **Cunningham's Motors** (☎ 789 7177) and **Karamea Express** (☎ 782 6617) run to **Westport** (1½hr.; M-F 8:20 and 8:10am, Karamea Express also Sa 8:10am Oct.-Apr.; $15). For accommodations, your first resort should be the **Last Resort** on Waverly St., a 7min. walk west from the center of town. It has two restaurants and reading lights in the airy dorms, but does not provide kitchen access. (☎ 782 6617; last.resort@xtra.co.nz. Internet. Dorms $20; twins and doubles $50-60; doubles with bath $75-140.) With psychadelic murals, loud music, and thrift-store furniture, **Punga Lodge** is on Waverly St. (☎ 782 6667. Dorms $15; doubles $40.) The **Karamea Information and Resource Centre,** on Bridge St., has information on Kahurangi and sells hut passes. (☎ 782 6652. Open daily 9am-5pm; in winter M-F 9am-5pm, Sa 9am-1pm.) Other local services include: a **Four Square** (☎ 782 6701; open M-Th 8:30am-6pm, F 8:30am-8pm, Sa-Su 9am-noon, until 5pm in summer); **petrol stations,** at Market Cross near the visitors center; **police** (☎ 782 6801), on Wharf St.; **Karamea Medical Centre** (☎ 782 6737); **internet access** at the visitors center ($2.50 per 15min.); and **postal facilities** at the Karamea Hardware Store (☎ 782 6700; open M-F 8am-6pm, Sa-Su 9am-noon). There is **no bank or ATM** in Karamea.

CANTERBURY

A spacious farmland nurtured among the shadows of the majestic
Southern Alps, Canterbury quenches the thirst of all types of travelers. Serious skiers flock to the treeless heights of the slopes, while summer visitors seek out the charms of the Banks Peninsula and nearby beaches. With green
belts both within its towns and beyond their limits, Canterbury draws equally from
its cosmopolitanism and provincialism—providing trendy cafes alongside natural
wonders, all in the agricultural center of the South Island.

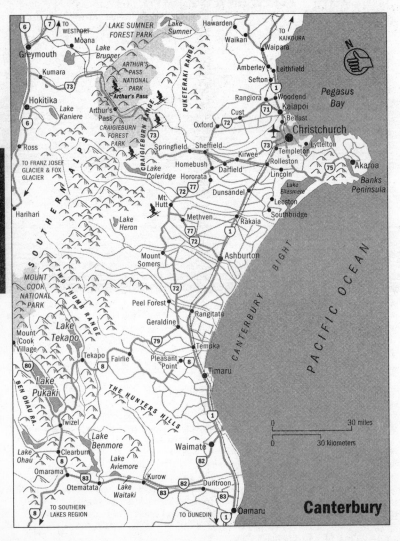

⚆ CANTERBURY HIGHLIGHTS

SLOPE down the **Southern Alps** to hit some of the nation's finest skiing (see p. 280).

SCOPE the scene in vibrant **Christchurch,** from Gothic architecture to botanic gardens to eclectic street performers (see p. 263).

STARE at some of the most breathtaking scenery in the world on the famed train ride through **Arthur's Pass**—getting there is *all* the fun (see p. 279).

DARE to ascend to formidable **Mt. Cook National Park,** which challenges thrill-seekers with its dramatic peaks, demanding walks, and majestic glaciers (see p. 284).

CHRISTCHURCH ☎03

Although this Garden City (pop. 300,000) remains closely bound to its English roots, it has a flamboyant tilt that could only be Kiwi. Named after Oxford's Christ Church College, the stone Gothic Revival churches and meeting houses that front the grassy, willowed banks of the Avon River are reminiscent of British sensibilities. Christchurch itself is more bohemian, nurturing a vibrant community of artists and artisans who instill a proud cultural spirit. Foreigners flock to Christchurch's countless seasonal festivals, when street entertainers, ethnic food stalls, and even a wizard (see Pay no Attention p. 270) clog Cathedral Sq. and the nearby Arts Centre.

✈ INTERCITY TRANSPORTATION

Flights: The **Christchurch Airport** is 9km from the city on Memorial Ave. and is served by **Air New Zealand, Qantas,** and many Asian and South Pacific carriers (☎374 7100). Flights go to **Auckland** (1½hr.; 1 per hr.; $230-500, check with a local travel agent about limited $89 one-way fares to Auckland) and **Wellington** (45min., 1 per hr., $130-592). **Air New Zealand,** 549 Colombo St., has frequent flights. (☎363 0600, 0800 737 000.) Open M-F 9am-5pm, Sa 9:30am-1pm. Great discounts can be procured by booking ahead (see **Transportation: Flights,** p. 39). The Airport "A" bus ($4) departs from the airport and Cathedral Sq. twice an hr. during the day, and once every hr. in evening. **Super Shuttles** (☎365 5655) to downtown cost about $12; a taxi is $20-25.

Trains: To reach the **train station,** located 3km from Cathedral Sq., head away from town on Riccarton Ave., turn left on Deans Ave., right onto Blenheim Rd., then left on Clarence St. Taxis to town cost about $12, though several hostels offer a free shuttle from the station. **Super Link Shuttle** (☎355 1111) does free pick-up from several centrally located backpackers to connect with the **TranzAlpine** run to **Greymouth** (4½hr., 9am, $61-87) via **Arthur's Pass** (2½hr., $43-62). **TranzScenic** (☎0800 802 802) runs daily to: **Invercargill** (9hr., 8:15am, $88-125) via **Dunedin** (5¾hr., $55-79); and **Picton** (5¼hr., 7:30am, $54-77) via **Kaikoura** (3hr., $31-44). Some TranzScenic trains have a designated **backpackers' car** and most offer substantial discounts (20% or more) to students and those who book ahead (see **Transportation: Trains** p. 39).

Buses: InterCity and **Newmans,** 123 Worcester St. (☎379 9020, 0800 686 862) and **Great Sights** (☎0800 808 226) run daily to **Queenstown** (5¾hr., 4-5 per day, $45-123) via **Mt. Cook** (5hr., $35-70) or **direct.** InterCity also runs to: **Dunedin** (6½ hr., 2-3 per day, $24-48); **Nelson** (8hr., 7:15am, $51-69) via **Kaikoura** (2¾hr., $14-28); and **Wanaka** (7hr., 2 per day, $65-130). Check with the visitors center for other destinations. **Alpine Coaches** (☎0800 274 888) and **Coast to Coast** (☎0800 800 847) traverse the South Island to Greymouth (4½hr., $35) via **Arthur's Pass** (2½hr., $25) **Atomic Shuttles** (☎322 8883, www.atomictravel.co.nz), **Southern Link Shuttle** (☎358 8355), **South Island Connections** (☎366 6633), or **East Coast Express** (☎0508 830 900) also run shuttles.

Hitchhiking: Though *Let's Go* does not recommend it, thumbers report success from the city outskirts, where urban traffic is steady. Those heading north often take the **Rangiori** bus and ask the driver to be dropped off on Hwy. 74, while those heading south take the **Hornby** bus (#83 or #84). Hitching west toward Arthur's Pass is made a reasonable prospect by taking the **Hornby** #84 bus to the Yaldhurst Roundabout. The best bet for hitching to Akaroa seems to be the **Halswell** bus (#7). Hitching south to Dunedin is best done along Main South Rd. (SH1); taking the #5 bus gets you to **Templeton.**

✦ ORIENTATION

Christchurch's flat grid of streets stretches in every direction from **Cathedral Square,** the city's heart, where food stalls and artisans congregate beneath the bell tower of **Christchurch Cathedral.** From there, cobblestoned **Worcester Blvd.** continues east through **Latimer Square** and west, over the **Avon River,** to the **Gothic Arts Centre** buildings, the **Canterbury Museum,** and the extensive **botanic gardens.** The city's central thoroughfare, **Colombo St.,** lined with wool and jewelry souvenir shops, runs north-south through the square. Arcades and plazas extend out from the **City Mall,** the pedestrian walkway one block south from the Cathedral where Cashel St. would be. North of the Cathedral, **Victoria Square** fronts both the town hall and the domineering Park Royal hotel. The shallow **Avon River** runs through the square, and is followed along much of its route by **Oxford Terrace** and **Cambridge Terrace.** Central Christchurch is bordered to the west by the gigantic **Hagley Park,** to the north and east by residential suburbs, and to the south by **Moorhouse Ave.,** the boundary of the industrial area. Don't be surprised to see prostitutes about, especially from Cambridge Terrace to Cashel St. and along Manchester St. north of Gloucester.

⊏ LOCAL TRANSPORTATION

Public Transportation: The **Bus Information Centre** (☎366 8855), at the corner of Colombo and Lichfield St. (Open M-F 7:30am-5:40pm, Sa 9am-5pm, Su 10:30am-4:50pm. Buses depart roughly every 30min. from 6am to 10:50pm, depending on time of day and route. Fares are calculated by zone and tickets are purchased on board. If you are going to more than 1 sight, a **Big Red Bus Pass,** good for a full day of travel on Red Buses, is quite economical. $5, families $10. Available at the visitors center or on board. **The Shuttle** is a **free** service that sends out a fleet of bright yellow buses each day to circle the city center every 10min. Get a route map at the visitors center.

Taxis: Choose from **First Direct** (☎377 5555, 0800 505 550), **Gold Band** (☎379 5795), and **Blue Star** (☎379 9799) for **24hr.** service.

Car Rental: The major car-rental companies are all in town, but for cheaper deals, try **Atomic Rentals** (☎322 8883), which rents from about $25 per day with unlimited mileage; the $750 credit bond is standard ($1000 if under 25). **Pegasus,** 127 Peterborough St. (☎365 1100; fax 365 1104); **Rent-a-Dent,** 132 Kilmore St. (☎365 2509, 0800 736 823); **Ace Rentals,** 237-239 Lichfield St. (☎366 3222, 0800 202 029, fax 377 4610); and **Shoestring Rentals** (☎385 3647; fax 385 3694) offer comparable rates. The **AA office,** 210 Hereford St. (☎379 1280, 0800 500 222) sells excellent road maps and dispenses sage traveling advice. Open M-F 8:30am-5pm.

Bike Rental: Trailblazers (☎366 6033) on the corner of Oxford Terrace and Armagh St., has standard mountain bikes. $5 per hr., half-day $15, full-day $20. Hours are variable, but generally open M-F 9am-6pm, Sa-Su 10am-5pm. **Cyclone Cycles,** 245 Colombo St. (☎332 9588) has bikes with suspension. Half-day $30, full-day $40. **City Cycle Hire** (☎0800 343 848) is open daily and offers half-day hires for $20 and full days for $30. **Free bicycle storage** (bring your own lock) is available in the Lichfield St. carpark, at **City Self Storage,** between Oxford Terrace and Colombo St. Open M-Th 7:30am-7:15pm, F 7:30am-11:45pm, Sa 9am-5:30pm, Su 10am-4:30pm.

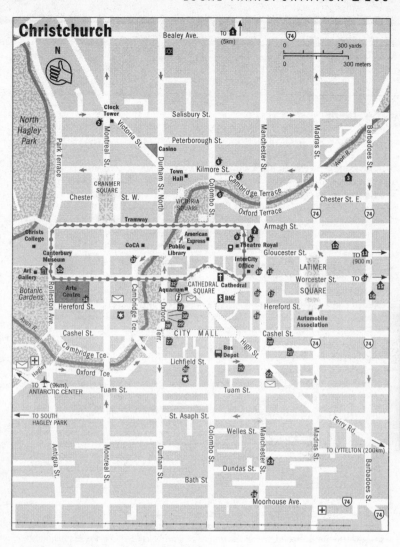

Christchurch

🏠 **ACCOMMODATIONS**
City Central YHA, 7
Coker's (VIP), 23
Frauenreisehaus, 16
Foley Towers, 3
New Excelsior, 22
The Old Country House, 13
Rolleston House YHA, 35
Stonehurst (VIP), 12
Vagabond Backpackers, 15
Top Ten Holidy Park, 1

🍴 **FOOD**
Alva Rados, 11
Blue Jean Cuisine, 18
Death by Chocolate, 5
Dux de Lux, 34
Il Felice, 26
Ironside House, 2
Memphis Belle, 14
Oxford on Avon, 6
Pak N' Save, 24
Penang Noodle House, 17

Pronto Nachos Cafe, 8
Raj Mahal, 10
Sala Thai, 4
Santonni Greek Ouzeri, 33
Thai Tasty, 9
Topkapi Turkish Kebab, 19

🍸 **NIGHTLIFE**
Azure, 28
The Bog, 27
The Boulevard, 31
DiLusso, 29
The Holy Grail, 32
Loaded Hog, 20
Platinum, 25
Sammy's Jazz Review, 21
Viaduct, 30

⚡ PRACTICAL INFORMATION

Visitors Center: Christchurch & Canterbury Visitor Centre (☎379 9629; fax 377 2424), is in the Old Chief Post Office Bldg. in Cathedral Square. Open M-F 8:30am-6pm, Sa-Su 8:30am-5pm; in winter M-F 8:30am-5pm, Sa-Su 8:30am-4:30pm. Additional offices (☎353 7774), are located in the domestic and international terminals of the airport. Open daily 7:30am-8pm.

DOC: 133 Victoria St. (☎379 9758). Open M-F 8:30am-4:30pm.

Budget Travel: STA Travel, 90 Cashel St. (☎379 9098), in City Mall. Open M-F 9am-5:30pm, Sa 10am-1pm. **Budget Travel,** 683A Colombo St. (☎366 6032). Open M-Th, F 8:30am-5:30pm.

Maps: Mapworld (☎374 5399, 0800 MAPWORLD), corner of Manchester and Gloucester St., has the best selection. Open M-Th 8am-6pm, F 8am-8pm, Sa-Su 9am-4pm.

Currency Exchange: BNZ (☎353 2532), in the glass and steel building in Cathedral Sq., provides MC/V cash advances and exchanges money (M-F 9am-4:30pm).

American Express: 773 Colombo St. (☎365 7366, 24hr. ☎0800 656 660). Mail held for 30 days for card members and AmEx traveler's check holders. No commission; good exchange rates. Open M-Tu and Th-F 9am-5pm, W 9:30am-5pm.

Bi-Gay-Lesbian Organizations: Gay Information Line (24hr. ☎379 3990); **Gay Information Collective** (☎/fax 379 9493).

Emergency: ☎111

Police: Cathedral Sq. Kiosk (☎379 0123). Open Su-W 8am-midnight, Th-Sa 8am-2am. **Main branch** (☎379 3999), at the corner of Hereford St. and Cambridge Terrace.

Hotlines: Lifeline (☎366 6743) offers 24hr. counseling; **Victim Support** (☎379 6767); **AIDS Hotline** (☎0800 802 437); **New Zealand AIDS Foundation** (☎379 1953); **Disability Info,** 314 Worcester St. (☎366 6189). Open M-Th 9am-4:30pm, F until 4pm.

Medical Services: Bealey Ave. After-Hours Surgery, 931 Colombo St. (☎365 7777). Open 24hr. **Christchurch Public Hospital** (☎364 0640), on the corner of Oxford Terrace and Riccarton Ave.

Internet Access: E-Caf, 28 Worcester Blvd. (☎365 6480) in the Arts Centre, offers deals with the cafe downstairs. $3 per hr., free 15min. with purchase of coffee. Open daily 8am-11pm. **E-Caf@Farmers,** 767 Colombo St., has cheap rates. Open M-Th 9:30am-6pm, F 9:30am-9pm, Sa 9:30am-6pm, Su noon-5pm.

Post Office: (☎353 1899), entrances at Hereford St. and the square. Poste Restante. Open M-Th 8am-6pm, F 8am-8pm, Sa-Su 10am-4pm.

🏠 ACCOMMODATIONS

While Christchurch has few of the charmingly quirky gems found in the smaller towns of the South Island, there are plenty of stately Victorian houses throughout the city that have been converted into hostels, B&Bs, and hotels.

WORCESTER STREET AND SOUTH

🏴 **Vagabond Backpackers,** 232 Worcester St. (☎379 9677), 5 blocks east of the Cathedral. An extremely popular house with a modern interior, stylish kitchen, TV lounge, and quiet location close to the city. Good selection of free videos. Book at least a week ahead. Dorms $14-16; singles $28; twins and doubles $40.

🏴 **Frauenreisehaus: The Homestead,** 272 Barbadoes St. (☎366 2585; fax 366 2589), past the Cathedral on Worcester Blvd., hang a right on Barbadoes St. Women are fortunate to have this **female-only** backpackers to themselves. An excellent collection of videos and music, free use of bikes, fresh mint in the garden for tea, free laundry, and a warm towel to use while you wash. Internet $4 per hr. on your honor. Reception 8:30am-10:30pm. Book ahead. Dorms $15; singles $25; twins $34.

New Excelsior Backpackers (NOMADS), 120 Manchester St. (☎366 7570; fax 366 7629, newexcel@ihug.co.nz), at the corner of High and Manchester St. Thirsty travelers will rejoice in the above-bar location. Internet. Reception 7am-8pm. Dorms $15-20; singles $35; twins $40; doubles $45, with bath $55. $1 *Let's Go* discount.

Coker's (VIP), 52 Manchester St. (☎379 8580; fax 379 8585). Winning our award for most whimsical charm in Christchurch, this reincarnated hotel retains the ornately carved wooden ceilings from 1875. Key deposit $20. Internet. Reception 24hr. Dorms $17.50; singles $40-45; twins $45; doubles $48-50.

Rolleston House YHA, 5 Worcester Blvd. (☎366 6564; fax 365 5589; yhachrl@yha.org.nz), at the corner of Worcester Blvd. and Rolleston Ave., across from the Arts Centre. You can hardly get closer to the city's cultural heart, with the Arts Centre, cafes, and museums right outside your door. Reception 8-10am and 3-10pm. Dorms $16-18; twins $42. Non-members $3 more.

NORTH OF WORCESTER STREET

▓ **The Old Country House,** 437 Gloucester St. (☎381 5504), several blocks east up Gloucester St., at the corner of Stanmore Rd. Herb garden out back, and frequent home-baked goodies. Free pick-up from Cathedral Sq. Reception 8-10am and 5-8pm. Internet. Dorms $15-17; twins and doubles $40; quads $17 per person.

Foley Towers, 208 Kilmore St. (☎366 9720; fax 379 3014; foley.towers@back pack.co.nz). Take Worcester Blvd. east to Madras St., go left, and then right on Kilmore St. Rooms line the extensive garden. Most have sinks, but a quick duck outside is required to reach the loo. Internet. Linen charge $2 for whole stay. Key deposit $10. Reception 9am-9:30pm. Dorms $14-16; twins and doubles $38, with bath $44.

Stonehurst (VIP), 241 Gloucester St. (☎379 4620; fax 379 4647; accom@stone-hurst.co.nz), east on Gloucester St. 3½ blocks from Colombo St. The bar at reception has Happy Hour, with $5 beers daily from 5-7pm. Internet. Reception 24hr. Dorms $16-19; singles $40; doubles $45; accommodation for groups as well. VIP $1 off.

City Central YHA, 273 Manchester St. (☎379 9535; fax 379 9537; yhachch@yha.org.nz), near Armagh St. Central, modern, and ultra-clean with tremendously helpful staff. Snug but bare rooms have that YHA feel. Reception 7am-10pm. Pool table. Internet. Dorms $20; singles $40; twins and doubles $46, with bath $56.

Meadow Park Top 10 Holiday Park, 39 Meadow St. (☎352 9176; fax 352 1272). Drive north 10min. from the city center on Sherborne St., which becomes Hwy. 74 and runs by the park about 5km from town. A sprawling complex with swimming pool, trampoline, and spa ($8 per 30min.). Reception 8am-10pm. Cabins for 2 $36, extra person $10; tourist flats for 2 from $52, extra person $11; tent and powered sites from $11 per person, children $5; funky hexagonal "kozy kiwi cottages" $60 for 2, $15 extra adult.

◘ FOOD

Many restaurants are concentrated on **Colombo St.,** north of Kilmore St., and on **Manchester St.,** south of Gloucester St. Cafes are often the best bet for hearty breakfasts and lunches (generally with lower prices), and there's always pub food to be found. Vendors in **Cathedral Sq.** sell a range of kebabs and stir-frys around lunchtime; on weekends they take over a corner of the Arts Centre. The **Pak 'N Save,** at the corner of Moorehouse Ave. and Manchester St., is the cheapest of the several megamarkets clustered a few blocks from Cathedral Sq. (Open M-W 8:30am-9pm, Th-F 8:30am-10pm, Sa 8:30am-8pm, Su 8:30am-8pm.)

WORCESTER STREET AND SOUTH

▓ **Memphis Belle,** 391 Worcester St. (☎389 4590), several blocks east of Manchester St. near the corner of Stanmore Rd. Calzones ($13.50) and exquisite thin-crust pizzas (small $7.50-8.50, large $20-22). If you like the meal, just walk into the kitchen to let Shayne and Serena know. Open Tu-Th 5-9pm, F-Sa 5-10pm, Su 5-9pm.

CANTERBURY

Il Felice, 56 Lichfield St. (☎366 7535) serves Italian cuisine in boisterous environment. Freshly made pastas ($17) and mains ($26-28) are worth a splurge, as portions more than make up for the expense. Reservations recommended. Open M-Sa 6pm-late.

Blue Jean Cuisine, 205 Manchester St. (☎365 4130). Whichever meal you choose, it's a safe bet that you won't leave hungry. The noise level loudly confirms the restaurant's popularity. So hip, your bill comes in a CD case. Lunch $6.50-17.50, light meals $11-13, dinners $16-23. Open M-F 11am-late, Sa-Su 5:30pm-late.

Alva Rados (☎365 1644), corner of Worcester and Manchester St. Sangria pitchers, mega-nachos, and multicolored blankets put a Hispanic spin on the wood and iron decor. Light meals from $12.50, mains $12.50-20. Open Tu-Su 6-9pm.

Dux de Lux, 41 Hereford St. (☎366 6919), at the Arts Centre. Serves only vegetarian and seafood dishes ($15-22) meant to be washed down with 1 of 7 house brews. Internet. Open daily 11:30am-late.

Topkapi Turkish Kebab House, 185a Manchester St. (☎379 4447). In this tiny piece of Turkey, kebabs and falafels are prepared windowside ($5-10). Open M-Tu 11:30am-10pm, W-Th 11:30am-10:30pm, F 11:30am-late, Sa 3pm-late.

Penang Noodle House, 172 Manchester St. (☎377 2638). The decor may be simple, but you'll be impressed by the food. Try the $5 lunch special on M and W-F. Open M-F 12:30-2:30pm and 5:30-10pm, Sa 5:30-10pm, Su 5:30-9pm.

NORTH OF WORCESTER STREET

▩ **Raj Mahal** (☎366 0521), at the corner of Manchester and Worcester St. Terrible puns aside, authentic Indian music wafts through this colorful dining room. Choose from several tandoori ($15-20) and vegetarian ($14.50-16) dishes. Takeaways all $13. Open M-Sa 5:30pm-10pm, Su 5:30pm-9:30; takeaway from 4:30pm.

▩ **Thai Tasty,** 10/129 Gloucester St. (☎379 7540). Tucked inside the Gloucester Arcade, you won't find it much cheaper, friendlier, faster, or Thai-tastier than this, with 20 $5-6 meals on the menu, and 30 more ranging from $7-9. Open in summer daily M-Sa 10:30am-10pm; in winter until 9pm.

Pronto Nachos Cafe, 8 New Regent St. (☎366 4676). Enormous nachos ($3.20-8.80) and tasty chicken burritos ($9) are served with fresh, homemade guacamole. Open M-Sa 11am-9pm.

Death by Chocolate, 209 Cambridge Terrace (☎365 7323). North on Colombo St. and turn right onto Cambridge Terrace. The namesake dessert ($16) could fill 2, and the "Multitude of Sins" ($24 for 2) is enough to inspire a gastronomic orgasm. Peruse the picture book before choosing from the scrumptious menu. Open Tu-Su from noon-late.

Santorini Greek Ouzeri (☎379 6975), at the corner of Gloucester St. and Cambridge Terrace. A fun-loving family restaurant with big Greek dinners ($22). Patrons are encouraged to dance on wine casks and the conga lines have even been known to invade the kitchen. Open Tu-Sa 6pm-late.

Sala Thai (☎365 5447), at the corner of Colombo and Kilmore St., takes pride in its unpretentious atmosphere. The wide range of Thai and Lao dishes encourage branching out from pad thai. Mains $13-18. Open daily noon-9:30pm.

Ironside House (☎365 6999), at the corner of Montreal and Salisbury St. Wonderful food is served in an elegant and historic setting. Pasta of the day is $13 and most mains run $13.50-22.50. Dinners are pricier. Open M-F 11am-late, Sa-Su from 9am (kitchen closes 2:30-6pm).

Oxford on Avon & Riverview, 794 Colombo St. (☎379 7148), at the corner of Colombo St. and Oxford Terrace. The pinnacle of Kiwi pub food—carved meats, veggies, and creamy cakes—served cafeteria-style. Lunch ($11-17) from 11:30am and dinner, often with daily specials ($16). Open daily 6:30am-late.

CANTERBURY

THE JOY OF YEAST What little joy our lives would have without yeast! No bread. No wine. No beer. And, by extension, no brewer's by-products. And without the by-products, to the shock and horror of millions, there would be no **Marmite,** the salty, yeasty brown paste with the look, consistency, and taste of spreadable bullion. Contrary to popular belief, you don't need to have been weaned on the stuff to truly enjoy it. The trick is to remember: 1) it's not sweet, and 2) it's *not* meant to be slathered across the bread. Tourists always smear it on like peanut butter, sending them to the nearest sink. Instead, scrape the tiniest bit across hot buttery toast. It's even rumored to prevent hangovers—true Kiwis eat Marmite.

⌘ CAFES

Reasonably priced, and with consistently good food, Christchurch's cafes are a good breakfast or luncheon option.

▨ **The Coffee House,** 290 Montreal St. (☎365 6066). Near the Arts Centre. Shelves and shelves of tins house an enormous selection of teas and coffees ($2.50-4.50) and provide pleasant torture for the indecisive. Open M-F 7:30am-late, Sa-Su 8am-late.

▨ **Le Cafe** (☎366 7722), on Worcester Blvd. in the Arts Centre. The cream of several cafes cached in the Gothic crannies of the Arts Centre, Le Cafe is always busy, always lively, and almost always open. The iced chocolate drink ($4) will make you tremble with delight (or a sugar high). Dinners $10-15, breakfast $7.50-12.50. Open Su-Th 7am-midnight, F-Sa 7am-2am.

▨ **Main Street Cafe,** 804 Colombo St. (☎365 0421). At the corner of Salisbury St. Hippie-ish bar/cafe/restaurant with a changing menu offers creative vegetarian and dairy-free options. Dinners from $16-17. Open daily 10am-late.

Java Cafe (☎366 0195), at the corner of High, Manchester, and Lichfield St. Hot chocolate served in jam jars ($3), a variety of bagels with just as many toppings ($2-5), and the massive vegetarian planet burger ($10) are a few all-day dining options. Open daily 7:30am-late, Th-Sa 24hr.

▣ ENTERTAINMENT

Christchurch has several excellent art cinemas and a professional theater company; check the back page of *The Press* for a full current listing. The **Court Theatre** at the Arts Centre, has two theaters running some of New Zealand's best professional repertory productions. (☎366 6992. Adults generally $27, students generally $20.) The **Theatre Royal,** 145 Gloucester St. (☎366 6326), is the forum for touring musicals and ballet companies. The **Repertory Theatre,** 146 Kilmore St. is a community theater running five plays a year. (☎378 8866. Tickets about $15.)

Gamblers can try their luck at the 24hr. **Christchurch Casino,** at Victoria and Durham St. While it may resemble an overgrown parking garage from the outside, the gaming room and cafes feature tasteful balconies and chandeliers. (☎365 9999. Free nightly transpo. No jeans or sneakers. Must be 20 to gamble. Open daily.)

FESTIVALS. Christchurch hosts an amazing number of festivals for a city its size. Check out **www.bethere.org.nz** for a relatively comprehensive listing of festivals in Christchurch and elsewhere in New Zealand. In November, **Showtime Canterbury** hits the city with its concerts, fireworks, and parades. Since 1983-84, **Summertimes** has been one of the most popular festivals in Canterbury, bringing a series of concerts and theater performances to the city over the course of the summer season, as well as a huge "teddy bear picnic" (www.summertimes.org.nz). After the New Year, the **International Buskers Festival** brings nutty street entertainers from around the world to the city in one of the wackiest outdoor festivals in the world. The **Festival of Flowers** blooms every

February, bedecking Cathedral Sq. with a floral carpet (www.festivalofflowers.co.nz, Feb. 15-24 in 2002). It includes garden competitions, street decorations, and visits to private gardens. Summer is also the season for outdoor opera and rock concerts, a **Wine and Food Festival** in February, and **Adventure Canterbury** in April, a two-week festival celebrating Canterbury's adrenaline activities. The **Christchurch Arts Festival** runs at the end of July in odd years, with multimedia performing arts and exhibitions (www.artsfestival.co.nz). Every August the **Montana Christchurch Winter Carnival** (www.wintercarnival.org.nz) celebrates the ski season, with imported snow (part of Cathedral Sq. is even covered with makeshift drifts and huge snow sculptures).

▨ NIGHTLIFE

On weekends a university crowd crams the clubs, bars, and saloons until mid-morning. Cruise the end of the **City Mall** by the Avon and up and down action-packed **Manchester St.** for after-dark hot spots. The **After Midnight Express** gets post-revelry partyers home safely, running through the central city and to selected suburbs. (☎0800 733 287. Runs Sa and Su mornings hourly from midnight-4am. $4.)

▨**The Bog,** 82 Cashel Mall (☎379 7141). This ain't your grandpappy's Irish pub. Live music (W-Sa from 9:30pm) and DJs get a young crowd going on the dance floor until the wee morn. Open daily 10am-late.

▨**The Loaded Hog** (☎366 6674), on Manchester St. at Cashel St. The lines are long because bartenders always pour an excellent lager at this homebrew chain. Bar snacks $5-12. Live jazz Tu from 8pm. DJs Th from 8pm, F-Sa from 9pm. Open M-F 11am-late, Sa 10am-3am, Su 10am-late.

The Holy Grail Sports Bar, 99 Worcester St. (☎365 9816). Don't pass up the chance to watch an All-Blacks game at this recently converted movie theater. When the big game is over, watch yourself groove on the dance floor in full cinematic glory. Live DJ Th-Sa. Open daily 11am-late.

Viaduct, 136 Oxford Terrace. (☎377 9968), on the Avon. Well-dressed 20-somethings pack into this dimly lit bar. Long lines on weekends. Open daily 10:30am-late.

Di Lusso (☎377 9968), adjoining Viaduct on the Avon, has the city's latest hours, often staying open until 8am on weekends. Dark and velvety and blue fishtanks glow. Open daily 6pm-very late.

Dux de Lux, 41 Hereford St. (☎366 6919). By the Arts Centre. It's unclear whether it's the enormous old house, the 3 separate bars, or the 7 freshly brewed beers that can be credited with attracting the students, but they certainly come in droves. Live jazz Tu. Punk, funk, rock, or reggae W-Sa. Open daily 11am-late.

The Boulevard (☎374 6676), at the corner of Oxford Terrace and Hereford St., is a cafe by day, but come the late evening hours, the floor swells with those who would dance while singing to classic radio hits. Open Su-Th 8am-late, F-Sa 8am-5am-ish.

Platinum (☎377 7891), on Lichfield St., across from Cashel Plaza. Dance floor holds a gyrating posse of gay and gay-friendly locals. Occasional live DJs and drag shows. Open M-F 4:30pm-late, Sa-Su 7pm-late.

Azure, 128 Oxford Terrace (☎365 6088). Brave the dance floor and gyrate to cutting-edge house funk, or watch from one of the arching alcoves. Open daily 11am-late.

Sammy's Jazz Review, 14 Bedford Rd. (☎377 8618) a block east of Manchester St. A touch of class amid lavish brick in the courtyard and inside. Live jazz nightly (8-11pm weeknights, 7:30pm-1am F-Sa). Open M-Sa 5pm-late, F-Sa 7:30pm-1am.

PAY NO ATTENTION TO THE LITTLE MAN BEHIND THE CURTAIN King of Christchurch's motley array of eccentrics, **The Wizard** makes his presence known daily in summer, around noon in Cathedral Sq. You may flee disgusted, which means that the pointed cap- and cape-bearing Wizard has won the day, still, he's a strikingly intelligent orator and entertainer. In and out of season you can find The Wizard on the web (www.wizard.gen.nz).

CANTERBURY

☉ SIGHTS

OUTDOOR SIGHTS

CHRIST CHURCH CATHEDRAL. This looming 1865 Gothic Revival Cathedral, and centerpiece of Christchurch, is an exercise in juxtaposition, combining stones quarried and hewn in Canterbury with hulking natural roots from native matai and totara. Inside, ornate stained-glass windows imported from England abut Maori *kai kai* (flax) weavings. You can even climb the 134 steps of the Cathedral's tower for a view of the city. (☎ 366 0046. Admission free. Tours M-F 11am and 2pm, Sa 11am, Su 11:30am. $3, children $1. Tower climb $4, children $2. Camera permit $2.50.)

AVON RIVER. Walk west down Worcester Blvd. and you'll cross the lovely river Avon, which meanders through the city under willows and arched bridges. Boating on the Avon is an enchanting experience. Tours depart frequently from Worcester Blvd., **Punting on the Avon** or **Punting in the Park** (Avon ☎ 379 9629; $15 per 30min., $10 per 20min. Park ☎ 366 0337; $7.50-20, depending on number of passengers.)

BOTANIC GARDENS. These free public gardens feature one of the country's best arrays of indigenous tree and plant life, with 10,000 different species sharing 30 hectares of land. 450acre **Hagley Park,** with jogging tracks and rugby fields, surrounds the gardens on three sides. (Gardens open daily from 7am.)

ARCHITECTURAL TOURS. Benjamin Mountfort conceived many of the Gothic Revival stone and brick structures in the 1860s and 1870s that today lend the city its distinctive architectural character. At the visitors center pick up a copy of the *Christchurch Central City Walks* pamphlet that details three walks past churches, government houses, and statues along the banks of the Avon. The brightly painted, arched wooden ceiling, magnificent stained-glass windows, and long neo-Gothic hallways of the **Provincial Council Bldgs.,** at Gloucester St. and Cambridge Terrace, have yet to be noticed by most tourists, or even by many locals. (Open M-Sa 10:30am-3:30pm, Oct.-May also Su 2-4pm.) For more comprehensive commentary, contact the **Personal Guiding Service** or **Private Garden Tours** through the visitors center.

MUSEUMS

CANTERBURY MUSEUM. One of the best regional museums in the country, it is home to a diverse range of exhibits, including a panoramic ode to the moa, maori artifacts, and an interesting history of Antarctic exploration. (Beyond the Arts Centre on Rolleston Ave. ☎ 366 5000. Open daily 9am-5:30pm; in winter 9am-5pm. Free.)

ROBERT MCDOUGALL ART GALLERY. Specializing in New Zealand and British painting, several galleries of permanent and temporary exhibitions, ranging from local works to traveling collections, radiate from a central, columned foyer. (Around the other side of the Canterbury Museum. ☎ 365 0915. Open daily 10am-5:30pm; in winter 10am-4:30pm. Free, with guided tours 11am-3pm.)

CENTRE OF CONTEMPORARY ART (COCA). This tribute to Kiwi modernity is an independently supported gallery of innovative modern works with both rotating and permanent exhibitions. (66 Gloucester St., a block toward the Avon from the Arts Centre. ☎ 366 7261. Open Tu-F 11am-5pm, Sa-Su noon-4pm. Free.)

SCIENCE ALIVE. This hands-on science experience also includes a climbing wall and New Zealand's highest vertical slide. It can often surprise and enlighten adults as well. (On Moorhouse Ave., near Manchester St. ☎ 365 5199, www.science-alive.org.nz. Open M-F 9am-5pm, Sa-Su 10am-6pm. $6, children under 5 free.)

OTHER DOWNTOWN SIGHTS

▨ ARTS CENTRE. Formerly the University of Canterbury, the Gothic Revival complex now houses cafes, art studios, shops, the Court Theatre, and two cinemas. Some of the university remains, however, and visitors can walk into **Ernest Rutherford's laboratory** to see where he first experimented with high-frequency magnetization of iron. On weekends craftsmen and clothiers practice the science of persuasion, selling goods in the outdoor market, while ethnic food stalls crowd the back courtyard. *(Bordering the Botanic Gardens on the east and stretching over an entire city block toward the city. ☎363 2836, www.artscentre.org.nz. Guided tours depart from the Arts Centre Information Centre, near the end of Worcester Blvd. M-F 11am, $5.) Take the 1hr. guided tour (with free samples) at the* **Fudge Cottage Kitchen,** *in the Arts Centre (☎363 2836; tours at 2pm M-F, $5, bookings recommended; Open daily 10am-5pm).* The **Arts Annex,** in the Arts Centre, exhibits contemporary sculpture and multimedia works. *(10am-4:30pm. Free.)*

KIWI BONE CARVING STUDIO. A lovely spot to create your own art; drill, chisel, and sand your own necklace for only $40. *(103 Worcester St., near the Cathedral. ☎377 8942; www.bonecarving.co.nz. Allow 3hr. Open daily 9am-5pm; later in summer.)*

SOUTHERN ENCOUNTER AQUARIUM. This recent addition to Christchurch's cultural gems is provoking all sorts of underwater applause. The plastic-wrought walls (designed by the same firm that created rockwork for *Xena*) evoke local rock formations, and unique South Island sea creatures. The eels are fed at 11am, the salmon and trout at 1pm, and the marine fish at 3pm; short films on South Island wildlife run continually in the theater. *(Right in Cathedral Sq., enter via the visitors center. ☎377 3474. Open daily 9am-7pm. $12.50, children $6.)*

OUTLYING SIGHTS

Although there is certainly plenty to do downtown, some of the area's most worthwhile attractions lie just outside the downtown area; most are accessible by a short bus ride from the city center. The **City Circuit Bus** (☎332 6012) runs two loops around outlying sights. For all the goods the **Top Attractions Booklet,** available at the visitors center, is a handy crib sheet for local sights.

■ **NGA HAU E WHA NATIONAL MARAE.** The "Marae of the Four Winds," this national *marae* provides an excellent window into Maori culture and history. The building itself represents the body of Maui, who fished the North Island out of the sea using his grandmother's jawbone (see p. 55); it is this hook that is symbolized by the popular jade or bone hook carvings. The flax ornamentation and painted carvings of ancestors are each uniquely symbolic, and a range of fascinating myths are associated with them. An outstanding guided tour plus an evening concert is available, as is a complete *hangi* (meal, see p. 64), tour, and concert. *(250 Pages Rd. East of Christchurch; take bus #5 from Cathedral Sq. ☎0800 456 898. Guided tour $27.50, children 5-15 $16.50; hangi, tour, and concert $60/$33.)*

■ **INTERNATIONAL ANTARCTIC CENTER.** Let's face it, this is as close as you'll probably ever get to the coldest, driest, windiest continent on earth. Educate yourself with interactive exhibits that include a "snow and ice experience" room, kept at -5°C (about 24°F) and stocked with snow to simulate an Antarctic spring. The multitude of concise, engrossing short videos and the up-close looks at live deep-sea critters housed in sub-freezing aquariums will make you the life of any cocktail party where people want to talk about penguins. Or take a behind-the-scenes tour of the international center of a genuine Antarctic Hagglund. *(Take the A bus or drive to the airport, head north around Hagley Park, and follow the signs. ☎358 9896, www.iceberg.co.nz. Open daily 9am-8pm; in winter 9am-5:30pm. $16, children $8, YHA discounts families $39. Antarctic Hagglund tour $20, in winter $15; children $12/$8.)*

WILDLIFE RESERVES. Willowbank maintains extensive walk-through aviaries and a nocturnal kiwi house. The exceptionally rare and exceptionally ugly *kune kune* pig roams freely, forcing inquisitive peacocks into fence-jumping routines. *(North of the city off Gardiners Rd., accessible by car or the City Circuit Bus. ☎359 6226. Open daily 10am-10pm. $14, students $12, children $6.)* **Orana Park** is a complete African plains park with lions, zebras, rhinos, a variety of savannah animals, native birds, and the ageless tuatara. *(18km from the city, north off Johns Rd. A shuttle (return $15) departs from the visitors center at 12:30pm. ☎359 7109. Open daily 10am-4:30pm. $12, children $6.)*

⚠ OUTDOOR ACTIVITIES

ON THE GROUND. In good weather, catch the free bus out to **Port Hills;** the **Mt. Cavendish Gondola** departs from the visitors center every 2hr. starting at 10am. (☎384 0700; more frequently in summer). The #28 Lyttelton bus also runs regularly. Take the gondola or walk up the steep bridle path (about 1hr.) to the top for a view encompassing Christchurch, the distant Southern Alps, and Lyttelton Harbour. (return $14, students $10, children $7.) Once at the summit, you can choose from numerous **walking tracks** or hurtle down on your mountain bike. **The Mountain Bike Adventure Company** will bring you and a rented bike up the gondola so you can cruise down after riding up. (☎0800 424 534. $40 including gondola ride. Book at the visitors center.)

FARTHER AFIELD. If you've got a car or bike, continue along the summit road to reach **Godley Head,** a rugged promontory of grassy paths and sheer cliffs overlooking the austere Pacific, with superb stargazing at night. In the other direction along Summit Rd., down Dyers Pass Rd., is the **Sign of the Takahe,** one of three Gothic mansions built as a stopping point for travelers decades ago. The Takahe offers a magnificent view of the lights of Christchurch and the Canterbury Plains. (Along Summit Rd., down Dyers Pass Rd. Take the #2 Cashmere bus (runs during the day only) into the hills. ☎332 4052.)

HOT AIR BALLOONING. Hot air balloon enthusiasts flock to the vast flatness of the Canterbury plains. Join **Up Up and Away** or **Aoraki Balloon Safaris** for a leisurely float. Aoraki often leads higher-flying trips from Methven that afford better mountain views. (Up Up and Away ☎358 9859; $200, with champagne. Aoraki ☎302 8172, 0800 256 837; $200-275, with champagne breakfast.)

OTHER AIRBORNE PURSUITS. Tandem skydiving with **Christchurch Parachute School,** at Wigram Aerodome, brings you back to earth after a harrowing free fall. Or, paraglide from the Gondola down to Sumner with ⚑**Phoenix Paragliding, Tandem Paragliding,** or **Nimbus Paragliding,** experiencing an exhilarating descent of near weightlessness. (Christchurch Mobile ☎025 321 135. $245. Phoenix ☎326 7634; www.paragliding.co.nz. Tandem ☎385 4739. Nimbus ☎326 7922; from $95.)

HORSE TREKS. Equestrians have many options for exploring the Canterbury countryside; some of the best trips are run by **Longspur Lodge,** on the road to Akaroa. Other companies that run horse treks include **AlpineHorse Safaris,** which does single- and multi-day horse tours. (Longspur ☎329 0005; 1¼hr.; $30; 2hr. $40; Return transport $20. AlpineHorse ☎314 4293.)

ON THE WATER. There are several local aquatic activities. **Jet Thrills** leads fast-paced river jet boating adventures, while **Waimak Alpine Jet** leads longer trips into the Waimakariri Canyon. **Rangitata Rafts** leads full-day trips over Class 4 and 5 rapids from September through May. **Canterbury Fishing Adventures** takes you out on nearby rivers for some good angling. (Jet Thrills mobile ☎025 387 485; $45, children $30; free pick-up. Waimak ☎318 4881. Rangitata ☎0800 251 251. $130. Free pick-up. Canterbury ☎0800 484 485. Half-day from $140 with 4 people, full-day from $200.)

🔖 DAYTRIPS

LYTTELTON. Clinging to the sloping hills bordering the industrialized Lyttelton Harbour, suburban Lyttelton (pop. 4,000) is Canterbury's major port and a pleasant escape from the city. Just 15min. from the city via the Tunnel Rd. (bus #28), the port shelters a compelling mix of far-flung sailors and bohemian locals, blending seamlessly amid small cottages, oddball curiosity shops, and cafes lining the main strips of London St. and Norwich Quay. The best way to truly enjoy Lyttelton's picturesque setting is by getting out and **walking** it. Grab a map from the visitors center and head up the Bridle Path to the Mt. Cavendish Gondola, or take the Major Hornbrook Track or the Chalmers Track to the ⚑**Crater Rim Walkway.** Many people choose to drive to a point along Summit Rd., which runs alongside much of the walkway, and take a short day-tramp. From Crater Rim, you can look onto the Canterbury Plains and see as far as the Southern Alps and Kaikoura on a clear day. You can then walk across to the gondola, back down to Lyttleton, or over toward Sumner and down to the beach.

Affirming Lyttelton's determined refusal to conform, the **Lyttelton Timeball Station** once communicated Greenwich Mean Time to the boats in the harbor so they could accurately gauge their longitude and remains one of just five in the world that still works. (☎328 7311. Usually open in summer daily 10am-5pm; in winter Su-Th only. $2.50.) Not afraid to get out among the wildlife, **Christchurch Wildlife Cruises** take dolphin- and shag-lovers on a 2hr. journey from 17 Norwich Quay into the harbor, where Hector's Dolphins and other forms of life are often encountered. (☎328 9078, 0800 436 574; www.blackcat.co.nz. $39 per adult. Bookings essential.) **Sea Cruises Ltd.** runs a similar service at a comparable price (☎328 7720). If you want to see the dolphins while simultaneously learning to sail a 1903 Gaff Yawl, check out **Jack Tar Sailing Co.** (☎389 9259, 0800 253 2663).

The **Visitors Center,** 20 Oxford St., between London St. and Norwich Quay, has self-guided walking tours (maps $1) as well as internet access for $2 per 15min. (☎328 9093. Open daily 9am-5pm.) Budget accommodations in Lyttelton are few and far between, but backpackers are fortunate to have **Tunnelvision,** a blue building at the corner of London St. and Canterbury St. (☎328 7576. Closed July-Aug. Dorms $14-16, twins $18 per person; doubles $20 per person.) The **Volcano Cafe and Lava Bar,** at the corner of London and Canterbury St., is difficult to miss. Big portions and tasty coffee are major draws, although the price puts it in the upper range of a backpacker budget. (☎328 7077. Most dinners $15-25, with cheaper bar snacks available. Bar open daily 5pm-late, restaurant from 6pm.) Next to the **Supervalue** on London St. (☎328 7038; open daily 8am-9pm), bright signs lead the way to **Wunderbar.** Follow them down the stairs, through the parking lot, and up the ramp—it's worth the walk. Illuminated mannequins in lingerie and neckties and a doll-head lamp cast light on the velvet seats and tribal masks along the bar, as music from scratchy vinyl LPs wafts overhead. In back, the aptly named **Backroom Bar,** a shimmering cabaret stage complete with a Saturn-shaped disco ball, opens Thursday to Saturday for dancing, live music, and cabaret shows. (☎328 8818. Open M-F 5pm-3am, Sa-Su 3pm-3am.)

SUMNER. Surfers and sun worshippers flock to Sumner (accessible by bus #31 or #32), Christchurch's summer beach-resort town. Those seeking a bit more seclusion continue on to **Taylor's Mistake,** a beach popular with surfers on the other side of the town. **Cave Rock,** near town, is a funky natural grotto accessible at low tide; beware of sudden surges if you choose to venture inside. If you'd rather the Pacific Ocean from stunning heights, call **Phoenix Paragliding,** based in town (☎326 7634; mobile 025 332 794; www.paragliding.co.nz). Lessons are $165 per day, and tandem flights are $120.

You can feel trendy, look stylish, enjoy a great view, and score a tasty meal, all at one place—**Cafe Rock,** 22A Esplanade, opposite the Cave Rock. Bask in the sun on the patio as you sample one of the special pastas ($17) or salads ($6-17). Live music Thursdays after 8pm. (☎326 5358. Open daily from 9am.) Restart your motor after a beachside stroll with a cuppa from bright yellow **Coffee Culture** along the main street. (☎326 5900. Open M-F 7:30am-late, Sa-Su 8:30am-late.) The town is budget–challenged, but **Marine Tavern** (☎326 6609), a well-vacuumed rock'n'roll and sports bar at 26 Nayland St., is in the process of opening up a backpackers.

AKAROA AND THE BANKS PENINSULA ☎03

Magical and old-fashioned, the French-named streets and *maisons*, historic homes, craft shops, and the fishing harbor of the Banks seem worlds away from Anglicized and urbanized Christchurch, despite the mere 85km that separate the two. Cyclists, hikers, and equestrians alike gravitate to Akaroa, for a serene, if provincial, getaway. Proud to be residents of Canterbury's oldest European town, Akaroans are quick to tell a tale or two about their lengthy heritage. Although there's no longer a French speaker to be found on the peninsula (French tourists aside), the cheese factory and winery are testaments to the area's cultural legacy.

TRANSPORTATION. The **Akaroa Shuttle** travels between the Akaroa and Christchurch visitors centers daily. (☎0800 500 929. Nov.-Apr. 2-3 per day, May-Oct. 1-2 per day; $17, return $30). The **French Connection** offers commentary and stops at the cheese factory and departs from the Christchurch visitors center daily at 9:30am (less frequently in winter), leaving the same day about 3:30pm from Akaroa's main wharf. (☎366 4556. $19, return $38, backpackers discount.) Hop on the **mail run** to see the most remote reaches of the peninsula; inquire at the visitors center. (☎304 7207; 304 8600; mobile 025 355 249. M-Sa departs 8:20am returns 1pm. $20.) Although *Let's Go* does not recommend it, **hitchhiking** is possible to and from Christchurch, as most traffic goes all the way to Akaroa; most thumbers take the #7 Halswell bus from Cathedral Sq. Hitchers heading back to Christchurch have the best luck just outside the township, at the bottom of Old Coach Rd.

ORIENTATION AND PRACTICAL INFORMATION. Running past the foliage on the banks of shallow Lake Ellesmere and through several tiny towns, **SH75** winds southeast for 75min. down from Christchurch to the harbor of Akaroa. The road traverses the now-extinct Akaroa volcano and its hairpin curves should not be taken lightly. The town itself, with most of the food and accommodations, sits on Rue Lavaud and Beach Rd. along the water.

Akaroa's **Visitors Centre,** 80 Rue Lavaud, has information on local accommodations, activities, and tracks. (☎/fax 304 8600. Open Oct.-Apr. daily 9:30am-5pm; May-Sept. 10am-4pm.) Other local services include: the **post office,** next door to the visitors center (☎304 7701; open M-F 8:30am-5pm); **BNZ,** which changes money (☎304 7050; open M-F 9am-4:30pm); the **police** (☎304 1030); the **hospital** (☎304 7023); a **pharmacy** (☎304 7002); and the **library,** 141 Rue Jolie, which provides **internet access** (☎304 8782; open M-F 10am-4pm, Sa 10am-1pm).

ACCOMMODATIONS AND FOOD. Built by a Spaniard in 1860, **Chez La Mer Backpackers,** 50 Rue Lavaud, still exudes Old World charm with its herb garden, gazebo, endearingly uneven floors, and free muesli. (☎/fax 304 7024; chez_la_mer@clear.net.nz. Reception 8:30am-10pm. Dorms $16; singles $25; twins and doubles $40, with bath $45.) **Bon Accord Backpackers** has a cheerful owner who welcomes all to stay and use the fully-equipped communal kitchen, den, and small porch. (☎304 7782; bon-accord@xtra.co.nz. Dorms $16; double $40.) A tempting alternative to the backpacker scene is **Akaroa Top 10 Holiday Park,** on Morgans Rd. at the northern outskirts of town. Nestled in the hills, the clean heated cabins offer beautiful views of the harbor, the hills, and the town all at once. (☎/fax 304 7471; akaroa.holidaypark@xtra.co.nz. Standard units from $42; kitchenette units from $48; self-contained units from $60; on-site caravans from $32; powered sites $10 per person; non-powered sites $9 per person.)

Several Akaroa eateries gain inspiration from the French, and unless you adore pub food and pies, they're worth the extra dollars. The **Dolphin Cafe & Bar,** at 6 Rue Balguerie, sits right on the harbor and is cheerfully decorated with fishing and boating artifacts. The TV is actually housed in a window from the sunken Greenpeace vessel, the *Rainbow Warrior* (see p. 110). Lunches run $12.50-19.50. (☎304 7658. Open daily 11am-9:30pm, lunch starts at noon; later hours in summer.) **Bully Hayes,** 57 Beach Rd. on the waterfront, has gourmet lunches for $10.50-15.50; evening cuisine runs a bit more. Choose from the sunny room with large windows and a bay view or the darker, fire-warmed back room. (☎ 304 7533. Open daily 9am-late.) The **Four Square,** on Rue Lavaud across from the museum, fills your grocery needs. (Open M-Sa 9am-6pm; in summer Su 9am-2pm.)

SIGHTS AND ACTIVITIES. There are numerous ways to get up-close and personal with area wildlife. **Dolphin Experience** takes you swimming with rare Hector's dolphins. (☎304 7726, 0508 365 744. 3hr. $75, children $50; spectators $50/ $15.) **Akaroa Harbour Cruises,** on the main wharf, showcases much of the harbor, including the seal and cormorant colonies. (☎304 7641, 0800 436 574. 2hr. $33, children $15.) **Akaroa Seal Colony Safari** takes you in an air-conditioned coach up over the crater, and down the outer slopes to the Pacific Ocean, where fur seals await. (☎ 304 7255; mobile 025 942 070. 2½hr. $50, children $30. Max. 6 people.) **Bluefin Charters** (☎ 304 7866) will take you fishing in the harbor (3hr., $50), or on a half-day trip around the Peninsula (8hr., $500 for boat). They also run cruises and dolphin-watching trips ($35). For the do-it-yourself adventurer, inquire about kayak hires from **Akaroa Boat Hire.** (☎ 304 8758. $35 per day.) **Mount Vernon Lodge** (☎ 304 7180) can arrange **Horse Treks** from $10 per 30min. **Mountain bikers** can rent bikes at **Akaroa Village Inn** (☎ 304 7421; $12 per hr., $30 per day) or at **Chez la Mer** ($15 per day).

If you find the convergence of Maori, British, and French cultures confusing, the **Akaroa Museum,** at the corner of Rue Lavaud and Rue Balguerie, has some informative exhibits detailing the cultural history of the region. (☎ 304 7614. Open in summer daily 10:30am-4:30pm, in winter 10:30am-4pm.) **Barry's Bay Cheese** shows visitors the wheys of cheese-making on alternate days from October-April. (☎ 304 5809; fax 304 5814.) Outdoor enthusiasts, take heart, numerous tracks depart from Akaroa, from the 2- to 4-day coastal **Banks Peninsula Track** to shorter day-hikes of varying difficulty levels through bush, and up the volcano. Fees are required for the Banks Peninsula Track, as the path traverses private property and accommodations are along the way. Inquire at the visitors center for details and maps.

CANTERBURY SKIING ☎ 03

The ski fields in the Southern Alps get downright crazy in winter, with ski fever breaking out just as surely as kids busting out of school for summer. The slopes of Canterbury offer great runs, less glitz, and in some cases cheaper rates than the tourist-heavy southern lakes and are much more likely to attract a Kiwi rather than international following. In addition to traditional commercial fields, several club fields open their slopes to the public. For detailed information on ski fields, check out www.nzski.com, www.snow.co.nz, or pick up the complimentary annual *Brown Bear* guide at the beginning of July (www.brownbear.co.nz).

▓ SKI TRANSPORTATION

Several companies, including some inevitable mid-season newcomers, shuttle the 90min. drive from Christchurch; check in at the Christchurch visitors center for current departures. As a jumping off point, **The Ski Shuttle** runs regularly from Christchurch to **Mt. Hutt** and to **Porter Heights** on demand. (☎ 324 3641. Return $40; students $32.) Similarly, **Snowline Tours** runs from your door to **Mt. Hutt, Broken River, Porter Heights, Mt. Cheeseman, Mt. Olympus,** and **Craigieburn Valley.** (☎ 0800 766 954. Return $42-45; students $38, no special student rate to Mt. Olympus.) Bring snow chains if you're driving; in some cases expect a walk from the parking lot.

▓ SKI FIELDS

While none of these clubs is as popular as nearby Mt. Hutt (see below), each has its own character and loyal following. To stay practically atop the runs, most club fields offer overnight accommodations, and all but Mt. Hutt (30min. from Methven; see below) are only 30min. from the comfortable backpackers in Arthur's Pass (see p. 279). Additionally, each of these clubs offers lessons and packages, but they do not hire equipment unless noted. If you plan on skiing for a number of days or in a number of locations, you may want to consider the **NZ Superpass.** The Superpass allows you to purchase a number of coupons (from $122 for 2 days) which can be used for lift passes on Queenstown and Canterbury ski fields, or on other activities. For more details, check out www.nzski.com.

Porter Heights (☎ 318 4002; snowphone 366 7766, ext. 6; www.porterheights.co.nz), a 1hr. drive from Christchurch. Claims the longest vertical drop. Lift pass $46, students $38; M 2-for-1 adult passes. Ski hire $25. Snowboard hire $40.

Temple Basin (☎377 7788; snowphone 366 7766) has some of the best snowboard terrain in New Zealand, with a 50min. walk from the parking lot to the field. Lift pass $34. Ski hire $30 per day. Snowboard hire $40. Room and board $39.

Craigieburn Valley (☎365 2514; snowphone 366 7766; www.craigieburn.co.nz) is demanding, but excellent. Lift pass $38; students $25. Room and board $45.

Broken River (☎318 7270; snowphone 366 7766, ext. 3) requires a 25min. walk. Lift pass $35; students $30. Room and board $35.

Mt. Olympus (☎0800 686 596; snowphone 366 7766) is known for light powder and cool mornings. Lift pass $30; students $20. Bottom hut $15 per night.

Mt. Lyford (☎315 6178) is known for its natural pipe and good board-learning terrain. Lift pass $40; university students $35; high school students $25.

Mt. Cheesman (☎379 5315; snowphone 366 7766) has a reputation for being family-friendly. Lift pass $42; youth $24. Lift pass, room and board $110; students $98. Ski hire $25, students $20. Snowboard hire $40/$35.

METHVEN AND MT. HUTT ☎03

The modest farming town of Methven (pop. 1500) swells every winter with skiers and snowboarders. The salmon-rich Rakaia and Rangitata Rivers frame the countryside, irrigating a landscape for sheep grazing, stud farming, and cropping. Recently, the town played host to the "Lord of the Rings" technical and construction crew, who were working to film scenes at nearby Mt. Potts.

⻌ TRANSPORTATION. Most transport in Methven either arrives from or departs for Christchurch. As a concession to the ski beast, the **InterCity/Newmans** team (☎379 9020) runs from Christchurch to the **Methven** visitors center (1½hr., 8:20am, $20) and back again (4:55pm). Other similar options include Southern Link's **Ski Link** (☎358 8355) and **Methven Travel** (☎0800 684 888) which drop by the **Christchurch airport** on the way. To shake things up a bit, InterCity/Newmans also runs to **Queenstown** via **Aoraki/Mt. Cook** (9hr.; 9:05am; $78, summer express $46). The **Leopard SkiBus** runs to **Mt. Hutt** from Methven. (☎302 8707. Departs from the Mt. Hutt Snow Centre down Main St. from the Methven visitors center at 8am, 10, and noon; return $20, students $16.)

◼◼ ORIENTATION AND PRACTICAL INFORMATION. SH77 becomes Main St. in town and makes a crossroads with Forest Dr./Methven Chertsey Rd. Most services and accommodations lie within a 5min. walk of the **Visitors Information Centre,** south of the crossroads on Main St., which doubles as a booking agent for transport and activities. (☎302 8955, 0800 764 444; fax 302 9367. Internet. Open daily 9am-5pm; in winter 7:30am-8pm.) **Big Al's,** at the crossroads, is the one-stop adventure shop, renting a variety of clothing and accessories. (☎302 8003; fax 302 8093; www.bigals.co.nz. Ski hire $27; snowboard hire $39; mountain bike hire $28 per day, $8 per hr.; fishing gear hire $8 per day. Open daily in winter 7:30am-7:30pm.) **Wombat's Ski Shop** has similar prices. (☎302 8084. Open daily in winter 7:30am-6:30pm.) The **Boarding House,** on Forest Dr. near the center of town, specializes in snowboards, and also has an indoor skateboard park. (☎ 302 9661; www.boardinghouse.co.nz. $30-37 per day. Open daily in winter 8am-7pm.) **Ski and board shops off the mountain offer cheaper rental deals.** Other services include: the **BNZ,** on Main St. (open M-F 9am-4:30pm); a **Westpac ATM** on The Mall; the **police** (☎302 8200); the **Methven Medical Centre,** opposite the visitors center (☎302 8105; open M-F 9am-5:30pm; weekend clinics June-Oct. also); and the **post office,** in Gifts Galore on Main St. (☎302 8463; usually open M-F 8am-5pm, though hours vary).

⌐ ACCOMMODATIONS. Lodges line the streets of Methven, though many accommodations close in the summer. Price ranges notwithstanding, shares in town are similar; all have waxing racks and somewhere to put your skis. The **Alpenhorn Chalet,** 44 Allen St., the third left past the pubs on Main St. from Forest Dr./Methven Chertsey Rd, stands out from the rest. The glass-enclosed solarium with spa and view of Mt. Hutt combines with central heating and a glowing rimu kitchen to welcome you in. (☎302 8779. Free laundry. Dorms $22, in summer $15; doubles $50/$39.) The rooms at the **Snow Denn Lodge (YHA),** at the corner of McMillan St. and Bank St., may be a bit pricier than other budget accommodations, but you might want to consider splurging; full-linened beds, continental breakfast, spa, and spacious lounges. (☎302 8997; snowdenn@xtra.co.nz. In winter bunks $30-40, singles $40, doubles/twins $40-70; cheaper rates and YHA discounts in summer.) The cozy **Mt. Hutt Accommodation Limited: Bedpost,** 177 Main St., occupies a small complex of brick houses near the center of town. Laundry and linen are free. (☎/fax 302 8508; beds@xtra.co.nz. Bunks $16-18; twins and doubles $20.) Turn right down Main St. from the visitors center, right again onto South Belt, and left onto Wayne Place to reach **The Ski Hut/Redwood Lodge,** 5 Wayne Pl. The Redwood Lodge is more rustic and crowded than the Ski Hut, but rooms in either of the two bungalows should be booked in the same office. (☎/fax 302 8964. Reception 24hr. Dorms $18-22; twins and doubles $25-35. Rates lower in summer.) **Skiwi House,** 30 Chapman St., is a half-block up Chapman St., which begins behind the visitors center and runs parallel with Forest Dr. A brightly painted suite of bungalows and a narrow lounge compose the lively Skiwi House. (☎302 8772; fax 302 9972. Shares in winter $18, $15 in summer; doubles $44/$36.)

⌐ FOOD. Many bars in town serve hearty pub fare during daylight hours (see **Nightlife** below). The urban **Cafe 131,** 131 Main St., is plushly appointed and set up to feed the refined ski set that regularly purchases sandwiches from $4. (☎302 9131. Open daily 9am-4pm; in winter 7am-5pm.) **Eagle Rock Cafe & Bar,** in the Value Tours Building on Main St., offers very good, yet unpretentious dining options. (☎302 8222. Mains $14-22.50. Open Th-Tu from 5pm.) Luxury and charm, however, await at the stone fireplace at **SkiTime,** down Racecourse Rd. Tasty mains run $13-25.50. (☎302 8398. Open daily 5pm-late.) **Four Square Discounter,** on McMillan St., has fresh produce. (☎302 8144. Open daily 7am-9pm.)

⌐ NIGHTLIFE. Pubs are dependable year-round, but upscale bars may shut tight when the days lengthen. Color-coded for easy recall, the **Blue Pub** (☎302 8046), announces its azure self at the crossroads. The **Canterbury Hotel** (☎302 8045, known to locals as the **Brown Pub**) lies just across the road. In broad terms, blue is for skier and brown is for local, but visitors to both enjoy the reasonable pub fare ($9-15). The nightly $10 roast at the Brown Pub deserves special kudos. The **Steelworx** (☎302 9900), a block down Forest Dr., and the **Last Post Saloon** (☎302 8259, open from 5pm), opposite the visitors center, are popular theme bars with character if not extreme originality.

◪◪ ACTIVITIES. With the longest season and best snowcover in New Zealand, **Mt. Hutt** is the main reason that crowds flock to Methven. The 2075m summit looks down upon 365 hectares of beautiful powder, 42 hectares of snow-making, and views reaching into the heart of the Southern Alps. The challenging terrain is suitable for all abilities and a sweet half-pipe beckons boarders. (☎302 8811; snowphone 0900 99 766 or 366 7766. Lift passes $65; students $48. Usually open May-Oct.) If your plan *is* skiing you should consider the **NZ Superpass** see p. 276.

Those seeking immersion in nature will find no shortage of **scenic walks** in the Methven area. If you are in for a longer haul, head for the 1687m **Mt. Somers Summit** (return 7hr.) or the geologically intriguing **Rakaia Gorge Walkway** (return 3-4hr.), which passes through forest and shrub and allows inspection of several coal mine shafts. The **Scotts Saddle Track** (return 5hr.) leaves from the carpark in the Awa Awa reserve, at the end of McLennan's Bush Rd., and climbs 1000m to views of Mt. Hutt for significantly less than the price of a lift ticket; all you pay is effort.

To satiate the needs of adrenaline seekers, **Planet Argo** (☎302 8464, 0800 2746 386, www.southern-x.co.nz) takes adventurers on a half-day excursion on 6-wheel and 8-wheel ATVs ($60 per person). The company also has a small paintball court ($25 per person), and has been known to combine the two activities. Also nearby, at the Mt. Hutt Ski Area Car Park, is the cleverly marketed **Mt. Hutt Bungy** (☎302 9969; www.mthuttbungy.com), which claims to have "New Zealand's highest bungy" only because the edge is the highest above sea-level.

ARTHUR'S PASS ☎03

Snaking through the towering Southern Alps, Arthur's Pass is a haven for skiers and trampers; major ski areas rise to glory within 30min. The tramping in the 230,000 alpine and sub-alpine hectares of Arthur's Pass National Park and nearby Craigieburn Forest Park is beautiful, challenging, and uncrowded year-round. In winter, it is possible to find the road through the pass (SH73) closed due to snow, but the TranzAlpine rail trip through the mountains, considered one of the world's best, is reliable. Amenities are scarce, so it is best to bring groceries.

◨ TRANSPORTATION. The aptly named **TranzAlpine** line, run by **TranzScenic** (☎0800 802 802), bridges Canterbury and Westland with Arthur's Pass at its center. Travel over gorges, river valleys, and alpine fields to **Christchurch** (2hr., 4:30pm, $62) or **Greymouth** (2hr., 11:30am, $39); cheaper fares are available with student card and when booked ahead. Departing from the Tearooms, **Coast-to-Coast** (☎0800 800 847) runs daily bus service to **Christchurch** (2½-3hr., 3:30pm, $25); **Greymouth** (1½hr., 11am, $20); and **Hokitika** (1½hr., 11am, $20). **Alpine Coach** (☎0800 274 888) charges the same rates ($2 cheaper to Greymouth) but departs for **Christchurch** at 10am and for **Hokitika** (2hr.) via **Greymouth** at 5pm.

◪ PRACTICAL INFORMATION. The **Arthur's Pass Visitor Information Centre** and **DOC office**, 200m from the train station on the way to the village, is one of the few buildings in town. (☎318 9211; fax 318 9210. Open daily 8am-5pm; in winter 9am-12:30pm and 1:30-4pm.) The **police** (☎318 9212) are on the main road, across Rough Creek, south of town. A tiny **post office** sits just past Oscar's Haus Cafe (open M-F 9:30-10am). For local **breakdown service** call ☎318 9266.

◪ ACCOMMODATIONS AND CAMPING. Mountain House Backpackers, on the main drag near the visitors center, has a great view of the pass from the comfortable lounge. A true tramper's rest, there are ice-axes, crampons, sleeping mats, and more for hire. (☎318 9258; mountain.house@xtra.co.nz. Reception 10-11:30am and 5:30-7pm; sign-in booking otherwise. Bunks $16; twins and doubles $45; tent sites $9.) The **Sir Arthur Dudley Dobson Memorial YHA,** across the street, commemorates the first man to survey Arthur's Pass in 1864 with a handsome mural in the lounge of this clean and peaceful hostel. (☎318 9230. Reception 8-10am, 5-7pm and 8-9:30pm; sign-in booking otherwise. Bunks $15; doubles $36. Non-members $4 more.) There are simple **DOC tent sites** and a day shelter opposite the visitors center. (Toilets and water in summer. $4 per person.) **Klondyke Corner,** 8km toward Christchurch on SH73, provides free roadside camping with pit toilets; river water must be treated before drinking. There are two other **free campsites,** with pit toilets and untreated water. **Hawdon Shelter** is 27km toward Christchurch on Mt. White Rd., and **Kelly Shelter** is 17km toward Greymouth.

🍴 **FOOD. Oscar's Haus Cafe** serves sandwiches ($3.50), beer and wine, and vegetable-packed mains from $9. (☎318 9234. Open daily 9am-5pm; in winter 10am-4pm.) Behind the gasoline pumps, **Arthur's Pass Tearooms** serves pastries, packaged sandwiches, and carries a small selection of groceries. (☎318 9235. Open daily 8am-7pm; until 9:30pm in summer.) Amid the alpine decor and tourist crowd of **The Chalet Restaurant and Bar,** on the right a few minutes past the hostels, patrons can decide between the bar and dining room, and menus to match. Light meals by the hearth run $2-12, while mains (from $19) are served along polished wooden tables. (☎318 9236. Open 11:30am-2pm and 6-7:30pm; in summer until 8:30pm.)

🥾 **OUTDOOR ACTIVITIES. Arthur's Pass National Park** and the adjacent **Craigieburn Forest Park** enjoy a diverse terrain, from gorges to ascents and from alpine meadows to riverbeds, allowing for both easy walks and demanding tramps in a compact area. Overnight trampers in either area should be aware that local weather can be volatile, and rivers can rise swiftly. As there are no bridges in the parks, and overnight huts cannot be reserved, trampers should check with the **Arthur's Pass Visitor Centre and DOC office** for hut ticket purchase (free to $10), weather reports, and track conditions before leaving. Whatever your destination, emergency overnight gear is essential—and don't feed the keas!

Pick up an informative brochure ($1) for a self-guided **historic walk** of the consistently peaceful village (1½hr.), which includes directions to original tunnelers' huts on the main road.

Among the leisurely tramps, the **Devil's Punchbowl Waterfall Trail** (return 1hr.) begins just past the **Chalet Restaurant** and leads to an arresting view of the falls. A beautiful spot near the start of the trail rewards early birds with a view of the sunrise over the mountains. A number of great day hikes are clustered around the **Craigieburn Environmental Centre** (2km off of SH73, about a 30min. drive east of Arthur's Pass village), where travelers can find picnic sites, camp sites, and shelter. Get trail information (brochure with map $1) from the Arthur's Pass Visitor Centre. The **Cass-Lagoon Saddle** (return 2-3 days) is a popular summertime tramp (beware of avalanches in winter) and one of the easier overnight hikes. Farther east, dayhikers can explore the limestone formations of the **Castle Hill** basin, though local Maori request that climbers stay off the rocks to respect their *tapu* status. A few minutes closer to Arthur's Pass, the **Cave Stream Scenic Reserve** awaits amateur but careful spelunkers bearing polypropylene and torches; expect to get wet in the flowing cave-water that can reach waist height. Both are located off of SH73, a 45min. drive east of Arthur's Pass, 7km past the turn-off to Craigieburn headquarters.

With a variety of ski fields within a 30min. drive, Arthur's Pass is a base camp for serious skiers. Inquire at the visitors center for conditions; weather is often unpredictable, so bring chains for any car you intend to drive to a ski field carpark or lodge. For details on slopes and rentals, see **Canterbury Skiing** (p. 276).

SOUTH CANTERBURY ☎03

Speckled with small agricultural outposts, the unending Canterbury plains slowly blend into the coastal climes of Timaru. Heading inland, the plains give way to mountain passes which lead to an area known as the Mackenzie Country. This area has remained an agricultural region where serene beauty provides welcome relief from the bustle of cities to the north and south. The mighty Aoraki/Mt. Cook lies in majestic repose at the northern end of Lake Pukaki, and in the heart of the Southern Alps, mountains everywhere are reflected in Tekapo, the basin's most famous lake. Covered with tussock grassland and sheep paddocks, and dotted with brilliant lakes against a backdrop of incomparable mountain scenery, southern Canterbury is ruggedly pastoral.

TIMARU   ☎03

With pleasant botanic gardens and beautiful ocean vistas, Timaru (pop. 26,000) beckons with an honest charm. First named Te Maru, meaning "place of shelter," Timaru once provided water and rest for Maori hunters. Today, an artificial harbor built in 1877 protects the international fishing fleet and rigs full of sheep bound for Asia. The wharves also shelter Caroline Bay from rough seas, making it popular with beachgoers in the summer.

▛ TRANSPORTATION. TranzScenic (☎688 3597) leaves daily for **Christchurch** (2hr., 3:11pm, $39) and **Invercargill** (7hr., 10:25am, $91) via **Dunedin** (3½hr., $44). Buses run by **InterCity** leave from the train station for **Christchurch** (2½hr., 3-4 per day, $28) and **Dunedin** (3hr., 3-4 per day, $32) via **Oamaru** (1¼hr., $17). For taxi service, try **Timaru Taxis** (☎688 8899) or **Budget Taxis** (☎688 8779). Several **shuttles** provide alternative service to and from Dunedin and Christchurch. **Hitchhikers** report the base of the highway up to Aoraki/Mt. Cook is a good place to catch a ride to the mountains, although *Let's Go* does not recommend it. Otherwise, SH1 north or south of town is considered the easiest place to grab a ride.

▛ ORIENTATION AND PRACTICAL INFORMATION. Midway between Christchurch and Dunedin, Timaru slopes down from the foothills of the Central Alps to the sea, just south of the road to Aoraki/Mt. Cook. Tranquil **Caroline Bay** is a 15min. walk from the visitors center along Stafford St., while the **Botanic Gardens** are a 20min. walk in the opposite direction on Stafford St., which becomes King St.

From the train station, head left to the **Visitor Information Centre**, 2 George St., in the old lava-built Landing Service Building, where you'll find free maps, local bus schedules, self-guided walking tours, and information on regional events. Also approach the visitors center for **DOC** information, various **shuttle** schedules, and other bookings. (☎688 6163; fax 684 0202. Open M-F 8:30am-5pm, Sa-Su 10am-3pm.) Other services include: **ATMs** along Stafford St.; the **police** station (☎688 4199), at North and Barnard St.; **pharmacies** along Stafford St.; the **hospital** (☎684 4000), on High and Queen St.; **internet access** for $1 per 5min. at **Bay City Internet**, 47a Stafford St. (☎688 6554; open M-F 9am-5:50pm); and the **post office,** at Books and Moore (☎686 6040; open M-Th 8am-5:30pm, F 8am-7pm, Sa 9am-2pm).

▛ ACCOMMODATIONS AND FOOD. Comfortable, well-equipped triples are the norm at **Timaru Backpackers (YHAe)**, 42 Evans St. In addition to a kitchen, the common space includes a lounge area with TV. Call the owner for pick-up, as the uphill walk from the train station is tough. (☎684 5067; fax 684 5706. Shares in spacious motel rooms $17; singles $25; twins/doubles $40; self-contained units for 2 $40.) At **Timaru Selwyn Top 10 Holiday Park,** an extensive camp facility 2km outside of town on Selwyn St., the 100 powered sites sit by a gently burbling creek. You can't beat the video games, TV lounge, immaculate shower blocks, and free access to neighboring Highfield Golf Club. (☎684 7690. Tent sites $19 for 2; power sites $21 for 2; cabins and flats for 2 $35-58; motel units for 2 $70; extra adult $10-13.)

For stellar coffee and food at non-astronomical prices zip off to **Red Rocket,** located at 4a Elizabeth St. adjacent to Chalmers Church off Sophia St. Red is the color of the day, and pizzas ($11.95-16.95) with names like "meat-eorite shower" and "astronomic gastronomic apricot chicken" await you. (☎688 8313. Open M-W 10am-10pm, Th 10am-11pm, F-Sa 10am-midnight, Su 11:30am-10pm.) Roosters watch from their stained-glass perches in the windows of **The Coq and**

Pullet, 209 Stafford St. The mammoth blueberry muffins ($2.50) are a good start to any day. (☎688 6616. Open M-F 7am-4pm, Sa 10am-1pm, Su 11:30am-1:30pm.) Over the hill toward Caroline Bay via Stafford St., the cozy wine bar **Boudicca's,** 64 The Bay Hill, keeps mainly Middle Eastern selections such as falafel-stuffed pitas (small $5, large $8) and beef satay kebabs ($9.50) on its all-day menu. (☎688 8550. Open daily 11am-late.) **The Loaded Hog,** 2 George St., in the Landing Service Building by the visitors center, is a trendy microbrew chain that serves as the late-night hot spot for a young crowd. Bite into the $5 lunch specials (noon-2pm) and wash them down with a $4.50 pint of Hog's Head Dark. (☎684 9999. Open daily 11am until late.)

⬛📷 SIGHTS AND ACTIVITIES. A major fixture of the South Islander's diet, Timaru's own beer is produced in massive vessels at **DB Brewery,** Sheffield St., using their patented continuous fermentation method. If you can, sample just one of the 55 million liters produced here. (☎688 2059. Tours M-F at 10:30am. Free, but call for reservations. No sandals.) The **Aigantighe Art Gallery,** 49 Wai-iti Rd., is just up the hill from SH1 and features a collection of paintings dating from early colonial New Zealand to the present. Gaelic for "at the house," Aigantighe (EGG-and-tie) also showcases sculptures from an international Stone Carving Symposium on the manicured grounds that overlook Timaru's rooftops and Caroline Bay beyond. (☎688 4424. Open Tu-F 10am-4pm, Sa-Su noon-4pm. Free.) From Boxing Day (Dec. 26) until mid-January, the bay area hosts a grand **Christmas/New Year Carnival** that draws crowds to its concerts and contests.

The **Timaru Botanic Gardens,** a 20min. walk south along Stafford St. (which becomes King St.), include rare plant species, ponds flitting with ducks, and grassy knolls fit for a picnic. A wide track runs through the gardens and lures walkers, joggers, and cyclists. **Caroline Bay** and its shallow sweep of sand bustle in the summer months—the reclaimed park contains an **aviary** swarming with technicolor parakeets, an open stage, miniature golf during the summer, and a host of other activities (housed in a historic mansion dating back to 1908). The **Benvenue Cliffs** on the far side of the beach are the best place for a view of the harbor. Today, memorial plaques nailed to a post commemorate lost ships.

TEKAPO ☎03

Encircled by majestic Southern Alpine peaks, the milky turquoise waters of Lake Tekapo lap gently against the smooth pebble beaches of the Tekapo village. The tiny stone church perched on the edge of the lake is powerful in its simplicity. With a moon casting shadows off the pines, and a great swath of stars arching across the horizon, Tekapo's luminous nights complement the serenity of the day. Resting almost exclusively on SH8, Tekapo may be the most glorious road stop ever.

▐ TRANSPORTATION. InterCity (☎0800 777 707), **Southern Link Shuttles** (☎358 8355), and **Atomic Shuttles** (☎322 8883) all run buses daily to **Christchurch** (4hr., $20-42) and **Queenstown** (5½hr., $20-55). Stop by the **Shell Station** on SH8 for prices.

■📷 ORIENTATION AND PRACTICAL INFORMATION. Tekapo is centered along **SH8,** which crosses the dam controlling the Tekapo River, and the central village is clustered around the Shell Station on SH8. The Kiwi Treasures shop in the village functions as the **visitors center.** (☎/fax 680 6686. Open daily 8am-8pm; in winter 8am-6pm.) In emergencies, call the **police** (☎680 6855). There are **no banks** in Tekapo, although the Shell Station has an **ATM,** and the visitors center has EFTPOS and exchanges credit card checks. The **Alpine Inn** (☎680 6848) changes money but takes a substantial commission. Book your **bus** and stock up on **groceries** from the **Shell Station** (☎680 6809). The **post shop** is next to the visitors center and has **internet access** for $12 per hr. (☎680 6861. Open M-Sa 8:30am-5pm, Su 9am-5pm.)

⌐ ACCOMMODATIONS. The **Tekapo YHA** is on Simpson Ln., past the pub on the west side of town. The lounge has massive windows, providing a soulful panorama of the lake. Bike and fishing rod hire is available. (☎680 6857; fax 680 6664. Reception 8-10am, 5-6:30pm, and 8-9:30pm. Dorms $15-16; twins $19 per person; tent sites $9. Nonmembers $3 more.) Up Aorangi Crescent, across from the tavern, is the recently-renovated **Tailor-made Tekapo Backpackers**, 9-11 Aorangi Crescent, with three spacious buildings and two stone BBQs on landscaped grounds. (☎680 6700; tailor-made-backpackers@xtra.co.nz. Linen $2. Internet. Dorms $16; twins and doubles $36, with shower and linen $48; triples and quad $18 per person.) Cyclists are fortunate to have the **Peddlers Paradise**, 1 Aorangi Crescent (the first house on the left), all to themselves. The rooms are spare, but with lake and mountain views for just $12 per night, they're a steal. (No bookings—go to the visitors center or just show up. Cyclists only. Open Oct.-Apr. Tent sites $8. Cash only.)

◖ FOOD. Restaurants and takeaways cluster around the Shell Station on SH8. **Kohan Restaurant,** in the Alpine Inn complex, has a generous array of sushi ($8-16), and their seared salmon steaks are widely renowned. Kohan is planning a move, but with its fabulous reputation, one will only have to ask to find its new location. (☎680 6688. Dinners from $10. Open daily 11am-2pm and M-Sa 6-9pm.) **Reflections,** at the western end of the village, has won cuisine awards for its meat dishes; if you're game, there's beef, lamb, venison ($21-24), and a stunning glimpse of Lake Tekapo and the mist-enshrouded mountains. Lunches cost, and dinners start from, $10; cheaper meals can be had at the adjoining tavern. (☎680 6808. Happy Hour M-Th 7-8pm, F-Sa 5-6pm and 8-9pm. Open daily 11am-late, restaurant from 7am.) **Robin's Cafe & Bar,** next to the visitors center, provides stunning views at cheaper costs, and takeaway service as well. (☎680 6998. Open daily 8am-8pm.) The **Bread Crumb Bakery,** on the main road, sells huge loaves of pizza bread ($4.50), as well as pies and baked goods. (☎680 6655. Open daily 6am-6pm; in winter 7am-5pm.)

◖◪ SIGHTS AND ACTIVITIES. If you have a few extra minutes, stroll across the bridge and down to the **Church of the Good Shepherd,** a tiny interdenominational church of wood and stone constructed in 1935. There are beautiful views of the lake and surrounding countryside from the interior windows. Longer walks in the area include the popular 2½hr. circuit up **Mt. John,** through pine forest and up to the observatory (it begins past the motor park, near the ice-skating rink along the lake's western side). A circuit track to **Cowan's Lookout** leaves from the far side of the bridge, and reveals comparable views of Mt. John in about an hour less. Follow the green and yellow stakes through the fields and over to the rocky shore and the church. If you became truly fascinated with Mt. John, it may be worthwhile to return at night for an entirely different look at Tekapo. **Star Watching** takes visitors on a trip throughout the galaxy in which constellations, galaxies, and planets are pointed out through the massive telescope on Mt. John. Most tours are in Japanese, but some are in English. (☎680 6565. 1¾hr., $35. Min. 4 people.)

To adventure Tekapo, **Lake Tekapo Adventures & Cruises** leads 4WD safaris into the hills surrounding the peaks and does cruises along the Lake. (☎0800 528 624; www.laketekapo.co.nz. 1½hr, $30-50.) Combine the two, and after cruising to the mouth of the Godley River take the 4WD to one of the three huts on the way to the Godley Glacier. This overnight trip costs $168, with an additional hut cost of $30. **Kiwi Express,** on the main road, rents kayaks (1hr. $10, each additional hour $5), golf clubs ($15; green fees at the nearby club are $10), and mountain bikes (half-day $10; full-day $15). They also do bookings for local activities and have internet access. (☎680 6224. Open daily 9am-6pm; in winter 9-10am and 3:30-5:30pm.)

One of the nearest ski fields is small, family-operated **Mt. Dobson** in Fairlie. One-third of the mountain is devoted to beginners, while the rest of the mountain is streaked with intermediate and some black diamond runs. (☎685 8039; www.dobson.co.nz. Lift tickets $30-42; students $24-30. Rentals $22.) Another ski field in Tekapo, is **Roundhill Ski Area**, providing gently undulating slopes that are perfect for beginners or those with children. (☎680 6977; www.roundhill.co.nz. Lift tickets $30-40; beginners $20-25; students $18-30; children $8-14. Ski rental $22-28, children $12-15.) Or, take a scenic 50min. flight with **Air Safaris** over Lake Tekapo to the Godley, Franz Josef, and Fox Glaciers, to Aoraki/Mt.Cook, and back over the Tasman Glacier. The flight includes a commentary sheet to follow along and even circles Aoraki/Mt. Cook for those who want the best view. The plane can also drop you off at the Aoraki/Mt. Cook. (☎0800 806 880. $220.)

AORAKI/MT. COOK NATIONAL PARK

With one-third of its area permanently snow-covered, Aoraki/Mt. Cook National Park and its jagged peaks have an austere and spectacular profile. Notoriously capricious weather and frequent avalanches make this one of the most dangerous regions in New Zealand. Dark lateral moraines and milky blue glaciers give an otherworldly flavor to the desolate landscape: a silence interrupted only by the screeching calls of the world's only mountain parrot, the kea. With 25 peaks over 3000m and a few hundred over 2000m, the highest peak in New Zealand (Aoraki/Mt. Cook), and the longest glacier in Australasia (Tasman), Aoraki/Mt. Cook National Park is near the top of the bottom of the world.

AT A GLANCE

AREA: 70,696 hectares.

CLIMATE: Severe weather patterns; especially dangerous in winter.

FEATURES: Highest mountains, largest glacier coverage (40%). No forest, but alpine plants and wildlife.

HIGHLIGHTS: Aoraki/Mt. Cook, the tallest mountain in New Zealand.

GATEWAYS: Aoraki/Mt. Cook Village is located within the park; Twizel is outside.

CAMPING: Accommodations available in the Village; 17 backcountry huts.

FEES & RESERVATIONS: Inform DOC of plans and check for necessary hut passes.

MT. COOK VILLAGE   ☎03

At the end of SH80, a 45min. drive from Twizel, the buildings of tiny Aoraki/Mt. Cook Village (pop. 120, in summer 300) are nestled in the heart of Aoraki/Mt. Cook National Park. Not just anyone can live here; residents must be employed by DOC or one of the local accommodations. To many Maori, the highest mountain in New Zealand represents the most sacred of ancestors, and a recent agreement with the national government has placed restrictions on the mountain's use. Climbers must turn back before reaching the summit, and all references to the mountain must place the Maori name before the English one.

▐ **TRANSPORTATION.** You can book **bus** transport with **InterCity** (☎0800 777 707); the schedule is flexible. Buses usually depart daily from the Hermitage and the YHA for **Christchurch** (5½hr., 12:45pm, YHA discount) and **Queenstown** (4hr., 2:45pm, YHA discount) via **Twizel**. **Great Sights** (☎358 9029) and **Grey Line** (☎0800 800 904) also run through Aoraki/Mt. Cook on their way between Christchurch and Queenstown. Both depart for **Queenstown** at 2:20pm and for **Christchurch** at 2pm; Great Sights (with full commentary) is $58, while Grey Line (no commentary) is $40. **High Country Shuttles & Tours** (☎0800 435 050) runs between Twizel and Aoraki/Mt. Cook. (Departs Twizel 7am and 1pm; departs Aoraki/Mt. Cook 10am and 4:30pm. In winter runs only on demand. $15, return $20.) For exploring the park, the Hermitage rents **mountain bikes** for tracks open to cyclists.

PRACTICAL INFORMATION. The **Aoraki/Mt. Cook Visitor Centre,** near the Hermitage, is the place to book activities, check track conditions, and check-in and out for all trips in the park. If the weather doesn't allow a good glimpse of the mountains, you are assured of one through the $2.50 visitors center's 20min. audio-visual presentation. (☎435 1186; fax 435 1080. Open daily 8:30am-6pm; in winter 8:30am-5pm.) The nearest doctor and pharmacy are located in Twizel. Head to the **Hermitage** (☎435 1809) for the **post office, grocery store, internet** ($10 per hr.), and **currency exchange** (24hr.). There is a self-serve **petrol** pump that accepts Eftpos, but no international credit cards. Pick up the phone at the pump to reach a Hermitage staff member, who will help you purchase with cash or international credit card. Consider bringing enough food, gas, and cash to avoid the high prices in Aoraki/Mt. Cook altogether.

ACCOMMODATIONS AND FOOD. With comfy couches, sauna, and a great video collection, the **Mt. Cook YHA** builds a cozy lodge atmosphere. (☎435 1820; fax 435 1821; yhamtck@yha.org.nz. Internet, some groceries, and lockers available. Reception 8-10:30am, noon-3pm, and 5:30-9:30pm; in winter 8-10am, 5-6:30pm, and 8-9pm. Dorms $21; twins $29 per person; doubles $32 per person. Nonmembers $3 more.) In summer, the **Hermitage** opens vacant chalets equipped with a TV and kitchenette for backpackers. (☎435 1809, 0800 801 111; fax 435 1879. Reception 24hr. Open mid-Sept. to mid-May. $20.) At the end of the Hooker Valley Rd. is the **White Horse Hill Camping Area** with on-your-honor sites ($5).

Food options in town are extremely limited. The **Chamois Bar,** in the Glencoe wing of the Hermitage, offers bar meals 5pm-10:30pm, and drinks until midnight (until 1am Th-Sa). In the main area of the Hermitage, the **Hermitage Coffee Shop** is open in summer from 7:30am-5:30pm, and in winter from 10am-5pm.

OUTDOOR ACTIVITIES. The peaks, glaciers, and ice cliffs of Aoraki/Mt. Cook National Park draw visitors from all over the world. Those traveling on a shoestring rather than a belay rope can taste glacial terrain with the many short day walks in the area. The most popular walk is the **Hooker Valley** (return 4hr. from the village) with a beautiful viewpoint and two swing bridges. The strenuous uphill climb up to **Red Tarns** (return 2hr.) rewards exertion with exhilarating views down into the Hooker Valley and up into the cloud-piercing Alps. Slightly milder, the **Kea Point Walk** (return 2hr.) leads through scraggly gorse to a lookout over the Mueller glacier, with Mt. Sefton's azure ice falls in the background. The only feasible overnight tramping option is the 3-4hr. route to **Mueller Hut** ($18). The rest of the huts in the park ($8-18) are accessible only to experienced climbers, and serve as bases for technical ascents. Always check in with DOC if you are planning a trip.

The Hermitage and the YHA have information on (and also book) several tours. In the summer, **Glacier Explorers** runs a boat tour of the Tasman Glacier that glides past the icy blue cliffs jutting over the lake. (☎435 1077. 2½hr.; $75, YHA $55, children $35.) **Alan's 4WD Tours** travel over rough terrestrial terrain to the Tasman Glacier. (☎435 1809. $75, children $35, YHA members $65.) The **Helicopter Line** (☎435 1801, 0800 650 651) has a 20min. flight with a snow landing ($138, YHA $128), as well as several longer—and more expensive—options. **Air Safaris** flies the airplane "Grand Traverse," guaranteeing a window seat and good commentary along the way. (☎0800 806 880. 50min.; $220, $195 if booked through visitors center; children $140; YHA 10% discount.) **Mt. Cook Ski Planes** runs the popular Flight Spa 1 with gorgeous views of Murchison and Tasman Glacier and a glacier landing in-between. If you are lucky, your pilot may do some plane skiing as he takes off from the hangar. (☎435 1026, 0800 800 702. 40min.; $240, YHA $223.) Some planes work with the heli-hikes, heli-skiing, and heli-mountain biking, although the prices rocket well over $500.

The small family ski field of **Ohau,** between Twizel and Omarama, is not far off. The field has plenty of beginner runs and a good number of intermediate and advanced slopes as well. The Hopkins and Huxley Wings offer $16 budget accommodations. (☎438 9885. Lift passes $40, students $28. Rental $25, student $20.)

CANTERBURY

THE WEST COAST

The towering Southern Alps bound the region to the east and form a geological wall a mere 40 to 50km from the Tasman Sea. The combination of snow-capped peaks, endless green bush, and pounding waves are the scenery of the West Coast. With all that beauty, it's no wonder that over 80% of the region is government-owned, set aside in various national parks, forest parks, and scenic reserves.

⛏ WEST COAST HIGHLIGHTS

CHIP AWAY with ice-axe in hand on **Fox** or **Franz Josef Glacier** (see p. 296).

GET BLOWN AWAY by the pancake rocks and blowholes of **Punakaiki** (see p. 289).

THROW YOUR CARES AWAY in the tiny, seaside outpost of **Okarito,** where worries neither enter nor leave (see p. 296).

⬛ TRANSPORTATION ON THE WEST COAST

West Coast travelers should keep in mind that there are no banks or supermarkets on the long stretch between Hokitika and Wanaka, and petrol stations are often few and far between. **Hitchhiking** through the West Coast has a bad reputation, and *Let's Go* doesn't recommend it. As usual, however, those with patience (and good rain gear) report success. Daily **buses** also provide a dependable way to travel.

WESTPORT   ☎ 03

Westport's lifeblood has always been its river, its gold, and its coal. A 19th-century gold-rush town, the original Westport washed away in a flood in 1872. Gold fever subsided, but the town soon bounced back to boomtown size thanks to the coal mining, shipping, and fishing that took its place. Westport also tames the tempestuous Buller River, which now provides thrilling rafting and springtime whitebait fishing. Cape Foulwind and the Tauranga Bay seal colony are also close by.

⬛ TRANSPORTATION

InterCity (☎379 9020) heads daily from Craddock's Energy Center/Caltex Garage, 197 Palmerston St. near Rintowl St., to: **Fox Glacier** (6¾hr., 11:20am, $64) via **Punakaiki** (1hr., $19), **Greymouth** (2hr., $24), and **Franz Josef** (6hr., $59); and **Nelson** (3¾hr., 4pm, $47). **East West** (☎789 6251, 0800 500 251) runs daily from Craddock's to **Christchurch** (4½hr., 8am, $44). **Karamea Express** (☎782 6617) departs from Craddock's and runs to **Karamea** (1½hr.; Oct.-Apr. M-Sa, May-Sept. M-F; 11:30am; $15). **Cunningham's Motors,** 179 Palmerston St. (☎789 7177), heads to **Karamea** (2½hr., M-F 3pm, $15), stopping to drop off mail at various points along the way. **White Star Passenger and Freight Service** (☎789 6200) departs for **Christchurch** (6hr., Su-F 10:05am, $40) and **Nelson** (6hr., Su-F 10:05am, $40). **Atomic Shuttles** (☎789 6658) departs daily from the visitors center for **Greymouth** (2hr., 3:30pm, $20) and **Nelson** (5½hr., 9:40am, $30). For a lift in town, call **Buller Taxis** (☎789 6900).

✦ ⓘ ORIENTATION AND PRACTICAL INFORMATION

The **Buller River** marks Westport's western border. Two blocks east, the main drag **Palmerston St.** runs parallel. **Brougham St.** intersects Palmerston near the center of town. The **Westport Visitor Information Centre and DOC Office,** 1 Brougham St., cheerfully answers queries. (☎789 6658. Open daily Jan.-Feb. 9am-7pm; Mar.-Dec. 9am-5pm.) Other services include: **House of Travel,** 196 Palmerston (☎ 788 8120; open M-F 8:30am-5pm); **banks** lining Palmerston St. (generally open M-F 9am-4:30pm); **bike**

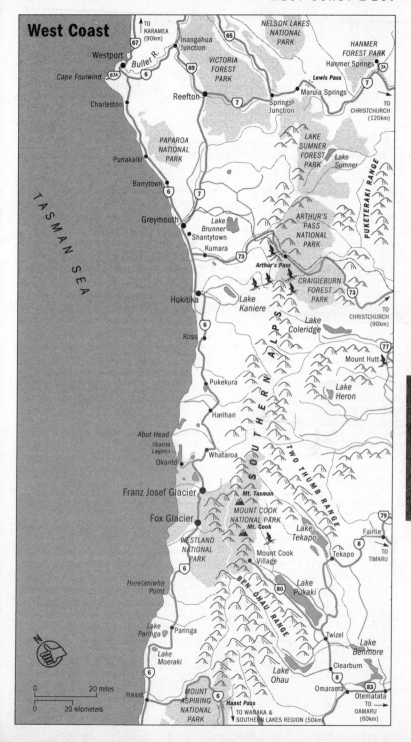

West Coast

TO
KARAMEA
(90km)

67

Westport

Buller R.

Cape Foulwind 67A

Charleston

Inangahua
Junction

65

69

6

VICTORIA
FOREST
PARK

Reefton

7

Springs
Junction

Maruia Springs

Lewis Pass

HANMER
FOREST PARK

Hanmer Springs 7A

7

TO
CHRISTCHURCH
(120km)

PAPAROA
NATIONAL
PARK

Punakaiki

Barrytown

6

7

LAKE
SUMNER
FOREST
PARK

Lake
Sumner

Greymouth

Lake
Brunner

Shantytown

Kumara

73

Arthur's Pass

ARTHUR'S
PASS
NATIONAL
PARK

CRAIGIEBURN
FOREST
PARK

73

TASMAN SEA

Hokitika

Lake
Kaniere

Lake
Coleridge

TO
CHRISTCHURCH
(90km)

77

Ross

6

Mount Hutt

Pukekura

Lake
Heron

Harihari

Abut Head

Okarito
Lagoon

Okarito

Whataroa

Franz Josef Glacier

Mt. Tasman

Fox Glacier

Mt. Cook

MOUNT COOK
NATIONAL PARK

WESTLAND
NATIONAL
PARK

6

Mount Cook
Village

Lake
Tekapo

Fairlie

79

Tekapo

8

TO
TIMARU

Heretaniwha
Point

Lake
Paringa

Paringa

Lake
Moeraki

6

80

Lake
Pukaki

Twizel

Lake
Benmore

Clearburn

Lake
Ohau

8

Omarama

83

Otematata

TO
OAMARU
(60km)

N

0   20 miles

0   20 kilometers

Haast

MOUNT
ASPIRING
NATIONAL
PARK

6

Haast Pass

TO WANAKA &
SOUTHERN LAKES REGION (50km)

SOUTHERN ALPS

TWO THUMB RANGE

PUKETERAKI RANGE

BEN OHAU RANGE

WEST COAST

rental at **Beckers Sportsworld,** 204 Palmerston St. (☎788 8002; $15 per day; open M-F 8:30am-5pm, Sa 9:30am-12:30pm); **police** (☎789 7339), on Wakefield St.; **Buller Pharmacy,** 160-162 Palmerston St. (☎789 7629; open M-Th 8:30am-5:30pm, F 8:30am-6pm, Sa 9:30am-12:30pm); **Buller Medical Centre,** 45 Derby St. (☎789 7309); **internet access** at the **public library,** on Brougham St. across from the visitors center (☎789 7235; $8 per hr.; open M-Th 10am-5pm, F 10am-6:30pm, Sa 10:30am-1pm); and the **post office,** on the corner of Palmerston and Brougham St. (☎789 7799; open M-F 8am-8pm, Sa 9am-6pm).

ACCOMMODATIONS

Bazil's Hostel, 54 Russell St. (☎789 6410), backing the clock tower. With your back to the visitors center, head left to the first intersection and take a left; Bazil's is in the middle of the block. Soft beds and a toasty lounge mean it's often full—Kiwi Experience stays here almost every night. Dorms $17; twins and doubles $40; camping $10.

Robyn's Nest (formerly Nancy's Hostel), 42 Romilly St. (☎789 6565; robyns.nest@xtra.co.nz). Head left from the visitors center and take a left at the first intersection; after 3 blocks, take a right on Pakington for 3 blocks. Robyn moved in last year and has set about restoring the Victorian house and garden to their original charm. Internet access $3 per 30min. Dorms $16; doubles $35; camping $8.

Marg's Traveller's Rest (YHA), 56 Russell St. (☎789 8627), next to Bazil's. Every two dorms have their own kitchen and common room. Dorms $18, in winter $16; twins and doubles $45/$38; powered RV sites for 2 $18/$16; camping $8. YHA $1-2 off.

TripInn, 72 Queen St. (☎789 7367; tripinn@clear.net.nz). Go left from the visitors center 2 blocks on Brougham to Queen and take a right. Big but quiet, with lots of common space. Video library. Dorms $15-16.50; twins and doubles $40; camping $10.

Westport Holiday Park, 37 Domett St. (☎789 7043; fax 789 7199). With your back to the visitors center, head left for 7 blocks, then take a left onto Domett St. Friendlier and better kept than most. Dorms $13.50; tent sites for 2 $16, powered sites for 2 $18; cabins for 2 $32, with bath $44.

FOOD

Most of Westport's dining choices (think takeaways) line Palmerston St. One sweet spot is **Mandala's Restaurant, Bar, and Coffee House,** 110 Palmerston St., where the ingredients are fresh and the portions gigantic. (☎789 7931. Eleven-layer burger $12. Open daily 7am-late; May-Sept. 8am-5pm.) **Bailie's Bar,** 187 Palmerston St., is nothing flashy, but nightly backpacker meals (grill-your-own burger and a 12oz. Steinlager for $10) can be tough to turn down. (☎789 7289. **Internet** $3 per 15min. Open M-Th 3pm-late, F-Su 11:30am-late.) Otherwise, just hit the **New World,** 244 Palmerston St. (Open M-F 8am-8pm, Sa-Su 9am-6pm.)

SIGHTS AND ACTIVITIES

The famed West Coast limestone **cave formations** are truly a regional highlight. **Norwest Adventures** offers trips through Westport's share of these wonders. Their "Underworld Rafting" adventure inner tubes through the rapids, glowworm grotto, stalactites, and stalagmites that characterize the Styxian river that flows, underground, through the **Metro Cave** system. (☎789 6686, 0800 116 686. 4-5hr. $105. Min. age 10.) With newly slimmed wallets, the more adventurous can squeeze through narrow passages and abseil down a 120-foot hole on their "Adventure Caving: Te Tahi" trip (4hr., $220, min. age 16).

The **Buller River,** the third largest in New Zealand (and the largest free from damming or other hydraulic alteration), provides plenty of **rafting** excitement, from mellow floats to raging whitewater expeditions. Ultra-professional **Ultimate Descents** (see p. 260), based in nearby Murchison, navigate the river by raft, by kayak, and by sledge. They also arrange trips to waters so remote one has to helicopter in. (☎523 9899, 0800 748 377; www.rivers.co.nz. 2hr. trip $95. Full-day $145.) **Buller Adventure Tours** (☎789 7286, 0800 697 286) also works out of Murchison and, like their neighbor, operates tours on the Buller's rougher waters (half-day $85, full-day $120). The company offers jetboating (1½hr., $60) and horse trekking (2hr., $45). **Burning Mine Adventures** (☎789 7277, mobile 025 275 3553) conducts mountain bike trips (4hr., $45), tours of the Stockton Opencast Mine (4hr., $45) and whitewater kayaking for beginners ($75).

The Westport area also harbors several beaches with swimming areas; **Carters Beach,** 6km from town, stretches from Cape Foulwind to the mouth of the Buller River, and **North Beach,** 4km from town, stretches along Craddock Dr. to the north end of the Buller. Just 16km out of town, **Tauranga Bay** is famous for some of the best **surfing** in New Zealand and the **seal colony** that makes its home here. The **Cape Foulwind Walk** (return 3hr.) provides an opportunity to see the seal colony from above as well as other great views. Try your luck **fishing** for whitebait (a West Coast delicacy) around the Buller River (Sept. 1-Nov. 15; no license needed).

Finally, head to **Coaltown,** a historical museum and replica coalmine, south on Queen St. across the railway tracks. (☎789 8204. Open daily 9am-4:30pm. $6, students $4, children $3.) A drive along the 120km **Buller Coalfields Heritage Trail** hits the other highlights of Westport's coal mining history. Release your social athlete on a beer made from a 16th-century recipe at the organic **Miner's Brewery,** 10 Lyndhurst St. off Palmerston. (☎789 6201. Tours M-Sa 11:30am and 1:30pm. $5.)

PAPAROA NATIONAL PARK ☎03

Waves crash with thunderous claps against the layered rocks, drenching the expectant sightseers clustered in their bright, crayon-colored raincoats. At last the waves strike just right, the blowholes spray high into the air, and the cameras click away in a fury of photographic zeal. Sharing smiles, the tourists congratulate each other on capturing that once-in-a-lifetime (or at least once-in-an-hour) shot of **Punakaiki.** Between Greymouth and Westport on SH6, the incredibly popular "pancake rocks" and blowholes are the highlights of the water-carved landscape of Paparoa National Park; the largest chunk of lowland rainforest in New Zealand.

AT A GLANCE

AREA: 30,000 hectares.

CLIMATE: Temperate coastal climate and high rainfall.

FEATURES: Lowland rainforest and limestone and mudstone rocks.

HIGHLIGHTS: Pancake rocks, Dolomite Point.

GATEWAYS: Park in Punakaiki, located near Westport and Greymouth, along SH6.

CAMPING: Accommodations and camping allowed in Punakaiki.

FEES & RESERVATIONS: Only individual accommodation and camping fees.

WEST COAST

TRANSPORTATION. Punakaiki is the main town of the Paparoa region. **Buses** stop near the visitors center. **InterCity** (☎768 7080) passes through Punakaiki daily en route to **Greymouth** (45min., 12:50pm, $9), and to **Nelson** (4¾hr., 3pm, $56-61) via **Westport** (1hr., $18), pausing long enough to allow riders to witness the explosive blowhole action and grab a bite. **Atomic Shuttles** (☎768 5101; $20 return) and **Greymouth Taxis** (☎768 7078) also run from Greymouth ($25 roundtrip, min. 3 persons).

 WHEN TO GO. Punakaiki can be visited year-round. Be sure to visit the pancake rocks during high tide as the blowholes are exceptional.

⁊ PRACTICAL INFORMATION. The **Punakaiki Visitor Centre,** on SH6 across from the blowholes, dispenses all park info—it is not a booking agent. (☎731 1895, after hours ☎0800 222 233; fax 731 1896. Open daily 9am-6pm; in winter 9am-4:30pm.) The nearest **petrol** stations are 35-60km away, but the Wild Coast Cafe, beside the visitors center, keeps a small emergency supply. The **police** can be reached at ☎768 1600. The cheapest **Internet access** in town is at the Beach Hostel ($9 per hr.).

⌂🏠 ACCOMMODATIONS AND FOOD. Punakaiki's accommodations are scattered along SH6. If you're coming by bus, ask the driver to drop you off at your destination or you're in for a long walk. The **Punakaiki Beach Hostel,** on the corner of Webb St. and Dickenson Parade, is a 15min. walk from the visitors center with the ocean on your left. Somewhat cramped but comfortable rooms open onto a magnificent beach. (☎731 1852; fax 731 1152. Free pick-up. Internet. Dorms $18, in winter $16; twins and doubles $40-44.) The **Te Nikau Retreat,** Hartmount Place, is a 30min. walk north of the visitors center; call for free pick-up. Several separate buildings connect through the rainforest. (☎731 1111. Internet. Dorms $16; doubles $40, with bath $45; motel units $55-60; tent sites $12.50.) Next door to the Beach Hostel, **Punakaiki Beach Camp** has a range of pleasant cabins as well as tent sites. (☎731 1894. 2-person cabins $26-33; tent sites $8.50, powered sites $10.) For limited groceries and takeaway, stop by **Wild Coast Cafe,** near the visitors center. (☎731 1873. Open daily 8am-7:30pm; in winter until 6pm.) For an evening drink, the **Punakaiki Tavern,** on SH6 by the Beach Hostel, is usually packed, and has an international musical instrument collection for twiddling. (☎731 1188. Open daily 8am-midnight; in winter M-Th 10am-10pm, F-Sa 10am-midnight, Su 10am-10pm.)

◎🏃 SIGHTS AND ACTIVITIES. The **Punakaiki blowholes** and mysterious 350-million-year-old **pancake rocks** are at the end of the **Dolomite Point Walk** across from the visitors center, "downtown" (return 20min.; wheelchair accessible). If possible, check the tide schedule before planning your visit—the blowholes are practically nonexistent at low tide. The 🏃**Trumans Track** (15min.) off SH6 3km north of the visitors center, heads out to a dramatic viewpoint at the ocean's edge, and at low tide the beach and rocks can be explored; keep your eyes peeled for starfish! Grab a flashlight to explore the **Punakaiki Cavern,** 500m north of Punakaiki, to the right of SH6. The **Punakaiki Pororari Loop** (return 3hr.) winds through the stretch of rainforest from the Punakaiki River to the Pororari River (check in advance to see if the river can be crossed). More rugged trekkers can explore the **Inland Pack Track** (27km, 2-3 days), which began as a safe alternative to the pitfalls of coastal travel during the 1860s gold rushes. Get full trail information and check-in at the **Punakaiki Visitor Centre** before you go; stay on the track as there are no huts, and numerous sinkholes. **Punakaiki Canoe Hire,** 1km north of the visitors center beside the tavern, has guides and rents canoes for paddling in the Pororari Gorge. (☎731 1870. 1hr. $15, each additional hour $5.) **Coast and Mountain Adventures** will guide you through the wilderness or set you up to scale high Paparoa limestone. (☎731 1853. 2-3 hr. nature walk $35, rock-climbing $55, overnight trek $135.) Call **Paparoa Horse Treks** to view the pancake rocks from horseback, or take a longer trip through the Punakaiki River Valley. (☎731 1839. 1-2hr., $30-50. Closed in winter.)

GREYMOUTH   ☎03

After the gold rush of the late 1800s, Greymouth's timber, coal, and fishing resources facilitated its growth into the biggest town on the West Coast. Besides being in the heart of extraordinary tramping, caving, and rafting terrain (there are at least 14 rivers in the vicinity), Greymouth is the western terminus of the Trans-Alpine railroad, one of the most breathtaking routes in the world. Those voyaging through Westland instead should pause here to stock up on groceries, cash, and gear, as small towns south and north have little.

Greymouth

ACCOMMODATIONS
Kainga-ra YHA Hostel, 5
Global Village Backpackers, 8
Noah's Ark Backpackers, 4
The Railway Hotel, 7

FOOD
Bonzai Pizzeria, 1
Raceway Carvery, 3
Smelting House Cafe, 6
Supervalue Supermarket, 2

▐ TRANSPORTATION

Trains: TranzScenic (☎ 0800 802 802). The **TranzAlpine** leaves daily for **Christchurch** (4hr.; 2:25pm; $87, with student card $70) via **Arthur's Pass** (2hr.; $39, students $31). Half-price "supersaver" fares sometimes available if booked in advance.

Buses: InterCity (☎ 768 7080) heads from the railroad station daily to **Fox Glacier** (4hr., 1:50pm $37) via **Hokitika** (40min., $11) and **Franz Josef** (3½hr., $37); and to **Nelson** (6hr., 1:50pm, $67) via **Punakaiki** (40min., $8) and **Westport** (2hr., $20). **Atomic Shuttles** (☎ 768 5101) is usually cheaper and runs south every day to: **Queenstown** (10½hr., 7:30am, $75) via **Hokitika** (30min., $10), **Franz Josef Glacier** (3hr., $25), and **Fox Glacier** (3½hr., $25). **Coast-to-Coast** (☎ 0800 800 847) runs to **Christchurch** (5hr., 1pm, $35) via **Arthur's Pass** (2hr., $20). **Alpine Coaches** (☎ 762 5081, 0800 274 888) goes daily to **Christchurch** (4hr., 8:30am, $35) via **Moana** (30min., $14) and to **Arthur's Pass** (1½hr.; $18, daytrips $30).

Taxis: Greymouth Taxis (☎768 7078). Runs to **Shantytown** ($23 return), **Hokitika** ($15), and **Punakaiki** ($25 roundtrip, min. 3 persons).

Car Rental: Budget (☎768 4343) is at the train station. **Half Price Rental,** 170 Tainui St. (☎768 0379), and **Hertz,** 92 Tainui St. (☎768 7379), are in town.

Bike Rental: Mann Security and Cycles, 25 Mackay St. (☎768 0255), and **Cole's Sports World,** 53 Mackay St. (☎768 4060; half-day $10, full-day $20).

✳ 🔃 ORIENTATION AND PRACTICAL INFORMATION

From the steps of the **Greymouth Railway Station** the main drag, **Mackay St.,** runs left to the town center and right to the Grey River behind the massive "Great Wall" down **Mawhera Quay.** Greymouth happily metropolises on Mackay and **Guinness St.**

Visitors Center: Promote native flora by purchasing seeds at the **Greymouth Information Centre** (☎768 5101; fax 768 0317), on the corner of Herbert and Mackay St. Also a booking agent. Open daily 9am-6pm; in winter M-F 9am-6pm, Sa-Su 10am-6pm.

Currency Exchange: Banks cluster around the intersection of Tainui and Mackay St. and are generally open M-F 9am-4:30pm. Almost all have **ATMs.**

Police: 47 Guinness St. (☎768 1600), at the corner of Tarapuhi St.

Medical Services: Check with **Mason's Pharmacy,** 34 Tainui St., for the number of the on-duty doctor. (☎768 7470. Open M-Th 8:30am-5pm, F 8:30am-6 or 7pm.) **Greymouth Hospital** (☎768 0499) is located on High St. 1km south of the town center.

Internet Access: Available at the **visitors center** for $2 per 10min. **DP-1 Cafe,** 108 Mawhera Quay, charges $6 per hour for those staying at Backpackers ($8 for others).

Post Office: (☎768 0123), on Tainui St. Open M-F 8:30am-5pm, Sa 10am-12:30pm.

▐ ACCOMMODATIONS

▨ **Global Village Backpackers,** 42-54 Cowper St. (☎768 7272, 0800 542 636; fax 768 7276). Walk down Tainui St. away from town, bear right onto High St., take a right down Franklin St. then a left on Cowper St. Rooms upstairs are inviting with international decor. Call for free pick-up. Free hot drinks, kayaks, bikes, and fishing rods. Linen $2. Dorms $16; twins $40, in winter $25; doubles $42.

Kainga-ra YHA Hostel, 15 Alexander St. (☎768 4951), around the corner from Noah's, and minutes from the train station. The hillside manor, formerly a residence for men of the cloth, commands an impressive view of the coast. Dorms $15-17; twins and doubles $40. Single sex dorms available. Wheelchair accessible unit.

Noah's Ark Backpackers (VIP), 16 Chapel St. (☎/fax 768 4868, 0800 662 472). Turn left off Mackay St. onto Tainui and cross the tracks; Chapel St. runs uphill to the left. The friendly owners, pets, and resident bus crowd conspire to keep things lively. Dorms $16; twins and doubles $40; tent sites $10 per person.

Neptune's, 43 Gresson St. (☎768 4425), along the Greymouth Great Wall by the old rail tracks. A former fishermen's pub and motel has been refitted into a deep-sea wonderland. Free bubblebath and spa. Dorms $16; singles $30; doubles and twins $40.

The Railway Hotel (☎768 4023), on Mawhera Quay. Clean and pleasant budget rooms above the happening bar. Breakfast $10. Singles $20.

TO PECK AND DESTROY Mother Nature's saboteur, the sharp-beaked **kea** is one of New Zealand's native birds—and a bloody nuisance. Among their notorious hobbies, keas enjoy casing carparks in search of unattended bike seats. They also steal food, untie shoelaces, feast on camping and skiing equipment, and rip windshield wipers to shreds. In fact, keas are one of the largest causes of rental car damage in New Zealand, so be wary of leaving cars unattended in kea-infested lots, or be prepared to pay the costly consequences.

FOOD

Restaurants and cafes line Mackay St., while takeaways crowd along Tainui St., down sidestreets, and in malls. The **Supervalue Supermarket** is between Guinness and Mackay St. below Herbert St. (☎ 768 7545. Open M-Tu 8am-6:30pm, W 8am-7pm, Th-F 8am-8:30pm, Sa 9am-7pm, Su 9am-5pm.)

Smelting House Cafe, 102 Mackay St. (☎ 768 0012). Creative, mouth-watering hot meal selections ($6-8.50) and sandwiches ($3-4) rotate daily. Open daily 8am-4:30pm; in summer until 5pm.

The Railway Hotel (☎ 768 7023), on Mawhera Quay. The best deal in town is a $3 all-you-can-eat BBQ of sausage, salad, onions, and bread (vegetarian option $5; nightly from 6pm). Open daily 11am-late.

Bonzai Pizzeria, 31 Mackay St. (☎ 768 4170). International newspapers cover the walls of this busy joint. Small pies from $11.50, large from $17.50; ample breakfast and non-pizza menu. Open daily 7am-late.

Raceway Carvery, 20 Herbert St. (☎ 768 4013), in the Union Hotel. Walk from the rail station to the end of Mackay St. and turn left onto Herbert. The carvery's $10 roast plus two courses is a local institution. Open M-Th 11:45am-2pm and 4:45-8pm; F-Su until 9pm; breakfast M-Su 7:30-9am.

SIGHTS

Founded to quench the thirsts (and empty the pockets) of gold rushers, ▨**Monteith's Brewing Company,** on the corner of Herbert and Murray St. (a block off Tainui St. about 10 minutes from town), produces between 30,000 and 60,000 liters of beer each day. Monteith's informative tour gives visitors a 30min. chance to taste the rainbow (from Black to Original Gold to Celtic Red) that has Kiwis raving. (☎ 768 4149. Tours M-Th 10, 11:30am, and 2pm; F 2pm. Book ahead. $5.)

For a more traditional approach to settler history, visit **Shantytown,** 11km south of Greymouth on SH6. Re-creating an 1880s gold rush town, Shantytown has its own post office, sawmill, working steam train, horse and cart rides, and gold mine. (☎ 762 6634. Open daily 8:30am-5pm. Admission $10.50, with panning $13.50; children $7.50.) To get to Shantytown, **Kea West Coast Tours** will pick you up from your digs and liven up the ride with running commentary on regional history. (☎ 768 9292, 0800 532 868. 3hr., daily 10am and 2pm. Return $32.) **Greymouth Taxis** also runs with less talk for less dough. (☎ 768 7078. 10:15am, 12:15pm, and 2:15pm. Return $23. Min. 2 people.) Locals highly recommend a self-guided tour of the **Brunner Mine Site** (1hr.), just north of town on Route 11 past Taylorville, and the **Woods Creek Track** (45min.), with gold mining and flora infoboards (bring a torch to explore the glowworm-inhabited tunnels), south of town near Shantytown. Pick up a brochure at the visitors center ($1). To wander farther, Kea runs tours to **Punakaiki** (4hr., 9am and 2pm, return $40) and to the **glaciers** and **Lake Matheson** (full-day, 8:30am, $165, min. 2 people).

ACTIVITIES

If Greymouth had a motto, it would probably be, "Water, water everywhere, so hop into the drink." One way or another, most of the town activities involve water. **Dragon's Cave Rafting,** operated by **Wild West Adventures,** runs a caving trip in the **Taniwha Caves.** The half-day excursion includes a beautiful 30min. rainforest hike and ends with a slick water slide and a dip in the hot spa back at headquarters. (☎ 768 6649, 0800 223 456. $105, pick-up and drop-off included.) **Eco-Rafting Adventures,** run out of the DP-1 Cafe, plans custom day or multi-day trips for kayaks or rafts on low-grade to Class V rapids, including extreme heli-rafting adventures. (☎ 768 4005. Half day $70, full day $120, heli-rafting from $190 per day.) **On Yer Bike!** runs 4WD farm bike tours through the bush on demand; the wetter, the better.

(☎762 7438. 1hr. $45, 2hr. $80.) **Dolphin Watch,** run by **Dolphin Adventure Tours,** brings you by kayak or boat to the dolphin areas and shag nesting sites off the coast of **Point Elizabeth.** (☎768 9770, 0800 929 991. 2hr. or 3-4hr. trips; $67 for trips down the Grey River, $87 for sea kayaking or trips with dolphin swimming.) The nikau palms on the coast can be seen along the **Point Elizabeth Walkway** (return 3hr., tide dependent); travelers without a car will need to take a taxi or catch a ride out. To walk, go past the rail station inland, across the bridge, turn left down Bright St., and turn right along the coast on Domett Esplanade toward the trailhead (return 2hr.).

About 30min. east of Greymouth lies the trout fishing of **Lake Brunner** and the avian attractions of Moana. (Alpine Coaches stops at Moana, at the edge of the lake; see **Transport** above.) Swim, kayak, or canoe among the white herons *(kotuku)* on the lake before bedding down at the campground at the Moana end of the lake. The **Moana Hotel** hires fishing rods at the pub and rents rooms. (☎738 0083. Dorms $14-16.) **Lake Brunner Boat Hire** will set you up with a kayak or a fishing dinghy. (☎738 0291. Kayaks $30 per half day, students $40 per day. Dinghies $15 per hr., 4hr. min.)

HOKITIKA ☎03

Once the largest port in New Zealand, Hokitika (ho-kuh-TEEK-uh) is no longer a bustling center of activity. Today it is famous for its abundance of crafts; virtually all of New Zealand's jade is quarried within a 20km radius of the town. If you spend more than just an afternoon in Hokitika, enjoy a long beach-combing meander and a potentially magnificent sunset over the Tasman Sea.

▐▌ TRANSPORTATION. InterCity (☎755 8557) drops off at **Hokitika Travel Centre,** 60 Tancred St. (☎755 8557). InterCity heads daily to **Nelson** (7hr., 12:45pm, $62) via **Greymouth** (45min., $11) and **Westport** (3hr., 12:45pm, $27); and to **Fox Glacier** (3hr., 3:05pm, $33) via **Franz Josef** (2½hr., $33). **Coast-to-Coast** (☎0800 800 847) goes to **Christchurch** (4½hr., 1:05pm, $35) via **Arthur's Pass** (2½hr., $15). **Atomic Shuttles** (☎768 5101) runs daily to: **Greymouth** (30min., 5pm, $10); **Queenstown** (10hr., 8am, $65) via **Franz Josef** (2½hr., $20); **Fox** (3hr., $25).

▐▌ PRACTICAL INFORMATION. The **Westland Visitor Information Centre** is in the Carnegie Building on the corner of Tancred and Hamilton St. (☎755 6166. Open daily 8:30am-6pm; in winter M-F 9am-5pm, Sa-Su 10am-2pm.) The local **DOC** is on Sewell St. near the river. (Open M-F 8am-4:30pm.) Other services include: an **ANZ** at the post office, and an **ASB,** 99 Revell St., both with **ATMs** (open M-F 9am-4:30pm); the **police,** 50 Sewell St. (☎755 8088); **Westland Medical Centre,** 54 Sewell St. (24hr. ☎755 8180); **internet access** at the Westland District Library, 36 Weld St. ($2 per 15min.; open M-F 10am-5pm, Sa 9am-noon); and the **post office,** on Revell St. (open M-F 8:30am-5pm, Sa 10am-12:15pm).

▐▌▐▌ ACCOMMODATIONS AND CAMPING. If you decide to stay overnight, try the ▨**Blue Spur Lodge,** 5km out of the city on Hampden Rd. turning to Hau Hau Rd. Overlooking Mt. Cook and the Southern Alps, the welcoming wood lodge is as private as backpackers get. The 100-acre property offers a 1hr. bushwalk and an open gold mine tunnel where guests can pan for treasure using the lodge's free equipment. Kayak trips are also available, with free transport to and from Lakes Kaniere and Mahinapua. (☎/fax 755 8445; bluespur@xtra.co.nz. Free bikes. Dorms $17; doubles $42, with bath $50.) Or stay with the "Mad Kiwi" (his real name is Gordon) at **The Jade Experience Backpackers,** 197 Revell St. Right on the beach, the house only holds 5 people and a couple of wwoofers (see **WWOOF** p. 52), but staying a night might get you a discount on the jade carving lesson. (☎755 7612. Dorms $15; doubles $35.) **Mountain Jade Backpackers,** 41 Weld St., near the clock tower, is a cheerful place to rest your head. From the mermaid peeking into the showers ("oh behave!") to the sheep surveying the bunkroom,

Got ISIC?

ISIC is your passport to the world.

Accepted at over 17,000 locations worldwide.
Great benefits at home and abroad!

To apply for your International Student, Teacher or Youth Identity Card
CALL 1-800-2COUNCIL
CLICK www.counciltravel.com
VISIT your local Council Travel office

Bring this ad into your local Council Travel office and receive
a free Council Travel/ISIC t-shirt! *(while supplies last)*

the hostel shows its colorful sense of humor. (☎755 8007, 0800 838 301; fax 755 7804. Single-sex dorms $16; doubles $40.) A short walk from the center of town, **Beach House Backpackers (VIP),** 137 Revell St., has a beachfront location. Despite being a tad chilly in winter, the place is still tidy and the folks are friendly. (☎0800 755 6859. 15min. free Internet. Dorms $16; twins and doubles $40; tent sites $10.) Lake Kaniere, 23km from town, has **DOC campground**s with water and toilets ($4 donation). There's another 10km south of town at Lake Mahinapua with water, toilets, and fireplaces ($4 donation).

◘ **FOOD.** A local spot popular for its cheap lunch ($5.50-9.50) and all-day breakfast, the **Filling Station Cafe,** 111 Revell St., will recharge your batteries. (☎755 8344. Open daily 7:30am-9pm; in winter 8:30am-8:30pm.) A heaping help-ing of Chinese at **Wong's Wok Cafe 'n' Restaurant,** 41 Weld St., downstairs from Mountain Jade Backpackers, is easy on the wallet, but hard on the biceps. The winter special of soup, entree, main, and dessert is just $16. (☎755 6444. Open daily 8:30am-late.) While it appears to be a standard cafe from the outside, a cuppa at **PR's Cafe and Restaurant,** on Tancred St., will be anything but dull. (☎755 8379. Open daily 8am-4pm; in summer also from 6pm-late for dinner.) **Cafe de Paris,** a few doors down, is a bit pricier. (☎755 8933. Lunch $7-15. Open daily 7:30am-midnight, in winter from 8:30am.) Stock up on groceries at **New World,** 116 Revell St. This is the last supermarket north of Wanaka and has the best prices you will find before then. (☎755 8390. Open M-W and Sa 8am-6:30pm, Th-F 8am-8pm, Su 9am-6pm.)

◕◪ **SIGHTS AND ACTIVITIES.** Hokitika is renowned for the expertise of its greenstone, woodworking, and glass-blowing artisans. In spite of the touristy kitsch that accompanies the sale of crafts, there are finely worked and reasonably priced pieces in Hokitika, and, if nothing else, the demonstrations showcase con-siderable skill. **Westland Greenstone,** 34 Tancred St., has jade pendants, pins, and paperweights for sale. (☎755 8713. Open daily 8am-5pm.) **Quades House of Wood,** located across the street, has a large, expensive wooden turtle with a removable shell. (☎755 6061. Open daily 8:30am-5pm.) The **Hokitika Glass Studio,** 28 Tancred St., exhibits glass artistry ranging from a whimsical penguin chess set to elephants and dainty flowers. (☎755 7775. Open daily 9am-5pm.) All three shops allow visi-tors to view the artisans at work. To become the artisan yourself, ring Gordon (☎755 7612) out at Jade Experience Backpackers for a **carving lesson** and piece of jade. Carvings begin at $80 and usually require all day.

The **Glowworm Dell** illuminates Hokitika after hours. A 30min. walk north of Hok-itika on SH6 by the right side of the road displays phosphorescent larvae separated from groping hands by a chain link fence. **Lake Mahinapua** is rife with walking tracks and picnic areas, and **Lake Kaniere** draws nature lovers to its stands of rimu, tussock grassland, and subalpine scrub. There is no public transport from Hoki-tika to the lake, but **Hokitika Cycles and Sports,** 33 Tancred St., rents bikes for $20 per day and offers a last chance to fix your bike before heading south. (☎755 8662. Open M-F 8:30am-5pm and Sa morning.) Tranquil weather often calls for an equally calming activity such as a paddle boat cruise from **Scenic Waterways** into the picturesque Lake Mahinapua. (☎755 7239. 1½hr., $20.)

No matter how wet the weather, you can fish to your heart's content at **West-land's Water World,** 55 Sewell St. (☎755 5251. Open daily 9am-6pm; in winter 9:30am-4pm. $10, students $8.) The **West Coast Historical Museum,** on the corner of Tancred and Hamilton St. will dole out leaflets for a Hokitika heritage walk. (☎755 6898. Open daily 9:30am-5pm; in winter Sa-Su 10am-2pm.) The **National Kiwi House** displays endangered kiwis and sundry aquatic creatures. Audio-visual "Who Killed the Kiwi" is included with admission. (☎755 8904. Open daily 9am-7pm. $8, children $4.) Visitors for the weekend of March 9, 2002, have a chance to sample possum, whitebait, snail, venison, and even kangaroo at the **Wild Foods Festival.**

WEST COAST

OKARITO   ☎ 03

On the edge of the 3240-hectare Okarito Lagoon, this tiny seaside community offers serenity and scenery unmatched along the coast. Certainly not known for its tourism or vast population (20), Okarito is famous instead as a habitat for a vast diversity of bird species. Some travelers use the town—just 28km north of Franz Josef Glacier and 13km off SH6—as a retreat from the over-touristed glaciers.

Okarito's treasure is its lagoon and the wildlife that goes with it—the best way to experience these is by getting out on the water. **Okarito Nature Tours** can supply kayaks, a map, and even a bird book to explore their well-marked routes. (☎753 4014. Half-day $40, full-day $50; guided trips from $65.) Okarito also has several beautiful hikes. The **Okarito Trig Trail** (return 1hr.), leads uphill through kahikatea and rimu rainforest to a viewpoint. The **Coastal Walk** (return 3hr.) wanders through the bush above the shoreline.

Coaches stop (by request) at the turn-off to Okarito on SH6; it's a common place to hitch or a long walk into town. Alternatively, **The Royal Okarito** will pick up guests from the turn-off, or even from Franz Josef for stays of two nights or more. This generosity typifies the Royal's atmosphere—stuffed animals and hot water bottles warm the beds. (☎753 4080; royalokarito@hotmail.com. Free breakfast and laundry. Potluck dinners several times a week. Dorms $18; doubles $44; self-contained unit $60.) The **Okarito Campground** has unpowered-only sites. Cottages for 4-8 people are available; book in advance. (Hostel beds $10; contact Suzie Clapperton for details ☎753 4124. Tent sites $5 per person, children $1; cottages $50; contact Tony and Rose-Anne Gray of the Royal Okarito for details.) There are **no shops** in town, so bring food, insect repellent, and other necessities with you.

FRANZ JOSEF AND FOX GLACIERS

Finding yourself face-to-face with several billion cubic meters of solid blue ice moving several meters a day is typical when visiting Fox and Franz Josef. In fact, that's precisely why tourists flock to these gargantuan glaciers. The twins are extraordinary not only because of their size and speed of advance (or retreat), but also because they descend almost into the rainforest, only 12km from the Tasman Sea. The glaciers' unique location, sandwiched between the sea and the Southern Alps in a temperate rainforest region, accounts for the massive 20 to 30 meters of snowfall that bury the top of the glaciers each year and ensures that they will long outlive any tourist impertinent enough to attempt to conquer them.

Fox and Franz Josef Glaciers are part of the 117,547-hectare **Westand National Park**, which contains a feast of hikes and bushwalks highlighting native biota. There are many ways to explore the glaciers: a hands-on hike on the glacier itself or a birds-eye helicopter tour are the most popular. Pressed for time, the hurried and harried traveler must often choose between Fox and Franz Josef Glaciers. Franz Josef Glacier, although smaller, may be more impressive than its icy neighbor, and therefore more popular. Fox Glacier has a longer walk through rainforest and moraine to reach the ice. The town of Fox Glacier is slightly less commercial than its twin and refreshes with more bucolic views and relaxed locals.

FRANZ JOSEF GLACIER   ☎ 03

Lying 140km south of Hokitika and 27km north of Fox Glacier, Franz Josef Village exists but for the grace of its massive glacier. With large Lake Mapourika nearby and more tourist outfitters, Franz is the destination of most tour groups and the backpacker buses. Slip down to the river for a picnic to escape the crowds.

▐ TRANSPORTATION

The **Glacier Shop** in the Alpine Adventure Building is the local agent for **InterCity** (☎752 0131). Daily buses head north to **Nelson** (10hr., 9:30am, $81) via **Hokitika** (3hr., $33), **Greymouth** (4hr., $41), and **Westport** (6½hr., $52). This bus connects with the **TranzAlpine** service to **Christchurch** in Greymouth. There is also a daily southbound bus to **Queenstown** (8hr., 8am, $54) with stops in **Fox Glacier** (45min., $8), the **Copland Track** (1hr., $13), and **Wanaka** (6hr., $65). Ask for discounts, as student and saver fares are often available. **Atomic Shuttles** (☎752 0738), booked at the Glowworm Cottages, provides northbound service to **Greymouth** (3hr., $25) via **Hokitika** (2hr., $20) and southbound to **Queenstown** (7½hr., 10:30am, $50) via **Fox Glacier** (30min., $10), **Haast** (3½hr., $30) and **Wanaka** (6hr., $40). The pick-up for both shuttle companies is at the coach stop on Main Rd. near the Cheeky Kea Cafe.

▐ ORIENTATION AND PRACTICAL INFORMATION

Running through the center of town, **SH6,** known as Main Rd., is the location of most of the town's services—backpackers are located on parallel **Cron St.,** also known as **Back St.** The **Franz Josef Visitor Information Centre** and **DOC office,** on the south edge of town on SH6, have displays on the ecological devastation wrought by possums (and, consequently, a possum pelts for sale; see **Possum Problems** p. 71). (☎752 0796; fax 752 0797. Open daily 8:30am-6pm; in winter 8:30am-noon and 1-5pm.) There are **no banks or ATMs** in town; the **Mobil Station,** near the center of town on SH6, will cash traveler's checks and advance cash on credit cards in summer and pending cash in winter. It is also the **post office.** (☎752 0725. Open daily 7:15am-10:15pm; in winter 8am-6pm.) Cheap **Internet access** is available at Cafe Franz in the Alpine Adventure Building on Main Rd. ($8 per hr. Open 8am-6pm.) **Ice Flow Arts,** down Main St. from the Mobil station rents bikes. (☎752 0144. Bikes $6 per hr., $18 for a half-day. Open daily 9am-10pm; until 6pm in winter.)

▐ ACCOMMODATIONS AND FOOD

Look for the roof-scaling mountaineers atop cozy **Chateau Franz (VIP),** 8 Cron St. Grab a round of pool ($1) or relax in the free spa pool. (☎752 0738. Internet. Reception 8am-8pm. Check-out 10am. Dorms $17; twins $37; doubles $40. VIP $1 off.) **The Glowworm,** at the other end of Cron St., could be its freshly built twin, were it not for its slightly smaller size. (☎752 0172. Dorms $17-20; singles $38; doubles $45.) The **Franz Josef YHA** is next door to Chateau Franz on Cron St. A game at the pool table and the hokey pokey ice cream for sale before nightly video screenings are a pleasant end to a glacier-filled day. (☎752 0754; fax 752 0080. Reception 8-10am, 4:30-6:30pm, and 8-9pm; extended hours in summer. Check-out 10am. Bunks $18; twins and doubles $40; camping $8.50. Nonmembers $3 more.) The clean and spacious **Montrose,** just opposite on Cron St., has vastly expanded its facilities and now hides a spa. (☎752 0188. Reception 8am-1pm and 4:30-7pm. Dorms $16; twins $36; doubles $40; tent sites $5 per person. Wheelchair accessible.) Join the Kiwi Experience at **Black Sheep Lodge.** Although it's a fair walk from the center of town, it has a big TV with a collection of Hollywood's finest. (☎752 0007; fax 752 0023. Internet. Reception closes at 8pm. Dorms $17; twins and doubles $44. VIP $1 off.) Tent sites at the **Franz Josef Holiday Park** are beside the Black Sheep. (☎752 0766, 0800 435 6733. $9; powered sites $10 per person.)

In a swinging setting just up from the petrol station, **The Blue Ice Cafe** serves a nice pizza-and-pint special ($12-16) one would happily order again if not distracted by the free pool table. (☎752 0707. Open 11am-late.) **Beeches,** in the center of town, makes a high-quality lunch menu available until 5:30pm (burgers $4) and makes 4-6pm a truly happy two hours with $2.50 beers. (☎752 0721. Open 7am-late.) **The Cheeky Kea Cafe,** right next door, pleases budgeteers with a Saturday evening all-you-can-eat feast (6-8pm, $17.50). (☎752 0139. Open 7am-8pm.) A limited range of pricey groceries are provided at the **Fern Grove Food Centre,** on Main Rd. (☎752 0731. Open 7:45am-6:30pm; until 10pm in summer.)

NIGHTLIFE

Although there are only a few who have enough energy to head out after a long day on the ice, there are a few pubs in town that satiate the urge for a frosty brew. **Batson's Tavern,** at the far end of Cron St., has both a bar and a bottle shop for relaxing at home. (☎752 0740. Open from 4pm.) The **Franz Josef Glacier Hotel,** at the north edge of town, has a similar setup with a blazing fire in winter that is guaranteed to warm all limbs that you haven't already lost to frostbite. (☎752 0729. Open from 4pm in winter, from 2pm in summer.)

ACTIVITIES

ON THE GLACIER
The best way to appreciate the size and majesty of the glacier is up close and personal. The following companies run a variety of trips to Franz Josef and provide all equipment, but no nourishment.

THE GUIDING COMPANY. This young but well respected operation leads both half- and full-day walks on the glacier. If you feel up to five or six hours on the ice, pack a lunch and opt for the full-day trip. As the guides lead the way, chipping steps with an ice-axe, no less brave and sure-footed hikers explore narrow crevasses, cavernous tunnels, and gorgeous glacial pools. The company also runs a fantastic full day of ice-climbing on the glacier, suitable for beginners and experienced climbers alike. (☎752 0047, 0800 800 102. Book ahead in summer as trip size is limited, and report 30min. in advance. Half-day hike 3½hr., daily 9:15am and 2pm, $40. Full-day hike 7-8hr., daily 9:15am, $80. YHA 10% off on hikes. Ice climbing 9:15am, $150.)

FRANZ JOSEF GLACIER GUIDES. This older company serves a young backpacker bus crowd, making for lively interaction and a little spring on their icy glacier steps. The half- and full-day walks go for the same rates as above, but this operation doesn't offer ice-climbing trips. (In the Helicopter Line/Franz Josef Glacier Guides Building on Main Rd. ☎752 0763, 0800 484 337; fax 752 0102.)

HELI-HIKING. This high-flying adventure is a terrific way to explore the glacier. Significantly more expensive than day hikes, a heli-hike deposits visitors atop the glacier, eliminating the trek to the terminal face, but provides less ice time to explore and gain confidence. Both guiding companies run trips. (3hr., around $200.)

SCENIC FLIGHTS
SKYDIVING. Professional and friendly, **Skydive New Zealand—Fox and Franz Josef Glaciers** is a small operation that provides a pre-jump scenic flight with views of three glaciers, Mt. Cook, Mt. Tasman, and the Tasman Sea. Lost in the magnificence of the Southern Alps, you'll almost forget your original reason for climbing to 12,000 ft.—almost. Bring a small camera for some unbeatable shots as you fall. (☎0800 751 0080. Book in advance. 9000 ft. $225, 12,000 ft. $265. Weather dependent.)

BY HELICOPTER. Four different helicopter companies operate from Franz Josef, none of which operate in questionable weather. It pays to book ahead, especially in peak season from Jan.-Mar. All operators offer similar prices (and essentially the same tried-and-true routes) except for **Mountain Helicopters,** who provide a cheaper option as they are not licensed to land on the glacier. (☎0800 369 423; from $90.) **Fox and Franz Josef Heliservices** (☎752 0764, 0800 800 793), **Glacier Southern Lakes Helicopters** (☎752 0755, 0800 800 732), and the **Helicopter Line** (☎752 0767, 0800 807 767) have offices on the Main Rd. (Tours of the Franz Josef Glacier, Fox Glacier, Tasman Glacier, and Mt. Cook range from $130-270, depending on flight duration and package chosen.)

BY PLANE. Air Safaris offers a "Grand Traverse" airplane tour. It does not include a snow landing, but it covers a greater area than the helicopter flights. *(☎ 752 0716, 0800 723 274; fax 680 6740. 45min., $220.)* **Aoraki Aero Company Ltd.** is the only plane permitted to land on the glaciers, although it also runs flights without landings. *(☎ 752 0714. Flights with landings from $230; without landings from $190.)*

LESS SLIPPERY WALKS

GLACIER VALLEY WALK. This stroll leads right to the terminal face of the glacier and approaches the gargantuan ice cube without paying the hefty guided price-tag. From there it's a hike along the Waiho River Bed (return 2hr. if you include a switchback trip up Sentinel Rock); observe markings and be careful. *(From the visitors center turn right, cross the bridge, and follow the signs. Allow an hour to walk to the end of the access road, or drive the 4km.)*

ALEX KNOB WALK. On a clear day, this tramp, accessible when it's not snowed under, leads to breathtaking views from the ridge. This walk is best attempted before lunch as clouds usually roll in each afternoon. *(Return 8hr.)*

CANAVAN'S KNOB. Another walk to take on a clear day, the high points along the way rise above the silverfern and rainforest to deliver views of both the glacier and the coast. *(Off SH6, 2km south of town. Return 40min.)*

ST. JAMES ANGLICAN CHURCH. The glacier view from the altar window of this church is so beautiful that it was showcased on a 1946 peace stamp that was issued to celebrate the end of World War II. *(A pleasant jaunt down SH6; turn onto the path at the right before the bridge; the church is through the brush at the end of the path.)*

GUIDED BUSHWALKS. Kamahi Tours leads guided trips in the Franz Josef and Okarito area. If you wish to approach the glacier, but not scale it, Kamahi runs a two-hour tour to the base of the glacier complete with commentary about area history and geology. *(☎ 752 0699, 752 0793. Trips range from 1hr. to full-day. 2hr. trip, $25.)*

OTHER ACTIVITIES

ALPINE ADVENTURE CENTRE. "Flowing West," a 20min. movie shown daily, catapults the viewer across glacial rivers, through tangled rainforest, over the Southern Alps, and finally out onto the glaciers. Much cheaper than a helicopter flight, this is a fine wet weather alternative well worth the price. *(☎ 752 0793. Up to 4 per day, guaranteed to show daily at 5pm. $10, children $5.)*

WHITE HERON SANCTUARY TOUR. This ecotour brings a limited number of visitors to observe breeding pairs of white herons. Sacred to the Maori, these birds breed only in New Zealand. *(☎ 0800 523 456. Operates from Whataroa, a 30min. drive north of Franz Josef. Summer only. Book ahead. 2½hr., $89, children $40.)*

LAKE MAPOURIKA. The lake is stocked with brown trout and Quinnat salmon, and the nearby bush is rife with chamois and possums; fishermen and hunters can get licenses from DOC. For a guided trip, call **Chris Morris** *(☎ 753 4177)* or contact **Ferg's Kayaks** across from the Glowworm Cottages on Cron St. *(☎ 752 0230, 0800 423 262. 3½hr. lake tour by kayak with digital photos of you on the lake $45.)*

A JADED PERSPECTIVE Greenstone (*pounamu*, or **jade**) has long been considered a precious mineral. Created millions of years of ago at the same time the Southern Alps were rising from their fault, greenstone is found primarily in Westland and around Lake Wakatipu. Today, factories in Westland excavate, chip, and carve the opaque emerald stone for everything from touristy trinkets to flowing works of art. In ancient times (and even up to the present), the Maori used greenstone for tools and *tikis* (carved figurines), as well as for weapons and religious purposes. Famed worldwide for its wide range of coloration, *pounamu* was renowned among the Maori (who knew it by over a dozen different names) for its tremendous spiritual value—it was believed to retain and even magnify a person's *mana*, or spiritual power.

FOX GLACIER   ☎03

Twenty-seven kilometers south of Franz Josef on SH6, Fox Glacier is a diminutive
village near a massive glacier. Normally visited only after a visit to Franz, Fox
offers a refreshingly less commercial atmosphere, a profoundly serene environment, and the tranquil quicksilver reflections of nearby Lake Matheson (New
Zealand's most photographed lake).

▐ TRANSPORTATION

InterCity (☎ 751 0701) leaves from **Alpine Guides** and heads north daily to **Nelson**
(11hr., 8:45am, $82) via **Franz Josef** (45min., $7), **Hokitika** (3½hr., $39), **Greymouth**
(4½hr., $45), and **Westport** (7hr., $60). They also travel southward daily to **Queenstown** (7hr., 8:45am, $52) via the **Copland Track** (20min., $8) and **Wanaka** (5hr., $48).
Prices listed are with a student and YHA discount of at least 20%; book ahead in
summer. From Ivory Towers, or your doorstep by request, **Atomic Shuttles** (☎ 768
5101) runs daily to **Greymouth** (3½hr., 2pm, $25) via **Franz Josef** (1hr., $10) and **Hokitika** (3hr., $25), and to **Queenstown** (7hr., 11am, $50) via **Haast** (3hr., $25) and
Wanaka (5hr., $35). **Mac's Shuttle** will run you all over if you just ask. (☎ 751 0712.
Prices vary. One way to **Lake Matheson** or **Glacier** access path $12 per person;
Gillespie's Beach, return $50.) **Around Here Rentals** (☎ 751 0821) rents wheels to
explore the region for $35 for a half day, $65 for full. **Fox Glaciers Motors** is the last
stop to fill up for 120km. (☎ 751 0823. Open from 8am-7:30pm; until 6pm in winter.)

✳▐ ORIENTATION AND PRACTICAL INFORMATION

Running through the center of town, **SH6** is known as Main Rd. It heads north over
three hills to Fox's comrade Franz Josef, south to one trailhead of the **Copland
Track,** and then to **Haast** (121km). Cook Flat Rd. leads south from the center of
town to wonderful views of the mountains over town. The famous reflecting **Lake
Matheson** (6km) and seal-colonized **Gillespie's Beach** (20km) are located down
Lake Matheson Rd., which is off Cook Flat Rd.
   The **Fox Glacier Visitor Information Centre** and **DOC office** is located on SH6 north of
the main village. (☎ 751 0807; fax 751 0858. Open daily 8:30am-6pm; in winter 9am-
4:30pm.) In the center of everything, **Alpine Guides,** on Main Rd., is the headquarters for the glacier guides and serves as a **post office** and **currency exchange.** (☎ 751
0825. Open daily 8am-9pm; in winter 8:30am-5:30pm.) Coin-operated **Internet** can
be found at the **Ivory Towers Backpackers** ($2 per 10min.).

▐▐ ACCOMMODATIONS AND FOOD

The majority of accommodations are located on Sullivans Rd. and Cooks Flat Rd.,
both of which veer off Main Rd. near the center of town. Without a doubt, the best part
of ▐**Ivory Towers,** Sullivans Rd., is the company. A large dining room, TV lounge, garden,
porch, and free spa pool are conducive to mingling. (☎/fax 751 0838. Bike hire. Reception 8am-8:30pm. Dorms $17; singles $30; twins and doubles $42.) Next door to Ivory
Towers, the **Fox Glacier Inn and Backpackers** combines standard rooms and a kitchen
with a popular local bar. You can get another session with a glacier guide or master
without ever leaving the building. (☎ 751 0022; fax 751 0024; foxglacierbackpack-
ers@xtra.co.nz. Hot showers must be paid for in $0.10 installments. Dorms $17; doubles $45; triples $54; tent sites $9 per person.) The **Fox Glacier Hotel,** on Cook Flat Rd.
just off Main Rd., offers privacy and beds that are softer than pudding. (☎ 751 0839.
Reception 7am-10:30pm; in winter until 8pm. Budget twins $25 per person.)
   Eating options in town are few but tasty; kitchens tend to close by 8:30pm in
winter, so plan accordingly. The **Cook Saddle Cafe and Saloon,** Main Rd., has American favorites like barbecued ribs ($18.75), a bar, and breakfast until 3pm. (☎ 751
0700. Open daily 10am-1:30am; in winter from noon.) Just a few doors down, **Cafe
Neve** serves fantastic meat dishes for a price. (☎ 751 0110. Open daily 9am-late; in
winter from 4pm.) On Main Rd. in the same building as Alpine Guides is **The Hob-
nail Cafe,** a simpler dining option. Pack up lunch before your trip to the glacier (fri-

tatta $5.50), or enjoy one of the light dishes after you get back. (☎ 751 0005. Open daily 7:30am-4pm; in winter 8am-3 or 4pm.) The only grocery is the small **Fox Glacier General Store**. (☎ 751 0829. Open daily 8am-8pm; in summer 7:30am-9pm.)

🗒 ACTIVITIES

ON THE GLACIER

ALPINE GUIDES. This is the only company that leads **guided walks** up Fox Glacier. The half-day trip begins with a steep and relatively lengthy ascent through the rainforest before stepping out onto the top of the glacier in view of the mountains. If a morning walk isn't offered due to party size, an afternoon one will be. If you can afford it, the **heli-hike** is a great way to avoid the rainforest trek and maximize ice time. Ice-climbing trips are also available. (☎ 751 0825, 0800 111 600; fax 751 0857. *Half-day 3½ hr., 9:15am and 1:45pm, $39. Full-day 6hr., 9:15am, $65. Heli-hike 3hr., 2 per day, $180. Ice-climbing 8am, $150. Min. party sizes apply on all trips. Book ahead.)*

SCENIC FLIGHTS

SKYDIVING. Skydive New Zealand-Franz Josef and Fox Glaciers combines a professional attitude, an adventuresome spirit, and unbeatable surroundings to make taking the plunge surprisingly carefree. Unlike many operators, Skydive New Zealand encourages you to bring your own (small) camera to document your fall. (☎ 0800 751 0080. *9000 ft. $225, 12,000ft. $265. Book ahead.)*

BY HELICOPTER. For scenery without the plunge, three helicopter companies provide trips ranging from 20-50min., and most include a snow landing. **Fox and Franz Josef Heliservices** (☎ 751 0866, 0800 800 793) can be booked at Alpine Guides. **Glacier Helicopters** (☎ 751 0803, 0800 800 732) and **Helicopter Line** (☎ 751 0767, 0800 807 767) have offices on Main Rd. If these offices are unattended, telephone their toll-free lines to reach them in Franz Joseph. *(Tours of glaciers cost between $130-280. Book ahead, especially in summer.)*

LESS SLIPPERY WALKS

GLACIER VIEWS. The **Chalet Lookout Walk** (1¼hr.; turn off onto Glacier View Rd. 2km south of town) yields a fantastic peek of the town's namesake, while the Fox Glacier Valley Walk (1hr.; take a left on the road to the glacier just south of town before the Fox River Bridge) follows the path taken by the guided glacier walks and leads directly to the terminal face itself.

LAKE MATHESON WALK. This walk offers unparalleled shots of Mt. Cook and Mt. Tasman in one of the most photographed reflecting lakes. Views are best in the morning and evening, when the water is undisturbed by wind; arrive 15-20min. before sunrise and walk to the nearest lookout point for some unadulterated New Zealand serenity. *(6km out of town on Cook Flat Rd. Return 3hr.)*

SHORT JAUNTS. The **Minnehaha Walk** gives a great sampling of Westland's rainforest as it wanders across bridges, over small trickling creeks, and through tall moss-covered trees surrounded by huge ferns and other primitive plants. *(Return 20min.)* Though not nearly as impressive as the display in Hokitika, there are indeed glowworms in Fox. *(At the corner of Sullivans and Main Rd. $2 in honesty box.)*

COPLAND TRACK. Connecting Westland National Park to Mt. Cook National Park, this 17km tramp should only be attempted by experienced and prepared hikers, though the first leg is a manageable one for hot pool lovers willing to overnight in the spacious hut at the **Welcome Flat Hut Pools.** *(Trailhead 26km south of Fox Glacier. InterCity and Atomic Shuttles make stops daily at 8:45am and 11:45am, respectively. See DOC office for track details and conditions.)*

GILLESPIES BEACH. Travelers willing to venture out to the beach can stroll for some two hours along the shore of the Tasman. The **Seal Colony Walk,** at the Gillespies Beach, leads to an endearing huddle of seals at Waikowhai Bluff. *(20km from Fox Glacier. Transport available from Mac's Shuttle. Seal Colony Walk return 3hr.)*

THE SOUTHERN LAKES

The Southern Lakes region bellows through fjords and lakes deeply scoured by glaciers. From the plummeting majesty of Milford Sound in Fiordland to the soaring peaks of Mt. Aspiring National Park, the peerless landscape entices visitors again and again to some of the most famous and spectacular walks in the world. Those seeking thrills rather than quiet meditation will rejoice in the riotous explosions of commercial Queenstown. Shock yourself awake with a dose of adventure by careening down slopes, rafting through canyons, or bungying off perilous heights. A land of superlatives where every lake revels in its distinct character and every valley is more breathtaking than the last, the Southern Lakes never fail to inspire.

▨ SOUTHERN LAKES HIGHLIGHTS

RUSH Queenstown, never-ending fun, with bungy jumping, skydiving, skiing, biking, and rock-climbing by day, and marathon bar-hopping by night (see p. 302).

SLOW DOWN for the striking and incomparable beauty of **Milford Sound,** which can be explored by boat, kayak, or plane (see p. 322) or relax lakeside in soporific **Wanaka** (see p. 313).

SET A STEADY PACE in **Fiordland** and **Mt. Aspiring National Parks** for some of the world's most glorious tramping (see p. 319 and p. 318).

QUEENSTOWN   ☎ 03

Although the gold-rush days are over, Queenstown has yet to lose its glitter. Street lamps twinkle along the lake as adrenaline addicts, worn from a day of thrills, begin a night of hard partying. The quips of other Kiwis about Queenstown's loss of character are tinged with equal doses of truth and jealousy, but the verdict is in, and Queenstown still has both small-town charm and indisputable raw beauty.

⌗ TRANSPORTATION

Flights: The **airport** is 6km east of town in Frankton. Take **The Shopper Bus** (☎ 442 6647) from the McDonald's on Camp St. (every hr. from 7:15am, $8) or **Super Shuttle** (☎ 442 3639, 0800 727 747; $8). Taxis to the airport are $15. **Air New Zealand** (☎ 441 1900, 0800 737 000) and **Quantas New Zealand** (☎ 442 6161, 0800 800 146) both have flights to: **Auckland** (3hr., 4-6 per day, from $367) via **Christchurch** (1hr., 4-6 per day, from $180); and **Wellington** (2hr., 3-4 per day, from $279). Several airlines do scenic flights to **Milford Sound** (40min.; 2 per day; $215, stand-by $95, including cruise $245-79), including **Air Fiordland** (☎ 442 3404) and **Milford Sound Scenic Flights** (☎ 442 3065).

Buses: InterCity (☎ 442 5628), departing from Camp St. beside the central tourist office, and the **Atomic Shuttles** (☎ 442 8178) and **Southern Link** (☎ 358 8355) head to **Christchurch** (7-11hr., 4-5 per day, $45-50) and **Dunedin** (4hr., 4-5 per day, $29-30). **Topline Tours** (☎ 442 8178) heads to **Te Anau** (2hr., 1-3 per day, $32) and **Southern Land Travel** (☎ 442 0099) to **Invercargill** (2¾hr., 8:30am, $38). Atomic Shuttles, InterCity, Southern Link, and **Wanaka Connexions** (☎ 0800 879 926) head to **Wanaka** (1¾hr., 4-5 per day, $15-22).

Regional Shuttles: The Information & Track Centre, 37 Shotover St. (☎ 442 9708), books trips to the **Routeburn** and **Greenstone and Caples Tracks** (1-2hr., 2 per day, $30), and to **Milford Sound** (5hr., 2 per day, $64) via **Te Anau** (2-3hr., $29); and from the end of Routeburn to Milford Sound, back to Queenstown ($149). Open daily 7am-9pm. **Backpacker Express** (☎ 442 9939) runs shuttles from Queenstown to **Glenorchy**

(in summer 8am, on demand in winter; $15) and from Glenorchy to the start of the **Routeburn, Greenstone and Caples,** and **Rees-Dart tracks** (in summer 9:30am, 1:15pm, on demand in winter; $15). They also run a **boat** from the Dart Valley end of the Rees-Dart Track ($60) and a **4WD** trip from the Dart Valley to Glenorchy ($20).

Ski Shuttles: Ski Shuttle (☎442 4630) runs daily to: **Cardrona** (1½hr., return $30); **Coronet Peak** (45min., 4 per day, return $25); **The Remarkables** (45min., 4 per day, return $25); and **Treble Cone** (2hr., return $30). **Kiwi Discovery** (☎442 7340) shuttles to the ski fields. **AA Alpine Taxis** (☎442 6666) runs to Coronet Peak for $17.

Local Buses: The **Shopper Bus** (☎442 6647) runs between most accommodations and the town center ($2.50) every hr., and to **Frankton** ($3) and the **airport** ($8).

Taxis: Alpine Taxis (☎442 6666) and **Queenstown Taxis** (☎442 7788, 0800 788 294) have **24hr.** service.

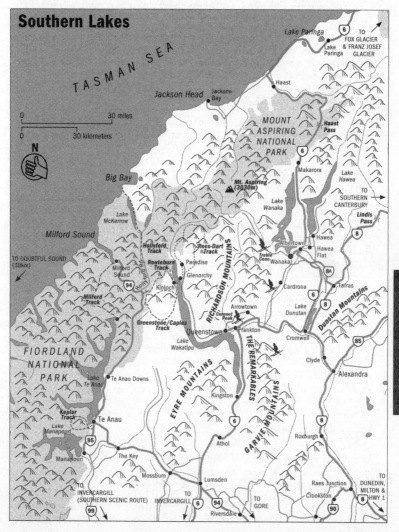

Southern Lakes

Car Rental: Pegasus Rental Cars (☎442 7176, 0800 442 7176), at the top of the Mall, offer cars from $35 per day, with insurance and unlimited mileage for rentals of 4 days or more. Open M-F 9am-6pm, Sa 9am-9pm. **Network Car Rentals**, 34 Shotover St. (☎442 7055), has cars from $49 per day plus mileage. Open daily 8am-6pm. **Queenstown Car Rentals**, 26b Shotover St. (☎442 9220), has cars from $49 per day and unlimited mileage after 2 days. Open daily 8am-6:30pm. Must be 21 to rent.

Hitchhiking: Though *Let's Go* does not recommend it, thumbers say getting to Glenorchy requires walking along the lake beyond the rotary at One Mile Creek. Hitching to Milford is an unlikely prospect; it involves taking the Shopper Bus to Frankton and walking past the airport along the road to Te Anau.

✦ ORIENTATION

Queenstown's smaller satellite towns include **Glenorchy** (45min.) to the west and **Arrowtown** (30min.) to the north. Queenstown itself is very compact. Booking agencies, bars, and gear rental stores line **Shotover St.** Shopping boutiques and restaurants are concentrated on **Beach St.** and **The Mall**, both of which run parallel to Shotover St. Hovering above Queenstown, the lights of the **Skyline Restaurant** resemble a spaceship. The spine of **The Remarkables** mountain range runs south down the east side of **Lake Wakatipu**, and **Coronet Peak** eyes the lake over the town's north shoulder.

▨ PRACTICAL INFORMATION

Visitors Center: The official source of info in town is the **Queenstown Visitor Information Network** (☎442 4100, 0800 668 888; fax 442 8907), at the Clocktower Centre. Open daily 7am-7pm; in winter 7am-6pm.

DOC: (☎442 7935; fax 442 7934), 37 Shotover St., beside the **Information & Track Centre.** Open daily 8:30am-5pm; call ahead for winter hours.

Currency Exchange: There are **ATMs** all over. **BNZ** (☎442 5013) on Rees St., has good exchange rates. Its **Bureau de Change** is open M-F 9am-8pm, Sa-Su 10am-8pm. **ANZ Postbank**, on Beach St. near the waterfront, has similar rates. Open M-F 9am-4:30pm.

Ski and Snowboard Rental: Outside Sports & Doctor Bike (☎442 8883), at the top of The Mall, offers the best selection. Ski, boot, and pole hire $30 per day; snowboard and boot hire $35; bike hire from $35 per half-day. YHA 5% discount. Open daily 8am-10pm; in winter 7am-10pm. **Bad Jelly** (☎442 4064), on Camp St., has slightly cheaper rates on boards and boots ($35 per day), and skis, boots, and poles (from $23 per day). Open June-Nov. daily 8am-10pm. The **Information & Track Centre**, 37 Shotover St. (☎442 9708) also provides basic equipment at "backpacker" rates.

Tramping Gear: Alpine Sports, 28 Shotover St. (☎442 7099; open M-Sa 9:30am-6pm, Su 10am-6pm) and **Information & Track Centre** 37 Shotover St. (☎442 9708; open daily 7am-9pm, until 8pm in winter) rent equipment at identical prices: tents $10 per day, packs $5, sleeping bags with liner $5. **Outside Sports & Doctor Bike** (☎442 8883) hires and sells tramping gear. Open 8am-10pm; in winter daily 7am-10pm.

Police: 11 Camp St. (☎442 7900).

Medical Services: Wilkinson's Pharmacy (☎442 7313), is on Rees St., at the foot of the Mall. Open daily 8:30am-10pm; in winter daily 8:30am-9pm. The **Queenstown Medical Centre** (☎442 7301), is at the corner of Shotover and Stanley St.

Internet Access: Budget Communications, O'Connell's Mall, 2nd fl. (☎441 1562). Daily $4 per hr. specials 9-11am and 9-11pm. Open daily 9am-11pm.

Post Office: Camp and Ballarat St. Open M-F 8:30am-8pm, Sa 9am-8pm.

▨ ▨ ACCOMMODATIONS AND CAMPING

Catering to honeymooners and broke ski bums alike, Queenstown has a staggering array of places to stay, with B&Bs and hostels springing up endlessly like mushrooms after rain.

SOUTHERN LAKES

Queenstown

ACCOMMODATIONS

Black Sheep Backpackers, 19
Bumbles Hostel, 17
Creeksyde Top Ten Holiday
  Park, 2
Deco Backpackers, 16
Hippo Lodge, 3
The Last Resort, 4
Pinewood Lodge, 1
Queenstown Lakeview Holiday
  Park, 15
Queenstown YHA, 18
Thomas' Hotel, 11

FOOD

Alpine Food Center, 5
Habebes Lebanese, 10
Happy Wok, 6
Ken's Noodle House, 7
Wholefoods Café, 12

PUBS

Pog Mahone's, 9
Rattlesnake, 14
Winnie Bagoes, 8
The World, 13

TO CORONET PEAK
SKI FIELD (13km),
ARROWTOWN (18km),
& SKIPPER'S CANYON/
PIPELINE BUNGY

TO (6km)
& WANAKA

Queenstown Hill
Recreation Reserve

Queenstown Hill Walkway

Frankton Arm

Ben Lomond
Scenic Reserve

Skyline
Chalet

Skyline
Gondola

Kiwi & Birdlife
House

Pipeline
Bungy

The
Station

Wilkinson's
Pharmacy

Town
Pier

Queenstown Bay

Queenstown
Gardens

Ice Skating
Rink

Lake Wakatipu

TO GLENORCHY
(44km)

Hamilton Rd
Gorge Rd.
Boundary St.
Robins Rd.
Memorial St.
Isle St.
Brecon St.
Hay St.
Man St.
Shotover St.
Camp St.
Athol St.
Rees St.
Cow Ln.
Church St.
Ballarat St.
Beach St.
Earl St.
Marine Parade
Lake St.
Lake Esplanade
St. Omer
Park
Thompson St.
Brunswick St.
Glasgow St.
Lomond Cres.
Anderson Heights
Weaver St.
Turner St.
Hallenstein St.
Melbourne St.
Stanley St.
Coronation Dr.
Sydney St.
Brisbane St.
Hobart St.
Adelaide St.
Kent St.
York St.
Edinburgh St.
Dublin St.
Sydney St.
Earl St.
Frankton Rd.
Panorama Tce.
Veint St.
The Terrace
Park St.
Peninsula St.
Frankton Rd.

100 yards
100 meters

N

Frankton Arm

SOUTHERN LAKES

▨ **Bumbles Hostel,** 2 Brunswick St. (☎442 6298, 0800 428 625). From the visitors center, walk left down Beach St. until the lakeside; it faces the water at the Brunswick St. and Lake Esplanade. Spacious and modern dorms have kitchenettes. Linen $1. Reception 7:30am-8pm. Dorms $18; twin bunks $40; twins and doubles with linen $45.

▨ **Deco Backpackers,** 52 Man St. (☎442 7384; fax 442 6258). From the visitors center, walk left up Camp St., take a left on Man St., and go up the hill; it's at the end of Man St. on the left. With two lounges, nice views, and free pick-up, you'll relish the extra delights. Reception 8am-2pm and 4-8pm. Dorms $18; twins and doubles $42; tent sites (summer only) $10 per person. 4 nights for the price of 3 or $2 off your first night Sept.-Oct. and Apr.-May; in winter discounts for stays of at least a week.

Thomas's Hotel, 50 Beach St. (☎442 7180; fax 441 8417; the.cat@xtra.co.nz). Go left down Shotover St., the first left on Rees St., then the first right. A gluttonous tabby, the hotel's namesake, runs this waterfront hotel. Kayak hire. Reception 7am-9pm. Dorms $19; hotel singles $79; twins and doubles $60-$89; triples $99.

The Last Resort (☎442 4320; fax 442 4330), from Beach St., walk one block up Camp St., past the Station, and turn right on Memorial St. Within stumbling distance of the bars, this hostel has a warm feel with a video collection. Reception appears to be open whenever staff decides to man the desk. 4-bed dorms $20.

Queenstown YHA, 88-90 Lake Esplanade (☎442 8413; fax 442 6561; yhaqutn@yha.org.nz), left down Shotover St. along the lakefront away from town (10min.). The friendly staff is the best for making adventure bookings with discounts. Internet. Reception 6:30am-10pm. Book ahead in summer and in winter peak times. Dorms $20; doubles and twins $44-60. Nonmembers $3 more.

Hippo Lodge, 4 Anderson Heights (☎/fax 442 5785; bookings@hippolodge.co.nz). A 5min. walk to town or a 15-20min. walk back up the hill to a commanding view of Queenstown. The self-contained cabin is a steal for small groups or couples seeking privacy. Reception 8:30am-1pm and 3-8pm. Dorms $19; twins and doubles $47.

Black Sheep Backpackers (VIP), 13 Frankton Rd. (☎442 7289; fax 442 7361). Turn right from the visitors center, follow Camp St. to the end, and head up the short trail in the park and cross over to Frankton Rd. Owned by Kiwi Experience, this isn't the place for space or peace. Internet. Reception 24hr. Dorms $18, with VIP $17; doubles $50.

Pinewood Lodge, 48 Hamilton Rd. (☎442 8273, 0800 746 396; fax 442 9470; rgreig@xtra.co.nz). Head left up Camp St. from the visitors center, follow Robins Rd. around to the right, and then left on Hamilton (10min.). Find relaxed seclusion in varied cabins with spa, trampoline, darts, and 8-ball. Bike hire available. Reception 7am-9pm; in winter 8am-9pm. Dorms $18; singles $30; twins and doubles $45; tent sites (summer only) $10 per person. Wheelchair accessible.

Queenstown Lakeview Holiday Park (☎442 7252; fax 442 7253; reception@holiday-park.net.nz), on Man St. across the street from Deco Backpackers. Reception 8am-10pm; in winter 8am-9pm. Cabins for 2 $40, extra person $15; double tourist flats $70, extra person $15; tent and powered sites $11 per person.

Creeksyde Top Ten Holiday Park, 54 Robins Rd. (☎442 9447; fax 442 6621; creeksyde@camp.co.nz). Go up Camp St., right on Robins Rd. (5min.) Reception 7am-9:30pm; in winter 8am-8pm. Lodges for 2 $42-46, extra adult $13, extra child $11, linen $5; tent sites $13 per person.

◖ FOOD

Backpackers shouldn't have to look far to find a good crumb at a low price or a big meal without stripping your wallet. **Alpine Food Center,** on upper Shotover St., is the largest and busiest supermarket. (☎442 8961. Open M-Sa 8am-8pm, Su 9am-8pm.)

▨ **Habebes Lebanese** (☎442 9861), on the Rees St. Arcade near the waterfront. Tucked away off the street. Add your choice of tabouli and salads to the scrumptious lamb pita ($7.50) for a messy delight. The apricot orgasm ($2.50) will certainly inspire climax. Open daily 11am-6pm.

▓ **Wholefoods Cafe** (☎ 442 8991), on the Plaza Arcade between upper Shotover and Beach St. Soup and homemade bread ($6) or refried bean enchiladas ($6.50)make the grade and used book exchange provides food for thought. Open daily 8am-5pm.

Happy Wok, 8 Shotover St. (☎ 442 4415), facing the parking lot of the Alpine Foodcentre. Even the alien-head-bedecked restroom can't distract you from the authentic Thai food served here. Pad Thai and curry dishes $9.50-13. Open daily from 11:30am.

The World (☎ 442 5714), on upper Shotover St. An Indian restaurant serving chicken *tikka masala* ($11) and vegetarian meals from only $8. Happy Hour 5-8pm and 10:30-11:30pm. Come back for the nightlife. Open daily 4pm-2:30am.

Ken's Noodle House (☎ 442 8628), on Camp St. between Shotover and Beach St. Friendly Ken serves up bowls of authentic Japanese noodles ($6 and up) and small plates of sushi ($6). Open M-Sa 11:30am-9pm. Cash only.

Joe's Garage (☎ 442 5282), on Camp St. next to the post office. A slick and funky venue where weathered outdoor operators go for a cup. Located (according to publicity) between a rock and a hard place, provides serious coffee rescue, breakfasts (yogurt and muesli $5) and sandwiches (pesto and bruscetta $3). Open daily 7am-5pm.

🎵🎭 ENTERTAINMENT AND NIGHTLIFE

Queenstown's concentrated nightlife rocks with backpackers fresh off the slopes and bungy cords and activity operators who just can't get enough madness. For a quieter evening, **movies** are shown in the tiny Embassy theater, on The Mall. (Movieline ☎ 442 9990. $11, students and YHA $8.) Relieve the munchies late into the night at the **Jazz Bar,** a Camp St. cafe that occasionally turns into a street party (open 8am-4am). Pick up a free copy of *The Source* at cafes and bars to see what the DJs are spinning for the week. For a drink without the noise and hassle of the local bars call for free delivery provided by **Ring-a-Drink** (☎ 0800 863 746).

▓ **Queenstown Maori Concert and Feast** (☎ 442 8878) on Memorial St. This impressive modern Maori buffet and concert is well worth the price. The entertainment is slightly showy but professionally done with authentic Maori Haka, songs, stick games, and warm hospitality. Dining 7-8:30pm; concert 8:30-9:30pm. $45; children $25.)

▓ **The World,** 27 Shotover St. (☎ 442 5714). Other bars have big nights, but The World never stops spinning. Backpackers flock here for an early drink, a cheap meal, a night of hard partying, or often all three. DJs daily from 10pm. Arcade games downstairs. Drink specials 5-8pm and 10:30-11:30pm. Open daily 4pm-2:30am.

▓ **Pog Mahone's,** 14 Rees St. (☎ 442 5382). A classy Irish pub where you can sit outside on the patio or the balcony for a view of Lake Wakatipu and the Eyre Mountains. If anyone asks you where you're going, just say "Kiss my ass!" (that's what Pog Mahone means in Irish). Usually live music daily from 9:30pm. Open daily noon-2:30am.

Rattlesnake, 14 Brecon St. (☎ 442 9995). Outrageous but inspiring decor would make even the staunchest Texan giggle like a schoolgirl. DJs nightly. Open daily from 5pm.

Winnie Bagoes (☎ 442 8635), in the heart of The Mall. The party spills out to the balcony into the open air as they pull back the retractable roof. If you get the munchies, there's the house ale ($2) and half-priced cocktails all night. Open daily noon-2:30am.

⛷️🏂 OUTDOOR ACTIVITIES

Queenstown is known for its thrills and breathtaking scenery; if you want to ride, jump, walk, or glide through spectacular wilderness, this is the place.

PLANNING

Budgeting for Queenstown activities can seem despairingly impossible. Most activities sound exciting and cost plenty. For **cheaper activities,** we recommend frisbee golf, the luge, gold panning in Arrowtown, hiking the Ben Lomond or Queenstown Hill, ice skating, and a 4WD trip into Skippers Canyon. To maximize your money, consider buying a **pre-packaged** combo which can save you up to $100

THE HISTORY OF BUNGY Bungy started with Pacific Islanders, who were jumping off towers for hundreds of years with nothing more than vines tied to their feet. In the 1970s, the Oxford University Dangerous Sports Club tried some jumps, when AJ Hackett heard about this new "sport" and collaborated with fellow downhill skier Henry Van Asch to develop modern bungy jumping. They opened the world's first bungy site at Kawarau Bridge outside Queenstown, and made quite a splash with an Eiffel Tower jump in 1987. Fifteen years and over a million jumps later, Queenstown is recognized as the world's bungy-jumping mecca. A serious rivalry exists between AJ Hackett and the other bungy outfit in town, Pipeline, as they try to out-spectacular each other like Las Vegas hotels. Existential enlightenment during your bungy jump is unlikely, but something will probably go to your head (be it adrenaline or all your bodily fluids).

on the more expensive activities. Combos include anywhere from two to five activities including helicopter flights, bungy jumps, jetboat rides, 4WD tours, and rafting trips. One of the best deals is the ◾Skippers Grand Slam (see below).

There are many other combos available at booking agencies. **The Station,** at Shotover and Camp St., is gigantic; many activities depart from there. (☎442 5252. Open daily 7am-9pm; in winter 8am-8pm.) **The Information and Track Centre,** 37 Shotover St., is geared to backpackers and very well informed about transport to local tracks and ski fields, tramping conditions and outfitting, as well as all the major Queenstown activities. (☎442 9708. Open daily 7am-9pm; in winter 7am-8pm.)

BUNGY JUMPING

PIPELINE BUNGY. New in 1994 with the promise of the highest jump, Pipeline wooed a skeptical Queenstown with its 102m plunge from a restored pipeline bridge over Skippers Canyon. In a stunningly scenic and historic gold-mining locale on the Shotover River, Pipeline offers activities in and around the canyon, including a gold mining museum. The **Skippers ◾Grand Slam** package includes jet boating, bungy jumping, 4W driving, zipping over the canyon on the flying fox wire, and is a thrilling way to spend 3½-4hrs of your day. *(27 Shotover St., next door to AJ Hackett. ☎442 5455, 0800 286 491; www.bungy.co.nz. Skippers Canyon 6 trips per day; one jump $140, including 4WD transport along the crazy road to the bridge and humorous commentary along the way. Drive to the canyon only $45; drive, museum, goldpanning and jet boating, $89. Drive, Jump, Jet, and Flying Fox (Grand Slam) $199.)*

AJ HACKETT. The original name in bungy now operates four Queenstown jumps. **The Ledge,** at the top of the gondola, may be the most unique jump—the 47m fall looks a lot farther at night with the lights of Queenstown twinkling below. The 43m **Kawarau Bridge,** the world's first bungy bridge, can submerse you in the river below. The newest addition to Hackett's bungy madness is the ◾ **Nevis Highwire Bungy,** the country's highest at 134m. Operating from a mostly glass gondola suspended by wire cables between two mountains over a canyon, it's almost impossible to avoid looking down, so enjoy the sweet anticipation—an opportunity to commune deeply with the mountain gods. Or, sample all three jumps in Hackett's **Bungy Thrillogy.** *(Office in the Station. ☎442 7100, 0800 286 492; www.ajhackett.com. The Ledge $110, including gondola ride and t-shirt. Open daily 11am-7pm; in winter 5-9pm. Kawarau Bridge 3 trips per day; $125, including transport and t-shirt. Nevis Highwire $174, including transport and t-shirt. Thrillogy $229. Open daily 8am-8pm; in winter 8am-7pm.)*

JETBOATING

SKIPPERS CANYON JET. Working with Pipeline Bungy, this trip combines history, breath-taking river scenery, and thrills as it cruises 16km past the precipitous walls of the old gold-mining canyon, under suspension bridges, and past abandoned pioneer settlements. Combo deals with a bungy jump are available. *(☎/fax 442 5455, 0800 226 966. Several trips per day; $85, including transport from the Pipeline Bungy office on Shotover St., a guided tour of the museum, and gold-panning.)*

SHOTOVER JET. Less personal, Shotover is the most popular. Skimming impossibly close to the rock walls and over waters as shallow as 10cm, the speedboats swivel and twist at 70kph. *(Pick-up from The Station every 30min.; otherwise, drive 15min. up the road toward Arrowtown to Shotover Canyon. ☎442 8570, 0800 746 868. $75, children $35. YHA 10% discount. Combinations with scenic helicopter ride and skyline gondola, movie, and luge, $159.)* Shotover also runs the ◼**Dart River Jet Safaris** *(☎442 9992),* which offers more remote trips through the river valleys north of Glenorchy (see p. 312).

RAFTING AND RIVER SPORTS

In addition to jetboating and spectacular views, the Shotover and Kawarau Rivers also nurture various innovative whitewater adventures. The Shotover has more consistent Class IV rapids and rides through the man-made 170m Oxenbridge Tunnel, but the Kawarau has a few wild sections (including the 400m Chinese Dog Leg, New Zealand's longest commercial whitewater segment).

RAFTING. Queenstown Rafting *(☎442 9792; fax 442 4609),* **Extreme Green Rafting** *(☎442 8517),* and **Challenge Rafting** *(☎442 7318)* run half-day trips on the Shotover and Kawarau mornings and afternoons. *(Shotover River $119. Kawarau River $99-109.)* Slightly more in-your-face, **Serious Fun River Surfing** operates a heart-pumping 7km Kawarau River boogie-board experience. *(☎442 5262. 4hr., $119 with training. Summer only.)* **Mad Dog River Boarding** runs similar trips on the Kawarau at slightly cheaper rates. *(☎442 7797. $109. Twice daily Sept.-May.)*

CANYONING. 12 Mile Delta leads exciting abseiling and canyoning trips, which plunge into pools, rappel into ravines, and slide down chutes: not for those with fears of heights, water, or very hard rocks. Ask about a new Routeburn canyoning trip in isolated park territory fed by mountain snow-melt. *(☎0800 222 696. Half-day $105; 6hr. Routeburn trip $180. 16 yr. minimum age. Summer only.)*

SKYDIVING AND OTHER AERIAL ACTIVITIES

SKYDIVING. For those who like to look down on skiers, Queenstown is one of the best places in the world. **Skydive Tandem** will pick you up, fly you 3100m, drop you tandem until you reach your terminal velocity, and then let you float down between Lake Wakatipu and The Remarkables. *(☎021 325 961. 3½hr.; $245.)*

SCENIC FLIGHTS. For slower aerial sightseeing, **Air Wakatipu** runs 20min. flights of the scenic and acrobatic varieties. *(☎442 3048. Scenic flights from $49.)* **The Helicopter Line** has 20min. Remarkables trips. *(☎442 3034. $152, including a snow landing.)* **Over The Top** has 20min. flights over The Remarkables, a longer 40min. flight with snow landing, and more expensive options to Milford or to remote rivers for fly fishing. *(☎442 2233. 20min. From $99 for 3 persons or more. 40min.; $175.)*

ZIPLINES. The newest rush is **Fly by Wire,** a personal craft swinging you on an attached wire like a pendulum up to 170kph. *(☎442 2116. $129).* If you're at Skippers Canyon and feel like warming up for your bungy jump, or prefer a relaxing glide over the canyon to a stomach-jerking dive into it, try the **Flying Fox,** a 250m zipline that reaches speeds of 70kph, as you watch others on the Pipeline. *(Run by Pipeline Bungy: various packages are available. Flying Fox $79. Flying Fox and bungy jump $184. Flying Fox and Skippers Canyon Jet $129. "Grand Slam" bungy, boat, and Flying Fox $199.)*

OTHER AERIAL ACTIVITIES. Aerophiles should try **paragliding:** a relaxing, exhilarating tandem ride from above the Skyline Gondola over Queenstown. Various companies at the top charge roughly $160 for about 10min. in the air. Try **Cloud Nine Tandem Paragliding,** run by Tim, one of the owners of Deco Backpackers *(☎025 326 732 or 442 6289).* For a faster, wilder ride try **Sky Trek Tandem Hang Gliding,** a 15-25min. flight from Coronet Peak or The Remarkables *(☎442 6311, 2hr., $145),* or ◼**AntiGravity Hanggliding** *(☎0800 426 445, 1½hr., $160)* whose tandem fliers have won international flying competitions and set national records. **Paraflights** attaches you to a boat and lifts you to 300ft. as you cruise around Lake Wakatipu. *(☎442 8507. $69.)*

ON THE SLOPES

From June to September **skiing** and **snowboarding** take over Queenstown as enthusiasts flock to **Coronet Peak** and **The Remarkables.** Lift passes and transport are cheaper in town, particularly when part of a package. An ISIC card is not valid for student deals; another **student ID** is necessary. The roads to the mountains usually require chains; shuttles are a safer option. (See **Transportation** p. 302) If you plan on skiing for a number of days or in a number of locations, you may wish to consider the **NZ Superpass,** available from nzski.com. The Superpass allows you to purchase a number of coupons (from $54 per day) which can be used for lift passes on Queenstown and Canterbury ski fields, or on other activities. For more details check the website or check in at the ski desk in The Station.

CORONET. Bigger and closer to Queenstown, Coronet has a longer season, offers weekend night-skiing (a great budget deal), and contains two half-pipes. Its slopes are suitable for all levels of skiers and boarders, particularly intermediate skiers. *(Office in The Station. Lift pass $68, students $56, children $34. Night-skiing lift pass (valid F or Sa 4-10pm) $35, children $25; no student rate.)*

THE REMARKABLES. This ski field usually has better snow conditions. It also has a wider beginner area and gets more sun. Its slopes cater to skiers and snowboarders of all skill levels, as well as to cross-country skiers. Students will appreciate the cheaper rates. *(Office in The Station. Lift pass $65, students $48, children $32.)*

FARTHER AFIELD. Although Wanaka is more conveniently situated, skiers and snowboarders frequently stay in Queenstown and catch morning shuttles to **Cardrona,** or make the longer drive to **Treble Cone.** Cardrona is 30km closer, has several slopes for intermediate skiers, and is a popular choice among families; its four half-pipes also make it a favorite for snowboarders. Treble Cone has the longest vertical rise of the ski fields in the Southern Lakes and has challenging slopes mostly for intermediate and advanced skiers, as well as a half-pipe for snowboarders. *(For more information on both ski fields, see **Wanaka: Outdoor Activities,** p. 317)*

OFF-ROAD

4WD TOURS. The walls and precipitous road through **Skippers Canyon,** constructed during the gold-rush days, now attract 4WD tours that give the fantastic drive a historical perspective. **Skippers Grand Canyon Ltd.** will take you on the rugged, windy road into the canyon, then on a jetboat ride that combines history and fast-paced thrills, gives you a view of the bungy jumping and the Flying Fox, and an opportunity to pan for gold. *(☎442 5455. 3-4hr., 3 per day, $85. Flying Fox $39 more, Pipeline Bungy $105 more.)* **Outback Tours** *(☎442 7386)* and **Nomad Safaris** *(☎442 6699)* have morning and afternoon tours into Skippers Canyon and up to the historic mining settlements of Macetown and Seffertown. *(2hr., $59; 4½hr., $75.)*

BIKING. In the summer, **Gravity Action** runs half-day **mountain biking trips** to the canyon twice daily; they drive you up Coronet Peak and let you coast down through creeks and over gravel. *(☎442 9708. $65; various Pipeline Bungy activities available for add-on.)* Wild, off-road two- and four-wheel biking treks through the canyon and elsewhere are available through **Offroad Adventures.** *(☎442 7858. 3hr.; $175, including gold panning.)* One especially good trip on your own is the 20km ride past Lake Hayes to Arrowtown, where you can stop to check out the historic Chinese settlement, pan for gold, or continue up the rugged 13km 4WD track to Macetown. *(Rides start 12-15km out of Queenstown toward Glenorchy.)*

ON THE LAKE

T.S.S. EARNSLAW. For decades, steamships were the only form of transport across the lake to Glenorchy and to the area's various sheep stations. Today, only the revamped **T.S.S. Earnslaw** remains. While the lake traverse is tradition, the 10am, noon, 2, and 4pm ☏**farm cruises to Walter Peak** with scrumptious afternoon tea are highlights. Once there, you can watch sheep shearing and a sheep dog demonstration, ride Duncan the Highland Bull, or enjoy a horse trek. The pricey dinner cruise involves a lamb and pavlova dinner followed by a rollicking farm show. *(Cruises depart from the summer wharf at the end of Shotover St. ☎ 442 7500, 0800 656 503. Glenorchy cruise $34, children $15. Walter Peak cruise 3½hr.; $52, children $15; horse trek only in summer. Dinner cruise 4hr.; 6pm; $88, children $44.)*

OTHER ACTIVITIES. The lake comes alive in summer with **waterskiing, jetboating, fishing,** and **water taxis** to secluded picnic spots—just ask at any booking office.

WALKS AND HORSE TREKS

The DOC office and the Information and Track Centre nextdoor sell a handy guide, entitled *Wandering in the Wakatipu* ($6), that gives detailed guidance on walks in and around the Queenstown-Arrowtown-Glenorchy area. Shorter tracks on the way to Glenorchy offer less-trodden native forest experiences (some suitable for mountain biking or trail running).

BEN LOMOND. One of the most difficult and rewarding treks is the climb to the top of ◪**Ben Lomond.** Mt. Aspiring and an entire panorama of peaks can be seen from the steep summit on a clear day. *(Check with DOC before attempting as the tramp goes through potentially dangerous alpine areas. Return 6-8hr. 3-4 hr. just to saddle.)*

QUEENSTOWN HILL TIME WALK. A less arduous climb leads you through thick forest to the peak of Te Tapunui, where you can enjoy a breathtaking 360° view of The Remarkables, Cecil Peak, and Lake Wakatipu. *(To get to the trailhead follow the Mall away from the Lake until you reach Hallenstein St., turn right, then left onto York St.; the trailhead is on the left side half a block past Kent St. Return 2-3hr.)*

HORSE TREKS. A few stables operate near Arthur's Point in the valley and include trips through farmland, foothills, and saddle tracks. Full-day trips are only in the summer. **Moonlight Stables** provides transportation and afternoon fishing. *(☎ 442 1229. 1½hr. $60; full-day $150, including lunch and fishing.)* **Shotover Stables** also provides transportation. *(☎ 442 9708. 1¾hr. $55; full-day $140, including lunch.)*

OTHER SIGHTS AND ACTIVITIES

ABOVE QUEENSTOWN. The **Skyline Gondola** goes up to the restaurant and pricey bar for panoramic views of the lake, including Coronet Peak. While the gondola runs all day, it is especially beautiful at ◪sunset. *(☎ 442 7860. Open daily 9am-9pm. Return $14, children $5.)* Better yet, walk the **One Mile Creek Trail** *(1hr. uphill)*, which starts along the lakefront toward Glenorchy, past the YHA, and passes through a canyon and pine forest to Skyline (where you can catch the gondola down). At the top, watch **Kiwi Magic,** a 30min. surround-sound visual experience about a bumbling American exploring New Zealand with a happy-go-lucky tour guide. *($8, students $5, children $4.)* By the top of the gondola, the ◪**Skyline Luge** may look tame, but its sharp turns and steep straightaways are exciting when you're crouched on a steerable plastic cart, racing past grandmas and friends alike. *(☎ 442 7860. $4.50 per ride; 5 rides $16, with return gondola $26. Open daylight hours in peak summer season.)*

KIWI AND BIRDLIFE PARK. The complex includes a nocturnal kiwi house, a range of native parakeets and ducks, and the head-bobbing **black stilt** *(kaki)*, the world's rarest wading bird (numbering around 150 in the wild). Proceeds support captive breeding programs. *(At the base of the gondola. ☎ 442 8059. Open daily 9am-7pm; in winter 9am-5pm. Feedings daily 4pm; in winter 11am. $10.50, children $4.)*

CLIMBING. Mountain Works runs introductory rock climbing courses in the summer, beginning ice-climbing in the winter, and multi-day guided ascents. *(17 Shotover St. ☎ 442 7329, 0508 summit. Rock climbing from $149. Ice-climbing from $175.)* **Independent Mountain Guides** offers similar instruction in rock climbing and can lead you on a full-day traverse of The Remarkables or a snow-shoed climb to Coronet Peak. *(☎ 025 352 005. Call ahead for prices.)*

SOUTHERN LAKES

OTHER ACTIVITIES. At the end of the boardwalk, secluded views of the lake can be seen from the **Queenstown Gardens.** With a track looping out onto the peninsula fitness stations scatter along the path. There's ice skating at the **Fun Centre.** (☎ 441 8000. 2hr.; $12, children $7.50. Skate hire $3.) Within chirping distance of the birdpark, **Queenstown Mini Golf,** 28 Brecon St., is a good and affordable family activity. (☎ 442 7652. Open daily 9:30am-dark. $7; children $5.)

ARROWTOWN   ☎ 03

William Fox and a small band of miners pulled some 230 pounds of gold from the Arrow River in 1862, precipitating the development of Arrowtown and its satellite towns. The region comes to life in April with the brilliant colors of the changing trees and the annual **Autumn Festival** (last weekend of Mar.), when visitors descend on the town for a parade, live music, and street performers. At the end of Buckingham St. is the historic **Chinese Settlement,** a series of mud-walled huts and signs that give a brief explanation of the former inhabitants and their lifestyle. A 9oz. and other special nuggets sit in a case at **The Gold Shop** on Buckingham St. (Open daily 8:30am-5:30pm.) If you've caught gold fever and don't want to leave Arrowtown without a little adventure and some gold to boot, you can join up with one of the **Golden Fox Tours.** These 1½hr. tours explain the history of the Chinese settlement, followed by some gold panning. (☎ 025 416 083. 1½hr. Oct.-Apr. only. $20, children $10. Longer tours available; call ahead for reservations.)

Several **tracks** for walking and mountain biking depart from the settlement, though they can be very slippery in winter. (The museum/visitors center has information on the tracks, though most are sign-posted from the Macetown Rd. out of town.) The **Arrowtown Lodge** leads guided walks. (☎ 442 1101. Trips from $40-120.) The **Macetown Road** is a rigorous 13km track upriver to another ghost town, along which many tracks begin and end. Ask for a map at the visitors center, or take a 4WD tour with **NOMAD Safaris.** (☎ 442 6699. $75. Summer only.)

To access Arrowtown, the **Arrow Express** runs to **Queenstown** with insightful commentary from outside the museum. (☎ 442 1900. 25min.; 5 departures per day; one way $10, return $18.) **The Double Decker Bus** also runs 3hr. sightseeing trips from Queenstown via Lake Hayes and the Bungy Bridge to Arrowtown. (☎ 442 6067. Departs 10am and 2pm, return $27.) The **Lakes District Museum** has impressive exhibits and simultaneously serves as a **visitors center** for local information and bookings. Pick up explanatory brochures and local trail maps here. (☎ 442 1824. Open daily 9am-5pm. Museum admission $5, children $0.50.)

GLENORCHY   ☎ 03

Surrounded by frosty peaks reflected in the head of Lake Wakatipu's azure waters, Glenorchy sits in a magical setting 48km north of Queenstown, where **Fiordland National Park** (see p. 319) and **Mt. Aspiring National Park** (see p. 318) meet. The tiny pastoral community is encircled by sheep stations and summer hikers eager to undertake the **Routeburn Track** (see p. 369), **Greenstone and Caples Tracks** (see p. 380), the **Rees-Dart Track** (see p. 378), or one of the shorter, but celebrated, valley walks. Queenstown's hype seems decades away from this diminutive hamlet, which claims the dubious honor of housing New Zealand's smallest library (2-person capacity). The slow, quiet lifestyle of Glenorchy's 200 inhabitants demonstrates that the Queenstown region harbors more than transient pleasures.

▐▌ TRANSPORTATION. Backpacker Express (☎ 442 9939) has shuttles to and from Queenstown every few hours in summer and once daily in winter ($15). **Dart River Jet Safaris** (☎ 442 9992) may give you a ride if there's room in the bus (2 per day, $14). The road is a winding 45min. drive along the side of Lake Wakatipu; some choose to hitch, although the road is sparsely traveled except for tourists.

▸ PRACTICAL INFORMATION. The **Glenorchy Store,** at the Holiday Park on the way into town, is the **visitors center** and provides limited groceries. (☎442 7171. Open M-Sa 8:45am-6pm, Su 9am-5:30pm; in winter M-F 9am-5pm, Sa 9:30am-4pm.) The **DOC office,** at the end of Main Rd., has up-to-the-minute weather, hut, and trail condition reports as well as some basic camping supplies. (☎442 9937. Open daily 8:30am-4:30pm; in winter closed Sa-Su.) The **post office** in the Mobil station is at the end of town. (☎442 9913. Open daily 8am-6pm; in winter M-Sa 8am-5pm.)

▸ ACCOMMODATIONS AND FOOD. The old-fashioned **Glenorchy Hotel,** on Mull St., is run by a spunky crew of happy heartlanders. Beds in the small bunkhouse abut an Oregon woodstove and canary-yellow kitchen; the hotel rooms are more comfortable. Book ahead in the summer. (☎442 9902, 0800 453 667; fax 442 9912. Bunks $15; single, double, and triple rooms $79.) The **Glenorchy Holiday Park** has an array of options. (☎442 7171; fax 442 7172. Bunks (summer only) $13; cabins $15 per person; tent sites $8, powered sites $9.)

The **Glenorchy Cafe,** opposite the Mobil station, serves delectable pastries (ginger crunch $2.50) and light meals (chicken, brie, and mushroom foccaccio $8.50). A vintage LP collection (great Tom Waites and Bob Dylan selection) entices *Let's Go* researchers and other itinerants to linger. (☎442 9958. Open daily 8am until late.) At the bar and restaurant of the **Glenorchy Hotel** the Kitchen Sink Burger ($9.50, comes with everything but the sink) and the Sunday Roast ($10.50) are good budget choices. (Open daily 8am until late.) At the **Glen-Roydon Cafe-Restaurant,** you can choose from assorted light meals ($3-8), or one of the larger pasta dishes ($10-15). (☎442 9968. Open daily from 8am-9pm. Bar open until late.)

▸ OUTDOOR ACTIVITIES. **Dart River Jet Safaris** is a fast-paced foray up the Dart River, past Mt. Earnslaw and into the heart of Mt. Aspiring National Park. The trip enters the UNESCO South West New Zealand World Heritage Area, which contains flora and fauna descended from the creatures that once inhabited the ancient supercontinent of Gondwanaland. The jet boats spin, grind, and fly up the pebbled braids of the Dart River, stopping at scenic **Routeburn Valley.** A unique combination of speed and scenery, the 2½hr. excursion cruises through exceptional scenery, and might be worth the price to jet-boat virgins. (☎442 9992. Daily 9am, 1, 3pm; in winter 9am, 12:30pm. $125, children $62.50. Leaves 1hr. earlier and costs $14 more from Queenstown.) Otherwise, a hike through the river valley is a more economical option. **Fun Yaks** combines tranquil inflatable canoe rides downstream with jetboating upstream. Wetsuits are included, and the personal crafts allow paddlers to explore an otherwise inaccessible gorge, while still letting the river do most of the work. (☎0800 386 925. 6hr. Departs Glenorchy at 10:15am, in winter 11:45am. $179, children $98. Leaves 45min. earlier from Queenstown.) **High Country Horses** (☎442 9915) and **Dart Stables** (☎442 5688, 0800 474 346), on the road next to the motor park, offer guided and unguided tours from casual saunters to gallops through the breathtaking valleys. (Trip prices range greatly depending on duration, $50-750.)

Glenorchy is the gateway to several stunningly scenic tramps. The **Routeburn Track,** 26km from town (see p. 369), crosses the road to Milford. The **Greenstone and Caples Tracks** (see p. 380) form a loop from the far side of Lake Wakatipu, accessible by car or boat. Finally, the **Rees-Dart Track** (see p. 378) loops through two glacier-filled river valleys. Other short hikes abound in nearby **Mt. Aspiring National Park** (see p. 318).

WANAKA ☎03

Wanaka staunchly resists the pressures that would mold it into a second Queenstown, and thereby wins the hearts of backpackers everywhere. Its skiing, summer watersports, and speedy ventures remain surprisingly inconspicuous, while its nightlife is pleasantly present without defining the Wanaka experience. Wanaka is as adrenaline- or tranquility-intensive as you choose.

SOUTHERN LAKES

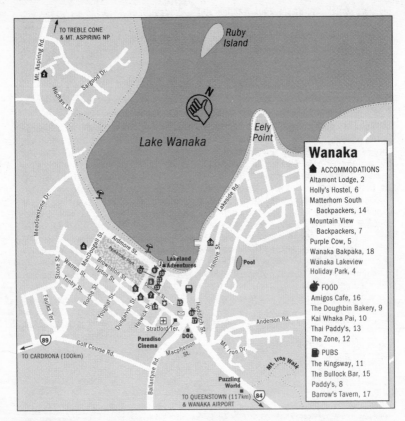

TO TREBLE CONE
& MT. ASPIRING NP

Ruby Island

Lake Wanaka

Eely Point

Meadowstone Dr.

Stone St.
Warren St.
Tenby St.
Faulks Ter.

MacDougall St.
Brownston St.
Upton St.
Roche St.
Youghal St.
Dungarvon St.

Ardmore St.
Pembroke Park
Helwick St.

Stratford Ter.
Paradiso Cinema
DOC
Ballantyne Rd.
Macpherson St.
Stratford Ter.

Lakeland Adventures

Lismore St.

Lakeside Rd.

Anderson Rd.

Mt. Iron Dr.

Mt. Iron Walk

Pool

89
TO CARDRONA (100km)
Golf Course Rd.

Puzzling World

TO QUEENSTOWN (117km)
& WANAKA AIRPORT
84

Wanaka

🏠 ACCOMMODATIONS
Altamont Lodge, 2
Holly's Hostel, 6
Matterhorn South
  Backpackers, 14
Mountain View
  Backpackers, 7
Purple Cow, 5
Wanaka Bakpaka, 18
Wanaka Lakeview
  Holiday Park, 4

🍎 FOOD
Amigos Cafe, 16
The Doughbin Bakery, 9
Kai Whaka Pai, 10
Thai Paddy's, 13
The Zone, 12

🍺 PUBS
The Kingsway, 11
The Bullock Bar, 15
Paddy's, 8
Barrow's Tavern, 17

▛ TRANSPORTATION

Buses: Most buses and shuttles leave from **The Paper Place** on Upper Ardmore St., which also acts as a booking agent. **InterCity** (☎443 7885) runs to: **Christchurch** (9½hr., 8:40am, $95) via **Mt. Cook** (3½hr., $57); **Franz Josef Glacier** (5½hr., 10:15am, $86) via **Fox Glacier** (5hr., $64); and **Queenstown** (2hr., 2pm, $26). **Southern Link** (☎443 7885) goes to **Christchurch** (6½hr., 1:40pm, $40). The Link also runs to **Dunedin** (4hr., 9am, $30) and **Queenstown** (2hr., 4:20pm, $15). **Wanaka Connexions** (☎0800 879 926) shuttles to **Queenstown,** daily at 7, 10am, and 2pm (1½hr.; $25, return $40). Running 3 shuttles from **Queenstown** to **Wanaka** each day as well, they are your best bet for a daytrip. **Atomic Shuttles** (☎443 7885) goes just about anywhere you would want to go, including: **Christchurch** (7hr., 2pm, $40); **Dunedin** (5½hr., 2pm, $30); **Greymouth** (9hr., 9:15am, $65) via the **West Coast** (Fox and Franz Glaciers and Hokitika); **Invercargill** (4½hr., 2pm, $35); **Queenstown** (1½hr., 4pm, $15). Many of these companies charge $5-15 extra to transport skis, snowboards, and mountain bikes. Book InterCity and other shuttles at the YHA or **Paper Place**, 84 Ardmore St. (☎443 7885; open daily 7:30am-6 or 7pm, Sa-Su 7:30am-4pm). **Edgewater Adventures,** 59a Brownston St. (☎/fax 443 8422; open daily 8am-6pm; in winter 7:30am-7pm), also books transport as well as activities.

Shuttles: Shuttles run frequently from Wanaka to the ski slopes as well as to Mt. Aspiring trailheads. **Alpine Shuttles** (☎443 7966) and **Mount Aspiring Express** (☎443 8422), make trailhead runs that cost anywhere from $5 to the Mt. Roy tramp to $25 to Raspberry Creek, the Mt. Aspiring National Park gateway. Book ahead to ski slopes with **Alpine Shuttles** (return $22), **Edgewater Adventure** (☎443 8422; return $22), **The Bus Company** (☎443 8775; return $19), or **Goodsports** (☎443 7966; return $22). The following shuttles go to Treble Cone only: **Ski Shuttles** (☎443 9327; return $20), **Flying Bus** (☎443 9193; return $18), and **Snow Limo** (☎0800 621 000; return $15). Always ask about multi-day, season, group, and backpacker discounts. **Wanaka Connexions** (☎443 8237) runs shuttles out to the Wanaka Airport.

Car Rental: Apex Car Rentals (☎442 8040, 0800 531 111) has cars from $49 per day or from $39 per day on rentals of 4 days or more.

Taxis: Wanaka Taxis (☎443 7999) operates late most nights. An airport run is $20.

Hitchhiking: Although *Let's Go* does not recommend it, hitchhikers report consistent success out to the slopes, though shuttles are a reliable alternative and a must for Mt. Aspiring. At the west edge of town, the Cardrona/Queenstown-bound gather at the southwest corner of Pembroke Park (at Brownston and McDougall St.) and those going to Treble Cone at the northwest corner (at Ardmore and McDougall St.). Those heading up the coast wait past the DOC office on upper Ardmore St.

🛈 PRACTICAL INFORMATION

Visitors Center: Lake Wanaka Visitor Centre (☎443 1233) is in the waterfront log cabin on Lower Ardmore St. Open M-F 9am-5:30pm; in winter M-F 8am-4:45pm, Sa 9:30am-3:45pm. The **DOC** office (☎443 7660) is on Upper Ardmore St. Open in summer daily 8am-4:45pm; in winter M-F 8am-4:45pm and Sa 9:30am-4pm.

Currency Exchange: National Bank (☎443 7521), on Upper Ardmore St., and **Westpac Trust,** 15 Helwick St. (☎443 7817), have **ATMs.** Hours vary from M-F 9am-4:30pm.

Equipment Hire: Rentals on the ski fields are rather expensive and the gear is not exceptional. **Sun & Snowbusiness,** 103 Ardmore St. (☎/fax 443 8855), rents quality carver skis, boots, and poles for $25-30, and snowboards and boots for $35. **Good Sports** (☎443 7966), on Dunmore St., rents winter gear for comparable prices, as well as a range of gear for other sports and camping. Fishing rods $10 per day. Sleeping bags $7.50 per day. Tents $10-15 per day. Open daily 8am-5pm; in winter 7:30am-7:30pm. Most hostels rent bikes (from $6 per hr.) and kayaks (from $25 per half-day).

Medical Services: Wanaka Pharmacy (☎443 8000; after-hour mobile 025 487 870), Helwick St. Open M-Sa 8:30am-7pm, Su 4:30pm-7pm. **Aspiring Medical Center,** 28 Dunvargon St. (☎443 1226). **24hr.**

Police: 28 Helwick St. (☎443 7272).

Internet Access: Budget Communications, 38 Helwick St. (☎443 4440). $6 per hr.; $5 per hr. 7-10pm. Open daily 10am-10pm.

Post Office: 39 Ardmore St. (☎443 8211). Open M-F 8:30am-5:30pm, Sa 9am-noon.

🏠🏞 ACCOMMODATIONS AND CAMPING

In winter, the long-term ski and snowboard bunnies move in, often filling more than half of the hostel beds for weeks and months at a time; it is essential to book ahead. In summer, the excellent facilities are more sparsely graced by trampers escaping the Queenstown rush.

🏵**Matterhorn South Backpackers,** 56 Brownston St. (☎443 1119; fax 443 8379), on the corner of Helwick and Brownston St., at the top of the town. The back porch offers privacy; clean motel units next door share a new kitchen and TV lounge. Reception 8am-9pm; in winter 8am-8pm. Dorms $17-20; twins and doubles $40-65.

Wanaka Bakpaka, 117 Lakeside Rd. (☎443 7837). From the foot of Upper Ardmore St., Lakeside Rd. rings the lake on the right; it is a 5min. walk from town. Relative seclusion, the kayaks are the added touch. Linen $3. Key deposit $10. Reception 8:30am-8:30pm; in winter 8am-8pm. Dorms $17-18; singles $17; twins $40; doubles $44.

The Purple Cow, 94 Brownston St. (☎443 1880, 0800 772 277; fax 443 1870; stay@purplecow.co.nz). The open fire compensates for the snug kitchen. Bike and kayak. Linens $3. Reception 8am-10pm. Dorms $18; twins and doubles $45.

Mountain View Backpackers (☎443 9010), on Brownston St. between Helwick and Dunvargon St. A clean and cozy fit, the new hostel in town wins accolades by Foosball. Reception 9am-noon and 4-8pm. Dorms $17; doubles $45.

Altamont Lodge (☎443 8864), more than 2km west out of town along Ardmore St. The ski-lodge atmosphere pervades, enhanced by the free spa pool and ski-tuning room. Linen $5. Reception 8am-9pm. Singles $30; doubles $48, extra person $11.

Holly's Hostel, 71 Upton St. (☎443 8187). With a sunny lounge areas, Holly's offers a home-style stay with heated dorms. Bike and kayak hire. Reception 8am-7pm; in winter until 6pm. Dorms $17; twins and doubles $42, in summer $40. Wheelchair accessible.

Wanaka Lakeview Holiday Park, 212 Brownston St. (☎/fax 443 7883), at the west end of Brownston St., past Pembroke Park. This motor camp is large and near town. Dorms $12; cabins for 2 $32, extra person $13; tent and powered sites $10 per person.

▐ FOOD

The true-value budget meal hides. However, the **New World,** on Dunmore St. is easy to find. (Open daily 8am-8pm.) **Soul Food: Organic Oasis** on the Pembroke Mall off of Dunmore St., proffers organic produce and whole foods. (☎443 8297. Open daily 10am-6pm.)

▓ Kai Whaka Pai (☎443 7795), on the corner of Ardmore and Helwick St., facing the lake. Enormous and creative sandwiches on foccaccia bread and light meals are served all day ($7-23). Open daily 8am-midnight.

The Zone (☎443 9220), on Pembroke Mall off of Dunmore St. Hang in the mall with Wanaka's climber crowd while sipping a smoothie from fresh-squeezed products ($5). Veggie Vishnu Curry $14; salad bowls $6 or $8.50. Open daily 8am until late.

The Doughbin Bakery (☎443 7290), on Ardmore St., on the lakefront. A cheap place for takeaways or the 3am munchies. Shop open daily 7am-6pm; takeaway midnight-7am.

Thai Paddy's, 21 Dunmore St. (☎443 7640), serves generous portions of Thai cuisine, just a hop, skip, and jump from Paddy's pub. Open daily 6am-11pm. Hours may vary.

Amigos Cafe (☎443 7872), on Upper Ardmore St. The owner fries his own tortillas and makes his own salsa. Combo platters from $15. Open daily from 5:30pm.

♫ ▐ ENTERTAINMENT AND NIGHTLIFE

In winter the skiers have to leave the mountain at 4pm and in summer trampers and adrenaline-philes often roll back into town the same time. For a relaxing night, many stop by ▓**Paradiso Cinema,** 3 Ardmore St., Wanaka's one-of-a-kind movie theater in town hall. (☎443 1505. $10, children $6.) Whatever their sport of choice, backpackers make a go of it on the weekends, packing bars that are silent any other time of the week.

The Kingsway, 21 Helwick St. (☎443 7663), is where the town is going later. Pool tables, drink specials, and DJs—this place has the works. Open daily from 5pm.

The Bullock Bar (☎443 9258), on Ardmore St. beside the BP station, is the *only* place to watch Rugby Union; pull up a stool. The combination of horse betting, meat raffles, and a bottle store next door draw an eclectic crowd. Open daily from 11am.

Paddy's, 28 Dunmore St. (☎443 7640), behind Thai Paddy's. Combining MTV and the All Blacks, this bar is a curious mix of genres and clientele. "Paddy" often picks up his guitar to play motley and rousing rock tunes. Open daily from 4:30pm.

Barrow's Tavern, 20 Ardmore St. (☎443 8616), at the top of Brownston St., is home to weekly specials, $4 jugs, and a mostly-male rugby crowd. Open M-Sa from 11am.

👁 SIGHTS

Puzzling World 3km out of town opposite Mt. Iron, is the famous creation of a man from Wanaka; everyone goes. The world's first two-story, mind-screwing maze, and a hall of chasing faces, you may get lost and never leave. (☎ 443 7489. Open daily 8:30am-5:30pm. $4, with maze $7; children $3, with maze $4.50. Maze only $5, children $3.)

The **Wanaka Beerworks** (☎ 443 1865) is a micro-brewery that produced top prize winners (Brewski and Tall Black) at the 2000 New Zealand International Beer Awards. A tour costs $5 and lasts about 5min., but the buzz from the brew keeps you happy much longer. The air-oriented activities are clustered around the brewery in the Sky Show Centre. The **New Zealand Fighter Pilots Museum** lauds the men and crafts that flew during the world wars. (☎ 443 7010. Open daily 9am-4pm; until 6pm in late Dec. to late Jan.) Transportation to the airport (including the Sky Show Centre and the Wanaka Transport Museum) is available through **Alpine Shuttles** (☎ 443 7966) and **Wanaka Connexions** (☎ 443 8237. Return $12.)

🎿🏔 OUTDOOR ACTIVITIES

SKI FIELDS

Two main ski fields are accessible from Wanaka, each with its own advantages—ask around to score some sweet deals on transport, tickets, and rentals. Keep in mind, that any money you may save will disappear in the cafeteria. An ISIC card and another **student ID** is necessary for student deals. Conditions between the ski fields vary, and snow reports are posted in town and accommodations in the morning.

CARDRONA. With half of its patrons coming from equidistant Queenstown, Cardrona is a more family-oriented field, with wide, sunny slopes perfect for learning and money-saving beginner deals. *(Ski Field 34km away. Wanaka office 18 Dunmore St., just west of Helwick. Ski Field ☎ 443 7341. Office ☎ 443 7411. Office open daily in season 8am-6pm, Sa 8am-noon. Lift pass $60, students $50, children $30.)*

TREBLE CONE. This field has the longest vertical rise in the Southern Lakes and contains more skiable terrain than anywhere else on the South Island. Runs are generally steeper and more difficult than at Cardrona—beginner ski bums will have bruised bums. *(Ski Field 43km away. Wanaka office on the waterfront, east of Helwick St. Ski Field ☎ 443 7443. Office ☎ 443 9327. Office open daily in season 7:45am-12:30pm and 3:30-6pm. Lift pass $57, students $48, children $28.)*

ON THE WATER

Beautiful Lake Wanaka and the rivers that feed it are fished and played upon in all ways imaginable. And, although it may seem that way, not all watersports in Wanaka are adrenaline-powered. **Lakeland Adventures,** on the wharf, rents everything you need for a calming morning on the lake. (☎ 443 7495. Kayak hire $10 per hr. Double kayak hire $20 per hr.)

CANYONING. Deep Canyon Experience runs intense canyoning trips daily in summer, which involve abseiling down waterfalls to natural rock waterslides as well as basic climbing; be sure to bring your swimsuit, sturdy outdoor footwear, and an intrepid attitude. *(☎ 443 7922; mobile 025 204 9296. Nov.-Mar.; $165, including lunch.)*

KAYAKING. Alpine River Guides runs whitewater trips for both beginner and experienced paddlers on many rivers in the area. *(☎ 443 9422. $120, all gear provided.)*

SLEDGING. Challenging the dominance of whitewater rafting, **Frogz Have More Fun** has a thrilling alternative. Careening through the rapids on your own personal "sledge" (a cross between a raft and a kickboard) is literally the most in-your-face way to conquer the river thus far. *(☎ 443 9130. 4hr., Nov.-Apr. 2 per day, $109.)*

JET BOATING. It wouldn't be the Southern Lakes region without a few opportunities to rip through water only a few centimeters deep. **Clutha River Jet** *(☎ 443 7495)* and **Wanaka Jet** *(☎ 0800 538 7746)* shoot up the Clutha River through both shallow rapids and deep pools. *(2½hr., $60.)*

FISHING. Lakeland Adventures, conveniently located at the wharf, hires gear. (☎443 7495. *Fishing rod hire $12 per day.*) Fishing gear and one-day fishing licenses are available from **Good Sports** on Dunmore St. (☎443 7966. *License $13-$50. Fishing rod hire $10 per day, including tackle.*) Inquire at the visitors center for a list of local trout and flyfishing guides, but be prepared to pay at least $200 for a half-day of fishing. Or just talk up your skills at the pub and see who takes you out next morning.

ADVENTURE ACTIVITIES

SKYDIVING. If you're into breaking wind at 3000m with a jumpmaster strapped to your back, **Tandem Skydive Wanaka** is more than happy to oblige. Their motto, "You call, we fall" is an apt description; keep your head up to see gorgeous lake and mountain views. (☎443 7207. *$225, including 20min. scenic flight and pick-up.*)

PARAGLIDING. If you scoff at the word tandem, surrender yourself to **Wanaka Paragliding.** After you've mastered the basics during a full-day course on the grassy slopes of Mt. Iron, you are ready to fly solo. Once you are certified, it's just $15 to soar down any time you like. (☎443 9193. *Full-day course $188.*)

MOUNTAIN BIKING. Alpine Mountain Biking takes the uphill battle out of cycling by transporting riders to some of the country's highest terrain, either by van or helicopter, so they are well rested and ready to enjoy themselves all the way back down. (☎443 8943. *Heli-bike Treble Cone $215; Mt Alpha $195. Prices include bike hire.*)

HORSE TREKS. run daily through New Zealand Backcountry Saddle Expeditions (☎443 8151) and Lake Wanaka Saddle Adventures (☎443 7777), with treks through the surrounding countryside. (*2hr., $50, must provide own transport.*)

WALKS

Not just for the frugal, tramping abounds around Lake Wanaka and the surrounding mountains. Each of the treks requires transportation; while you can ride your own bikes there, you can't ride them up. **Alpine Shuttles** (☎443 7966), in the morning, and **Mount Aspiring Express** (☎443 8422), at 9:30am and 2:30pm, run daily from October to May. (*Diamond Lake $10; Mt. Roy $5.*) As always, the DOC office has up-to-the-minute information on track conditions.

SHORT HIKES. The **Diamond Lake Walk,** through glacially carved terrain, is one of the prettiest short hikes in New Zealand. (*Trailhead is signposted from Mt. Aspiring Rd., 25min. out of Wanaka on Ardmore St. Return 3hr. Inaccessible July-Sept.*) Beginning along the south side of the bay, the **Waterfall Creek Walk,** also known as the **Millennium Walkway,** is a perfect short trip for novice mountain bikers looking for quiet views of Lake Wanaka. (*Return 1½hr., 4hr. with Millennium extension.*)

MOUNTAIN HIKES. The tramp up **Mt. Roy** delivers views of Mt. Aspiring National Park, including glimpses of the very large rock known as the Matterhorn of the South. (*The marked trailhead is off Mt. Aspiring Rd. about 6km from Wanaka. Return 5-6hr.*) In the other direction, a shorter hike ascends **Mt. Iron** in pursuit of local vistas. (*2km from Wanaka. Return 2hr.*)

MT. ASPIRING NATIONAL PARK ☎03

AT A GLANCE	
AREA: 355,543 hectares.	**GATEWAYS:** Wanaka, Queenstown, Glenorchy, Te Anau.
CLIMATE: Pleasant climate in summer, dangerous conditions in winter.	
	CAMPING: Established camping areas, backcountry huts.
FEATURES: Haast River, Humbolt Mountains, and Red Hills "mineral belt."	**FEES & RESERVATIONS:** Hut Pass necessary for Routeburn Trek.
HIGHLIGHTS: Superb views and extreme terrain.	

The craggy, snow-covered peaks of Mt. Aspiring National Park are the center of the Te Wahipounamu South West New Zealand World Heritage Area. Of the park's 100-odd glaciers and 13 peaks over 2500m, Mt. Aspiring (3027m) is the perfectly pyramidal pinnacle. With the mellow Greenstone and Caples and the challenging Rees-Dart Tracks within reach of Glenorchy or Queenstown and walks up the Matukituki accessible from Wanaka, the park attracts a variety of trampers. Most activities, hikes, and scenic flights are run out of the gateway towns of **Glenorchy** (see p. 312), **Queenstown** (see p. 302), and **Wanaka** (see p. 313). Even far-off **Te Anau** (see p. 324) takes part, as an access point for Fiordland's and Mt. Aspiring's shared **Routeburn Track** (see p. 369). The **Rees-Dart Track** (4-5 days, 54km) travels over the Rees and Dart River Valleys, crowned with glaciers galore. A one day side trip up to the Cascade Saddle can afford one of the most mind-numbing views in New Zealand. The **Greenstone and Caples Tracks** (4-5 days, 50km) passes cattle grazing in paradise, where green mountains overlook the golden meadows of the valley floor (see p. 380).

> **WHEN TO GO** The park is much safer in the summer months as the winter can get extremely cold in the high altitudes and tracks become more dangerous. Many trails have few hut wardens and weather conditions such as thick snow and freezing wind can make trekking more difficult.

FIORDLAND NATIONAL PARK   ☎ 03

A great, glacier-scoured valley, green with beech trees and brimming with waterfalls that spill into the sea, Fiordland is New Zealand's largest national park. From Milford Sound to the wild southern coast, this wet and living wilderness, part of the renowned Te Wahipounamu World Heritage Area, features over 500km of trails, including three Great Walks. The lush scenery comes at a price, however—Fiordland's precipitation seldom ceases: it rains more than 200 days of the year. The winter brings precipitation issues of its own in the form of frequent avalanches—even the beech trees sometimes roll down mountainsides. Nevertheless, in any season, ageless power and natural grandeur unfold along the roadsides and speak from deep within the park's wild core.

AT A GLANCE

AREA: 1,251,924 hectares.

CLIMATE: Extreme weather in winter, but warm temperatures in summer.

FEATURES: Deep fiords, waterfalls.

HIGHLIGHTS: The largest park in New Zealand. Home to the Milford Track.

GATEWAYS: Te Anau, Manapouri.

CAMPING: Backcountry huts.

FEES & RESERVATIONS: Hut passes necessary; tramps need advanced bookings.

TRANSPORTATION

Only one paved road penetrates Fiordland National Park: SH94, otherwise known as the **Milford Road** (see p. 321), which runs north from Te Anau to Milford Sound. Nevertheless, the park's three Great Walks—the **Routeburn** (see p. 369), **Milford** (see p. 370), and **Kepler Tracks** (p. 374)—make Fiordland shuttle central. Assault on the park usually begins from Te Anau or Queenstown—see the **Transportation** sections under each walk's header for more specific information.

ORIENTATION AND PRACTICAL INFORMATION

Fiordland occupies most of New Zealand's southwest corner. The fjord-studded coastline forms its western edge; roads run along much of its eastern border. **Te**

SOUTHERN LAKES

Anau (see p. 324) is by far the area's most convenient and developed tourist center, with **supermarkets, banks,** and the only **ATMs** in the region. Some people also explore Fiordland from sleepy **Manapouri** (see p. 326) or **Tuatapere** (see p. 348), while others use Queenstown as their base. Fiordland's **DOC Visitor Centre** sits on the lakefront in Te Anau, and comes equipped with a crack staff, small museum, and the **Great Walks Booking Desk** (see p. 355).

GEAR AND STORAGE. To enjoy the splendor of Fiordland, one must be prepared to battle the demonic sandflies and torrential rain. DOC sells indispensable heavy-duty **plastic pack liners** ($4) to keep gear dry. As for sandflies, see p. 25 for preventive measures. Rent from **Bev's Tramping Gear Hire,** 16 Homer St., Te Anau; her **Great Walks Package** (3-4 days, $80) includes everything, except boots, that an unprepared tramper could need. (☎ 249 7389. Open daily Oct.-May 9am-12pm and 6-8pm; in winter on demand.) **Te Anau Sports World,** in the town center, has a more limited selection of equipment for hire. (☎ 249 8195. Open daily 9am-9pm; in winter M-F 9am-6pm, Sa 9am-noon.)

Finally, **PLBs** (Personal Locator Beacons) are excellent emergency precautions. You can rent them from the **Mobil Station** in Te Anau for $20 per week. (☎ 249 7247. Open daily 7am-8pm.) **Te Anau Motor Park,** near the DOC office, stores extra luggage ($1-5); in fact, most area accommodations store gear for little or no charge.

 WHEN TO GO. Though the tramps and walks within the Fiordland National Park can be enjoyed year-round, extreme winter weather conditions necessitate experience and appropriate hiking equipment; winter in the Fiordland backcountry can be avalanche intensive, life endangering, and comfort free. February brings the best hope for good weather, while March has the best shot at a solitude-and-sunshine combination. From late April to October, the Milford (see p. 370), Routeburn (see p. 369), and Kepler Tracks (p. 374) lose their Great Walk status and use regular track and hut passes; in these months there is neither wood nor fuel in the huts, the valleys get little to no sunlight, and snow and ice can make the tracks impassable.

OUTDOOR ACTIVITIES

The **Routeburn Track** (2-4 days, 32 km) runs high above the tree line, skirting grand valleys and overlooking great mountain ranges (see p. 369). **The Milford Track** (4 days, 54km) is heralded as "the finest walk in the world," running through two green glacier valleys and over a spectacular mountain pass. Sheer rock faces are watered by countless cascades, including Sutherland Falls, the highest in New Zealand (see p. 370). **The Kepler Track** (3-4 days, 67km) is the most easily accessible of the Great Walks, running along awe-inspiring ridgetops high above Lake Te Anau and descending into dense forest alongside Lake Manapouri (see **The Kepler Track** see p. 374 and **Lake Manapouri** p. 326). The **Hollyford Track** (56km, 4 days oneway) starts at the Lower Hollyford road-end off the Milford Road (see p. 321) and penetrates lush lowland forest before reaching the sea at Martin's Bay. The route's low altitude makes it less scenic than other tracks, but far safer to walk in the wintertime. **Fiordland Tracknet** (☎ 249 7777) runs on demand to the roadside trailhead ($37). Many Kiwis regard the **Dusky Track** (84km, 8-12 days) as the ultimate challenge. Downpours and whiteouts can strand trampers for days at a time, if they aren't already up to their armpits in mud. All the same, the Dusky's popularity is growing, thanks to a strange brew of masochism, glorious mountain vistas, and unrealistic expectations. To hike the Dusky safely, you really need an emergency radio or PLB (see **Gear and Storage** above), a party of at least four, surplus food, and ample experience. **Fiordland Travel** (☎ 249 6602, 0800 656 501) transports trampers to the track's northern trailhead at Lake Manapouri ($27); **Lake Hauroko Tours** (☎ 226 6681) does the same at the southern end ($60). **Waterwings Airways** (☎ 249

7405) flies in and out of Supper Cove ($183 one-way), a hard-core possible addition to the standard track. **Huts** along both the Hollyfield and the Dusky cost $5 per night year-round; they have tank water and toilets, but no cooking stoves. At the opposite end of the spectrum, Fiordland also hosts a number of lovely **daywalks** and other outdoor excursions; see coverage of Te Anau (see p. 324), Manapouri (see p. 326), the Milford Road (see p. 321), and Tuatapere (see p. 348) for details.

THE MILFORD ROAD

Getting there is half of the Milford Sound experience. From Te Anau to the Sound, the 119km (3hr. with stops) Milford Road climbs through Fiordland National Park past staggeringly beautiful valleys, lakes, and creeks. Pick up a guide to the sights for $1 at the **DOC office;** Fiordland Travel has a less extensive guide for free. In winter, definitely stop at the DOC office in Te Anau to see if the road is passable, or if tire chains are required (chains can be rented locally for about $25; when required, vehicles without them are subject to fines). After all, the stretch of road near the Homer Tunnel is the most avalanche-prone piece of highway on earth—an average of one avalanche per day in winter keeps a full-time clearing crew stationed near the tunnel very busy. Te Anau provides the only reliable services for Milford Sound and the road. There are no **gas stations** before Milford. Several tour operators clog the length of the narrow road on their way to and from Milford Sound (see below for details). To avoid most of the tourist-bus traffic in the summer try leaving Te Anau before 8am or after 11am. There are 12 handsome **DOC camping sites,** most with pit toilets, picnic tables, fire pits and fresh water access, along the route ($5 per person, self-register). From Te Anau, the road runs beside Lake Te Anau through sheep stations before entering the red and silver beech forest of Fiordland National Park. Traversing the classic U-shaped **Eglinton Valley,** the road runs through wide expanses

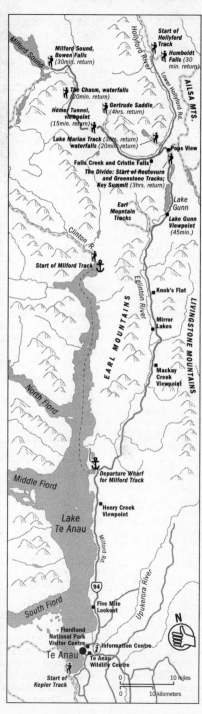

SOUTHERN LAKES

of golden grassland veined with creeks beneath the impressive backdrop of the Earl and Livingstone Ranges. Stop at **Mirror Lakes** to reflect on the tussocked swamp and teal ducks beyond the pools, or take a bathroom break in **Knob Flats** (where the toilet-to-inhabitant ratio is 35 to 1), with displays on avalanches and native bats (one of the only pre-human kiwi mammals). **Lake Gunn,** farther down the road, harbors a 45min. walk through the moss-covered glory of the forest. Beaches and fishing spots abound, and you can often see the trout you're trying to nab loafing in the water.

A shelter at **The Divide** marks the starting point for the **Routeburn Track** (see p. 369) and **Greenstone and Caples Tracks** (see p. 380). From here, the staggering valley views of the **Key Summit** (return 3hr.) make a great day-hike; a spot about 25 minutes along the track allows for views of both the road and a waterfall. Meanwhile, the road continues past a lookout and over **Falls Creek,** where **Christie Falls** is visible from the roadside. Turn right on **Lower Hollyford Road** to reach the track to **Lake Marian** (return 3hr.), which threads through lush rainforest and past waterfalls to an idyllic picnic spot. The eerie **Homer Tunnel** is next on the main road; constructed in 1953 (but having the appearance of a dwarf's lair from a Tolkien novel) the tunnel still has no internal lighting. Drivers must turn on headlights and take off sunglasses to navigate through its 945m of darkness. After emerging on the other side of the mountain, hairpin turns down Milford Valley lead to the **Chasm,** where a boardwalk (return 10min.) spans the **Cleddau River** and its surreal, water-carved clic rocks. Just beyond the Chasm lies the haunting Milford Sound itself.

MILFORD SOUND ☎03

Mystical and dramatic, Milford Sound rests in the middle of Fiordland National Park. A marine reserve since 1993, the fjord brims with life, from unique waterline flora to bottlenose dolphins, fur seals, and the occasional Fiordland crested penguin. Sheer cliffs and snow-capped summits surround the Sound and its photogenic focal point, the rugged Mitre Peak. Waterfalls cascade from dizzying heights—at 146m, Stirling Falls is among the most spectacular—and grow and multiply after heavy rain. Barely marred by a century of eager eyes (walks to the area were guided as early as the 1890s), Milford Sound retains a majesty despite the cruise ships and swarm of scenic flights.

TRANSPORTATION. The variety of tour options to Milford Sound is staggering—in peak season, as many as 70 buses head up the Milford Road in the morning and back in the afternoon. Daytrips depart Queenstown or Te Anau early in the morning and don't return until evening; book well in advance and bring lunch with you—or prepare for high-priced mediocrity. Daytrippers to Milford should try to get an early start as it sometimes clouds over on summer afternoons, while the morning fog in winter usually burns off by late morning. The following coach-cruise combos operate daily in the summer (Oct.-Apr.) and at least a few times a week during the rest of the year.

The friendly, tongue-in-cheek local guides from **Trips 'n' Tramps** run small (max. 12 people) tours from **Te Anau;** some of their trips allow several hours for tramping along the Routeburn Track. (☎249 7081. From $105, children from $50.) Another smaller option (max. 22 people), the **BBQ Bus,** based in Queenstown, stops its commentary for bush walking and a barbecue lunch. (☎442 1045. $149, YHA/VIP $129, children $75, 2 adult/2 child family package $373.) **Kiwi Experience** (☎442 9708) and Magic partner **Kiwi Discovery** (☎442 7340) offer comparable daytrips from **Queenstown** ($129; Kiwi Experience also has a $67.50 child price) and one-way sector fares along the road (Kiwi Discovery's are a few dollars cheaper: **Queenstown** to **Te Anau** $30, **Te Anau** to **The Divide** $20, **The Divide** to **Milford Sound** $15). **Fiordland Travel** also offers large-scale excursions. (☎249 7416, 0800 656 501. From Queenstown $170-185, children $85-$95; from Te Anau $100-120, children $51.50.) **InterCity's Mil-**

ford Experience offers similar service. (☎249 7559. From Queenstown $160, children $84; from Te Anau $90, children $36.) Rosco's Sea Kayaks, Fiordland Wilderness Adventures, Tawaki Dive, and some of the scenic flight operators also offer packages that include transport to and from **Te Anau;** see **Activities,** below for more on these. **Hitchhikers** report success getting to and from Milford Sound, although *Let's Go* does not recommend it.

⌐ ACCOMMODATIONS AND FOOD. Milford Sound's hit-and-run style of tourism doesn't encourage a proliferation of overnight options; the **Milford Sound Lodge** is the only budget joint. The rooms are serviceable, the giant track map in the lounge is extremely helpful, and the recently revamped restaurant serves sophisticated meals. (☎249 8071; milford.sound.lodge@xtra.co.nz. Restaurant open daily 7-9am, noon-2pm, and 6-8:30pm; mains $10.50-17. Internet. Dorms with 6-11 beds $18; 4-bed dorms $20; doubles $46; tent sites $8, powered sites $12.)

⚡ OUTDOOR ACTIVITIES. Boat tours are the most popular way to see the Sound. **Fiordland Travel** sends out eight boats per day in the summer and at least three per day year-round. (☎249 7419, 0800 656 501. 1¾hr.-2½hr. $45-53, children $10.) Two of their summertime (Oct.-Apr.) boats have a 10% YHA discount: the intimate, tugboat-esque *Friendship* and the *Milford Wanderer* sailboat. Both boats pose more character than many of the other vessels plowing the Sound; both also offer relaxed **overnight trips** that include a hearty dinner, breakfast, and kayaking ($145, children $72.50). **Red Boat Cruises** runs a fleet of modern red-hulled cruise boats. (☎441 1137, 0800 657 444. 1¾-2¾hr. Oct.-Apr. 8 departures per day 9am-3pm, May-Sept. 5 departures per day 11am-1:30pm; $45-$60, children $10-18, 10% YHA discount.) **Mitre Peak Cruises'** boats feature underwater portholes and a maximum capacity of 60 passengers. (☎249 8110. 1¾-2¼hr.; 3-4 trips per day 10am-5:15pm. $45-60, children $25, 10% YHA discount.) **Milford Deep,** the **underwater observatory** that floats more than 8m below the surface of the Sound, allows visitors a peek ($20, children $13) at cool critters like black coral and snake stars, which grow much closer to the surface here than elsewhere thanks to the light-repelling layer of fresh water that Fiordland's heavy rainfall leaves on the Sound. Most cruises can drop people off here—Red Boat Cruises offers the best price ($60) for those who want to combine a tour and an observatory visit. Milford Deep also runs its own shuttles from the boat terminal. (☎249 9442, 0800 326 969. Open daily 8am-5pm. $40, children $20.)

Of course, **kayaking** may be the best way to comprehend the Milford Sound's vast scale. **Rosco's Sea Kayaks** (☎0800 476 726) runs kayak tours early in the morning, late in the afternoon, and even after dark ($49-89), as well as daytrips ($99) that include transport to and from Te Anau. Operating out of Te Anau, **Fiordland Wilderness Experiences** offer coach-kayak-coach tours. (☎249 7700, 0800 200 434. $95, from Milford Sound $75, not always available in winter.) Meanwhile, **diving** in the Sound allows first-hand encounters with black coral and other Creatures of the Reasonably Deep; **Tawaki Dive** runs great personalized excursions from Te Anau with a maximum of four people. (☎249 9006. 12hr. trip, 4-5hr. cruise. $220, $175 from Milford Sound, $45 without gear rental; winter trips on demand.)

Breathtaking **helicopter** and **flightseeing** tours may make you inhale deeply, but getting high is expensive. **Waterwing Airways** (☎249 7405) sends seaplanes from Te Anau on round-trip flights over the Sound (1hr. $215), as does **Air Fiordland** (☎249 7505; 70min.; $199). Air Fiordland also runs a posh flight-cruise-flight combo from Queenstown or Te Anau ($245-$280). **Milford Sound Helicopters** (☎249 8384) take off straight from the Sound; trips range from a 10min. hover over the Sound ($110) to a thrill-packed 50min. excursion that flies around the Sound, takes in Sutherland Falls, and lands on Tutoko Glacier ($325).

TE ANAU ☎ 03

"Walking capital of the world," Te Anau (tee-AH-now, 3000) draws more than its fair share of happy trampers and is a compromise between the unpeopled expanse of Fiordland National Park and the commercial buzz of Queenstown. Beyond the milling mallards on the rubble shore of Lake Te Anau, green mountain ranges soar to alpine heights, sending a siren song to outdoor enthusiasts of all stripes.

⌷ TRANSPORTATION

Buses: Book bus transport at the **Air Fiordland** office, in town center. **Topline Tours** (☎0508 832 628), heads daily to: **Christchurch** (10hr.; 8am; $116, YHA $93) via **Dunedin** (4½hr.; $58, YHA $46); and **Queenstown** (2hr.; 10am; $35, YHA $25). **Spitfire Shuttle** (☎249 7505) goes daily to **Invercargill** (2½hr.; 8:30am; $39, backpackers $34). **Catch-a-Bus** (☎471 4103) runs daily to **Dunedin** (1pm, $39). For transport links to **Milford Sound** see p. 322.

Taxis: Tracknet (☎249 777).

Car Rental: Major chains book through local travel agencies. **Te Anau Rentals** (☎249 8365; mobile 021 612 061), is on the road to Milford. $40 per day plus a charge per km. Courtesy pick-up from town. Open M-F 8:30am-5pm, on call Sa-Su.

Bicycle and Kayak Rental: Fiordland Bike Hire (☎249 7211) at the mini-golf course on Mokonui St. near the town center has bikes available. $5 per hr., $20 per day. Mountain bikes $8 per hr., $25 per day. Open daily 10am-dusk; in winter on demand. **Fiordland Wilderness Experiences**, 66 Quintin Dr., (☎249 7700), rents kayaks for Lake Te Anau, Lake Manapouri, and Doubtful Sound. $45 for 1 day, $155 for 4-5 days. **Lakeland Boat Hire** (☎249 8364), on the lake, has all sorts of hire. Kayaks $10 per 30min. Canoes $8 per 30min. Dinghies $5 per 30min.

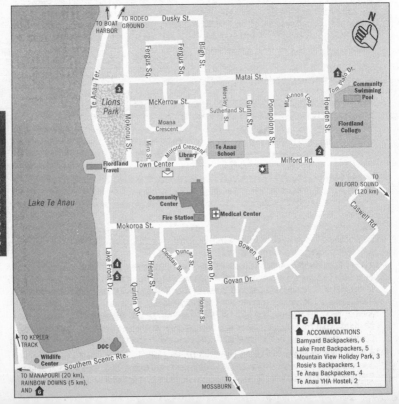

Te Anau

🏠 ACCOMMODATIONS
Barnyard Backpackers, 6
Lake Front Backpackers, 5
Mountain View Holiday Park, 3
Rosie's Backpackers, 1
Te Anau Backpackers, 4
Te Anau YHA Hostel, 2

Hitchhiking: Traffic to Milford Sound usually consists of sightseers who rarely pick up hitchers. Although *Let's Go* does not recommend it, hitching is nearly impossible in winter, but those who try often head out early and walk to where the houses end on the road to Milford Sound. Getting to Manapouri or Queenstown is reportedly much easier; most thumbers walk to where the roads begin south of town.

⚜🛈 ORIENTATION AND PRACTICAL INFORMATION

The short main drag of the **town center** runs perpendicular to the lake and **Lakefront Dr.** The **Southern Scenic Route** runs west beyond the DOC office (left as you face the water) toward **Manapouri** (20km), while **SH94** runs inland toward **Mossburn** and points east. The **Milford Rd.** heads through town, branching off from the town center and away from the lake to **Milford Sound** (120km). Shops are concentrated in the town center, while booking agencies and tour operators are on Lakefront Dr.

Visitors Center: The **Te Anau Visitor Information Centre** (☎249 8900), an appendage of **Fiordland Travel** (see **Booking Offices** below). Open daily 8:30am-6pm; in winter 8:30am-5pm.

DOC: (☎249 7924; fax 249 7613), 3min. drive from the town center, on the corner of Lakefront Dr. and the Manapouri-Te Anau Rd. Regional office for **Great Walks**, tramping information, and the Milford Rd. Open daily 8:30am-5pm; in winter 8:30am-4:30pm.

Booking Offices: Air Fiordland (☎249 7505) is in the town center. Open daily 7:30am-8pm; in winter 8:30am-5:30pm. **Fiordland Travel** (☎249 7416) is at the end of the town center. Open daily 7:30am-9pm; in winter 8am-7pm. **T.A. Travel and Information Centre** (☎249 7516), opposite Fiordland, is open daily 8am-7pm; in winter 9am-5pm.

Tramping Gear: Bev's Tramping Gear Hire, 16 Homer St. (☎249 7505), rents packs and sleeping bags $20 each for 3-4 days. Open daily 9am-noon and 6-8pm. **Sports World,** (☎249 8195) in the town center. Open daily 9am-9pm; in winter 9am-6pm.

Currency Exchange: Westpac Trust (☎249 7824), in town center, boasts the only **24hr. ATM.** Bank open M-Tu and Th-F 9am-4:30pm, W 9:30am-4:30pm. **BNZ** (☎249 7826), has an **ATM.** Open M-F 8:30am-7pm, Sa-Su 8:30am-6pm; in winter closed Su.

Police: 196 Milford Rd. (☎249 7600).

Pharmacy: Te Anau Pharmacy, 60 Milford Rd. (☎249 7134), has advice and a range of products. Open daily 8:30am-9pm; in winter M-F 8:30am-6pm, Sa and Su 9am-6pm.

Medical Services: 24hr. doctor (☎249 7007).

Internet Access: e.stop internet Connexion, in the town center, $2 per 14min. **Pop Inn Cafe,** two doors along the lake to the east of Fiordland travel, $3 per 15min.

Post Office: (☎249 7348), at **Paper Plus.** Open M-F 8:30am-8pm, Sa 9:30am-6pm.

🏠📷 ACCOMMODATIONS AND CAMPING

Rosie's Backpackers, 23 Tom Plato Dr. (☎249 8431). Head up Milford Rd., turn left on Howden St., and right on Tom Plato Dr. A secluded home bordering sheep paddocks, Rosie's is a real homestay. Reception after 3pm; free pick-up in town. Book ahead. Dorms $18; doubles $40.

Lake Front Backpackers Lodge (☎249 7974; fax 249 7973), next door to Te Anau Backpackers is furnished in a similar—but slightly more mature and elegant style. Internet. Reception in summer only 8am-8pm. Dorms $17-18; doubles $44-55.

Barnyard Backpackers, 80 Mt. York Rd. (☎/fax 249 8006; rainbowdowns@xtra.co.nz), 8km from Te Anau toward Manapouri. Ranch-style accommodations in the hills, with terrific views of Fiordland. Reception 8:30am-8:30pm; on call 24hr. Dorms $17; twins and doubles $44. Discounts on horse treks and excursions.

Te Anau YHA, 29 Mokonui St. (☎249 7847; fax 249 7823). Friendly, witty, and knowledgeable staff know Te Anau back and front. A clean and placid haven. Reception 8am-9pm; in winter 4-8pm only. Dorms $17; twins and doubles $42; non-members $3 extra.

Te Anau Backpackers Lodge, 48 Lakefront Dr. (☎249 7713; fax 249 8319). A backpackers with huge easy chairs, and a communal atmosphere. Spa. Internet. Reception 7:30am-9:30pm; in winter 8:30am-7:30pm. Dorms $17-18; twins or doubles $42-44.

Te Anau Mountain View Holiday Park (☎249 7462), on Te Anau Terrace. From town center, turn right along the waterfront. Clean as Fiordland mountain water and recently refurbished, this is an award-winning holiday park. Reception 7:30am-9pm. Standard cabins for 2 $44, with bath $70, extra person $14; tourist flats $85; motel units $98; tent sites $12, powered sites $12. Off-season rates negotiable.

🄵 FOOD

If you're in need of groceries, **Supervalue** in the town center, has the best selection. (☎249 9600. Open M-F 8am-7pm, Sa 8:30am-7pm, Su 10am-6pm.)

La Toscana (☎249 7756), in the upper end of the town center. About as Italian as you can get in New Zealand, with hanging wine bottles, high wooden benches, and Mediterranean memorabilia. Cheesy thin-crust pizza ($8.50-17.50) and red wine (from $5 a glass). Free delivery. Open daily 5:30-10:30pm; in winter Tu-Su 5:30-9pm.

The Olive Tree Cafe (☎249 8496), halfway up the town center. Like offerings of peace, the Olive Tree serves up homemade goods made daily. Foccaccia sandwiches with salad ($8.50) and evening pastas from $12. Open daily 9am-9pm.

The Ranch (☎249 8801), in the town center. A popular pub with a huge open fire and garish iced beer lights. The $15 menu is a good feed, as are Sunday roasts ($10). Pick up a free drink voucher from your hostel. Bands on weekends. Happy Hour with $1 drinks daily 8-9pm. Open daily 11am-1am; in winter M-F 2pm-late, Sa-Su 11am-late.

🄾 OUTDOOR ACTIVITIES

As a starting point for three of New Zealand's **Great Walks** (see p. 358), Te Anau could entertain the outdoor enthusiast for months on end. Walk along the shore away from town (15min.) and past the DOC office to reach the **Wildlife Center,** where you can commune with some of the earth's rarest birds; native owls, parakeets, and kea reside in natural caged habitats. The perilously endangered takahe is an especially beautiful and sobering sight. Continue around the lake about two hours (or grab a shuttle) to reach the **Mt. Luxmore Track.** The tramp along a section of the **Kepler Track** (return 8-10hr.) offers fabulous lake and mountain views. Pick up an infosheet guide to Te Anau walks.

Te Anau got its name from the **Te Ana-u Glowworm Caves** (some say it is Maori for "caves of rushing water"). Limestone walls worn away by 15,000 years of acidic waters have formed impressive caverns housing a spectacular glowworm grotto (see **Starry Night,** p. 149). As you meander by pontoon through the blackness of the watery grotto, it feels as if someone collapsed the galaxy and turned the stars blue-green. Located across the lake, cave tours are run a few times daily by **Fiordland Travel.** (☎249 7416, 0800 656 501. $44-51, children $15.) **Sindbad Cruises** takes aspiring sea dogs for a sail on the largest body of freshwater in the South Island, **Lake Te Anau,** on the hand-crafted and crimson-sailed gaff ketch *Little Ship Manuska*. (☎249 7106. $45.) **Rainbow Downs** runs **horse treks** through the rainforest from stables located between Te Anau and Manapouri. (☎249 8006. 1hr. $25, 2hr. $45. Pick-up $5 more.) Most charters run fishing trips, and plenty of locals lead guided **hunting** and **fishing excursions;** inquire at the visitors center.

Scenic flights out of Te Anau cover the entire Southern Lakes region. **Waterwings Airways,** on the waterfront, runs a variety of floatplane flights. (☎249 7405. 10min.; $43, children $26.) **Air Fiordland** (☎249 7505) has a fantastic Doubtful Sound excursion (40min.; $150, children $90), while **Southern Lakes Helicopters** (☎249 7167), also on the lakefront, has a range of trips, some of which include snow landings and hike-down options (from $90). Finally, Te Anau boasts an impressive number of well-known hikes in the surrounding **Fiordland National Park** (see p. 319).

MANAPOURI ☎03

The fog-shrouded peaks of the Hunter and Kepler mountain ranges preside with alpine majesty over the tiny, quiet town of Manapouri, nestled on the beech-clad banks of breathtaking Lake Manapouri. Lush rainforests and rugged white-capped mountains reflect on the cool waters of this stunning "lake of the sorrowing heart," widely regarded as the most beautiful in New Zealand. Although tourist ventures are beginning to take hold, Manapouri remains a pristine gateway to the remote Doubtful Sound (see p. 322) and the magnificent Kepler Track (see p. 374).

TRANSPORTATION. Fiordland Travel (☎249 6602, 0800 656 502) sells standby tickets on tour buses heading north at the end of the day (5:15-5:30pm; Te Anau $6, Queenstown $45). **Spitfire Shuttle** (Te Anau ☎249 7505) leaves for: Invercargill (2¼hr.; daily 8:45am, in winter M-F only; $34) via Tuatapere (1¼hr., $20) and Riverton (1¾hr., $30); and Te Anau (15min.; daily 3:15pm, in winter M-F only; $10). Though *Let's Go* doesn't recommend it, **hitchhikers** report that getting a ride to Te Anau is easy, though buses are better for getting back to Manapouri again.

PRACTICAL INFORMATION. The town lies just west of the junction of the Southern Scenic Highway and SH95, 20km south of Te Anau (see p. 324), where you'll find the nearest **police station, doctor, bank,** and **DOC office. Visitor information** is provided by **Fiordland Travel** and **Adventure Charters** (see below). The **post office** is inside **Hay's Manapouri Store** (see below).

ACCOMMODATIONS AND FOOD. ⚡**Possum Lodge** is among the top-rated hostels in the country despite being named after the noxious marsupial pest (see **Invasions** and **Possum Problems** p. 70). Big brown floor pillows and forest green bedsheets create a lived-in feel. (☎249 6660. Laundry $2. Book a week ahead in summer. Closed late June-early Sept. Bunks $17; twins and doubles $37.) **The Lakeview Motor Inn,** on the road to Te Anau, offers heaps of backpacker rooms with a superb view and a motel ambiance. (☎249 6652. Dorms $20; full rooms $60-70.) Next door, the refreshingly weird **Manapouri Lake View Motels and Motor Park** has a vintage pinball machine in the game room. (☎249 6624; fax 249 6699. Cabins for 2 $33; motel rooms $65-95; tent sites for 2 $18, powered sites for 2 $19.) The **Beehive Cafe and Bar,** adjoining the Lakeview Motor Inn, is the only grog stop in town and has internet access. (Open M-Sa 11am-3am, Su noon-2pm; in winter M-Sa 2pm-3am, Su noon-10pm.) At the main crossroads, **Hay's Manapouri Store** has two aisles of basic items; next door is the bright **Cathedral Cafe,** with a lake view and tasty mains from $11. (☎249 6619. Store and cafe open daily May-Sept. 7am-5:30pm; Oct.-Apr. 7am-7pm or later in peak season.)

SIGHTS AND ACTIVITIES. Captain Cook was skeptical that there would be wind to return his ship to sea, so he skipped over **Doubtful Sound** in 1770, leaving only the name as his legacy. Rounded hills carved by ancient glaciers mark the entrances to over 100km of waterways. Inaccessible by road, Doubtful Sound leaves its silence and serenity to the pods of dolphins and Fiordland crested penguins that call it home. **Adventure Charters**, next to the store, runs an 11hr. **cruise and kayak tour** of Doubtful Sound ($165, overnight $225), and cruises ($85 per hr.) and kayak rentals on Lake Manapouri ($40 per day) and Doubtful Sound (2-day $195). Transport ($10) is available from Te Anau for the carless, but book ahead. (☎249 6626. Open daily 8:30am-5:30pm; variable in winter.)

Fiordland Travel (☎249 6602, 0800 656 502), at the end of the road, offers extensive full-day trips around Doubtful Sound, including a tour of the **Manapouri Power Station;** turbines at the end of a 2km tunnel beneath the earth's surface generate power from plummeting lake waters. After a lake cruise and an overland jaunt with knowledgeable ecological commentary, the tour heads through 40km of Doubtful Sound to the **Tasman Sea** before returning to Manapouri. (Oct.-Apr. 3 tours per morning; May-Sept. 9:45am. $185, children $45.) There are also summer cruises to the power station only. Bring your own lunch or pay the expensive penalty. (12:30pm. A whopping $52, children $15.)

A variety of 1-3 day tracks in the area offer inexpensive—and relatively uncrowded—immersion in the grandeur of Fiordland. The **Circle Track** (return 3hr.) promises excellent lookouts of the Hope Arm of the lake, Mt. Titiroa, Manapouri, and Te Anau. Two huts ($5) are also available for longer hikes; pick up a pamphlet from Adventure Charters or the DOC office in Te Anau—**Adventure Charters** rents rowboats ($5 per person), which are necessary to cross the Waiau River from Pearl Harbor in Manapouri as all tracks begin on the far side.

SOUTHERN LAKES

OTAGO AND SOUTHLAND

With rugged coastlines bordering rural towns and farms, Otago and Southland retain their early pioneer spirit. Plentiful marine life draw thousands to the Otago Peninsula, which teems with fur seals, sea lions, dolphins, albatross, and rare penguins. The isolated beaches and soaring rock formations of the Catlins coast are relaxing, while Stewart Island's even more remote beauty beckons. A Scottish temperament gives a rollicking flavor to the university pub town of Dunedin (Scottish for Edinburgh), where Guinness and rowdy camaraderie invigorate urban life.

◪ OTAGO AND SOUTHLAND HIGHLIGHTS

GET LOST in the quiet, rugged beauty of the **Catlins,** "New Zealand's best-kept secret" (see p. 340).

GET VOYEURISTIC on the **Otago Peninsula,** an ecological wonderland, home to seals, penguins, and other squawking birdlife (see p. 330).

GET NOWHERE on **Stewart Island,** remote even by Southland standards (see p. 351).

GET ROWDY in youthful **Dunedin**—a quintessential college town elevated by a passion for beer and rugby (see below).

OTAGO

DUNEDIN   ☎03

"The people here are Scots. They stopped here on their way home to heaven,
thinking they had arrived."
— Mark Twain

Undoubtedly, the original Scottish settlers would be proud to see that Dunedin has been transformed without losing its spirit. While statuesque whitestone buildings and galleries preserve the European heritage of this harbor port, Dunedin's student population (peaking the town at 120,000) ensures that the Scottish pub culture continues to thrive. With its precipitous hills (Baldwin St. is the steepest street in the world) and magical harbor, Dunedin is deeply inscribed on Otago's historical and industrial heart.

▐ TRANSPORTATION

Flights: The **airport** is 30min. south on SH1. **Air New Zealand,** corner of Princes St. and the Octagon (☎479 6594; 0800 737 000), flies one-way to **Auckland** (2¾hr.; $452-600, YHA standby 50% off of regular fares, ISIC holders $268) and **Wellington** (2hr.; $315-416, YHA standby 50% off of regular fares, ISIC holders $184), often via **Christchurch** (45min.; $225-296, YHA standby 50% of regular fares, ISIC holders $102). From the airport, **taxis** to the city center will cost at least $10.

Trains: The **train station** (☎477 4449; fax 477 4953) is located at the bottom of Stuart St. Open M-F 8am-5pm, Sa-Su 9am-2:30pm. **TranzScenic** goes daily to **Christchurch** (5½hr., 11:45am, $55-79) via **Oamaru** (2½hr., $21-30) and **Timaru** (3½hr., $31-44) and to **Invercargill** (3¼hr., 2pm, $39-55). A scenic way to get to **Queenstown** is to make a bus connection after taking the **Taieri Gorge Train** (☎477 4449; about $99).

Otago and Southland

Buses: InterCity, 205 St. Andrew St. (☎474 9600), runs to: **Ashburton** (4½hr., 4-5 per day, $21-42); **Christchurch** (6hr., 4-5 per day, $28-55) via **Oamaru** (1½hr., $13-24) and **Timaru** (3hr., $15-30); **Invercargill** (3-4hr., 1-2 per day, $20-40); and **Queenstown** (4¼hr., 1 per day, $27-53). **Shuttles** traverse the same routes, often for less and more frequently in summer; **Atomic Shuttles** (☎322 8883) is cheap and reliable.

Public Transportation: 4 **bus** companies depart from the Octagon ($1.10-$3.70).

Taxis: Stands on High St. off Princes St., and on St. Andrew and Hanover St. off George St. Call **Dunedin Taxis** (☎477 7777), **City Taxis** (☎477 1771), **Otago Taxi** (☎477 3333), or **Call-a-Cab** (☎477 7800).

Car Rental: In addition to the major national chains, rental companies include: **Inner City Rentals,** 99 Crawford St. (☎477 3017), which rents cars from $28 per day and $0.28 per km; and **Jackie's,** 23 Cumberland St. (☎477 7848).

Bike Rental: Cycle Surgery, 67 Stuart St. (☎477 7473), at the corner of Cumberland St., $25 per day. Open M-F 8:30am-6pm, Sa 9:30am-3:30pm, Su 10:30am-3:30pm.

Hitchhiking: Although *Let's Go* does not recommend it, hitchhikers often take a bus from the Octagon out of the city. Those heading north usually take the Pine Hill bus ($1.50), while those heading south take the Mosgiel bus to Kenmont ($3.70).

✦ ORIENTATION

Dunedin is easily navigable and organized around the **Octagon,** where a statue of Robert Burns presides over the city center in front of the gothic revival spires of St. Paul's. **George St.** extends roughly north toward the University of Otago and is Dunedin's main commercial shopping thoroughfare; it becomes **Princes St.** south of the Octagon as it nears most of the backpackers. Pubs are mostly scattered on and southeast of George St. between the Octagon and the University. **Stuart St.** heads down the hill directly toward the train station and Otago Harbour. The Otago Peninsula extends from the southeastern part of the city.

▨ PRACTICAL INFORMATION

Visitors Center: Visitor Information Centre, 48 The Octagon (☎474 3300; fax 474 3311), to the right of the soaring clock tower of the limestone **Municipal Chambers** building. Open daily 8:30am-6pm; in winter M-F 8:30am-5pm, Sa-Su 9am-5pm.

DOC: 77 Lower Stuart St. (☎477 0677), on the first floor of the Conservation House. Open M-F 8:30am-5pm.

Budget Travel: STA Travel, 32 Albany St. (☎474 0146; fax 477 2741), a block down from George St. Open M-F 9am-5pm, Sa 10am-1pm.

Currency Exchange: Banks dot George and Princes St., most with **ATMs. Thomas Cook** (☎477 1532), on the corner of George St. and Andrews St. Open M-F 8:30am-5pm, Sa 10am-2pm. The visitors center exchanges money outside these hours.

Bi-Gay-Lesbian Organizations: Gay/Lesbian Support Group (☎477 2077) meets Tu 5:30-7:30pm for women, W 5:30-7:30pm and F 7:30-10pm for men.

Police: 25 Great King St. (☎477 6011).

Medical Services: The **pharmacy** is at 95 Hanover St. (☎477 6344). Open M-F 6am-10pm, Sa-Su 10am-10pm. **Urgent Doctors** (☎479 2900) is next door and open daily 24hr. **Dunedin Public Hospital** is at 201 Great King St. (☎474 0999).

Internet Access: Shooters, 109 Princes St. (☎477 8650), has access at the bar ($5 per hr.). Open M-Th noon-late, F noon-5am, Sa 2pm-5am, Su 3-8pm. The **Arc Cafe** (see **Cafes** below) has 25min. of free access without purchase.

Post Office: (☎477 3517). At the corner of Princes and Rattray St. Poste Restante. Open M-F 8:30am-5:30pm.

🏠🏨 ACCOMMODATIONS AND CAMPING

Edwardian hotels, former churches, and rambling homes converted into backpackers provide Dunedin with an impressive array of budget accommodations. Most are found within a 10min. walk of the Octagon. Book in advance when there's a big rugby game. Check-out is 10am unless otherwise noted.

Elm Lodge, 74 Elm Row (☎474 1872). Head up Rattray St. to Brown St., then uphill to Elm Row; the backpackers is a few yards to your right. More homey than most of the other backpackers in town. Internet. Free pick-up and drop-off. Laundry $4. Key deposit $5. Reception 8am-10pm. Dorms $15-16; doubles $36.

Aunty's Backpackers Lodge, 3 Union St. (☎474 0708; 0800 428 689; fax 474 0715; auntys@xtra.co.nz). Take George St. 5 blocks from the Octagon and turn left on Union St. Conveniently located near the University, the public garden, and the pubs. Owner (and ex-Otago Highlander) takes guests out to local rugby matches. Internet. Free pick-up and drop-off. Mountain bike hire. Laundry $2. Reception 8am-8pm. Check-out 10:30am. Dorms $16-18; singles $25; twins and doubles $20 per person.

Chalet Backpackers, 296 High St. (☎479 2075). Take Princes St. to High St. and then up the hill. Free pick-up. You can't even tell it was once a hospital. Free pick-up. They will wash and dry your laundry just like mom ($5). Reception 8am-10pm; in winter 9am-9pm. Dorms $16; singles $30; doubles $40. Cash only.

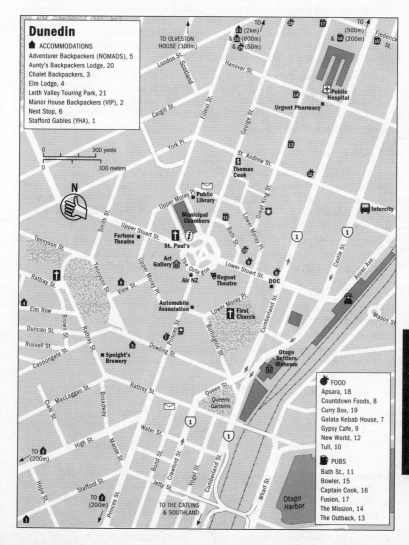

Dunedin

➤ ACCOMMODATIONS

Adventurer Backpackers (NOMADS), 5
Aunty's Backpackers Lodge, 20
Chalet Backpackers, 3
Elm Lodge, 4
Leith Valley Touring Park, 21
Manor House Backpackers (VIP), 2
Next Stop, 6
Stafford Gables (YHA), 1

🍎 FOOD
Apsara, 18
Countdown Foods, 8
Curry Box, 19
Galata Kebab House, 7
Gypsy Cafe, 9
New World, 12
Tull, 10

🍺 PUBS
Bath St., 11
Bowler, 15
Captain Cook, 16
Fusion, 17
The Mission, 14
The Outback, 13

OTAGO

Stafford Gables (YHA), 71 Stafford St. (☎474 1919). Take Princes St. up several blocks to Stafford St.; it will be on your left. You could get lost exploring the nooks and crannies of this supposedly haunted old jaunt. Internet. Reception 8am-noon, 1:30-3:30pm, and 5-10pm; in winter 8-10am and 7:30-10pm. Dorms $16; singles about $28; doubles $40. Book in advance in summer.

Manor House Backpackers (VIP), 28 Manor Pl. (☎477 0484; 0800 477 0484; fax 477 8145). Six blocks down Princes St. and to the right. A juxtaposition from the cozy atmosphere and the beer cans lining the foyer. Free pick-up. Internet. Reception 8:30am-10pm; in winter til 8pm. Dorms $15-16; twins and doubles $40. VIP $1 off.

Next Stop, 2 View St. (☎477 0447; fax 477 0430; nextstop2@hotmail.com). Go right on Moray Pl. from Princes St. and then left on View St. Relatively bare but spotless rooms ring the two-story common space. Indoor smoking area. Internet. Laundry $3-4. Reception 8:30am-10pm. Dorms $15-17; singles $30; twins and doubles $19 per person.

Adventurer Backpackers (NOMADS), 37 Dowling St. (☎/fax 477 7367; 0800 422 257), 2 blocks from the Octagon down Princes St., then up Dowling St. Pool table, fireside couches, and breadmaking machine add to ski-lodge atmosphere. Reception 8am-9pm. Key deposit $10. Internet. Dorms $16; singles $32; twins $18 per person; doubles $38; triple $51. NOMADS members get $2 off first night.

Leith Valley Touring Park, 103 Malvern St. (☎467 9936), 2km from the city. Take George St., then turn left on Duke St. and continue up to Malvern St. A small, secluded park on Leith Stream with access to trails. Reception 9am-9pm. Caravan and tent sites $10 per person, minimum charge of $12; caravan doubles $30, $22 for 1; tourist flats $60 for 2, extra person $12.

■ FOOD

Catering to budget-conscious students, Dunedin overflows with cheap quality eats. For a quick grab outdoors, look for the **Khmer Satay-Away** stand that appears around lunch time on the Octagon. Markets include **Countdown Foods** at Cumberland and Stuart St. (open daily 8am-10pm) and **New World** on Cumberland between St. Andrew St. and Hanover St. (open daily 7am-11pm).

Tull, 29 Bath St. (☎477 5331), off Lower Stuart St. This hippie ode to Jethro Tull rates its 25 sinful triumphs according to decadence (desserts $7.50-15). Bottomless homemade soups ($5) are a fabulous deal, and the distinctive French bread sandwiches, called "flutes" in homage to Tull's Ian Anderson, are enormous and delicious ($6.50-8.50). Open M-Th 11:30am-11pm, F from 11:30am, Sa from 5:30pm.

Apsara, 380 George St. (☎477 4499), opposite Albert Arms. The big Cambodian noodle soups ($5-8) warm you from the inside out, and the curry veggies with coconut milk served over rice ($5) revitalize the taste buds. Open daily 11am-9pm. Cash only.

Curry Box, 442 George St., (☎477 4713) opposite Knox Church. Very good Indian fare that's easy on your wallet. Mains $10-13. Open for lunch M-F 11am-2:30pm, and dinner M-Sa 5pm-9:30pm.

Tangente, 111 Moray Place, (☎477 0232), left off Upper Stuart St. a block past the Octagon. Sip latte from a giant multi-colored goblet as you "celebrate our humanity" at this bright, family-friendly designer cuisiner. Mains $11.50-24.50. Open Su-Th 8am-3:30pm, F-Sa 8am-10pm.

Gypsy Cafe, 126 Lower Stuart St. (☎025 280 1559). This small and eccentrically-decorated cafe offers flavorful dinners for $6.50-7.50. Open daily 7am-9pm.

Galata Kebab House, 126 Princes St. (☎474 1444), 2 blocks from the Octagon. Enjoy music and Turkish decor as you choose from kebabs in pita ($6.50-9) or over rice ($12.50-14.50). The pita lunch special ($5-6.50) and special vegetarian kebabs ($5.50-8) are exceptional. Open daily 11am-10:30pm, often later F-Sa.

CAFES

Cafes are hot in Dunedin (heck, McDonald's even has a McCafe), and you'll find more than cappuccino-sipping artists crowding these hangouts.

■ **Percolater,** 142 Lower Stuart St. (☎477 5462), just below the Octagon. With less self-consciously displayed character than many of the others in town, this cafe makes its mark with excellent coffee and food. Internet. Open Su-Th 9am-11pm, F-Sa 9am-late.

■ **Arc,** 135 High St. (☎474 1135), a block up from Princes St. You can't beat the 25min. of free internet, even without purchase. Choose coffee or beer to go with your veggie meal. Frequent live music in the back room (often cover charge). Open M-Sa noon-late.

Fuel, 21 Frederick St. (☎477 2575), a block from George St. One of Dunedin's stylish all-purpose cafes, Fuel packs it in during the day with posh eats, and at night with its lounge, bar, and pool table. W $2 pints. Open M-F 7:30am-late, F-Sa 10am-late.

Mazagran, 36 Moray Place (☎477 9959), above Princes St. Try one of their special coffee blends which taste familiar—Mazagran roasts and grinds for a number of the other cafes in Dunedin. Open M-F 8am-6pm, Sa 9am-2pm.

ENTERTAINMENT

The Fortune Theatre Company, on upper Stuart St. and Moray Pl., puts on a number of professional shows throughout the year. (☎477 8323. Box office open M-F 10:30am-5pm, longer on performance nights. Tickets around $25, students $15.) The palatial **Regent** in the Octagon, hosts an International Film Festival in July and August and several traveling shows throughout the year. (☎477 8597. Box office open M-F 8:30am-5pm, Sa 10:30am-1pm; $10-11, students $8.) The **Metro Cinema,** one block up Harrop St. from the visitors center, behind the Municipal Chambers, shows foreign and independent films. (☎474 3350. $10, students $8.50, seniors $7; matinees before 5pm $7.) Check the *Otago Daily Times* for screenings, or pick up a copy of *Fink* at most cafes for entertainment listings.

NIGHTLIFE

As a university town, Dunedin has its fair share of standard student hangouts; in recent years the variety of dance venues, alternative clubs, and Irish pubs has multiplied considerably. Keep your eyes peeled for other nightlife venues as well.

■ **Captain Cook** (☎474 1935), at the corner of Albany and Great King St. Even North Islanders have stories about this quintessential varsity pub with pool and a throbbing dance floor upstairs. Sports fans watch the big screens in the outdoor garden. W $1 drinks 8pm-midnight. Open M-Tu 11am-10pm, W-Sa 11am-3am, Su 11am-6:30pm.

Fusion (☎477 2575), located through the Fuel Cafe on Frederick St. Often overflowing with students in the leopard-print lounge or amid the loud pumping music of the club. There is a smaller room through the freezer door upstairs; if you are nice to the bartenders, you may be able to visit. Open W-Sa 9pm-very late (often 3 or 4am).

The Mission (☎477 1637), corner of Great King St. and Hanover St. A throbbing dance floor where pews used to stand and gyrating bodies flood the dais. The party mainly gets going on weekends, around 1am. Open M-Sa 9pm-very late.

The Outback, 101 Great King St. (☎477 4414). Clean-cut college cruisers congregate for classic cuts on the dance floor. Extensive selection, including an array of bar food.

Bath St., 1 Bath St. (☎477 6750). Alternative types flock to the burgundy leather couches and laser-lit dance floor, as do some of the hottest DJs (W-Sa). Cover $3-5. Open W-Sa from 10pm. The water gets hot around 1am.

Bowler (☎477 5272), on Malcom St. just off Frederick St. A standard student hangout, it draws huge crowds, as do Wet W (drinks $2 until midnight) and cheap handles ($2-3). Open M-Sa 11am-late, Su noon-10pm.

◉ SIGHTS

OTAGO MUSEUM. This extensive museum takes an in-depth look at the material culture and natural history of Otago, including a full-size Maori war canoe and a room full of Chinese clothing. The museum's **Discovery World** has hands-on science exhibits that will enthrall children, as well as free internet access to enthrall visitors of all ages. *(Down the hill on Great King between Albany and Union St. ☎477 2372, www.otagomuseum.govt.nz. Open M-F 10am-5pm, Sa-Su noon-5pm. Recommended donation for museum $5. Discovery World admission $6, students $4, children $3.)*

CHURCHES. The Gothic Revival churches established by early Scottish residents are worth a look, especially the **First Church of Otago,** with its rose windows and wood-ceiling sanctuary. (Down Moray Pl. from Princes St.) **St. Paul's** in the Octagon has the only **stone-vaulted ceiling** in New Zealand, an organ with 3500 pipes, and the most impressive flying buttresses in the city. For those who can't get enough stone churches, **St. Joseph's Cathedral** (at the corner of Rattray and Smith St.) and **Knox Church** (at the corner of George and Pitt St.) are also worthwhile.

OLVESTON. Astonishingly, this perfectly preserved historic home (built in 1904) still feels lived in. All the clocks in this Edwardian mansion still run, and even the 1926 Frigidaire still works. The benefactor's will stipulated that anyone could tickle the ivories of the 1906 Steinway grand piano, so feel free to play. *(42 Royal Terrace. Take George St. to Pitt St., then follow Royal Terrace until you see it on the right. ☎477 3320. Tours at 9:30am, 10:45, noon, 1:30, 2:45, and 4pm. $11, under 15 $3.)*

OTHER ARCHITECTURE. The Scottish Edwardian architecture of Dunedin's **railway station** is spectacular, and is rivaled only by the black and white facade of the **University of Otago's main hall,** down St. David St., which is spectacular at night.

OTAGO SETTLERS MUSEUM. This eclectic and Art Deco former bus station entices visitors with the promise of a ride on an old penny farthing (turn-of-the-century bicycle) and a look at the early portraits in the gallery. The museum keeps records and photos of immigrants available for public viewing. *(31 Queens Garden, down Dowling St. ☎477 5052. Museum open M-F 10am-5pm, Sa-Su 1-5pm. $4, students and YHA/VIP members $3, children free. Immigrant records open M-F 10am-1pm. $10.)*

BEHIND THE TARTAN. Daily tours depart from the Highland Room in Roganos Restaurant, next to the visitors center. Knowledgeable guides take you on a walking tour of the city, all the while relating historical anecdotes and pointing out Victorian and Edwardian architecture. *(☎474 3300. Leaves daily at 10am. $20, children 11-17 $10, children 7-10 $5, under 7 free.)*

ON A FIRST NAME BASIS

Beer, a staple of the New Zealand diet, is a matter of pride for most Kiwis. The most popular drinks are Steinlager (a Steiny), DB Draught, and Export Gold. Tui and Canterbury Draft (DB) on the North Island and Speight's and Monteith's on the South are also good choices. But don't be surprised if the classics go by unfamiliar names:

Double. A standard shot to Brits and Americans; if asked, that's what you want.

7oz. A denomination to avoid, unless the bartender is your best friend. 7oz. in a glorified shot glass.

12oz. Commonly called a "thirteen," nearly 13oz. of frosty brew in a tapering glass. A bar standard.

Handle. Also called a pint, though it's not quite 16oz. For the thirsty.

Jug. The American "pitcher," about 2½ pints.

Schooner. A rare promotional monster in a 1½L glass. Jump at the opportunity.

DUNEDIN PUBLIC ART GALLERY. Home to a Renaissance collection with several good pre-Raphaelite works, this gallery showcases both colonial and modern New Zealand exhibitions. The spare foyer in the lobby is impressive in itself, with the iron spiral staircase of the original building hanging two stories down. *(In the Octagon. ☎ 474 4350. Open daily 10am-5pm. Regular exhibits free.)*

DUNEDIN HERITAGE TOUR. See the city in style, via a bright red double-decker bus. 1½hr. tours depart from the visitors center at 10am and 3:30pm daily. The same company also provides transportation to Larnach Castle, leaving the visitors center daily at noon. *(Run by Citibus Newton, ☎ 477 5577; www.transportplace.co.nz.)*

🔷 ACTIVITIES

SPEIGHT'S BREWERY. Judge the "Pride of the South" for yourself with free samples after the tour. A 1½hr. tour takes you through the history of beer-making. The building is built over a well, from which water for the beer is drawn. The water is the best in town, and thirsty post-rugby match locals line up at the outside tap to sip to their hearts' delight (of water, that is). *(Turn right onto Rattray St. from Princes St., you can't miss the protruding barrel. ☎ 477 7697. 4 tours per day F-Sa, with an additional 7pm tour M-Th. Bookings essential. $12, student $10.)*

TUNNEL BEACH. Among the best of local walks, the Tunnel Beach track is only accessible at low tide. When it is above water, the hike leads through a century-old tunnel onto a cliff-backed beach with sea caves carved into the walls. *(To reach the beach take the Corstophine bus from the Octagon to Stenhope Crescent, then walk down Blackhead Rd. Walk return 1hr. Inaccessible Sept.-Oct.)*

TAIERI GORGE RAILWAY. If you're tired of being on your feet, ride on the train through the hinterlands of Dunedin's pioneer history. The railway precariously flies through tunnels and over viaducts to Pukerangi over spectacular gorges and through native forests. *(☎ 477 4449. Departs from the railway station Oct.-March 2:30pm, April-Sept. 12:30pm. $53, students $42.40.)*

MT. CARGILL. A 4km track through a former tree-planting scheme brings a panoramic view of the harbor. Another 1hr. tramp will take you to the volcanic spires of the **Organ Pipes**. *(Normanby bus to Norwood St.; walk to Bethunes Gully. Walk 3½hr. return.)*

BOTANIC GARDENS. Established in 1863, Dunedin's gardens are arguably the best in the country. The **Rhododendron Festival** is world-renowned in botanic circles. The large aviary with native birds, including the kea, draws similar interest from ornithologists. Continuing from the Botanic Gardens, with a car, **Signal Hill** is a great place to admire the stars and the twinkling lights of the city below. *(Gardens: Take any city bus from the Octagon down George St. or walk from the University on Leith St. Signal Hill: Accessible off Opoho Rd. on the northern side of the botanic garden.)*

BIKING. A great **bike path** follows Thomas Burns St., which runs into Wharf St., toward the Otago Peninsula—look for blue and white signs. *(To access the path, cross the foot bridge to the right of the train station.)*

HORSEBACK RIDING. You can explore the beaches to the south of Dunedin with a 2hr. ride from **Bums 'n' Saddles**, 8min. from the Octagon. *(☎ 488 0097. $25. Transport arranged.)* **Trojan Riding** offers longer gallops on the coast of Karitane north of Dunedin. *(434 Coast Rd. ☎ 465 7013, 025 298 2588. Half-day $49, full-day $99, after-work special $39.)* Trojan offers free pick-up for groups of four or more. Or, take the bus from the Bowling Green Hotel at the corner of Frederick and Cumberland St.

WHITEWATER RAFTING. Those who would rather move swiftly through water than plod over land will enjoy **Silver Peaks Tours**, a 4-6hr. whitewater adventure on Class 3 rapids. *(☎ 489 6167. From $60, students from $50, children from $40.)*

OTAGO PENINSULA ☎ 03

Serene Otago Peninsula is as popular for its penguin and albatross colonies as Dunedin is for its museums and pubs. Stretching over 20km from the city, the peninsula has incomparable opportunities to experience an amazing ecology. Yellow-eyed penguins, fur seals, sea lions, and royal albatrosses claim the peninsula's many weather-worn inlets, beaches, and promontories. Dramatic **Taiaroa Head** drops off onto seal-covered crags and great swaths of billowing kelp. The beaches teem with bird activity even before the penguins waddle ashore in the evening.

◨ TRANSPORTATION. The best way to experience the peninsula is by car. **Portobello Road,** the sinuous coastal route along the bay, is full of treacherous curves—even the locals who know the road often don't drive it. If you decide to take a tour, there are many well-operated ones from which to choose. **Back to Nature Tours** has smaller, more intimate, tours than its competition, with a very knowledgeable tour guide, Les. Free binoculars allow you to see nature in action. The tour ends at Sandfly Beach where the yellow-eyes waddle up the cliff. (☎ 0800 477 048; www.backtonaturetours.co.nz. 5hr.,; in summer daily 2pm, in winter daily 1pm; $43.) **Elm Wildlife Tours** also provides small (max. 10 people), in-depth walking wild-life excursions, going to a private beach that no other tour can visit. This company is especially popular with the backpacker bus crew. (☎ 0800 356 363. 6hr.; daily 3pm, in winter 12:30pm; about $43. Free pick-up.) **Newton Tours** (☎ 477 5577) offers an array of packages to the sights ($20-35, plus entry fees to attractions), as do many other carriers, though some run only in summer.

▮◨ ACCOMMODATIONS AND FOOD. If you decide to stay over at the peninsula rather than daytrip, **homestays** are a possibility. Most cost about $50 per night per person; the visitors center in Dunedin will provide brochures, recommendations, and bookings. One farmstay that beats the cost curve is the **McFarmers Backpackers,** 774 Portobello Rd., a cozy former pottery studio that provides stunning views of the harbour, as well as free boats and canoes, and bikes for hire. (☎ 478 0389, 025 206 0650. Dorms $15; doubles $35; tent sites $10 per person. Closed in June.) **Penguin Place,** right next to the Yellow-eyed Penguin Reserve, has sparsely furnished rooms with terrific views of the bay. (☎ 478 0286. Book ahead. $15 per person.) **Portobello Village Tourist Park** in Portobello is a peaceful, verdant expanse midway between Dunedin and the albatross colony. It is a good starting point for exploring the peninsula by bike. (☎/fax 478 0359. Reception 8am-10:30pm. Half-day bicycle hire $15, full-day $25. Bunks $15-25; tent sites $9, powered sites $10; tourist flats $65.) Food options on the peninsula are limited, but one standout is the **1908 Cafe,** 7 Harrington Point Rd. in Portobello. The rotating dinner menu can be pricey (mains $22-28), but lunch options are cheaper ($7-18), and chef Ian will happily tailor menu items to your tastes, appetite, and budget. (☎ 478 0801. Open in summer daily noon-2:30pm and 5pm-late, bookings recommended. Winter hours are variable, but almost always open on weekends.)

◧ BIRD WATCHING. At the **Taiaroa Royal Albatross Colony** (☎ 478 0499; www.albatrosses.com), you'll learn that these massive birds, immortalized by poet Samuel Coleridge, are not merely seagulls with pituitary problems. Taiaroa is unique as the only mainland albatross colony on earth; these majestic wanderers fledge and rear their young here, then circumnavigate the globe without landing until they return. Entrance to the **Albatross Centre** which houses extensive displays and live TV coverage of the birds' activities is free, but the educational tour and observatory distance viewing is rather steep ($23, in winter $18; children $9/11). **Monarch Wildlife Cruises** runs a jolly skiff from Wellers Rock near the head, 45min. from Dunedin, and provides the best way to view the massive chimney roosts and rare cormorants that coexist there. (☎ 477 4276. 2 per day; $25, children $13.)

Rare yellow-eyed penguins (*hoiho*) have, with a little human assistance, recolonized Penguin Beach just beyond Taiaroa Head. Speed through a maniacal camouflaged trench system at the ▨**Yellow-eyed Penguin Conservation Reserve,** 40min. from Dunedin and 2min. from the Albatross Centre, to view these sleek divers from just a few meters away. Clearly refusing to place a premium on privacy, their monogamous devotion only goes so far; see **Bisexual Penguins** above. (☎478 0286. 1½hr. tours run every 30min.; Oct.-Apr. from 8am, May-Sept. 3pm until dark; $27, children $12. Book ahead in summer.) Those with slim wallets and big binoculars may appreciate penguin viewing (best in late afternoon) at **Nature's Wonders,** a few minutes down the road. (☎0800 246 446, fax 478 0714. Entry fee $10, children $5.) Give yourself a self-guided viewing, or pay extra for an all-terrain ARGO tour of the wildlife (ARGO prices currently under negotiation). Open daily 10am-dark, but earlier viewings of penguins heading out to sea are possible with advance booking.

◙ **SIGHTS.** To get up close and personal with Otago's rocky coastline, try sea kayaking with **Wild Earth Adventures Ltd.** and do one of their many guided trips. (☎473 6535; 0800 699 453; www.nzwildearth.com. Prices from $49.)

1.5km up a dirt road from town in Portabello sits the **New Zealand Marine Studies Center** run by the University of Otago. Doubling as a research center for budding marine scientists and as an educational aquarium accessible to the public, the small display areas give a hands-on exposure to the local marine animals and ecosystems. (☎479 5826; www.otago.ac.nz/MarineStudies. Open daily noon-4:30pm. $7, children $3, family pass $14.) For the historically inclined, **Larnach Castle** is a 43-room architectural marvel, though the story behind the castle may be even more interesting than the building itself. The virile Mr. Larnach (with six children by his first wife alone) eventually married his third wife when he was 60 (though she was 35). When she ran off with his second son, Larnach committed suicide in the Parliament building in Wellington. Take a self-guided tour through the inlaid mahogany, teak, and kauri foyer up the only hanging Georgian staircase in the Southern Hemisphere. The view of Dunedin and the entire peninsula from the battlements is incomparable. To reach the purportedly haunted castle, take the Otago Road Services city bus from Stand 5 outside **New World** on Cumberland St. to the Company Bay stop ($2.50) and walk up the hill, or catch the noon tour from the visitors center ($30, children $15). **Citibus Newton** also provides transportation from the Dunedin visitors center to the castle (☎477 5577). Halfway down the peninsula and 3km up the winding Castlewood Rd., the aptly named **High Cliff Road** is an alternate route with views of the south side of the peninsula. (☎476 1616. $12, children $4.50. Garden access $6, children $2.) A mode of transport more befitting a stately visit, **Castle Discovery Horse Treks,** based in Broad Bay, embarks upon a 3hr. trip to Larnach Castle twice daily. (☎478 0796; 0800 467 738. 9:30am and 1:15pm; $45, students $35, child $30; includes castle entrance fee.)

OAMARU ☎03

Penguins. While the rest of the country must count sheep to fall asleep, the folks in historic Oamaru (pop. 12,400) picture the nightly return of their penguins. Although known primarily for its blue penguin colony (the smallest penguins in the world), visitors to this town can easily spend a day browsing antiques and collectables in the whitestone historic district. With historical and ecological attractions and the nearby boulders at Moeraki, you'll find Oamaru a convenient and pleasant stop along the Otago coast.

◪ **TRANSPORTATION. TranzScenic** leaves daily from the station on Humber St. for **Christchurch** (3hr., 2:10pm, $39-55) and **Invercargill** (6hr., 11:30am, $57-81) via **Dunedin** (3hr., $21-30). **Buses** leave the bus stop at Eden and Thames St. (☎434 8716). **InterCity** and cheaper options head to **Christchurch** (4½hr., 4-5 per day, $20-40) and **Dunedin** (2¼hr., 3-4 per day, $15-22). The **Oamaru Mini-Coach** (☎439 4765) also services **Dunedin** (3hr., M-F 8am, $20). The **Atomic Shuttle** (☎322 8883) goes to **Christchurch** (4pm, $25). Although *Let's Go* does not recommend hitching, **hitchhikers** report heading up Severn St. to the edge of town to catch a lift south. The upper end of Thames St. is reportedly the best place for a ride north, but it's a hard walk with a backpack.

▲⚡ ORIENTATION AND PRACTICAL INFORMATION. Coming from Timaru to the north, SH1 follows Thames St. into the heart of downtown Oamaru. From the visitors center, go left onto Itchen St. and then follow Tyne St. around to the right to reach the **historic precinct.** Continue on Tyne St. and make a left on Waterfront Rd. to get to the **Blue Penguin Colony.** The **Visitor Information Centre,** 1 Thames St., is on the left side of Thames St. just after the train tracks. By car, continue straight after SH1 veers right onto Severn St.; walking from the train station, go up one block, turn left onto Thames St., and continue 10min. The visitors center has maps, information, and **DOC information.** (☎ 434 1656; fax 434 1657. Open M-F 9am-6pm, Sa-Su 10am-5pm; in winter M-F 9am-5pm, Sa-Su 10am-4pm.) The **BNZ,** 149 Thames St., with **ATM** is one block left from the bus station. (Open M and Th-F 9am-4:30pm, Tu-W 9:30am-4:30pm.) Other services include: the **police station** (☎ 434 5198), off Severn St.; the **hospital** (☎ 434 8770), on Devon St., follow Severn St. past the police station and turn right on Cross St.; **internet access** at the **visitors center** ($2 per 10 min.) and **Small Bytes Computer,** next to the bus stop (☎ 434 8490; $10 per hr.; open M-F 9am-5pm, Sa 10am-12:30pm); and the **post office,** at Severn and Thames St. (☎ 434 7884; open M-F 8:30am-5pm, Sa 9am-noon.)

▮▮ ACCOMMODATIONS AND CAMPING. Those who brave the uphill trek from the visitors center to **Swaggers Backpackers,** 25 Wansbeck St., will be rewarded with a cheery manager and the warmth of an 80-year-old home. (☎ 434 9999. Pick-up after 5pm. Reception 8-10:30am and 5:30-10pm; self check-in during the day. Checkout 10:30am. Reservations in summer. Dorms $15; singles $25; twins $34. Cash only.) The **Red Kettle Hostel (YHA),** at the corner of Cross St. and Reed St., has a red kettle perched on the white picket fence that surrounds this simple, spotless, seasonal hostel with a large common area. (☎/fax 434 5008. Reception 8-10am and 5:30-10pm. Closed July-Aug., but call for specific dates. Two coed dorms and one female-only dorm $15; twins and doubles $34. Nonmembers $2-3 more.) The **Oamaru Gardens Top 10 Holiday Park,** up Chelmer St., is a short walk from the center of town, with a bridge to the botanic gardens and a small grocery store next door. It's great for tent sites. (☎ 434 7666; 0800 280 202; fax 434 7662. Laundry $2. Reception 8am-10pm; in winter 8am-8pm. Cabins $22 for 1, $32 for 2; kitchen units $31/$44; self-contained units $39/$52; chalets $49/$62; tent sites about $9 per person.)

▯ FOOD. Many of Oamaru's most popular eateries also double as bars and the center of the nightlife. And, on the flip side, most nightlife attractions also serve bar food and heartier lunchtime fare. The vegetable quiche and salad ($6.50) at **Emma's Cafe,** 30 Thames St., combine about as many herbivorous treats on one crowded plate as you could handle. (☎ 434 1165. Open Tu-F 9am-6pm, Sa 9am-5pm, Su 10am-5pm.) "Eat, drink and be merry for tomorrow you diet," quotes the menu at the **Last Post,** 12 Thames St. The winter lamb shanks ($11) are served piping hot, while breakfast lovers will be thrilled to see all their favorites served for dinner on the mixed grill ($12). (☎ 434 8080. Live music on weekend nights. Open Su-Th 11am-10pm, F-Sa 11am-midnight.) **Woolworth's,** across from the BNZ on Thames St., fills all your grocery needs. (☎ 434 8127. Open M-F 7:30am-9:30pm, Sa-Su 7:30am-8pm.

▮ NIGHTLIFE. A block from the visitors center on Thames St., **Annie Flannagan's** is a traditional Irish bar serving up typical bar food (many meals under $10) and, more importantly, drink (pints $4). With its live music on Friday and Saturday nights—AF's is the place to be. (☎ 434 8828. Open M-Th 11:30am-10pm, F-Sa 11:30am-1:30am, Su noon-10pm.) See the other side of Oamaru at the **Criterion Hotel,** 3 Tyne St., an English-style pub in the historic precinct. You won't find Emerson's London Porter pulled from an oak barrel (pints $4.50), pickled eggs ($1), or the hearty Ploughman's Lunch ($7.50) anywhere else in town. (☎ 434 6247. Open M-Th 11:30am-10pm, F-Sa 11:30am-midnight or whenever the singing stops, Su 11:30-4pm.) As the penguin wearing shades on the sign says, "It's damn hot" at

The Penguin Entertainers Club, tucked away behind Harbour St. in the historic precinct. This semi-secret music-lovers hideout draws top blues, jazz, folk, and rock musicians who stop in for a night on their way to Dunedin; call ahead to find out what's playing. Friday night is club night. (☎437 1251. No food served. Call for semi-secret directions; semi-secret cover charge varies.)

🄾🄲 **SIGHTS AND ACTIVITIES.** Let's be frank: you came to see penguins. And see penguins you shall. You can reach the **Oamaru Blue Penguin Colony** either by heading south from the center of town to Waterfront Rd. or via **Coast Line Tours,** which provides transport and entrance for the penguin viewing attraction for those too tired to waddle there under their own power. (☎439 5265; mobile 021 118 8906; or the Oamaru visitors center ☎434 1656. $15.) Make sure to arrive well before dusk so you can catch the timid Lilliputians struggle up the rocks, gather to recuperate, and head to their burrows. Flash cameras are not permitted, but bring warm clothes and binoculars. (☎433 1195. Viewing $8, students $6, under 15 free.)

In order to see the larger rare **yellow-eyed penguins** head to Bushey Beach. You can drive down Bushey Beach Rd. or take a $15 tour to both penguin colonies through **Coastline Tours.** Only 400 breeding pairs remain on the mainland (they are also found at Katiki Point near Palmerston, near Dunedin, and Balclutha).

While Oamaru's attractions center around its penguins, there's more than enough to fill a day in town. The **Historic Precinct,** with its mix of stately restored whitestone buildings and dilapidated facades, surrounds Harbour and Tyne St. where the **Sunday market** opens from 10am-4pm. You can view the work of local artists at the **North Otago Art Society Gallery** (open F-Su 1:30-4pm), browse in the antique and second-hand book shops, or take the 1hr. **historic tour** from the visitors center for a look inside some of the unrestored structures ($7.50, students $4, under 15 free). Charming and well-kept, the **North Otago Museum** (open M-F 1-4:30pm, Sa 10am-1pm, Su 1-4:30pm; free) and the **Forrester Gallery** on the main street (open M-F 10:30am-4:30pm, Sa 10:30am-1pm, Su 1-4:30pm; free) make worthwhile rainy day activities. Great on sunny days, **Oamaru Gardens,** on Severn St., features a wide walkway, rhododendron and rose gardens and the Summerhouse, a romantic spot that has been the site of more than one marriage proposal.

MOERAKI BOULDERS   ☎03

The small hamlet of **Moeraki** and the nearby 60-million-year-old **Moeraki Boulders** lie about 40km south of Oamaru. One of the oldest European settlements in New Zealand, **Moeraki** itself is a sleepy fishing village just south of the boulders. Early European visitors to the famed site snatched up the smaller boulders for themselves; only 1-2m high giants remain. Scientifically known as **septarian concretions,** the 50-odd stones started out as bits of animal or plant matter on which successive layers of calcite grew, eventually forming four-ton boulders. Lime crystals at the core attract and condense earthly matter, so their perfect roundness is due to this process rather than the molding power of the sea. The boulders, the largest of which took four million years to develop, are best viewed at low tide.

To reach the boulders on your own, simply follow the turn-off signs about 1km north of Moeraki on SH1. The 30min. drive between Oamaru and Moeraki can be made either by SH1 or the less-traveled Coast Rd. If you choose to take Coast Rd. you'll wind over rolling hills through countryside overlooking the ocean. At the end of SH1 you can either take the free public access road, which will leave you about a 300m walk from the boulders, or you can park by the **Moeraki Boulders Restaurant** (☎439 4827) and pay a $2 access fee. The restaurant looks out in three directions: at the boulders, the ocean, and Moeraki. For a moderate price (sandwiches from under $4) you can get simple food and a great view. If coach transport is necessary, **Coast Line Tours** (☎439 5265; or Oamaru visitors center ☎434 1656) runs out of Oamaru, but can arrange a tour from Moeraki to see the boulders. Tours usually last from 1:30-4:30pm and cost $30 from Oamaru. **Oamaru minicoaches** and **InterCity buses** will take you near the boulders or Moeraki (specify which you prefer), but leave you with a 3km walk to town on SH1.

BISEXUAL PENGUINS Yellow-eyed penguins are bi. Pairs some-times remain monogamous, but infidelity is common and a Ross occasionally paddles away with a Joey as eagerly as he might with a Rachel. Of course, distinguishing the sexes in the world's rarest penguins is a bit difficult, as neither gender leaves anything hanging out as a clue. Researchers originally thought that the male stayed on top during coupling, but who's really to say? Perhaps the penguins have as tough a time telling as we do. Maybe it's just free love. Regardless, spring is always a very stimulating season on the Peninsula.

Along the Coast Rd. you'll pass ▨**Coastal Backpackers,** a couple of cozy bunk-houses on a 20-acre family farm. If you call, the owner will pick you up from either Oamaru or Moeraki. Choose from bikes, canoes, kayaks, and surfboards, or take the short walk to the beach to see Hector dolphins; then have a home-cooked dinner and dessert with the family for only $10. (☎439 5411; fax 439 5242; seaside@coastalbackpackers.co.nz. Dorms $15; doubles $30; tent sites $8. Cash only.) The **Moeraki Motor Camp,** within walking distance of the boulders, contains a range of sites that overlook the peaceful cove. It offers a playground with a small trampoline, a grocery with a wine and beer license, and petrol for your thirsty car. (☎439 4759. Check-out 11am. Quiet hours 11pm-7am. Tent sites $9.50 per person; standard cabins for 2 $25; tourist flats for 2 $60-65; motel units $68 for 2.)

THE CATLINS ☎03

A coastline of untouched beaches, promontories, and ancient forests amid sheep paddocks and turnip patches—the Catlins region lives up to its reputation as the best-kept secret in New Zealand. Cliffs dotted with native bush drop into swirling Antarctic waters, while rare penguins waddle across white sand beaches. With a bit of exploring, you may discover a private inlet shared only with sea lions. Its remoteness is tempered by cordial coastal villages; there are few places in New Zealand where civilization can be so close and yet seem so distant.

▐ TRANSPORTATION IN THE CATLINS

The **Southern Scenic Route (SH92)** runs 172km through the Catlins from Balclutha to Invercargill; anyone driving through the Catlins would do well to buy a detailed map. Twenty-three kilometers of the road between the Curio Bay cutoff and Papatowai are unsealed; allow 40min. to 1hr. to drive this portion of the road. A car or mountain bike (and strong lungs) is the best way to take in the coast at your own pace. Although several tours run through the area, the ever-changing tides make it rare for the bus to arrive at the right time to enter **Cathedral Caves** (see p. 343). **Kiwi Experience's Bottom Bus** departs from Dunedin on a 10hr. backpacker-oriented tour. The bus drops off in Riverton at the end of the day, or in any of the towns along the way. (☎442 9708. Runs M, W, F, and Sa at 7:30-8am; fewer runs in winter. $89, free pick-up.) **Catlins Coaster** runs similar trips with experienced guiding staff and wildlife viewing licences from Dunedin to Invercargill. (☎0800 304 333. Daily in summer, in winter on demand. Min. 5 people. Departs Dunedin 8 or 11:15am $90; VIP, ISIC, and YHA $10 discount on regular rates. $199 with overnight farmstay, $10 discount applies.) Tours are also available from Queenstown or Te Anau ($125) with an option to include a return flight to Stewart Island ($245). **Catlins Mini Tours** allows you to choose your own destinations. (☎/fax 415 8686. Pick-up from Dunedin or Invercargill at 10am. Min. 2 people $60 each, $50 each for 4 or more.) Another option is **Catlins Natural Wonders,** which runs daytrips from Dunedin, Balclutha, Owaka, and Invercargill. (☎418 1798; mobile 025 985 941. $65-85.) More comprehensive overnight tours are available through **Catlins Wildlife Trackers,** which runs from Balclutha. (☎415 8613; 0800 228 546. M, W, and Sa 10am. $270.) Though *Let's Go* doesn't recommend it, **hitchhiking** through the Catlins is said to be feasible in summer, but more difficult in winter when there's little traffic.

🔼 PRACTICAL INFORMATION

There are **no banks** between Balclutha and Invercargill. There are plenty of secluded **camping sites** and superb, albeit limited and expensive, accommodations in the Catlins (booking ahead is vital during the summer).

BALCLUTHA ☎ 03

Balclutha is the "big city" of the Catlins, being the only convenient place between Dunedin and Invercargill to get groceries, withdraw money, or enjoy urban conveniences. Located at the junction of SH1 and SH92, 30km from Owaka and 56km from Papatowai, Balclutha has the most accessible resources for Catlins-bound travelers, and many of its services cater to the whole region. The **Clutha Information Centre** is at 63 Clyde St. (☎418 0388; fax 418 1877. Open M-F 8:30am-5pm, Sa-Su 9:30am-3pm.) Stock up on groceries at the **New World** down Lanark St. at the corner of Clyde St., a block before the bridge. (☎418 2850. Open M-F 8:30am-7pm, Sa-Su 9am-6pm.) Other Balclutha services include: **banks** with **ATMs** along Clyde St.; a **BP station** on Clyde St. (☎418 0034; open M-F 7am-10pm, Sa-Su 7:30am-10pm); the **police**, 47 Renfrew St., two blocks down from Clyde St. (24hr. ☎418 0203; open M-F 8am-5pm); and **Clutha Health First,** 3-7 Charlotte St., also accessible from Clyde St., which serves as the region's hospital (24hr. ☎418 0500; open M-F 8am-5pm).

KAKA POINT, NUGGET POINT, AND ROARING BAY ☎ 03

The Catlins' coastline is its claim to fame, with fine sand beaches and jutting headlands where sea lions bask on the rocks amid squawking colonies of birds. Start exploring at **Kaka Point,** 12km north of Owaka on a well-marked road off the Southern Scenic Route. The sandy swath at Kaka arcs toward **◪Nugget Point,** 8km south down a winding gravel road. The little lighthouse (the most southern in the world) is a 10min. jaunt over the blue-green waters toward the fragmented islets that give the point its name. Fur seals, elephant seals, and hooker sea lions frolic on the waterlogged crags—the only place in New Zealand that these creatures coexist. On the road to Nugget Point, **◪Roaring Bay** is home to yellow-eyed penguins that hop up the cliffs in the two hours before sunset. Their amiable socializing can be viewed from a hide above the beach. For more structured trips, **Nugget Tour Boat Charters** (run by the owners of Nugget View Motels) give one- to two-hour wildlife excursions to view local marine life. (☎412 8602. 2hr. trips from $50; other options include 5hr. fishing trips on the high seas among the albatrosses for $100.)

 Kaka Point Stores has groceries, takeaways, a bar, and the **post office. The Point Cafe,** in the same complex, affords oceans views, pleasant ambiance, and a sole and salad dinner for $14. (☎412 8800. Open daily 8am-8:30pm.) At **Nugget View Motels,** 11 Rata St., relax in luxury in one of the four-star modern rooms with a king-size bed and a spa, or in a budget suite with full facilities overlooking the ocean. (☎412 8602; fax 412 8623. Reception 24hr. Doubles $60-$150.) A path through lush native bush leads to tiny **Fernlea VIP Backpackers,** off Moana St. directly beyond the store. Overlooking the bay, the lounge and doubles share good views. (☎412 8834. Linen $2. Reception 8am-10pm. Bunks $15; alcove doubles $30. Cash only.) **Kaka Point Camping Ground** has two simple cabins, although you'll miss the ocean views. (☎412 8818. Self-registration. Singles $15; doubles $25, extra person $10; caravan sites for 1 $10, for 2 $15; tent sites $10, $15. Cash only.)

FROM KAKA POINT TO OWAKA

Beyond Kaka Point, follow the sign for **Tunnel Hill** on the main road to experience a five-minute walk through an abandoned railway tunnel. Turn off your flashlight for a spooky experience; the track is quite flat and smooth. Farther along the Southern Scenic Highway, fur seals and sea lions congregate on the beach at **Cannibal Bay** or at the dunes at **Surat Bay** (see below). Surat Bay is a shorter drive from the Southern Scenic Route, but it's not accessible by car at high tide (regardless of tides, it's a 30min. walk from Cannibal Bay). Though human bones were once discovered at Cannibal Bay, it's more likely that the unlucky chap was killed in a battle than eaten by cannibals.

OTAGO

OWAKA ☎ 03

Just 25km south of Balclutha (see p. 341), Owaka (o-WACK-a; pop. 400) is one of the few places that actually pass for towns in the Catlins. Stock up here on petrol, supplies, and small-town hospitality.

⚐ PRACTICAL INFORMATION. The **visitors center** at the **Catlins Diner** offers area maps, accommodation listings, farmstay information and bookings, and a $2 **DOC** pamphlet on regional flora and fauna. (☎/fax 415 8371. Open M-F 6:30am-8:30pm, Sa-Su 10am-5pm.) **Helen's Dairy** has light meals and operates a **post office** (☎415 8304; open M-Sa 7am-8pm), while **Niles Four Square** has provisions (☎415 8201; open M-Th 8:30am-5:30pm, F 8:30am-7pm, Sa 9am-5pm, Su 10am-3:30pm; in winter closes Sa and Su at 1pm). Other services include: a **Shell petrol station** that is also an **AA service station** and the last cheap gas until Invercargill (☎415 8179; open M-Th 7:30am-6pm, F 7:30am-7:30pm, Sa 9am-1pm); local **police** at the west end of town (☎415 8056; after-hours calls are directed to the Balclutha police); a **pharmacy,** 26 Waikowa Rd. opposite the police station (☎415 8109; open M-Th 8:45am-5:30pm, F 8:45am-7pm; also Th 7-9pm); the **Catlins Medical Centre,** 29 Main Rd. (24hr. ☎415 8006); and Internet access at the **Internet Cafe,** opposite the grocery (☎ 415 8030; open M-F 9am-5pm, Sa 9am-noon; $2 per 15min.).

⚏⚏ ACCOMMODATIONS AND FOOD. The brightly colored period rooms of the ◪**Catlins Retreat Guesthouse,** 27 Main Rd., have dried flowers in the hearth. Even without roaring fires, this place is a hot pick. Backyard garden vegetables are free to guests energetic enough to pick them. **Blowhole Backpackers,** across the street at 24 Main Rd., is owned by the same couple and offers similarly pleasant surroundings. (☎/fax 415 8830; catlinsbb@xtra.co.nz. Dorms $15; double $40. B&B accommodations at the retreat: single $45; double $75.) **Catlins Backpackers,** at the diner, has laundry facilities, TV, and a kitchen with a cappuccino machine. For those seeking more comfort, the spacious motel accommodations upstairs are the best deal in town. (☎415 8392. Bikes. Reception M-F 6:30am-8:30pm, Sa 8am-8:30pm, Su 9am-8:30pm. Simple dorms $14, in winter $12; tent sites $6. Motel doubles $55, extra adult $11, extra child $8.) Follow the signs from Owaka to reach the sunny **Pounawea Motor Camp,** by an estuary on the Catlins River. The Pounawea Bush Walk begins from the campground, and the trills of song birds will greet you in the morning. You can also hire canoes ($5) to explore the birdlife along the waterway. (☎/fax 415 8483. Reception 24hr. Cabins $15 per person; tent sites $8 per person; caravan sites $8.) Across the bay from the motor camp, the **Surat Bay Lodge** is a low-key backpackers right on the water's edge, only a bay's arm away from the ocean and a substantial sea lion colony. Follow the signs from the Surat Bay Rd. (☎415 8099. Dorms $17; twins $40; doubles $45.)

The pub adjoining the **Owaka Inn** has pool, darts, and an early Happy Hour (M-F 5-7pm). It's an authentic place to enjoy a hot meal or toss back a few cold ones with the old-timers. (Mains $10-15. Open daily from 11am.) For a cold brew by a toasty fire, mosey on into the incongruously modern **Lumberjack Bar and Cafe.** A three hundred gram rump steak or venison runs $18-21. Entrees start at $7.50. (☎415 8747. Open daily noon-2pm and 6pm-late.)

⚑ OUTDOOR ACTIVITIES. Ten minutes from town, **New Zealand sea lions** lounge, bray, and butt heads along the beach in **Surat Bay.** The sea lion colony, whose numbers swell to 40 in the winter, makes up a substantial percentage of a "mainland" population of 100; the rest are chilling in Antarctica. **Surat Bay Lodge** (see below) is positioned just a few hundred meters from the lions and will rent canoes to explore the surrounding estuary for $8.50 per hour. The Owaka region also has some of the best brown trout rivers for **fishing** in the country.

FROM OWAKA TO PURAKAUNUI ☎ 03

From Owaka to **Ratanui** (5km south) keep an eye out for the signs to **Jack's Blow-hole.** More accurately called a slurp hole, the deep depression is connected to the ocean (200m away) by caves (walk the easy 30min. paddock track to reach it; visit at high tide for most dramatic viewing). Once back on the highway, another side trip leads up the Owaka Valley through forests along the **Catlins River Gorge.** Get a ride to the top of the **Catlins River Track,** a well-maintained tramp through unspoiled beech forest and over three suspension bridges (5hr. one-way). When the trout are biting, this is the place to catch 'em; you may even see the yellowhead or Mohua bird along the way. The track is accessible from a number of points, including the following trailheads: the "Wisp"; the Wallis Stream (1hr. down river from the Wisp); and Frank's Creek (1½hr. from Wallis Stream). There are bathrooms at the top of the track, but no camping; the **Tawanui campsite** ($4 per person) at the track's base also has bathrooms.

PURAKAUNUI BAY AND FALLS ☎ 03

Local beach cows munch kelp on the sand of **Purakaunui Bay** (a surfing beach for the brave-hearted). The mist from crashing waves lends a magical effervescence to the view from the popular **DOC campsite** ($4 per site; with bathrooms). To reach it, take the rough road south of Ratanui. A few kilometers farther south on the scenic route is the turn-off to **Purakaunui Falls** (follow the signs toward Maclennan). The walk to the falls (10min. from the car park) is as spectacular as the multi-tiered cascades themselves. A little luxury is available at the **Greenwood Farmstay,** a warm, sophisticated B&B with meticulously gardened grounds 2km closer to Owaka. Call for pick-up from Owaka. Co-owner Alan will take you out farming with him if you ask. (☎415 8259. Dinner $27.50. Rooms, including a queen with day room and suite, $85. Cash only.)

PAPATOWAI ☎ 03

Papatowai Beach is gorgeous—crashing waves, mist rising off the sand, cliffs visible farther down the coast, and an estuary flowing through the dune forest. Papatowai is well worth a stop, whether you intend to canoe or kayak in the estuary or simply want a scenic picnic. Follow the signs off the main road to reach the ▧**Hilltop Backpackers.** The rugs, glowing wood stove, lavish modern kitchen, and the tub all invite instant relaxation. Canoes, bikes, surfboards, boogie boards, and wetsuits are available. (☎/fax 415 8028. Reception 24hr. Dorms $20; doubles with an incomparable beach view and thick bed covers $45. Cash only.) The **Southern Secret Motel** has luxurious one-room apartments that share a view of the road and sheep-laden fields. (☎/fax 415 8600 or 415 8830. 24hr. reception. Rooms $75; in winter $65.) The **Papatowai Motels and Store** has gas, groceries, and spacious, pleasant rooms behind the store. (☎/fax 415 8147. Reception and store open daily 8:30am-7pm; in winter Su-Th 9am-6pm, F-Sa 9am-7pm. Doubles $65, extra adult $12, extra child $8.) The **Papatowai Motor Park** is behind the store in a bushy area filled with birds. (☎415 8500; fax 415 8503. Reception 8:30am-9:30pm. Basic dorms $12; cabins for 2 $20-30; tent sites $6 per person; caravan sites $7 per person.)

South of Papatowai, the road becomes gravel and winds to **Florence Lookout** and a spectacular view of **Tautuku Beach.** Backed by olive and rusty hues of the native forest, Tautuku may be the best of the Catlins' remarkable beaches. Turn off for **Lake Wilkie** and its 20min. boardwalk a bit farther down the hill. Don't miss the **Cathedral Caves** turn-off, 16km from Tautuku, a highlight of the Catlins. The two 30m-tall mouths of the caves are only accessible at low tide; check a tide table at the visitors center or your accommodation before making the half-hour trek down under dripping tree ferns and kamahi trees to **Waipati Beach** and the caves. (Gates open 2hr. either side of low-tide. Admission $5 per car and 2 adults, extra person $1; trampers $2.) Just after the caves turn onto Rewcastle Rd. for the 30min. walk through the beech forest to the **McLean Falls.**

OTAGO

WAIKAWA, CURIO BAY, AND SLOPE POINT ☎03

Continue towards **Invercargill** via **Tokanui** on the main road, or turn back onto gravel toward **Waikawa** some 20km beyond the Cathedral Caves. The **Waikawa Dolphin Information Centre**, which acts as a **visitors center**, is located in a trim old church in the center of Waikawa and has displays on the area's marine mammals. Its small cafe serves snacks, and the center does bookings for daytime and twilight dolphin viewing tours. (☎246 8444; 0800 377 581. Dolphin cruises daily 10am, 1pm, and 3pm for $50; twilight cruises 5:30pm, $75. Center open daily Oct.-Apr.) Across from the visitors center, **Waikawa Holiday Lodge** provides spartan, immaculate rooms with metal frame bunks. (☎246 8552. Reception 24hr. Dorms $17; twins and doubles $40.)

   Porpoise and **Curio Bays** are each a 30-minute drive from Waikawa along an unsealed road. Just past the Slope St. turnoff, ▓**Curio Bay Backpackers** is a comfortably furnished cottage right on the Porpoise Bay Beach. (☎246 8843. Dorms $18; doubles and twins $36.) At the point of a craggy coastal peninsula, the **Curio Bay Campground** (☎246 8897) has somewhat exposed tent sites and very basic facilities ($4 per person), powered sites ($15 per night), and non-powered sites ($10 per night). On the other side of the point lies **Curio Bay**, situated by the 180-million-year-old ▓**petrified forest** visible on the rocky coast at low tide. Among pools of bead-like seaweed and unhinged bull kelp are the mineralized trunks of tall, ancient trees. From the turn-off at Porpoise Bay, follow signs to **Slope Point**, the southernmost tip of the South Island. The lighthouse is a 10min. walk from the road markers; you'll pass **Pope's Place** on the way. This sheep farm and spacious hostel is run by friendly Jeanette Jack and sports gorgeous and colorful gardens. (☎/fax 246 8420. Reception 24hr. Reservations recommended. Dorms $15; doubles $35. Cash only.) **Waipapa Point**, the site of the worst maritime disaster in New Zealand history (the wreck of the SS *Tararua* in 1881), is 20 km from Pope's Place past **Otara** toward **Invercargill**.

SOUTHLAND

INVERCARGILL ☎03

Invercargill surprises travelers prepared to quickly transfer through to Stewart Island or Fiordland National Park. Despite its population of 53,000 Invercargill retains a small-town feel, and the outstanding cinema is often crowded on nights and weekends. A great place to hire gear or a car, stock up on groceries and supplies, Invercargill provides backpackers a holiday from being on holiday.

▐ TRANSPORTATION

Flights: The **airport** is 2.5km west of the city. Take Dee St. south as it becomes Clyde St. and follow the signs on the roundabout to the airport. Or, take **Spitfire Shuttle** (☎214 1851; $5). A taxi to the airport costs $8. **Air New Zealand** and **Ansett New Zealand** fly frequently to **Auckland** (from $350) and **Christchurch** (from $180).

Trains: The **train station** (☎214 0598) on Leven St. behind the clock tower. **TranzScenic** goes daily to **Christchurch** (9hr., 8:25am, $88-125) via **Dunedin** (3hr., $39-55).

Buses: InterCity (☎214 0598) leaves the train station daily for **Christchurch** (9hr.; 8:45am; $85, YHA $68) via **Dunedin** (3hr.; $40, YHA $32). **Atomic Shuttles** (☎322 8883) has cheaper fares to **Christchurch** (2pm, $48) and **Dunedin** ($23). **Spitfire Shuttle** (☎218 7381) runs to **Te Anau** (2½-3hr.; 12:50pm; $39, YHA $34). **Southern Air Land Travel** (☎216 0717) goes daily to **Queenstown** (3hr.; 2:15pm; $38, YHA $35), as does Atomic Shuttles ($35). Call for booking and pick-up. **Bottom Bus** (☎442 9708) also runs to **Te Anau** and **Queenstown** (daily 6pm; in winter M, W, Sa only; $39-59). **Campleton Passenger Shuttles** (☎212 7404) runs to **Bluff** (5 per day, $10).

Public Transportation: (☎218 7108). Buses serve the suburbs M-F every hr. ($1.20). Most depart from near the library on Dee St.; the visitors center has schedules.

Taxis: Blue Star (☎218 6079) and **Taxi Co.** (☎214 4478) run **24hr.**

Car Rental: Among other smaller operations, **Pegasus,** 61 Bond St. (☎214 3210; 24hr. 0800 803 580) has cheap rental cars from $35 per day, plus long-term rates. **First Choice Rent-a-car** (☎214 4820) and **Intercity Rentals** (☎214 5179) are both in budget range, the latter offering rentals from $39 per day on longer term rentals, or $28 per day without mileage, with free pick-up.

AA: 47-51 Gala St. (24hr. ☎218 9033; fax 214 0246). Open M-F 9am-5pm.

Bike Rental: Wensley's Cycle Centre, 53 Tay St. (☎ 218 6206). Mountain bikes $12-20 per day. Open M-Th 8am-5:30pm, F 8am-9pm, Sa 9:30am-12:30pm.

Hitchhiking: Though *Let's Go* does not recommend it, those heading toward Queenstown are said to take the Waikiwi bus (#10) from the library up North Rd. as far as possible to Westlans Rd. and then walk to the city. For Dunedin, hitchhikers take the Hawthornedale bus (#4), from Tay St. and Lithgow St., as far as it goes.

◼✱🛈 ORIENTATION AND PRACTICAL INFORMATION

From the train and bus station, cross **Leven St.** and pass through **Wachner Pl.** under the **clock tower** to enter downtown. **Dee St.,** Invercargill's main thoroughfare, runs to the right toward **Bluff** and the **Catlins,** and to the left toward **Queens Park** and **Queenstown.** North of the city, it becomes **North Rd.** Across from the clock tower, **Esk St.** is the main shopping center. **SH1** from Dunedin cuts through the city via **Tay St.** and ends on Dee St.

Invercargill

🏠 ACCOMMODATIONS
Backpackers Riverside, 1
Invercargill YHA, 2
Lorneville Holiday Park, 3
Southern Comfort Backpackers, 4

🍴 FOOD
Natural Ice Cream Cafe, 9
Tillerman's Cafe, 6
Pak 'N Save, 12
Robert Harris Cafe, 7
Zookeepers Cafe, 11

🍺 PUBS
Louie's, 5
Players, 10
Sugar Shack, 13

SOUTHLAND

Visitors Center: The Invercargill Information Centre (☎214 6243) is on Victoria Ave, just off of Gala St., inside the massive white pyramid. From Wachner Pl., go left up Dee St., take a right at McDonald's onto Gala St., and the center is 2 blocks down on the left. Open M-F 9am-7pm, Sa-Su 10am-7pm; in winter until 5pm.

DOC: (☎214 4589), State Insurance building, 7th floor, Don St. Open M-F 8am-5pm.

Currency Exchange: BNZ (☎218 9179), at Esk and Kelvin St. Open M-F 9am-4:30pm.

Police: 117 Don St. (☎214 4039).

Pharmacy: Mills Pharmacy (☎214 4249) on the corner of Don and Kelvin. Open M-Th 9am-5:30pm, F 9am-9pm, Sa 10am-1pm.

Medical Services: Urgent Doctor, 103 Don St. (☎218 8821). Open M-F 5-10pm; on call 24hr. Sa-Su and holidays. The **Southland Hospital** (☎214 5735) is on Kew Rd.

Post Office: 51 Don St. Open M-F 8:30am-5pm, Sa 10am-1:30pm.

Internet Access: Available at the **public library** (☎218 7025) on Dee St. $2 per 15min. Open M-F 9am-8:30pm, Sa 10am-1pm. **Gordon's Data Services,** 124 Dee St. (☎0800 222 225) $2 per 15min. Open M-F 10am-5:30pm, Sa 10am-noon.

🏠 ACCOMMODATIONS AND CAMPING

🛏 **Southern Comfort Backpackers,** 30 Thomson St. (☎218 3838), treats you like only a fine bourbon could. From the visitors center, turn right down Victoria Ave., then take a right on Thomson St. The fire-warmed living room and the spotless, ultra-modern kitchen make you feel like a houseguest. Free bikes. Linen $3. Reception 8am-10pm. Book ahead. Dorms $17; doubles $40. Cash only.

Backpackers Riverside Guesthouse, 70 Filleul St. (☎218 9207; 0800 736 323), just off Dee St., overlooking the Waipati River. Park behind the Asthma Society at the corner of Filleul and Dee St. Free pick-up and bikes. Dorms $15; cabins $10 per person; single $32, double $39; B&B $40/$55. Cash only.

Invercargill YHA, 122 North Rd. (☎215 9344; fax 215 9382), 3km up Dee St., that changes to North Rd. just over the bridge. Clean but unexciting. Reception 8-10am, 5-7pm, and 8:30-10pm; in winter 8-10am and 5:30-8:30pm. Dorms $15; twins $34; doubles $36.

Lorneville Holiday Park (☎235 8031), 10km from town. Take Dee St. (which becomes North Rd.) toward Queenstown and then turn right on SH98, in the direction of Dacre/Gore. This sunny caravan park delivers. Tourist flats from $58; on-site caravans $32; tent and powered sites $9.50 per person. Cash only.

🍴 FOOD

Restaurants are scattered in the city (near Dee St.), and many double as bars. Additionally, a new cafe scene is beginning to develop. The **Pak 'N Save market** is at 95 Tay St. (☎214 4864. Open M-Tu, Sa 9am-7pm, W-F 9am-9pm, Su 9am-6pm.)

The Zookeepers Cafe, 50 Tay St. (☎218 3373). Animals are the cafe's primary theme. Sip a bottomless coffee ($2.50) or select from several beers on tap. Snacks $6-8; mains $10-20. Open M-Sa from 10am, Su from 11am.

Tillerman's Cafe, 16 Don St. (☎218 9240), has brick walls clad in classy modern art. Lunch is an affordable indulgence—the baked potato and salad option is only $7. The bar upstairs features a wide range of bands Th-Sa nights. Open M-F noon-2pm and 6-10pm, Sa 6-10pm. Bar open daily 6pm-late.

New Zealand Natural Ice Cream Cafe, 59 Esk St., makes its own waffle cones. Those with heartier appetites will appreciate the luscious kebabs ($4-5.50); either way Natural is sure to please. Open M-F 9:30am-5:30pm, Sa 10am-2pm.

Robert Harris Cafe, 75 Dee St. (☎214 1914), this pleasant cafe, right downtown, has a wide selection of meals and healthier baked goods. Healthy start (yogurt, fruit, and granola) for $7.50. Open M-F 7am-5pm, Sa 8:30am-2:30pm, Su 9am-2pm.

PAUA POWER Of the 144 types of abalone (shellfish) found around the world, the New Zealand paua boasts the most brilliant peacock shades, as well as a hefty price tag. On the South Island there is a strict harvest quota of 400 tons; a one-ton permit costs $100,000. Harvested by fishermen who free-dive up to 10m to pry the crustaceans from rocks, paua can live up to 100 years and grow up to 220cm in size. Much of New Zealand's catch ends up in Asia among the festivities for Chinese New Year. Like a fingerprint, each shell is unique. Ground, polished, and lacquered paua run $10-20—a small price for a shell that took 20-50 years to create.

ENTERTAINMENT AND NIGHTLIFE

The **Movieland 5 Theatre,** 29 Dee St. (☎214 1110; $10, students $8 after 5pm and week-ends; $7 before 5pm weekdays), the cafe/bar **Tillerman's** (see **Food** above) provides the local entertainment Thursday to Saturday. *The Plot,* a weekly calendar posted at most venues, advertises DJs and live music. **Players,** 25 Tay St., has pool tables for a quick game. (☎218 1857. Tables $8-10 per hr. Open M-W noon-11pm, Th-Sa noon-1am.) The **Sugar Shack,** 77 Don St., sets the mark for the Invercargill party style with a cavernous interior done up like a tropical village. (☎218 6125. Drink specials Th-F and DJs W-Sa. Open W-Sa 4pm-late.) **Louie's,** on Dee St., is an upscale tapas bar with white sloping walls and leather banquettes. (☎214 2913. Open from 6pm.)

SIGHTS

The **Southland Museum and Art Gallery,** at the city end of Queen's Park, is in the same gleaming white pyramid as the visitors center. The highlight is the tuatarium, a live exhibit of the nocturnal reptiles that once roamed all of New Zealand. The Roaring 40s gallery upstairs describes New Zealand's subantarctic islands and the megaherbs that thrive there, supremely adapted to the severe conditions. The dynamic slide show includes strobe lightning and may be as close as you can get to the restricted-access isles. **Queen's Park** itself is well worth a visit to the roses with names like "New Dawn," and "Madame de Port." On a clear, cool night, view the stars at the **Observatory** next to the visitors center. (☎218 9753. Museum open M-F 9am-5pm, Sa-Su 10am-5pm. By donation; slideshow $2, children $0.50. Observatory open W 7pm-9pm. $0.50 admission includes slideshow.)

FROM INVERCARGILL TO TUATAPERE

When heading to or from Te Anau and Invercargill consider taking the ✺**Southern Scenic Route.** While the inland route passes through the service towns of Lumsden and Mossburn, the Southern Scenic Route takes an equally efficient but more enjoyable path replete with ocean vistas and mountain panoramas before heading inland and upland to Te Anau. The stretch of road from Riverton to Tuatapere is dotted with small towns, a handful of motor parks and taverns, and innumerable bays and inlets with great surfing and paua shells.

TRANSPORTATION

The **Kiwi Experience Bottom Bus** runs from Invercargill to Te Anau with an overnight stay in Riverton. (☎442 9709. Daily 6pm; in winter M, W, and Sa only.) **Spitfire Shuttles** runs in both directions. (☎214 1851, 249 8077. Departs Invercargill daily 1pm, Te Anau daily 7:45am; in winter departures M-F only; $39. Te Anau to Tuatapere or Tuatapere to Invercargill $20 each. Inquire about backpackers discounts.) Though *Let's Go* doesn't recommend it, **hitchhiking** along this stretch of the Southern Scenic Route is reportedly a good prospect in summer, but uncertain in winter.

RIVERTON   ☎03

One of New Zealand's oldest towns, Riverton (pop. 1850) is a seaside retreat. **Riverton Rocks,** over the bridge and a few kilometers along the coast, is a popular sheltered swimming beach with views of Invercargill and Stewart Island. Harvest your own mussels and enjoy them at the picnicking area. Many short paths to beaches and unusual rock formations like the precarious Balancing Rock start at the **Aparima River Road** bridge. The **Maori Craft Centre,** 130 Palmerston St., is worth a look, with handwoven bullrush (*raupo*) and flax creations on display. (☎234 9965. Open M-Sa 9am-5pm, Su noon-6pm). The **Wallace Early Settlers Museum,** 172 Palmerston St., opposite the Supervalue, displays an impressive collection of Riverton stock—a mint condition fire engine, portraits, Maori feather blankets, and other esoterica. The **visitors center** is located in the museum. (☎234 8520. Open daily 10am-4pm.)

At the tastefully refurbished **Riverton Rock Backpackers** you'll find a TV lounge with free tea and coffee. (☎234 8886; 0800 248 886; fax 234 8816. Reception 9am-noon and 4-7pm. Dorms $19.) The owners run another backpackers at **The Globe Hotel** next door. Reservations are essential in summer and advisable in winter since the Bottom Bus stops here. (☎234 8527. Linen $1. Reception 1pm-late at the bar. Dorms $17; singles $30; twins and doubles $40. VIP $1 off.) The **Beach House Cafe and Bar,** 126 Rocks Highway, a 10min. drive from town on the way to the Rocks, is a popular cafe on the cliffside offering mains from $8.50 and Internet access. (☎ 234 8274. Open daily 10am-late; in winter Tu-Su 10am-late.) **The Nostalgia Country Cafe,** 108 Palmerson St., serves intriguing pies for lunch (venison or chicken-and-apricot pie with salad $10) in a cool, surrealistic, sailing-themed setting. (☎234 9154. Open M-F 10:30am-3:30pm and 6pm-late.) **Aparima Tavern,** across the bridge, opens its bistro on weekends. (☎234 8502. Open Sa-Su 6-9pm.) Other local services include: the **National Bank** (open M-F 9am-4:30pm); **Riverton Pharmacy,** 168 Palmerston St., (☎234 9999; open M-F 9am-5:30 or 6pm); the **medical center,** (☎234 8209; open M-F 8:30-5pm; on call after hours); and the **Riverton Supervalue** and the **post office** across the street and down a bit from the hotel (both open M-Th 7:45am-6:30pm, F 7:45am-8pm, Sa 9am-7pm, Su 9:30am-4:30pm).

OREPUKI   ☎03

From Riverton, the Southern Scenic Route traverses open country past the Longwood Range to Tuatapere. **Colac Bay,** a former Maori settlement 10km beyond Riverton, is a popular surfing beach with a tavern, holiday park, and tent sites. Through the summer mist in **Te Waewae Bay,** which suddenly appears over the hill 15km farther on, you can sometimes see Hector's dolphins or an occasional right whale spouting off. Look out for windblown macrocarpas as you pass through **Orepuki** (pop. 150). Originally located at **Monkey Island** (or **Te Puka a Takatimu,** meaning "anchor stone of Tatuatea's great canoe"), this gold-mining town was relocated three times to satisfy prospectors—follow signs from the highway when you reach the mouth of the Waiau River. Nearby at **Orepuki Beach** you can find tiny, low-grade gemstones amid the grains of sand, and some hopefuls still pan for gold.

TUATAPERE   ☎03

A small logging and sausage town (pop. 700) situated halfway between Invercargill and Te Anau, Tuatapere (tua-TAP-ery) is an undiscovered base for the tramps and wilderness activities in the area, including forays into Fiordland National Park. Though Tuatapere means "a meeting place between two ridges" in Maori, some local legends have renamed it "the hole in the bush," because the town was cut out of a thick forest. Nowadays locals like to call it "land of the last light" because the town is the last in New Zealand to see the sun go down.

⟨⟩ TRANSPORTATION AND PRACTICAL INFORMATION. The **Spitfire Shuttle** (☎249 7505 or ☎218 7381) runs at 9:30am to **Invercargill** and at 2pm to **Te Anau** (daily; in winter M-F; $20). Tuatapere's **Visitors Center & Bushman's Museum** is south of the bridge over the **Waiau River** and sells **hut passes.** (☎226 6399. Open daily 9am-5pm; in winter 10am-3:30pm. Museum entrance by donation.) **Tuatapere Health and Gift,** across from the DOC field office, doubles as the **post office.** (☎226 6999. Open M-F 9:30am-5:30pm, and F 7-9pm.)

⟨⟩ ACCOMMODATIONS AND FOOD. The **Waiau Hotel,** south of the town center, has pleasant, private rooms in a building dating from 1909. (☎226 6409. Breakfast $10. Singles $40, with bath $45; doubles $55, with bath $60.) More budget-oriented and far less glamorous lodging can be found at **Five Mountains Holiday Park and Hump Track Backpackers,** north of the bridge. The rooms are clean, basic, and crowded. (☎226 6148. Linen $5. Free laundry. 24hr. reception next door in the private residence. Dorms $10-15; private rooms for 2 $30; tent sites $10; powered caravan sites $15.) Better camping sites can be found down by the river past the Domain though the cabins there are starkly basic.

The **Waiau Hotel** (see above) has full meals from $12.50, takeaway, and a cafe with delicious home cooking and baking. (Open daily. Hours vary.) **Dowling's Discounter's** perennial takeaways generally range from $10. (☎226 6250. Open daily 8am-8:30pm.) Although Dowling's may have a better selection, **Western Foodmarket,** north of the river, is cheaper. (☎226 6292. Open M-Th 7am-7pm, F 7am-8:30pm, Sa 7am-5pm, Su 9am-4pm.)

⟨⟩ SIGHTS AND ACTIVITIES. Though the **Tuatapere Scenic Reserve** no longer houses the ancient tuataras that once prospered, it is now home to towering beeches. Grab an informative pamphlet from the visitors center and follow the signs to the Domain for the **Tuatapere Walkway** (return 1½-2hr.). Mountain biking along the old logging roads to Lake Hauroko (roughly 40km west of Clifden) and down winding Borland Rd. to **Lake Monowai** is very popular. Tuatapere is also home to the annual **Wild Challenge** (☎226 6568), a 35km whitewater kayak, 30km run, and 32km bike race held the second Saturday in January. If you're only a minor masochist, the **Waiau Grunt** (13km kayak, 8km run, 20km bike) may be more appealing. Brimming with tourists in season and out, the **Giant Totara Tree Loop,** 30km northwest of Tuatapere on the edge of Dean Forest, has trees up to 1000 years old. To get there, take Clifden Lake-Hauroko Rd. via Motu Bush Rd.

Some of the most exciting tours in Tuatapere are onboard jetboats that fly over **Lake Hauroko** and down the rock-strewn rapids of the **Wairaurahiri River. Wairaurahiri Wilderness Jet** (☎225 8174; 0800 270 556) and **Wairaurahiri Jet** (☎236 1137; 0800 376 174) both run full-day trips (around $130; book ahead). **Lake Hauroko Tours** connects with **Spitfire Shuttle** to provide access to the **Dusky Track.** (☎226 6681. M, Th, and on demand; $50 per person.) The visitors center has details on guided walks, helicopter tours, and other services in remote Fiordland.

Tuatapere is the endpoint (or beginning point) for the **Dusky Track,** a rugged 8-day walk for experienced trampers (parts of the track may be done in smaller 3-4 day trips with fly-in service). The town is also a departure point for the walk to the **Percy Burn Viaduct,** the largest wooden viaduct in the world (36m high and 125m long), and the **South Coast Track,** which follows a former logging tramway. The viaduct walk requires two nights at Port Craig Hut, a former school, to reach the viaducts that were once constructed for timber transport. The track begins 28km from Tuatapere at **Bluecliffs Beach,** at the signposted road on the north side of town. The newest addition to the region's walks is the **Hump Ridge Track,** a three-day, 53km loop through beach, bush, and mountain areas that is slated to open in late 2001 (check with the visitors center for track status).

CLIFDEN ☎ 03

North of Tuatapere, 17km along the road to Te Anau, the hamlet of Clifden is known for its **limestone caves,** located 1km up the road after the lime works on the route toward Winton. Prospective spelunkers should pick up a map in Tuatapere and bring a flashlight; the caves are cramped in places, and sometimes flooded, so if you decide to go, be extremely careful. Walk the **suspension bridge,** completed in 1902. Downstream, the protruding cliff face looks like the profile of a legendary Maori maiden thwarted in love who leapt off the precipice. From Clifden, the road heads through the Waiau River valley as the inaccessible Takitimu mountains to the east and the distant heights of Fiordland to the west are occasionally visible over the foothills.

BLUFF ☎ 03

As the departure point for the ferry to Stewart Island (see p. 351), seaside Bluff (Invercargill's peninsular port town) also marks the beginning (or end) of SH1. Bluff lies at the tip of a long spit of land 27km south of the city. Though fishing and shipping industries dominate the port, it's still worth looking around here on the way to Stewart Island. The **Paua Shell House,** 258 Marine Parade, is renowned for the thousands of lacquered and colorful shells that line its walls. (☎212 8262. Open daily 9am-5pm.) If you're waiting to catch the ferry, the **Bluff Maritime Museum,** on the pier, is a good place to learn about the region's history. (☎212 7534. $2; seniors and students $1. Open M-F 10am-4:30pm, Sa-Su 1-5pm.)

The **Campbelltown Passenger Service** runs between Bluff and Invercargill. (☎212 7404. M-F 5 per day, Sa-Su 2 per day; $10, round-trip $20. Bookings required.) At Bluff's **visitors center,** 74 Gore St. inside Foveau Souvenirs, Arts, and Gifts, Yvonne and Jim will answer your queries. (☎212 8305. Open daily 9am-5pm.) With the recent closure of the town's bank, Eftpos withdrawals at the **Service Centre** on Gore St. are the only way to get cash; some backpackers and bars will also provide this service. (Open M-F 9am-4:30pm.) Other services include: the **medical centre,** behind the camping ground (☎212 7337; open M-F 8:30am-5pm; after-hours information available by phone); and the **post office** next door (☎212 8759; open M-F 9am-5pm, Sa 10am-7pm). For backpackers, **Flynn Club's Hotel,** on Gore St., is weathering in the tradition of the grandest European hotels. (☎212 8124. Reception in the adjacent bar. Budget rooms $15; singles $30; doubles $60. Suite for 7 available.) **The Tanti B&B,** on Marine Parade at the end of Gore St., provides cabins and doubles at reasonable rates. (☎212 8886. Doubles $50-65; triples $75; cabin accommodation for 6 $60-75.) **Bluff Backpackers and Hunting Lodge,** on Gore St., is another amiable backpackers, with a large suite of rooms. (☎212 8074; mobile 025 207 7301. Reception 8am-6pm. Dorms $14.) Groceries are available at the **Four Square.** (Open M-W 8am-6pm, Th-Sa 8am-7pm, Su 9am-6pm.)

TRAGICALLY DELICIOUS Named for its strangely sheeplike flavor, muttonbird (or sooty shearwater, or titi) is a delicacy enjoyed primarily on Stewart Island and in Invercargill. Today, it can only be harvested by Rakiura Maori, who move onto the offshore Muttonbird Islands for the annual hunt, which dates back hundreds of years. By day, when the adult birds are out foraging, harvesters push sticks down titi burrows and scoop the baby birds out. By night, they hunt by torchlight, capturing the juveniles as they emerge from the holes. Immediately killed by a bite to the head or a whack to the ground, the birds are dipped in hot wax, cooled, plucked, and stored in bags made of rubbery bull kelp. The annual harvest begins on April 1, and ends with the collection of up to 250,000 birds—a major source of food and income. To ensure a sustainable harvest, the kill area must be rotated at least every two years, since titi migrate all the way up to Siberia and back to the burrows of their birth. If you eat muttonbird, you know it came from this harvest.

STEWART ISLAND ☎03

Maori legend has it that when Maui fished up the North Island from his South Island canoe, Stewart Island was his anchor stone. Named *Rakiura* in Maori, "the place of glowing skies" sees fiery red sunsets in summer and the eerie *aurora australis* in winter. Muddy tracks and remote beaches retain the wild flavor of a land where kiwis still vastly outnumber Kiwis. Of Stewart Island's 1683 square kilometers, 90% are DOC-managed as reserve lands, with 8% owned by the Rakiura Maori and 2% in other private hands. Bird life abounds, with wood pigeons noisily swooping through town, rarer birds thriving on rat-free Ulva Island, and droves of penguins and muttonbirds crowding beaches. The island's 350-odd (or 350 odd) residents cluster in the fishing village by Halfmoon Bay, gracefully weathering 290 days and 1500mm of rain per year. They insist, with good reason, that you haven't seen New Zealand until you've experienced their beech-free forests, pristine beaches, and quiet lifestyle.

▮ TRANSPORTATION

Flights: Southern Air (Oban ☎219 1090, Invercargill ☎218 9129) flies a 9-seat prop plane to and from **Invercargill** (20min.; 3 per day and on demand; $75, return $140; standby $50, return $90). Only 15kg per person will be carried on a single flight—extra gear must be flown over separately. Southern Air runs a free shuttle from the Stewart Island airstop to **Halfmoon Bay. Spitfire Shuttle** (☎214 1851) runs between **Invercargill** and the **airport** (on demand; $5 one-way if alone, $3 per person for 2-10 passengers). Flights to Stewart Island are much faster and almost as economical as taking the ferry.

Ferries: Foveaux Express (☎212 7660) runs a catamaran between Bluff and Halfmoon Bay (1hr.; 2 per day in summer, 1-2 per day in winter; $45, return $84, children half-price). Alternatively, the record for swimming the strait is 9hr. and 41min. **Campbelltown Passenger Service** (☎212 7404) makes ferry drop-offs and pick-ups between **Bluff** and **Invercargill** (30min., 5 per day, $10). Secure parking at the Bluff ferry terminal costs $5 per night; alternately, park in front of the Bluff Police Station.

Taxis and Rentals: Oban Taxis and Tours (☎219 1456) hires **mopeds** (from $20 per hr.), double **motor scooters** (from $25 per hr.), and **cars** (half-day $50, full-day $70; includes mileage and petrol), and runs a **taxi** service (on-call daily 7:00am-10pm).

✦ ▮ ORIENTATION AND PRACTICAL INFORMATION

Stewart Island lies about 35km across the **Foveaux Strait** from Bluff, the nearest mainland town. The island's primary human settlement is tiny **Oban**, also known by its location at **Halfmoon Bay. Elgin Terrace** curves along the bay, while **Ayr St., Main Rd.,** and **Horseshoe Bay Rd.** branch inland; nothing in town is farther than a 15min. walk. **Golden Bay Rd.** crosses to **Paterson Inlet** in the South (10min.) and Horseshoe Bay Rd. and Elgin Terrace lead along the water to quiet beaches and coves.

Visitors Center: The **Visitor Centre** (☎219 1218) is on Main Rd. in the same building as the **DOC office** (☎219 1130). Both open M-F 8am-7pm. **Luggage storage** available (large lockers $5). Activity info and bookings are handled by the **Stewart Island Adventure Center**, on the wharf (☎219 1134; open daily 7:15am-about 7pm; in winter 7:15am-6:30pm), or by **Stewart Island Travel**, on Main Rd. (☎219 1269; open daily 9am-5pm; in winter 10am-3pm).

Bike Rental and Tramping Gear Hire: Innes's Backpackers (☎219 1080), on Argyle St. rents bikes ($10 per day) and camping equipment.

Currency Exchange: There are **no banks** and **no ATMs** on the island.

Police: (☎219 1020), on Golden Bay Rd.

Medical Services: District nurse (☎219 1098; 0800 100 776) on Argyle St.

SOUTHLAND

Internet Access: Justcafe (☎219 1208) has access for $14 per hr. Open Dec.-Mar. daily 8am-10pm.

Post Office: Run by **Southern Air** (☎219 1090), on Elgin Terrace. Open M-F 7:30am-6pm, Sa-Su 9:30am-5pm; in winter M-F 8:30am-4:45pm, Sa-Su 8:30am-4:45pm.

ACCOMMODATIONS AND CAMPING

Oban's range of character-laden accommodations is impressive. The visitors center/DOC office is very helpful with bookings, and has listings with photos; call ahead in summer and bring a sleeping bag (in most cases).

The rooms and the lounge with pool table, TV, and kitchen are knit together with boardwalks at **Stewart Island Backpackers**, on Ayr St. (☎219 1114. Reception M-Sa 8:30am-7pm, Su 9am-7pm; in winter M-Sa 8:30am-7pm, Su 8:30am-6:30pm. Dorms $14; backpacker doubles $32; twins and doubles $60.) **Michael's House Hostel** overlooks Dundee St., off Ayr St. Michael is a good-natured and garrulous fisherman and his home is as welcoming and weather-worn as the man. (☎219 1425. Call ahead. $15.) **The View,** up steep Nichol Rd. past the Southern Air office is a homestay with fantastic harbor views. (☎219 1328. Linen $5. Doubles $40. Cash only.) **Joy's Place,** on Main Rd., offers beds in the comfort of a rather small but still abode; a small cabin double is available behind the house. (☎219 1376. Linen $2. $15; double or twins $40. Call ahead.) **Deep Bay Cabin** is a 25min. trek from town, on Deep Bay; but call for a pick-up and then enjoy the outdoor shower and ready-made aviary in this isolated bush-cabin, proximate to several walking tracks. (☎219 1219. $15 per person with sleeping bag.) Some single women travelers have reportedly felt uncomfortable at **Jo and Andy's B&B** and **Innes' Backpackers. Ferndale Campsite** (☎219 1176), off Horseshoe Bay Rd., has showers ($2) and grassy tent sites ($8) with spankin' pine-hewn bathrooms, newly manicured grounds, and lovely hothouses with terrific bay views. Just across the wharf, before Tendale on Horseshoe Bay Rd., airy **Dave's Place** has a sunny lounge with another view of the bay. (☎219 1427. No linen or advance bookings. Dorms $15.)

FOOD

Dr. Britt's pottery-filled and earth-toned **Justcafe,** on Main Rd., is a mellow and tasteful island-on-an-island, serving quality java. (☎219 1208. Espresso $3.50. Open Dec.-Mar. daily 9am-6pm; in winter noon-3pm.) Brass plates adorn the walls of the comfortable **South Sea Hotel Restaurant and Pub,** where locals mingle to tell stories about (and drink like) fish. The $12 Wednesday roast is a budget dream. (☎219 1059. Restaurant open daily 7-9:30am, noon-2pm, and 6-9pm; in winter 7-9:30am, noon-1pm and 6-7:30pm. Pub open from 11am till "as late as necessary.") The **Church Hill Cafe and Bar,** 36 Ramaki Rd., sits beside the church at the top of the hill, behind the wharf. The food is a bit dear, but the views and atmosphere are delightful. (☎219 1323. Open daily from 10:30am; in winter W-Su from 11:30am.). For late night dining, try the **Kai Kart,** a mobile purveyor of cheap take-away (burgers $5.95), and (amazingly) several sit-down meals in the evening (Rumpsteak meal $14.80); the cart is now lodged on Ayr St. (Open Tu-Su noon-2pm and daily 5-10pm.)

Lettuce Inn, a block up Main Rd., provides fresh fruits and vegetables, meats, and bulk foods in summer. (☎219 1243. Open M, W, and F noon-7pm; Tu and Th 9am-7pm; Sa-Su 10am-7pm; in winter M-Sa noon-6pm, Su 2-6pm.) **Ship to Shore,** on Elgin Terrace, sells a decent array of foodstuffs, with a strait-inspired price hike. (☎219 1069. Open M-F 8am-6:30pm, Sa-Su 9am-6:30pm; in winter M-F 8am-5:30pm, Sa-Su 10am-4pm.)

OUTDOOR ACTIVITIES

The Rakiura Track (2-3 days, 36km) far removed from the mainstream, and winds entirely through lush forest (see p. 375). Easy day walks lead right out of Oban. **Observation Rock,** a 15min. walk up and beyond Ayr St., affords prime sunset views over Paterson Inlet. The 3hr. return walk to **Ackers Point,** east of town, is a great option for summer dusks, as hundreds of muttonbirds fly in to nest. Quiet, sandy swimming beaches are close to town along any coastal road; more day hike details can be gleaned from DOC.

For more serious trampers, the challenging **North West Circuit Track,** which continues from the Rakiura Track (see below), rewards trampers with uncut forests, lots of mud, a chance to scale the highest point on the island (Mt. Anglem, 980m), the well-named dunes of Ruggedy Beach, and best of all, a very strong chance of seeing multitudes of kiwi along the wild west coast. The walk takes 10-12 days, not including the 3-4 day **Southern Circuit,** and is the best tramp to tackle if you have the time. Backcountry huts ($5) have running water and toilets, but no cooking stoves; tenting is free.

Between December and February, DOC conducts its **Stewart Island Summer Visitor Programme,** including an evening slideshow ($3) and guided trips to the gloriously predator-free **Ulva Island** in Paterson Inlet ($27.50, children $15; advance bookings essential.) Otherwise, **Seaview Watertaxi** (☎219 1014), **Stewart Island Watertaxi** (☎219 1394), **Rakiura Waterways** (☎219 1414), and **Seabuzz** (☎219 1282) also make the bird-intensive trip (return $25, $20 per person for 2 or more; advance booking essential). Seabuzz leads glass-bottom boat trips to the salmon and mussel farm, as does **Taliskee Charters** (☎219 1151). On alternate evenings, **Bravo Adventure Cruises** runs a cruise and bushwalk to see wild brown kiwi near the mouth of Paterson Inlet; with a 98% kiwi-spotting success rate to date, this is the surest way to behold the flightless icons without trekking the North West Circuit. (☎219 1144. 4hr., $60; max. 15 people. Bookings essential.)

Water activities in Stewart Island are as original as its residents; speak with booking agents to see what types of trips are running. It is good to have flexible plans as schedules vary widely. **Completely Southern Sea Kayaks** (☎219 1275) rents boats ($40 per day) and runs guided paddles around Paterson Inlet and further afield (from $60 per day). **Stewart Island SEALS** (☎219 1180) takes divers ($70-90) and snorkelers ($50) out for daytrips; overnight options are also available ($165-230, gear not included). **Lo Loma** (☎219 1425), **Mareno Excursions** (☎219 1023), and **Taliskee Charters** (☎219 1151) run diving trips as well. **Oban Taxis and Tours** (☎219 1456) rents two-tank scuba gear ($100 per day) and snorkeling sets ($40 per day); they also run daytime bus tours (1½hr.; $18, children $9) and sunset rides (Dec.-Feb.; 2hr.; $25, children $12.50). To hire a fishing charter, contact **Fish 'n' Trips;** Michael emerges from the hostel and puts his own fishing on hold to give novices a chance. (☎219 1425. Half-day $50 with a 6-person min.) Local naturalist and eccentric raconteur graybeard(s) **Sam and Billy the Bus** do their own offbeat tour of Stewart Island's road-accessible sights. (☎219 1269. 1½hr.; $18, children $9).

To flex your mental muscles after a day of touring, play **chess** as gulls wheel above, waves crash, locals go about their business, and the children of tourists frolic around you at Oban's giant waterfront board.

SOUTHLAND

TRAMPING

Backpacking, trekking, bushwalking—whatever you call it back home, it's called tramping in New Zealand. With all the national parks, forest parks, scenic reserves, and other protected areas in New Zealand, it is no surprise that the opportunities for overnight wilderness excursions are practically limitless. Hundreds of well-maintained tracks are scattered across New Zealand. New Zealand's 9 most spectacular and popular tramps (including one canoe trip) are classified as **Great Walks** and are run by DOC under a separate administration.

GREAT WALK	LENGTH	DURATION	DIFFICULTY	HIGHEST POINT
Lake Waikaremoana Track	46km	3-5 days		1186m
Tongariro Northern Circuit	44.5km	3-4 days		1800m
Whanganui River Journey	145km	5 days		N/A
Abel Tasman Coast Trek	51km	3-5 days		150m
Heaphy Track	82km	4-6 days		915m
Routeburn Track	33km	2-4 days		1280m
Milford Track	54km	4 days		1150m
Kepler Track	67km	3-4 days		1200m
Rakiura Track	36km	3 days		300m

⚠ DEPARTMENT OF CONSERVATION

The **Department of Conservation (DOC),** or Te Papa Atawhai, is an unparalleled resource with the lowdown on the seasonal availability and safety of hikes, the regulations and practicalities of adventuring in New Zealand, maps, and more. Offices are all over New Zealand in every large city, most small towns, and near virtually every protected wilderness area. The staff has information and advice on current track conditions and weather forecasts and an intentions book. Nearly every Great Walk requires trampers to provide their information in this book before starting the track, especially in the winter. Most city DOC offices will sell hut passes and assist with hut bookings, however often only for those tracks nearby. For most tracks, DOC also produces a $1 brochure with a basic but adequate map and track information. Detailed topographic maps are $11-13.50. The main DOC office is located at P.O. Box 10420, Wellington (☎04 471 0726; fax 471 1082; www.doc.govt.nz). For more information on Great Walk Passes and bookings see below.

🚶 HUTS AND CAMPING

HUTS. New Zealand's tracks are home to a well-developed **backcountry hut system.** Cabins are essentially an overnight accommodation, and can be found on virtually every developed track in New Zealand. The huts were created for three reasons: to increase safety for trampers, to reduce the environmental damage caused by camping and tramping off-trail, and to provide the opportunity for meeting fellow trampers. There are four categories of huts, the first of which includes mattresses, water, cooking facilities, fuel, and a warden. Category 4 huts, are shelters with extremely limited facilities. More equipped huts cost $5-10 per night, while a Category 4 hut is free of charge; purchase tickets at DOC offices or from park rangers. Extensive trampers can purchase an Annual Hut Pass for NZ$65; children under age 12 stay for free, ages 12-17 are half-price. However, those who prefer alternate accommodation can camp on almost all tracks. There is usually a small charge for camping near huts; camping at a distance from the track is free where permitted, though often difficult because of heavy foliage.

CAMPGROUNDS. Like huts, there are three categories of DOC campgrounds: serviced, standard, and informal. Serviced grounds include flush toilets, tap water, kitchen, showers, laundry, and usually electricity. Standard have toilets, water supply, and some type of vehicle access, while informal have limited facilities, sometimes only a water supply. Prices of grounds depend on the facilities offered and range from $2-10 with informal grounds free of charge. Fees are collected by camp wardens or the local agent. Camping is not allowed outside designated sites on Great Walks. For more information see www.nzcamping.co.nz.

GREAT WALK PASSES. Most walks require a **Great Walks Pass,** except in winter when many revert to the backcountry hut pass system. Due to an increase in traffic, most walks require booking in advance in the summer (Nov.-Apr.), especially the **Abel Tasman, Milford,** and **Routeburn** tracks. DOC offices provide **Great Walks Camping** or **Hut Passes** for overnight tramping in the summer. Each pass is specific to a track and has an expiration date. They can be used at any time before this date, but do not guarantee a bunk; these passes permit the actual trekking. The process of booking with a DOC office has increased for many popular tracks. This system restricts visitor numbers and guarantees an actual bunk at a hut. An **annual** Great Walks Hut Pass can be purchased for $65, but bookings for individual tracks are still required. Contact the DOC **Great Walks Booking Desk,** PO Box 29, Te Anau (☎ 03 249 8514; fax 249 8515) for further information.

CAMPING AND HIKING EQUIPMENT

WHAT TO BUY...

Good camping equipment is both sturdy and light. Camping equipment is generally more expensive in Australia, New Zealand, and the UK than in North America. If you bring your own camping equipment with you into New Zealand, make sure it is clean, as customs officials will check used equipment upon arrival.

Sleeping Bag: Most sleeping bags are rated by season ("summer" means 30-40°F at night; "four-season" or "winter" often means below 0°F). They are made either of **down** (warmer and lighter, but more expensive, and miserable when wet) or of **synthetic** material (heavier, more durable, and warmer when wet). Prices range US$80-210 for a summer synthetic to US$250-300 for a good down winter bag. **Sleeping bag pads** include foam pads (US$10-20), air mattresses (US$15-50), and Therm-A-Rest self-inflating pads (US$45-80). Bring a **stuff sack** to store your bag and keep it dry.

Tent: The best tents are free-standing (with their own frames and suspension systems), set up quickly, and only require staking in high winds. Low-profile dome tents are the best all-around. Good 2-person tents start at US$90, 4-person at US$300. Seal the seams of your tent with waterproofer, and make sure it has a rain fly. Other tent accessories include a **battery-operated lantern,** a **plastic groundcloth,** and a **nylon tarp.**

Backpack: Internal-frame packs mold better to your back, keep a lower center of gravity, and flex adequately to allow you to hike difficult trails. **External-frame packs** are more comfortable for long hikes over even terrain, as they keep weight higher and distribute it more evenly. Make sure your pack has a strong, padded hip-belt to transfer weight to your legs. Any serious backpacking requires a pack of at least 4000 in^3 (16,000cc), plus 500 in^3 for sleeping bags in internal-frame packs. Sturdy backpacks cost anywhere from US$125-420—this is one area in which it doesn't pay to economize. Fill up any pack with something heavy and walk around the store with it to get a sense of how it distributes weight before buying it. Either buy a **waterproof backpack cover,** or store all of your belongings in plastic bags inside your pack.

Boots: Be sure to wear hiking boots with good **ankle support.** They should fit snugly and comfortably over 1-2 pairs of wool socks and thin liner socks. Break in boots over several weeks first in order to spare yourself painful and debilitating blisters, and spray them with a waterproofing agent.

Other Necessities: Good raingear may seem expensive, but it is a worthwhile invest-ment. Raingear in two pieces, a top and pants, is far superior to a poncho. **Synthetic** layers, like those made of polypropylene, and a **pile jacket** will keep you warm even when wet. When camping in autumn, winter, or spring, bring along a **"space blanket"** which will help you to retain your body heat and doubles as a groundcloth (US$5-15). Plastic **water bottles** are virtually shatter- and leak-proof. Large collapsible **water sacks** will significantly improve your lot in primitive campgrounds and weigh practically noth-ing when empty (though they are bulky and heavy when full). Bring **water-purification tablets** for when you can't boil water, unless you are willing to shell out money for a por-table water-purification system (around US$35). Although most campgrounds provide campfire sites, you may want to bring a small **metal grate** or **grill** of your own. For those places that forbid fires or the gathering of firewood you'll need a **camp stove** (the clas-sic Coleman starts at US$40) and a propane-filled **fuel bottle** to operate it. Also don't forget a **first-aid kit, pocketknife, powerful insect repellent, calamine lotion, toilet-ries, toilet paper, moleskin, sunscreen, biodegradable soap, duct tape** and **water-proof matches** or a **lighter.**

...AND WHERE TO BUY IT

The mail-order/online companies listed below offer lower prices than many retail stores, but a visit to a local camping or outdoors store will give you a good sense of the look and weight of certain items.

Campmor, 28 Parkway, P.O. Box 700, Upper Saddle River, NJ 07458 (US ☎888-226-7667; elsewhere US ☎+1 201-825-8300; www.campmor.com).

Discount Camping, 880 Main North Rd., Pooraka, South Australia 5095, Australia (☎08 8262 3399; www.discountcamping.com.au).

Eastern Mountain Sports (EMS), 327 Jaffrey Rd., Peterborough, NH 03458, USA (☎888-463-6367 or 603-924-7231; www.shopems.com)

L.L. Bean, Freeport, ME 04033 (US and Canada ☎800-441-5713; UK ☎0800 891 297; elsewhere, call US +1 207-552-3028; www.llbean.com).

Mountain Designs, P.O. Box 1472, Fortitude Valley, Queensland 4006, Australia (☎07 3252 8894; www.mountaindesign.com.au).

Recreational Equipment, Inc. (REI), Sumner, WA 98352, USA (☎800 426-4840 or 253-891-2500; www.rei.com).

YHA Adventure Shop, 14 Southampton St., London, WC2E 7HA, UK (☎020 7836 8541). The main branch of one of Britain's largest outdoor equipment suppliers.

WILDERNESS SAFETY

> **EMERGENCIES.** For all emergencies that occur tramping call ☎111

Stay warm, stay dry, and stay hydrated. The vast majority of life-threatening wil-derness situations can be avoided by following this simple advice. Be prepared by always packing raingear, a hat and mittens, a first-aid kit, a reflector, a whistle, high energy food, and extra water for any hike. Dress in wool or warm layers of synthetic materials designed for the outdoors; never rely on cotton for warmth, as it is absolutely useless when wet. On any hike, however brief, you should pack enough equipment to keep you alive should disaster befall. Always fill out the **intentions form** at the nearest DOC office (and any huts along the way) before undertaking a hike; also let someone know when and where you are tramping, whether it's a newfound friend, your backpackers, or a local hiking organization. Always get updates on the latest **weather forecasts** from the local DOC. Weather patterns can change instantly, especially in the more volatile mountainous areas. If the weather turns nasty on a day-hike, turn back immediately. Before undertaking overnight or longer hikes, in particular, always check with the nearest DOC office about the hike's weather and safety rating, as well as the availability of huts along the track; be sure to fill in the DOC's intentions book. A good guide to outdoor survival is *How to Stay Alive in the Woods*, by Bradford Angier (Macmillan, US$8).

See p. 25 for info about outdoor ailments such as giardia and insects. **Mosquitoes** are most active in the summer from dusk to dawn; the ever-present and ever-annoying **sandflies** make their home in bushy and grassy areas, and are especially populous in the southern parts of the South Island. To guard against both, wear long pants (tucked into socks) and long sleeves, buy a bed net for camping, and use insect repellent. Unlike mosquitoes, sandflies cannot bite through clothing, so even very light layers are an effective deterrent. As a further precaution, soak or spray your gear with permethrin, which is licensed in the US for use on clothing. Natural repellents can also be useful: taking vitamin B-12 pills regularly can eventually make you smelly to insects, as can garlic pills. Still, be sure to supplement your vitamins with repellent. Calamine lotion or topical cortisones (like Cortaid) may stop insect bites from itching, as can a bath with a half-cup of baking soda or oatmeal.

FURTHER READING AND WEB RESOURCES

Whether novice or expert, you can visit your nearest outdoors equipment store or bookstore to find publications and general info on camping and adventuring in New Zealand, or contact an outdoors publication company. Specific New Zealand titles, such as *101 Great Tramps in New Zealand*, by Pickering and Smith or *Adventuring in New Zealand*, by Margaret Jefferies provide good broad surveys of the New Zealand outdoors. Similarly, **GORP** (the Great Outdoor Recreation Pages; www.gorp.com) provides information on outdoor activities in New Zealand and a number of useful links. For **topographical maps** of New Zealand, contact **Map and Chart Center**, 32 Goodshed Rd. (Private Bag 903), Upper Hutt, New Zealand (☎04 527 7019; fax 527 7246; mapcentre@terralink.co.nz). Once in New Zealand, you can buy topographical maps from local DOC offices.

 ENVIRONMENTALLY RESPONSIBLE TOURISM The idea behind responsible tourism is to leave no trace of human presence. A campstove is a safer (and more efficient) way to cook than using vegetation, but if you must make a fire, keep it small and use only dead branches or brush rather than cutting vegetation. Make sure your campsite is at least 150 ft. (50m) from water supplies or bodies of water. If there are no toilet facilities, bury human waste (but not paper) at least four inches (10cm) deep and above the high-water line, and 150 ft. or more from any water supplies and campsites. Always pack your trash in a plastic bag and carry it with you until you reach the next trash receptacle. For more information, contact one of the organizations listed below.

Earthwatch, 3 Clock Tower Place, Suite 100, Box 75, Maynard, MA 01754 (US ☎(800) 776-0188; info@earthwatch.org; www.earthwatch.org).

Ecotourism Society, P.O. Box 668, Burlington, VT 05402 (US ☎(802) 651-9818; ecomail@ecotourism.org; www.ecotourism.org).

EcoTravel Center: www.ecotour.com.

National Audobon Society, 200 Trillium Ln., Albany, NY 12203 (US ☎(518) 869-9731; www.audobon.org).

Tourism Concern, Stapleton House, 277-281 Holloway Rd., London N7 8HN (UK ☎020 7753 3330; www.tourismconcern.org.uk).

GREAT WALKS

The 13 National Parks of New Zealand comprise over 10% of New Zealand's total area, almost 3 million hectares of land. Most have historical and spiritual significance for the Maori and each are unique with different terrain, climate, weather, and highlights. Parks are open year round and visitation does not require a permit. DOC provides each well-designed and maintained park with a visitors center complete with representatives, maps, and displays. All Great Walks lie within National Parks and are maintained by DOC. Though DOC designates which tracks are considered Great Walks, their specification lasts a period during the year varying from track to track; it is called the track's Great Walk season. Walks within parks range from leisurely day hikes to week-long overnights requiring crampons, ice picks, and climbing equipment in the winter. Track facilities range from basic camping grounds to Category 1 huts (see **Huts and Camping** p. 354). The DOC's fantastic system of Great Walks allows people of all ages and fitness levels to enjoy the beauty of New Zealand.

■ LAKE WAIKAREMOANA

LAKE WAIKAREMOANA TRACK SEGMENTS	DISTANCE	TIME
Onepoto Trailhead to Panekiri Hut	8.8km	5hr.
Panekiri Hut to Waiopaoa Hut and Campsite	7.6km	3½hr.
Waiopaoa Hut and Campsite to Marauiti Hut	12.1km	4½hr.
Korokoro Campsite		1¼hr.
Maranui Campsite:		2½hr.
Marauiti Hut		30min.
Marauiti Hut to Waiharuru Hut and Campsite	6.2km	2hr.
Waiharuru Hut and Campsite to Hopuruahine Trailhead	10.5km	3½hr.
Tapuaenui Campsite		1¼hr.
Whanganui Hut		1hr.
Hopuruahine Landing		35min.
Hopuruahine Trailhead		40min.

With its vast tangles of native trees and kiwis crying through the night, the Lake Waikaremoana (WIE-kah-ray-moe-AH-nah) Track in **Te Urewera National Park** (see p. 173) affords an ideal opportunity to experience New Zealand's bizarre biology. Much of the track cuts through dense bush along the lakefront, where another hooting bird or azure inlet is never far off. But then there's the occasional wide-open marshland, where long grasses bend with the breeze and humming insects drown out most other sounds. And who could forget spectacular Panekiri Bluff, with its sweeping panoramas out over one of New Zealand's most beautiful lakes? Nevertheless, the Lake Waikaremoana Track remains, first and foremost, a mellow walk in the woods.

Trailheads: Trampers can begin at either **Onepoto** (which hits the toughest climb right off the bat), a 20min. drive south of the visitors center and 500m off SH38, or **Hopuruahine** (which leaves Panekiri Bluff for when one's pack is lighter), 1km off SH38 a 30min. drive north of the visitors center.

Transportation: Waikaremoana Guided Tours (☎837 3729) shuttles trampers between the Waikaremoana Motor Camp and **Onepoto** ($15), **Hopuruahine Landing** ($15), **Waiopaoa Hut** ($80), **Korokoro Campsite** ($80), **Marauiti Hut** ($70), and **Waiharuru Hut** ($70). Though *Let's Go* does not recommend it, hitchhiking to and from the trailheads is a cheaper but far more time-consuming endeavor.

Seasonality: It's possible to complete the track year-round, but it gets awfully boggy and cold in winter. The best weather generally lasts from mid-Oct.-Mar.

Huts and Campsites: 5 huts and 5 campsites. **Booking system** required year-round. The Aniwaniwa Visitor Centre, SH38, Private Bag 2213, Wairoa (☎837 3722) handles phone and postal reservations. Huts $14, under 18 $7; camping $10, under 18 $5. Untreated water, wood or gas heating stoves, and toilets.

Gear: A **stove, fuel,** and **matches**.

Storage: Free at the Waikaremoana Motor Camp store.

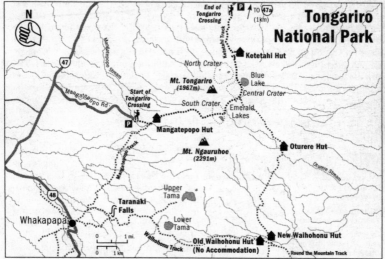

ONEPOTO TRAIL HEAD TO PANEKIRI HUT. The Onepoto Trailhead does not announce itself as such, but the small trail beside the DOC sign in the grassy field just off SH38 is indeed the start of the Lake Waikaremoana Track. After passing a small shelter, the trail briefly follows a wide grassy track until it reaches a fork for **Lake Kiriopukae** (return 20min.). The lake can be a nice picnic spot but is otherwise not worth visiting. From the fork, the track makes a calf-burning 600m ascent up **Panekiri Bluff.** A gauntlet of roots leads through wind-wracked forest, which every so often parts to reveal (weather permitting) a fresh vista of the lake waters far below. The steepest section comes within the first hour, after which the incline mellows some as it winds up the ridge of the Panekiri Range. There is **no water** on this section of the trail; trampers should pack well over two liters to prevent dehydration. The highest bunch of beds on the track, tall-ceilinged **Panekiri Hut** (1180m; 36 beds) perches on a ridge with a two-way view: the lake lies to the north, while the Hawke's Bay region's cleaved hills roll into the southern horizon.

PANEKIRI HUT TO WAIOPAOA HUT AND CAMPSITE. From Panekiri Hut, the track drops steadily, often steeply, passing plenty of tree ferns, tea trees (kanuka), and mossy rock walls. Snug **Waiopaoa Hut** (21 beds) sits at the base of the bluff; nearby **Waiopaoa Campsite** lies by a frog-filled inlet. As with all of the track's lakefront campsites, sandflies mar this otherwise lovely spot.

WAIOPAOA HUT AND CAMPSITE TO MARAUITI HUT. A flat stretch of lakeside track leads to the turn-off for the stunning **Korokoro Falls** (return 1hr.), where hundreds of rivulets gush down a vertical stone slab. **Korokoro Campsite** lies on a lagoon shortly after the turn-off for the falls (head right after the bridge). From the campsite, the track follows some reasonable ups and downs above the shoreline. Past a private hut and the DOC warden's quarters sits **Maranui Campsite,** with a choice inlet view and surrounding bluffs. **Marauiti Hut** (22 beds) waits on the other side of a peninsular hill, on the edge of a cove perfect for fishing or swimming.

MARAUITI HUT TO WAIHARURU HUT AND CAMPSITE. Beyond Marauiti, the track continues to undulate gently, as does its surface—this is the muddiest part of the tramp. Super-posh **Waiharuru Hut** (40 beds), the nicest hut north of the Routeburn, features separate kitchen and bunkroom buildings, a gas heater, washrooms, and wide porches overlooking the lake. Adjacent **Waiharuru Campsite** borders what could almost be called a beach.

WAIHARURU HUT AND CAMPSITE TO HOPURUAHINE TRAILHEAD. A kilometer past the Waiharuru complex, the track runs a steep 100m over the **Puketukutuku peninsula.** On the other side of the hill, sites at the otherwise undistinguished **Tapuaenui campsite** are well segregated by shrubbery. Largely flat hiking along some of Waikaremoana's most striking inlets leads to **Whanganui Hut** (18 beds), which rests next to a creek but has minimal lake access. The subsequent walk to **Hopuuahine Landing** (where Waikaremoana Guided Tours picks up its passengers) is brisk and undaunting, as are the remaining kilometers through grassy fields and up a river valley to the **Hopuruahine Trailhead.**

◤ TONGARIRO NORTHERN CIRCUIT

TONGARIRO NORTHERN CIRCUIT SEGMENTS	DISTANCE	TIME
Whakapapa Village to Mangatepopo Hut	8.5km	2½hr.
Mangatepopo Hut to Emerald Lakes Junction	7.7km	3½hr.
Emerald Lakes to Ketetahi Hut (Road End) or Oturere Hut	9.3km or 3.3km	3½hr. or 2hr.
Emerald Lakes Junction		3½hr.
Ketetahi Hut (Crossing)		1½hr.
Ketetahi Road End (Crossing End)		1½hr.
Oturere Hut (Circuit)		2hr.
Oturere Hut to New Waihohonu Hut	8.5km	3hr.
New Waihohonu Hut to Whakapapa Village	15.5km	5hr.
Tama Lakes Junction		3hr.
Taranaki Loop Junction		1hr.
Whakapapa Village		1hr.

Winding around the park's trinity of volcanoes, the Tongariro Northern Circuit in the **Tongariro National Park** (see p. 190) unveils the area's unique otherworldly landscape—in depth. A landscape pocked with steaming vents, technicolor lakes, and bizarre rock formations, it trembles in the shadows of Mt. Ngauruhoe's perfect cone, Mt. Tongariro's jumbled mass, and Mt. Ruapehu's slumbering snow-covered hothead. The Tongariro Crossing, from Ngauruhoe's daunting loft to the unreal colors of Red Crater and the Emerald Lakes—from the lifeless, blackened earth on the way up to the soft tussocked slopes of the way down—the Crossing is one head-spinner of a hike. Acclaimed as the best one day hike in the country, the Northern Circuit's highlights are not exclusive to that stretch. Beyond where the two part ways, the Circuit leads to a field of lava flows, each as intricate as any sculpture, a tranquil (if mystifyingly solitary) patch of native forest, the Tama Lakes, and the Taranaki Falls. The Tongariro Northern Circuit is one of the country's most breathtaking walks, and it's worth hiking the whole track.

Trailheads: Start from **Whakapapa Village,** the **Mangatepopo** road-end (6km off SH47), the **Ketetahi** road-end (1km off SH46), or **SH1.** Most begin and end in Whakapapa Village. To **avoid the crowds on the Crossing,** consider spending a night at Mangatepopo Hut the night before. The first shuttle buses don't drop off passengers until almost 8am, so early risers will be ahead of the pack all day.

Transportation: Alpine Scenic Tours (☎07 386 8918, mobile 025 937 281) cycles among the **trailheads, Turangi, National Park Village,** and **Whakapapa Village** (1-3 per day; return $20). **Tongariro Track Transport** (☎07 892 3716, mobile 021 256 3109) runs daily Oct.-Apr. from **National Park Village** (departs 7:45am) and **Whakapapa Village** (departs 8am) to **Mangatepopo** (return $15, under 16 or over 65 $10), and picks up at **Ketetahi** (4:30 and 6pm). Some area hostels also run on-demand shuttles in the summer. **Hitchhiking** to any of the trailheads is usually difficult, and *Let's Go* does not recommend it. Leaving a **car** unattended is a bad idea—the Mangatepopo and Ketetahi car parks are among the country's most unsafe.

Seasonality: Harsch conditions due to high altitudes and extreme exposure. Winter is a technical tramp necessitating equipment and experience. Dec.-Mar are safest; Feb. most stable weather patterns.

Huts and Campsites: Four 26-bed **huts.** Late Oct.-early Jun., on-site wardens, gas cookers, and require a **Great Walks pass** ($14-18). **Tent plots** ($10-$12). Late Jun.-early Sept. backcountry ticket system (huts $10, tent sites $5).

Gear: Raincoat, fleece or wool layer, water, lunch, sunscreen, and chocolate. In winter ice pick and crampons.

Storage: Whakapapa Visitor Centre $3 per bag.

WHAKAPAPA VILLAGE TO MANGATEPOPO HUT. The section of track from Whakapapa Village to **Mangatepopo Hut** crosses several streams and affords memorable views across tawny tussock to the volcanoes. However, it is extremely rutted and can get very muddy in adverse weather, so some folks skip this section. The hut itself, 25min. from the Mangatepopo road-end, faces Mt. Tongariro, Mt. Ngauruhoe, and the ridge that connects them. Its vistas stretch west to Mt. Taranaki and the Tasman Sea; sunsets here are intense.

MANGATEPOPO HUT TO EMERALD LAKES JUNCTION. From the hut, a faint spur path leads to the wispy waterfalls of **Soda Springs** (return 15min.). The track up the ridge is quite steep, but the climb's over in less than an hour. At the top, cold winds blow across **South Crater,** a Mars-like world scoured almost clean of plant life. A side trip leads up the great **Mt. Ngauruhoe** (2291m; ascent 2hr., descent 45min.), whose summit yields the all-encompassing views one expects at 2291m. Much of the climb is unmarked, but if you follow the rocks on the way up and the scree on the way down, it's unlikely you'll get lost. The main track continues across South Crater's flat expanse, then ascends another steep ridge to the rim of steaming **Red Crater.** From here, a well-marked spur route leads very gradually to the peak of **Mt. Tongariro** (1967m; return 1½hr.). Meanwhile, the main track skirts Red Crater's edge and climbs to the track's highest point (1886m), where first views of the limpid Emerald Lakes reward the work. It's just a quick, steep scree-run down to their scenic and (we have to say it) smelly shores.

EMERALD LAKES TO KETETAHI HUT (ROAD END) OR OTURERE HUT. At the **Emerald Lakes Junction,** just beyond those amazing green pools, trampers completing the Northern Circuit have a choice. They can head north to Ketetahi Hut or veer southeast to Oturere Hut. A ½hr. off the main circuit, **Ketetahi** offers thrilling views of Lakes Rotoaira and Taupo, but the Crossing crosses its front porch—literally—so the place turns into a major thoroughfare on pleasant afternoons; the nearby Ketetahi Hot Springs are on private land and off-limits. Past the hut, the track drops rather steeply, the surrounding vegetation changes from tussock to podocarp forest, and eventually the Ketetahi road-end appears (2hr.). Heading toward Oturere from the junction, the track drops steeply into a valley strewn with chunks of lava that have hardened into cool shapes and pinnacles. Several waterfalls cascade down the cliffs that cradle this fascinating area, exposing layers of ash, lava, and sediment. The Circuit cuts a relatively flat path across the valley floor, at the end of which, on a ledge overlooking a waterfall and stream, sits **Oturere,** generally the quietest hut—and the best at which to catch a stunning sunrise.

OTURERE HUT TO NEW WAIHOHONU HUT. Beyond Oturere, the track winds over a series of sand and gravel hills studded with the occasional wind-whipped treelet. After about two hours, the path crosses a river to enter honest-to-gosh forest, ascends through cool beeches to a view-filled ridge, and descends again through forest to **New Waihohonu Hut,** which stares Mt. Ruapehu straight in the face. Those who reach the hut with energy to spare can head a bit farther along the main track, then follow signposts to the **Ohinepango Springs** (return 1hr.), where exquisitely tasty (and freezing cold) water bubbles straight out of the ground.

NEW WAIHOHONU HUT TO WHAKAPAPA VILLAGE. Just a bit beyond New Waihohonu a spur trail leads to century-old **Old Waihohonu Hut** (return 6min.), which is unlivable and filled with decades of tramper graffiti. The track rises and falls only slightly (but repeatedly) as it continues through stream-fed tussockland to the turn-off for the Tama Lakes: **Lower Tama** (return 20min.), a shining blue pool couched in a canyon far below; and crescent-shaped **Upper Tama** (return 1½hr.), which lies steeply uphill amid wind-buffeted vistas that sweep far beyond the park. The final stretch forks about an hour short of Whakapapa Village; an upper route travels through more tussock terrain, while the equidistant, forested lower route goes past the brilliant 20m **Taranaki Falls.**

WHANGANUI RIVER JOURNEY

WHANGANUI RIVER JOURNEY	
SEGMENTS	DISTANCE
Cherry Grove to Whakahoro Hut	**57km**
Ohinepane Campsite	22km
Poukaria Campsite	14km
Maharanui Campsite	17km
Whakahoro Hut	4km
Whakahoro Hut to Mangapa-papa Marae	**40.5km**
Mangapapa Campsite	11km
Ohauora Campsite	16km
John Coull Hut	10.5km
Mangapapapa Marae	3km
Mangapapapa Marae to Tieke Marae	**25.5km**
Mangawaiiti Campsite	6km
Mangapurua Landing and Campsite	9km
Tieke Marae	10.5km
Tieke Marae to Pipiriki Landing	**21.5km**
Ngaporo Campsite	12.5km
Pipiriki Landing	9km

Not only is the Whanganui River Journey the only **Great Walk** over water, but **Whanganui National Park's** (see p. 209) Great Walk also provides an outdoor experience unique to New Zealand. Those who paddle between the river's steep banks will meet rapids, an endless number of green, worried-looking goats, and hundreds of waterfalls. Moreover, the journey passes numerous reminders of its long human history, from the Lombardy poplars planted by missionaries to the iron moorings used by steamers headed upstream. The tramp also has a living legacy in its two *marae*, Tieke and Mangapapapa, both of which welcome overnight guests.

Trailheads: Heads downstream from **Cherry Grove,** near Taumarunui, to **Pipiriki** landing.

Transportation: On-river transport, **Bridge to Nowhere Jets** runs upriver from Pipiriki to its namesake. (☎06 385 4128. Return 4hr. $70, children under 10 $35, under 3 free.)

Seasonality: Dec. and Jan. and weekends are most busy. The water gets cold and the weather gets rainier Jun.-Sept., making crowds a non-issue and experience a must.

Huts and Campsites: Oct.-Apr. DOC charges a flat fee of $25 for paddlers spending 2-6 nights anywhere (be it hut or campsite) on the river ($35 for those who don't buy the pass before starting the journey). 1-night passes are available (jetboaters $10, children $5. canoeists $6, children $3.) The huts have water and cooking facilities; the campsites have small cooking shelters and usually have water, but no stoves. May-Sept. huts revert to the backcountry ticket system ($10 per night), and camping is free. The 2 *marae* dispute the pass system and receive only voluntary donations.

Gear: Check out the *Guide to the Whanganui River* that describes the river and its rapids in detail ($9 from DOC). Outfitters: **Tieke Canoes** (☎06 385 4128. 5 days $50 per person, 3 days $30 per person); **Plateau Outdoor Adventure Guides** (☎0508 752 832. kayaks 5 days $130 per person, 3 days $110 per person; canoes 5 days $650, 3 days $390; min. 4 people.); **Wades Landing Outdoors** (☎07 895 5995; mobile 025 797 238. kayaks $130 for 5 days, $115 for 3; canoes $140-150 per person for 5 days, $125-140 per person for 3.); **Blazing Paddles** (☎07 895 8074; 5-day kayak or Canadian canoe rental $134 per person, 3-day rental $113 per person). **Te Whare Ponga Trust,** based in Wanganui but owned by a Maori family from the Whanganui River, runs **guided tours** offering insight into the river's spiritual and historical significance (☎06 343 9627. $160-200 per person per day, 10 person min. Canoe rental $25 per person per day.)

Storage: Most outfitters can also hold onto extra gear.

CHERRY GROVE TO WHAKAHORO HUT. This two-day leg covers the vast majority of the journey's rapids. Paddlers begin near Taumarunui at **Cherry Grove,** where the Ongarue and Whanganui rivers meet. Roads and grazing farm animals surround the introductory stretch of river. Large, lawn-like **Ohinepane Campsite**

provides the first opportunity to stop and camp. The next two campsites, **Poukaria** and **Maharanui,** feature flat ground and lush bush and tend to be quieter than the road-accessible Ohinepane. Between these rise the imposing carved **niu poles,** where Hau Hau warriors used to pray before embarking for battle. Also road-accessible, **Whakahoro Hut** (16 beds) is a homey old schoolhouse blessed with electricity; the grassy field outside makes a perfect tent pitch. Unfortunately, reaching this former *pa* site is no easy task for those already on the river—it involves a 600m upriver paddle (to a landing past the bridge) and then a 500m uphill climb.

WHAKAHORO HUT TO MANGAPAPAPA MARAE. From Whakahoro on, dramatic cliffs steady the flow of the river. Somewhere before the next hut hunches **Taniwha Rock,** on which legend dictates that travelers must place a sprig of green or risk the wrath of the river's guardians. However, as few people remember which rock is Taniwha, most paddlers take their chances. Stairs of rounded stone lead up to grassy **Mangapapapa Campsite,** but it's easier to land by the less romantic wooden ones a few meters down river. **Ohauora Campsite** lies across the river from **Tamatea's Cave,** named for a former temporary inhabitant (who was also the first man to explore the whole river), which exhibits a small glowworm show by night. Roomy **John Coull Hut** (30 beds) sports plenty of burners and natural history tidbits. The next possible rest stop, unmarked **Mangapapapa Marae,** is a bit hard to find— watch for a leftward bend in the river, with a sheer white bluff on the right and a wide beach with a faint path leading uphill on the left. The tiny and tidy *kainga* (village), which has a centuries-old legacy at this site, was reestablished in 1996. As of this writing, the *marae* has no permanent residents, though any and all visitors are welcome to visit, pitch a tent, or even sleep inside (provided, of course, that they leave everything as they found it). However, community elders do plan to return by early 2002; if you'd like to stay at Mangapapa, leave advance notice with Patrick (☎ 06 385 8258), who can give you an update on the current situation.

MANGAPAPAPA MARAE TO TIEKE MARAE. At **Mangawaiiti Campsite,** marked "CAMP-SITE," a long staircase leads above the river to some beautiful plots, all set about with ponga trees. **Mangapurua Campsite** rests on the river's right bank across the water from **Mangapurua Landing,** which is on the left bank. From the landing, an easy walk of 30-40 minutes leads deep into the bush, opening onto an astounding view of the ponga canopy, with a tannin-stained stream far below, and in the middle of it all, a perfectly ordinary concrete bridge. This **Bridge to Nowhere** is the last remnant of an isolated WWI rehabilitation settlement, which officially failed in 1942. Back on the water, the river leads to the well-marked **Tieke** (TEE-ehh-kee) **Marae,** a hospitable settlement hosting a rotating roster of caretakers who urge guests to make themselves at home in the kitchen, on the mattresses in bunk room, or atop the beautiful lawn. Reestablished in 1993 and larger than Mangapapa, Tieke functions primarily as a community center for Whanganui Maori families, though recently it has been working with DOC to create a new sleeping house and kitchen for passing paddlers. Across the river, the unrelated, privately owned Raumanui Campsite charges $5 a camper.

TIEKE MARAE TO PIPIRIKI LANDING. This final stretch holds several of the journey's largest rapids. Set between two rather choppy sections, **Ngaporo Campsite** makes for nice, well-perched tenting, framed by sheer gray rock faces. By the time **Pipiriki Landing** appears at journey's end, the native forest has again yielded to cleared sheep fields.

⚑ ABEL TASMAN COASTAL TRACK

One of New Zealand's best-loved and most-walked tramps, the easygoing Abel Tasman Coast Track in the **Abel Tasman National Park** (see p. 254), is as stunning as it is colorful. Emerald forests give glimpses of turquoise through the trees, until, eventually, those trees open onto azure bays and the park's famous golden beaches. The Coast Track's lingering pockets of private enterprise and occasionally maddening crowds may not please wilderness-hungry trampers, but its scenery remains scintillating and accessible.

ABEL TASMAN COASTAL TRACK		
SEGMENTS	DISTANCE	TIME
Marahau Trailhead to Anchorage Hut and Campsite	**11.5km**	**3hr.**
Tinline Creek Campsite		30min.
Appletree Bay Campsite		40min.
Stilwell Bay Campsite		25min.
Akersten Bay Campsite		10min.
Watering Cove Campsite		1hr.
Anchorage Hut and Campsite		15min.
Anchorage Hut To Bark Bay Hut	**9.5km**	**2½hr.- 3hr.**
Torrent Bay Estuary Campsite (time depends on the tide)		20min. -1hr.
Torrent Bay Township		20min.
Medlands Beach Campsite		1½hr.
Bark Bay Beach Campsite		15min.
Bark Bay Hut and Campsite		5min.
Bark Bay Hut to Awaroa Hut	**11.5km**	**3-4hr.**
Tonga Quarry Campsite		1hr.
Onetahuti Beach Campsite		20min.
Awaroa Hut and Campsite: via inland route or via Awaroa Lodge		2½hr. or 1¾hr.
Awaroa Hut to Totaranui Campground	**5.5km**	**1½hr.**
Waiharakeke Campsite		40min.
Totaranui Campground		50min.
Totaranui Campground to Wainui Carpark	**13km.**	**3¾hr.**
Anapai Campsite		45min.
Mutton Cove Campsite		45min.
Whariwharangi Hut and Campsite		1hr.
Wainui Campsite		1¼hr

Trailheads: Marahau in the south and **Wainui Carpark** in the north. An intermediate point at **Totaranui** is also car-accessible, and **water taxis** (see **Transportation** below) can make any point a start or finish.

Transportation: Abel Tasman Coachlines (☎548 0281) between Motueka and Marahau (30min.; Nov.-Apr. 3 per day, May-Oct. 2 per day; $7) and between Takaka and Wainui carpark (30min.; Nov.-Apr. 2 per day, May-Oct. 1 per day; $7); **Kahurangi Bus Services** (☎525 9434) does the same Nov.-Apr. only: Motueka-Marahau (3-4 per day, $7), Takaka-Wainui (1 per day, $8). Though *Let's Go* does not recommend it, **hitchhiking** to or from Marahau is easier than from Wainui carpark. The latter is easiest within an hour on either side of low tide, when one can cut across Wainui Bay to a busier stretch of Abel Tasman Dr. Inside the park, **water-taxis** service the track's coastal sections, heading north from **Marahau** to **Torrent Bay** (30min.-1hr., $17-18), **Bark Bay** (40min.-1½hr., $20-21), **Onetahuti Beach/Tonga Bay** (45min.-1¾hr., $23), **Awaroa Bay** (1½hr.-2¼hr., $27-30), and **Totaranui** (1¼hr.-3hr., $29-30), then looping back. On calm days, some travel beyond Totaranui on demand (usually min. 2 people). The following run daily: **Abel Tasman Aqua Taxi** (☎527 8083, 0800 278 282) has the fastest boats and departs Marahau Oct.-Apr. 9, 10:30am, noon, and 1:30pm and May-Sept. 9am and 1:30pm; **Abel Tasman Enterprises** (☎528 7801, 0800 223 582) departs May-Sept. 9am and noon, Oct.-Apr. 9am; **Abel Tasman Seal Swim and Water Taxi** (☎0800 527 8136; departs Nov.-Apr. 8:45am and 1pm); **Marahau Beach Camp** (☎527 8176, 0800 808 018) departs Oct.-Apr. 9am and 1:30pm; **Abel Tasman Water Taxis** (☎528 7497, 0800 423 397) departs Nov.-Apr. 9, 10:30, 11:30am, 1, 1:30, 2:30pm.

Tides: It is possible to cross **Awaroa Inlet** on foot only within 2hr. on either side of low tide (though Awaroa Lodge runs a launch across M-F 1hr. before high tide, $5). **Onetahuti Beach** has a river best crossed within 4hr. on either side of low tide. **Tide tables** posted at area visitors centers and in each hut.

Seasonality: Christmas and Easter are the busiest.

Huts and Campsites: 4 **huts** on a **booking system**, Oct.-Apr. ($14). DOC accepts bookings starting July 1 for the following season. May-Sept. still require a **Great Walks pass** but it is not necessary to book a spot in advance ($13-10). The track's 21 **campsites** require a Great Walks pass year-round ($9-7). All huts and most campsites have toilets and taps.

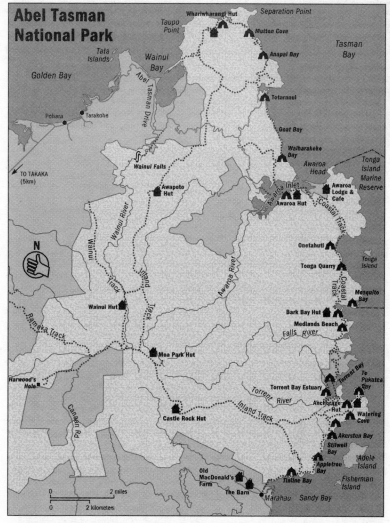

Abel Tasman National Park

Golden Bay
Tata Islands
Wainui Bay
Tasman Bay
Taupo Point
Wharwharangi Hut
Separation Point
Mutton Cove
Anapai Bay
Pohara
Tarakohe
Totaranui
TO TAKAKA (5km)
Abel Tasman Drive
Wainui Falls
Goat Bay
Waiharakeke Bay
Awaroa Head
Awapoto Hut
Awaroa Inlet
Awaroa Lodge & Cafe
Awaroa Hut
Tonga Island Marine Reserve
N
Wainui River
Inland Track
Awaroa River
Onetahuti
Tonga Quarry
Tonga Island
Coastal Track
Wainui Hut
Ramaka Track
Bark Bay Hut
Medlands Beach
Falls River
Mesquito Bay
Moa Park Hut
Harwood's Hole
Camban Rd
Torrent River
Torrent Bay Estuary
Torrent Bay
Te Pukatea Bay
Anchorage Hut
Watering Cove
Castle Rock Hut
Inland Track
Akersten Bay
Stilwell Bay
Adele Island
Appletree Bay
Fisherman Island
Old MacDonald's Farm
Tinline Bay
The Barn
Marahau
Sandy Bay
0   2 miles
0   2 kilometers

Gear: A stove, fuel, matches, insect repellent, and waterproof sandals. Check out the "Abel Tasman National Park **Free Map.**" Rent gear from **White Elephant** or **Twin Oaks Cottage** in Motueka (see p. 253) or **Old Macdonald's Farm** in Marahau.

Storage: Most accommodations store for free. **Kahurangi Bus Services** charges $5 per bag for transport between Motueka and Takaka.

MARAHAU TRAILHEAD TO ANCHORAGE HUT AND CAMPSITE. Beginning at the southern end of the park, the track proceeds past the unremarkable trailside grass that marks **Tinline Creek Campsite** (15 sites), down to the long and lovely beach at **Appletree Bay Campsite** (15 sites). **Stilwell Bay Campsite** (3 sites) is on a nice beach, but high tide can create an access problem. Shortly thereafter a switchback descent to **Akersten Bay Campsite** (5 sites) offers terraced sites among trees next to a small beach. From here, the track rises to a ridge, giving some stunning sea views of **Anchorage Bay.** A steep side trip down the other side of the ridge leads to the excellent sites of **Watering Cove Campsite** (10 sites), right on the beach. The main track descends more gradually to a wide, golden, and often rather busy arc of sand, with the modest **Anchorage Hut** (24 bunks) nearby. The wide field next door is **Anchorage Campsite** (50 sites), a veritable tent town with drying lines and heaps of taps. Both Anchorage Hut and Campsite have taps that dispense **filtered drinking water** from October to April.

About a 10min. walk from Anchorage Campsite is the secluded **Te Pukatea Bay Campsite** (10 sites), on a perfect golden crescent hemmed by lush headlands. There's no water on-site, but the sublime sunrise makes up for any inconvenience. It was here and at nearby **Pitt Head** that Te Rauparaha's forces slaughtered the local Ngati Apa in 1828, taking few prisoners and burying no bodies.

ANCHORAGE HUT TO BARK BAY HUT. To continue toward Bark Bay from Anchorage without doubling back up the ridge go all the way to the western edge of the beach, where a signpost points to the high-tide route (1hr.) and low-tide route (20min.) to Torrent Bay Estuary. A side trip off the high tide route, **Cleopatra's Pool** (return 20min.) sees water spill down a rocky chute into a magnificent pebble-bottomed swimming hole.

Neither **Torrent Bay Estuary Campsite** (6 sites) nor nearby **Torrent Bay Campsite** (10 sites) are terribly ideal—the former overlooks a mudflat half the time, while the latter is in a grove of pines. Near Torrent Bay Campsite a path leads to the densely forested upstream portion of the **Falls River** (return 3hr.). Tiny **Torrent Bay Township** is most notable for its **public telephone** with free local calls. Back in the wilderness, **Medlands Beach Campsite** (6 sites) offers sandy plots framed by a gorgeous combination of estuary and surf. **Bark Bay Campsite** (40 sites) is a crowded, kanuka-filled monster, though the bay is big and beautiful. Just before the spacious rooms and freshwater shower of the inland **Bark Bay Hut** (25 bunks), the miniscule **Bark Bay Hut Campsite** (5 sites) is hidden, yet only paces off the track. Both Bark Bay Hut and Bark Bay Beach Campsite have **filtered drinking water** from October to April.

BARK BAY HUT TO AWAROA HUT. The track crosses Bark Bay estuary (an alternative high-tide route goes around the inlet) and then winds steadily up and over a small peninsula before hitting **Tonga Quarry Campsite** (20 sites), which features a stream, a nice white stretch of sand, and some big blocks of stone from the old quarry days. Another brief up-and-over breaks onto the huge, golden arc of **Onetahuti Beach,** host to the ample **Onetahuti Campsite** (20 sites) and, all too often, scores of buzzing water taxis. The track runs the length of the beach until, after about 20min., it crosses a river at the northern end that can rise chest-high at high tide (see **Essentials: Tides** p. 364 for more on timing your crossing).

Heading back inland, the track climbs gently toward the **Awaroa Lodge**, a swank resort and restaurant that runs a **barge** across Awaroa Inlet for those anxious to continue their tramping, no matter what the tide. (☎528 8758. Barge M-F 1hr. before high tide; $5. Restaurant open daily 7:30-10am, 11:30am-2:30pm, and 5:30-8:30pm. Burger $17, soup $12. Free toilets and drinking water. Hot shower $5, sauna $10.) Even those not interested in the barge can pass through this posh slice of civilization en route to **Awaroa Inlet;** the route takes an hour less than the main track, though at high tide it navigates a waist-deep stream. Simple **Awaroa Hut** (25 bunks) and the hard-packed dirt of neighboring **Awaroa Campsite** (18 sites) sit beside the inlet, which becomes a pebbly and crossable mudflat within two hours on either side of low tide. Change into sandals even at dead low tide; there are always lingering streams to ford.

HEAPHY TRACK		
SEGMENTS	DISTANCE	TIME
Brown Hut to Perry Saddle Hut	17km	5hr.
Aorere Shelter		3hr.
Perry Saddle Hut		2hr.
Perry Saddle Hut to Gouland Downs Hut	8km	2hr.
Gouland Downs Hut to Saxon Hut	5km	1½hr.
Saxon Hut to Mackay Hut	14km	3hr.
Mackay Hut to Lewis Hut	13.5km	3½hr.
Lewis Hut to Heaphy Hut	8km	2½hr.
Heaphy Hut to Kohaihai carpark	16.5km	4½hr.
Katipo Shelter		2hr.
Scotts Beach Campsite		1½hr.
Kohaihai carpark		1hr.

AWAROA HUT TO TOTARANUI CAMPGROUND. After the inlet, the track turns inland again before it comes to the grassy plots and long nearby beach of **Waiharakeke Campsite** (10 sites). The track then passes a couple of huge beech trees and stunning Goat Beach before emerging into the caravan sprawl of Totaranui (see **Accommodations and Food**).

TOTARANUI CAMPGROUND TO WAINUI CARPARK. Comprised of hillier terrain than other parts of the track, lined with majestic beaches, and featuring superior overnight options, this section is arguably the Coast Track's most beautiful. It also attracts fewer day-trippers, since the water taxis rarely venture north of Totaranui. **Anapai Bay Campsite** (4 sites) lies next to a beach fringed by fluted rock faces, its sites concealed inside a dense canopy of windswept kanuka. **Mutton Cove Campsite** (20 sites) also sits alongside an elegant beach, though unsightly felled pines mar its plots. From Mutton Cove the track forks for an extra loop around **Separation Point** (return 1hr.), a walk through kanuka-clad hillsides that leads to a lighthouse with misty vantages of Farewell Spit, the North Island, and the occasional fur seal. The main track descends gradually to **Whariwharangi Hut** (20 bunks), an old two-storey farmhouse with freshwater showers and the fields of **Whariwharangi Campsite** (20 sites) outside. The rugged beach nearby may have seen the first brutal Maori-Pakeha encounter upon Abel Tasman's arrival to New Zealand (see p. 56). Only one very large (but very scenic and gradually graded) hill stands between Whariwharangi and the carpark.

⚡ HEAPHY TRACK

The longest of the overland Great Walks, the Heaphy Track in the **Kahurangi National Park** (see p. 259) is also the most diverse. It traverses no fewer than four completely different ecosystems as it winds from east to west: mountain beech forests, flat and tussock-tufted expanses (or "downs"), primary podocarp forests, and the palm-intensive beachgasm at journey's end. For the past century, environmentalists have managed to keep the proposed road that would connect Collingwood and Karamea in the planning stages. Though the issue has returned to the table in recent years, for now the Heaphy provides a glimpse of Kahurangi's still largely unexplored natural richness.

Trailheads: Brown Hut, 28km southeast of **Collingwood** (see p. 258) and **Kohaihai Carpark,** 16km north of **Karamea** (see p. 260); most start at Brown Hut.

Transportation: Bickley Motors (☎525 8352) runs Oct.-Apr. daily from Takaka to the trailhead (1¼hr., 10am, $22) via Collingwood; the bus departs the trailhead at 12:15pm. **Kahurangi Bus Services** (☎525 9434) runs earlier in the day (departs Takaka 9:30am, trailhead 11:15am; $20). **Farewell Spit Tours** (☎524 8257) runs on demand any time between Brown Hut and **Collingwood** ($15). **Karamea Express** (☎782 6916) runs Oct.-Apr. daily between Karamea and Kohaihai (departs Karamea 1:45pm, departs Kohaihai 2pm; $5) and on demand year-round ($25 up to 5 people, $5 per additional person). **Karamea Taxis** (☎782 6757) runs any time on demand ($25 up to 4 people, $6 each additional person). **Hitching** to either trailhead can be difficult, as there is no through traffic; though *Let's Go* doesn't recommend it, patient hitchers report success.

Seasonality: Dec., Jan., and Feb. are the busiest; Mar. and Apr. have mildest weather.

Huts and Campsites: 7 huts, 5 of which (Perry Saddle, Saxon, Mackay, Lewis, and Heaphy) have gas cookers. Oct.-Apr. requires **Great Walks pass** ($14). May-Sept. reverts to backcountry hut system ($10). DOC officially permits tenting at 3 **campsites** along the track's coastal section ($7 year-round), though each hut has an adjacent cluster of boggy sites (meant for overflow when the huts are full).

Gear: Rain gear, waterproof pack liner, insect repellent. Brown Hut, Gouland Downs Hut, and the campsites require **cooking equipment.** The closest **camping gear shops** are in Motueka (see p. 253), and Westport (see p. 286); the White Elephant (see p. 254) in Motueka rents basic gear.

Storage and Baggage Transport: Most area accommodations store gear. Local visitors centers can arrange luggage transport between the trailheads (label destination prominently). Generally, it costs $5 for each change-of-hands (e.g. Collingwood to Westport $10, Collingwood to Karamea $15).

BROWN HUT TO PERRY SADDLE HUT. Brown Hut (20 bunks), just 5min. from the carpark at the track's eastern end, sports a large fireplace and free local phone calls but lacks cooking facilities. From here the track follows a broad path, climbing steadily but gently up the **Aorere Valley,** past dense beech forest and the occasional sweeping mountain view. Most of the climbing is done by **Aorere Shelter,** a three-walled affair with a grand view, water, and a toilet. About 10min. beyond the shelter, a spur trail leads to **Flanagan's Corner** (915m; return 7min.), the highest point on the track, with a sweeping panorama of the upper Aorere Valley and surrounding mountains. A gradual ascent leads to **Perry Saddle Hut** (26 bunks), perched on the edge of the valley and offering still more good views. From here, experienced hikers can climb **Mt. Perry** (return 2hr.)— the trail is unmarked and rather rough, but the views are the best yet; there are directions in the national park binder in the hut. On clear nights, the track around Perry Saddle is a promising place to hear or even see the spotted kiwi.

PERRY SADDLE HUT TO GOULAND DOWNS HUT. About an hour after Perry Saddle Hut, the trail leaves behind the patches of beech and opens onto the **Gouland Downs,** the beginning of the track's most exposed section. Windswept grass stretches to the horizon, punctuated only by tiny carnivorous sundews or the odd shoe tree. **Gouland Downs Hut** (10 beds) is the smallest and most bare on the track, with a warm stone hearth but no gas burners. The tent sites are unremarkable, but they're the grassiest you'll find between Aorere Shelter and Lewis Hut. Just a few hundred meters farther awaits a Tolkien-esque forest, full of bizarre moss-shrouded rock formations, caves, and arches. Several beautiful streams that wind through and around the limestone.

GOULAND DOWNS HUT TO SAXON HUT. The track traverses the western end of Gouland Downs, gradually re-entering beech forest; **Saxon Hut** (16 beds) sits amid decent scenery, offering one cozy room with gas cookers and a fireplace. The campsites here can get extremely wet.

SAXON HUT TO MACKAY HUT. The track winds gradually uphill, in and out of forest and the **Mackay Downs.** This area can flood quite seriously during heavy rain, and the inconsistent boardwalking means wet feet during any degree of downpour. Past many-textured variegated mosses, **Mackay Hut** (26 beds) features flush toilets and views down to the sea.

ROUTEBURN TRACK		
SEGMENTS	DISTANCE	TIME
Routeburn Shelter to Routeburn Falls Hut	**8.8km**	**2-4hr.**
Routeburn Flats Hut and Campsite		1½hr.
Routeburn Falls Hut		1½hr.
Routeburn Falls Hut To Lake Mackenzie Hut and Campsite	**11.3km.**	**5hr.**
Harris Saddle Shelter		1½hr.
Lake Mackenzie Hut and Campsite		3½hr.
Lake Mackenzie Hut and Campsite to The Divide	**12km**	**4-5½hr.**
Lake Howden Hut		3hr.
The Divide		1¼hr.

MACKAY HUT TO LEWIS HUT. From Mackay it's all downhill to the sea. As the elevation decreases, the forest changes from beech to rimu and tree fern. By the time **Lewis Hut** (20 bunks) comes into view, the bush has thickened and diversified, the beautiful nikau palm has appeared, and rata lace the hillsides with red (in summer). Lewis Hut sits at the junction of the Heaphy and Lewis Rivers and features flush toilets. **Sandflies** begin to appear here: be warned.

LEWIS HUT TO HEAPHY HUT. After Lewis, the vegetation grows more extreme. Epiphytes (plants that grow from another tree's branches) drip from giant rata, the tree ferns grow taller and taller, and after traversing four long swing bridges the track finally reaches the sea. Cheery **Heaphy Hut** (20 bunks) holds court by the mouth of the Heaphy River; highlights include a large fireplace, flush toilets, and stellar views on all sides. Its adjacent campsite is excellent: wide and grassy with a well-kept shelter. Out front there's a beach littered with driftwood, an ideal spot to watch high tide's waves surge upstream the otherwise lazy Heaphy, or the sun set over the angry Tasman Sea.

HEAPHY HUT TO KOHAIHAI CARPARK. This palm-filled stretch of track runs entirely along the coast and is almost totally flat. (NB: the surf is ferocious; riptides make the water too dangerous for swimming.) **Katipo Creek Campsite** has a small number of tent sites, an aging shelter, and a toilet, but no water. Shortly after the shelter **Crayfish Point,** floods frequently—use the cliff-side path except within two hours on either side of low tide. There are tide tables posted at Kohaihai and Heaphy Hut. The longest stretch of sand before Kohaihai is **Scotts Beach;** those on an excursion from the carpark need go no farther to enjoy the track's sublime coast. Flax and nikau palms ring **Scotts Beach Campsite,** which lies within earshot of the waves. From here, the track does its only real coastal climbing as it skirts **Kohaihai Bluff** before reaching the carpark. At Kohaihai there waits a shelter, a phone for ringing a ride, and a free campground (it's not part of the Great Walk system), with water, toilets, and a great view of the bluff.

ROUTEBURN TRACK

Lying half within **Fiordland National Park** (see p. 319) and half within **Mt. Aspiring National Park** (see p. 318), the Routeburn is the shortest of the Great Walks, and among the most spectacular. A razor-sharp bushline slices across these mountains, and the track delves through either side, passing thick forests and blue-green waterways. And then there are the vistas, at least on clear days: valley views, mountain views, glacier views, and even a far-away seascape. True, the Routeburn Track receives second billing after the Milford, but it's really an arbitrary battle for superiority between the two incredible hikes.

Trailheads: The Mt. Aspiring side of the track begins at **Routeburn Shelter,** 24km north of Glenorchy. The Fiordland side begins at **The Divide,** on the Milford Road 84km north of Te Anau (). Trampers can walk the track in either direction.

Transportation: Both **Backpackers Express** (☎442 9939) and **Upper Lake Wakatipu Tours** (☎442 9986) run between **Routeburn Shelter** and **Glenorchy** (30min., $15) or **Queenstown** (1¼hr., $30) 2-3 times a day. **Tracknet** (☎249 7777, 0800 483 2628) makes the most frequent trips to and from **The Divide** (to or from **Te Anau** 1½hr., $22; to or from **Milford Sound** 30min., $16). Although *Let's Go* does not recommend it, patient **hitchhikers** report success getting to or from The Divide; those who've tried to hitch to or from Routeburn Shelter, on the other hand, advise hitching hopefuls to have a back-up plan—since the Shelter isn't on the way to anywhere, the Backpackers Express and Upper Lake Wakatipu shuttles are sometimes the only traffic heading there from Glenorchy.

Seasonality: Year-round, however winter requires more experience and appropriate equipment. May-Nov. are very dangerous.

Huts and Campsites: Late Oct.-late Apr., the 4 huts and 2 campsites operate on the **booking system**. Dec. and Jan. are busiest, Nov., Mar., and Apr., are slower. In summer, all have gas cookers, taps, and flush toilets ($35 per night). 50% discount on a third night's stay in either the Lake Howden or Routeburn Flats Hut. Campsites have toilets and cooking shelters, but no stoves ($12). **Trampers must pick up their hut and campsite passes from a DOC office either the day before or by 2pm the day they start the track.** In winter (late April-late Oct.), the gas is removed from the huts, hut fees revert to backcountry ticket system ($10 per night); camping is free.

Gear: Appropriate winter gear necessary: ice axe, crampons, and appropriate clothing. **Topline Tours** (☎249 7505, 0508 832 628) transports **extra gear** between Te Anau and Queenstown ($5 per bag).

Storage: Most accommodations will oblige.

ROUTEBURN SHELTER TO ROUTEBURN FALLS HUT. From **Routeburn Shelter,** a gradual ascent over and along various charging blue streams leads to the turn-off (return 10min.) for **Routeburn Flats Hut** (20 beds), which fronts a dramatic tus-socked valley and the gentle Routeburn River. Fifty-odd campsites lie secluded among tall grasses, well away from the hut. The **North Branch Routeburn** (return 4hr.), a flat-ish but barely marked valley sidetrip, begins across the river and affords great views of Mt. Somnos and Mt. Nereus. Back on the main track, much steeper now, the trail ascends through the ferned and forested flanks of the Routeburn Valley's southern side. As the obvious landslide sites can attest, this stretch is at risk for avalanches, particularly in the winter but also in early and late summer. Just at the edge of the treeline perches **Routeburn Falls Hut** (48 beds), a wood-paneled palace with snazzy furniture, two separate bunkrooms, and a balcony overlooking the valley.

ROUTEBURN FALLS HUT TO LAKE MACKENZIE HUT AND CAMPSITE. This is the Routeburn's most awesome stretch, and its most exposed and potentially hazardous; observe the advice of DOC staff. (It's also strewn with large, ankle-con-demning rocks—though many are purple or pink, so watching where you walk isn't at all boring.) Initially very steep, the track passes the neighboring guided walkers' hut and roaring **Routeburn Falls** before leveling out a bit. It winds under craggy moss-encrusted peaks, then edges above **Lake Harris.** Around a few more bends, **Harris Saddle Shelter** contains toilets, emergency equipment, and tasty-look-ing food for the guided walkers. From here, a steep and poorly marked side trip leads to the top of **Conical Hill** (return 1½hr.), where on a clear day the 360° pan-orama encompasses crinkly ridges, unnamed glaciers, and valleys stretching as far as the Tasman Sea. Meanwhile, the main track sidles along the mountainside above the **Hollyford Valley** and gradually descends along the exposed Hollyford face, exposing greater views with every step. Once **Lake Mackenzie** comes into sight, the trail drops steeply to **Lake MacKenzie Hut** (48 beds), another back-country grand hotel. Step outside to see up the lake to **Emily Peak.** The campground—nine astroturf sites ringed by green trees—lies 100m farther along the trail.

LAKE MACKENZIE HUT AND CAMPSITE TO THE DIVIDE. A steep ascent brings trampers to the bushline. Easing back down, the track weaves through the naturally pastoral **Orchard,** a patch of pioneering ribbonwood trees, and, almost an hour later, passes the thundering 80m **Earland Falls;** there's an emer-gency bridge downstream in case the falls are in flood. **Lake Howden Hut** (28 beds) sits on the shores of its namesake; the junction for the **Greenstone Track** is right outside. A 20min. hike along the Greenstone leads to the **free Green-stone Saddle Campsite,** which sports a toilet but no shelter or water. (see **Green-stone and Caples** p. 380) Back at the Lake Howden junction, the track ascends to the turn-off for **Key Summit** (return 1hr.), a popular day-hike for those cruis-ing the Milford Road. A self-guided nature walk up top provides a view-enhanced crash-course in high-altitude botany and glacial geology. The main track zig-zags down to **The Divide,** where there are toilets and shelter.

▶ MILFORD TRACK

New Zealand's Holy Grail of hikes, the astounding Milford Track in the **Fiordland National Park** (see p. 319) opened in 1888 and soon became world famous. "The fin-est walk in the world!" gushed obscure but oft-quoted Victorian poet Blanche Baughan in a London paper. Since then, over a century of wide-eyed walkers have traversed the Milford's brief alpine pass and beech-lined, waterfall-laced valleys—a corner of Fiordland in all its glory. Today, DOC estimates that 12,000 people walk the track each year, and despite the high cost, tight regulation, occasional floods, and frequent downpours (the track has an average annual rainfall of 8000mm), it remains a singular experience in most trampers' memories.

Trailheads: The track begins at Glade Wharf at the northern tip of Lake Te Anau and ends at Sandfly Point near Milford Sound (p. 322). Both places are accessible only by boat.

Transportation: Tracknet (☎249 7777, 0800 483 2628) runs from the DOC office in Te Anau to the boat launch at **Te Anau Downs** (25min.; 9:45am and 1:15pm; $12, under 14 $8), connecting to the boat run by **Fiordland Travel** (☎249 7416, 0800 656 501) that heads across Lake Te Anau to **Glade Wharf** (1hr.; 10:30am, $38, under 14 $15; 2pm, $50, under 14 $15). From Sandfly Point, **Red Boat Cruises** (☎441 1137, 0800 657 444) runs boats to **Milford Sound Launch Terminal** (20min.; 2:30 and 3:15pm; $22.50, under 14 $12.50), where you can catch Tracknet's 3 or 5:15pm bus to **Te Anau** (2hr.; $37, under 14 $24.50). The **Great Walks Booking Desk** (see **Great Walk Passes** p. 355)

MILFORD TRACK		
SEGMENTS	DISTANCE	TIME
Glade Wharf to Clinton Hut	3.5km	1hr.
Clinton Hut to Mintaro Hut	16.5km	5½hr.
Hidden Lake		3hr.
Bus Stop Shelter		1hr.
Mintaro Hut		1½hr.
Mintaro Hut to Dumpling Hut	14km	6hr.
MacKinnon Pass Shelter		2½hr.
Quintin Hut		2½hr.
Dumpling Hut		1hr.
Dumpling Hut to Sandfly Point	18km	5hr.
Mackay Falls and Bell Rock		1¾hr.
Great Gate Shelter		2hr.
Sandfly Point		1¼hr.

can arrange these. From Sandfly Point, it's also possible to paddle into Milford Sound with **Rosco's Sea Kayaks** (☎0800 476 726; 2pm; $20, $49 with bus transport to Te Anau) or **Fiordland Wilderness Experiences** (☎249 7700, 0800 200 434; 2:30pm; $49, including bus transport to Te Anau); kayaking takes 20-30min. **Sinbad Cruises** (☎249 7106) organizes a **sail-paddle-bus** round-trip from Te Anau ($110). Though *Let's Go* does not recommend it, **hitchers** set out very early or try to catch rides the day before in order to make the early boat the first morning of the tramp; returning to Te Anau, some report that it's effective to beg rides from people getting into their cars in the Milford Sound parking lot. Tracknet shuttles **extra gear** from Te Anau to Milford Sound ($5 per bag).

Seasonality: See **Routeburn: Seasonality** p. 369.

Huts and Campsites: 6 huts: 3 for guided walkers (probably not you) and 3 for independent walkers (you). Huts are expensive, $105 with spacious common areas, flush toilet annexes, and rows of gas cookers (matches necessary but not provided). Each independent hut with its own DOC warden. Late Apr.-Oct. (the low season) has fuel for fires, flush loos, and fees revert to backcountry hut system ($10 per night). **Trampers must collect their hut passes from a DOC office either the day before or by 11am on the day they start the track.** Camping on the Milford Track is not permitted.

Bookings: Unlike any other track in New Zealand, the Milford is entirely scripted: not only must you book in advance, but you **must stay in a designated hut each night.** DOC allows 40 unguided trampers to start the track each day. It's possible to do day hikes from Te Anau and Milford Sound, but you will not reach the best scenery in such a short time. **Milford Track Guided Walks** (☎441 1138, 0800 659 255; fax 441 1124) charges $1300-1600 a head for the privilege of cooks and hot showers in upscale accommodations. **Applications** to walk the Milford independently are first-come, first-served, starting **July 2** for the following season (late Oct.-late Apr.; Dec. and Jan. fill up fast). If full, put your name on the **waiting list**—DOC will alert the freshly eligible by fax or email; couples and solo trampers have the best chances (see **Great Walk Passes** p. 355). Calls to the Booking Desk to inquire about cancellations can also sometimes yield a last-minute spot for those flexible on dates.

Gear: See **Routeburn: Gear** p. 369

Storage: Most accommodations will oblige.

TRAMPING

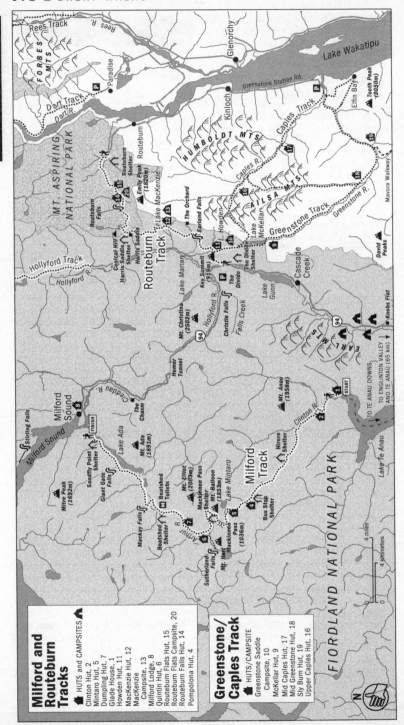

Milford and Routeburn Tracks

▲ HUTS and CAMPSITES

Clinton Hut, 2
Mintaro Hut, 5
Dumpling Hut, 7
Glade House, 1
Howden Hut, 11
MacKenzie Hut, 12
MacKenzie
    Campsite, 13
Milford Lodge, 8
Quintin Hut, 6
Routeburn Flats Hut, 15
Routeburn Flats Campsite, 20
Routeburn Falls Hut, 14
Pompolona Hut, 4

Greenstone/ Caples Track

▲ HUTS/CAMPSITE

Greenstone Saddle
    Campsite, 10
McKellar Hut, 9
Mid Caples Hut, 17
Mid Greenstone Hut, 18
Sly Burn Hut, 19
Upper Caples Hut, 16

Rees Track
FORBES MTS
Rees R.
Paradise
Dart Track
Dart R.
MT. ASPIRING NATIONAL PARK
Hollyford Track
Hollyford R.
Routeburn Falls
Conical Hill
Harris Saddle
Harris Saddle Shelter
Routeburn Shelter
Emily Peak (1820m)
Lake MacKenzie
The Orchard
Earland Falls
Lake Howden
Routeburn Track
Lake Marian
Mt. Christina (2502m)
Key Summit (919m)
The Divide Shelter
The Divide
Hollyford R.
Christie Falls
Falls Creek
Lake Gunn
Cascade Creek
Homer Tunnel
The Chasm
Cleddau R.
Milford Sound
Stirling Falls
Mitre Peak (1692m)
Sandfly Point Shelter
Giant Gate Falls
Lake Ada
Mt. Ada (1691m)
Boatshed Toilets
Mackay Falls
Boatshed Shelter
Arthur R.
Mt. Elliot (2003m)
Quintin Shelter
Mt. Balloon (1853m)
MacKinnon Pass
Sutherland Falls
Mt. Hart
MacKinnon Pass (1036m)
Lake Mintaro
Bus Stop Shelter
Clinton R.
Mt. Anau (1958m)
Hirere Shelter
START
TO TE ANAU DOWNS
TO ENGLINTON VALLEY AND TE ANAU (65 km)
Lake Te Anau
FIORDLAND NATIONAL PARK
Milford Track
Milford Sound
FINISH
94
Glenorchy
Lake Wakatipu
Greenstone Station Rd.
Kinloch
Caples Track
Caples R.
Elfin Bay
Tooth Peak (2045m)
HUMBOLDT MTS
AILSA MTS
Greenstone Track
Greenstone R.
Lake McKellar
Lake Howden
Mavora Walkway
David Peaks
Knobs Flat
EARL MTS
4 miles
4 kilometers
N

GLADE WHARF TO CLINTON HUT.
The first day out is the shortest and the flattest, passing under tall, slender beech trees and the occasional totara. Just shy of the hut, the boardwalked **Wetlands Walk** (return 10min.), leads to carnivorous sundews, explanatory plaques, and a great view out over the bog. **Clinton Hut** is a corrugated outdoor mansion near the clear Clinton River. Those on the morning boat will probably reach the hut very early in the afternoon and can take a dip in some nearby swimming holes.

CLINTON HUT TO MINTARO HUT.
Flat and slightly inclined tramping through beechy bush begins the second day's walk along the Clinton River. In dry conditions, the route fords various small rivers; in wet conditions, the route fords various mid-sized rivers; in very wet conditions, this section of the track may well become a river. After several hours,

KEPLER TRACK		
SEGMENTS	DISTANCE	TIME
Control Gates to Brod Bay Campsite	5.6km	1½hr.
Brod Bay Campsite to Mt. Luxmore Hut	8.5km	3½-4½hr.
Mt. Luxmore Hut to Iris Burn Hut.	18.6km	5-6hr.
Mt. Luxmore Hut to Forest Burn Shelter	8.3km	1½hr.
Forest Burn Shelter to Hanging Valley Shelter	4.5km	1¾hr.
Hanging Valley Shelter to Iris Burn Hut	5.8km	1¾hr.
Iris Burn Hut to Moturau Hut	17.2km	5-6hr.
Moturau Hut to Rainbow Reach	6.2km	1½-2hr.
Shallow Bay Junction		40min.
Shallow Bay Hut		20min.
Rainbow Reach		50min.
Rainbow Reach to the Control Gates	10.9km	2½-3½hr.

the track begins to wind through open stretches. Massive cliff faces rise from either side of the valley, and a new view of a waterfall, mountaintop, or glacier awaits over every little rise. A handmade sign points the way to the dramatic but carnivorous-eel-infested **Hidden Lake** (return 5min.); a safer and equally lovely swimming hole lies just a few minutes farther up the track. The way gets rougher and steeper just before passing the dank **Bus Stop** shelter and remains so as it approaches **Mintaro Hut**. A cozy two-story affair, Mintaro could hardly occupy a more imposing location: step out of the front door, staring up at the 800m rock face that towers over **Lake Mintaro**, and get ready for tomorrow. Access to the lake is 100m past the hut turn-off on the main track.

MINTARO HUT TO DUMPLING HUT. Day three is the most taxing and the most incredible, given clear skies. Twenty minutes after departing Mintaro Hut, the track makes a switchbacked ascent (the Mile 15 marker indicates the halfway point) to **MacKinnon Pass,** where spectacular scenery makes tired legs an afterthought. Vast glacial valleys spread in either direction, while kea circle over the monument to Quintin MacKinnon, the Scotsman who discovered the pass and first guided people over it. Up and over another rise (20min.) waits the **MacKinnon Pass Shelter,** a cheerless but safe place sheltering gas cookers and a loo with a view. Heading back down, the track winds beneath a cliff topped by the **Jervois Glacier,** where wispy waterfalls dissolve into mist before they reach the ground; if it's been snowing, the track may detour onto a rougher, but avalanche-safe, "emergency track." Once the trail enters the trees, a powerful series of waterfalls replaces the magnificent mountain scenery—behold the **Arthur River** beginning its journey to the sea. At **Quintin Hut,** the next guided walkers' accommodation, independent trampers can stash their packs under an overhang while they wander down the spur trail (return 1½hr.) that leads to the base of the monstrous, three-tiered, 580m **Sutherland Falls,** the highest waterfall in New Zealand and the fifth highest in the world. The crash of water into water blows out enough mist to drench anyone within 10m, to say nothing of those who venture behind the torrent. One more hour leads down to **Dumpling Hut;** the boardwalked section just before this backcountry manor hosts hundreds of glowworms.

DUMPLING HUT TO SANDFLY POINT. The final day's flat tramping passes the toilets and taps of the guided walkers' **Boatshed Shelter** shortly before reaching **Mackay Falls** and resonant **Bell Rock** (keep a torch handy to check out the water-carved interior). The shelter near **Great Gate Falls** makes a good lunch stop; from here, the track passes splendid valley views and glimpses Lake Ada as it nears **Sandfly Point.** Here, an enclosed shelter protects trampers from the point's namesake as they await transport to Milford Sound. To get the boat from Sandfly Point to Milford Sound (see **Transportation** above), trampers should depart Dumpling Hut between 8 and 9am; those on the 2:30pm boat will reach the Sound in time for afternoon cruises.

■ KEPLER TRACK

Initially opened in 1988 to relieve pressure on the Milford and Routeburn Tracks, the Kepler Track in the **Fiordland National Park** (see p. 319) more than holds its own. Not only does this track pass breathtaking ridgetops and ancient beech forests, but it's the most accessible Great Walk in the system; you can set out on foot from the middle of Te Anau, without any transportation costs or reservations, and loop right back a few amazing days later.

Trailheads: The track forms a loop, beginning and ending at the **Control Gates** at the southern end of Lake Te Anau. The Control Gates can be reached from the DOC center via a brief (45min.) walk through the Te Anau Wildlife Centre. Most walk in a counter-clockwise direction.

Transportation: Fiordland TrackNet (☎ 249 7777) runs from **Te Anau Holiday Park** (see p. 324) to the **Control Gates** ($5) and to **Rainbow Reach** ($9). (10-15min. In summer 8:30, 9:30am, 2:45, 4:45pm; in winter on demand. Pick-up from Rainbow Reach at 10am, 3, 5pm.) **Sinbad Cruises** (☎ 249 7106; mobile 025 408 080) between Te Anau and Brod Bay, departing daily at 9 and 10:30am; **Lakeland Boat Hire** (☎ 249 8364) departs at 8:30 and 9:30am (both one-way $15, same-day return $28).

Seasonality: See **Routeburn: Seasonality** p. 369.

Huts and Campsites: With gas cookers and live-in wardens during the summer ($20 per night, 3 nights $50); tent site quality varies as noted ($9). In winter, when gas and wardens are removed, the huts revert to the backcountry system ($10 per night).

Gear: See **Routeburn: Gear** p. 369

Storage: Most accommodations will oblige.

CONTROL GATES TO BROD BAY CAMPSITE. From the Control Gates, which regulate the level of Lake Te Anau for the greater glory of hydroelectric power, the track sidles easily into sandy and swim-worthy Dock Bay. Farther along the lakeshore, the long beach of Brod Bay has a toilet, several sheltered campsites, but unpurified lake water.

BROD BAY CAMPSITE TO MT. LUXMORE HUT. The track steadily climbs a series of switchbacks past great limestone bluffs (remnants of an ancient sea floor), through a lichenologist's paradise of thick-trunked beech trees, and suddenly breaks out into golden alpine tussocks with views all around (try to time your assent to catch the fabulous sunrise here). A little further, **Mt. Luxmore Hut** (60 beds) is a veritable mountain chalet with perhaps the best location of any hut in the Great Walk system. The South Fiord of Lake Te Anau and the Hidden Lakes sparkle far below, while in the distance hulk the Murchison Mountains, the last natural habitat of the fantastical takahe. The hut's famous and long-serving warden has plastered the walls with flower photos and pressed leaf specimens. Nearby are the spooky **Luxmore Caves,** where at least two flashlights per person are the wisest bet. Mt. Luxmore is a fine day-hike destination, and an ideal place for waiting when inclement weather bashes plans for the next stretch.

MT. LUXMORE HUT TO IRIS BURN HUT. In this astounding alpine section, the track steeply ascends for about an hour until emerging just below the summit of **Mt. Luxmore** (1472m). A 10min. scramble brings you to the top for a 360° panoramic view of the region, with knife-edged arretes spreading everywhere. The track then descends to **Forest Burn Shelter,** a spare affair with avalanche equipment and a rainwater barrel. **Hanging Valley Shelter** is much the same, but getting there's the prize: the track follows the crest of several humped ridges, where fair weather brings awe-inducing mountain views, and foul weather brings dangerously harsh winds. An extremely steep plunge back into the beeches follows a worthwhile lookout (return 5min.) over a full panorama of hanging valleys and green promontories. **Iris Burn Hut** (60 beds) is somewhat cramped, with serviceable tent sites about 200m away. From the hut, a side trip leads to the 10m **Iris Burn Waterfall** (return 45min.).

IRIS BURN HUT TO MOTURAU HUT. The track briefly ascends past the hut, before opening into the **Big Slip,** a testament to Too Much of a Good Thing. Here, in 1984, heavy rains sent a nice-sized chunk of mountain screaming down, obliterating the local tree population. Back in the intact forest, the track provides a reasonably level walk to **Moturau Hut** (40 beds) by the shores of Lake Manapouri with a large communal area, a spiral staircase, and great sunsets.

MOTURAU HUT TO RAINBOW REACH. Beyond Moturau Hut lies the turn-off to Shallow Bay Hut (6 beds), a small and unserviced hut with a dunny (toilet) and a whole shore of free camping out back. Not part of the Great Walks system, this hut is cheap ($5). From the turn-off, the Kepler winds through bogland, crosses the Forest Burn River, and then reaches the swing bridge that leads to Rainbow Reach and its accompanying shuttles.

RAINBOW REACH TO THE CONTROL GATES. This seldom-traveled stretch closes the loop back to the Control Gates, hugging Fiordland's forested border and promising a variety of views and a good chance to see parakeets or fish for trout.

▚ THE RAKIURA TRACK

Cruising along a boardwalk almost entirely below the bushline, the Rakiura Track on **Stewart Island** (see p. 351) lacks the spectacular flash boasted by more view-festooned Great Walks. There's plenty to delight the birdwatcher or botanist, though, from numerous silver-throated tui to exquisite hanging orchids. The track is too close to the dogs and development of Halfmoon Bay to support many kiwi, but the beaches are clean and vital regardless.

Trailheads: The DOC office is at the center. From the office, Main Rd. leads west about 2km to the **Kaipipi Rd.** section of the track. The other proper trailhead is at **Lee Bay,** about 5km from town; just across from the wharf, Horseshoe Bay Rd. runs north to Lee Rd., which deadends at this trailhead.

Transportation: It's an easy walk, but **Oban Taxis and Tours** (☎ 219 1456) offers a shuttle service ($18) as does **Stewart Island Travel** (☎ 219 1269. $15).

THE RAKIURA TRACK		
SEGMENTS	DISTANCE	TIME
Town to Port William Hut	**12km**	**4-5hr.**
Lee Bay Trailhead		1½hr.
Maori Beach Campsite		1½hr.
track junction		40min.
Port William Hut		30min.
Port William Hut to North Arm Hut	**12km**	**5-6hr.**
track junction		45min.-1hr.
Lookout Tower		3½hr.
North Arm Hut		1-1½hr.
North Arm Hut to town	**12km**	**4-5hr.**
Sawdust Bay Campsite		1½-2hr.
town		2¾-3hr.

Seasonality: Year-round, though the island's southern location means limited daylight hours during the winter. Torrential rain is never out of season.

Huts and Campsites: 2 huts have running water and pit toilets, but no cooking facilities (there are woodstoves, but not always wood). 3 camping areas have similar amenities. **Great Walks tickets** (huts $10; camping $6) can only be bought at the Oban DOC office.

Gear: Essentials include a cooking stove, toilet paper, and, of course, rain gear. **Ship to Shore**, **Stewart Island Travel,** and **Innes's Backpackers**.

Storage: Most accommodations store for free. DOC office has lockers ($5 per day).

TOWN TO PORT WILLIAM HUT. As you face the harbor in Halfmoon Bay, the road to **Horseshoe Bay** (a.k.a. Horseshoe Bay Rd.) heads off to the left. Past the local abalone farm, at Horseshoe Bay's northern end, Lee Bay Rd. branches off for 1km to its lovely, undeveloped namesake; from here the track begins in earnest. Skirting the coastline, the track soon reaches **Little River**, where the sandy mouth provides a low-tide walking option. Further on, **Maori Beach** is an excellent daytrip. The campsite here has a few grassy spots, a basic shelter, water, and an outhouse. Just beyond the campsites lurks a **big rusty boiler,** relic of a 1920s sawmill, and favorite backcountry accommodation for school kids ever since. At the western end of the beach, a swing bridge crosses a wide tidal estuary before climbing to a junction. The right fork leads north to **Port William Hut** (30 beds), with a low-tide route over eroded stones and polychrome seaweeds. The hut area is a laid-back place, with blue cod off the rocks, a hammock shaded by exotic gum trees, and campsites nearby. Five minutes before the hut, just prior to the wharf, is the junction for the **North West Circuit**.

PORT WILLIAM HUT TO NORTH ARM HUT. Back at the track junction, the right fork steadily ascends over extensive boardwalking and two swing bridges, eventually reaching the spectacular **Lookout Tower**. It's amazing what a difference 5m can make: a lush canopy of rata, rimu, and spindly inaka rolls down to Paterson Inlet, with minor mountains in the distance and birdsong nearby. About halfway to the hut, a junction branches off to the other side of the **North West Circuit**. The **North Arm Hut** (30 beds), set a ways above the water, has a decent-sized common area and two rooms of bunks; camping is not permitted.

NORTH ARM HUT TO TOWN. The last section of the track undulates across boardwalked stairs to **Sawdust Bay Campsite,** a simple shelter by scraggly trees with a nice bayside location (and a great potential for mud). After passing a small spur to the subtly lovely **Kaipipi Bay,** the track becomes the old **Kaipipi Road,** which leads out of the forest along roadways back into town.

OTHER RECOMMENDED TRACKS

There are plenty of other tramps in New Zealand that rival even the Great Walks for natural splendor and typically have fewer people. Though DOC has not designated these walks as "Great Walks" they have the same range of terrain and difficulty and just as much appeal.

◙ QUEEN CHARLOTTE TRACK

Trumpeted for green-and-blue beauty, the **Queen Charlotte Track** in **Marlborough Sounds** (see p. 239) is a pleasant outdoor experience, if not a rugged wilderness adventure. Along its vista-filled path above the Queen Charlotte and Kenepuru Sounds, signs of development abound—sheep graze on either side, boats buzz through the waters below, and a string of private accommodations welcomes weary travelers. Thanks in large part to this proximity to civilization, the Queen Charlotte is the only track in New Zealand where even trampers on a budget can have their gear transported for them (see **Essentials: Gear** below). It is also one of the country's best trails for **mountain biking.**

Trailheads: The track runs between **Ship Cove** in the east and **Anakiwa** in the west; water taxis and luggage transport encourage traveling from east to west.

Transportation: Ship Cove is accessible only by boat. **The Cougar Line's Round Trip Track Pass** ($48) includes drop-off and pick-up at any two points along the track and unlimited pack transfers. **Endeavor Express** round-trip ($35, with limited pack transfers), as well as a **pack transfer pass** ($10). Anakiwa lies 4km off Queen Charlotte Dr.; **hitchhikers** may walk that distance before a ride comes along, but once on the main road it's an easy 21km to Picton or 15km to Havelock, though *Let's Go* does not recommend it.

Seasonality: Year round. The section between Ship Cove and Kenepuru Saddle **closes to mountain bikes Dec.-Feb.**, the busiest walking season. **Droughts** can present the largest obstacle to traveling the trail; due to extreme fire risk, much of the track closed during the first half of 2001.

Campsites & Accommodations: 7 DOC campsites vary widely in amenities and seclusion ($5 per night). Numerous **private seaside establishments** provide a variety of dorms and double rooms.

Gear: Water taxis transport packs and overnight gear to any campsite or accommodation by the water (see **Transportation** above). Stove and food.

Storage: Most accommodations in Picton store for free; the visitors center charges $4 per bag per night.

QUEEN CHARLOTTE TRACK		
SEGMENTS	**DISTANCE**	**TIME**
Ship Cove to Resolution Bay Cabins	4.5km	1½hr.
School House Bay Campsite		1¼hr.
Resolution Bay		15min.
Resolution Bay Cabins to Endeavour Resort	10.5km	2¼hr
Furneaux Lodge		2hr.
Endeavor Resort		15min.
Endeavour Resort to Noeline's	13km	3½hr.
Camp Bay Campsite		3hr.
Punga Cove Resort		10min.
Homestead Backpackers		13min.
Noeline's		7min.
Camp Bay Campsite to Portage Hotel and Cowshed Bay Campsite	20.5km	6hr.
Bay of Many Coves Campsite		2½hr.
Black Rock Campsite		1¾hr.
Portage Hotel and Cowshed Bay		1¾hr.
Portage Hotel and Cowshed Bay Campsite to Mistletoe Bay Reserve	7.5km	2½hr.
Lochmara Lodge Turnoff		1½hr.
Mistletoe Bay Reserve		1hr.
Mistletoe Bay Reserve to Anakiwa	12.5km	3hr.
Te Mahia Resort		15min.
Anakiwa		2¾hr.

SHIP COVE TO RESOLUTION BAY CABINS. Ship Cove's **Captain Cook Monument** commemorates the many weeks the great navigator spent anchored here on five separate visits, harvesting scurvy-fighting grass for his crew and flogging those who refused it. As the track climbs steeply over a small saddle, it passes through the walkway's finest primary forest. Five minutes off the track, **School House Bay Campsite** has spare and sloping sites on Resolution Bay. Farther downhill, life flows slowly at the rambling bungalows of **Resolution Bay Cabins,** where the shop is always open, if better stocked in the summer. (☎579 9411. Linen $10. No electricity. No kitchen for campers or dorm residents. Free use of kayaks. Basic bunks $20; cottages $50-85; campsites $8.)

RESOLUTION BAY CABINS TO ENDEAVOUR RESORT. Past Resolution Bay, the track undulates along to **Furneaux Lodge,** where tidy lawns slope down to the sound and cozy bargain accommodations pop up despite the upscale atmosphere. (☎579 8259. Restaurant. Rowboat $10 per hr. Kayaks $15-20 per hr. Dorms $18; doubles $25; campsites Feb.-Nov. $8.50, Dec.-Jan. $10.) Just past the lodge turnoff, the **Waterfall Walk** (return 1hr.) leads through tall rimu-filled forest to a small cascade. The area's other accommodation option is **Endeavour Resort,** where a library and games room offers escape from uninspiring quarters. (☎579 8381. Free use of canoes. Dorms $25; double cabins $65-95.)

ENDEAVOUR RESORT TO NOELINE'S. At the head of Endeavor Inlet, a steep spur trail climbs into the bush to great views by the long-unused **antimony mines** (return 3½hr.). As the main track rounds **Big Bay**, its surroundings alternate between towering tree ferns and developed grazing land. From here, a side trail leads to three excellent and completely dissimilar accommodation options; all are also road-accessible. **Punga Cove Resort** offers fun-filled luxury, with a pool, spa, and beach-side trampoline. (☎579 8561. Restaurant. Kayaks $15 per hr. Dorms with linen $35.) Funky **Homestead Backpackers** occupies a great 1908 house, with sunny deck dorms ($18), gypsy-themed caravans ($17 per person, no power), romantic doubles ($40-60)—and a fire-warmed outdoor bathtub. (☎579 8373. Closed May-Sept.)

Up one last little hill, **Noeline's** is a fresh and intimate place with four beds and wide views, where charming world-traveler Noeline and Penny, the possum-catching lapdog, disarm guests with beaming hospitality and grandmotherly care. (☎579 8375. Linen $5. 2-bed dorms $18.)

CAMP BAY CAMPSITE TO PORTAGE HOTEL AND COWSHED BAY CAMPSITE. Trampers can reach **Kenepuru Saddle** via a 15min. scramble from Camp Bay Campsite or a slightly longer and easier route up the road from Homestead Backpackers. From the saddle, the track travels through scrubby vegetation before reaching the steep spur to **Eatwells Lookout** (15min.), a nearly 360° panorama. A half hour of rolling track later, the **Bay of Many Coves Campsite** has lofty sea views and bumpy, kanuka-sheltered plots. Boat companies will not be able to deliver packs here until Kiwi ingenuity perfects a high-precision baggage cannon.

From here, the track encounters some of its most beautiful trademark vistas, which encompass both Queen Charlotte and Kenepuru Sounds. **Black Rock Campsite,** another boat-inaccessible spot, has small, grassy sites, plus a handsome cooking gazebo that overlooks Kumutoto Bay and Picton.

It's all downhill to **Torea Saddle,** where paddlers through the years have found it wise to carry their canoes between Queen Charlotte and Kenepuru. A 10min. walk down the road north of the saddle sits the snazzy **Portage Hotel** (☎573 4309), with its restaurant, swimming pool, and flashy dorms ($25). Nearby, **Cowshed Bay Campsite** is a bayside but caravan-heavy complex with major road access. Water-taxis don't deliver gear to the campsite or the hotel, since they front Kenepuru (rather than Queen Charlotte) Sound; the hotel picks up luggage from a nearby drop-off for its guests (return $4).

PORTAGE HOTEL AND COWSHED BAY CAMPSITE TO MISTLETOE BAY RESERVE. The track traverses many switchbacked ups and downs and passes the steep turnoff to 🖪**Lochmara Lodge** (one-way 40min.), which sits on more than 10 acres of native bush, with hammocks and tree carvings scattered throughout. Free use of sea kayaks, windsurfer, rowboat, fishing and snorkeling gear, and a rope swing over the water makes for fun-filled days; a guitar, spa ($2 per ½hr.), and resident glowworms take care of the nights. (☎573 4554; lochmaralodge@xtra.co.nz. Tiny shop. Closed June-Aug. Dorms $20; tents with mattress and pillow $18; doubles with bath $60; self-contained cabins $100 for 2, each extra person $20; campsites $15.) A sidetrip to **Hilltop Lookout** (return 40min.), which showcases great views over Kenepuru Sound, begins 30min. farther along the main trail. Another relatively steep sidetrack descends past fungus-blackened beeches to the **Mistletoe Bay Reserve** (one-way 20min.), a DOC campsite on a small and quiet bay. In addition to a grassy flat for tents, the reserve maintains three ramshackle cottages with full kitchens ($10 per person; contact the **Picton DOC office** (p. 236), for reservations). Several short trails explore the forest from here.

MISTLETOE BAY RESERVE TO ANAKIWA. Beyond the trail junction for Mistletoe Bay, the track follows the road. Down a side road, the tropical-themed **Te Mahia Resort** has a backpacker room with its own piano. (☎/fax 573 4089. Dorms $25; doubles $90; campsites $12.50.) Meanwhile the main track follows Mistletoe Bay's lovely length before descending to **Davies Bay Campsite,** situated on an estuary. About 45min. of relatively level walking later, teeny **Anakiwa** marks the finish line; the small, plain **Anakiwa Backpackers** sits right by the end of the track. (☎574 2334. Closed Apr.-Nov. Dorms $15.)

◪ REES-DART TRACK

As grandiose as any Great Walk, the Rees and Dart Tracks in **Mt. Aspring National Park** (see p. 318) form a glorious loop through two river valleys, both lined with living glaciers. The track passes a great diversity of landscapes, including beech forests, subalpine herbfields, grassy flats, and manmade pastures. This is not an unduly easy walk, as many streams are unbridged and much of the path is invisible—poles and cairns make better friends than often misguided footprints. With two stunning daytrip alternatives beyond the main loop, the Rees-Dart richly rewards an increasing flow of trampers.

Trailheads: Tracks begin at road ends north of **Glenorchy** and meet at **Dart Hut.**

Transportation: Backpacker Express (☎ 442 9939) runs from **Glenorchy** (9:30am daily in summer) to the **Rees Track trailhead** at Muddy Creek carpark (30min., $10), and will go all the way up to **25 Mile Hut** (1½hr., $20). They also serve the **Dart Track trailhead** at Chinaman's Bluff (1hr., departs **Glenorchy** 12:30pm, $20), and will pick up at **Sandy Bluff** via jetboat ($50). **Upper Lake Wakatipu Tours** (☎ 442 9986; mobile 025 333 481) is similar. Both operators run between **Glenorchy** and **Queenstown** ($10).

Seasonality: May-Nov. is dangerous. Avalanches and heavy snowfall make it extremely treacherous, and the Upper Snowy Creek swingbridge is removed to avoid avalanche damage. Those attempting to cross the creek in winter must have alpine experience and be handy with an ice axe and crampons.

Huts and Campsites: Huts ($10 per night) except for the 25 Mile Hut ($3). Huts include heating, taps, and toilets; none have cooking stoves. Camping is free in forests and grassy flats, but discouraged between Shelter Rock Hut and Dart Hut.

Gear: The **Glenorchy DOC Office** (see p. 312) sells a small supply of gear, including stoves. Te Anau (see p. 324) and Queenstown (see p. 302) have a wider selection. **Chlorine tablets** or other **water purification** measures are crucial, since gut-wrenching giardia (see p. 25) has been detected on the track.

Storage: Many hostels will oblige. **Topline Tours** (☎ 249 8059, 0508 832 628) transports extra gear between Te Anau and Queenstown ($5 per bag).

REES TRACK		
SEGMENTS	**DISTANCE**	**TIME**
Muddy Creek carpark to 25 Mile Hut	6km	2-3hr.
25 Mile Hut to Shelter Rock Hut	10.5km	4-5hr.
Shelter Rock Hut to Dart Hut:	9km	5-7hr.
Rees Saddle	4km	3-4hr
Dart Hut	4km	2-3hr.
Dart Hut to Cascade Saddle	8km	5hr.

DART TRACK		
SEGMENTS	**DISTANCE**	**TIME**
Dart Hut to Daleys Flat Hut	15.5km	8½-12½hr.
Whitbourn Valley junction	1.5km	30min.
Whitbourn Glacier	5km	2-4hr. one-way
Daleys Flat Hut	14km	6-8hr.
Daleys Flat Hut to Chinaman's Bluff	14.5km	4-6hr.
Sandy Bluff	4.5km	1-2hr.
Chinaman's Bluff	10km	3-4hr.

MUDDY CREEK CARPARK TO 25 MILE HUT. This stretch of the Rees Valley—sometimes avoidable by shuttle, though not regularly serviced—can be a swampy walk along a lightly marked track. The mountain peaks are imposing, but only get better. The grungy and character-laden **25 Mile Hut** (8 beds), maintained by the Otago Tramping and Mountaineering Club as a base camp for Mt. Earnslaw, has six well-loved bunks and a stone hearth.

25 MILE HUT TO SHELTER ROCK HUT. The Lovely Lennox Falls quickly come into view across the valley; about two hours later, a swingbridge leads into Mt. Aspiring National Park proper. Winding in and out of beech forest and grassy slip sites, the track reaches **Shelter Rock Hut** (20 beds) a snazzy two-building abode on the east side of the river. Take care where the track crosses gullies above the bush; these are avalanche paths and can be dangerous, especially with the late snows in spring and early summer.

SHELTER ROCK HUT TO DART HUT. This is the loop's most challenging stretch, with steep inclines and faint markings (i.e. rock piles). The track climbs steadily through alpine vegetation until it hugs a bluff for the extremely steep (but brief) ascent to the **Rees Saddle.** The main track makes a tricky descent through even more diverse plant zones before hitting a cozy campsite. Just across Snowy Creek is **Dart Hut** (20 beds), with three rooms, a central stove, and separate toilets.

DART HUT TO CASCADE SADDLE. Dart Hut is a popular base for daytrips up to the spectacular Cascade Saddle. Any stretch of crummy weather can flood the area with anxious, view-hungry trampers awaiting the sun. The track to the Saddle begins at the campsite across Snowy Creek. As one follows the Dart River upstream, it disappears into the gray and terminal moraine, which then gives way to the exposed ice of Dart Glacier itself. The track then leads along the lateral moraine, high above the glacier's current melted level, and then climbs steadily to the prize: **Cascade Saddle.** On the far side, Cascade Creek roars into the beech-clothed Matukituki Valley, while snowy Mt. Aspiring towers in the distance; on the near side, Dart Glacier tumbles down blue icefalls from an amphitheater of rock. It's possible to camp on the Saddle, though whipping winds and naughty kea (see p. 71) threaten tent integrity.

If you intend to cross to the **Mt. Aspiring Hut,** allow 8-10hr. and bring years of experience. This is an alpine route and can be dangerous even in summer. The area's side creeks can rise quickly in rain and melt. Consult DOC for track details.

DART HUT TO DALEYS FLAT HUT. From the main track, a seldom-traveled spur leads across some difficult but beautiful country to the **Whitbourn Glacier.** Half an hour past Dart Hut it drops steeply to the Dart River, crosses a swingbridge, and scrambles through grass and forest to thick subalpine scrub. The track is difficult to see through the shrubs, which fortunately make great handholds. Eventually the track hits open flats, where a profusion of tiny plants spreads alongside the froth-ing Whitbourn River. Snowfields and waterfalls ring the lonely valley, which leads right up to the gritty snout of the Whitbourn Glacier itself, along the Whitbourn track. Meanwhile, the main track becomes less strenuous across the wide Cattle Flat, where grassy terraces are framed by still more legions of glaciers. **Daleys Flat Hut** (20 beds) is very spacious, with an idyllic riverside setting marred only by abundant sandflies.

DALEYS FLAT HUT TO CHINAMAN'S BLUFF. From the hut, it takes about an hour to reach some small, sandy bluffs that are *not* **Sandy Bluff.** The real McCoy is a walk away, by the signs for jetboat pick-up. From here, the jetboats zoom along the otherwise tranquil river, as the track runs up and over **Chinaman's Bluff,** beyond which lies the road. There is a road to Paradise car park (2½hr. one-way).

◪ THE GREENSTONE AND CAPLES TRACKS

This peaceful and pastoral pair stretches around impressive mountain peaks and through cow-filled river valleys. While a tiny corner of the loop lies inside **Mt. Aspiring National Park** (see p. 318), most of it falls within the Wakatipu Recreational Hunting Area. Deer season is from April-September, though shooting is prohibited within 100m of tracks or on farmland; a license is required. Black fallow deer are the most common animal on the track, although there are white fallow deer, chamois, and cattle who, unabashedly grace grassy fields with their pies.

> **Trailheads:** The two tracks form a loop between Fiordland National Park and the Glenorchy area, which can be entered from the west via **The Divide**, midway between Milford and Te Anau, or from the east via the **Greenstone Station** road-end (42km from Glenorchy).
>
> **Transportation:** Backpacker Express (☎ 442 9939) runs from the motor park in Gle-norchy (see p. 312) across Lake Wakatipu to this road-end. (30min.; departs **Gle-norchy** daily Nov.-Apr. 9:30am and 1:30pm, departs **trailhead** 10am and 2pm; in winter runs on demand; $15.) They have a $15 special between the Routeburn and the Greenstone and Caples within one day, and also travel to **Queenstown** ($15). **Upper Lake Wakatipu Tours** (☎ 442 9986; mobile 025 333 481) is the same.
>
> **Seasonality:** Thick snow and a lack of hut wardens make the winter season more chal-lenging than the summer, but the track is considered reasonably safe year-round.
>
> **Huts and Campsites:** All of the huts (except for the tiny $5 Sly Burn) cost $10 per night year-round and provide coal stoves, water taps, outhouses, and a weather report; none offer cooking burners. **Mid Caples** and **Mid Greenstone Huts** have two bunkrooms flank-ing a small, central kitchen room; **Upper Caples** and **McKellar Huts** are identical one-room jobs. Camping is free and easy, permitted at least 50m away from huts, or any-where within the bush or bush edge, but not on open flats (private land).

Gear: The **Glenorchy DOC Office** (see p. 312) sells a small supply of gear, including stoves. The outdoor shops of **Te Anau** (see p. 324) and **Queenstown** (see p. 302) have a much wider selection. **Chlorine tablets** or other water purification measures are crucial, since gut-wrenching giardia (see p. 25) has been detected on the track.

Storage: Most hostels will oblige. **Topline Tours** (☎ 249 8059, 0508 832 628) will transport gear between Te Anau and Queenstown ($5 per bag).

THE GREENSTONE AND CAPLES TRACK		
SEGMENTS	DISTANCE	TIME
Road-end to Mid Caples Hut	7.5km	2-3hr.
Greenstone and Caples Junction		30min.
Mid Caples Hut		2¼hr.
Mid Caples Hut to Upper Caples Hut	7.5km	2-3hr.
Upper Caples Hut to Lake McKellar Junction	7.5km	3-5hr.
McKellar Saddle		2-3hr.
Lake McKellar Junction		1-2hr.
Lake McKellar Junction to The Divide	6km	1-2hr.
Greenstone Saddle Campsite		30min.
Lake Howden Hut		30min.
The Divide		45min.
Lake McKellar Junction to McKellar Hut	3km	1-2hr.
McKellar Hut to Mid Greenstone Hut	13km	4-6hr.
Mid Greenstone Hut to road-end	14.5km	3¾-5hr.
Sly Burn Hut	5km	1hr.
Greenstone and Caples Junction	8km	2¼hr.
Road-end	1.5km	30min.

ROAD-END TO MID CAPLES HUT. From the parking area at the end of the road, the track leads past the confluence of the Greenstone and Caples Rivers. Do not cross the river at the bridge for the Lake Rere track; keep to the downstream left bank (true left bank), until you reach the swingbridge posted for the Greenstone track. The Caples Track branches off to the right alongside the river through beech forest until reaching the swingbridge to **Mid Caples Hut** (12 beds). This two-wing number has great views of fields, streams, and faraway peaks.

MID CAPLES HUT TO UPPER CAPLES HUT. The track weaves between beech forest and grassland replete with lovely mountain and river views before reaching the **Upper Caples Hut** (20 beds, space for camping). The rugged **Steele Creek Route** is accessible from the hut 20min. back up the track, and is a highly unmarked, untrodden, and unforgiving path (8-10hr.) to **Mid Greenstone Hut** (see below), essentially bisecting the Greenstone and Caples loop.

UPPER CAPLES HUT TO LAKE MCKELLAR JUNCTION. Through moss and filmy ferns, the track ascends steeply but briefly before breaking onto the grasslands and misty mountain vistas of **McKellar Saddle,** conical Mt. Christina and the Darron Mountains beckoning on the horizon. This root-entangled stretch is the steepest on the Greenstone and Caples: strenuous going up, and slippery and potentially dangerous going down to the junction at **Lake McKellar.**

LAKE MCKELLAR JUNCTION TO THE DIVIDE. The northbound fork leads past the stream-fed, rocky, and free **Greenstone Saddle Campsite** (toilet, no tap) before joining the Routeburn Track at **Lake Howden Hut.** From here, you can head down to the **Milford Road** (see p. 321), or set off along the Routeburn.

LAKE MCKELLAR JUNCTION TO MCKELLAR HUT. From the junction, the track follows the lake edge past lichen-encrusted beeches and officially out of Fiordland National Park to **McKellar Hut** (20 beds), a one-roomer in the shadow of McKellar Saddle.

MCKELLAR HUT TO MID GREENSTONE HUT. Through the forest, meadows, and cow herds, the track crosses a swingbridge over the Steele River, a half-hour shy of **Mid Greenstone Hut** (12 beds). Besides its great valley view and forested tent sites, this hut boasts a genuine bovine skull on its commode.

MID GREENSTONE HUT TO ROAD-END. From the main track a brief (10min.) detour leads across a stunning gorge to the tiny **Sly Burn Hut** (4 beds) and a grassy field of potential tent sites. This is one end of the **Mavora-Greenstone Walkway** (51km, 4 days), which leads south to an unsealed offshoot of SH94. Back on the Greenstone it's another rolling, blue-pooled riverside stretch back to the Caples junction and the carpark.

FIJI (VITI)

HISTORY AND CURRENT EVENTS

IMPORTANT EVENTS

c. 2000 BC
The Lapita people arrive in Fiji; over the next few thousand years they and their descendants populate ¼ of the globe's surface using only stone age technology—an achievement unrivalled in human history

1643
Dutch explorer Abel Tasman sights Nukubasaga and the peaks of Taveuni, becoming the first European explorer to see Fiji

1774
On his second voyage in the Pacific, English explorer James Cook sails from Tonga to Vatoa in the southern Lau Group; sights but never actually encounters any Fijians

1789
Captain William Bligh and 18 of his men sail through the "Cannibal Islands" en route to Jakarta, pursued by several canoes full of angry Fijians

VITIAN PRE-HISTORY

The history of Fiji is both colorful and violent—modernization that took millenniums to achieve in Europe has been squeezed into just 200 years of contact with Westerners, but ancient Fijian culture and tradition remain unchanged in many ways. Fiji is actually the Tongan term for the islands—Fijians called their home Viti. European explorers and merchants heard tales of Fiji from the Tongans long before ever laying eyes on the islands; somehow the foreign name stuck.

The Fijian archipelago was first settled c. 2000 BC. Most scientists agree that the **Lapita** people began a massive outward migration in open wooden outriggers from somewhere in the area of Papua New Guinea. Migration to the Fijian Islands continued in waves over the next few thousand years, with the most recent arriving from Melanesia c. AD 1000-1800.

CONTACT WITH EUROPEANS

Fiji was "discovered" by Europeans relatively late compared to many nearby archipelagos. While the Dutch explorer **Abel Tasman** was the first European to sight Fiji on his way to Australia and New Zealand, **Captain James Cook** first came ashore in 1774 after visiting Tonga to the east. Having heard tales from the Tongans of the ferocious nature and cannibalistic tendencies of their western neighbors, a cautious Cook rowed ashore, glanced around, left some nails, and quickly returned to the safety of the *Resolution*. His reports bolstered the only slightly exaggerated European image of Fiji as the "Cannibal Islands." The first accurate charting of Fiji was made by **Captain William Bligh** as he and 18 of his men (after being kicked off the *Bounty* in the famous mutiny) sailed their dinghy through the islands.

While Fijian goods had long ago entered European and American markets via Tongan traders, it wasn't until the early 1800s that Fiji became an important trade center, producing **sandalwood** and **bêche-de-mer** (sea cucumber, an Asian delicacy). However, as merchant ships began to deal directly with the Fijians, many chiefs actively exploited their own people in this production to gain modern weapons; the supply of both quickly dried up. With the eruption of chaotic internal fighting during the mid-1800s, many chiefs became extremely concerned about losing control of Fiji. Eventually recognizing that foreign rule was inevitable, these chiefs elected to embrace what they perceived as the lesser of the colonial evils. They officially ceded Fiji to Great Britain in 1874.

Internal political pressures in Britain began to force **Sir Arthur Gordon,** Governor of Fiji from 1875-80, to try to make his colony self-sufficient. His solution was to import **indentured laborers** from India to work the sugar plantations. These workers, known as **girmitiyas,** signed five-year contracts, however few returned to India upon completion of their terms. Over 60,000 Indians were brought to Fiji between 1879 and 1919. They often labored under horrendous conditions, and were subject to gross human rights violations at the hands of supervisors. Public pressure gradually mounted to put an end to the indentured servitude, and the practice was officially outlawed in January, 1919. The tide turned in the 20th century as Indo-Fijians became quite economically successful, controlling over 70% of the nation's wealth by the late '90s. This economic inequality sowed the seeds of the racial conflict that troubles the islands to this day.

In the years following World War II Fiji found itself in a period of rapid democratization. However, as the political system developed, it incorporated the deep-seated racial division between indigenous Fijians and Indo-Fijians—the distribution of seats in Parliament was limited by racial quotas, and the main political parties were based on race, with the **Alliance Party** representing indigenous Fijians and the **National Federation Party (NFP)** chiefly supporting Indo-Fijian interests.

A gradual and peaceful transition to **independence** from Great Britain ended successfully on October 10, 1970, and was accompanied by a new constitution that preserved Fiji's racial segregation in politics. The first post-independence election was won by the Alliance, and **Sir Ratu Sir Kamisese Mara (Ratu Mara)** became Prime Minister. He remained in power until 1987, winning every election.

POLITICAL UPHEAVAL: THE '80S, '90S, AND TODAY

In April 1987, a coalition of Indo-Fijian parties upset the faltering Alliance Party. Many indigenous Fijian leaders felt threatened due to the increase in elected Indo-Fijians, and extremist nationalists began a campaign of protest and destabilization. Indigenous Fijian army leader **Lieutenant Colonel Sitiveni Rabuka** stormed parliament on May 14 in a bloodless coup that ousted the fledgling government. Claiming that he was acting in the interest of all indigenous Fijians, Rabuka suspended the constitution and proclaimed himself head of a military government. Although he was eventually convinced to step down in favor of an interim government, Rabuka remained in control of the army and police, and staged a second coup in September. This time he dissolved the old constitution and declared Fiji a republic, renouncing its status as a member of the British Commonwealth. **Ratu Mara** was appointed by Rabuka as Prime Minister of the new interim government.

Rabuka officially made the move from the military to politics when he ran for Prime Minister in 1992, a position that he won and held until May, 1999. The foundation upon which Rabuka built his government was shaky at best. The 1990 constitution was extremely racist and discriminatory towards Indo-Fijians, and many saw it as an institutionalized assurance of the political dominance of indigenous Fijians. From requiring an indigenous Fijian majority in the House of Representatives to imposing a Christian-based compulsory Sunday observance (the remnants of which tourists experience each weekend), the system preserved or accentuated the racially divided political system. Pressure for constitutional reform came to a head with the adoption of a vastly more democratic constitution in 1997.

FIJI

1800
US schooner *Argo* is wrecked; surviving crew bring a devastating epidemic to Fiji, killing many indigenous inhabitants

1808
US ship *Eliza* sinks. Swedish sailor "Charles Savage" makes his way to Bau and becomes Fiji's most influential beachcomber

1813
Overharvesting finally depletes sandalwood supplies in Fiji. Beachcomber Charles Savage is killed in an ambush and his skull is made into a ceremonial kava cup

1820
Large-scale bêche-de-mer production under the principal direction of American merchant ships begins

1850
The final explosion of bêche-de-mer production comes to an end as sea cucumbers become increasingly hard to find

1870
'Blackbirding', the frequent kidnapping of other South Pacific peoples into forced labor in Fiji's sugar industry, is finally brought to an end

1871
Ratu Seru Cakobau, chief of Bau, declares himself the Tui Viti (King of Fiji)

Oct. 10, 1874
Fiji becomes a British colony. Virtually all chiefs signing the Deed of Cession are from the eastern parts of Fiji—many western chiefs opposed the annexation. An outbreak of measles claims the lives of 40,000 Fijians, over a third of the population

1877
The Fijian capital moves from Levuka, on the island of Ovalau, to Suva, in Viti Levu, where it remains to this day

1879
Indentured Indian laborers first brought in large numbers to work on the sugar plantations

1919
Indentured labor officially comes to an end, most laborers voluntarily choose to remain in Fiji

Oct. 10, 1970
Fiji gains independence from Great Britain. Sir Ratu Sir Kamisese Mara appointed Prime Minister

THE *OTHER* OTHER WHITE MEAT
During the 17th-19th centuries, fantastic stories of Fijian cannibalism abounded in impressionable Europe. Amazingly, most of these notions were highly accurate—the practice of eating enemies was commonplace in Fijian society by the time Europeans arrived. In a society rooted in ancestor worship, consuming a rival's flesh was the ultimate token of disrespect, dooming his soul for eternity. Often an arm or leg would be cut from a live victim, cooked, and eaten before his eyes—sometimes he would be forced to try a piece. Many powerful chiefs were infamous for their love of the "long pig." While cannibalism gradually died out as Christian missionaries (many of the early ones were eaten) won converts, the practice persisted through the early 1800s.

In the May 1999 elections a coalition of Labour and Indo-Fijian parties took the reigns from Rabuka. **Mahendra Chaudhry,** an Indo-Fijian, became Fiji's first non-indigenous Prime Minister. The country braced itself for the protests and chaos that had followed the 1987 election, but no violence erupted—until exactly one year later.

On May 19, 2000, the anniversary of Chaudhry's election, failed businessman and indigenous Fijian **George Speight** and a group of gunmen stormed the House of Parliament, taking Prime Minister Chaudhry and several other Ministers hostage and proclaiming a new all-indigenous government. Speight expected that popular anti-Indian sentiment would lead Fijians to support him, but after a 56-day standoff with the military he negotiated a return of the hostages and was later taken into custody. At the time of publication, he was standing trial for charges including treason, which is punishable by death.

The military restored order by placing an interim government into power under banker **Laisenia Qarase** on July 4, 2000. The country has experienced relatively little conflict since. The major exception was an attempted rebellion by Speight-supporting soldiers on November 2, 2000, in which eight soldiers died and ten were injured.

The government's legitimacy has been shaken by a High Court ruling that Qarase's interim government is illegal—however, new (and legal) elections were planned for August 28, 2001. All major parties will contest the election, including the new breakaway **Labour Unity Party (LUP),** which claims to be non-racial and interested in the good of all Fijians. However, the LUP may only have the effect of dividing Indo-Fijian voters and delivering the election to the nationalist Fijians.

FIJIAN CULTURE
THE PEOPLE

Fiji's population of 830,000 only inhabit 100 of the 320 islands that comprise the nation; 70% call Viti Levu home. Slightly more than half of the population are indigenous Fijians, while over forty percent are of Indian descent, many the great-great grandchildren of *girmitiyas* (see p. 382). Fijian, Hindi, and English are the principal languages.

Christianity, Hinduism, and Islam are the predominant religions. Coinciding largely with racial divisions, most indigenous Fijians are Christian (Methodism being the largest denomination), while most Indo-Fijians are Hindu. A smaller Muslim following is comprised mostly of Indo-Fijians.

VITIAN TRADITIONS

The relatively late arrival of foreign influence to Fijian shores has allowed a strong preservation of cultural traditions despite modernization. Although more barbaric practices such as cannibalism (see *Other* **Other White Meat** p. 384) are no longer practiced, Fijian society still roots itself in ancient customs.

The traditional Fijian tribes are based on a hierarchical system of several **mataqali** (extended family units claiming common ancestry). The importance of lineage is even reflected in architecture; the highest house within each village is traditionally the temple for worship of the *kalou vu* (ancestor-gods), with the chief living in the less-prominent, second tallest house.

While Christianity has been strongly established, some villagers still retain animistic beliefs, claiming dependent relationships with aquatic creatures. These include the ability to chant and call upon sharks and turtles.

SPORTS. Fijians, like Kiwis, are rabid sports fanatics. Rugby, soccer, and cricket are the most popular contests, and broadcasts of overseas tournaments are listened to religiously. At the time of publication, the Fiji National Rugby Team was ranked 11th in the world in international competition. The most famous Fijian athlete today is golfer and Lautoka native **Vijay Singh**. Recently ranked as high as 6th in the world, Singh is known as the "best Asian golfer in the world."

CLOTHING. Traditional Fijian dress consists of a *liku* (grass skirt) for women and a *malo* (loincloth) for men. Since the arrival of conservative Christianity, dress codes in villages have called for less exposed skin—long dresses or *sulus* (sarongs) are the norm for women, while men now commonly wear a sulu and a t-shirt. Indo-Fijian women tend to wear a long *sari*. In the more urban areas Western-style clothing predominates.

GIFT GIVING. An important traditional Fijian concept is **sevusevu.** Basically this is the practice of giving a gift in return for (and with full expectation of) some sort of favor—the recipient of the gift cannot refuse to perform the favor (this causes many problems with modern materialism). While yaqona root is the most common item to give a Fijian, the greatest gift one can receive is the **tabua,** a sperm whale's tooth. Length and thickness determine the value of the present. It is doubtful visitors will see a tabua given; laws now protect the whales.

FIJIAN VILLAGE ETIQUETTE. Correct and respectful entrance to a Fijian village is essential. Usually, visitors do not enter a village without a guide or permission; to wander in is extremely rude. **Dress conservatively;** do not wear shorts or a hat. A **sulu** (sarong) is always considered appropriate, and is light and easy to carry. Women should never bare their shoulders and should wear pants, below-the-knee skirts, or a sulu. Lone female travelers have had mixed experiences when visiting villages; if you are traveling solo your best bet is to enter with a group.

Apr., 1987
Dr. Timoci Bavadra's Indo-Fijian Labour/National Federation Party coalition defeats Ratu Mara's Alliance Party

May-Sept., 1987
Sitiveni L. Rabuka leads two military coups, declares himself ruler and severs Fijian ties with the British Commonwealth

Dec., 1987
Ratu Mara appointed Prime Minister of interim government

June, 1992
Rabuka becomes Prime Minister

July, 1998
New Constitution supported by President Ratu Mara comes into effect

Sept. 30, 1997
Fiji re-enters the British Commonwealth

May 19, 1999
Mahendra Chaudhry leads a Labour coalition to victory and becomes Fiji's first Indian Prime Minister

May 19, 2000
George Speight takes over the House of Parliament with armed supporters, taking PM Chaudhry and others hostage

May 20, 2000
Ratu Jope Seniloli sworn in by Speight and his men as "president"

FIJI

Upon entering the village be prepared to present the **Turaga ni Koro** (head of the village, chief) with a gift. **One kilogram of kava root** is both appropriate and common ($20). You will usually be brought to his home to present the gift. It will then be ground and you will be expected to take part in the kava ceremony. Be prepared to answer a lot of personal questions.

When invited into a **bure**, leave your shoes outside and stoop slightly upon entering; to stand upright inside is poor manners. If you are invited to spend the night indoors, stay. Pitching a tent outside a home indicates that you see that home as unfit for sleeping. When visiting with one family, do not accept invitations to eat or sleep with other families; politely decline explaining that you are a guest of another family. Remember to speak softly as loud voices are a sign of anger, and be sure not to touch a Fijian on the head, as this is an ultimate token of disrespect. Be cautious with compliments or praise for objects, as a Fijian may feel obligated to give you something as a gift even if they cannot afford to. Note that village water must be treated before drinking (see **Food- and Water-borne Diseases** p. 25).

To show your appreciation for a family's hospitality if you spend the night, you may want to give each member of the family a useful gift of an appropriate value. If you would like to give more, ask the family what they might enjoy and purchase it; a bag of groceries **(powdered milk, sugar, bread, tea)** is greatly appreciated by large families. It is often tempting to reward villagers with a **tip** after visiting. An understanding of the communal nature of a Fijian village, however, suggests that a personal reward, especially money, is not necessarily in keeping with custom. *Let's Go* recommends giving things that can be shared, like **books** or clothing (such as a **tee-shirt**) to individual hosts or guides; it's even better to present the added gift during an appropriate time to the chief and the village as a whole, when both your gratitude and generosity can be shared with everyone. It's much more Fijian that way.

Be sensitive when taking photographs, and never take pictures of a kava ceremony without explicit permission. Never wander a village alone; only explore with an adult or child as your guide. While your experience in each village will differ, it is a general rule that the farther you get from cities, the greater the emphasis tradition will receive. Fijians greatly appreciate respect for their customs; the more respectful and pleasant you are, the more enjoyable your stay will be for everyone involved.

FOOD AND DRINK. Contemporary Fijian fare presents a mixed plate of indigenous Fijian, Polynesian, Indian, Chinese, and Western cuisine. Like most countries, Fiji has been infected by Western fast food, but this has yet to displace traditional cuisine in villages. Traditional Fijian food is typical of South Pacific islands and includes **tavioka** (cassava, tapioca), **dalo** (taro) roots, and seafood in **lolo** (coconut cream). **Mango, pineapple**, and **guava** are seasonal fresh fruits. Meat is also eaten with dalo roots after being fried and is often served in lolo. A delicious traditional dish called **kokoda** consists of raw fish marinated in lime juice and lolo. One of the stranger Fijian delicacies is the tail of the **balolo worm**—twice a year the worm fills its tail with sperm and releases it to float to the surface of the sea, only to be snatched up by the Fijians who hunt them on the surface.

An evening in a Fijian village will expose you to true authentic Fijian cuisine. In the popular **lovo** banquet, food is wrapped in banana leaves and cooked over hot stones in an underground oven. A lovo is often accompanied by *meke* (see **Dance** below). While tap water in some areas of Fiji may be potable, it is always safest to drink bottled water. Soft drinks and alcohol are also available; most alcohol is imported from Australia or New Zealand. The most distinctive Fijian beverage is definitely **kava** (see **I Can't Feel My Lips** p. 388).

THE ARTS

HANDCRAFTS. Fijian women weave ceremonial **kuta mats** from the leaves of the pandanus tree. **Masi (tapa),** taken from the paper mulberry tree, is also a common material for mats. Many villages are famous for their **pottery,** both contemporary and ancient—some artifacts date from as early as 1290 BC. Fijian men have traditionally created **wood carvings,** ranging from clubs, spears, and cannibal forks to sophisticated outrigger canoes and intricately detailed *tanoa* (kava bowls).

FILM. Though Fiji has not supplied many movie stars, it has been the site of many sets, its untouched environment, splendid climate, and pristine beaches having lured filmmakers from all over the world. Undoubtedly the most infamous films shot in Fiji are **Brooke Shields'** breakthrough performance in the 1979 classic *The Blue Lagoon* and its 1992 reprise *Return to the Blue Lagoon*, both of which take place on **Turtle Island** in the Yasawa Group. If you go anywhere near the island you will surely be reminded of this countless times by helpful locals.

DANCE. The traditional dance of Fiji is called **meke.** Usually a narration of tales of ancestors and past wars, *meke* serves as the sole means of transmission for Fijian legends, and as such is crucial for the continuation of village identity. Each tribe has its own movements and dialect, all set to singing, chanting, and the beat of the **lali** (a type of drum hollowed from a tree trunk).

FLORA AND FAUNA

Most of Fiji's plants and animals are Indo-Malayan. Europeans' first impression of Fiji was that it was covered by nothing but mangroves growing on salt mud flats, coconuts, lush rainforests, and bamboo. Today just over half of the islands are still covered with rain forest and this is rapidly diminishing as forests are destroyed to make way for agriculture and development. Since 1960 over 15% of Fiji's forests have been cleared, resulting in extreme erosion and environmental degradation.

Fiji's islands are home to over 3000 identified plant species. Many are used as resources for food, medicine, and building materials. **Ota** are the ferns found in Fiji; some are edible, but are primarily used in the construction of *bures* (traditional Fijian houses). **Dakua** (Fijian kauri) and **yaka** are the most prevalent timber woods, although foreign pine planted for market export is becoming common. The most edible root crops are **tavioka, dalo,** and of course **yaqona.**

As in New Zealand, indigenous mammals in Fiji are few; only six species of bat and a small grey Polynesian rat are indigenous. Human immigrants from Polynesia introduced dogs and pigs, while all other mammals arrived within the last 200 years. Cattle and horses were brought by missionaries; settlers brought sheep. In an attempt to control Fijian pests, foreign pests were introduced. For example, the mongoose was imported to eat snakes and rats in the cane fields and is now a menace. In contrast, thousands of birds, over 100 species in all, are indigenous to Fiji, including a variety of parrots, honey-eaters, fantails, owls, ducks, rails, cuckoos, large swamp fowl, and kingfishers.

Fiji has about 20 species of land reptiles, four species of turtle, and four species of sea snakes, mostly harmless. The most common snake is the **Pacific boa,** while the sole venomous terrestrial snake is the **bolo.** Coastal **seasnakes** are also poisonous, but rare. Reptiles and amphibians, including lizards, giant toads, and frogs,

Fiji Islands

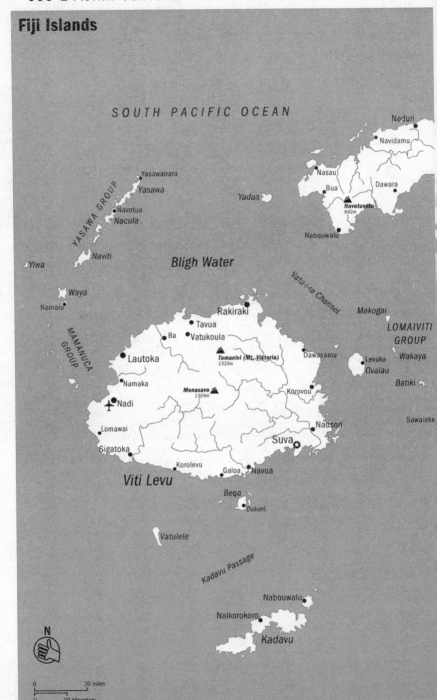

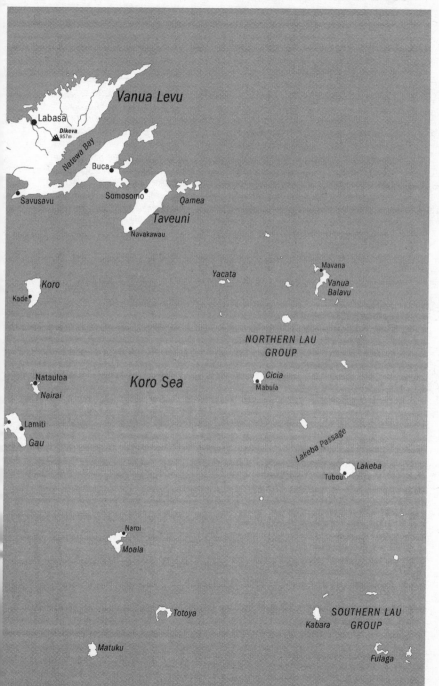

are a common sight. The crested iguana, thought to have floated over from South America on vegetation, is endangered and not often spotted.

Fiji's waters contain hundreds of species of coral, sea fans, sea sponges, and fish; diving in Fiji is among the best in the world. Many marine mammals, including dolphins, pilot whales, and sperm whales, swim in the azure waters, and divers often report seeing sharks, mantas, and bill fish

BURNT IN BEQA Walking on hot rocks is painful, but for the people of **Beqa Island** (BENG-ga p. 406) it's a soulful, sole-scorching tradition. According to legend, one day the great chief **Tui Qalita** accidentally captured **Tui Namoliwai,** leader of the *veli* band of lilliputian spirit gods who inhabit the Namoliwai River. The tiny Tui pleaded with the taller Tui for release, promising to magically make him the best fisherman, warrior, or wealthiest man in the village. Since the taller Tui was already a superstar, he chose instead to have power over fire. He tested the talent by *vilavilairevo* ("jumping into the oven"; placing one's feet on white hot coals). Tui Walita's descendends, the **Sawau** people, today serve as the *bete* (BAY-tay; priests) of the firewalkers. The *bete,* who abstain from sex and coconuts for a month before a ceremony, go to the same stream to prepare for a *vilavilairevo* ceremony by collecting the *drau ni balabala,* tree ferns used as firewalkers' anklets, and by calling to the *veli* and placing little twigs across streams and holes to allow the mini-men to follow to the village and watch over the hot feat. A pit is dug, stones are fired for half a day, and the *vilavilairevo* begins. Kitschy imitations of this amazing tradition can be seen in hotels throughout Fiji.

VITI LEVU

In the dart game of budget travel, you've hit the board with Viti Levu, Fiji's largest and most commercially important island. Getting a bullseye isn't the object of this game, however; most resources, services, accommodations, and attractions lie along the Kings and Queens Roads, which encircle the perimeter of Viti Levu. The interior is mainly undeveloped and untouristed except for a few breathtakingly gorgeous highland villages. The western half of the island is home to Fiji's primary international airport and therefore sees the most tourist action. The Coral Coast in the south offers exquisite beaches and easy transportation, making it another popular destination. The northern parts of Viti Levu are rarely visited by most tourists, and thus provide a rough glimpse into Fiji's agricultural side. While the eastern half is home to the capital Suva, the largest city in all of Fiji, recent political instability has kept most tourists away; however, the harsh beauty and deep history of the region are a unique draw that shouldn't be missed.

▧ VITI LEVU HIGHLIGHTS

LOOK OUT from the summit of Fiji's highest peak, Mt. Batilamu, in the heart of **Koroyanitu National Heritage Park** (see p. 409).

LOOK BACK thousands of years of Fijian tradition as you participate in a kava ceremony in **Navala Village** (see p. 407).

LOOK GOOD in your wetsuit as you windsurf the Bligh Waters north of **Nananu-i-ra** (see p. 402).

▨ TRANSPORTATION

International Flights: Almost all international flights to Fiji arrive at **Nadi International Airport,** 15min. by car outside Nadi on the Queens Rd. Carriers include **Air New Zealand, Qantas Airways,** and **Air Pacific;** each runs multiple flights each week, sometimes every day. Average flight times from the following hubs are: **Auckland** 3hr.; **Frankfurt** 22¼hr.; **Honolulu** 6½hr.; **L.A.** 10hr.; **London** 21½hr.; **Sydney** 3¾hr.; **Tokyo** 8½hr.

Domestic Flights: Domestic carriers include **Sunflower Airlines** (☎ 723 555, 723 016; fax 720 085, 723 611; www.fiji.to) and **Air Fiji Ltd.** (☎ 473 155; fax 400 479; www.airfiji.net). Both service more than a dozen Fijian destinations, including **Labasa, Mana, Ovalau, Savusavu, Suva,** and **Taveuni. Island Hoppers** (☎ 720 410; fax 720 172), based at the Nadi airport, provides superfast helicopter transfers throughout Fiji. (20min. flight from **Coral Coast** to **Mamanucas** US$115. Min. 2 people. All transactions in US$.) **Turtle Airways** (☎ 721 888; fax 720

SUNSET EXPRESS BUSES (DAILY)		
SUVA-LAUTOKA	STOPS	LAUTOKA-SUVA
8:45am/4pm	Suva	9:30am/3:15pm
11:10am/6:25pm	Sigatoka	9:50am/3:35pm
12:20pm/7:35pm	Nadi	10:10am/3:55pm
12:30pm/7:45pm	Nadi Airport	11:20am/5:05pm
12:50pm/8:05pm	Lautoka	1:35pm/7:20pm
Fares $1-10 open-air, $2-11 A/C		

FIJI EXPRESS BUSES (DAILY)		
SUVA-NADI	STOPS	NADI-SUVA
8am	Suva	6pm
9am	Pacific Harbor	5pm
9:55am	Warwick Hotel	4:05pm
10:35am	Sigatoka	3:25pm
10:45am	Fijian Resort	3:15pm
11:55am	Sheraton Denarau	2:05pm
12:15pm	Nadi	1:35pm
12:30pm	Nadi Airport	1:30pm
A/C Fares $6-27		

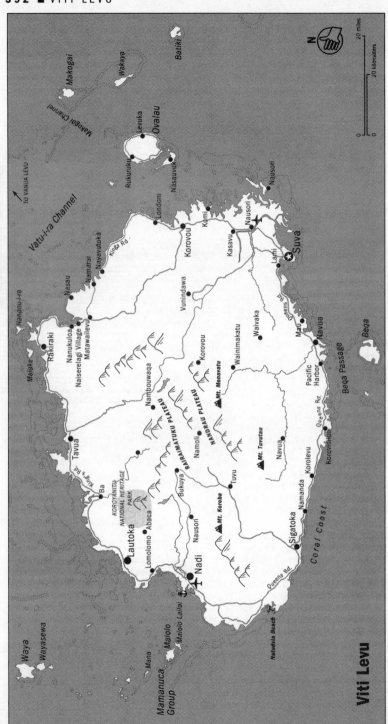

Viti Levu

095; www.turtleairways.com) offers seaplane transfers (West Viti Levu to Mamanucas $109; Yasawa to Tavewa $79.)

Buses: Sunset Express (☎382 811, Nadi ☎720 266, Lautoka ☎668 276; fax 320 769) and **Fiji Express** (contact United Touring Ltd. ☎722 811, 722 821; fax 720 389, 720 107) both have express service to many cities in Viti Levu; **Pacific Transport Ltd.** (Nadi ☎700 004) runs the most buses at the lowest fare (14 daily; $0.42-10.36). The tables below detail schedules and fares.

| PACIFIC TRANSPORT LTD. BUSES | | | | |
| SUVA-LAUTOKA | | | LAUTOKA-SUVA | |
STAGE	EXPRESS	STOPS	EXPRESS	STAGE
Departs 7:30, 8, 9am, 1:30pm, (Sa-Su 3:30pm, M-F 4:30pm)	Departs 6:45, 8:30, 9:30am, 12:10, 3pm, (F 5:30, 6pm)	**Suva**	Arrives 11:20am, 12:05, 1, 5, 8:35, 10:20pm, (F 9:50, 10:20pm)	Arrives 1:25, 2:55, 3:25, 6:55pm (Sa-Su 9:30pm, M-F 10:20pm)
8:30, 9, 10am, 2:30pm, (Sa-Su 4:30pm, M-F 5:30pm)	7:35, 9:15, 10:20am, 1, 4:05, 6:35pm, (F 6:50pm)	**Navua**	10:35, 11:20am, 12:15, 4:15, 7:50, 9:35pm, (F 9:05, 10pm)	12:30, 2, 2:30, 6pm, (Sa-Su 8:35pm, M-F 9:25pm)
8:50, 9:20, 10:20am, 2:50pm, (Sa-Su 4:50pm, M-F 5:50pm)	7:50, 9:30, 10:35am, 1:15, 4:05, 6:35pm, (F 6, 7:05pm)	**Pacific Harbor**	10:15, 11, 11:55am, 3:55, 7:30, 9:15pm, (F 8:45, 9:40pm)	noon, 1:30, 2, 5:35pm, (Sa-Su 8:10pm, M-F 8:55pm)
11, 11:30am, 12:30, 4:55pm, (Sa-Su 6:55, M-F 7:55)	9:35, 11:!5am, 12:20, 3, 6, 8:20pm, (F 7:50, 8:45pm)	**Sigatoka**	8:45, 9:10, 10:25am, 2:25, 6, 7:45pm, (F 7:15. 8:10pm)	10:10, 11:40am, 12:10, 3:45pm, (Sa-Su 6:20pm, M-F 7:05pm)
12:35, 1:35, 2:30, 6:30pm, (Sa-Su 8:30pm, M-F9:30pm)	10:50am, 12:40, 1:35, 4:15, 7:15, 9:35pm, (F 9:05, 10pm)	**Nadi**	7:20, 7:50, 9am, 1, 4:40, 6:20pm, (F 5:50, 6:50pm)	8:25, 9:25, 10:25am, 2pm, (Sa-Su 4:35pm, M-F 5:20pm)
12:50, 1:55, 2:50, 6:50pm, (Sa-Su 8:50pm, M-F 9:50pm)	11:05am, 12:55, 1:50, 4:30, 7:30, 9:50pm, (F 9:20, 10:15pm)	**Nadi Airport**	7, 7:25am, 12:40, 4:20, 6pm, (F 5:30, 6:30pm)	7:55, 8:55, 9:55am, 1:30pm, (Sa-Su 4:10pm, M-F 4:55pm)
Arrives 1:30, 2:35, 3:30, 7:30pm, (Sa-Su 9:30pm, M-F 10:30pm)	Arrives 11:35am, 1:30, 2:20, 5, (7:55 to Ba), 10:20pm, (F 9:50, 10:45pm)	**Lautoka**	Departs 6:30, (7am from Ba), 12:10, 3:50, 5:30pm (F 5, 6pm)	Departs 7:15, 8:15, 9:15am, 12:50pm, (Sa-Su 3:30pm, M-F 4:15pm)
N/A	Arrives 8:40pm	**Ba**	Departs 6:15am	N/A

NADI

The band strumming guitars in the airport will sing it, the salesmen teeming the streets hawking swords and seashells will shout it, and almost every other local in Nadi will undoubtedly announce, upon seeing a tourist, the spirited greeting "Bula!" As Fiji's major air traffic hub, Nadi fits the phrase welcoming, quite literally, most tourists to the islands. The friendliness may seem a bit purposeful, however, as it becomes clear that every taxi driver and resort representative vies for attention and business with their words. Most travelers move on quickly from this urban center to more idyllic destinations.

▐ TRANSPORTATION

Buses: Local open-air buses are cheap and frequent, making them the primary means of transportation for most locals; they can even be waved down from the side of the road. Fare from the airport to Nadi proper is $0.70; the bus stop at the airport is immediately outside the gate and across the street on Queens Rd. Local buses do not adhere to a strict schedule ("Fiji Time" being the reason and the excuse). **Sunset Express** (☎382 811, Nadi ☎720 266, Lautoka ☎668 276; fax 320 769) and **Fiji Express** (contact United Touring Ltd. ☎722 811, 722 821; fax 720 389, 720 107) both have express service to many cities in Viti Levu; **Pacific Transport Ltd.** (Nadi ☎700 004) runs the most buses at the lowest fare (14 daily; $0.42-10.36). See **Transportation** p. 391 for schedules and fares. All buses leave from the **Nadi Airport** outside the Arrivals gate, and from the **bus station** in Nadi proper, behind the market on Hospital Rd. across from the post office.

Car Rentals: Hertz, Avis, Budget, and a slew of other car rental companies have offices in the Arrivals Concourse of the Nadi airport. Despite the competition, rentals are expensive; most economy-class cars start at more than $50 per day.

Taxis: While many **taxis** have meters, just as many do not, and work on a **fixed price** system. Prices for tourists may vary wildly from prices for locals, however. Discussing a price before committing to the trip, and even haggling a bit, is common practice. It should cost no less than $6 and no more than $10 to get from the airport to Nadi proper. Many drivers charge more for driving down dirt and gravel side roads. Taxis coming back from a destination charge a **return fare,** the same as bus fare, and pick up as many passengers as possible; you've spotted one if it's half-full, honks at pedestrians walking along the road, and pulls over when you wave it down. The same system works for large 12-person **van carriers.** These to a certain extent, and **truck carriers** (with canopied flat beds and no seat belts) to a larger extent, serve remote villages and less-traveled areas along with more common routes. Fare for both should be cheaper than taxis and often match bus fares; fares in truck carriers are almost always negotiable.

Scooter/Motorcycle Rentals: Beat Motorcycle & Rentals (☎/fax 721 471, mobile 949 383), halfway to the airport on the Queens Rd. near Ed's Bar, hires scooters and motorbikes from $10 per 2hr. or $33 per day.

✦ ORIENTATION

If you picture the island of Viti Levu as the face of a clock with Rairaimatuku and the Nandrau Plateaus at the center, Nadi rests squarely at nine o'clock. The city and its environs curve 9km along **Nadi Bay** from the **airport** to the **city center** on **Queens Road,** whose final downtown stretch is often referred to as **Main St. Denarau**

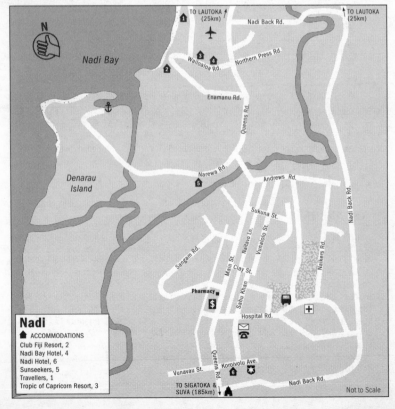

Nadi

▲ ACCOMMODATIONS
Club Fiji Resort, 2
Nadi Bay Hotel, 4
Nadi Hotel, 6
Sunseekers, 5
Travellers, 1
Tropic of Capricorn Resort, 3

Not to Scale

Island, just west of the city on **Narewa Rd.,** is nestled in the Bay and serves as the port for most tourist vessels headed for the Mamanuca and Yasawa Groups. North of the city, **Queens Rd.** heads 24km to **Lautoka,** and to the south 197km to **Suva.**

PRACTICAL INFORMATION

Visitors Center: Fiji Visitors Bureau, Arrivals Concourse in the Nadi Airport (☎ 722 433, 721 721; fax 720 141), is open to meet all international flights. Beware that many travel agents in downtown Nadi and in hotels masquerade as "official" visitors centers.

Banks: Many banks with **ATMs** and currency exchange services line the Queens Rd. in downtown Nadi. **ANZ** has **24hr.** branch in the Airport. Most banks are closed on Su.

American Express: Tapa International Ltd. (☎ 722 325; fax 721 427), the AmEx representative in Fiji. Branch in the Nadi Airport is open M-F 8:30am-5pm, Sa 9am-12pm.

Luggage Storage: Nadi Airport has **lockers.** Most hotels will store bags for a small fee.

Emergency: ☎ 000 throughout Fiji; **FVB Tourist Helpline:** ☎ 0800 721 721.

Police: Nadi Police Station (☎ 700 222) is at the end of Koroilovu Ave. off Queens Rd. on the south side of Nadi City. There are police posts in every section of Nadi, including **Namaka** (☎ 722 222) and the **Airport** (☎ 722 355).

Pharmacy: Thakorlal's Pharmacy, 347 Main St., (☎ 705 514; fax 705 517) is clean, well-staffed, and can fill prescriptions. Open M-Sa 8am-6pm, Su 10am-2pm.

Medical Services: The best care is found at the **Lautoka Hospital** (see p. 397) or a **private clinic;** the **Namaka Medical Center** (☎ 722 288; fax 723 926; mobile emergency 922 288; open M-Sa 9am-10pm, Su 9:30am-5pm; AmEx/MC/V and most travel insurance accepted) and the **Shortlane Medical Center** (☎ 725 707; fax 722 888; mobile emergency 955 151; open M-F 8am-5pm, Sa 8am-1pm; AmEx and some travel insurance accepted) are both on the Queens Rd. near the MH Supermarket in Namaka.

Internet Access: Connections can be brutally slow. **Cybernet Space Cafe** ($0.10 per min.; open M-Sa 8am-9pm, Su 10am-8pm) and **CyberCafe** (☎ 702 226; $0.10 per min.; $4 per 70min.; Sa $3 per hr., 10min. free per hr.; open M-Sa 8am-10pm, Su 9am-10pm) are both in Sharma's Arcade on Main St. **Internet Planet,** on Grey Rd. and Queens Rd. next to the Bounty Restaurant near Wailoaloa Rd., provides web access for $0.20 per min. (☎ 725 130. Open M-F 8am-9pm, Sa-Su 9am-9pm.)

Post Office: The **main** post office is in downtown Nadi behind the Civic Center arcade, across from the bus terminal. Poste Restante. Open M-F 8am-4pm, Sa 8am-noon. There is an office in Nadi Airport, and a roadside **stamp shop** and post box next to Proud's and the ZigZag Cafe (open M-F 8am-1pm and 2-4pm, Sa 8am-12pm).

ACCOMMODATIONS

Nadi Bay Hotel (☎ 723 599; fax 720 092; nadibay@is.com.fj), on Wailoaloa Rd. off Queen's Rd. halfway between the airport and Main St., packs blue pool, pink restaurant, and yellow sun into a prism of a place. Happy Hour 5-7pm at restaurant. Internet. Prices include breakfast. Dorms $15; private dorms $18; singles $44, with bath $82; doubles $52/92; Other options available. Stay 6 nights, 7th free. AmEx/MC/V.

Tropic of Capricorn Resort, 11 Wasawasa Rd. (☎ 723 089; fax 723 050), off Wailoaloa Rd. is just a year old and still shines. The white tiles, metal-framed blue-linened beds, and small maple kitchen seem brand new. Dorms $15; quads $45; doubles $95.

White House Visitor's Inn, 40 Kennedy Ave. (☎ 700 022; fax 780 468). Manager Joe will make you feel like one of his own. Your only chore: wash the dishes after eating free breakfast bread. 4-bed dorms $10; singles $25; doubles $30; $5 for A/C. Cash only.

Sunseekers (☎ 701 655; fax 702 047), 1km west on Navewa Rd. Turn a blind eye to the green pool and dingy floors; instead, nestle into clean sheets and dream of the islands. 6- and 10-bed dorms $8.80; singles $33, with A/C $38.50; doubles $38.50/$48.50.

Kon Tiki (☎ 722 836), off Votualevu Rd. 3km east of the airport. Tidy spartan rooms overlook cane fields. 5-bed dorms $11; singles $22; doubles $33. Cash only.

Travellers (☎ 723 322, 724 441; fax 720 026; beachvilla@is.com.fj), at the end of Wasawasa Rd. off Wailoaloa Rd. Spacious lounge and smallish rooms with clean beds. Free email. 4-bed dorms $11; singles $33, with A/C $40; doubles $40/$55. Stay 7 nights, 8th free. AmEx/MC/V.

▐ FOOD

Mama's Pizza (☎ 720 922), in the Colonial Plaza Mall in Namaka, serves the best slices in town ($6.50-$18.95). Open 10am-11pm. MC/V.

Skyway Restaurant & Takeaways (☎ 700 204) in the Civic Center on Main St., is where the locals munch on Indian fast food. Veggie curry $2.60. Open M-Su 7:30am-5pm.

Chefs: The Corner (☎ 703 131) is like a New York diner with pink booths and mirrored walls, but with curry instead of kosher corned beef. Lamb with ginger ($9), fish'n'chips ($6), and espresso ($2.50) hit the spot. Open M-Su 8am-5pm, 6-9pm.

Chefs: The Edge (☎ 703 131), in Jack's Handicrafts, is the bistro-style middle son. A complete menu of curries and continental fare ($9-25). Open daily 9am-10pm.

Chefs (☎ 703 131), behind Jack's handicrafts, the suave eldest sibling, has had time to mature. Dishes like crab and pumpkin soup ($10) and crepes suzette ($10) go well with an aged wine. Open daily 11am-2pm for lunch, 6-10pm for dinner.

The Highlands (☎ 702 929), at the corner of Koroilovu Ave. and Main St. is a typical Nadi fast food joint, except the food is hot, the service friendly, and the prices listed (thus making them the same for both tourists and locals). Open 10am-11:30pm.

◉ ♫ SIGHTS AND ENTERTAINMENT

Sri Suva Subrahmanya Swami Devasthanam, known as the **Swami Temple,** shines with color at the south end of Main St. Bright pinks, blues, and greens dominate the ornate concrete sculpture of this Hindu temple, opened in 1994 after two years of labor by dozens of Indian *silpi* (craftsmen). Check out the paintings of various Hindu deities, especially Murugan, the god of Nature. Visitors must dress neatly and modestly, leave their shoes at the entrance, and refrain from eating any non-vegetarian food, smoking, or drinking alcohol on the day of the visit. (☎ 700 016, fax 703 777. Open M-Su 5am-1pm and 3:30-8pm.) The **Novelty Movie Theater,** upstairs in the Civic Centre on Main St., shows $3 movies from Hollywood and Bollywood daily at 10am, 1:30, and 8pm, with added shows at 4:30pm on T and Th, while **Galaxy 2 Cinema** (☎ 700 176), 1st right south of the bridge on Main St., shows $3 Bollywood films daily at 10am, 1:30, and 8pm—great for those who understand Hindi.

▐ NIGHTLIFE

Ed's (☎ 724 650), on Queens Rd. just north of Wailoaloa Rd., is the bar at the top of everyone's list. A central location draws locals and tourists for music, company, and beer ($2.50 stubby), while **The West Coast Grill** (same location and ☎) feeds the bunch with Thai mussels ($9), and burgers ($6). Open daily 5pm-1am.

Planter's Club (☎ 750 777), in the Sheraton Fiji on Denerau Island at the end of Navewa Rd. The shroud of the Sheraton ensures a tidy and controlled atmosphere at this small bar. Wooden dance floor and DJ. Beer $4.50. Open Th-Su 8pm-1:30am.

▙ ACTIVITIES

DIVING: Inner Space Adventures (☎/fax 723 883), on Wasawasa Rd. at the end of Wailoaloa Rd. offers a range of dives. (1-tank $99; 2-tank $130; dive daily for $30 after $350-699 PADI course. Hotel pick-up and gear included.)

GOLF: Nadi Golf Club, at the end of Wailoaloa Rd. between the airport and the Bay. The first club in Nadi has 150 members. (☎ 722 148. Ladies' day Th, competition day Sa 70 par. Open daily 7am-6pm for non-members. Buggy rental $3; clubs $20; greens fee $15.) **Fiji Macambo Golf Course & Shop,** at the Fiji Macambo Hotel on Votualevu Rd. 2km east of the airport, is a modern, Western-style course on top of Namaca Hill. (☎ 722 000. $11 greens fee. Open daily 10am-6pm.)

DON'T BE SUCH A SWORD LOSER Upon arriving in Fiji tourists quickly fall into two categories: those who *don't* buy swords from street vendors, and those who do and regret it. Nadi and Suva both teem with guys pressing to shake your hand, get your name, quickly carve it into the handle of a shoddy sword, sell it to you for loads of moolah, then quickly walk away as the sword breaks and you cry. It happens every day. Avoid these men and their evil scamming ways, and remember—even if they carve your name in a sword, you don't have to pay for it.

JET BOAT. Shotover Jet Fiji, in Port Denarau, takes fast and wild ½hr. rides around Denarau and up the Nadi River in 12-person jet boats. (☎750 400, fax 750 666, reservations@shotoverjet.com.fj. $69, children $25; hotel pick-up included.)

LAUTOKA

Lautoka looked lovely to the mutinied Captain Bligh of *HMS Bounty* fame when he spotted it from his dinghy in 1789; today it proves a rewarding respite for those escaping the tourist traps of nearby Nadi. The second largest city in Fiji, Lautoka is a worker's town inundated by industry, home to a large fishing port, a distillery, a lumber and woodchip export plant, and the Colonial Refining Company, which starts buzzing with its sugar high every June when cane shuttles in on trolley tracks from the fields. Travelers benefit from the scene—shopping is good and prices fair (i.e. much lower than in Nadi) in both clothing stores and the market.

▸ TRANSPORTATION

To get to Lautoka, the top-end **express buses** run by **Sunset Express** (☎382 811, Nadi ☎720 266, Lautoka ☎668 276; fax 320 769), **Fiji Express** (contact United Touring Ltd. ☎722 811, 722 821; fax 720 389, 720 107), and **Pacific Transport Ltd.** (Nadi ☎660 499, 700 004; Suva see p. 411) are quick and inexpensive; see **Transportation** p. 391 for schedules. Open-air **local buses** take longer, stopping at every bus shelter and village along the way, but come along main roads every 15min. during the week. 12-person **vans** often wait during the early morning in certain areas of the bigger cities for transfers to other big cities; they leave when they fill up, charging $20 a head from Suva to Lautoka. A private **taxi** from Nadi Airport takes 30min. ($20); local taxis and carriers are plentiful and cheap (if you're not afraid to bargain).

✦❔ ORIENTATION AND PRACTICAL INFORMATION

24km north of Nadi Airport the **Queens Road** ends at the outskirt entrance of Lautoka, where it splits into **Navutu Rd.** and **Drasa Rd.** Navutu splits again before joining **Nadovu Rd.** and becoming **Vitogo Parade** in the city center. Vitogo Parade runs parallel to **Naviti St.,** the four-block main drag. Drasa Rd. bypasses this central shopping district and spits north-bound vehicles onto the **Kings Road.**

Banks: All major banks with **ATMs,** including **ANZ** (open M-Th 9:30am-3pm, F 9:30am-4pm), are at the western entrance of Vitogo Parade and Naviti St. near the post office.

Police: Lautoka Police Station (☎660 222) is off Drasa Rd., across from Yawini St. just south of Churchill Park. **Ambulance** administrative calls are ☎660 399.

Pharmacy: Thakorlal's Pharmacy, 103 Vitogo Parade (☎664 645, 664 044; fax 665 946), right near the park. Open M-F 8am-6pm, Sa 8am-1pm.

Medical Services: Lautoka Hospital (☎660 399), at the end of Hospital Rd. off Thomson Crescent, or **private clinics** such as the **Bayly Clinic,** 5 Nede St. (☎665 133, 664 599, mobile 953 197; open M-F 8am-4:30pm, Sa 8am-1pm) and **Dr. Gounder Suman Lata** (☎662 334, mobile 953 603; fax 662 332; goundersds@is.com.fj) on Vakabale St.; both accept travel insurance and major credit cards. As always, the best modern care is found in Suva (see p. 412), and all persons with major injuries or illness should seek attention there after initial contact with local heath services.

Internet Access: Cyberzone Netcafe, 159 Vitogo Parade (☎651 675) has the lowest rates in town. Su special $0.10 per hr. Open M-Sa 8am-7:30pm, Su 10am-2pm.

Post Office: ☎660 022; fax 664 666. On Vitogo Parade. Open M-F 8am-4pm, Sa 8am-noon. Poste Restante. Post Shoppe next door.

ACCOMMODATIONS

Lautoka has many affordable accommodations; however, many of them rent by the hour, and are used by prostitutes. Travelers should avoid the **Mon Repo Back-packers,** where professional ladies offer their services with the rooms. The **Diamond Hotel** is noisy and suffers from excessive bugs and litter. The following are some of the better choices in town.

Cathay Hotel (☎660 566; fax 660 136; cathay@fiji4less.com, www.fiji4less.com), on Tavewa Rd. across from the Northern Club, has TV, a courtyard pool, and the best dorm deals in town: clean and spartan 3- and 4- bed rooms are $11, with A/C $16. Singles $31.90, with A/C $41.80; doubles $39.60, with A/C $48.40. AmEx/MC/V.

Lautoka Hotel, 2-12 Naviti St. (☎660 388, 660 126; fax 660 201). Clean and basic rooms all have bath and fan, and most have A/C, fridge, and a sitting area. Restaurant/nightclub downstairs. 2-bed dorm $15; singles $25; doubles $30-59. AmEx/MC/V.

Sea Breeze Hotel, 5 Bekana Ln. (☎660 717; fax 666 080). Feel ocean wind through a chain-link fence; despite seeming a bit like a city tenement, the lush courtyard and big blue pool make the place pretty pleasant. Authentic mattresses and clean baths. Singles $33, with A/C $40; doubles $37/$45. AmEx/MC/V.

Hotel 2000 (☎666 546; fax 667 476), on Tavewa Ave., opened in June 2001 fit for the new millennium. The 6 rooms are sparkling new, with 1 double and single bed each, big bathrooms and new wood furniture; though this may be standard motel fare in other countries, it seems like big news in Lautoka. Continental breakfast included; room service available. Kava, post, and liquor store. All rooms $55. AmEx.

FOOD AND NIGHTLIFE

Ganga's Vegetarian Restaurant (☎662 990), at the corner of Yasawa and Naviti St. Tiny milk-and-sugar *barfi* ($0.40, mango is especially good) sooth after spicy samosas and chutney. 3-scoop ice cream $1.80. A/C. Open M-F 9am-4:30pm, Sa 9am-1:30pm.

Pizza Inn, The Corner Cafe, and the **Sea View Restaurant,** 2 Naviti St. (☎664 592), are all practically the same operation in the Lautoka Hotel. Partitions separate the more expensive Sea View from the others, which have lunch specials like chicken fried rice ($3), club sandwiches ($4), and small cheese pizzas ($5). Open daily 8am-9:30pm.

Fins (☎664 777), in the Waterfront Hotel at the end of Marine Dr. and the corner of Shirley Park, is modern and sleek. Steamed mussels $14.50; pine nut and pumpkin ravioli $12.75. Open daily 6:30am-10pm. AmEx/MC/V.

MH Foodcourt (☎662 999), in the back of the MH Supermarket at the corner of Vidilo St. Relax in a wicker chair with roast chicken and chips ($3.70) near Housewares in Aisle 3. Open M-F 9am-5pm, Sa 9am-1pm.

Jolly Good (☎669 980), under a big-top tent at the corner of Naviti and Vakabale St., across from the Market. The loud radio and constant flux of locals is a circus of activity. Chinese chicken spring rolls $0.80; "x-large" slush $2. Open M-Sa 8am-10pm.

The Northern Club (☎660 184), Yanduli Rd. off Tavewa Ave., is a quiet, members-only club (tourists welcome) with tennis facilities and a large lounge, bar, porch, and pool tables. Sip beer in a big comfy chair ($1.45) Low-priced restaurant on site. Generally very quiet. Open M-W and Sa 8am-10pm, Th 8am-11pm, F 8-midnight, Su 8am-8pm.

Hunters Inn (☎660 388l), at the corner of Tui and Naviti St. next to the Lautoka Hotel, floods with youngbloods hunting for a large mix of musical styles. Feast on the bounty. Open M-W noon-9pm, Th-Sa noon-1:30am.

Coco's (☎668 989), at the corner of Vidilo and Naviti St., is a dark disco playing popular music from reggae to techno. F Bula Night. Open Tu-Sa 8pm-1am. $1.50 stubby during 5-7pm Happy Hour applies upstairs at the **Rooftop Bar** (open Tu-Sa 5-11pm).

👁 🎢 SIGHTS AND ACTIVITIES

Aside from the usual diversions of visiting the market and exploring the city, there is little to do immediately in Lautoka. The 9-hole **Lautoka Golf Club** (☎613 411) off Tavakubu Rd. south of the city, lets guests play for less than $5 on the course where internationally-ranked golfer Vijay Singh got his start. The **Village Four Cinema** shows English and Hindi movies in constant rotation in its four theaters ($4), with late-night showings on F and Sa.

GARDEN OF THE SLEEPING GIANT. Originally the collection of *Perry Mason* actor Raymond Burr, this rambling rainforest garden and nursery at the foot of the "Sleeping Giant" mountain contains three dozen types of Asian orchids. Elephant ears, hibiscus, flowers growing out of coconuts, and free juice and pawpaws. *(6½km north of Nadi Airport on Wailoko Rd.; look for the small arrow sign. ☎723 418. Open M-Sa 9am-5pm, Su 9am-noon. Adults $9.90; children age 5-15 $4.90; families $24.90.)*

VISEISEI VILLAGE. This is perhaps the most touristed and groomed of any Fijian village; set on cut grass and banked by the sea, the picturesque village has been visited by Queen Elizabeth II, Princess Margaret, and Prince Charles. Village members are royalty too; the current chief was made President of Fiji after the coup in 2000, and is also the Tui (king) of three nearby villages. One Sunday each month services are held at the John Wesele Methodist Church; coming early means visitors won't have to struggle to hear the hymns, most of which are original English Methodist songs translated into Fijian and spiced up with a bit of rhythm over the years. *(9½ km north of the airport, at the foot of Vuda Point.)*

VUDA POINT. According to legend the first Melanesians came to Fiji in a canoe called *Leaunitoni*, landing on a rock called Nalamu ("to pierce"); the seafarers moved a few meters south and settling at Viseisei. Now called Vuda Point, this site is popularly considered the first landing spot of the Fijian people. Though fraught with significance, visitors here can find neither proof nor monument; picnics are a nice alternative. *(Walking along the beach from Viseisei or take the road on the hill 2km north of the village—look for signs to Anchorage Resort—which leads 3km past the oil tanks to a sandy road; from here walk through a cane field between 2 freshwater ponds to get to the Point. The local bus comes infrequently, less than 1 per hr. on weekdays.)*

KINGS ROAD

While fertile farming land and tourist resorts stretch south along the Queens Road from Suva to Lautoka, northern Viti Levu along the Kings Rd. is mostly agricultural and industrial land. Rolling hills and mountain backdrops stand in contrast to seaside vistas on the north coast, while eastern cow towns sit tight together along the dirt stretch of the road. Visitors rarely get as much direction as the cattle; with fewer services, visitors avoid being herded along established tourist routes.

✈ INTERCITY TRANSPORTATION

Hiring private transport in the form of **taxi** or **rental car** is by far the easiest way to get around the Kings Rd., especially for quick sightseeing; **taxis** are plentiful in most northern and eastern towns. A cab from Lautoka to Suva takes more than 4hr. and costs over $100; each leg of the Lautoka-Ba-Tavua-Rakiraki section takes about 30min. and costs $15-30. Slower buses are the only cheaper option; **Pacific Transport Ltd.** (Nadi ☎700 004) runs the only A/C express bus to **Ba** (see **Transportation** p. 391 for schedule and fares). Local buses also run between **Lautoka, Ba, Tavua, Rakiraki,** every **eastern village, Korovou,** and **Nausori** before reaching **Suva** (5 transfers per day; about $3 for each leg of the Lautoka-Rakiraki section). The dirt portion of the Kings Rd. takes almost 2hr. by car, and almost 3hr. by bus ($5). **Carriers** are an alternative (depart dependent on market times F-Sa 5-9am and 4-7pm, $10-20). See **Interior Highlands** p. 406 for info on treks to the interior of the island.

BA

Recently placed off the main stretch of the Kings Rd. by the construction of a new bridge, **Ba** (pop. 13,000) is also off the tourist track. Local interests such as horse races at the track, the nationally competitive soccer team, and the Rarawai Sugar Mill are the few attractions for visitors, although the real draw of Ba is its location as a base for interior village towns, including **Navala** (p. 407) and **Bukuya** (p. 408). The **bus station** is at the entrance to town across from the rotary and the Mobil station. For **ATMS,** try the **Exchange & Finance Fiji Ltd.** (☎670 766; open M-F 8:30am-5pm, Sa 8:30am-1pm), **ANZ, Westpac,** or **Bank of Baroda,** all on the main drag (open M-Th 9:30am-3pm, F 9:30am-4pm). Other services include: the **police station** (☎674 222) on the corner of Koronubu and Kula St. east of the rotary in the center of town; the **ambulance** (☎674 108); Dr. Patel Nima Jayant (☎/fax 674 121, residence 670 195) in nearby Varoka; the **Western Pharmacy** (☎674 561; fax 670 158; open M-Sa 8am-6pm); the **post office** on Nareba St. (☎674 341; fax 670 066; open M-F 8am-4pm, Sa 8am-12pm); and **internet access** at **Venus Stationary 2000** (☎676 342; fax 670 183; $0.30 per min., $15 per hr). The **Town Square Cinema** (☎674 048) only shows Hindi films. English speakers can strain to understand on Super Tuesdays for $2.

The only accommodation is **Ba Hotel,** on Banks St. near Varoka St., which offers 10 foam-mat beds in a tight dorm; the toilet is *in* the shower. Family rooms are nicer. (☎674 000; fax 670 559. Dorms $10; singles $44; doubles $55; family $66.) The hotel **restaurant** is small and mediocre (lemon chicken or sandwiches $5), while the bar hawks cheap beer. **Chand's Restaurant,** on Main St., has fast food downstairs and seated eats upstairs—the best and only choice for sit-down food ($3-8) besides the hotel. (☎670 822. Open M-Sa 11am-6:30pm.) **Abby's Cake Shop,** across from the bus station, sells simple baked goods. (☎575 822. Open daily 7am-6pm.) The **New World Supermarket** is behind the bus stand at the town entrance. (☎674 600. Open M-F 8am-5pm, Sa 8am-1pm.)

TAVUA

Similar to Ba, Tavua is an agricultural town with a large Indian population and a sizable sugar industry. Of more interest may be the Yaqara cattle station between here and Rakiraki, which has over 4000 cows, nearby Vatukoula, home of the Emperor Gold Mining Company since 1931. The Monasavu Dam in the southern highlands controls much of the river flow in the region. None of this can be visited, however. The town serves as a launching pad for inland treks. Outfit yourself at the **market,** at the edge of town across from the bus station on the Kings Rd., which is the biggest in the area. **Caboni Beach** provides a seaside respite 20min. farther along King's Rd. toward Rakiraki; ask directions from local bus drivers for the dirt access road. Town services include: the **police station** on the hill (☎680 222); the tiny **hospital** (☎680 444); the **Excel Pharmacy** (☎/fax 680 108, after-hours 681 179; open M-F 8:30am-5:30pm, Sa until 1pm); and the **post office** on Nasivi St. just west of the police station (☎680 239; fax 681 435; open M-F 8am-4pm, Sa 8am-12pm).

The only place to stay in town is the **Tavua Hotel,** at the top of the hill off Nabuna St. A grand old 1930s Colonial, this fine building is the best choice along the Kings Rd. for inexpensive lodging. While the dorm is tight other options are spacious, with big beds, real mattresses, and clean bathrooms. BBQ pits, a pool, and a bar/nightclub under construction. (☎680 522; fax 680 390. Dorms $25; singles $33; doubles $44. A/C $22 more.) The **restaurant** serves decent food. Breakfasts are only $5; dinners range from $12-16. **Lee's Hot Bread Takeaway & Restaurant** is a cafeteria-style fast-food joint. Veggie curry $2.80. (☎681 888. Open M-Sa 8-2am, Su 2-8pm.)

RAKIRAKI

The northernmost town in Viti Levu, Rakiraki is most often used by budget travelers on route to Nananu-i-ra (p. 402). The only tourist sight in town is **Udre Udre's Tomb,** the resting place of a former Tui (chief) from the 19th century; each stone piled around his tomb represents the head of one of the 800 people infamous Udre killed and devoured before his own death. Brains were considered a delicacy fit only for the chief's tongue, so Udre Udre was required to eat each without using his hands—a very messy proposition.

While the town and the small surrounding region are referred to as Rakiraki, the one-block, two-street downtown area is properly called **Vaileka**, and is reached by a 1km turn-off from the Kings Rd. at the rotary split and police post (the sign reads "Vaileka"). The downtown area is a small ring of shops surrounding the market, bus station, police station, and post office. The Kings Rd. continues 12km after the turn-off to the Wananavu Beach Resort and Ellington's Wharf, both with jetties for boat transfers to Nananu-i-ra. Rakiraki is an agricultural town similar to Tavua and Ba. The most interesting thing about it may also be the most scary; the **water** in the area was deemed non-potable seven years ago after a major mainline contamination, and though locals now drink it, **visitors are still warned to avoid tap water.** Ironically, the major bottling plant for Fiji Mineral Water is just north of the city. Other services include: **emergencies** (giardia-related and otherwise) ☎ 000; the **police** ☎ 694 222; the **ambulance** ☎ 694 368; Dr. Naidu Ram ☎ 694 284; and the **post office** in Vaileka ☎ 694 060.

The only budget accommodation option is the **Rakiraki Hotel,** a cozy hostel 5km east of Vaileka on the Kings Rd. Rooms surround an airy shed with a central barn-like sitting room. Each room has two beds and porthole windows with clean private baths. (☎ 694 101; fax 694 545. Singles $35, with A/C $49.50; doubles $44, with A/C $66. AmEx/MC/V.) The best chow in the area are the restaurants at the Rakiraki (full meals from $11) and at the posh **Wananavu Beach Resort** (6km from Vaileka at the end of a 3km dirt road; signs near bus stop on the Kings Rd. direct visitors). Though beyond budget prices, the main lodge's restaurant, bar, and veranda are like a millionaire's treehouse—visit for a drink and a stroll to enjoy the ambience. (☎ 694 433; fax 694 499. AmEx/MC/V.) The **Rakiraki** serves full meals from $11. The **Wananavu's** ever-changing menu includes grilled tuna sandwiches ($12) and Thai egg rolls ($9).

Ellington's Wharf, 9km east of Vaileka and down a short access road, is where most boat transfers depart for Nananu-i-ra, as well as Vanua Levu and other islands. Aside from specific resort-run transfers to Nananu-i-ra (see p. 402), the **Safari Lodge** (☎ 693 333; fax 693 366; safarilodge@is.com.fj) and **Watersports Adventures** run **licensed** and **safety-equipped boats** for transfer ($11 per person, 2 person min.) and activity purposes (see **Nananu-i-ra: Activities** p. 403), and should have a backpacker resort up and running on Ellington's by May 2002. They stock a small store with basic foods on the Wharf. The jetty at Wananavu is also often used as a pick-up point for boat transfers; arrangements should be made with specific lodgings on Nananu-i-ra, and permission may be needed from the Wananavu.

NAISERELAGI VILLAGE

About 25km south of Rakiraki along the Kings Rd. is **Naiserelagi Village** and its **Catholic Mission,** site of the famous **Black Christ** mural in the St. Francis Xavier Parish. The fresco, painted in 1962 by French artist Jean Charlotte at the request of then-caretaker Monsignor Franz Wagner (former singing tutor to the Von Trapp tots of *Sound of Music* fame), depicts the story of Christ with traditional Fijian motifs. Martyred St. Peter Chanel, the first Fijian Catholic Priest Father Mataca, a *tanoa* bowl symbolizing the Eucharist, breadfruit, and a man offering Christ a *tabua* (the highest Fijian token of respect; see p. 385) are pictured.

NAUSORI

Nausori is home to Fiji's second largest airport, which thrives largely on domestic travel from Nadi to Suva; it is located 4km east of town on Wainibokasi Rd., accessed from the rotary near the market and the Rewa Bridge on the southern edge of town. **No public buses** stop there, but **taxis** charge a reasonable rate ($5). There is an **ANZ** and a **Colonial Bank** with **ATMs** on Main St. (open M-Th 9:30am-3pm, F 9:30am-4pm). The **Rewa Pharmacy** is on Main St. near the market. (☎ 478 235; fax 400 134; mobile 977 916. Open M-Sa 8am-6pm.) Considering Nausori's proximity to Suva's first-class medical care, any emergencies should be directed there (see p. 412); **Goundars Medical Clinic** (☎ 400 850; mobile 99 850) on Main St. is otherwise capable. The **police station** (☎ 477 222) is just south of the rotary on Court St. next to the **post office** (☎ 477 745).

Nausori's proximity to Suva, its absence of tourist services, and its lack of top accommodations give reason enough not to stay here unless completely forced to. Whereas the **King's Hotel** hosts a raucous and rowdy bar and night-

VITI LEVU

club and its rooms are used primarily by prostitutes. The only other place in town, the **Riverside,** is reasonably clean and can adequately serve travelers in a pinch, although it has no phone. When coming from Suva and the southern end of town, take the first left after the Shell Station, then the first right behind the block of Main St. buildings; the Riverside is the third house on the left. (Doubles $25, $140 per week.) A great place to eat is **Jay's Restaurant & Takeaway** on Main St., one block north of the market. Waves of hungry locals wash through this cafeteria for quality Indian fast food and loads of sweet treats. (☎476 614. Open M-Sa 6:30am-5pm. Basic groceries for sale.)

NANANU-I-RA

Just off the northeastern shore of Viti Levu from Rakiraki, 870-acre Nananu-i-ra gives budget travelers several great choices of accommodation; this established island destination allows travelers to chase the sun without the hordes of other bores who do the same. Eight beaches, strong winds and coral, and a lack of Fijian culture means that this is primarily an activity-based island where diversion, athletic and otherwise, is the name of the game.

 TRANSPORTATION. Most transfers leave from **Ellington's Wharf** in Rakiraki, though when making reservations with any of the hostels on the island, you may be able to arrange pick-up at the Wananavu (see p. 401), which has a restaurant for pre-transfer meals. The **Safari Lodge** (☎693 333; fax 693 366; safarilodge@is.com.fj) and **Watersports Adventures** are the least expensive, running **licensed** and **safety-equipped boats** ($11 per person, 2 person min.). Check with **Beachcomber** (☎661 500, 723 828; fax 664 496; beachcomber@is.com.fj; www.beachcomberfiji.com) to see if the *Lagi Lagi* still comes through twice weekly from **Nadi** and **Lautoka** ($50).

 ORIENTATION AND PRACTICAL INFORMATION. Three of the four budget accommodations on triangular Nananu-i-ra are clustered near the southern tip at a point between Wainimolona and Lomanisue Bays, where the interior is skinny enough to allow a short walk to the Mile Long Beach on the eastern side. Walking north along this beach is the quickest way to get to **Mokusiga's Island Resort,** an upscale establishment whose back entrance is marked with a sign reading *Sa Tabuna Lakdeke;* the front of the resort has a private jetty. North of this area the island gets thicker, and the interior is primarily privately-owned subdivided property. There is **no police, post office, emergency** medical facility, or **bank** on the island (you may need cash—call ahead to hostels to find if they have a credit card machine *and* if it's working). There are **phones** at all hostels, and most charge for local calls. The **Mokusiga Resort** may have the most resources to deal with an emergency, though any serious medical problems should be taken to **Suva** (p. 410).

 ACCOMMODATIONS. The three hostels grouped near the southern tip (Betham's, MacDonald's, and Charlie's) are similar in room style and meals; activities and transfers can be shared among them (for appropriate fees, of course), though this may be limited in high season. Renting a private **home** is sometimes affordable for a group, though getting the information and a good rate may necessitate knowing a local; give Warren at the Safari Lodge a try for more info, as well as the Fiji Visitors Bureau, which may have new brochures. Also keep a keen eye out for the **Safari Lodge** itself, which should have new accommodations on Ellington's Wharf and the north side of Nananu-i-ra, both with loads of activities.

Betham's Beach Cottages (☎/fax 694 132, 0800 684 132; www.bethams.com.fj), is under (relatively) new management, and the influence subtly shows; rooms practically scream "I'm clean!" Lockers $1 per day, $5 per week. $10 key deposit. Snorkeling $10 per day, kayaks $5 per hr. **Robb's Shop** sells groceries. Reserve dinner meals ($15-20) by noon. 6- and 10-bed dorms with kitchenette $16.50; cottages $75. MC/V.

MacDonald's Cottages (☎694 633; fax 694 302), is strikingly similar to Betham's. Snorkeling to One Beach $15; lovo night $17. Dinner is usually curry or fish dishes for about $12; order before 4pm. Lunch menu includes $3.50 sandwiches and $12-15 pizza. 6-bed dorms $16.50; bures for 1 or 2 $71, $9.90 each additional person.

Charlie's Place (☎694 676), is the smallest hostel on the island, but has the most space per person in 3 hilltop huts. Clean white bathrooms and spacious kitchenettes thanks to a low number of guests. Laundry $5. Snorkeling $10 per day or $15 per 2½hr. tour. Fishing $20 per hr. Transfers $18 return. No food available. Dorms $16.50; huts for 1 or 2 $66, $8 each additional person.

⬛🅵 FOOD AND NIGHTLIFE. The food available at hostels is described under the accommodations listings above. The **Safari Lodge** stocks a small store with basic groceries on the Wharf, and both Betham's and MacDonald's have their own mini-marts, but buying food and supplies in Rakiraki provides more options and lower costs. There is occasionally an Indian man wandering the hostel area on the island selling curries, roti, and samosas for under $3. Close in distance but not in price range, **Mokusiga's Island Resort** (☎694 449; fax 694 404) serves fresh specials all day every day from an ever-changing blackboard menu. Nightlife usually involves some sort of communal intoxication at **Mokusiga's Bar** or at **Betham's** or **McDonald's;** avoid the (minor) island markups and be a cheap drunk by snagging booze duty-free before going offshore.

🅲🅼 BEACHES AND ACTIVITIES. Most of the island's privately owned interior can't be walked through, though it can be circumnavigated by beach; the total trek takes about 6hr. Of the eight beaches, the nicest are **Mile Long** and **One Beach** (OH-knee). Reach Mile Long Beach by the short path between Betham's and Charlie's; One Beach is similar, though a bit wider and with better sunset views.

The **Bligh Waters** are far off the north shore, with good breaks for surfing closer in. Frequent strong winds make **windsurfing** the activity of choice. While most windsurfers bring their own equipment, the **Safari Lodge** hires boards ($20); contact them for availability. The Lodge also has four sailing vessels, sea kayaking ($9), snorkeling ($15), and fishing gear on Ellington's Wharf, and should soon be able to provide services on the island as well. All of the backpackers listed above offer snorkeling gear. **Ra Divers,** based on the island, is PADI-certified with a full range of introductory and higher level courses available. (☎694 511; fax 694 611. Introductory course $175, full package rental $25; successive dives $75.) **Crystal Divers** (☎694 747; fax 694 877; www.crystaldivers.com) has its base in Rakiraki, but dives on Nananu-i-ra with similar services and prices.

THE CORAL COAST

Traffic along the Queens Road between capital Suva and capitalistic Nadi is flanked to the north by fertile farmland and to the south by the region's namesake attraction—over 100km of fantastic soft coral. Though the Coast tends to be wetter than western parts of Viti Levu, the bevy of tourist spots, beautiful location, and quality surfing and diving are wonderful for the more resort-minded traveler.

SIGATOKA AND POINTS WEST

Lying a third of the way between Nadi and Suva at the mouth of the Sigatoka River, Sigatoka (SING-uh-toke-ah) is surrounded by more important places. However, with a handful of notable attractions and a relaxed service industry for tourists, Sigatoka makes a pleasant and convenient base for exploring the Coral Coast.

🅴 TRANSPORTATION. Buses from **Sunset Express** (Nadi ☎720 266, 382 811; Suva fax 320 769), **Fiji Express** (contact United Touring Ltd. ☎722 811, 722 821; fax 720 389, 720 107), and **Pacific Transport Limited** (☎660 499, Nadi 700 004) all serve Sigatoka; See **Transportation** p. 391 for schedules and fares. Open-air **public buses** comes quite frequently, though they make many stops. 12-person **vans** and **taxis** often wait during the early morning for transfers to large towns and cities.

🅴🅿 ORIENTATION AND PRACTICAL INFORMATION. Gas stations and a handful of **shops** line the stretch of Queens Rd. east of the rotary and the bridge, where town-bound traffic splits off north onto Sigatoka Valley Rd. Market Rd., which circles the market and bus station, is the location of the majority of businesses, including the **banks** and **supermarkets.**

VITI LEVU

The **police** (☎007 or 500 222) are on Water Supply Rd., off Queens Rd. west of the rotary; reach the **ambulance** at ☎500 264. **Medical emergencies** should be directed to the Suva Private Hospital (see **Suva: Practical Information** p. 412), or **Gerona Medical & Surgical Clinic**, on the third block of shops on Valley Rd. (mobile 975 003. Open M-F 8:30am-4pm, Sa 8:30am-1pm; night clinic open daily 6:30-8pm.) **Care Chemist** is in Market Square. (☎520 393. Open M-F 8am-6:45pm, Sa 8am-4:30pm, Su 10am-12pm.) The **post office** is across from the police station. (☎500 321. Open M-F 8am-4pm, Sa 8am-12pm.) **T-Wicks Fiji Ltd.** (☎520 928) has **internet access** ($15 per hr.); **Le Cafe** (see **Food** below) has similar prices. Four major **banks** in the immediate downtown area have **ATMs.** (Open M-Th 9:30am-3pm, F 9:30am-4pm.)

▐ ACCOMMODATIONS. Club Masa, down a 3km dirt road 3km west of Sigatoka (look for signs, or take the thrice-daily Kulukulu bus from Sigatoka), attracts surfers, loungers, jokers, and tokers—those who like being elevated can't do any better. Prices include 3 meals per day. (☎500 643. Board rentals $25. Horseback riding $20 per hr. 10-bed dorm $30; cabins $40; family room $60; camping $18. Cash only.) The **Hotel Riverview,** on the town side of the rotary, is a boarding house in classic small-town style. (☎520 544; fax 520 016. 3-bed dorm $15; singles $35; doubles $45; add $5 for A/C. Cash only.) The **Sigatoka Club,** on the ocean side of the rotary, is primarily a bar with a large local draw, but has rooms for rent and a large dorm. (☎/fax 500 026. Dorms $19; singles $25; doubles $38. MC/V.)

▐▐▐ FOOD AND NIGHTLIFE. Krispas Party Cake & Delicious Curry Shop, halfway down Mission Rd., is a tiny local haunt. $3 curries and fresh *roti.* banana bread $0.60. (☎500 445. Open M-Sa 8am-5pm.) **Lucky Corner,** at the southwest corner of the market, seats hordes at lunchtime. Chinese and Indian foods are in full force, including $0.80 fried eggs and $2.50 chicken fried rice. (☎520 275. Open M-Sa 8am-5pm.) **Le Cafe,** on the first block of Valley Rd., is the most tourist-geared spot in town, situated appropriately next to the duty-free trinket shops. (☎520 668; fax 520 864. Open M-Sa 8am-5pm.) The **H&M** on the corner of Valley and Market Rd., is open for groceries Monday to Saturday 9am-5pm. The **Sigatoka Club** draws locals with its chic '50s-era bowling alley feel. (☎/fax 500 026. $3.50 curries; $5 fried fish. Open M-Sa 10am-10pm, Su 10am-9pm.)

◙ SIGHTS. Enjoy great views of the eastern mountains from atop the finely sanded peaks of the 650-hectare **Sigatoka Sand Dunes;** archaeologists recently excavated over 50 skeletons from elaborate coral-mounded tombs dating from 5 BC. The Fijian government named the dunes its first national park in 1989, effectively protecting not only the burial sites, but also the 165 plant species found in the area's native casuarina and pandanus forests. The park entrance and visitors center is clearly marked 5km west of Sigatoka. (☎520 343; fax 520 243. $5 fee.) Frequent buses headed to Nadi from Sigatoka make drops at the park for $0.40; taxi fare should be $6. **Natadola Beach,** 4km west of Sigatoka and an additional 8km down bumpy Natadola Rd., is one of the most beautiful beaches on Viti Levu. The **Natadola Beach Resort** (☎721 002; fax 721 000; www.natadola.com) is quite high-end; they have a **phone** in case of an emergency, and a restaurant with $12 burgers. A local bus goes to the beach from Nadi via Sigatoka four times daily, dropping passengers 3km from the beach. If driving or biking, follow signs for the resort or for Robinson Crusoe Island, then take a left at the T about 6km further. The **Tavuni Hill Fort,** 4km north of Sigatoka near Naroro Village, is the ancient site of the first Tongan settlement in Fiji and is the only original "cannibal" village open to tourists. (Entry $6, $3 children. Carrier or taxi fare should be around $5; the local bus departs Sigatoka 7 times daily for $0.55. Walking from town takes 45min.; take the first left after the bridge onto Kavanagasau Rd., follow it along the river until it veers straight up the hill and reaches the fort—signs mark the route.) The **Ka Levu Center,** across from the Fijian Resort just west of Sigatoka, is a Fijian cultural museum introducing visitors to the basics of bure construction, pottery and weaving handcrafts, ancient and modern history of Fijians and Indo-Fijians, typical ceremonies, and traditional tools and weapons.

⛄️ VILLAGE VISITS AND DAYTRIPS. The women in two villages just north of Sigatoka show visitors the process and products of their handiwork. **Lawai Village** is 2km from town down Valley Rd., clearly marked with a large sign, and specializes in pottery made from clay collected from the hillside and river. The 1hr. demonstration costs $5, and visitors, welcome any time of day, should follow village rules and bring a *sevusevu*. The same applies for **Lakabuta Village,** 1km past Lawai and also clearly marked, which specializes in both pottery and weaving. Demonstration costs $5. Cab fare to both villages should be $3-4.

Despite its homeliness, to idle on **Robinson Crusoe Island** is to be in budget bliss. Twenty-five-acre Likuri, as it's called in Fijian, was possibly one of the first landing sites of the native Fijians. Opened in January 2001, the resort's beehive reception and bar, cramped toilets (with ingenious, if cold, bucket showers), and wood-shack dorm will benefit from planned additions and improvements. Transfer to the island, including bus ride from Nadi and boat ride from the Natadola Rd. Jetty, costs $40; the jetty is 3km off Queen's Rd. west of Sigatoka. Once on the island, **dive** with Aquatrek, **waterski** ($15 per 10min.), **snorkel** ($5), or **cruise** on the catamaran. If you want to extend your daytrip to a few days there are dorms and more private options, all with shared bath. Filling buffet-style meals, included in the room price, are very high quality, especially on the three days each week when the day-trippers ($79) come to join in the feast. (☎/fax 510 100; mobile 950 131; robinsoncrusoeisland@hotmail.com. Dorms $40; private bure doubles $45; twin/double lodges $55. Cash only.)

KOROLEVU AND SURROUNDS

27 km east of Sigatoka, Korolevu Town isn't much: it consists of a **bus stop,** a **phone booth,** and a **corner store** (open M-Sa 9am-5pm), meaning travelers on public transportation can buy food and call a ride when dropped off on their way to the one of the two budget resorts. The **police** post (☎530 122) is across from the corner store.

That the 🏖️**Beachouse** is popular is no secret; the lush gardens and beachfront locale are simple but humongous draws. The rooms are basic and clean; the loft dorms have more privacy. Food at the Beachouse's **Coconut Cafe** is excellent if a little pricey ($5.50 bowl of chips). Complimentary 4pm tea with homemade jam and fresh, hot scones and frequent free boat trips; free kayaks and bikes. (☎0800 530 530, 530 500; fax 450 400; beachouse@is.com.fj. 5-bed dorms $16.50; loft dorms $18-20; doubles $46; camping $8.80. Stay 6 nights, 7th free. MC/V.) Get to the **Waidroka Bay Resort** by turning up the hilly, oceanside dirt road 20km west of Pacific Harbor at the "Surf Frigate's Pass" sign. Huge lawn and private bay with full diving, fishing, and surfing facilities. The wood-floored bungalows are simple but clean. Full meal plan at the new restaurant is $38 per day. Diving costs $60 for 1 tank, $110 for 2, plus $15 equipment rental. Surfing (rentals available) on the six nearby breaks is for the experienced only (Frigate's Pass $45 with lunch; Mada Point & Pipe $20). Definitely a relaxed destination. (☎304 605; fax 304 383; waidrokaresort@suva.is.com.fj; www.dive-surf-fiji.com.fj. Dorms $18; lodge $54. Free kayaks and pick-up from bus in Korolev. MC/V.) **Vilisite's Place** is a crayon-box explosion of pink bedspreads, orange doors, and blue and green tiles. (☎530 054. Doubles $55; family room $70.) The abutting **restaurant** serves lunch sandwiches for under $3 and veggie curry for $4.40. (Open daily 8am-10pm. MC/V.)

It's easy to stay well-fed with the resorts above, but those who venture out find treats at the four restaurants of the lux **Warwick Hotel,** 6km west of the Beachouse: **Cafe Korovou** (☎530 634) caters to the $12.50 burger crowd; **Sanzami** (☎530 729) serves spicy tuna sushi ($4.25) and teppanyaki dinner ($27.50); **Papagallo** (☎530 632) presents pizzas, like margarita ($18.50) or veggie supreme ($19); while **Wicked Walu's** grills fresh seafood for around $25 on its own tiny island.

PACIFIC HARBOR

A product of wealthy developers and the booming '80s economy, Pacific Harbor in the town of Deuba (DOOM-ba) was supposed to be the all-in-one resort playground for Japanese, American, and Australasian tourists; financial (and political) fluctuations have left many of the upscale hotel rooms and stores empty. Still, quality accommodations and beckoning dive sites draw many a guest.

▣▶ ORIENTATION AND PRACTICAL INFORMATION. The town is nothing more than a strip of homes and resorts along the Queens Rd. 49km west of Suva, with a **gas station** and a few small **groceries** in tow. Frequent buses to and from Suva stop at the **police** post (☎460 222), one block west of the **post office** (where there is a public **phone**) and sprawling Kalevu Center. Access to most of the private homes, as well the **Pacific Safari Club, Dive Connection,** and **Club Coral Coast** (which all have signs) is via the rotary just beside the police post. There is **internet access** at the **Oasis Restaurant.** There are currently **no banks or ATMs** in town, though one or two may pop up in the bigger resorts soon.

⌂ ACCOMMODATIONS. Budgeteers at **Club Coral Coast** get tight rooms, small shared bathrooms, and kitchenette-closets, but can use the gorgeous lounge, pool, grass tennis court, weight room, and ping-pong table. Laundry $5. (☎450 421; fax 450 900. Dorms $25; singles $70; deluxe rooms $100. Amex/MC/V.) The **Pacific Safari Club** has large, quality rooms with showers, TVs, and kitchenettes. (☎450 498; fax 450 499. Dorms $25; singles $55; twins/doubles $70. MC/V.) The shop at **Dive Connection,** 16 River Dr., has a gorgeous apartment on its property, with a big bath, bigger kitchen, and biggest bedroom. Most people who stay are already dive clients, or quickly become them. (☎450 541; fax 450 539; mobile 920 541; dive-conn@is.com.fj. Apartment $30 for 1, $40 for 2, $55 for 3. Amex/MC/V.)

▢ FOOD. Kumaran's Restaurant & Milkbar, next to the Mobile gas station, is a busy little Indian place—especially at lunch, when $4 curries and $2 *dhal* are served up fresh and hot. (☎450 294. Open 8am-8pm daily.) The **Oasis Restaurant** attracts a local crowd with darts, a paperback library, web access, and a small busy bar. $7 burgers and fish 'n' chips; $16 fried walu or pakapaka. Internet $0.40 per min. (☎450 617; fax 450 199. Open daily 9:30am-11pm. MC/V.) The **Nautilis Restaurant,** in the center across from the police post, has $15 pizzas, $9.50 burgers, and $20 steaks; bar open til midnight. (☎450 022; fax 450 262. AmEx/MC/V.)

▣▶ SIGHTS AND ACTIVITIES. Only one corner of the **Cultural Center and Marketplace,** on the northern side of the Queens Rd. just east of the police post, survived from the '80s. Firewalking shows on the grand-bure stage used to occur daily, but now take place weekly. (☎450 177. Shows Th 2:30pm. $18, children $9.)

Most **dive** operators make the 35min. boat ride to **Beqa** (BEN-ga) or **Yanuca** (ya-NU-tha) **Island** from Pacific Harbor to start their exploration of **Beqa Lagoon,** where the waters teem with soft coral, gorgonian fans, coral heads, and fish of all varieties. **Dive Connection** does intro dives for $140, or two-tank boat dives for $130; all equipment and lunch included. (☎450 541; fax 450 539; mobile 920 541; dive-conn@is.com.fj; www.pacific-harbor.com/diveconn.) **Aqua-Trek,** based at the **Centra Resort,** dives off the *Aqua-Sport.* (☎/fax 450 324; aquatrekbeqa@is.com.fj; www.aquatrek.com. 2 dives $160; 4 dives $300; $15 gear per dive.) The **Centra Resort** (☎450 022; fax 450 262) has a full range of activities open to non-guests, including horseback riding ($15), reef fishing ($18), sailing ($10), windsurfing ($15), and canoeing ($10). **Rivers Fiji,** based in town, does reasonably priced sea kayaking and whitewater rafting adventures along the coast and up the Navua and Luva Rivers. (☎450 147; mobile 992 349; fax 450 148; riversfiji@is.com.fj; www.riversfiji.com. AmEx/MC/ V.)

INTERIOR HIGHLANDS

Travelers circling Viti Levu's royal road rarely sprinkle their plain vanilla itineraries with flavored journeys inland. The few who do find a cool, sweet treat: rocky roads dish out dollops of dewy rainforest, crunched by bits of thick grassland, and top it all off with remote highland villages, where all-natural, no-frills experiences with local culture can be sweeter than a cherry.

✖ TRANSPORTATION

Public **buses** visit all of the villages below, though unreliable schedules change frequently. Buses are most frequent on Friday and Sunday evenings, and during the day on Friday and Saturday. Inquire about service in the access towns listed in the introduction to each village. A more dependable mode of transport is canopied **carrier** trucks. For villages that do not have arrangements with specific carriers, find one in the access town (asking a village woman in the market about the carrier she takes is a good method, and may also secure your night's accommodation).

Most rental car companies will not rent to drivers headed far into the highlands. **Budget** (Nadi Airport 24hr. ☎ 722 753, 722 636; fax 722 053; www.budgetfiji.com), with eight offices on Viti Levu, is the only company to rent a low-end (and less expensive) hard-top 4WD; taking a 2WD vehicle on many of the interior roads is a very bad idea, especially in the wet season (or any time rain is expected). Ask carrier drivers or call the **Public Works Department** (☎ 700 389) or **Forestry Department** (☎ 661 085) for specific road conditions.

✺ ❷ ORIENTATION AND PRACTICAL INFO

There are **no police, postal,** or **emergency facilities** in any of the villages, although the **visitors center** in Abaca and the **guides** from Navilawa on the Mt. Batilamu Trek have **first-aid equipment.** There is a **phone** in Navala, and **radio communication** is available in Abaca and Navilawa, but only for emergency use. In all cases, the quickest way out if something goes wrong is by helicopter: Call **Island Hoppers** (see **Suva: Intercity Transportation** p. 410).

In all cases, follow village custom and dress requirements; bringing a *sevusevu* of kava (see **Village Etiquette** p. 385) is also necessary, except for day trips to Abaca in the Koroyanitu Park when hiking (and not visiting the village) is the only intended activity. As always, visiting a village **unannounced on a Sunday** (especially with the intention of staying) is a bad idea, though if it is necessary try to arrive early in the morning before Church services start (from 6-9am), or after they end (around noon); not only is it considered rude to interrupt Church, but it is also necessary to give villagers ample time (which they rarely have on Sunday when prayer and family are priorities) to prepare adequate food and accommodation.

NAVALA

In 1970, 100-year-old Romanu Nagate called a meeting of his fellow villagers in Navala, nestled deep within in the Ba Highlands, and told them to save the village from encroaching modernization (though perhaps not in those words). True to his wishes, the 100 villagers in this fascinating community continue to live only in traditional thatched-roof bures; not only does this make Navala unique, but it also makes this perhaps the most beautiful and picturesque village in all of Fiji.

☰ TRANSPORTATION AND PRACTICAL INFORMATION. Navala is most easily accessed from the coastal town of **Ba** (see p. 400). Buses to the village depart from the bus station on some days, usually around 6am and 6pm, though this changes frequently. There is no specific carrier service for tourists to the village, so inquiring in Ba about the villagers' transport (especially in the market) is a good idea. Alternatively, try calling the **single phone** in Navala (☎ 113 214) or **Boulou's Lodge & Backpacker Hostel** (☎ 666 644, wait for two beeps, then dial 2116) to see if arrangements can be made. A 4WD vehicle is necessary if driving; follow Rarawai Rd. from the central rotary in Ba around the bend near the sugar mill, and continue straight past several turnoffs until you reach the village 2hr. (26km) later. Have a strong heart; the road keeps going and going and going.

There is a one-time **entrance fee** to the village of $15, which also pays for the privilege of taking photographs, and can be given to the host family or to the Turaga-ni-koro (elected chief), Karoalo Vaisewa, who is rumored to have run track in the Olympics; Vaisewa is also the *tui*, or king, of the Qalitina people, enlarging his jurisdiction to two other nearby villages, Koroboya and Namau.

ACCOMMODATIONS AND FOOD. There are two options for accommodation in Navala. The best is to **stay with a family in the village** itself and eat all meals with them. Visitors can be matched with a family by the chief (usually after the *sevusevu* ceremony), but more often are claimed by the first villager they meet upon arrival. Be prepared to sleep on the woven-mat covered ground (a sleeping bag is a good idea) and eat mostly vegetables from the village farms. Outdoor toilets were installed last year. Though the bures are rustic, the experience of living with a family can be incredibly comfortable and comforting ($15 per person). The other option is in **Boulou's Lodge,** 1km past the village on the right when coming from the north. Boulou sleeps six guests in a house with real beds (meaning not just a floor), a connected bathroom, and a kitchen, or four guests in a nearby one-room bure ($35 per person; all meals included). His house is not *in* the village however, but instead on the edge of farmland in an overgrown front yard. Bringing food as a gift for the owners is a good idea. Boulou also offers horseback riding ($20), *bilibili* raft riding ($20), and a 2½hr. mountain trek ($10).

ACTIVITIES. Activities beyond making the village a temporary home (helping to cook and farm) include treks to lookout points, a nearby waterfall, or a number of other sights. Finding a villager or a group of children willing to accompany you (sometimes for a fee, sometimes free) is easy. Of note in the village itself are the school (where visitors may be able to guest teach), the students' tiny fish pond, and the first school teacher's grave. **Whitewater Rafting Adventures** (☎450 180; fax 450 549; discoverfiji@is.com.fj) does a day rafting tour from Navala, with transfers available from the Coral Coast, Nadi, and Lautoka; they may be able to meet up with rafters in Navala itself.

BUKUYA

Housing some 500 people in over 100 houses, Bukuya is the largest highland village in Fiji. With mass comes a sprawling mess, however, meaning that all beauty of a picturesque type is found on a trek *away* in the surrounding hills, while the more sentimental kind of beauty can be found in one's heart after the meaningful multicultural experience of a long village stay. The village *tui* is also the chief of five surrounding villages, namely Nasivisikoso, Tabalei, Nadevo, Navaga, and Tabuquto. He's also king of the ring, having won the Western Heavyweight Boxing Championship of Fiji in 1980 at the age of 24; the belts still line his walls. You won't have to see them by candlelight, because the village was recently given the comprehensive infrastructure upgrade of electricity by the US Army.

The village charges visitors anywhere from $130 for one night stays to $200 for five nights—the price may be entirely dependent on their whimsy and your bargaining skills. The chief generally assigns visitors a family to stay with. More consistently priced, and much cheaper, is **Peni's,** just on the western edge of the village. The four shoddy shared bures with outdoor concrete showers and bath go for $20-35; looking desperate and poor may get you a stay on the cheaper end. The three included meals are served in a large adjoining bure-lounge, where most folks tend to hang. Peni can also lead treks to the nearby **Lolo Waterfall** and organize activities like horseback riding and wild-pig hunting (all around $20).

The village is set at the intersection of two major highland roads, one coming 66km from southern Sigatoka and extending 36km to northern Ba, the other coming 41km from western Nadi. The village is most easily accessed from Ba by way of Navala. Public **buses** depart from the Ba station, and are the same ones which go to Navala (see p. 407). There is no specific **carrier** service for tourists to the village, so inquire at the market in Ba for the villagers' preferred transport. Alternatively, try finding Peni at the Coconut Inn in Nadi, where he tends to make a makeshift office, or call him (☎ 700 801, 113 212; mobile 248 890) to arrange $40 return transport departing Nadi. If driving, follow the directions to Navala but continue for 40min. It's also possible to access the village driving from Nadi, but the road tends to be in worse condition and is often flooded in rain. Ask for road conditions and directions from local bus drivers, police, and the Public Works and Forestry Departments (see **Interior Highlands: Transportation** p. 407).

KOROYANITU NATIONAL HERITAGE PARK

Set in the hills above Nadi and the Western shores, the Koroyanitu Park is home to more than half of Fiji's endemic flora and fauna, including the immense dakua makadre and the rare Naivati falcon, of which there are only 100 pairs left. Only two years ago, the park, also home to six highland villages, was threatened by potential burning and logging; various governments and their agencies (including the Native Land Trust Board, the South Pacific Regional Environmental Programme, and the New Zealand Official Development Assistance Programme) banded together to establish a community-based ecotourism enterprise, which would at once support the villagers *and* protect the surrounding environment. Abaca (below) and Navilawa's Mt. Batilamu Trek are the first fruits of their labor.

ABACA

In 1931 torrential rains drenched Viti Levu's highlands for two weeks, causing a great landslide that buried the village of Nagaga (meaning "cave," probably where everyone was hiding) and all but three of its villagers. Searching for a spot to establish a new village, the survivors came upon a rock etched with the letters A, B, and C (Abaca), which were interpreted to represent the words *ai vakatekivu* (beginning), *nulatawa mudu* (eternal life), and *cakacaka* (miracle work). Given a fresh start by government funds, self-sustaining Abaca (aum-BA-tha) now tells the world its story and provides visitors Grade A (not B or C) accommodation.

▨▧ ORIENTATION AND PRACTICAL INFORMATION. Abaca is 16km from Lautoka. **Vijendra** provides carrier transport to the village. (☎/fax 666 590, mobile 253 014. 30min.; $8 per person, $14 minimum) The local **Tavakubu bus** leaves Lautoka and takes passengers as far as the Abaca junction, a 40min. walk from the village, twice daily for less than a dollar. **Drivers** and **cyclists** should get specific directions from Vijendra or the visitors center; it's easy once you get to the Abaca junction (there are signs), but getting that far through the maze of Lautoka back streets is hard. **Entrance** to the park (and village) is $5.

The **Abaca Visitors Center** (☎ 666 644, after two beeps dial 1234) in the village arranges both daytrips and village or Nase stays. If the visitors center does not answer on the first try, try (try) again after 10min.; it is the only phone in the village, locked in an office, and the one woman with the key will most likely be running to answer it.

▨▧ ACCOMMODATIONS AND FOOD. The ▨**Nase Lodge** is an immaculate, modern, and high-ceilinged red-and-teal hut on par with the best budget accommodations in Fiji. Two spacious rooms with three bunks each (all with sheets, duvets, and mosquito netting) flank a central sitting room/dining and kitchen area that is outfitted with new wood furniture and adequate supplies. Potable rainwater feeds the sink, while clean but non-potable ground water feeds the one adjoining shower and toilet; **cold water only** means brisk highland freshness! Reservations are essential. (Beds $25; whole room for up to six people $80; whole lodge $150; camping $10 per person. Under 15 half-price. Village stays with a family $30 including all meals, under 15 half-price. With a bit of warning the village women can prepare **meals** for Nase or daytripping guests: breakfast $5, lunch $7, dinner $10.)

◙ **OUTDOOR ACTIVITIES.** There are two main treks: a 2hr. loop past the **Savui-one Waterfall,** which ascends through primeval cloud forest and returns past the roofed **Kokobula Scenic Viewpoint** through yellow grassland ($5 per person with a village guide); and a 4hr. return trek over **Mt. Batilamu** ($15 per person with a village guide). A 5min. walk from the village, a system of river rock pools flows past a lookout platform and over the **Verenu Falls.** Though the treks can be done with the map in the back of the village guidebook ($5) instead of with the village guides, it's recommended to employ one of the villagers; they provide information and a safe trip, while you support their ecotourism plan.

NAVILAWA

The Sleeping Giant's rocky repose casts a grand shadow over Navilawa, tucked in a pocket valley just west of the **Vatura Dam.** Lying at the geographic center of the area's volcanic activity, the village is bubbling with excitement after a successful start to its ecotourism enterprise. A town meeting hall has been built at the base of the village's giant boulder centerpiece (clay-oven kitchen, modern bath, and shower units alongside), while villagers have been trained as mountain guides and porters in preparation for the **Mt. Batilamu Trek,** a 2½-day guided jaunt from Navilawa over Mt. Batilamu and the Sleeping Giant to Abaca. While the cost of the trek is not exactly budget ($250 per person including all transport, accommodation, meals, guides, kava for *sevusevu*, and park entry fees), it is personal (limited to 8 people), unique, and one of the best ways to see the highlands. Trekkers sleep heavily on their first night in Navilawa after a full evening of kava-induced delirium, and sleep lighter the second, way up near the summit of Mt Batilamu in the "highest bure in Fiji"; the route there is rough and steep in sections (with secured ropes aiding the way) and not as groomed as some Western-style trails, but is still easily passable. The **Batilamu Trek Booking Office** (☎0800 729 455), based at **Tourism Transport Fiji** (☎723 311, fax 720 184) in the Aerotown Mall next to the Nadi Airport, takes reservations; talk to Emele Marama or Ana Navitio. 15% discount on bookings of four or more. As the project becomes self-sustaining and village infrastructure is bolstered, Navilawa may also be able to accommodate daytrippers and those interested in longer village stays.

SUVA

Now a mooring for small boats, Nubukalou Creek was the site of modern Suva's establishment by Australian sugar farmers in 1870. Their efforts soon wilted, and by 1882 speculators convinced the British that the peninsula was better suited for capital splendor than off-shore Ovalau's Levuka (see p. 424). Today Suva is still the capital, and unlike many decayed outposts of the British empire it retains its Colonial charm. Weathered government buildings and labyrinthine streets add a shot of flavor to the duty-free shops and cosmopolitan cafes.

⊠ INTERCITY TRANSPORTATION

Flights: There is **no airport** within Suva; **Nausori Airport** (☎478 344) handles the air traffic for the area. Most arriving flights are domestic, usually from Nadi, though **Air Pacific** (Nausori Airport office ☎478 859) offers infrequent service from **Sydney** and **Auckland. Turtle Airways** (☎721 888; fax 720 095; www.turtleairways.com) and **Island Hoppers** (☎720 410; fax 720 172) are more expensive options; see **Intercity Transportation** p. 393. There is **no public transportation** to Suva from the airport.

Buses: At least 6 local buses arrive daily from points north. Express buses by **Sunset Express** (☎382 811, Nadi ☎720 266, Lautoka ☎668 276; fax 320 769) and **Fiji Express** (contact United Touring Ltd. ☎722 811, 722 821; fax 720 389, 720 107) and **Pacific Transport Ltd.** (Nadi ☎700 004) serve points west (see **Transportation** p. 391 for schedules and fares), as do **Sunbeam** (☎382 122) and **UTC** (☎312 287).

Taxis: Van carriers and taxis congregate behind the **MH Supermarket** in the early morning to take loads of passengers west to Nadi and intermediary points ($15).

Ferries: Services to the outer islands arrive and depart from **Bau Landing**, 24km north of Suva. Taxis to Bau Landing from Suva (45min.) cost $2.25. **Patterson Brothers Shipping** (Levuka ☎ 440 125) runs a ferry-bus service between **Levuka** and **Suva** (5hr. total; bus Suva-Natovi, ferry Natovi-Buresala, bus Buresala-Levuka; M-Sa; departs Suva 2pm, Levuka 9am; $30 one-way, $60 return). **Leleuvia Island Resort** (☎ 301 584) operates a boat-taxi service between **Suva** and **Levuka** via **Leleuvia** on demand (30min., Levuka-Leleuvia; 30min. Leleuvia-Bau, landing on Viti Levu; 20min., Bau landing-Suva, on taxi; leaves Leleuvia for **Levuka** at 8:30am and for **Bau landing** at noon; leaves Levuka for **Leleuvia** at 10am and Bau landing for **Leleuvia** at 1pm; $35 Levuka-Suva one-way, $20 Leleuvia-Suva one-way, $15 Levuka-Leleuvia one-way). *Spirit of Free Enterprise (SOFE)*, operated by **Consort Shipping** (Savusavu ☎ 850 279), runs between Suva and **Taveuni** via **Koro Island** and **Savusavu** (22hr. total, 12hr. between Suva and Savusavu, 5hr. between Savusavu and Taveuni; departs Suva for Savusavu Tu 10pm and Sa 6pm; departs Savusavu for Suva M and Th 8pm, for Taveuni W and Su 10pm; departs Taveuni M and Th noon; $41 one-way between Suva and Taveuni, $38 one-way between Suva and Savusavu, $22 one-way between Savusavu and Taveuni). *Adi Savusavu*, operated by **Beachcomber Shipping** (Savusavu ☎ 850 266, 850 706), also runs between Suva and **Taveuni** via **Savusavu** (20hr. total, 11hr. between Suva and Savusavu, 5hr. between Savusavu and Taveuni; departs Suva Tu 10am and Th noon; departs Savusavu for Suva Su 7am and W 8pm, for Taveuni W and F 1am; departs Taveuni W and F 12:30pm; one-way between Suva and Taveuni $47 economy class, $67 first class; one-way between Suva and Savusavu $42/$62; one-way between Savusavu and Taveuni $22/$42). Both the *SOFE* and *Adi Sasusavu* offer cafeterias and motor vehicle berths.

✦ ORIENTATION

Suva sprawls over a 15 sq. km peninsula extending from the southeast corner of Viti Levu. **Edinburgh Drive** and **Foster Road** feed traffic into the north side of the city from the Kings and Queens Rd. respectively. The bus station, municipal market, and wharf are clumped along the water where the traffic pours in, edged to the east by **Rodwell Rd.,** the supermarkets, and hilly areas that are less friendly than the more cosmopolitan streets to the south. **Victoria Parade** starts its sweep one block south of the market near the post office, extending as the city's main drag to Thurston Gardens and past the majority of shops and the Government Buildings.

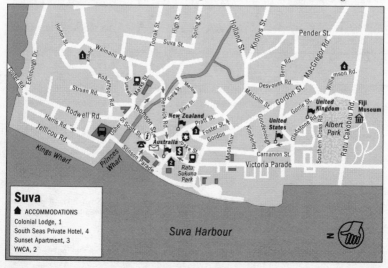

Suva

🏠 ACCOMMODATIONS
Colonial Lodge, 1
South Seas Private Hotel, 4
Sunset Apartment, 3
YWCA, 2

Suva Harbour

LOCAL TRANSPORTATION

Small downtown Suva is easily walkable. Most taxis use meters or have set rates for longer distances; **Regent Taxi** (☎312 100) is one of many companies with **24hr.** service. Find **vans** near the bus station, especially behind the MH Supermarket. **Beat Motorcycle & Rentals** (☎/fax 385 355, mobile 912 587), in Grantham Plaza off the Kings Rd., hires scooters and motorbikes from $10 per 2hr. or $33 per day; Suva traffic can be fast and vicious, and is **not recommended for beginner riders.**

PRACTICAL INFORMATION

The city center is generally well lit, though as always parks and other deserted areas should be avoided at night. Guard against **pickpockets,** especially around the markets. The suburbs and villages extending east of downtown for miles are hard to navigate and vary radically in safety.

Visitors Center: The **Fiji Visitors Bureau** (☎373 2133; fax 309 4720), on the corner of Scott and Thompson St.

Banks: The many downtown banks are generally are open M-Th 9:30am-3pm, F 9:30am-4pm. **Westpac,** 1 Thomson St. (☎300 666), and **ANZ,** 25 Victoria Parade (☎301 755), are best for changing money.

American Express: Tapa International Ltd., 25 Victoria Parade (☎302 333, 24hr. authorization line 217 689). Open M-F 8:30am-5pm, Sa 9am-12pm.

Maps: The **Department of Lands & Survey,** Room 10, Records and Reprographics Sub-section, Government Buildings, has numerous maps of Fiji. Enter via Gladstone St.

Women's/BGLT Organizations: The committed staff at **Women's Action for Change (WAC),** 33 Waimun Rd. (☎314 363; wac@is.com.fj), have a handful of initiatives including the Sexual Minorities Project, which works for BGLT rights and acceptance.

Groceries: The **Morris Hedstrom Supermarket (MH)** (☎311 811), across from the bus station, is open M-F 8:30am-5:30pm, Sa 8:30am-1pm.

Laundry: Wash and dry at the **Suva Electric Laundry,** 31 Knolly St. (☎301 442) for $4.

Emergency: Dial ☎000 nationwide. **St. John's Ambulance** (☎301 439). The Fiji Visitors Bureau's **24hr. Visitor Helpline** is ☎0800 721 721.

Police: Dial ☎007. **Central Station** (☎311 222) on the corner of Joske and Pratt St.; **Albert Park Police Post** (☎315 742) on Gladstone Rd. in the northeast corner of the park; **Suva Point Police Post** (☎307 057) at the bus station.

Crisis Lines: The **Women's Crisis Center** (☎313 300) takes calls for any issue, though primarily domestic abuse.

Pharmacy: The **Central Pharmacy** is open M-Th 8am-5:30pm, F 8am-6pm, Sa 8am-1pm at: 109 Cumming St. (☎301 877; fax 303 677) and in the Downtown Boulevard shopping center on Ellery St. (☎303 770; fax 303 677). The pharmacy at the **Suva Private Hospital** (☎313 495) is open M-F 8am-8pm, Sa 8am-6pm, Su 11am-1pm.

Hospitals: The Suva Private Hospital, 120 Amy St. east of downtown, was opened in February 2001, and has the best medical facilities in the country, including the **Amy Street Medical Center** (open **24hr.**), a **heli-pad** for air transfers, and a **recompression chamber** for divers. This is the place to be if you have any sort of major injury. (☎303 404; fax 303 456; healthcare@is.com.fj. MC/V.) The **Downtown Boulevard Medical Centre,** 33 Ellery St. (☎313 461, 313 355; emergency ☎320 321, 997 733; fax 302 423), in the Downtown Boulevard shopping center, also offers quality care. Open M-F 8:30am-5pm, Sa 8:30-11:30am.

Recompression Chambers: The best option is the facility at the **Suva Private Hospital** (see above). The **Fiji Recompression Chamber** (emergency ☎993 506, 995 500; administrative ☎305 154) is another decent operation.

Internet Access: The **Republic of Cappuccino** (see **Food** below), known as the "Rock," is by far the coolest place to get online. $0.20 per min. The **Alpha Computer Centre,** 181 Victoria Parade and in the Honson Arcade (☎300 211; fax 302 089; shelen@alpha.com.fj), charges $0.22 per min. or $0.20 per min. for more than an hour.

Open M-F 8am-6pm, Sa 9am-4pm, Su 10am-2pm. **CyberStation** (☎/fax 311 347; cyberstation@internet.com.fj), on Marks St. near Stuart St., charges $1 for login plus $0.10 per min. Open M-Sa 8:30am-9pm, Su 11am-9pm.

Post Office: 10 Thomson St. (☎302 022; fax 307 819; General Inquiries ☎0800 307 966; Express Mail Service ☎218 388, 0800 307 304; Post Shop ☎218 312). Poste Restante. Open M-F 8am-4pm, Sa 8am-noon.

ACCOMMODATIONS

The Raintree Lodge (☎320 562; fax 320 113; raintreelodge@is.com.fj; www.rain-treelodge.com), opposite the police post in Colo-i-Suva, 18km from Suva on Princes Rd. This system of wooden lodges seems like a millionaire's dream. Laundry service. Lockers. Kitchen. Excellent restaurant serves all meals ($6-25). Taxi from Suva $8; Saweni bus $0.85. Dorms $16.50; doubles $55; quads $96.25; camping $5 per person, children half price. More options available. AmEx/MC/V.

Colonial Lodge, 19 Anand St. (☎300 655, 313 366). Suzie and Joe serve fresh fruit, have a no-shoes-inside rule, hang laundry under the porch, and cook a $7 buffet dinner; their little quirks make the lodge a home. New bathrooms and showers. Car park and internet. No cooking facilities. 7-bed dorm (no bunks) $14.50; twins $40; doubles $28.

Sunset Apartment Hotel (☎301 799; fax 303 466), on the corner of Murray and Gordon St. While the dorm is dark, musty, and cramped, the other 3 stories of tidy, motel singles and doubles with own basic kitchenettes and private balconies have beautiful views. 12-bed dorm $9; single $42; double $50. More options available. MC/V.

South Seas Private Hotel, 6 Williamson Rd. (☎312 296; fax 340 236; south-seas@fiji4less.com), has long been used by backpackers and abused by southern winds; its once-beautiful Colonial facade is now feeling the wear. Office open 7am-11pm. Dorm $9.90; shared single $16.50; shared double $24; shared family $33; single or double with private bath $36.30. Cash only.

University of the South Pacific Lodge (☎212 614, 212 639; fax 314 827; usplodges@usp.ac.fj), 200m before the main university entrance when coming from Suva on Lacala Bay Rd., is best suited for those seeking longer stays. The gorgeous garden suites offer apartment-style comfort with immaculate baths, full kitchens, and space to breathe. Breakfast $4-6. Take the Lacala Bay/Natadola Stadium bus from Suva. Singles $39; doubles $59; $425 per month, negotiable weekly rates. MC/V.

The YWCA (☎304 829), in Sukuna Park between Stinson and Victoria Parade, has spartan women-only rooms inside its behemoth concrete belly. Shared baths are cleaned regularly, but see a lot of use. Transit rooms $10 per night. There are no cheaper weekly rates in town: singles $30; doubles $21; twins $24. Cash only.

FOOD

Old Mill Cottage Cafe, 49 Carnavon St. (☎312 134). Neither a mill nor a cottage, the locals treat this old house as both, milling about the big porch like it's their second home. Home-cooked specialties only encourage the behavior. One of the few places to find high quality traditional Fijian food ($1-6). Open M-F 7am-6pm, Sa 7am-5pm.

Hare Krishna Restaurants (5 in the area) are determined to spread vegetarianism and the word of the Bagavad Gita. Potato, bean, pumpkin, or curd curry ($1.20) are four of the savory options. Try them at: the corner of Pratt and Joske St. (☎314 154); in the FNPF Dolphin Foodcourt (☎304 930); on Cummings St. (☎304 238); at 82 Ratumara Rd. in the suburb of Samabula (☎386 333); or on Laucala Bay Rd. across from USP (☎311 683). Open M-F 9am-8pm, Sa 9am-3:30pm; at USP daily 8am-8pm.

Fong Lee Seafood, 293 Victoria Parade (☎304 233). On first blush this pink 1-room restaurant would get average marks; however, give it an A+ for fresh fish and a friendly staff—this place is a palace, regarded by locals as serving the best seafood in town ($5-20). Open M-Sa for lunch 11am-2pm, daily for dinner 6-10pm.

Bad Dog Cafe (☎312 968), on the corner of Victoria Parade and Macarthur St. Naughty puppies never had it so good: $7 bowls of pasta and meaty $8 burgers are more satisfying than any bone. Sa special on imported beers. Connects to Wolfhound and O'Reilly's Bar, listed below. Open M-W noon-10:30pm, Th-Sa noon-1am.

JJ's Bar & Grill, 9-10 Gordon St. (☎305 005), is a Western-style bistro serving $20 seared prawns and $14 chicken chimichonga in an intimate, relaxed atmosphere. Open M-Sa 11:30am-11:30pm. AmEx/MC/V.

The Dolphin Foodcourt (☎307 440), on Victoria Parade in the FNPF Building opposite the Shell Station, is busiest at midday, when the working set fills the spotless courtyard to eat lunch from the 8 fast-food restaurants serving typical Indian, Chinese, and Fijian fare. The best are **Hare Krishna** (☎304 930), the **Roti Shop,** and the **Viti Deli** (☎307 789). Most shops are open M-Sa 8am-9pm, some Su 10am-7pm.

The Republic of Cappuccino (☎300 333, 361 035), on Victoria Parade in the FNPF Dolphin Foodcourt, is the favorite coffee spot for expats, students, and other posh locals; most check email ($0.20 per min.) and nosh on a slice of $4 cake or $4.50 grilled veggie panini, while downing the requisite $2.50 cup-of-capp. Open M-Sa 8am-11pm, Su 10am-7pm.

▶ NIGHTLIFE

Traps, 305 Victoria Parade (☎312 922) It's easy to get lost here; doors from one bar lead to doors to another, connecting 4 dark, intimate rooms into 1 giant social scene. The post-work crowd fills up on $1.80 stubbies during 6-8pm Happy Hour weekdays, while a younger crowd takes over weekends. Open M-F 5pm-1am, Sa 6pm-1am.

O'Reilly's and **Wolfhound's,** 5 McArthur St. (☎312 884, 312 968), connected to the Bad Dog Cafe. While a thick brogue may be out of place, a thick Guinness and some Irish pride is not. A huge TV, pool tables, darts, and shamrocks comfort in predictable pub fashion. Tu Ladies Night; Th buy a beer and get a bargain $2.50 beef burger; Sa-Su 2-for-1 Lion Red. Open noon til late.

Birdland, 112 Carnavon St. (☎303 833) is a tiny, poster-plastered 2-room bar devoted to jazz and its heroes. Open daily 7pm-1am.

◉ SIGHTS

THE FIJI MUSEUM. The museum was unwittingly started by Sir William Allardyce in 1904 when he presented his collection of Fijian artifacts to the Suva town board. The subsequent formation of the **Fijian Society,** along with donations from private and government sources, eventually led to the museum charter. Today the museum has five galleries presenting different aspects of Fiji's culture and history, including: the **Taukei Gallery,** showcasing the culture of Native Fijians; the **Masi Gallery,** showcasing traditional crafts like rock paintings from Vatulele; the **Art and Natural History Gallery,** highlighted by Belcher paintings of birds and orchids; and the **Indian gallery,** tracing Indo-Fijian history. The reference library provides the unique service of allowing visitors to order reprints of any photo in their large historical collection, including many of the famous first images of "Fijian savages." *(On the eastern edge of the gardens, past the Government Buildings on Victoria Parade. ☎315 944, 315 043; fax 305 143; www.fijimuseum.org.fj. Museum open M-Sa 9:30am-4:30pm. Library open M-F 8am-4pm. Admission $3.30, children $0.50.)*

SUVA MUNICIPAL MARKET. While the market in Lautoka is the biggest in the country, the Suva Municipal Market may have the biggest variety of goods; villagers bring in their root crops and fish on Saturdays. A heap of fruit is generally $2; a bundle of fish $10; smoked octopus and crabs $20. The two **Handicraft Centers** around the corner cater almost exclusively to visitors, with heaps of woven mats and bags, wooden combs, printed *masi*, and other trinkets. If tempted, remember to bargain! *(Corner of Rodwell and Usher St. on the foreshore. The Handicraft Centers are both along Stinson Parade. Open M-Sa 8am-6pm.)*

THE OLD TOWN HALL. While it used to host performing arts events, today it draws considerable and varied attention; Greenpeace lobbies for the environment of the Pacific upstairs, while downstairs three restaurants vie for tourist attention. The middle Chinese spot, despite its flashy interior, tries to keep a low-profile these days and recover its reputation—a sting operation by police led to the biggest drug bust in recent memory in Fiji. *(On Victoria Parade, just opposite Gordon St.)*

VALE NI BOSE LAWA. Based on a traditional chief's *vale* (house), the Fijian Parliament is set on elevated grounds overlooking both land and sea. Visitors are rarely allowed in the building; instead, most (who get past the first security gate) are allowed to go as far as the large rotary for closer views. Calling ahead betters your chances. *(5km from Suva on Battery Rd. in Veiuto. The Suva Bus Company's Naseisei bus goes by at least 5 times daily. ☎ 305 811.)*

THE UNIVERSITY OF THE SOUTH PACIFIC. The USP was established in 1968 as the central institute for higher learning in the entire south seas. Most of the students at the four schools (Agriculture, Education, Natural Resources, and Social & Economic Development) are Fijian, though a large number come from the 11 other joint Pacific nations. The botanical gardens near the entrance make for a nice stroll. *(☎ 313 900.)*

BEACHES. Nukumarorika-i, otherwise known as **Mosquito Island,** lies just offshore near **Raffle's Tradewinds Hotel** (☎ 362 450) in Lami, 6km North of Suva on Queen's Rd. Visitors can arrange for a short boat transfer (costing a few dollars) to the island from the hotel. Swimming across is also possible; follow the locals' lead and do it at low tide, when wading eases the full 10min. swim. The small, pretty beaches on the island have some sea snakes and sand flies, but are much closer than **Deuba Beach,** 49km west and the only other option in the Suva area.

COLO-I-SUVA FOREST PARK. An anomaly in Fiji, Colo-i-Suva Forest Park (THOLO-ee-suva) is the only small, self-contained nature reserve with an official park staff and maintained hiking trails, showcasing an array of native wildlife. Well-suited for short day hikes, the 245-hectare park has 6.5km of trails, all starting from an entrance point and parking lot 2.5km down Kalabu Rd. from the main gate and visitors center. The **Waisila Creek** provides the biggest attractions, including three large swimming pools in the **upper pools** area (one with a rope swing), the **Waisila Falls** along the Falls Trail, and a system of small **lower pools** on the eastern edge of the park. The decrepit droptoilets, bure shelters and BBQ grates dotting the upper pools are not well maintained. Iron cooking sheets for the fire grates are available from the visitors center. Camping is not allowed in the park, though officials may let campers pitch tent behind the gate near Princes Rd.; a better choice is to camp at the **Raintree Lodge** (p. 413), 500m past the park across from the **police post.** No alcohol or weapons are allowed in park, and hikers are not allowed to clear trail brush with machetes. *(18 km northeast of Suva; follow Edinburgh Dr. from the north side of town to Princes Rd., then continue past the suburb of Tamavua; there are park signs. By bus, take the Tacirua Bus Company's Saweni for $0.85 from the Suva bus station, which runs every 20min. weekdays and every hr. evenings and weekends. Visitors Center ☎ 320 211; fax 320 380. Open M-Sa 9am-4pm. Admission $5, teenagers $1, children $.50.)*

🔼 ACTIVITIES

Suva Olympic Swimming Pool, 224 Victoria Parade (☎ 313 433, ext. 233) underwent renovation in July 2001. Adults swim for $1.10, children $.55. Rent a changing cubicle for $.22 with a $2 deposit. Open Apr.-Sept. M-F 10am-6pm, Sa-Su 8am-6pm; Oct.-Mar. M-F 9am-7pm, Sa-Su 6am-7pm.

Matthew Light (☎ 998 830) picks up experienced surfers during high tide from the seawall on the eastern edge of Suva and takes them to the reef breaks 10min. away, charging $20-25 for 4-5hr. No rentals available (yet), and not for beginners.

Wilderness Ethnic Adventure Fiji (☎ 315 730, mobile 928 731; fax 315 730; wilderness@is.com.fj; www.wildernessfiji.com.fj) rafts down the Navua River on full-day interior treks for $69, including BBQ lunch. $10 extra from Nadi.

OTHER ISLANDS

Much of the Fijian experience can be enjoyed on Viti Levu; however, those who truly want to appreciate the pleasures of paradise should grab a plane or hop a boat and head to any of the dozens of other islands in the archipelago. From the azure waters of the Blue Lagoon to the backpacker bacchanalia on Beachcomber to Taveuni's lush rainforest reserves, travelers of all stripes find inexhaustible enjoyment on Fiji's spectacular and diverse outlying islands.

☒ OTHER ISLANDS HIGHLIGHTS

GET WET with well-oiled movie stars in the **Blue Lagoon,** the Yasawa Group's most frequently advertised secret (see p. 420).

GET DEEP in the Somosomo Strait and experience diving ecstasy at the world-renowned **Rainbow Reef** (see p. 433).

GET SCANDALOUS on **Beachcomber Island,** the craziest and most luxurious backpacker mecca in the Pacific (see p. 418).

THE MAMANUCA GROUP

While Nadi may be the gateway to Fiji, the Mamanucas (mah-mah-NUTH-uhs) are possibly its most popular destination. The 30-odd islands that make up the Group rest securely like little lily pads along Viti Levu's Western shore, creating a 50km trail that tourists hop like frogs. The combination of established, relatively speedy transport and the islands' proximity to the mainland can bring hordes of amphibian visitors eager to mix sand, surf, and semi-seclusion. Unfortunately, all but two of the island resorts are only accessible to those with fat wallets.

✈ INTERISLAND TRANSPORTATION

Flights: Island Hoppers, based at the Nadi airport, provides speedy helicopter service to the Mamanucas. (☎ 720 410; fax 720 172. 20min. flight from **Coral Coast** to the **Mamanuca Group** US$115. Min. 2 people. All transactions in US$.) **Turtle Airways** provides seaplane transfers. (☎ 721 888; fax 720 095; www.turtleairways.com. **West Viti Levu** to the **Mamanuca Group** $109.)

Ferries: Port Denarau, at the end of Narewa Rd. near the Sheraton on Denarau Island in Nadi, is the departure point for most travelers headed to the Mamanucas. For transfers not docking directly on island jetties, water taxis from the islands provide the final leg, taking passengers from larger boats to the shore. Some boats also depart from **Lautoka Wharf** in downtown Lautoka off Waterfront Rd. To get to Mana Island, both Ratu Kini's and Mareini's (see **Mana Island: Accommodations and Food** p. 417) organize transport for around $70 return; it should be noted that the two operators *Let's Go* lists below have registered boats, life jackets, and other basic measures of safety and dependability. **South Sea Cruises** runs a variety of island transfer services. (☎ 750 500; fax 750 501. Departs **Denarau** for **Mana** and **Beachcomber** daily 9am, 12:15, and 3:15pm.) **Beachcomber** delivers guests to its own island resort (see p. 418) or **Treasure Island Resort** with courtesy transportation to the dock from area hotels. (☎ 661 500, 723 828; fax 664.496; www.beachcomberfiji.com. Departs **Denarau** or **Lautoka Wharf.** $69 return, under 16 $34.50; $40 one-way, under 16 $20. Transfer from Coral Coast $20 extra.)

ORIENTATION

Following a vague track northwest from Nadi, the small and numerous Mamanuca Islands include: Tavarua, Namotu, Naisali, Yakuilau, Malolo Lailai (Plantation Island), Malolo, Wading, Qalito (Castaway Island), Malamala, Navini, Vunivadra, Kadavu, Luvuka (Treasure Island), Tai (Beachcomber Island), Mana, Matamanoa, Nautanivono, Tavua, Monuriki, Monu, Yanuya, Tokoriki, Bekana, Thovuli, Nakumbu, Vomo, Yavurimba, Kadomo, Vomolailai, Vanua Levu Island (not to be confused with Vanua Levu, the second largest island in all of Fiji), Navadra, and Eori. The only islands of interest to budget travelers are **Mana** and **Beachcomber.**

MANA ISLAND

For travelers searching the high-priced seas of the Mamanucas for a low-cost alternative, Mana is like bread from heaven. Two backpacker resorts satiate budget-hunger with one of the cheapest options west of Nadi. Resort is a relative term; the budget price of Mana means comfort on a towel at Sunset Beach, but little more than the basics when the sun sinks and guests return to roost.

ORIENTATION AND PRACTICAL INFORMATION. Located only 30km west of Nadi, elbow-shaped Mana is home to the upscale, family-style **Mana Resort,** whose jetty and serenading staff greet disembarking passengers arriving with South Seas Cruises or Beachcomber. While the resort is technically private property reserved for its own guests, the beach encircling the island is public. To the east lie the two budget accommodations and a ramshackle shanty-town village for resort workers; the north side of the island is home to spectacular **Sunset Beach.** To the west of Mana Resort lies a short airstrip where **Island Hoppers** picks up passengers and persons in need of **emergency medical care.** Minor injuries may require boat transfer back to the mainland, for there is **no police, post, or medical presence** on the island. Bringing **cash** is recommended. There is a **public phone** at Meraeni's.

ACCOMMODATIONS AND FOOD. The two budget options are strikingly similar. The resemblance is fitting, considering they are run by two brothers who swear they've passed their competitive days and now work in cooperation. The hostels share a 50 sq. ft. patio and guests cross between the two freely. Both hostels have **snacks and drinks** for sale at their bars, **safety deposit** for valuables, ill-tempered **generators, rain water** for drinking (don't drink from the tap), can organize **surfboard** or **boat hire** from the local villagers, and offer transfer from Port Denarau ($40 one-way, $70 return). All prices include three meals daily. **Meraeni's Backpackers Inn,** on the right when entering from the beach, is the smaller of the two hostels. The rooms here are modest; rows of dripping candles lead from the lounge to the shared baths. (☎663 099. 2-4-bed dorms or 6-bed womens-only dorm $35; tiny doubles connected by an open ceiling with shared or private bath $77.) **Ratu Kini's Resort** lies straight ahead when entering from the beach. (☎669 143, airport office 721 959, mobile 936 455; fax 720 552; tkabu@is.com.fj. Bunks $35; double with shared bath $73-85; family room, bure, or deluxe double $110. MC/V 5% surcharge.)

ACTIVITIES. The beach near the hostels on the southern side of the island is nameless, and rightly so; it is a pithy little stretch compared to beautiful **Sunset Beach** on the northern side, accessible by a short path through the resort from the jetty, left past the airstrip, or by a longer path directly through the hostel properties. Circling the island on the beach takes 2½hr. **Snorkeling** close to shore yields a mix of pretty coral and bits of trash; both hostels rent equipment for $5. Swimming farther out to the break on the south side can take 40min. but rewards with views of sharks and Napoleon fish. Those with less endurance can hire a boat from the village for $10 to **Sand Bank Island,** a prime snorkeling spot 50m from shore. Those with deeper diving desires should check out the **Supermarket** or visit batfish in **Gotham City** with **Aqua-Trek,** the PADI outfit at Mana Resort. (☎669 309; aquatrek-mana@is.com.fj. 1 dive $80, 4 dives $300, night dive $95. Gear hire $15.)

OTHER ISLANDS

Trekking through the interior is a drier option. To reach the hills, walk east on the beach from the hostels to the first rocks and turn left on the path past the Sunday Church or take the longer path through the village; to reach the **lookout,** follow the signs through the resort. Thursday is **lovo night** at the hostels. Monday the **local kids** put on a show; visitors are always welcome to teach or speak at the school. $20 at Ratu Kini's buys **spear fishing,** a **medicine walk,** or a myth-filled **"legend" walk** to the eastern hills; **deep-sea fishing** will cost $35. Both hostels offer **island-hopping** safaris to Castaway, Malolo, Plantation, and Musket Cove Islands (1-day, $20).

Travelers should be aware that **bats** come out in the evening, especially on the northern beaches, and that a large number of **wild dogs** inhabit the island, especially in the area north of the hostels. When walking to the beach or into the hills it is advised to avoid running; the dogs tend to bite the rushed and scared.

BEACHCOMBER ISLAND

You don't need to search the sands with a fine-bristled pet brush to find this tiny 5-acre island completely covered by one resort. **Beachcomber** (☎ 661 500, 723 828; fax 664 496; beachcomber@is.com.fj; www.beachcomberfiji.com), just 17km northwest of Nadi, is popular, often packed, and precisely groomed like a pink poodle to be the ultimate resort and party spot for the backpacker (if not quite budget) set. In being so supremely organized with consistent, timely, and friendly service, the resort has also combed out the kinks of any actual Fijian culture, which may be a loss to travelers seeking more than pure hedonistic comfort. Circling the round island (known in Fijian as Tai) takes 10min., meaning no one is ever far from the **main lodge,** where most of the action takes place. **Reception** is located here, as are the **phone** ($2 surcharge), the island **shop,** and **first aid** to deal with any minor injuries. Major emergencies are dealt with off the island (Beachcomber can arrange boat transfer, or see **Island Hoppers** p. 391). Visitors can charge everything from activities to drinks to sunscreen to their room, meaning that **cash is not needed** (except for late-night *un*official kava parties). The 102-bed **Grand Bure Dorm** is packed, clean, and entirely subject to how loud and late guests tend to be. The shared baths see so much use they are rarely spotless, though the staff tries. Other options include swank lodges with private bath, standard self-contained bures, and super-swank, budget-busting premium bures. All prices include three meals daily. The massive buffet-style spread serves all palates with a consistent range of high-quality fare. If tummy-grumbles hit between meals, the sandwiches and snacks for sale at the bar are inexpensive; better yet, just gorge off the free never-ending supply of coconut slivers. (Dorms $75 each; lodges and bures $179-320. Laundry service available. AmEx/MC/V.)

Eating, lounging on the spacious cream-colored beach, and eating some more dominate the day scene, while drinking in the large lodge bar is the favorite night pastime (🍹**lemon margaritas);** the house band entertains all evening with a wide repertoire, including the inescapable *Beachcomber* song, while weekly fire-warrior and hula-highlights pepper drinking games with a bit of variety. For those willing to actually get out of the jacuzzi, the resort offers: free mini golf and glass-bottom boat viewing for the leisurely; jetskiing ($60 per 15min.) and parasailing ($60 solo, $85 tandem) for the thrill seekers, and wakeboarding, waterskiing ($28-32), windsurfing ($15), snorkeling (free with deposit), and volleyball for the athletic. Free sailing and windsurfing lessons. **Subsurface Fiji** offers dives to Namotu Passage, the B-26 Bomber plane wreck, and the *Salamanda* shipwreck, among the usual shark and fish sites. (☎ 666 738; fax 669 955; www.fijidiving.com. 1 dive $72, 3 for $264. Equipment rental $12 per dive. PADI courses available.)

THE YASAWA GROUP

Pristine white beaches fringed by palm trees, azure tranquil lagoons teeming with dazzling aquatic life, breathtaking vistas from rugged volcanic mountains—comprised of six large islands and a number of smaller ones stretching in an 80km line northwest of Viti Levu, the Yasawa Group (pop. 5000) has some of the most beautiful geography in all of Fiji. First charted by a US expedition in 1840, for many years the Yasawas remained one of Fiji's most isolated regions. Today they are a prime destination, and a plethora of budget resorts have appeared in recent years. Between snorkeling, fishing, diving, kayaking, hiking, and village visits, the Yasawas will be a highlight of any traveler's experience.

✈ INTERISLAND TRANSPORTATION

Turtle Airways offers daily seaplane service between **Turtle Airways Base,** located 20min. from Nadi Airport on Viti Levu, and the waters off **Tavewa Island.** (☎721 888; turtleairways@is.com.fj. 30min. Departs Nadi 8am, Tavewa 5pm. Min. 2 passengers. Book 24hr. in advance. $79 one way.) **South Sea Cruises** operates a high-speed 42-passenger boat daily between Denarau Marina in **Nadi** and a number of stops in the **Yasawa Group** via **Lautoka.** (☎750 500; fax 750 501; southsea@is.co.fj. 2-4hr. to Tavewa depending on number of stops. Departs Denarau 9am, Tavewa 1:30pm. To **Tavewa** $70 one-way, $135 round-trip; to **Waya & Waya Lailai** $50/95. $55 for inter-island transfer within Yasawa Group, call to arrange pick-up.) A number of **budget resorts** in the Yasawas run their own services, some of which are licensed and equipped with life jackets (contact the resorts directly to make arrangements). The quality and safety of these options can vary greatly—ask around to find the safest service, and always make sure a boat has proper safety equipment.

The most reliable option for transfers between the major islands in the Yasawa Group is the **South Sea Cruises** daily service to **Waya Lailai, Waya, Naviti,** and **Tavewa.** For transfers between nearby islands, the various resorts operate their own small boats (usually about $10 one-way); again, check for safety equipment.

✦⚡ ORIENTATION AND PRACTICAL INFORMATION

With a total area of 135 sq. km, the hilly Yasawas experience a relatively dry climate. For the most part unde-veloped and thus unspoiled nature at its best, the islands include moun-tainous **Waya** and **Waya Lailai Islands** in the south and, moving along a rela-tively straight line to the northeast, steep and rugged **Naviti Island,** oval-shaped **Matacawalevu Island,** rela-tively flat **Tavewa Island,** large **Nacula Island,** and northernmost **Yasawa Island,** the largest and the group's namesake. The vast majority of bud-get resorts are located in **Nacula Tikina** (a Tikina is a Fijian unit of local administration), the middle section of the Yasawas consisting of Nacula, Tavewa, Nanuya Lailai, Matacawa-levu, and Yaqeta. There are also a few budget resorts on Waya and Waya Lailai. Exclusive **Turtle Island** (Nanuya Levu), is also a part of Nacula Tikina, separated from Nanuya Lailai by a shallow strip of water that can be crossed on foot during low tide. Tur-tle Island and its neighboring islands in Nacula Tikina enclose the beauti-ful ▨**Blue Lagoon,** immortalized by the infamous 1980s movie of the same name featuring Brooke Shields.

Yasawa Group

N

Yasawa
Yasawa Island
Sawa-i-lau Island
Nacula
Tavewa Island
Nacula Island
Matacawa Levu Island
Nanuya Lailai Island
Nanuya Levu Island
Yaqeta Island
Somosomo
Naviti Island
Bligh Water
Waya Island
Waya Sewa Island
Kuata Island

0   5 miles
0   10 km

There is little in the way of the amenities and services in the Yasawas. Apart from the village nurses and community shops stocked with minimal provisions, there are **no banks, post offices, hospitals, ATMs** or **internet access** on the islands. **Electricity** is available during limited hours at some budget resorts, and a majority of the resorts use radio phones. Most resorts provide boiled rainwater, although some sell bottled water. There are no independent restaurants, bars, or nightclubs; most resorts include a complete meal package in their prices and provide nightly entertainment for their guests in the form of string serenades, kava ceremonies, and dance performances. **Cooking is not allowed at most resorts.**

WAYA AND WAYA LAILAI (WAYA SEWA)

Waya, about 7km long and 5km wide, is the tallest island in the Yasawas. Both Waya and Waya Lailai ("Little Waya," located south of Waya) offer spectacular views of the entire Yasawa Group from their hilltops. With friendly villages, lovely beaches, great diving and snorkeling, and challenging hikes, the southern section of the Yasawas are an attractive alternative to more central Nacula Tikina.

▐ TRANSPORTATION. South Sea Cruises (☎ 750 500; fax 750 501; south-sea@is.co.fj) drops off passengers at **Waya** and **Waya Lailai** on its daily scheduled service between **Nadi** and **Tavewa**. **Octopus Resort** runs a daily boat service (licensed 14-passenger boat with life jackets) to and from **Lautoka** (1hr.; departs Lautoka 9:30am, Octopus Resort 2pm; $50 one-way). Octopus and other resorts provide small boats for island hopping between Waya and Waya Lailai (usually $10).

▐▐ ACCOMMODATIONS AND CAMPING. Octopus Resort, on the northeastern side of Waya, is one of the best budget resorts in the Yasawas. Although slightly upscale, the luxurious sand, great snorkeling (free rental with a deposit), and world class diving are worth the money. Prices include breakfast and dinner. (☎ 666 337; fax 666 210; octopus_resort@yahoo.com. Laundry $5 per load. Reservations strongly recommended. Private baths in dorm and bures; shared bath for camping. Free beach shower. 5-bed dorm $45; double bure $110-$140; camping $35. MC/V/major currencies accepted.) **Adi's Place,** next to Yalobi Village, is a small no-frills establishment for those seeking a secluded stay immersed in Fijian village life. (Call the Cathay Hotel, Lautoka ☎ 660 566. Free beach snorkeling, hiking, and village visits. Prices include 3 meals per day. Communal bath for all guests. 12-bed dorm in a wooden hut $35; 3-room bure, max. 5 people, $40 per person; camping $25.) **Bayside Budget Resort,** a 10min. walk down the beach from Adi's Place and operated by Adi's brother Manasa, offers similar facilities and activities. (☎ 723 035; fax 721 981; sosene@is.com. Prices include 3 meals per day. Communal bath. 14-bed dorm $35; 2-room bure $35 per person; camping $25.)

▐ ACTIVITIES. Octopus Resort operates its own PADI dive shop, a branch of **First Divers.** (Firstdivers@is.com.fj. 1 tank $80; 2 tanks $140; $10-$20 less with own gear.) Guests at other Waya resorts can dive at Octopus or **Waya Lailai Resort** on Waya Lailai. Octopus also offers its guests: **guided village visits** (1½ hr., $18 per person including gift presented to the village chief), **reef snorkeling** (1½ hr., $15 per person), **night** or **daytime fishing** (2hr., $15 per person), guided **mountain hiking** with great views (2hr., $15 per person including packed lunch), and **island hopping** (whole day, $25 per person including packed lunch). **Adi's Place** and **Bayside Budget Resort** also offer reef snorkeling, hiking, and other activities at similar prices.

NACULA TIKINA

A closely-packed cluster of islands consisting of Nacula, Tavewa, Nanuya Lailai, Matacawalevu, Yaqeta, and Turtle Island (Nanuya Levu), this middle section of the Yasawas contains the world-famous ▓**Blue Lagoon** and is rapidly becoming the budget traveler's favored destination in Fiji.

TRANSPORTATION. Turtle Airways (☎721 888; turtleairways@is.com.fj) operates its daily service between **Nadi** and the waters off **Tavewa**, as does **South Sea Cruise** (☎750 500; southsea@is.co.fj). The various resorts on Tavewa and other islands provide transfers on small boats to and from the plane and the South Sea Cruise boat stop. **Coral View Resort** on Tavewa runs its own service to and from **Nadi** via **Lautoka** on a licensed 26-passenger boat. (Lautoka ☎669 316; Nadi 724 199; Tavewa 662 648; coral@is.com.fj. 6-7hr. M-Sa departs **Nadi** 9am, **Tavewa** 7am. $60 one-way, $100 round-trip. Equipped with life jackets.) For island hopping within Nacula Tikina, the various resorts provide small boats (usually $10).

NACULA

The third largest in the Yasawas (10km long and 3km wide), hilly Nacula is home to four villages. Ratu Epeli Vuetibau, the Tui Drola (high chief) of Nacula Tikina, lives in Nacula Village. With five budget resorts operating and more to be built in the near future, travelers will certainly find lodging to suit their needs.

ACCOMMODATIONS. All prices below include three meals daily. **Oarsman's Bay Lodge** and **Nalova Bay** sit by the exquisite beach on the southeastern side of the island. This new resort complex differs from the other resorts on the island in its modern design and the availability of hot water, electricity, and ceiling fans. (Book through Turtle Airways at ☎721 888. Laundry $4. Advance reservations recommended. 14-bed dorm $45; double bure with bath $130; camping $25. AmEx/MC/V/ traveler's checks accepted.) **Nabua Lodge** is a beachfront collection of bures on the southwestern side, next to Melbravo. (Lautoka ☎669 173. 6-bed dorm $35; double bure $77; camping $25.) **Melbravo** offers a similar experience. (Lautoka ☎650 616. 7-bed dorm $35; double bures $77; pre-pitched tent for 2 $30 per person; camping $25.) **Safe Landing** (due to be completed by December 2001) is on a silky beach at the southwestern tip of the island. (☎951 341. Free laundry. 6-bed dorm $34; double bure $70; camping $23.)

ACTIVITIES. All resorts on the island offer **snorkeling** at a modest rental fee ($2-5 per day), trips to Blue Lagoon for **sunbathing** and **fish-feeding** (about $10 per person), **fishing trips** ($10), visits to nearby **limestone caves** ($25), and **village visits** ($5-$12, usually including a kava ceremony and sometimes lunch). **Diving** is offered at **Tavewa Island Dive Center** and **Coral View Resort** (see **Tavewa: Activities** p. 422).

NANUYA LAILAI

Adjacent to Turtle Island, beautiful little Nanuya Lailai's rolling hills, mangroves, and white-sand beaches border the northern end of the Blue Lagoon. The southwestern corner of the island is the location of ⬛**Blue Lagoon Beach,** where cruise ships from Blue Lagoon Cruises and yachts from all over the world anchor for sunbathing, snorkeling, diving, and barbecues on the beach. Expect to be woken up in the morning by the sound of rooster cries and the flapping of chicken wings.

TRANSPORTATION. The daily services on **Turtle Airways** and **South Sea Cruises** (see **Interisland Transportation** p. 419) are the most reliable and safest modes of transportation. **Sunrise Lagoon** (Lautoka ☎951 341) and **Gold Coast** (Lautoka ☎651 580) on the island offer their own services on 14-passenger boats to and from **Lautoka** (2hr., $60 one-way), which guests staying at the other three resorts on the island can also use. All five resorts provide **small boats** for transfers to and from nearby islands (usually $5-$10).

ACCOMMODATIONS AND CAMPING. The five budget accommodations on the island's northern beach are similar, close to one another, and owned by members of the same extended family, offering a simple yet authentic Fijian experience. All offer laundry ($2-5 per load), a 10-30% *Let's Go* discount on bookings made directly, and universal access to services (radio phone, boat rides for fishing, cave trips, snorkeling, etc.). All prices include three meals daily. **Sunrise Lagoon** has a family-like atmosphere with electricity until 10pm. (Lautoka ☎951 341. 8-bed dorm $35; double bures $77; family bure $80; camping $28.) **Kim's Place** has a nice view from the hilltop at the back of the resort and an open-air tea house serving tea and cakes daily from 3:30-5:30pm for only $2.50 per person. (Call Sunrise Lagoon ☎951 341 or Gold Coast ☎651 580. 5-bed dorm $35; double bures $77; camping $25.) **Gold Coast,** the largest of the five resorts, has a large dining hall on top of the hill out back. (Lautoka ☎651 580. Electricity until 10pm. 12-bed dorm $35; double bures $77; camping $25.) **Seaspray Backpackers** provides a comfortable rest. (Lautoka ☎668 962. 8-bed dorm $35; double bures $77; camping $30.) **Al's Paradise** is the fifth and smallest resort. (Lautoka ☎973 800. 6-bed dorm $35; double bures $75; camping $25.)

⚑ ACTIVITIES. Guests staying at the five resorts have access to any activities offered among them, such as: **trips to the Blue Lagoon** ($10), **village meke trips** ($10), **cave trips** ($25), **fishing trips** ($10), **Honeymoon Island trips** ($10), and **snorkeling gear rental** ($5 per day). **Diving** can be arranged with **Tavewa Island Dive Center** or the dive shop at **Coral View Resort** on Tavewa Island (see below).

TAVEWA

One of the smaller islands of the Yasawa Group, Tavewa's hilly expanse measures a mere 3km long by 1km wide. It is the home of three long-established budget resorts and has lovely beaches on its southern and western sides; the best is on the southern side bordering the Blue Lagoon, next to Otto & Fanny's.

▤ TRANSPORTATION. The Turtle Airways seaplane lands on the waters just off the southern side. (See **Interisland Transportation** p. 419 for information on services offered by Turtle Airways and South Sea Cruises, and **Nacula Tikina: Transportation** p. 421 for Coral View Resort's services.) The resorts on Tavewa provide transfers to neighboring islands on their own small boats ($5-$10).

⌂⌂ ACCOMMODATIONS AND CAMPING. All of these resorts include three meals daily in their prices. **Coral View Resort** is the largest resort on the island. They have a dance performance and DJ music in the large dining hall nightly, except Sundays. (Lautoka ☎669 316; Nadi 724 199; Resort 662 648; after-hours 668 876; fax 669 312; coral@is.com.fj. Reservations recommended. Laundry $5 per load. Phone service and electricity. Afternoon tea hour daily 4-5pm, $2. One free resort activity daily. 15% discount on the first 4 nights if stay is longer and booked directly with the resort. Dorms $35; standard double bures $77; luxury double bures $88; camping $27.50.) **David's Place** is also large, with an excellent lovo buffet every Thursday and barbecues on Saturday. (Nadi airport ☎721 820; mobile 950 545. Reservations recommended. Electricity during limited hours. Laundry $5 per load. Phone service. Dorms $35-37; double bures $77-88; camping $27.50. MC/V 5% surcharge.) **Otto & Fanny's** is a bit pricier, but the owners are wonderful hosts and great storytellers. (Lautoka ☎/fax 661 462. Reservations recommended. Electricity in all buildings. Phone. Laundry $5 per load. 8-bed dorm $65; double bures with bath $140. MC/V/traveler's checks.)

⚑ ACTIVITIES. Those staying at **Coral View Resort, Fanny & Otto's,** and **Kingfisher Lodge** can go on **village trips** ($20 with lunch in the village), **cave trips** ($25), **hikes** (free), rent **snorkeling** gear ($5 per day with $20 deposit), or **dive** at Coral View Resort's PADI dive shop (1 tank $80, 2 tanks $130, introductory dive $125, min. 4-day open water course $450). **David's Place** offers similar activities at similar prices. **Tavewa Island Dive Center** (call West Side Water Sports in Lautoka ☎661 462; mobile 998 862), next to Fanny & Otto's, runs full-range PADI offerings for guests staying on Tavewa Island for prices similar to Coral View's.

MATACAWALEVU AND YAQETA

The oval-shaped Matacawalevu (4km long) and Yaqeta (further south) are sizable, hilly islands where budget resorts are beginning to develop. At present, only **Sunset Beach Resort** on Matacawalevu is open. (☎722 921. Hot water, fan, solar-powered electricity, phone. Double bures $140, includes 3 meals per day. MC/V.) Plans call for the construction of one more resort on the other side of Matacawalevu and two on Yaqeta. Activities provided by **Oarsman's Bay Lodge** (p. 421) on Nacula.

LOMAIVITI GROUP

Less touristed than the Coral Coast of Viti Levu or the popular resorts in the Mamanucas and Yasawas, the Lomaiviti ("central Fiji") Group is a pleasant surprise and excellent value for the budget traveler. Located in the geographical heart of the Fijian archipelago, the Lomaiviti Group consists of seven large islands (Ovalau, Gau, Koro, Wakaya, Batiki, Nairai, and Makogai) and a few small ones, with a total area of some 400 square kilometers that includes some of Fiji's best beaches.

⚜🛈 ORIENTATION AND PRACTICAL INFO

The few budget accommodations in the Lomaiviti Group are mostly on Ovalau. Most amenities and travel services such as **banks,** the **post office, grocery stores,** and **internet access** are concentrated in **Levuka** on the eastern coast of Ovalau and are **not available on the smaller islands** such as Leleuvia and Caqelai. The budget resorts on Leleuvia and Caqelai offer **drinking water** (boiled rainwater), limited **electricity,** and regular **phone service. Wakaya,** a privately owned island, is home to a superexclusive resort, the **Wakaya Club. Naigani** (Mystery Island) and **Namenalala** sport their own upmarket resorts. The budget resort on **Yanuca Lailai** (Lost Island) was closed at the time of writing.

OVALAU

The densely vegetated Lovoni Valley is situated at the center of Ovalau, the closest principal island of the Lomaiviti Group to Viti Levu. Moving towards the eastern coast, Nadelaiovalau (620m) rises from the flat bottom of a crater, providing a magnificent backdrop to the town of Levuka. As Fiji's first capital, Levuka has a strong sense of history. Most travelers dabble here before exploring nearby Lovoni village or heading offshore to snorkel, dive, and kayak.

✈ TRANSPORTATION

Air Fiji (Suva ☎313 666; Levuka ☎440 139; www.airfiji.net) flies twice daily between **Suva** and **Bureta Airstrip** (15min.; leaves Suva at 7:30am and 5:30pm, Bureta at 7am and 5pm; $47 one-way, $79 return). **Patterson Brothers Shipping** (Levuka ☎440 125), on Beach St. in Levuka, runs a ferry/bus service between **Levuka** and **Suva** (5hr. total; bus Suva-Natovi, ferry Natovi-Buresala, bus Buresala-Levuka; M-Sa; departs Suva 2pm, Levuka 9am; $30 one-way, $60 return). **Leleuvia Island Resort** (☎301 584) operates a boat-taxi service between **Suva** and **Levuka** via **Leleuvia** on demand (30min. Levuka-Leleuvia; 30min. Leleuvia-Bau Landing on Viti Levu; 20min. Bau Landing-Suva by taxi; leaves Leleuvia for **Levuka** at 8:30am and for **Bau Landing** at noon; leaves Levuka for **Leleuvia** at 10am and Bau landing for **Leleuvia** at 1pm; $35 Levuka-Suva one-way, $20 Leleuvia-Suva one-way, $15 Levuka-Leleuvia one-way). Within Ovalau, **carriers** (canopied open pickup trucks) depart when full (typically $1 within Levuka, $3 between Levuka and Lovoni). **Minibuses** connect **Bureta** and **Levuka** (1hr., $3 one-way). **Taxis** ($1.50 within Levuka) can be hired for $60 to go around the island. **Ovalau Watersports** (see **Activities** p. 425) in Levuka rents out **mountain bikes** (1hr. $5, half-day $10, full-day $15).

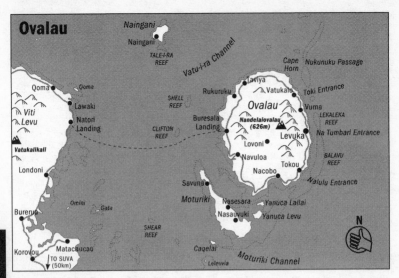

LEVUKA

Historical Levuka (pop. 3000), the site of the first European settlement in Fiji, was a wild spot in the South Pacific during the 1840s. Over 50 pubs and lodgings catered to the European population of whalers, beachcombers, runaway convicts, and speculators of all shades. Chosen as the capital of Fiji in 1874 for its accessible port, central location between Viti Levu and Vanua Levu, and proximity to the important island of Bau, Levuka still retains much of its colonial character.

✦ ⚡ ORIENTATION AND PRACTICAL INFORMATION

The town is located on a narrow coastal strip with the steep mountains as its backdrop and is easily explored on foot. Most shops and services are located along the waterfront on **Beach Street.** At the southern end of Beach St. is the **Pacific Fishing Company (PAFCO),** the town's main employer and the lifeblood of its economy. The **Community Center** (open M-F 9am-1pm and 2-4:30pm, Sa 9am-1pm) in the Morris Hedstrom building gives out **tourist information,** but it is better to check with **Ovalau Water Sports** (☎440 166) a few doors down Beach St. or at the **Royal Hotel** (☎440 024). **Colonial National Bank** (☎440 300; open M-Th 9:30am-3pm, F 9:30am-4pm) and **Westpac Bank** (open M-Th 9:30am-12:30pm and 1:30pm-3pm, F 9:30am-4pm), both on Beach St., exchange currencies and cash traveler's checks (Westpac also gives Visa cash advances).

Buy your groceries at **Gulabdas Supermarket** (open M-Sa 8am-7pm, Su 8am-1pm and 5-6pm) at the southern end of Beach St. **Gulabdas & Sons,** farther up Beach St., has a tiny **pharmacy.** (☎440 015. Open M-Sa 7:30am-6pm.) The **market** (open F 8pm-Sa 5pm), close to the Royal Hotel, sells fresh fish, fruit, and vegetables. The **hospital** at the northern end of Beach St. has an **ambulance.** (☎440 088. Open M-F 8am-4pm; nurse on duty 24hr.) The **police** (☎440 222) are at the corner of Garner Jones Rd. and Totogo Lane. **Internet** access is available at **Ovalau Watersports** (☎440 166. $0.30 per min. Open M-Sa 8:30am-3:30pm.) The **post office** (☎440 141; fax 440 633; open M-F 8am-4pm), at the southern end of Beach St., can send and receive fax/telegrams, Poste Restante mail, and Western Union. **Pay phones** are at the post office and several points along Beach St.

♠♞ ACCOMMODATIONS

▧**The Royal Hotel** (☎440 024; fax 440 174; royal@is.com.fj), on Langham St. close to Beach St., is the oldest continuously operated hotel in the South Pacific. Ceiling fans, historical photos, a century-old billiard table, and hibiscus flowers in polished brass vases give a Somerset Maugham flavor. Restaurant serves light meals ($1.50-$7.50). Laundry $5. Dorms $10; singles $18.70; doubles and twins $27.50; triples $35.20; quads $48.40; other options available. Traveler's checks accepted.

Mavida Guest House (☎440 477; fax 301 652), on Beach St., is well known for warm hospitality. Manager Rosie Patterson has a charmingly colorful personality. Free kayak rental. Breakfast included. Lunch and dinner each $6 per person. Laundry $5. 5- and 3-bed dorms $10; doubles $40; private rooms $15 per person.

Ovalau Holiday Resort (☎/fax 440 329), a few kilometers north of Levuka on a small bay, is good for a quiet, secluded stay. Free transport to and from Levuka. Restaurant. Snorkeling, reef fishing trip and kayak rental. 19-bed dorm $10.50; self-catering bunga-lows with bath $55-$66; camping $5. 20% *Let's Go* discount if booked directly.

♠▨ FOOD AND ENTERTAINMENT

Kim's Paak Kum Loong Wine & Dine (☎440 059), on Beach St., has a 2nd. fl. balcony view over the harbor that makes up for any lack of atmosphere. Great selection of tasty Chinese, Fijian, and European dishes. All meals $3.30-$9. Sunday evening buffet with dessert $13.20. Open M-Sa 7am-3pm and 5-9pm, Su noon-2pm and 6-9pm.

Whale's Tale (☎440 235), on Beach St., cooks up excellent light meals. The European menu with Fijian flare includes burgers ($7.70), sandwiches with salad ($4.40), stir-fry ($6.95), and 3-course dinner specials ($13.20). Try the tropical fruit smoothie ($3.30). Open M-Sa 11am-3pm and 5-9pm. Traveler's checks accepted.

Cafe Levuka (☎440 329), at the southern end of Beach St., serves decent Indian, Chinese, and European dishes (fish and chips $7, curries and Chinese $6-7, breakfast $2.50-$8). Open M-Sa 8am-2pm and 6-9pm.

Ovalau Club (☎440 507), next to Nasau Park and Town Council Hall, is the best bar in town. Established in 1904 as one of Fiji's oldest social clubs, the Club is open to any out-of-town travelers. $2-3 beer, $1.20 shots. Ask the bartender to show you the letter written by German sea raider Count Von Luckner during World War I. Open M-Th 4-10:30pm, F 2-10:30pm, Sa 10am-midnight, Su 9am-8pm.

♞ ACTIVITIES

▧**WALKING TOUR.** Within Levuka itself, a historical walking tour makes for a pleasant afternoon. Starting at **Cession Site** in Nasova (10min. walk south of PAFCO), three boulders commemorate the local signing of the Deed of Cession on October 10, 1874, Fiji's independence in 1970, and the centenary of the Deed of Cession in 1974. Across the street is the thatched-roof **Provincial Bure,** used by Prince Charles when he came to represent Queen Elizabeth during Fiji's transition to independence in 1970. Walking north past the PAFCO/Bumble Bee tuna cannery onto Beach St., the **old Morris Hedstrom company building (1868),** which was important in developing Levuka's early trade networks, now houses the town's museum, Community Center, and library. The modest museum displays pictures and tools illustrating Fiji's history, as well as weapons, tribal handicrafts, and shells. (Open M-F 9am-1pm and 2-4:30pm, Sa 9am-1pm; $2 suggested.) Further on, **Sacred Heart Catholic Church's** tall stone clock tower (late 1800s) hides the tranquil stone building of the **Marist Convent School** (1880) on Totoga Ln. Northward on Totoga Ln. stands the police station compound and the wooden buildings of the **original police station** (1920; Fiji's first police station) and **former prison.** Across Totoga Creek are the **Ovalau Club** (1904), one of Fiji's oldest social clubs, and the adjacent **Town Council Hall,** erected in 1898 to celebrate Queen Victoria's silver jubilee. The first **Masonic Lodge** in the South Pacific (1875) next door was unfortunately burned down in the wake of the May 2000 coup.

Cross the creek again, turn right onto Garner-Jones Rd., and **Levuka Public School,** founded in 1879 as Fiji's first public school, is on your left. At this point there is the option of a brief hike (20min. return) up to a **small waterfall.** To get to the waterfall, continue from the school towards the mountain following the stone path up the stairs and through a small village settlement. Sturdy shoes are needed to get down to the waterfall. The view of the ocean along the trail is spectacular.

Back on Garner-Jones Rd., turn left onto the bridge and go around Nasau Park on Church St. On the left are the 199 steps leading to **Mission Hill,** which presents another stunning view of the sea. Walk past the **Royal Hotel** (c. 1860) and left on Beach St. to reach seaside **Niukaube Hill,** site of the **First World War Memorial,** a white-washed monument in the form of an ionic stone column. King Cakobau's original Parliament House and Supreme Court once stood on this hill.

CINEMAS. Cinema Levuka shows Hollywood and Bollywood movies. *(On Beach St. Showtimes M-F 8pm; Sa 11am, 2, and 8pm; Su 2 and 8pm. Adults $3, under 12 $1.50.)*

DIVING. Ovalau Watersports offers fine diving near Wakaya Island and around Ovalau, including several unexplored sites. *(In the Ovalau Tours and Transport building at the southern end of Beach St. ☎/fax 440 166; dive@owlfiji.com. 2 tanks start at $130; open-water course $460; reef snorkeling $30; snorkeling gear rental $10 per day.)*

DAYTRIPS. Ovalau Watersports is also the agent for transfer and daytrips to **Leleuvia Island Resort.** Daytrips to **Caqelai Island** can be booked at the **Royal Hotel.** Another great day trip from Levuka is **Epi's Inland Tour** to Lovoni Village (also called Epi's Midland Tour; book at the Royal Hotel) at the bottom of the central volcanic crater. You can ride on the village truck to Lovoni or hike over the mountains from Levuka (5hr.; hiking boots needed; carry plenty of water). If you take the truck, Epi will take you to some waterfalls after lunch. During the hikes, Epi identifies various medicinal plants; he is most impressive when narrating the tragic history of his village. *(Leleuvia daytrip departs 10am, returns by 4pm; $35 per person, including lunch. Caqelai daytrip $30 per person, including lunch. Epi's Tour starts from Levuka at 11am and returns by 7pm M-Sa on demand; $25 per person, including lunch at Epi's home in Lovoni.)*

CAQELAI AND LELEUVIA

The closest you may ever come to seeing your tropical beach fantasy may be on Caqelai or Leleuvia. These tiny coral islands allure sunseekers and beach bums with every sort of temptation: luxurious golden sandy beaches, azure shallow water brimming with colorful fish, lush vegetation, and palm trees offering a cool reprieve from the sun. The area has some of the best fishing, snorkeling, and crab watching in Fiji. The islands are close to each other (5min. by boat), with Caqelai closer to Moturiki Island. Caqelai is owned by the Methodist Church on Moturiki, while Leleuvia belongs to the chiefs of Bau Island. **No alcohol is sold** on Caqelai, but guests may bring their own. Both resorts have **boiled rainwater** for drinking, **phones,** and **snack shops.** Caqelai runs its own boat service (canopied 15-passenger boat with life jackets) to **Levuka** (1hr; departs Caqelai 8:30am, Levuka 10am; $15 one-way; book at the resort or at the Royal Hotel in Levuka—see p. 425) as does Leleuvia (for info on boat services to and from Leleuvia see **Ovalau: Transportation** p. 423). Caqelai also has service to **Waindalice** and **Verata** on Viti Levu (1hr; departs Caqelai 8:30am, Waindalice 10am; $15-20 one way). Either resort will transfer you to the other ($10 return).

Caqelai Island Resort has spartan facilities (bucket water for showers) but organizes more activities for its guests than Leleuvia. Visitors can walk during low tide to nearby Snake Island. (☎430 366. Bare-bones 12-bed dorm $28; bures $30 per person; camping $24. Snorkeling gear rental $6 per day; reef fishing $5; village vis-

MISSIONARY IMPOSSIBLE The village of Lovoni on Ovalau was the last holdout against Bauan Chief Seru Cakobau's campaign to rule all of Fiji. After repeated defeats at the hands of the fierce Lovoni warriors, Cakobau resorted to trickery, sending a Christian missionary to invite the villagers to a feast of reconciliation. Accepting the gesture in good faith, the villagers arrived, laid down their arms, and started to party, only to be ambushed by Cakobau's warriors. Horribly tortured and sold into slavery, the villagers were allowed to return to their home only when Queen Victoria, the new ruler of Fiji, intervened several years later after hearing about their plight. Hear more about this fascinating story from Epi on his Lovoni Village tour (see above).

its to Moturiki $10 per person; and trips to nearby Honeymoon Island $15.) **Leleuvia Island Resort** offers slightly more creature comforts than Caqelai, like running showers and electricity in the dorm and bures. (☎301 584; Suva ☎301 799. 12-bed dorm $28; bures $32 per person, with bath $34; cabins with bath $36 per person; camping $23. Day trips to Honeymoon Island $10; snorkeling gear rental $10 per day; reef fishing $10-15; Sunday village visits $4. Packages at the PADI dive shop include: 1 tank $75; 2 tanks $110; open-water course $390.) Prices at both resorts include three meals per day.

VANUA LEVU

Volcanic activity thousands of years ago melded together several islands, creating strangely irregular Vanua Levu, Fiji's second largest island (5538 sq. km) and home to 20% of the Fijian population. A mountain range rises across the island, with the bulk of Vanua Levu's mountains concentrated near the southern coast. A relative lack of sandy beaches and hiking trails has prevented tourism from supplanting the sugar and copra industries; the northern and most populous town of Labasa (pop. 25,000) is home to mills and plantations but no amenities for travelers. However, many travelers do visit the island's southeastern coast for incredible diving, snorkeling, kayaking, and fishing. As it attracts more visitors, Vanua Levu's tourist infrastructure is beginning to grow accordingly.

OTHER ISLANDS

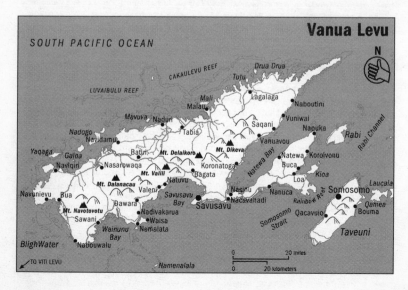

SAVUSAVU

A popular port for yachts traveling around the world, Savusavu (pop. 2000) is well-protected by a lovely harbor ringed with towering green mountains. An early European settlement that bustled with whalers and sandalwood, gold, and copra traders during the 19th century, Savusavu is now a relaxed town that only gets dressed up for a biennial yacht race from New Zealand. An extensively renovated copra shed serves as the yacht club and the hub of the town's tourist activity. Despite its calm and tranquil appearance, Savusavu sits atop a cauldron of geothermal activity—on a walk along the town's main road, visitors can sometimes see steam rising from a stream just off the sidewalk.

■ **TRANSPORTATION.** Savusavu is now well-connected by air and sea to **Viti Levu** and **Taveuni.** Most of Vanua Levu's roads are gravel, with the exceptions being the sealed road between Labasa and Sabusabu and sealed sections of the road between Labasa and Nabouwalu in the southwest. Plans are in place to seal the road from Savusavu to Buca Bay in the east, though only the portion reaching Mumu's Resort is scheduled to be completed by late 2001. **Savusavu Airport** is close to town; taxi transfer costs $2-3.

Flights: Air Fiji (Savusavu ☎ 850 173), with an office in the Copra Shed Marina on the main road (open M-F 8:30am-4:30pm, Sa 8am-noon), flies twice daily to **Nadi** (1hr.; departs Nadi 8am and 1pm, Savusavu 9:15am and 3:25pm; $148 one-way); **Suva** (45min.; departs Suva 9:30am and 2:30pm, Savusavu 10am and 3:30pm; $104 one-way); and **Taveuni** (20min.; departs Taveuni 10:10am and 2:10pm, Savusavu 9:10am and 1:40pm; $68 one-way). **Sun Air** (Savusavu ☎ 850 141), whose office is next to Air Fiji in the Copra Shed Marina (open M-F 8am-1pm and 2-5pm, Sa 8am-noon), flies twice daily to **Nadi** (1hr.; departs Nadi 8am and 12:30pm, Savusavu 10:40am and 2:40pm; $148 one-way) and **Taveuni** at about the same times and fares as Air Fiji.

Ferries: Spirit of Free Enterprise (SOFE), operated by **Consort Shipping** (Savusavu ☎ 850 279; on the main road opposite the Shell station; open M-F 8am-4:30pm), runs between **Suva** and **Taveuni** via **Koro Island** and Savusavu (22hr. total, 12hr. between **Suva** and **Savusavu,** 5hr. between **Savusavu** and **Taveuni;** departs Suva for Savusavu Tu 10pm and Sa 6pm; departs Savusavu for Suva M and Th 8pm, for Taveuni W and Su 10pm; departs Taveuni M and Th noon; $41 one-way between Suva and Taveuni, $38 one-way between Suva and Savusavu, $22 one-way between Savusavu and Taveuni). **Adi Savusavu,** operated by **Beachcomber Shipping** (Savusavu ☎ 850 266, 850 706; next to Air Fiji in the Copra Shed Marina; open M-F 8am-5pm, Sa 8am-1pm), also runs between **Suva** and **Taveuni** via **Savusavu** (20hr. total, 11hr. between Suva and Savusavu, 5hr. between Savusavu and Taveuni; departs Suva Tu 10am and Th noon; departs Savusavu for Suva Su 7am and W 8pm, for Taveuni W and F 1am; departs Taveuni W and F 12:30pm; one-way between Suva and Taveuni $47 economy class, $67 first class; one-way between Suva and Savusavu $42/$62; one-way between Savusavu and Taveuni $22/$42). On both the *SOFE* and the *Adi Sasusavu* there are cafeterias and spaces for motor vehicles. A new rapid boat service by Beachcomber Shipping, **Lagilagi** (100 passengers) links **Nadi** (Port Denarau) and **Savusavu** via **Lautoka** and **Beachcomber Island** (6hr. total; departs Nadi Tu and Sa 6am, Savusavu Tu and Sa 12:30pm; $90 one-way between Nadi and Savusavu). Aboard is an A/C lounge with bar. In addition to the above options, **Vishnu Holdings** offers a combined bus/ferry service between Savusavu and **Taveuni** via **Buca Bay** (Savusavu ☎ 850 276; 5hr. total, bus between Savusavu and Napuca in Buca Bay 3hr.; departs Savusavu daily 10:30am and 2pm; $15 one-way between Savusavu and Taveuni, $4 one-way between Savusavu and Buca Bay). If the small boat between Buca Bay and Taveuni doesn't have life jackets or radio communication, make sure you feel comfortable with the safety risk; do not get on if the weather looks threatening.

Buses and Taxis: Buses run to **Labasa** (3hr.; 7, 9:30am, 1:30, 2:30, and 4pm; $6 one-way). There are also services to **Nabouwalu** via **the Junction** on the way up to Labasa. The bus stand is on the main road next to the market and police post. To hire a taxi from

Savusavu to Labasa costs about $60 and takes about 4hr. The town is easily explored on foot, but a taxi ride anywhere in town costs only $1-1.50.

Car Rental: There is no car rental agency in town at the moment, but travelers may call the **Budget** office in Labasa (☎811 999) and receive a car in about a day. 4WDs available. Open M-F 8am-4:30pm, Sa 8am-noon

Bike Rental: Eco Divers-Tours (☎850 122), inside Copra Shed Marina on the main road, rents mountain bikes ($10 per half day).

⬛🛈 ORIENTATION AND PRACTICAL INFORMATION. Most services in Savusavu are located along **Lesiaceva Road** (simply called the **main road**) along the waterfront. Behind this thin strip of flat coastal land rise the peaks of **Saqayaya** (878m) and **Suvasuva** (1157m).

Banks: Westpac Bank (☎850 229; open M-Th 9:30am-3pm, F 9:30am-4pm), **ANZ Bank** (☎850 005; open M-Th 9:30am-3pm, F 9:30am-4pm) and **Colonial National Bank** (☎850 199; open M-F 8am-5pm) are all near the eastern end of town on the main road. ANZ and Westpac give cash advances on MC/V.

Police: ½km east of Savusavu on the main road (☎007); there is also a police post on the main road in town next to the market.

Pharmacy: There is no full-scale pharmacy, but a couple of supermarkets have a mini pharmacy section; try **J. Dayaram & Co.** (☎850 247; open M-F 8am-5pm, Sa 8am-1pm) diagonally across from the ANZ on the main road.

Medical Services: The **hospital** (24hr. ☎850 444) is several km east on the main road.

Internet Access: At **Plantation Real Estate,** across the main road from Copra Shed Marina (☎850 801; open M-Sa 8am-around 4pm; $0.35 per min.); **Savusavu Real Estate,** inside the Copra Shed Marina (☎850 929, 850 549; open M-F 8am-5pm, Sa 8am-1pm; $0.35 per min.); and the **Hot Springs Hotel** (☎850 195; $0.35 per min.).

Post Office: (☎850 310; fax 850 117). At the eastern end of town on the main road. Fax, telegram, pay phone, and Poste Restante. Open M-F 8am-4pm, Sa 8-11am.

🛏 ACCOMMODATIONS. The **Copra Shed Marina** on the main road has two spacious self-catering apartment units offering great views of the harbor. (☎850 457; fax 850 989. Reservations recommended. Laundry $7. 2-room with bath $90; studio $45. Discounts for longer stays.) The **Vatukaluvi Holiday House,** a 15min. drive from Savusavu on a hillside overlooking Koro Sea, is great for a secluded stay amid lush scenery. (☎850 143. Reservations recommended. 2-bedroom house for 6 with bath, kitchen, and deck $55.) For a funky stay with a wide range of rooms try **Mumu's Resort,** about 15km southeast of Savusavu on the coast. Diving, fishing, and other activities are arranged with Eco Divers-Tours (see **Activities** below). The bus from Savusavu (M-Sa 6 daily, Su 3 daily) is $1.30 and taxi is $15. (☎850 416; fax 850 402. Breakfast, lunch $10; dinner $20. Laundry $5. 6-bed dorm $15; doubles $12-60 per person. Traveler's checks accepted.) Although **Savusavu Bay Accommodation,** on the on the main road, lacks atmosphere, it has great views of the harbor. (☎850 100. Laundry $6. Doubles with bath, veranda, and fan $22; with A/C $40.)

AAAAAHHHH... Directly on the opposite side of the globe from Greenwich, England, the **180° meridian line** is the geographically accurate International Date Line. Running almost all of its course over the open waters of the Pacific Ocean, the meridian only crosses land in a few places—the frigid Chukotsky peninsula in eastern Siberia, and Vanua Levu, Rabi, and **Taveuni** in Fiji. The meridian neatly bisects the island of Taveuni; its inhabitants are both the first to see each new dawn and the last to see the sunset every day. This also makes Taveuni one of the only places in the world where you can pee on Wednesday and have it hit the ground on Tuesday.

OTHER ISLANDS

◪◩ FOOD AND NIGHTLIFE. On the deck at the **Captain's Cafe,** in the Copra Shed Marina, you get breakfast, sandwiches, and massive pizzas ($3-15) with great harbor views. (☎850 511. Open M-Sa 8am-9pm, Su 10:30am-9pm.) Recently-opened **Fale Tau's Daily Grind,** a few doors west of the Westpac Bank on the main road, offers international cuisine ($2.50-6), specialty coffees ($2-4), and plentiful purified water. (☎850 710. A/C and fan. Open M-Sa 7am-8:30pm.) **Seabreeze Restaurant,** in a concrete building next to Savusavu Bay Accommodation, has the friendliest staff around and massive servings at rock-bottom prices (curry, chow mein, and chop suey $3-5). For groceries visit **Morris Hedstrom (MH),** adjacent to the Shell station on the main road (open M-F 8am-5pm, Sa 8am-1pm) and the **town market,** next to the police post on the main road. (Open M-F 7am-5pm, Sa 7am-3pm.) The two watering holes in town are the **Savusavu Yacht Club** (☎850 685; inside Copra Shed Marina building; beers $1.50-2.50; open daily 10am-11pm) and the **Planters' Club** (☎850 233; beers $1.15-2.85; open M-Th 10am-10pm, F-Sa 10am-11pm, Su 10am-8pm) in the weatherboard building behind the wooden fence along the main road, which has gaming tables and a TV.

⛴ ACTIVITIES. Diving around the peninsula takes place in moored sites such as **Shark Alley, Big Blue, Whales Tale,** and **Alice in Wonderland,** notable for colorful soft corals and multitudes of fish. It is possible to access the dive sites of Rainbow Reef along the southeastern coast of Vanua Levu from the Savusavu area, but Rainbow Reef is best reached from Taveuni (see **Activities** p. 433). The two dive shops in the Savusavu area are the upmarket outfit at **Jean-Michel Cousteau Fiji Islands Resort** (☎850 188, fax 850 340; jmcfir@aol.com) and **Eco Divers-Tours,** a well-established PADI operation located in Copra Shed Marina building and headed by Curly Carswell, president of the Fiji Dive Operators Association. (☎850 122; fax 850 344; ecodivers@is.com.fj; www.skyboom.com/ecodivers. Open M-F 8am-5pm, Sa 8am-1pm. 2 tanks $130; open water course $495; Discover Scuba dive $126.) It also offers **kayak rental** (single $10 per hr., double $15 per hr.), **snorkeling boat trips** ($25 per person for a group of 2), **waterskiing/watersledding** ($40 per 30min.), tours of nearby **Naidi Village** (2-4hr., $20 per person), **sailboat rental** (14ft. catamarans $15 per hr.), **bay cruises** ($30 per person per hr., min. 4 people), and **mountain and rainforest tours** (3-5hr.; $40 per person, min. 2 people).

TAVEUNI

The third largest island in Fiji, Taveuni (435 sq. km) has every reason to be called the "Garden Island." Fiji's unique national flower, the tagimaucia, spreads its tendrils amidst rainbows of tropical blooms and the mist of stunning waterfalls and virgin rainforest. Relatively young volcanic formations have formed breathtaking ridges near the center. If natural splendor on land is not reason enough to visit, the world-renowned Rainbow Reef surely is, drawing experienced divers from around the globe. However, Taveuni's burgeoning ecological diversity only survives due to extremely high amounts of rainfall; be prepared for some of the wettest weather in Fiji.

⛵ TRANSPORTATION

Taveuni is well connected to Viti Levu and Vanua Levu by sea and air. A gravel road runs along the island's perimeter, except for the portion between Lavena and Navakawau in the southeast. The road can be impassable due to heavy rain; plan accordingly. Regularly scheduled bus services connect the **Naqara/Waiyevo** area with **Lavena** (via **Matei** in the north) and **Navakawau** (via **Vuna Point** in the south).

Flights: Air Fiji (Matei Airport ☎880 062 or Garden Island Resort ☎880 286; offices also in Krishna Brothers ☎880 051) flies twice daily between Taveuni and **Nadi** (1hr.; departs Taveuni 9:30am and 2:50pm, Nadi 8am and 1:30pm; $183 one-way) and between Taveuni and **Suva** (40min.; departs Taveuni 9:30am and 2:50pm, Suva 8am and 1:30pm; $131 one-way) and **Savusavu** (20min; departs Taveuni 10:10am and 2:10pm, Savusavu 9:10am and 1:40pm; $68 one-way). **Sun Air** (Garden Island Resort ☎880 286) offers two daily flights between Taveuni and **Nadi** (1hr.; departs Taveuni 9:45am and 2:10pm, Nadi 8:20am and 12:30pm; $183 one-way).

Ferries: See **Savusavu: Transportation** p. 428. The local **Beachcomber Shipping** agent is **Tima Ltd.** (☎880 261), in the fish market building across from Garden Island Resort. Open M-F 8am-4pm and some Sa mornings. The local **Consort Shipping** agent is **First Light Inn** (☎880 339), next to Garden Island Resort. Open M-F 8am-5pm, Sa 8am-1pm. Both the *Adi Savusavu* and the *SOFE* moor at the main government wharf in **Waiyevo** (the "Korean Wharf" just to the north is used for smaller boats). Finally, a combined boat/bus service between **Savusavu** and Taveuni via **Buca Bay** has recently been restarted, but may close down if business is slow. (☎880 134. 5hr.; departs Taveuni M, W, and F 9am; $15 one-way.)

Buses: Local bus service connects the **Waiyevo/Naqara area** with **Lavena** via **Matei** and **Bouma.** (2hr. total, 30min. Waiyevo to Matei, 30min. Matei to Bouma, 30min. Bouma to Lavena. Departs Waiyevo M-Sa 10am, noon, and 4pm, Su 4pm; departs Bouma for Lavena M-Sa 2 and 6pm, Su 5:30pm; departs Bouma for Matei M-Sa 6:30, 11:30am, and 2:30pm; departs Lavena M-Sa 6am, Su 8am; departs Matei for Waiyevo, Sa 9am. Tickets $0.60-1.80.) Buses also run 3 times daily M-Sa (1 on Su) between **Waiyevo/Naqara** and **Navakawau** via **Vuna Point** (times depend on road conditions—inquire at Naqara bus station; Waiyevo-Vuna Point $2.50 one-way).

Taxis: Taxis from Matei Airport to all local destinations cost $2; from the **Waiyevo/Naqara area** to **Matei Airport** $15; to **Vuna Point** $25-30; to **Matei-Bouma** $15-20; to **Bouma-Lavena** $10. Though expensive, hiring taxis may be cheaper than renting a car if more than 2 people split the cost. Book ahead on Su.

Car Rental: Garden State Price Point (see **Financial Services** below) in Naqara is the local **Budget** agent. 4WDs available.

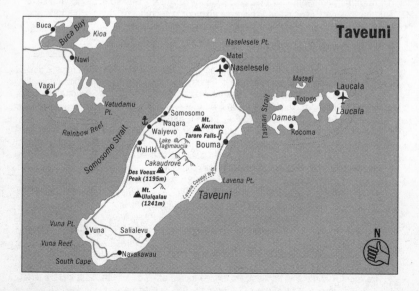

✳❓ ORIENTATION AND PRACTICAL INFO

While **Waiyevo** is the main administrative center and houses the **post office, police station,** and **hospital, Naqara** is Taveuni's commercial center with the island's only **bank,** a **shopping complex,** and a large **supermarket.** Somosomo, just north of Naqara, was the site of a rare 1986 meeting of the Great Council of Chiefs. The beaches and resorts of the three offshore islands lie to the northeast across the Tasman Strait.

Financial Services: Colonial National Bank (☎ 880 433), in the shopping complex in Naqara. Open M-Th 9:30am-3pm, F 9:30am-4pm. Cash advances on AmEx/MC/V are available with a 10% surcharge at **Garden State Price Point,** the mini-supermarket next door in the same shopping complex.

Groceries: Garden State Price Point (☎ 880 291; open M-Sa 8am-5pm, Su 8am-1pm) and **Kaba's Supermarket** (☎ 880 233; open M-F 8am-5:30pm, Sa 8am-1pm) in Naqara. All accept AmEx/MC/V.

Police: (☎ 880 222), in Waiyevo next to the post office. Matei airport also has a police post (☎ 880 224).

Pharmacies: All of the grocery stores listed above maintain mini-pharmacy sections with antiseptic and basic first aid materials.

Hospital: (☎ 880 444; same ☎ for ambulance), next to the police station in **Waiyevo.** Doctor/nurse on duty **24hr.**

Public Phones: Available at the airport, the post office, Bhula Bhai & Sons Supermarket in Matei, and several other points in the Naqara/Waiyevo/Wairiki area.

Post Office: (☎ 880 027), in Waiyevo next to the police station. Fax, telegram, and Poste Restante. Open M-F 8am-1pm and 2-4pm.

AROUND SOMOSOMO, NAQARA, WAIYEVO, AND WAIRIKI

Other than being a transit point for passengers on ferries that dock in Waiyevo, this area offers the quickest access to world-class diving at Rainbow Reef, good snorkeling, and sunbathing on Korolevu Island off Waiyevo. Wairiki Catholic Mission (est. 1907) is a beautiful stone cathedral set on a hill next to the mountains overlooking Somosomo Strait. The trailheads for hiking Des Voeux Peak and Lake Tagimaucia start nearby, and this area also contains most of Taveuni's shops and services (bank, grocery stores, post office, hospital, etc.).

⌂ ACCOMMODATIONS

First Light Inn (☎ 880 339), next to Garden Island Resort in Waiyevo, has fantastic doubles with bath, fridge, TV, phones, coffee-makers, and spacious interiors. Internet. Meals available at **Whathi Pokee Restaurant** next door. Reception M-Sa 8am-5pm, see security after hours. Doubles with fan $45, with A/C $55.

Kaba's Motel and Guesthouse (☎ 880 233; fax 880 202; kaba@is.com.fj), across from the shopping center, is the best option in Naqara. 24hr. electricity. Laundry $2-5. All rooms have fans and phones. Motel rooms with bath and TV: single $45; double $55; twin $60. Guesthouse rooms with shared bath, kitchen, and lounge area: single $25; double $35; twin $60. AmEx/MC/V/traveler's checks.

Garden Island Resort (☎ 880 286; fax 880 288; glennor@aquatrek.com, garden@is.com.fj), is a favorite for divers on package tours. All rooms have a balcony with ocean view. Boats depart twice daily for the fine sandy beach on nearby Korolevu Island ($10 per person; snorkeling gear rental $11 per day). Hiking and kayaking. Restaurant open daily 7-10am, 11:30am-3pm, 7-9pm. Laundry $5. 4-bed dorm with fan and bath $33; doubles with A/C and bath $146-184. AmEx/MC/V/traveler's checks.

Kool's Accommodation (☎ 880 395), a few doors opposite Kaba's Supermarket in Naqara. Rustic house with shared bath and kitchen. Snorkeling gear $15 per day. Free transfer to/from the wharf. Restaurant open daily 7am-7pm, may be closed in low season. Mr. Singh cooks for guests ($3-5 per meal). 3-bed dorms $10; doubles $30.

Sunset Accommodation (☎880 229), just across from the Korean Wharf in Waiyevo, is the most humble option. Breakfast $4, dinner $6. Activities arranged locally. The 3 tin-roofed houses share a kitchen and bath. Singles $15; doubles $30.

⚡ ACTIVITIES

IN THE WATER. The name ▓**Rainbow Reef** is sacred to dive enthusiasts the world over. Though this 30km reef is actually near the southeastern corner of Vanua Levu, it is best accessed from Taveuni across the Somosomo Strait. Especially renowned is the **Great White Wall,** a dive site where a 12m underwater tunnel leads to a dramatic dropoff and a 40m wall resplendent with white soft coral. Other well known sites include **Blue Ribbon Eel Reef** and **Annie's Bommie.** Because of the strong current, Rainbow Reef is best for experienced divers, but with the aid of a descent line beginners can also experience the underwater wonders. The Reef is a 20min. boat ride from **Aqua-Trek Taveuni Dive Center** (☎880 544; fax 880 288; www.aqua-trek.com) at Garden Island Resort. This well-established PADI operation (2-tank dive $165, open-water course $660, Discover Scuba course $148), with a teaching staff of 10, also offers **reef snorkeling trips** (snorkel gear not included) to Korolevu Island (10am and 2pm daily; $10 per person) and Rainbow Reef, where snorkelers explore a shallow protected reef separate from the dive sites (2hr.; 9am daily; $20 per person, min. 2 people). The Dive Center also rents out **snorkeling gear** ($11 per day) and **kayaks** ($11 per hour, $44 per day).

ON FOOT. For hikers, the marked trail up to **Des Voeux Peak** starts in Wairiki (6-8hr. return). **Lake Tagimaucia** is located just below and is visible from the Peak. The challenging trail to the Lake starts in Naqara (8-10hr. return; a guide, sturdy shoes, plenty of water, warm clothes, and a packed lunch are recommended; leave before 6am). The highlands are home to Fiji's national blossom, the **tagimaucia.** A red- and white-flowered creeper linked to local legends involving a little girl's tears of blood, it grows only above 2000 ft. and blooms between late September and late December. Garden Island Resort organizes hikes to the lake (inquire at the reception). Naveen Singh, the owner/manager at **Kool's Accommodation** (☎880 395) in Naqara, also organizes **hikes** to the peak (half-day; $120 for 4WD hire) and the lake (usually $20 per person) and trips to **Bouma Falls** (half-day, full-day including Lavena Coastal Walk; $15 per person plus entry fees to Bouma; min. 4 people) in his minivan. Garden Island Resort also organizes trips to the Falls and the Coastal Walk (park entry fee is $5 per person at both Bouma and Lavena).

OTHER ACTIVITIES. A fun natural attraction, the **Waitavala Waterslide** is about a 25min. walk up the hill from Garden Island Resort. This is a series of smooth rocks punctuated by water pools (the last large one at the bottom is swimmable). Heavy rainfall can make the slide very dangerous, so if you decide to go, exercise caution. The slide can also take a toll on the butt; heavy trousers help. Maps are available at Garden Island Resort reception. A 10min. walk south of Garden Island Resort leads to a shelter marking the **180° meridian line (International Date Line)**—see AAAAAHHHH... p. 429.

MATEI AND SURROUNDS

This residential area on the northern tip of Taveuni has the most, and best, budget accommodations and restaurants on the island. Despite the lack of sand on area beaches such as Beverly, many (especially those belonging to private resorts) are lovely and secluded. It is a 25min. ride from Matei to Bouma Falls and an additional 10min. to the Lavena Coastal Walk. There is a supermarket in town (Bhula Bhai & Sons), a police post at the airport, and payphones at the supermarket and airport. It takes 25min. to walk from the southwestern end of the area (near Lisi's Accommodation) to the southeastern end (near Tovutovu Resort).

🏠🏕 ACCOMMODATIONS AND CAMPING

Some of the private properties here have a cottage/bure/room for rent and the number of such establishments will undoubtedly rise as tourism increases. Just walk along the coastal road and see what has newly opened (or shut down).

■ **Todranisiga** (☎ 880 871), "a flaming ray of sun" in Fijian, is perched on a panoramic cliff located between Matei Point and Karin's Garden. Communal shower and sink. Camping in 4 large pre-set tents on the 5½-acre clifftop lawn. 4 people max.; mattress, sheets, pillows provided; $15 per person. Hip owner May is considering building bures soon.

Tovu Tovu Resort (☎ 880 560; fax 880 722; tovutovu@is.com.fj), the farthest from the airport southeast across from Viubani Island, is a 120-acre copra plantation. Attractive dorms are housed in a beautiful bure. Laundry $5. Reservations recommended. 8-bed dorms $15; bure with kitchen $75, bure without $65. AmEx/MC/V/traveler's checks.

Bibi's Hideaway (☎ 880 443), 20 beautifully landscaped acres across from Karin's Garden, are the work of James, an affable Fijian. A 5min. walk to dive shops and beach. All accommodations come with bath/kitchen. Meals prepared upon arrangement. Electricity 6pm-9pm (afterwards lantern). Reservations recommended. Camping is $25 per tent (2 people), with shower/kitchen. Cottage $90; double cottage $50-60; bure $80.

Little Dolphin Treehouse (☎ 880 130), across from Bhula Bhai & Sons supermarket. A cute studio setup, all self-contained (downstairs kitchen, bath, fridge) with an ocean-view balcony. Free fruit from the garden in season. Electricity 6pm-10:30pm. Snorkeling gear rental $10 per day, canoe $40. Studio $55.

Beverly Camping (☎ 880 684), on Beverly Beach next to Aquaventure dive shop, comes with free fruits and bedding in a wooded, shaded area. Communal bath and open-air thatched roof kitchen meet your basic needs. Plots $10.

🍴 FOOD

Coconut Grove Cafe (☎ 880 328), at Coconut Grove Beachfront Cottage across the road from the airport, is the best restaurant in town. Though a bit pricey (breakfast $3.50-7; lunch $7.50-16; dinner $13.50-19.50), the international menu includes fruit shakes ($3-4) and homemade banana/papaya bread ($3.50). Weekly *lovo* and *meke* nights $25. Take-aways. For dinner, order before 4pm. AmEx/MC/V.

Island Pizza Kitchen (☎ 880 083), next to Aquaventure dive shop. This new out-on-the-beach hangout is good at 5pm for a beer-in-hand sunset. The yummy pizzas are $12-15. Open daily 10am-2pm, 5-9pm.

Tovu Tovu Resort Restaurant (☎ 880 560). Enjoy mostly Fijian and European dishes (breakfast $2.50-7.50, sandwiches $5.50-6.50, dinner $7.50-15) on the oceanview veranda. Open daily 8am-2pm, 5-9pm. AmEx/MC/V/traveler's checks.

🏄 ACTIVITIES

Diving is provided by **Aquaventure Taveuni** (☎/fax 880 381; www.aquaventure.org; 2-tank with equipment US$76, open-water course US$276; PADI, NAUI, SSI) and the PADI **Swiss Fiji Divers** (☎/fax 880 586; www.swiss-fijidivers.com; 2-tank without equipment US$99, open-water course US$381, Discover Scuba dive US$150), which are located right next to each other. The latter is a high-powered setup offering all sorts of groovy electro equipment and instruction in German and French. Aquaventure also runs **reef snorkeling trips** ($10-40 per person, snorkeling gear rental $12 per day), rents kayaks (double kayaks $10 per hr., $60 per day; singles $10 per hr., $35 per day) and does bookings for the **Waitabu Marine Park Tour** and the **Vidawa Rainforest Hike.** Next door to Aquaventure is **Ringgold Reef Kayaking** (☎ 880 083), whose owner/manager Keni is the local guru for fishing trips—he also runs camping, kayaking, hiking, and horseback riding trips, and rents kayaks.

SOUTHERN TAVEUNI

A scenic 1hr. drive along the coast past Taveuni Estates from Waiyevo/Naqara area, Vuna and its environs have several budget accommodation options on a beautiful rocky waterfront (no worries, sandy beaches are just a few minutes away). The area has a very mellow vibe, even by Fijian standards (there are no shops or services other than a community grocery store), and some of the best snorkeling in Fiji. Very good diving can be found off Vuna Reef. The road from Waiyevo/Naqara is rough and can be impassable after heavy rains.

⌂⌂ ACCOMMODATIONS AND FOOD. Under new Dutch-Fijian management, **Susie's Plantation Resort,** a former copra plantation, is set on a beautiful lawn overlooking a rocky deep-water coastline. Facilities were being renovated/expanded at the time of writing. (☎880 125; susies@is.com.fj. Snorkeling gear hire $10 per day. Shared kitchen. Laundry $5. 24hr. electricity. Internet. Breakfast $3.50-7, lunch $7.50, 3-course dinner $13-15. 8-bed dorm $10; doubles $35-55; bures with bath $65-85; camping $10. MC/V/traveler's checks.) The **Vatuwiri Farm Resort** was established in 1871 by James Valentine Tarte as a copra plantation; this 2000-acre estate now produces beef, vanilla, and cocoa and is one of the biggest farms in Fiji. Steeped in colonial history, the busy staff of 100 workers offer guests an intimate glimpse into Fiji's rural past. (☎880 316; fax 880 314. Mealplan (fresh homegrown food) US$35 per day. Laundry $5 per load. Cottage with double bed and bath or room in the owner's homestead $55. MC/V/traveler's checks.) Find no-frills rooms in a spartan house at **Vuna Lagoon Lodge,** located farthest south. (☎880 627. Kitchen. Breakfast and dinner prepared on request ($5-15). Electricity 6-10pm. Laundry $5. 4-bed dorm $15; singles $30; doubles with bath $50.)

⌦ ACTIVITIES. Vuna Reef Divers (☎880 125; 1-tank $75, 2-tank $110, shore dive $40, PADI open-water $500; instruction also in German), at Susie's Plantation, is the primary dive operator and also runs **reef snorkeling trips** ($15 per person) and rents out **snorkeling gear** ($10 per day). **Susie's Plantation** organizes **horseback riding trips** to a nearby volcanic crater (half-day $35 per person), and guests at the plantation can follow **bush trails,** watching birds at leisure. **Vatuwiri Farm Resort** offers **fishing trips** ($15 per person), **guided horseback riding** ($35 per person), and **guided hiking** to the volcanic crater (half-day $15 per person). Remains of an old **village hill fortification** can be found on the Resort property, but the site is now quite overgrown and probably isn't worth the trouble. Finally, **Vuna Lagoon Lodge** also runs **horseback riding trips** ($35 per person) and rents out **kayaks** ($5 per half-day) and **canoes** ($10 per half-day).

EASTERN TAVEUNI

Most of eastern Taveuni is included in **Bouma National Heritage Park** (15,000 hectares), which contains 80% of Taveuni's pristine rainforest, the three stunning Tavoro waterfalls, and the gorgeous Lavena Coastal Walk. A conservation success story, the Park is the result of an agreement in the 1980s between the village communities of Waitabu, Vidawa, Korovou (Bouma), and Lavena, whereby the villagers ▧**rejected logging** in favor of eco-tourism as a means of generating income. Park entry fees go toward trail maintenance and to financing village projects and scholarships for children. Most tracks are on the coastal periphery except for the Vidawa Rainforest Hike, which leads into the heart of the forest.

A must-do while in Taveuni, the **Tavoro** (or **Bouma**) **Waterfalls** offer walking, hiking, and swimming. From the Park Visitor Centre in Bouma, it is an easy 10min. walk to the first and tallest (30m) waterfall, which has the largest swimming pool. The second fall (a bit smaller, but good for swimming) is a relatively easy 40miin. walk, which includes a stream crossing with the help of a rope. It takes an extra hour of more strenuous hiking along a less well maintained track to reach the third fall, smaller than the first two. (Visitor Centre ☎880 390. Entry fee $5 per person. Snacks and lunch available at the Centre; order lunch in advance for $10. Don't go beyond the first fall after heavy rain.) The falls can be done as a day trip by bus from either Matei or the Waiyevo/Naqara area (catch the first morning bus to Bouma; see **Taveuni: Transportation** p. 430).

The ⬛**Lavena Coastal Walk,** along the coastal boundary of Bouma National Park, has remote sandy beaches (Taveuni's best), lush rainforest, stunning waterfalls, pristine streams, and some surf action off the beaches. The marked trail starts from the **Lavena Visitor Centre** (☎ 116 801; pay the $5 entrance fee here) and continues along the coast past streams, two waterfalls, and over a suspension bridge before finally turning inland along **Wainibau Stream** and ending 50m downstream from the beautiful **Lower Wainibau Waterfalls.** Only the bottom of the falls is visible from this point. Although *Let's Go* doesn't recommend it, to reach the falls you need to swim upstream, which can be hazardous; don't swim if the water is murky—a sign of flooding—or if you can't see the rocks on the way upstream. The visitors center has four simple rooms, and lunch ($10) can be ordered here in advance. (1 double and 3 triples with shared kitchen and bath $15 per person. Electricity 6pm-11pm. Breakfast $7. Laundry $5.) There is a village store nearby with the usual canned food and drinks, but it is better to bring food from Matei.

Wainibau Stream at the southern end of Lavena Coastal Walk is the southern boundary of Bouma National Heritage Park; on the other side is the 4000-hectare **Ravilevu Nature Reserve,** farther south of which is the village of **Salialevu.** Halfway down the coast from Wainibau Stream is the 20m **Savulevu Yavonu Falls,** which plunges into the ocean (accessible by boat only; inquire at Lavena Visitor Centre).

Not to be outdone by Korovou (Bouma) and Lavena, the villages of **Waitabu** and **Vidawa** (a bit north of Bouma) have also organized eco-tourism projects such as the **Waitabu Marine Park** and the **Vidawa Rainforest Hike.** The Rainforest Hike is a challenging full-day hike. (Book at Bouma Visitor Centre ☎ 880 390. $60 per person, including transport to/from Matei, lunch, guide, and drinks.) Are you one of those people who picks up a book and immediately flips to the end so that you can read the last sentence first? *Why?*

PRUSSIAN ROULETTE
Ever the precocious young Prussian, 13-year-old **Count Felix von Luckner** ran away from home in 1894 for a life at sea. After various misadventures including stints as a kangaroo hunter and a boxer in Australia, von Luckner joined the Imperial German Navy during World War I. Given command of an old-fashioned sailing ship outfitted with modern guns, he managed to sink 14 enemy ships on his way to the Pacific, only to be wrecked in Tahiti by a tidal wave. Not one to be perturbed, he and five of his men jury-rigged a 6m boat out of the wreck and filled it with a ridiculous amount of weaponry, determined to capture the first vessel they met. Fortunately for everyone else, they never saw another boat, and after an amazing journey of over 2300 nautical miles in their tiny open boat the men finally landed on Wakaya Island near Ovalau. They were immediately arrested and sent to the police in Levuka, where townspeople still tell stories of how von Luckner could bend coins or rip telephone books in half with his bare hands. He later made several escape attempts from jail in New Zealand that earned him the nickname **Seeteufel** (German for "Sea Devil"). Von Luckner died of natural causes in 1966 at the age of 84.

APPENDIX

GLOSSARY OF KIWI ENGLISH

abseil: rappel
Aotearoa: "land of the long white cloud," the Maori name for New Zealand
ANZAC: Australia New Zealand Army Corps (p. 59). Anzac Day is a national holiday (April 25th).
All Blacks: the national rugby team; don't ever let on that you don't know exactly what this is
Aussie ("Ozzie"): Australian
bach ("batch"): Small, often beachside holiday house; known as a "crib" on the South Island
backpackers: hostel
basin: bathroom sink;
bathroom: room with a bath; not necessarily a toilet
belt bag, bum bag: hip pack, fanny pack ("fanny," should not be used in New Zealand; it's a slang word referring to female genitalia)
"big bikkies": big money, the big bucks
bikkies: cookies, crackers
biscuit: cookie
bottle shop: liquor store; the only place to buy beer besides a bar/club
bloke: man
bloody: all purpose curse
bonnet: hood of car
boot: trunk of a car
brasserie: trendy cafe
brekkie: breakfast
bugger all: very little
bum: one's rear-end; arse
BYO: bring-your-own alcohol
capsicum: green, red, or yellow peppers
caravan: trailer, mobile home
carpark: parking lot
cashpoint: ATM
chat up: to hit on (eg. "I'm going to chat up that girl")
cheeky: rude, impertinent
cheers: goodbye; thanks; excuse me; and just about anything else you can think of
chemist: drugstore, pharmacy
chilly bin: portable cooler
chips: french fries
chocka, chockablock: packed, crowded, busy, full
choice: good, proper, sweet
chunder: vomit
coach: bus that travels long distances; not a local bus
college: secondary school
concessions: senior citizens

crib: South Island version of "bach," vacation home
crisps: potato chips
cruisy: mellow, no worries
cuppa: cup of tea or coffee
dag: good guy/joker
dairy: convenience store
dear: expensive
Devonshire tea: afternoon tea and scones, often with whipped cream; see p. 67
DOC ("dock"): Department of Conservation (see p. 354)
domain: public park
doughnut: cream- and jam-filled sweet dough roll
duvet: comforter, inch-thick feather blanket
entree: appetizer
Enzed: New Zealand ("NZ")
fair go: opportunity; a shot
feed: a meal
filled roll: sub sandwich
filter coffee: drip coffee
flash: snazzy, upscale, smart, trendy, glam
flat: apartment
flat white: coffee: a long black with a dollop of milk
footie: soccer
footpath: sidewalk
for donkey's years: for a long time
fortnight: two weeks
get on the piss: get drunk
Godzone: New Zealand (from "God's own")
good as gold: fine, sure, great
good on ya: good for you, good job
gridiron: American football
grotty: dirty, run-down
ground floor: an American first floor (and first floor is second floor, etc.)
gumboots: rubber boots
hard case: tough to get to know
hire: rent
hockey: field hockey
hoe: to eat quickly
holiday: vacation
hoon: slob, jerk
hoover: to vacuum, or eat quickly
hottie: hot water bottle
jundreds and thousands: sprinkles
jandals: flip-flops
jersey, jumper: sweater
judder bar: speed bump
jugger: bloke, man
jumper: sweater
Kiwi: New Zealander; of or relating to New Zealand

kiwi: small flightless bird; the national symbol (never short for kiwifruit)
kiwifruit: a furry greenish-brown fruit
knickers: women's underwear
kumara: sweet potato
L&P: soda
lemonade: lemon-flavored carbonated soft drink
licensed: sells alcohol legally
lift: elevator
local rag: local newspaper
long black: espresso with hot water
long drop: outhouse
loo: toilet
main: main course of a meal
Mainland: South Island
Maori: the indigenous peoples of New Zealand
Marmite: yeast spread
mate: friend, buddy, pal
metal road: gravel road
milk bar: convenience store
nappy: diaper
no joy: no luck
not a problem: you're welcome;
note: currency bill
no worries: sure, fine
Oz, "Ozzie": technically "Aussie"; Australia, Australian
paddock: sheep pasture
Pakeha: person of European descent; foreigner
paper (university): class/course
petrol: gas
paua: abalone; a type of shellfish
pavlova: a creamy, fruity meringue dessert
pie: flaky pastry shell with a variety of fillings, usually with meat (mince)
pipi: clam-like shellfish
pissed: drunk
pissing down: raining hard
plate: potluck dinner
Pom: Englishman (often derogatory)
to post: to mail
pot plant: house plant
powerpoints: electrical hook-ups for tents or caravans
prawns: jumbo shrimp
push bike: bicycle
quai: "key"; a pier
queue: "Q"; a line of people
rag: local newspaper
rattle your dags: hurry upr
ap-jumping: abseiling face-first down a building

437

return: round-trip
to have a row: to fight
ring: call
rubber: eraser
rubbish: garbage, trash
salad: usually cucumber, carrots, beetroot; "with salad" means that these items come on a sandwich or burger; not a separate side salad.
scroggin: trail mix, gorp
sealed road: paved road
serviette: napkin
shagging: having sex
shares: shared rooms at an accommodation
short black: coffee, flat white without the milk; between an espresso and a long black
Shortland Street: New Zealand soap opera; constant hostel entertainment
shout: to buy for someone (eg. "I'll shout you a drink")
Simpsons, the: the best show on television; also, constant hostel entertainment
skivvies: turtle-neck sweater
skull: to chug (as in beer)
Sky TV: satellite television

snog: kiss or make out
snooker: a game similar to pool
strewth!: an exclamation; truly (from "God's truth")
stubby: small bottle of beer
sultanas: large raisins
suss out: to figure out
ta: thanks
TAB: shop to place bets without going to the tracks
take a sikkie: play hookey, pretend to be sick to skip work
takeaway: food to go, or a place that offers such
tariff: price
tea: hot drink; also refers to a full afternoon meal
that's all right, that's okay: you're welcome
tinny: lucky
togs: swimming suit
tomato sauce: ketchup; sold in small packets at restaurants
torch: flashlight
take the piss out of: to poke fun at someone

take the mickey out of: to ridicule
torch: flashlight
trainers: sneakers
transport: transportation; how dumb are you?
tyre: tire
uni: university
ute: pick-up truck ("utility vehicle")
varsity: university
Vegemite: Australian yeast spread
wanker: jerk
wedges: large, thick slices of deep-fried potato; often served with sour cream
wellies: rubber boots
woolies: winter clothes; long underwear
Xena: "Xena, Warrior Princess" a TV show filmed in Northland (see p. 67)
yob: see "hoon"
yonks: forever
zed: the letter "z"
zorb: to roll down a hill ina giant hamster ball

MAORI-ENGLISH DICTIONARY
(SEE ALSO **MAORI ARTS AND CULTURE, P. 63**)

ao: cloud
Aotearoa: Maori name for New Zealand
atua: gods or spirits
awa: river, valley
e noho ra: goodbye (said by the person leaving)
haere mai: welcome
haere ra: goodbye, farewell (said by the person staying)
haka: fierce war dance
hangi: underground Maori oven; also the meal
hapu: regional community
hau: wind
Hawaiki: mythical (?) ancient homeland of the Maori
hoa: friend
hongi: Maori welcome expressed by the touching together of noses; literally, the "sharing of breath"
hui: meeting
ika: fish
iti: small
iwi: tribe, people, nation
ka pai: thank you; excellent
kai: food
kainga: village, town
karakia: chants, prayer
karanga: chant of welcome
kei te pehea koe: how are you? (one person)
kia ora: hello, health, luck
koe: you (singular)
korero: stories
koutou: you (plural)
kumara: sweet potato; a Maori food staple

mana: prestige, power
manaia: bird men
manga: river, stream
manuhiri: guest
Maoritanga: Maori culture
marae: a meeting place, sacred ground
maunga: mountain
mauri: essence of a natural state
mere: greenstone warclub
moana: sea, lake
moko: traditional facial tattoo
motu: island
namu: sandfly
noa: counterpart to tapu
nui: big, large
ngai, ngati: prefix indicating tribe, people, or clan
ngaru: wave
o: of
ora: life, alive, healthy, safe
pa: fortified Maori village, often on a hilltop
Pakeha: person of European descent; foreigner
patu: club (weapon)
pohatu: stone, rock
poi: a dance involving twirling balls on the ends of strings
pounamu: greenstone
powhiri: formal welcome ceremony
puna: spring (water)
rangi: the sky, the heavens
roto: lake
rua: two
takiwai: translucent greenstone

tane: man
tangata: humans, people
tangata whenua: local Maori people; "people of the land"
taniwha: water spirit, demon
taonga: highly treasured
taparahi: weaponless dances
tapu: taboo, holy, sacrosanct
te: the
teka: peace offering
tena -koe: hello (to one person)
tiki: small carved figurine of a human in wood, stone, or greenstone; when hung around the neck, a heitiki
tino rangatiratanga: sovereignty, self-determination
tohunga: priest or specially learned men
tukutuku: woven reed panels frequently found in marae
umu: underground oven
wahi ngaro: lost aspects
wahine: woman
wai: water
waiata: traditional song, often of mourning or unrequited love; see p. 47
waka: canoe
wai: water
wero: challenge
whaikorero: welcome speech
whakama: ashamed; or guilty
whanga: bay, body of water
whanau: family
whare: house
whenua: ground, land

FIJIAN-ENGLISH DICTIONARY

CONSONANTS
b = mb
d = nd
q = ng
g = ng
c = th
VOWELS
a = as in "watch"
e = as in "Che Guevara"
i = as in "knee"
o = as in "rope"
u = as in "Et tu, Brute?"

au vinakata (aoo vina kahta): I want
bele: a green, always boiled
bia (bee-a): beer
bilo: bowl for kava
bula (mbula): hello
bulumakau: cattle
bure/vale (mburey/valey): thatched house
ca (tha): bad
cakacaka (thaka thaka): work
dalo: taro (like potato)
dua (ndua): one
dua tale (ndua ta lay): one more
gone (ngonay): child
gunu (goo noo): drink
ika (eekah): fish
ilavo (eelavo): money
io (ee-o): yes
ivi: Fijian chestnut
jaina: banana
kakana: food
kana: eat

kanikani: scaly skin due to excessive kava
kauta mai (ka ou tah my): bring
koli: dog
koro: village
kumala: sweet potato
kuro: pot
kuwawa: guava
lailai (lie lie): small
lako mai (la ko my): come
lako tani (la ko tanee): go
levu (layvu): big, many
lilia (leeah leeah): stupid
lolo: coconut milk
maca (matha): thanks for kava
manumanu vuka: bird
maqo: mango
marama: lady
marau: happy
masese: matches
matai (mahtye): smart
meke: traditional Fijian dance
na cava oqo (na thava on go): what is this
nanoa: yesterday
ni mataka: tomorrow
ni sa bula (nee sah mbula): greetings/hello
ni sa moce (ni sa moe-they): goodbye
ni sa yadra (ni sah yarn dra): good morning
nikua: today
niu (new): coconut
puaka: pig
rua: two
sa moce (sah more they): goodbye

seqa (senga): no
sevusevu: gift
sitoa (seetoah): shop
sulu: sarong
tabua: tooth of sperm whale
tagane (tahng-ahnay): boy, male
tavako: tobacco
toa: chicken
totoka (toe-toe-kah): handsome, beautiful
tulou (too low): excuse me
ura: freshwater prawn
uto: breadfruit
uvi: yam
vaka lailai (vaka lie lie): little
vaka levu: plenty
vaka malua: slowly
vaka totolo: quickly
vale/bure (valey/mburey): house
vale ni lotu (valey nee lohtoo): church
vale lailai (valey lie lie): toilet
vinaka (vee naka): thank you
vinaka vakalevu (vee naka vakalevoo): thank you very much
vivili: shellfish
vonu: turtle
yalewa (yah-lay-wah): girl, female
yalo vinaka (yarlo vee naka): please
yavusa: extended family group derived from one original person

CLIMATE CHART

The following chart shows the monthly rainfall and average low and high temperatures of several major destinations in New Zealand and Fiji during four representative months of the year.

Av. Temp. lo/hi Precipitation	January			April			July			October		
	°C	°F	mm	°C	°F	mm	°C	°F	mm	°C	°F	mm
Auckland	16/23	61/73	79	13/19	55/66	97	8/13	46/55	145	11/17	52/63	102
Bay of Islands	14/25	57/77	12	17/26	89/95	12	15/19	47/59	12	25/30	58/99	12
Christchurch	12/21	54/70	56	7/17	45/63	482	2/10	36/50	69	7/17	45/63	56
Dunedin	10/19	50/66	86	7/15	45/59	71	3/9	37/48	79	6/15	43/59	89
Napier	14/24	57/75	74	10/19	50/66	76	5/13	41/55	102	9/19	48/66	56
Nelson	13/22	55/72	73	8/18	46/64	81	3/13	37/55	89	7/17	45/63	78
Queenstown	10/22	50/72	82	6/16	43/61	71	1/10	34/50	78	5/16	41/61	88
Rotorua	12/24	54/75	90	9/18	48/64	119	4/13	39/55	145	7/17	45/63	116
Wellington	13/21	55/70	81	11/17	52/63	97	6/12	43/54	137	9/16	48/61	102
Nadi (Fiji)	23/32	73/90	299	22/31	72/88	163	18/29	64/84	46	20/28	68/82	103
Suva (Fiji)	24/31	75/88	315	23/30	73/86	390	20/27	68/81	142	22/28	72/82	234

INDEX

INDEX

INDEX

MAPS

ABOUT LET'S GO

FORTY-TWO YEARS OF WISDOM

For over four decades, travelers crisscrossing the continents have relied on *Let's Go* for inside information on the hippest backstreet cafes, the most pristine secluded beaches, and the best routes from border to border. *Let's Go: Europe*, now in its 42nd edition and translated into seven languages, reigns as the world's bestselling international travel guide. In the last 20 years, our rugged researchers have stretched the frontiers of backpacking and expanded our coverage into the Americas, Australia, Asia, and Africa (including the new *Let's Go: Egypt* and the more comprehensive, multi-country jaunt through *Let's Go: South Africa & Southern Africa*). Our new-and-improved City Guide series continues to grow with new guides to perennial European favorites Amsterdam and Barcelona. This year we are also unveiling *Let's Go: Southwest USA*, the flagship of our new outdoor Adventure Guide series, which is complete with special roadtripping tips and itineraries, more coverage of adventure activities like hiking and mountain biking, and first-person accounts of life on the road.

It all started in 1960 when a handful of well-traveled students at Harvard University handed out a 20-page mimeographed pamphlet offering a collection of their tips on budget travel to passengers on student charter flights to Europe. The following year, in response to the instant popularity of the first volume, students traveling to Europe researched the first full-fledged edition of *Let's Go: Europe*. Throughout the 60s and 70s, our guides reflected the times—in 1969, for example, we taught you how to get from Paris to Prague on "no dollars a day" by singing in the street. In the 90s we focused in on the world's most exciting urban areas to produce in-depth, fold-out map guides, now with 20 titles (from Hong Kong to Chicago) and counting. Our new guides bring the total number of titles to 57, each infused with the spirit of adventure and voice of opinion that travelers around the world have come to count on. But some things never change: our guides are still researched, written, and produced entirely by students who know first-hand how to see the world on the cheap.

HOW WE DO IT

Each guide is completely revised and thoroughly updated every year by a well-traveled set of nearly 300 students. Every spring, we recruit over 200 researchers and 90 editors to overhaul every book. After several months of training, researcher-writers hit the road for seven weeks of exploration, from Anchorage to Adelaide, Estonia to El Salvador, Iceland to Indonesia. Hired for their rare combination of budget travel sense, writing ability, stamina, and courage, these adventurous travelers know that train strikes, stolen luggage, food poisoning, and marriage proposals are all part of a day's work. Back at our offices, editors work from spring to fall, massaging copy written on Himalayan bus rides into witty, informative prose. A student staff of typesetters, cartographers, publicists, and managers keeps our lively team together. In September, the collected efforts of the summer are delivered to our printer, who turns them into books in record time, so that you have the most up-to-date information available for your vacation. Even as you read this, work on next year's editions is well underway.

WHY WE DO IT

We don't think of budget travel as the last recourse of the destitute; we believe that it's the only way to travel. Our books will ease your anxieties and answer your questions about the basics—so you can get off the beaten track and explore. Once you learn the ropes, we encourage you to put *Let's Go* down and strike out on your own. You know as well as we that the best discoveries are often those you make yourself. When you find something worth sharing, please drop us a line. We're Let's Go Publications, 67 Mount Auburn St., Cambridge, MA 02138, USA (feedback@letsgo.com). For more info, visit our website, www.letsgo.com.

Will you have enough stories to tell your grandchildren?

Yahoo! Travel

CHOOSE YOUR DESTINATION SWEEPSTAKES

No Purchase Necessary.

**Explore the world with Let's Go® and StudentUniverse!
Enter for a chance to win a trip for two to a Let's Go destination!**

Separate Drawings! May & October 2002.

GRAND PRIZES:

Roundtrip StudentUniverse Tickets

✓ Select one destination and mail your entry to:

☐ Costa Rica
☐ London
☐ Hong Kong
☐ San Francisco
☐ New York
☐ Amsterdam
☐ Prague
☐ Sydney

* Plus Additional Prizes!!

Choose Your Destination Sweepstakes
St. Martin's Press
Suite 1600, Department MF
175 Fifth Avenue
New York, NY 10010-7848

Restrictions apply; see offical rules for
details by visiting Let'sGo.com or sending SASE
(VT residents may omit return postage) to the address above.

Name:_____

Address:_____

City/State/Zip:_____

Phone:_____

Email:_____

Grand prizes provided by:

 StudentUniverse.com   Real Travel Deals